Denmark

Glenda Bendure
Ned Friary

LONELY PLANET PUBLICATIONS
Melbourne • Oakland • London • Paris

DENMARK

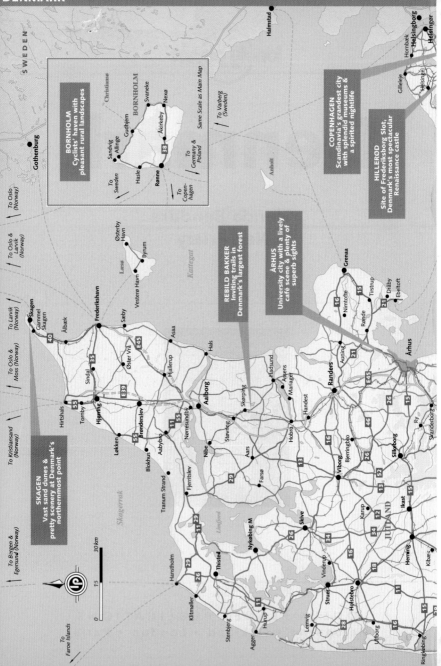

SKAGEN
Vast sand dunes & pretty scenery at Denmark's northernmost point

BORNHOLM
Cyclists' haven with pleasant rural landscapes

REBILD BAKKER
Inviting trails in Denmark's largest forest

ÅRHUS
University city with a lively café scene & plenty of superb sights

COPENHAGEN
Scandinavia's grandest city with splendid museums & a spirited nightlife

HILLERØD
Site of Frederiksborg Slot, Denmark's most spectacular Renaissance castle

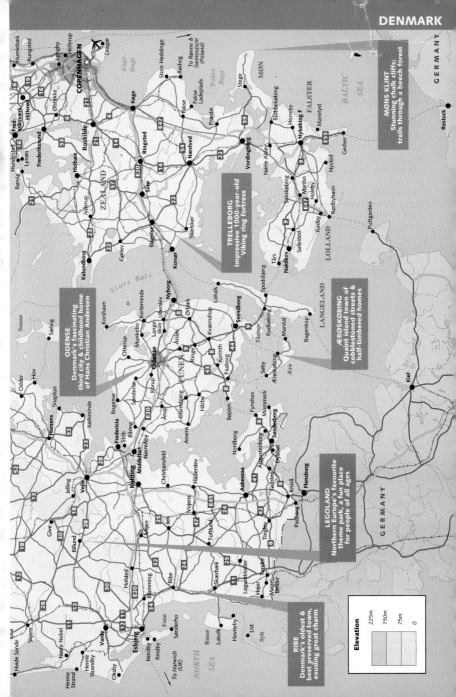

Denmark
2nd edition – June 1999
First published – July 1996

Published by
Lonely Planet Publications Pty Ltd A.C.N. 005 607 983
192 Burwood Rd, Hawthorn, Victoria 3122, Australia

Lonely Planet Offices
Australia PO Box 617, Hawthorn, Victoria 3122
USA 150 Linden St, Oakland, CA 94607
UK 10a Spring Place, London NW5 3BH
France 1 rue du Dahomey, 75011 Paris

Photographs
Many of the images in this guide are available for licensing from
Lonely Planet Images.
email: lpi@lonelyplanet.com.au

Front cover photograph
Classic Danish church tower, affording sweeping views of the North
Zealand landscape (Ned Friary)

ISBN 0 86442 609 7

Although the authors
and Lonely Planet try
to make the informa-
tion as accurate as
possible, we accept
no responsibility for
any loss, injury or
inconvenience sus-
tained by anyone
using this book.

Contents – Text

2 Contents – Text

NORTH ZEALAND   167

SOUTHERN ZEALAND   192

MØN, FALSTER & LOLLAND   215

BORNHOLM   232

FUNEN   251

Contents – Maps

CENTRAL JUTLAND

NORTHERN JUTLAND

MAP LEGEND – SEE BACK PAGE

MAP INDEX

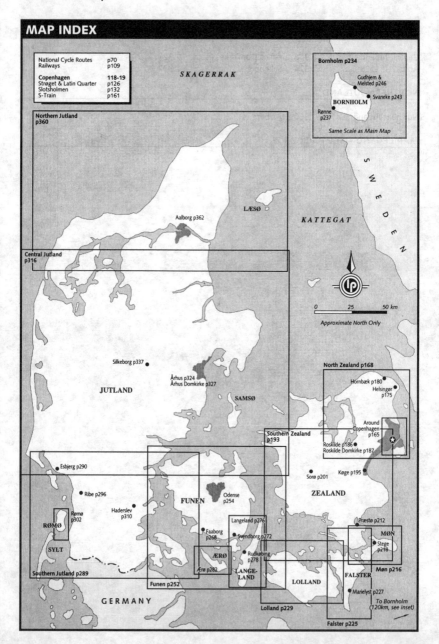

Bornholm p234

Gudhjem & Melsted p246

BORNHOLM

Svaneke p243

Rønne p237

Same Scale as Main Map

SKAGERRAK

Northern Jutland p360

LÆSØ

Aalborg p362

KATTEGAT

S W E D E N

Central Jutland p316

Silkeborg p337

Århus p324
Århus Domkirke p327

JUTLAND

SAMSØ

0   25   50 km

Approximate North Only

North Zealand p168

Hornbæk p180
Helsingør p175

Around Copenhagen p165

Southern Zealand p193

Roskilde p186
Roskilde Domkirke p187

Esbjerg p290

Køge p195

Ribe p296

Sorø p201

ZEALAND

Odense p254

Haderslev p310

FUNEN

Rømø p302

RØMØ

SYLT

Faaborg p268

Langeland p276

Svendborg p272

ÆRØ

Rudkøbing p278

Ærø p282

LANGE-LAND

Southern Jutland p289

Funen p252

Præstø p212

MØN

Stege p218

Møn p216

FALSTER

LOLLAND

Marielyst p227

GERMANY

Lolland p229

To Bornholm (120km, see inset)

Falster p225

The Authors

Glenda Bendure & Ned Friary

Glenda grew up in California's Mojave Desert and first travelled overseas as a high school AFS exchange student to India.

Ned grew up near Boston, studied Social Thought & Political Economy at the University of Massachusetts in Amherst and upon graduating headed west.

They met in Santa Cruz, California, where Glenda was completing her university studies. In 1978, with Lonely Planet's first book *Across Asia on the Cheap* in hand, they took the overland trail from Europe to Nepal. The next six years were spent exploring Asia and the Pacific, with a home base in Japan where Ned taught English and Glenda edited a monthly magazine. They now live on Cape Cod in Massachusetts – at least when they're not on the road.

Ned and Glenda have visited Denmark seven times in the past seven years, exploring the country extensively, on some trips using public transport and on others self-touring by car.

They are also the authors of Lonely Planet's guides to *Hawaii, Honolulu, Bermuda* and the *Eastern Caribbean* and they write the Norway and Denmark chapters of Lonely Planet's *Scandinavian & Baltic Europe*.

From the Authors

Thanks to Lillian Hess of the Danish Tourist Board in New York and to Mette Dahl-Jensen and Henrik Thierlein of the Wonderful Copenhagen Convention and Visitors Bureau for their kind assistance. We would also like to thank the helpful folks at Use It and at the many local tourist bureaus along the way who patiently answered questions and dug through their files.

Thanks also to Lise Kirkpatrick at the Danish Cultural Institute in Scotland; Thomas Østergaard at Nordsømuseet in Hirtshals; Svend Ravnkilde of the Dansk Musik Informations Center; Nina Skriver Dahl of the Danish Literature Information Center; Charlotte Christiansen of the Traffic Information Centre; Annette Nielsen of KVINFO in Copenhagen; Jette Sandahl, curator of Kvindemuseet in Århus; and Sarah Rothman and Thomas Hadrup in the information office of the Danish embassy in Washington DC.

Many thanks to the various travellers and friends we met along the way and to those who took time to write to us after we returned home, including Tove & Knud Bøjland, Trine & Birthe Bøtkjær, Gitte Hansen, Charlotte Hindle and Jan Buschardt, and a special thanks to Gudrun Rishede, Jens Philpsen and their son Svend for a cosy evening of wine and fireworks.

This Book

Denmark was first written by Glenda Bendure and Ned Friary in 1996.

From the Publisher

This second edition of *Denmark* was edited and proofed by Paul Bloomfield with help from Rhonda Carrier, Katrina Browning and David Rathborne. David Wenk coordinated the design and cartography, assisted by Tony Battle, Tom Fawcett and Michelle Lewis. Illustrations were drawn by Nicky Castle and Tamsin Wilson. Thanks are due to Lyndell Stringer for help with the colour map; Quentin Frayne for checking the language chapter; Leonie Mugavin, Jen Loy and Claire Hornshaw for work on the Getting There & Away chapter (Leonie also tweaked the health section); Paul Clifton for input on the sections for gay and lesbian travellers; and Lonely Planet Images for supplying photographs. Many thanks to Margit Klemmensen at the Danish Tourist Board in London for providing additional photos.

Thanks

Many thanks to the travellers who used the first edition and wrote to us with helpful hints, useful advice and interesting anecdotes. Your names follow:

Philip S Adey, Daniel Beaumont, Jes Bengtsson, Bo Bjoedstrup, Derek Blice, Dr R Bourne, R Brandwood, Paul Dalton, Melinda Drew, Anders Ekelund, Humphrey Evans, Steve Frandsen, Dave Fuller, Jen Gleave, Torben Grue, Joen Pauli Hansen, Mark Hoewisch, Virginia J Holoday, Line Holm Jensen, Deborah & Barry Hurwitz, Stephen Jacob, Peter Johnson, Sioned Lewis, Silvia Marinovova, Jeppe Mikkelsen, Bruno Moncorge, Giorgia Naccarato, Riccardo Nanni, Rasmus Nedergaard, Douglas M Nelson, Maire Ni Eafa, Urban Ocvirk, Brian Payne, Peter Sluijter, David Smoler, David Stifel, Stine Suhr, Chuck & Rebecca Theobald, Jantine Wijnja.

Foreword

ABOUT LONELY PLANET GUIDEBOOKS

The story begins with a classic travel adventure: Tony and Maureen Wheeler's 1972 journey across Europe and Asia to Australia. Useful information about the overland trail did not exist at that time, so Tony and Maureen published the first Lonely Planet guidebook to meet a growing need.

From a kitchen table, then from a tiny office in Melbourne (Australia), Lonely Planet has become the largest independent travel publisher in the world, an international company with offices in Melbourne, Oakland (USA), London (UK) and Paris (France).

Today Lonely Planet guidebooks cover the globe. There is an ever-growing list of books and there's information in a variety of forms and media. Some things haven't changed. The main aim is still to help make it possible for adventurous travellers to get out there – to explore and better understand the world.

At Lonely Planet we believe travellers can make a positive contribution to the countries they visit – if they respect their host communities and spend their money wisely. Since 1986 a percentage of the income from each book has been donated to aid projects and human rights campaigns.

Updates Lonely Planet thoroughly updates each guidebook as often as possible. This usually means there are around two years between editions, although for more unusual or more stable destinations the gap can be longer. Check the imprint page (following the colour map at the beginning of the book) for publication dates.

Between editions up-to-date information is available in two free newsletters – the paper *Planet Talk* and email *Comet* (to subscribe, contact any Lonely Planet office) – and on our Web site at www.lonelyplanet.com. The *Upgrades* section of the Web site covers a number of important and volatile destinations and is regularly updated by Lonely Planet authors. *Scoop* covers news and current affairs relevant to travellers. And, lastly, the *Thorn Tree* bulletin board and *Postcards* section of the site carry unverified, but fascinating, reports from travellers.

Correspondence The process of creating new editions begins with the letters, postcards and emails received from travellers. This correspondence often includes suggestions, criticisms and comments about the current editions. Interesting excerpts are immediately passed on via newsletters and the Web site, and everything goes to our authors to be verified when they're researching on the road. We're keen to get more feedback from organisations or individuals who represent communities visited by travellers.

Lonely Planet gathers information for everyone who's curious about the planet – and especially for those who explore it first-hand. Through guidebooks, phrasebooks, activity guides, maps, literature, newsletters, image library, TV series and Web site we act as an information exchange for a worldwide community of travellers.

Research Authors aim to gather sufficient practical information to enable travellers to make informed choices and to make the mechanics of a journey run smoothly. They also research historical and cultural background to help enrich the travel experience and allow travellers to understand and respond appropriately to cultural and environmental issues.

Authors don't stay in every hotel because that would mean spending a couple of months in each medium-sized city and, no, they don't eat at every restaurant because that would mean stretching belts beyond capacity. They do visit hotels and restaurants to check standards and prices, but feedback based on readers' direct experiences can be very helpful.

Many of our authors work undercover, others aren't so secretive. None of them accept freebies in exchange for positive write-ups. And none of our guidebooks contain any advertising.

Production Authors submit their raw manuscripts and maps to offices in Australia, USA, UK or France. Editors and cartographers – all experienced travellers themselves – then begin the process of assembling the pieces. When the book finally hits the shops some things are already out of date, we start getting feedback from readers, and the process begins again ...

WARNING & REQUEST

Things change – prices go up, schedules change, good places go bad and bad places go bankrupt – nothing stays the same. So, if you find things better or worse, recently opened or long since closed, please tell us and help make the next edition even more accurate and useful. We genuinely value all the feedback we receive. Julie Young coordinates a well-travelled team that reads and acknowledges every letter, postcard and email and ensures that every morsel of information finds its way to the appropriate authors, editors and cartographers for verification.

Everyone who writes to us will find their name in the next edition of the appropriate guidebook. They will also receive the latest issue of *Planet Talk*, our quarterly printed newsletter, or *Comet*, our monthly email newsletter. Subscriptions to both newsletters are free. The very best contributions will be rewarded with a free guidebook.

Excerpts from your correspondence may appear in new editions of Lonely Planet guidebooks, the Lonely Planet Web site, *Planet Talk* or *Comet*, so please let us know if you *don't* want your letter published or your name acknowledged.

Send all correspondence to the Lonely Planet office closest to you:

Australia: PO Box 617, Hawthorn, Victoria 3122
UK: 10A Spring Place, London NW5 3BH
USA: 150 Linden St, Oakland CA 94607
France: 1 rue du Dahomey, Paris 75011

Or email us at: talk2us@lonelyplanet.com.au

For news, views and updates see our Web site: www.lonelyplanet.com

HOW TO USE A LONELY PLANET GUIDEBOOK

The best way to use a Lonely Planet guidebook is any way you choose. At Lonely Planet we believe the most memorable travel experiences are often those that are unexpected, and the finest discoveries are those you make yourself. Guidebooks are not intended to be used as if they provide a detailed set of infallible instructions!

Contents All Lonely Planet guidebooks follow roughly the same format. The Facts about the Destination chapter or section gives background information ranging from history to weather. Facts for the Visitor gives practical information on issues like visas and health. Getting There & Away gives a brief starting point for researching travel to and from the destination. Getting Around gives an overview of the transport options when you arrive.

The peculiar demands of each destination determine how subsequent chapters are broken up, but some things remain constant. We always start with background, then proceed to sights, places to stay, places to eat, entertainment, getting there and away, and getting around information – in that order.

Heading Hierarchy Lonely Planet headings are used in a strict hierarchical structure that can be visualised as a set of Russian dolls. Each heading (and its following text) is encompassed by any preceding heading that is higher on the hierarchical ladder.

Entry Points We do not assume guidebooks will be read from beginning to end, but that people will dip into them. The traditional entry points are the list of contents and the index. In addition, however, some books have a complete list of maps and an index map illustrating map coverage.

There may also be a colour map that shows highlights. These highlights are dealt with in greater detail in the Facts for the Visitor chapter, along with planning questions and suggested itineraries. Each chapter covering a geographical region usually begins with a locator map and another list of highlights. Once you find something of interest in a list of highlights, turn to the index.

Maps Maps play a crucial role in Lonely Planet guidebooks and include a huge amount of information. A legend is printed on the back page. We seek to have complete consistency between maps and text, and to have every important place in the text captured on a map. Map key numbers usually start in the top left corner.

Although inclusion in a guidebook usually implies a recommendation we cannot list every good place. Exclusion does not necessarily imply criticism. In fact there are a number of reasons why we might exclude a place – sometimes it is simply inappropriate to encourage an influx of travellers.

Introduction

The world first took notice of Denmark a millennium ago when Danish Vikings took to the seas and ravaged vast tracts of Europe. Much has changed since then. These days Denmark is the epitome of civilised society, noted for its progressive policies, widespread tolerance and liberal social-welfare system.

The smallest and most southern of the Scandinavian countries, Denmark offers visitors an interesting mix of lively cities and rural countryside. The country abounds with medieval churches, Renaissance castles and well-kept 18th century fishing villages.

Copenhagen, Scandinavia's largest and most cosmopolitan capital, is home to renowned museums, a wealth of cultural

activities and a spirited music scene ranging from top operas to jazz festivals.

Denmark's historic treasures include the preserved bodies of 2000-year-old 'bog people', a scattering of Neolithic dolmens and a number of impressive Viking ruins. Denmark also boasts quaint towns lined with period half-timbered houses, an array of white-sand beaches and scores of unspoiled islands.

Denmark is a maritime nation, bordered to the west by the North Sea and to the east by the Baltic Sea. Most Danes live within a couple of kilometres of the coast, and no place in Denmark is more than an hour's drive from the sea. The only part of Denmark connected by land to continental Europe is the Jutland peninsula, with the

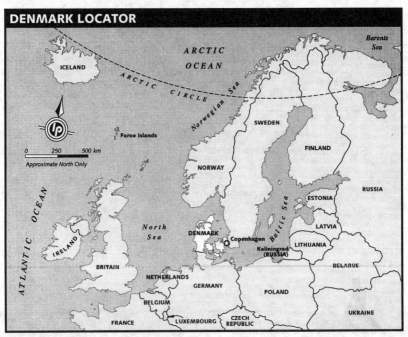

DENMARK LOCATOR

remainder of the country comprising some 400 islands.

While much of the coast of Denmark is dominated by dunes and heathland, most of the interior is given over to farmland.

Despite a few gentle hills here and there, Denmark is a largely flat country which, combined with an extensive network of cycle routes, makes it a great place to explore by bicycle.

Facts about Denmark

HISTORY

The Stone Age

There are indications that Denmark may have been inhabited by humans intermittently during the interglacial period, but the first permanent settlements were probably founded in around 12,000 BC. By that time the glacial ice, which once covered all of Denmark, had receded, exposing a low-lying tundra. The tundra's vegetation of lichen and mosses attracted drifting herds of reindeer, which were in turn followed by nomadic hunters.

A Stone Age culture developed that relied primarily on hunting but, as the climate gradually warmed and the tundra gave way to forest, the reindeer migrated farther north. Eventually the hunters were compelled to resettle near the sea and subsisted by fishing and catching sea birds and seals.

As time went on, Stone Age people began to grow more of their own food crops and by 4000 BC agriculture and the keeping of stock animals had become common practice. Woods were cleared by slash-and-burn methods and grain was sown in the resulting ash.

Villages developed around the fields and the villagers began to bury their dead in dolmens, a type of grave monument comprising upright stones topped by a large capstone; a number of these ancient dolmens can still be found in meadows today. There are no indications that social organisation extended beyond that of village life during the Stone Age.

The Bronze Age (1800-500 BC)

Bronze was introduced to Denmark in around 1800 BC, giving rise to a skilled society of artisans who used this pliable metal to make weapons, tools, jewellery and finely crafted works of art. Trade routes to the south were opened to maintain a supply of bronze; influences from as far away as Crete and Mycenae are found in Danish bronzeworks of the period.

In prehistoric Denmark, objects of great value were often buried in bogs as sacrificial offerings. One superb artefact from that era is the Sun Chariot, crafted in bronze 3500 years ago by followers of a sun cult and found by a farmer in a Zealand field in 1902. It's now on display at Nationalmuseet in Copenhagen, along with Bronze Age *lurs*, curved metal horns that were blown to call villagers to meetings and which are among the world's oldest surviving musical instruments.

The Iron Age (500 BC-800 AD)

Iron began to replace bronze in about 500 BC. Because iron ore was readily available domestically, long-distance trade trickled off during this period. Iron proved useful for creating ploughs to till fields and as a result large agricultural communities began to develop.

The linguistic and cultural roots of present-day Denmark can be traced back to the late Iron Age and the arrival of the Danes, a tribe that is thought to have migrated south from Sweden in about 500 AD.

Threat of the Franks

At the dawn of the 9th century Denmark was still on the outer perimeter of Europe when an expansion-oriented Charlemagne (768-814) extended the power of the Franks northwards to present-day northern Germany. Hoping to ward off a Frankish invasion of Denmark, Godfred, King of Jutland, reinforced an impressive earthen rampart that ran along the entire length of his southern border, all the way from the North Sea coast to the town of Hedeby (absorbed by present-day Schleswig, now part of Germany). However, the rampart, known as the Danevirke, was breached by the advancing Franks who combined their military adventures in Denmark with efforts to establish Christian missions. Both measures encountered widespread resistance from the Vikings.

To some degree the Viking expeditions – at least those that spread southwards – were a reaction to the powerful challenge posed by the Frankish Empire, which had changed the political and economic landscape of Western Europe.

Early Viking Era

Although unrecorded raids had probably been occurring for decades, the start of the Viking Age is generally accepted to date from 793 AD, when Nordic Vikings brutally raided Lindisfarne Monastery, off the coast of Northumbria in north-eastern England. Survivors of the Lindisfarne attack described the Vikings' sleek square-rigged vessels as 'dragons flying in the air' and the raiders as 'terrifying heathens'.

The early Viking raiders often targeted churches and monasteries, not for their religious significance but because they were rich repositories of gold and jewels. Because the churches also served as centres of learning, many invaluable documents, books and other cultural artefacts went up in flames during the raids. So fearsome were the Vikings that a special prayer was

Viking Fortresses

The remains of four Viking ring fortresses have been discovered in the Danish countryside. Two sites, the Trelleborg fortress in Zealand and the Fyrkat fortress near Hobro in Jutland, have been excavated and developed as sites of historic significance, with educational displays and reconstructed Viking-style buildings.

The other two fortress sites, which have been identified by archaeologists but not developed as tourist attractions, are the Nonnebakken fortress in Odense on Funen, and the Aggersborg fortress on the northern shore of the Limfjord in Jutland.

These Viking fortresses were constructed in a ring shape with thick earthen walls and gates at the four points of the compass. They were built using the Roman foot (29.33cm) as a unit of measurement and were mathematically precise and strikingly symmetrical. The long wooden stave buildings that once stood inside the walls were all of an equal measure and were clearly used as barracks for soldiers: there were no houses for nobility, as would have been found inside castle walls.

Although the purpose of these Viking camps is not entirely understood, it's now known that all were erected in the early 980s. Researchers, including Poul Nørlund, who excavated Trelleborg in the 1930s, once believed these impressive camps served as staging grounds for the invasion of England by King Sweyn I (Forkbeard). Current research, however, including the more precise dating (to 981) of the timbers used in the Trelleborg fortress, place the construction time far in advance of Forkbeard's raids on England in 993. Furthermore, most of the four base sites were not well located for naval purposes. In the case of Trelleborg, archaeologists now believe that the marsh streams that connect the camp with the sea probably weren't navigable in Viking times.

A popular current theory suggests that these fortified military camps may have been used by the monarchy to strengthen its domestic position, rather than being involved in Viking forays overseas. The massive earthen walls and moats of the fortresses certainly lend support to that theory, as they suggest a defensive function rather than an offensive one.

Whatever their exact function, the two excavated fortresses, at Trelleborg and Hobro, are intriguing places to visit, their perfectly symmetrical walls still intact after more than 1000 years.

introduced into British church services: 'From the fury of the Northmen, good Lord, deliver us'.

The Vikings were, by and large, adventurous opportunists who took advantage of the turmoil and unstable political conditions that prevailed elsewhere in Europe. In time their campaigns evolved from the mere forays of pirates to organised expeditions that established far-flung colonies overseas.

The Vikings came from Denmark, Norway and Sweden, and each group had its own dominant sphere of influence. The Swedes colonised the Baltic States, which became bases for expeditions deep into Russia, with Swedish Viking ships sailing as far east as the Caspian Sea. The Norwegian domain included Scotland, Ireland and the Shetland, Orkney and Hebrides island groups. It was a Norwegian explorer, Erik the Red, who colonised Iceland and Greenland; his son, Leif Eriksson, went on to explore the coast of North America.

The main area visited by the Danes was along the coast of Western Europe and in north-eastern England, with the first documented raid by Danish Vikings occurring in the year 835. In 845 a Danish fleet devastated Hamburg and in the same year other Viking raiders attacked Paris, successfully forcing its citizens to pay a hefty ransom in silver. With the concept of ransom established, Viking fleets began to terrorise other parts of the Frankish Empire.

In the 860s the French monk Ermentarius wrote:

The number of ships is growing. Endless flocks of Vikings keep pouring in. Everywhere the Christians are massacred, burned and pillaged. The Vikings take everything that comes their way. Nobody is able to resist them. They have captured Bordeaux, Périgeux, Limoges, Angoulême and Toulouse. Angers, Tours and Orléans have been annihilated. A countless fleet moves up the Seine and all over the country viciousness is growing. Rouen has been devastated, plundered and sacked. Paris, Beauvais and Meaux are captured, the strong fortress of Melun has been razed to the ground, Chartres is occupied, Evreux and Bayeaux plundered and all towns besieged.

Still, the Danes' main focus was on England, in part because it comprised a number of warring kingdoms, which made it a suitable target for conquest. By 850 Danish Vikings had established a settlement in Kent and in the years that followed sizeable groups of Danish colonists arrived. They soon came to control all of north-western England, although the Anglo-Saxon king Alfred the Great (871-899) successfully repelled their advances to the south and forced the Danes to accept a boundary that recognised his reign over the kingdom of Wessex.

Unification of Denmark

Denmark's lands, like the rest of Scandinavia, have a long history of being ruled by rival regional kings, although by the early 9th century Jutland (and parts of southern Norway) appears to have been more or less united under a single king. In the late 9th century a final move towards Danish unification occurred when warriors led by the Norwegian chieftain Hardegon conquered the Jutland peninsula; Hardegon then began extending his power base across the rest of Denmark.

The Danish monarchy, the oldest kingdom in Europe, can be traced back to Hardegon's son, Gorm the Old, who established his reign in the early 10th century, ruling from Jelling in central Jutland.

Gorm's son, Harald Bluetooth, took the throne in 950 AD and, during his 35 year rule, completed the conquest of Denmark. He also spearheaded the conversion of Danes to Christianity, partly to appease his powerful Frankish neighbours to the south who, a century earlier, had sent the Christian missionary Ansgar to build churches in the Danish towns of Ribe and Hedeby.

End of the Viking Era

Under the reigns of Harald Bluetooth's son Sweyn Forkbeard (985-1014) and grandsons Harald II (1014-18) and Canute the Great (1018-35), England was conquered and a short-lived Anglo-Danish kingdom was formed.

Danish Kings & Queens

The Danish monarchy dates back to Gorm the Old in the 10th century and has continued to the present day; the official name of the country is Kongeriget Danmark (Kingdom of Denmark). The monarchs, and the dates of their reign, are as follows:

Gorm (The Old)	?-950	Valdemar III	1326-30
Harald I (Bluetooth)	950-85	Valdemar IV (Atterdag)	1340-75
Sweyn I (Forkbeard)	985-1014	Oluf III (Håkonsson)	1376-87
Harald II	1014-18	Margrethe I	1387-96
Canute I (The Great)	1018-35	Erik VII (of Pomerania)	1396-1439
Hardecanute	1035-42	Christopher III (of Bavaria)	1440-48
Magnus (The Good)	1042-47	Christian I	1448-81
Sweyn II (Estridsen)	1047-74	John (Hans)	1481-1513
Harald II	1074-80	Christian II	1513-23
Canute II (The Holy)	1080-86	Frederik I	1523-33
Oluf I	1086-95	Christian III	1534-59
Erik I (The Kind)	1095-1103	Frederik II	1559-88
Niels	1104-34	Christian IV	1588-1648
Erik II	1134-37	Frederik III	1648-70
Erik III (The Lame)	1137-46	Christian V	1670-99
Sweyn III & Canute III		Frederik IV	1699-1730
(both claimed the throne)	1146-57	Christian VI	1730-46
Valdemar I (The Great)	1157-82	Frederik V	1746-66
Canute IV		Christian VII	1766-1808
(Son of Valdemar)	1182-1202	Frederik VI	1808-39
Valdemar II (The Victorious)	1202-41	Christian VIII	1839-48
Erik IV (Ploughpenny)	1241-50	Frederik VII	1848-63
Abel	1250-52	Christian IX	1863-1906
Christopher I	1252-59	Frederik VIII	1906-12
Erik V	1259-86	Christian X	1912-47
Erik VI	1286-1319	Frederik IX	1947-72
Christopher II	1320-26	Margrethe II	1972-

Canute the Great was the first true Danish king to sit on the throne of England, reigning in much the same manner as an English king except that he employed Scandinavian soldiers to maintain his command. The period of Danish rule in England ended when Canute's son Hardecanute died in 1042, after which the balance of power shifted to the English heirs of Alfred the Great. Many of the Danes who had settled in England stayed on to live under English rule.

There were a couple of later unsuccessful attempts by the Danes to reclaim England but the Viking era was clearly on the wane. The defeat of Norwegian Vikings by Harold II of England at the Battle of Stamford Bridge in 1066 marked the end of the Viking Age.

The Middle Ages

During the medieval period Denmark was plagued by internal strife, plots, counter plots and assassinations. Rival nobles, wealthy landowners and corrupt church leaders all vied for power and influence.

In 1060 King Sweyn II, wary of the influence of the bishop of Hamburg who ruled the Danish Church, divided Denmark into eight domestic dioceses and appointed his own bishops, all trusted members of the aristocracy.

Two decades later Sweyn's son, Canute II, introduced the first personal tax and sent heavy-handed bailiffs into the countryside to collect it. The resistance to the new tax was so widespread that in 1086 Canute was chased from Jutland by a band of rebellious farmers. He was eventually cornered in an Odense church and stabbed to death.

Following a brief period of stability the monarchy was again thrown into turmoil in 1131 when Knud Lavard, a nephew of the ageing king Niels, was coaxed into the forest and slain in cold blood by his cousin Magnus the Strong. Although Magnus, as Niels' oldest son, was the rightful heir to the throne, he feared that Knud Lavard's popularity as a war hero might put his cousin in a position to declare himself king.

The murder of Knud Lavard incited a civil war that resulted in the death of Magnus the Strong, Niels and five of his bishops. Knud's brother Erik Emune, who led the campaign against Magnus the Strong, ascended the throne in 1134 but his tyrannical rule ended abruptly with his assassination at a council meeting just three years later. The civil strife continued unabated throughout a series of brief reigns until Knud Lavard's son Valdemar finally took the throne in 1157.

King Valdemar I united the country, which was weary from civil war, and enacted Denmark's first written laws, known as the Jyske Lov (Jutland Code). With the cooperation of Bishop Absalon, the militaristic church leader from Roskilde, a series of successful crusades into eastern Germany were launched against the Wends, who had long raided the Danish coast with impunity.

Valdemar's successors enacted other laws that in some respects were quite

The Dannebrog

The Danish flag, the Dannebrog, is the oldest national flag in the world. Legend has it that in 1219, during an invasion of Estonia by Valdemar II (the Victorious), an imminent Danish defeat was reversed when a red banner with a white cross fell from the sky. A voice from the mist proclaimed that if the banner was raised, the Danes would win. The Danes followed the instructions, won their battle, and took this banner as their national flag.

Danes take great pride in their flag and display it whenever possible. There are strict rules connected with who may fly different versions of the flag and when; for example, it's illegal to fly the Dannebrog at night (although it's permissible to fly a pennant version after dark), and it must never touch the ground. A special swallow-tailed version belongs to the state, the royal family and the navy, and can only be flown by others with special permission.

progressive for their times. In 1282 Erik V signed a coronation charter outlawing imprisonment without just cause and agreed to hold an annual assembly of the *hof*, a national council. In 1360 Valdemar IV, under pressure from the hof, established the first supreme court and instituted a new and more powerful national council, known as the Rigsråd, comprising nobles and bishops.

The Kalmar Union

Dynastic ties formed during the 14th century formed the basis of a union between Denmark, Norway and Sweden. In 1363 Norway's King Haakon married Margrethe, daughter of the Danish king Valdemar IV. When Valdemar IV died in 1375 without a direct male heir, Oluf, the five-year-old son of Margrethe, was selected to become king of Denmark. In 1380, after King Haakon died, Oluf became the king of Norway as well.

It was actually Margrethe, not Oluf, who became leader of the two countries. Margrethe had assumed de facto control of the Danish Crown upon Valdemar's death and became the official head of state in 1387 after Oluf died before reaching majority.

In 1388 Swedish nobles rebelled against their unpopular German-born king, Albert of Mecklenburg, and turned to Margrethe for assistance. Sweden and Norway had long maintained royal ties and, indeed, prior to the selection of Albert, King Haakon had sat on the throne of Sweden as well as Norway.

The Swedes hailed Margrethe as their regent and in turn she sent Danish troops to Sweden, capturing Albert and securing victory over his forces.

In 1397 Queen Margrethe established an alliance between Denmark, Norway and Sweden, known as the Kalmar Union. A primary objective of the union was to counter the influence of the powerful Hanseatic League which had come to dominate the region's trade. Three decades earlier the Hanseatic League, from its base in northern Germany, had initiated a campaign of ransacking Danish coastal cities, stopping only after the Danish Crown agreed to pay an annual ransom and give the league a voice in Danish affairs.

In 1410 King Erik of Pomerania, Margrethe's grandson, staged an unsuccessful attack on the Hanseatic League; he then went on to exhaust the resources of the trinational government in a petty war at Denmark's border in southern Jutland. Erik's penchant for appointing Danes to public offices in Sweden and Norway further soured native aristocrats in those countries and in 1438 the Swedish council withdrew from the union, whereupon the Danish nobility deposed Erik.

Erik's successor, the Danish king Christopher III, promised to keep the administration of the countries separate and was accepted as king by both Norway and Sweden. The union continued to be a rocky one, however, marred by Swedish rebellions and a few fully fledged wars between Denmark and Sweden. In 1523 the Swedes elected their own king, Gustav Vasa, and the Kalmar Union was permanently dissolved. Norway, however, would remain under Danish rule for another three centuries.

The Lutheran Reformation

A pivotal power struggle involving the monarchy and the Catholic Church was played out during the Danish Reformation.

Frederik I ascended the throne in 1523, promising to fight heresy against Catholicism, but in an attempt to weaken the influence of Danish bishops he switched course and instead invited Lutheran preachers to Denmark. Their fiery messages against the corrupt power of the Catholic Church, which over the centuries had accumulated an ungodly amount of property and wealth, found a ready ear among the disenchanted.

After Frederik I died in 1533, the Catholic majority in the Rigsråd postponed the election of a new king, afraid that heir-apparent Prince Christian, Frederik's eldest son and a declared Lutheran, would favour the further spread of Lutheranism. Instead they attempted to position Christian's younger brother Hans as a candidate for the throne.

The country, already strained by social unrest, erupted into civil war in 1534. Mercenaries from the Hanseatic city of Lübeck, which hoped to gain control of Baltic trade by allying with Danish merchants against the Danish nobility, invaded southern Jutland and Zealand. By and large the Lübeckers were welcomed as liberators by peasants and members of the middle class.

Alarmed by the revolt against the nobility, the Rigsråd now threw its support behind Prince Christian and his father's skilful general, Johan Rantzau. Even the Catholic bishops, who realised the coronation of Christian would signal the end of the Catholic Church in Denmark, felt compelled to add their support rather than face the consequences of a peasant uprising.

In 1534 the prince was crowned King Christian III.

The rebellion raged strongest in Jutland, where manor houses were set ablaze and the peasants made advances against the armies of the aristocracy. Rantzau took control and quickly secured Jutland's southern border by cutting Lübeck off from the sea. He then made a sweeping march northward through Jutland, smashing the peasant bands in brutal fighting. Copenhagen, where merchants supported the uprising and the idea of becoming a Hanseatic stronghold, was besieged by Rantzau's troops for more than a year. Protected by its ramparts but totally cut off from the outside world, Copenhagen's citizens suffered widespread starvation and epidemics before finally surrendering in the summer of 1536, marking the end of the civil war.

With the war's end, Christian III took advantage of the opportunity to consolidate his power. He took a surprisingly lenient approach to the merchants and Copenhagen burghers who had revolted, and in turn they now pledged their allegiance to the Crown, seeing opportunities for themselves in a stabilised Denmark. On the other hand, the Catholic bishops were arrested and monasteries, churches and other ecclesiastical estates became the property of the Crown.

The Danish Lutheran Church was established as the only state-sanctioned denomination and was placed under the direct control of the king. For all practical purposes the church officials, appointed at the whim of the king, had become civil servants. They were now reliant upon the government for approval of their actions and for financial support.

Sharing power only with the nobility, the monarchy emerged from the civil war stronger than ever, buoyed by a treasury that was greatly enriched by the confiscated Church properties.

Wars with Sweden

No Danish monarch has made such a lasting impact on the Danish landscape as Christian IV (1588-1648), who succeeded his father, Frederik II, at the age of 10 and ruled for more than 50 years.

When Christian took power, Denmark held a firm grip on Baltic trade, providing strong export markets for Danish agricultural products and reaping handsome profits for landowners and merchants. With a robust economy and a seemingly boundless treasury at hand, the ambitious king established trading companies and a stock exchange, using this wealth to build new Renaissance cities, castles and fortresses throughout his kingdom.

A wealthy upper class prospered during the reign of Christian IV and many of Denmark's most lavish mansions, palaces and public buildings were erected during this period. There was also an awakening of the arts and sciences.

Unfortunately, the king's foreign policies weren't nearly as brilliant as his domestic undertakings. When the Swedes began to vie for greater influence in the Baltic, Christian, hoping to neutralise Swedish expansion, dragged Denmark into a protracted struggle known as the Thirty Years' War.

The war drained Danish resources and resulted in substantial territorial losses for Denmark. The king himself lost an eye to shrapnel when his flagship was attacked in battle. In a treaty of 1645, signed after a Swedish invasion of Jutland, the Baltic island of Gotland and two Norwegian provinces were handed over to the Swedes, while a second treaty signed in 1648 relinquished the western half of Pomerania and the bishoprics of Bremen and Verden.

In 1655 the Swedish king invaded Poland and, although the victory was swift, the Swedes found themselves bogged down trying to secure that vast country. Word of the Swedish troubles ignited nationalistic fervour throughout a Denmark that was seething for revenge. In 1657, Christian IV's successor, Frederik III, hoping to take advantage of the Polish situation, once again declared war on the Swedes. For the Danish government, itself ill-prepared for battle, it was a tremendous miscalculation.

Sweden's King Gustave, looking for an honourable way out of war-ravaged Poland, which had already been pillaged to the limit, gladly withdrew and readied his forces for an invasion of Denmark. He led his troops through Germany and into Jutland, plundering his way north.

In the winter of 1657 to 1658 – the severest winter in Danish history – King Gustave marched his soldiers across the frozen seas of the Lille Bælt between Fredericia and the island of Funen. His uncanny success unnerved the Danes and he proceeded without serious resistance across the similarly frozen Store Bælt to Lolland and then on to Falster.

The Swedish king had barely made it across the frozen waters of the Storstrømmen to Zealand when the thawing ice broke behind him, separating Gustave and his advance detachment from the main body of his forces. However, the Danes, who had amassed most of their troops in Zealand to protect Copenhagen, were in such a state of panic that they failed to recognise their sudden military advantage and, instead of capturing the Swedish king, they sued for peace and agreed to yet another disastrous treaty.

On 26 February 1658 the Treaty of Roskilde, the most lamented treaty in Denmark's history, was signed. The territorial losses were staggering, with Denmark's borders shrinking by a third. The Danes relinquished the island of Bornholm and lost the old Danish province of Skåne and all of its other territories on the Swedish mainland. Only Bornholm, which eventually staged a bloody revolt against the Swedes, would again fly the Danish flag.

Absolute Monarchy

Denmark emerged from the Swedish wars heavily in debt. In 1660 King Frederik III convened an assembly of nobles, clergy and burghers. The royal tax base had been compromised during the years of war during which the king had granted nobles and burghers (and the citizens of Copenhagen) exemptions from taxation in return for their war efforts. During the assembly, only the nobles steadfastly refused to relinquish their tax exemption, setting off a division between themselves and the other participants.

The clergy and burghers, egged on by Frederik III, resolved to clip the wings of the nobility, which over the years had secured for itself a disproportionate voice in government affairs. The Copenhagen gates were closed and the capital put under a state of siege until the nobles finally agreed to declare the charter by which they had assumed their powers of council to be null and void.

With the nobility no longer entitled to a central role in government, Frederik introduced the Act of Absolutist Succession, which conferred on the king and his heirs the unrestricted right of absolute rule. In 1665 the king enshrined the new system in an absolutist constitution called Kongeloven (The Royal Act), which was to stand as the Danish constitution for almost two centuries. In the spirit of the day, the exact content of the constitution was not made public at the time of its enactment and for nearly 50 years no copies were allowed to be printed. In its essence the document was simple enough: it declared the king to be the highest head on earth, above all human laws and inferior to God alone. Supreme legislative, judicial and military authority was placed solely in the hands of the king.

So concentrated were the royal powers under the new constitution that when Christian V ascended to the throne in 1670 as the first king to be anointed under absolute rule, it was decided that he alone had the authority to crown a king, requiring Christian to place the crown upon his own head during the church service.

Frederik III, effectively using his new powers to break the self-serving influence of the nobility, then established a predecessor to the civil service. The new bureaucracy was divided into departments that ran the foreign service, military affairs and commercial activities. Membership was open to the sons of privileged landholders but it was based upon wealth rather than noble lineage.

Crown holdings, consisting largely of manor estates and other Church properties that had been confiscated in the wake of the Reformation, were sold off en masse to satisfy the war debt.

The monarchy managed to rebuild the military and put up a reasonable fight in three more wars with Sweden (1675-79, 1699-1700 and 1709-20), but none of these campaigns enabled Denmark to regain its lost territories in southern Sweden. In the end it was the resistance of other countries (such as Holland) concerned that a more expansive Denmark could block their own access to the Baltic that ensured defeat for the Danes.

Throughout the rest of the 18th century the Danes and Swedes managed to coexist without serious hostilities, and there was even a degree of reconciliation when a Danish princess married the Swedish king Gustav III.

The Age of Reforms

The peace of the 18th century gave Denmark a badly needed economic boost and set the stage for political and social change. In 1784 the crown prince Frederik

---

Palace Follies

One of the pivotal players behind the early reforms of the 18th century was not a Danish king but a German doctor named Johan Struensee. In 1768 Struensee was appointed court physician to King Christian VII, who suffered from bouts of insanity. The doctor managed to win favour both with the ailing king, who granted Struensee broad powers of state, and with the 18-year-old queen, Caroline Matilda, who became Struensee's lover.

Emboldened by his assumed powers, the 34-year-old physician dismissed the prime minister and, over the next 16 months, succeeded in proclaiming some 2000 decrees in the name of the monarch. Contemptuous of the aristocracy, he applied the same laws to all citizens across class boundaries. The exploitation of peasants for the benefit of landlords was restricted and ill treatment in prisons, orphanages and poorhouses was outlawed. Trade barriers were lifted and money from the king's treasury was transferred to public sources for the support of new social endeavours.

Unfortunately for Struensee, he was ahead of his time – the French Revolution that would stir similar passions was still some 20 years away. Instead of broad support, Struensee elicited widespread resentment that was inflamed by unfounded rumours of his ill treatment of the ailing king. In actuality, however, it seems that the mad king had taken some comfort in being relieved of both his stately and marital duties.

In January 1772 a coup d'état was instigated at a palace ball and the conspirators, led by the queen mother, forced the king to sign a statement against Struensee, who was being arrested elsewhere in the palace. Unable to prove that Struensee had forcibly taken control of the government or even that he had been corrupt, the court instead condemned him to death for his illicit relations with the young queen, which it ruled to represent lese-majesty.

The queen, incidentally, had her marriage dissolved by a special court and was subsequently taken by a British frigate to England to live on the estate of her brother, King George III. Forbidden to take her young daughter (who was deemed to be Christian VII's heir although she was fathered by Struensee) with her to England, Caroline Matilda died a broken woman at the age of 24.

VI, then 16 years old, assumed control of the government. More benevolent and intelligent than his predecessors, Frederik VI brought progressive landowners into government and introduced a sweeping series of reforms. With the French Revolution brewing elsewhere on the continent, the government now took an interest in improving the lot of the Danish peasantry, who in centuries past had received scant attention from the powers that be.

Under the leadership of Frederik VI long-held feudal obligations were abolished, including those that had required peasants to reside within prescribed geographic boundaries and to provide compulsory labour in the domain of landlords. Large tracts of land were broken up and redistributed to the landless. The reforms extended to other areas and included the liberalisation of trade and the introduction of compulsory universal education for all children under the age of 14.

Despite these domestic reforms, Denmark found itself once again embroiled in the mire of international power struggles with the outbreak of the Napoleonic Wars (1796-1815).

The Napoleonic Wars

At the turn of the 19th century Britain, which dominated the seas, was not altogether keen on the growth of Denmark's foreign trade. In 1800, trying to counter potential threats posed by the British, Denmark signed a pact of armed neutrality with Sweden, Prussia and Russia. Britain regarded the act as hostile and in 1801 sent a naval expedition to attack Copenhagen, inflicting heavy damage on the Danish fleet and forcing Denmark to withdraw from the pact.

Denmark managed to avoid further conflicts and actually profited from war trade until 1807, when a new treaty between France and Russia once again drew the Danes closer to the conflict. The British, weary of Napoleon's growing influence in the Baltic, feared, without solid grounds, that the Danes might soon be convinced to place their fleet at the disposal of the French.

In September 1807, without attempting diplomacy, a British fleet unleashed a brutal bombardment upon neutral Copenhagen, setting much of the city ablaze and destroying its naval yard. The British then proceeded to confiscate the entire Danish fleet, sailing away with nearly 170 gunboats, frigates, transports and sloops. Ironically, the only ship left standing in Copenhagen harbour was a private yacht that the king of England had bestowed upon his nephew, Denmark's crown prince Frederik, two decades earlier.

Although the unprovoked attack was unpopular enough back home to have been roundly criticised by the British parliament, Britain nonetheless kept the Danish fleet. The British then offered the Danes an alliance – something that might have been accepted by Denmark a few months earlier but which, in the wake of the recent British assault, was now unthinkable. In October 1807 the Danes joined the continental alliance against Britain. In turn, Britain blockaded Danish and Norwegian waters, causing poverty in Denmark and outright famine in Norway. When Napoleon fell in 1814 the Swedes, by then allied with Britain, successfully demanded that Denmark cede Norway to them.

The Golden Age

Although the 19th century started out dismal and lean, by the 1830s Denmark had awakened to a cultural revolution in the arts, philosophy and literature. The times gave rise to such prominent figures as philosopher Søren Kierkegaard, theologian Nikolaj Frederik Severin Grundtvig and writer Hans Christian Andersen. It was the 'Golden Age' of the arts, with sculptor Bertel Thorvaldsen bestowing his grand neoclassical statues on Copenhagen and Christoffer Wilhelm Eckersberg introducing the Danish School of Art, which paid homage to everyday life.

Spurred on by new ideas and the rising expectations of a growing middle class, the

Crown was challenged by an unprecedented interest in democratic principles. Provincial assemblies were formed and, although their jurisdiction was nominal, they provided a vehicle for debate and gave rise to the formation of political parties. While the Crown vacillated on how far it wanted to take the democratisation of power, two growing factions – farmers and liberals – joined forces to form a united liberal party in 1846.

The powers of the absolute monarch were already on the wane when revolution swept across the continent from Paris to Germany in the spring of 1848. The new Danish king Frederik VII, under pressure from the liberal party, convened a national assembly to abolish the absolute rule of the monarchy and to draw up a democratic constitution.

The constitution, enacted on 5 June 1849, established a parliament with two chambers, Folketing and Landsting, whose members were elected by popular vote. Although the king retained a limited voice, legislative powers were now shifted to parliament. An independent judiciary was established and citizens were guaranteed the rights of free speech, religion and assembly. Denmark changed overnight from a virtual dictatorship to one of the most democratic countries in Europe.

Schleswig & Holstein

The duchies of Schleswig and Holstein in southern Jutland, which had long been under Danish rule, became restless during the nationalist fervour of the 1840s. Holstein, which was linguistically and culturally German, had already affiliated itself with the German Federation. Schleswig, on the other hand, was inhabited by people of both Danish and German heritage. When Denmark's new constitution threatened to incorporate Schleswig outright as an integral part of Denmark, the German population in Schleswig allied with Holstein and sparked a war against the Danes. The three year revolt didn't end until 1851, when Denmark agreed to accept the status quo rather than further tighten its bonds with Schleswig.

In 1864 the Prussian prime minister Otto von Bismarck declared war on a militarily weak Denmark and within a matter of months had captured Schleswig. Denmark's new border in southern Jutland was now drawn at the Kongeå river on the southern outskirts of Kolding. This further erosion of Denmark's domain opened the question of the very survival of Denmark as a nation. In the aftermath of the 1864 defeat, a conservative government took power in Denmark and retained it until the end of the century. Although reforms had come to a standstill, the conservatives oversaw a number of economic advances: the railway was extended throughout the country; Danish farmers found a ready grain market in Britain; and Denmark's major industries – shipbuilding, brewing and sugar refining – developed into maturity.

Early 20th Century

In 1901 the conservative landowners, who had long had a stranglehold on government, were ousted by the Venstrereformparti (Left Reform Party). The Venstrereformparti carried through a number of broad-minded reforms, including the application of the progressive principles of NFS Grundtvig to the education system and the revision of the constitution to extend the right to vote to women.

Denmark remained neutral during WWI. The northern part of Schleswig was returned to Denmark following a plebiscite that took place in 1920 under the accords of the Treaty of Versailles. In the period between the two world wars a social-democratic government emerged, passing landmark legislation that not only softened the effects of the Great Depression but also laid the foundations for a welfare state.

WWII

Denmark again declared its neutrality at the outbreak of WWII but, with the growing Allied presence in Norway, Germany became intent on acquiring advance coastal bases in northern Jutland.

In the early hours of 9 April 1940 the Germans crossed the frontier in southern Jutland and simultaneously landed troops at half a dozen strategic points throughout Denmark. A military airfield in Copenhagen was attacked and commando troops landed in the city, promptly taking the citadel. The German troops proceeded to Amalienborg Slot, where they met resistance from the royal guards. In the meantime the German envoy delivered an ultimatum, warning that if the Danes resisted Copenhagen would be bombed.

With German warplanes flying overhead, King Christian X and parliamentary heads hastily met at Amalienborg and decided to yield, under protest, to the Germans. The Danish government did manage to get assurances from the Nazis that Denmark would be allowed to retain a degree of internal autonomy.

The Danes, with only nominal military forces, had no capacity to ward off a German attack and little alternative but to submit. In all, the lightning blow lasted only a matter of hours, and before nightfall Denmark was an occupied country.

For three years the Danes managed to tread a thin line, basically running their own domestic affairs but doing so under Nazi supervision, until August 1943 when the Germans took outright control. The Danish Resistance movement quickly mushroomed. In October 1943, as the Nazis were preparing to round up Jewish Danes, the Resistance, using night-running fishing boats, quickly smuggled 7000 Jews, some 95% of those remaining in Denmark, into neutral Sweden.

Although the island of Bornholm was heavily bombarded by Soviet forces, the rest of Denmark emerged from WWII relatively unscathed.

Postwar Developments

Under the leadership of the Social Democrats a comprehensive social-welfare state was established in postwar Denmark. Al-though a tax revolt in the 1980s led to some revisions, those revisions in large part also assured the viability of the system, and Denmark still provides its citizens with extensive cradle-to-grave securities.

Denmark joined NATO in 1949 and the European Community (now the European Union or EU) in 1973.

The Danes have been hesitant to support expansion of the EU; indeed when the Maastricht Treaty, which established the terms of a European economic and political union, came up for ratification in Denmark in June 1992, Danish voters rejected it by a margin of 51 to 49%. After being granted exemptions from the Maastricht Treaty's common defence and single currency provisions the Danes, by a narrow majority, voted to accept the treaty in a second referendum held in May·1993.

In May 1998 Danish voters ratified the Amsterdam Treaty, which authorised the EU's institutional reforms to proceed, moving Denmark a step closer to European integration. Nonetheless, support for the EU continues to be tepid because many Danes fear the loss of local control to a European bureaucracy dominated by the stronger nations.

GEOGRAPHY

Denmark is a small country with a land area of 42,930 sq km, slightly larger than Switzerland.

The Jutland (Jylland) peninsula, where the 69km-long border with Germany is Denmark's only land connection to the European mainland, encompasses more than half of the land area, stretching 360km from north to south. In addition, Denmark has 406 islands, about 90 of which are inhabited. The capital city, Copenhagen, is on Zealand (Sjælland), the largest island. The next largest islands are Funen (Fyn), the twin islands of Falster and Lolland, and Bornholm.

Denmark is bordered to the west by the North Sea and to the east by the Baltic Sea. To the north, separating Denmark from Norway and Sweden, are the Skagerrak and

Iceland, Greenland & the Faroe Islands

When Norway broke its political ties with Denmark in the early 19th century, the former Norwegian colonies of Iceland, Greenland and the Faroe Islands stayed under Danish administration. Iceland became an independent state within the Danish realm in 1918, becoming completely independent in 1944.

The Kingdom of Denmark still includes Greenland and the Faroe Islands. The political situations of the two are not identical but both are essentially self-governing. The Faroe Islands have had home rule since 1948, Greenland since 1979.

In part because Denmark retains responsibility for their banking, defence and foreign relations, Greenland and the Faroe Islands each have two parliamentary representatives in the Danish Folketing. Unlike Denmark, however, neither Greenland nor the Faroe Islands is part of the EU.

Greenland is the world's largest island (if Australia is regarded as a continent), with a total area of 2,175,600 sq km (of which only 341,700 sq km is not under permafrost) and a population of 55,000. The Faroe Islands have a land area of 1399 sq km and a population of about 48,000.

If you want to learn more about these islands, an excellent source of information is Lonely Planet's *Iceland, Greenland & the Faroe Islands*.

Kattegat straits. Sweden is just 5km away at its closest point, across a narrow strait called the Øresund.

Most of Denmark is a lowland of fertile farms, rolling hills, beech woods and heather-covered moors. The country hasn't a single mountain; the highest elevation, at Yding Skovhøj in Jutland's Lake District (called Søhøjlandet), is a mere 173m.

There are numerous small rivers, lakes and streams. The largest lake is Arresø on the island of Zealand and the longest river is the 158km Gudenå in Jutland.

The coastline, which includes many inlets and bays, is 7314km in length. No place in Denmark is more than 52km from the sea.

CLIMATE

Denmark lies at a northern latitude stretching from 54° 34' to 57° 45', approximately the same as Moscow, central Scotland and southern Alaska. Considering its northerly location, it has a relatively mild climate, moderated by the effects of the warm Gulf Stream, which sweeps northward along the western coast.

In the coldest winter months of January and February, the average daytime temperature hovers around the freezing point – and while that may be cold, it's nearly 10°C above average for this latitude. Winter, however, also has the highest relative humidity (90%) and the cloudiest weather (with more than 80% cloud cover on an average of 17 days each month), both of which can make it feel much colder than the actual mercury reading.

From May to September there are about nine cloudy days a month and the humidity drops to a comfortable level of around 70% at noon.

Expect to see rain and grey skies in Denmark. Measurable rain falls on an average of 11 days in June (the month with the fewest rainy days) and 18 days in November, with the greatest amount of precipitation between July and December – although, when all's said and done, rain is fairly evenly spread over the year. During the most popular months for visitors (May, June, July and August) there's an average of 48mm, 55mm, 66mm and 67mm of rain, respectively.

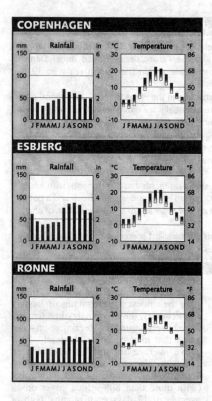

The normal mean temperature for Denmark is 2.1°C in March, 10.8°C in May, 15.6°C in July and August, 9.1°C in October and 1.6°C in December.

With its low-lying terrain and proximity to the sea, variations in climate throughout Denmark are minimal. There's a prevalent westerly wind, averaging 13 knots.

You can get a five day weather forecast in English from the Danish Meteorological Office at their Web site at www.dmi.dk or by calling ☎ 38 38 36 63.

ECOLOGY & ENVIRONMENT

The Danish environment is one that has been heavily exploited. In the early 19th century after centuries of deforestation and overgrazing, less than 4% of Denmark's land remained forested, and encroaching heathlands and meadows covered nearly 50% of the total land area. In the late 19th century much of that marginal heathland was turned into agricultural land, heavily reliant upon fertilisers and the alteration of waterways.

In all, about 20% of Danish farmland is at or near sea level, much of it on environmentally sensitive wetlands that have been made arable by draining the water with pumps. The landscape has been so intensely altered that only about 2% of Denmark's naturally winding streams remain intact, the rest having been artificially straightened.

Recent international trade agreements and EU quotas have brought an end to many agricultural subsidies for Danish farmers and the most marginal farmland is no longer economically viable. These conditions, along with a growing environmental awareness, have created a backdrop for the implementation of widespread restoration projects. Under a nature management act passed in 1990, the government has instituted an ambitious programme to restore wetlands, re-establish salt marshes and realign streams to their original courses. That same act called for the doubling of forest cover over the next 100 years.

On another front, Denmark has vowed not to build nuclear power plants. Instead, it's developed an extensive network of alternative energy sources, most notably wind power. Rows of sleek wind turbines are an increasingly common sight on the Danish landscape, particularly in breezy coastal areas. Denmark is also making strides in harnessing solar energy, with the construction in 1996 of Europe's largest solar power station on the island of Ærø.

Recycling is extensive, with more than 80% of all paper produced from used paper and roughly half of all waste recycled. Over recent decades many air-pollution levels, including those of sulphur dioxide, have dropped by nearly 50%, and since 1993 Danish businesses have been required to pay a tax based on their carbon dioxide emissions.

In 1971 Denmark created a cabinet-level
ministry to deal specifically with environmental matters, becoming the first
industrialised country to do so. The EU has
placed its European Environment Agency
in Copenhagen and the Danes have taken
an active role in promoting international
efforts to reduce pollution.

FLORA & FAUNA
Flora
About 12% of Denmark has tree cover but
primary forest is rare. Instead, most woods
are planted, the bulk of them having been
reforested either for conservation and recre-
ation purposes or for timber production.
Most of the commercial forests are now
planted with fast-growing conifers such as
spruce and fir.

Denmark's natural woodlands are largely
deciduous with a prevalence of beech and
oak trees. Other common trees found in
mixed woodlands are hazel, maple, pine,
birch, aspen, lime (linden) and horse chestnut. Elm trees are also common, but an
outbreak of Dutch elm disease that hit
Denmark in 1993 has devastated these
stately trees in many areas. In Copenhagen,
for example, virtually all of the city's estimated 10,000 elm trees contracted the
disease and most have been cut down.

Heath, bogs and dunes cover about 7% of
Denmark's land area and are particularly
common in western Jutland. In an effort
to stem coastal erosion, large tracts of the
dunes have been planted with lyme and
marram grasses, the deep root systems of
these species help to hold the sand in place.
Wild pink and white beach roses, of the
variety *Rosa rugosa*, are common on sand
dunes as well.

In the spring, cultivated fields of brilliant
yellow rapeseed flowers, a member of the
mustard family, are a particularly lovely
addition to the farm-belt areas.

In the summer, gardens throughout
Denmark are planted with the usual colourful mix of temperate-climate flowers. The
national flower is the marguerite, a white
daisy with a yellow centre.

Fauna
The loss of much natural wilderness habitat
to cultivated farmland has spelt the end
for numerous animal species in Denmark.
Approximately 30% of all mammal species
and breeding birds in Denmark are listed as
either threatened, vulnerable or rare.

Among the mammals that have disappeared are the elk, bear, wolf, wild boar and
beaver. The freshwater otter, which was
plentiful as late as the 1950s, is today the
most endangered mammal in the country,
with perhaps as few as 100 remaining.

The largest wild species still found is the
red deer, which can weigh over 200kg.
Denmark is also home to the roe deer,
fallow deer, wild hare, fox, squirrel, hedge-
hog and badger.

Nearly 400 bird species have been observed in Denmark; of these about 160
breed in the country. Some of the more
commonly seen birds include the magpie,

crow, sparrow, pigeon, coot, goose and duck.

The western coast of Jutland attracts migrating water birds and breeding waders such as the avocet, dunlin, ruff, redshank, lapwing and black-winged godwit. The gull-billed tern, which is a threatened species in Europe, breeds on the uninhabited fjord island of Fjandø, as do some of the country's largest colonies of the sandwich tern, arctic tern and black-headed gull.

The easternmost island, Bornholm, is home to relatively large numbers of rooks and nightingales and is a resting spot for migratory ducks and waders. The nearby Ertholmene Islands provide a bird refuge that hosts breeding eider ducks, razorbills, guillemots and other sea birds.

Birds threatened by extinction, mostly because of the destruction of their habitat, include the wood sandpiper, golden plover and black grouse, all once common birds of the heathland. The national bird is the swan, widespread in urban parks and suburban ponds throughout the country.

There are 68 indigenous species of butterfly, though many are rare; since 1950 nine species have vanished altogether. The national butterfly is the small tortoiseshell, a pretty brownish-orange butterfly with a blue fringe; it's common in all areas of the country from early July and is unusual in that it hibernates as a fully grown insect.

Eleven species of frogs and toads can be found in Denmark, including the common toad, green tree frog and fire-bellied toad; however, because of the loss of wetlands, amphibians have disappeared from approximately 50% of their breeding sites in the past 50 years. Efforts are being made to turn the situation around, most notably in Bornholm where 400 water holes have been restored to create a habitat for the green tree frog, whose breeding area on the island had diminished by 90%.

National Parks

Because Denmark does not have large expanses of wilderness, it's not surprising that it does not have a system of national parks.

Its largest contiguous area of woodlands is Rold Skov, a 77 sq km public forest that contains Denmark's only national park, Rebild Bakker.

Although sizeable tracts of wilderness don't exist, numerous state-administered nature conservation areas are spread around the country which collectively encompass about 4% of the nation's land area. These include beaches, coastal forests, heathlands and inland woods and lakes. Many are quite scenic and have been selected for some particular natural quality or historical significance. Most are crossed with hiking and biking trails and, although the majority can be walked in an hour or two, some areas are long and narrow and thus suitable for longer outings.

GOVERNMENT & POLITICS

Denmark is a constitutional monarchy with a single-chamber parliamentary system. The parliament, called Folketing, is responsible for enacting legislation. The prime minister leads the government with the assistance of cabinet ministers who head the various government departments. Queen Margrethe II, who has been on the throne since 1972, has a largely ceremonial role but her signature is required on the enactment of new legislation.

Honest as a Dane

Ever wondered what the least corrupt country in the world is?

Well, according to Transparency International, the answer is Denmark – which, in 1998, took the honours for the second year in a row. The Berlin-based anti-corruption watchdog organisation measures corruption through a combination of studies and public opinion polls.

For those keeping score, Finland, Sweden and New Zealand came in second, third and fourth, respectively, while Cameroon and Paraguay sit at the bottom of the list.

Denmark's Royal Family

Denmark's current monarch, Queen Margrethe II, was born on 16 April 1940, the eldest daughter of Frederik IX (1899-1972), who had no sons. As a result of a 1953 referendum that amended the sex-bias of the Danish constitution to allow women to succeed to the throne, Margrethe was proclaimed queen on 15 January 1972, the first female monarch of Denmark since 1396. Margrethe is a popular queen who has been credited with giving a fresh perspective to the Danish monarchy and minimising the privilege that has traditionally separated royalty from commoners.

In addition to performing her ceremonial roles as head of state, the queen is an accomplished artist. She has illustrated a number of books, including Tolkien's *Lord of the Rings*, and has also designed Christmas seals for UNICEF and stamps for the Danish postal service. The queen has been active in the theatre as well, designing costumes for a production of Hans Christian Andersen's *The Shepherdess and the Chimney Sweep* and creating both the sets and costumes for Det Kongelige Teater's ballet *Et Folkesage* (The Legend). Together with her French-born husband Prince Henrik, the queen translated Simone de Beauvoir's novel *Tous les hommes sont mortels* (All Men Are Mortal) from its original French into Danish.

Queen Margrethe and Prince Henrik have two sons. Crown prince Frederik was born in 1968 and, like his mother, is a graduate of Århus University, where he studied politics and law. Prince Joachim was born in 1969 and attended a smaller Danish college. Both princes did stints in the armed services following their graduation and have also undertaken work internships overseas – Joachim on a farm in Australia and Frederik at a Californian winery.

The minimum voting age is 18; parliamentary elections are held at least once every four years. The Socialdemokratiet (Social Democrats), Venstre (Liberals – a right-of-centre party) and Det Konservative Folkeparti (Conservative Party) are the three main political parties, though there are now close to a dozen parties represented in the 179 seat parliament.

The major parties are quite moderate and most parliamentary members linger near the centre; however, one noteworthy change in the political landscape is the emergence of the far-right Danish People's Party which, in the 1998 election, captured 13 seats on an anti-immigration, anti-EU platform. In a bit of a counterbalance, the other right-leaning party, Fremskridtspartiet (Progress Party), saw its representation drop from 11 delegates to just four during that election.

Socialdemokratiet, the largest party, is a moderate socialist party. It's founded on the belief in the right of guaranteed security to all in the form of extensive social-welfare programmes that are funded by high taxes. Socialdemokratiet first came to power in 1924 and has been in power, either alone or as part of a coalition government, for most of the time since then.

Since 1993 Poul Nyrup Rasmussen, the leader of Socialdemokratiet, has led the government under various left-centre coalitions. As prime minister, Rasmussen has attempted to minimise the boundaries between politicians and the general population. He attracted widespread attention in 1995 by joining a bicycle rally to Paris in protest of the resumption of French nuclear testing in the southern Pacific.

The main domestic issues revolve around reforming taxes in the hope of lowering the nation's 50%-plus income-tax rate, the highest in the EU. The latest tax reform initiatives focus on shifting from direct to indirect taxes by upping consumption taxes such as those levied on petrol and motor vehicles. In an attempt to capitalise on progressive environmental sentiments, many of the new taxes are being promoted as 'green taxes'.

In addition to having a national government, Denmark is divided administratively into 14 counties and 273 municipalities. Many government services, such as urban transport, health services and primary education, are administered at a local level.

ECONOMY

Denmark has the highest per-capita GNP in the EU and its citizens enjoy a high standard of living. It has a workforce of 2.9 million, divided almost evenly between men and women. Relative to other European countries the Danish economy remains strong, despite the fact that the government impounds almost half of its GNP for social services and transfer payments to the disadvantaged.

Recent changes in employment policy, including more liberal parental leave and enhanced job training programmes, have contributed to a reduction in the unemployment rate to 7%. Generous income-transfer payments, including early retirement pay, pensions and unemployment benefits, have buffered the financial impact on those without work.

Almost all government funding is derived from taxes: one-third comes from value-added tax (VAT) and taxes on petrol, alcohol and other dutiable items; 53% comes from income taxes; and a mere 3.7% is derived from corporate taxes. The government, although having a socialist slant on social welfare issues, is not involved in the ownership of capital; on the contrary, a number of state-funded services, including such basics as the ambulance and firefighting services, are provided by privately owned companies.

Nearly two-thirds of Denmark's land area is under cultivation. Of the country's 61,000 farms, the vast majority are still owned and operated by families. The average farm size is 43 hectares. Although family-operated, farms are highly mechanised and efficient, and 65% of their output is exported abroad.

Important crops include wheat, barley, sugar beet and rapeseed, which is used to make canola oil.

Livestock raising is also important. Denmark is the world's leading exporter of canned ham and Danish dairy farms supply the milk used to make the country's famous cheeses and butter cookies.

Fishing remains economically important. Denmark boasts the largest fish catches of any EU country, with a fleet of about 2700 trawlers. The main fishes caught for human consumption are cod, herring, sprat, mackerel and plaice, but about 20% of the catch is industrial fish used to produce fish oil and fish meal.

Danish industry provides roughly 20% of the nation's employment. Important industrial exports include beer, home electronics, furniture, silverware and porcelain. Food processing and the manufacturing of machinery are also significant industries. Denmark is self-sufficient for both oil and gas and since 1991 has been an exporter of these fossil fuels.

POPULATION & PEOPLE

Denmark's population is about 5.3 million, with 70% living in urban areas. The four largest cities are Copenhagen (1.4 million), Århus (265,000), Odense (184,000) and Aalborg (155,000).

Denmark is almost entirely inhabited by ethnic Danes, people of the Teutonic ancestry common to all of Scandinavian. Foreign nationals account for just 4.5% of Denmark's population, increased from 2% in 1984. More than 25% of foreign nationals come from Western Europe, particularly from Germany and the Nordic countries.

A relaxation of immigration policies during the economic expansion of the 1960s attracted 'guest workers', many of whom established a permanent niche, and there are now sizeable Turkish and Pakistani communities. More recent humanitarian policies, introduced in response to famine and war crises, have resulted in small Somalian and Ethiopian immigrant communities and there are a growing

What's in a Name?

Of the five million-plus Danes on the planet today, two-thirds have a surname ending in 'sen'. The three most common – Jensen, Nielsen and Hansen – account for 23% of all Danish surnames. Next, in order of frequency, are Pedersen, Andersen, Christensen, Larsen and Sørensen.

You may notice a trend here. The most common Danish surnames are derived from the most common given names with 'sen' suffixed on. This is because up until the mid-19th century most peasants and other rural folk did not have a permanent family name but simply added 'sen', meaning 'son', onto their father's first name. Thus if your father was Peder Hansen and your name was Eric, you would be known as Eric Pedersen.

number of refugees from the former Yugoslavia.

The average life expectancy for Danish people is 72.6 years for men and 77.8 years for women. There's been a sharp decline in the birth rate in recent decades and the population is expected to fall below five million by the year 2020. Currently only 21% of Danes are aged 17 or younger. The disparity between the age groups could bode poorly for the future of the social-welfare system because there will be progressively fewer people of working age supporting a proportionately larger number of pensioners.

EDUCATION

Education is free and nine years of schooling starting at the age of seven is compulsory. Preschool and kindergarten are optional; about two-thirds of children aged five and six attend.

About half of all Danish students who graduate from secondary school continue on to higher education. Slightly more than half of these graduates enrol in vocational programmes providing training in business,

nursing, maritime studies and other career-specific fields. Most others attend one of the five state-supported universities, of which the most elite is Copenhagen University (founded in 1479); the others are in Århus, Aalborg, Odense and Roskilde. Men and women are evenly represented in higher education, although female students tend to enrol in shorter courses than those chosen by men.

ARTS
Fine Arts

Prior to the 19th century, Danish art tended to revolve around formal portraits of the bourgeoisie, the aristocracy and the royal family. One of the most highly regarded portrait painters was Jens Juel (1745-1802).

Denmark's 'Golden Age' of the arts (1800-50) produced such luminaries as Christoffer Wilhelm Eckersberg (1783-1853), who depicted more universal scenes of everyday Danish life, and Eckersberg's student Christen Købke (1810-48), who was little known in his time but is now regarded as one of the most important painters of the era. The leading Danish sculptor of the day was Bertel Thorvaldsen (1770-1844), who re-created classical sculptures during a long sojourn in Rome and returned to Copenhagen to establish his own museum.

Another artistic movement was the Skagen school, which was active in the late 18th and early 19th centuries and which specialised in romantic seaside subjects with an emphasis on the effects of natural light. Leading Skagen painters included PS Krøyer, Michael Ancher and Anna Ancher.

The COBRA (COpenhagen-BRussels-Amsterdam) movement, which was formed in 1948 with the aim of exploiting the free artistic expression of the unconscious, had a significant impact on 20th century Danish art. One of its founders, Danish artist Asger Jorn (1914-73), achieved an international following for his abstract paintings, many of which evoke imagery from Nordic mythology.

DANISH MODERN DESIGN

Denmark has distinguished itself as a leader in the field of applied design, with a focus on cool clean lines, graceful shapes and streamlined functionality. These concepts have been applied to everything from coffeepots to the construction of concert halls.

Architecture

In the second half of the 20th century a number of Danish architects have taken a leading role in introducing new designs both at home and abroad. Perhaps the most influential of these is Jørn Utzon who, in the 1950s, took the basic elements of a California ranch house design and modified them into a popular style of suburban Danish house that can be found throughout Denmark today. These homes utilise an open floor plan and an abundance of windows and glass doors that are designed to merge indoor spaces with the outdoors and utilise precious sunlight during long winters. Utzon has also been responsible for designing a number of eminent public buildings in Denmark, such as a performing arts centre, Musikhuset Esbjerg, in Southern Jutland. His most monumental claim to fame, however, lies in Australia, where he designed the Sydney Opera House. Constructed in the 1960s, this striking waterfront building with its multiple shell design is one of the world's most famous and readily recognised landmarks.

Other notable contemporary Danish architects include Johan von Spreckelsen, who designed a European landmark, the huge cube-like La Grande Arche in Paris, in 1984, and Arne Jacobsen, who was an innovator in international modernism, producing Danish interpretations of the Bauhaus style. Some of Jacobsen's best-known works are additions at St Catherine's College in Oxford, England, and the Herrenhaus concert hall in Hanover, Germany, the latter created in collaboration with his partner Otto Weitling. Weitling himself has designed some significant European buildings, including the much-acclaimed Museum of Art in Düsseldorf in 1986.

Furniture

Danish architects place such great emphasis on 'form following function' that they typically design a room only after considering the styles of furniture that are most likely to be used there. Consequently it's not surprising that several Danish architects have crossed over to the field of furniture design, where their work has had an even broader impact.

Modern Danish furniture focuses on the practical refinement of style and the principle that design should be tailored to the comfort of the user. Kaare Klint, who both worked as an architect and founded the furniture design department at the Royal Academy of Fine Arts in Copenhagen, modified a number of chair designs to add functionality, developing the smooth, unadorned style that was to become the prototype of contemporary Danish furniture design.

In 1949 one of Klint's contemporaries, Hans Wegner, created the Round Chair; its fluid curving lines made it an instant classic and a model for many furniture designers to follow. So popular was the chair at the time that it appeared on the cover of a number of international interior-design magazines, helping to establish the first successful overseas export market for Danish furniture.

A decade later architect Arne Jacobsen created the Ant, a form chair designed to be mass produced, which became the model for the stacking chairs found in schools and cafeterias worldwide. Jacobsen also designed the Egg and the Swan; both are rounded, uncomplicated upholstered chairs with revolving seats perched on pedestal stands.

Danish design prevails in stylish lamps as well. Denmark's best-known lamp designer is Poul Henningsen, who in his work has

Right: Cross-fertilisation of ideas has borne fruit in Danish design: architect Arne Jacobsen turned his hand to furniture, resulting in the classic Egg chair.

emphasised the need for lighting to be soft, for the shade to cast a pleasant shadow and for the light bulb to be blocked from direct view. His PH-5 lamp, which he created in 1958, remains one of the most popular hanging lamps sold in Denmark today.

Silverware & Porcelain

The clean lines of industrial design are also evident in Danish silver, which combines aesthetics with function. Danish silverwork is highly regarded both at home and abroad, the chief design criteria being that the item is attractive yet simple, as well as easy to use. The father of modern Danish silverwork was the sculptor and silversmith Georg Jensen, who artistically incorporated curvilinear designs; his namesake company is still a leader in Denmark silverwork. Two of Jensen's students, Kay Bojesen and Henning Koppel, are also leading names in Danish silverwork.

One of the world's most famous sets of porcelain is the Flora Danica dinner service created by Royal Porcelain Manufactory (now Royal Copenhagen). No two pieces of this 1800 piece set are alike; each is hand-painted with a different native Danish wildflower or other plant, then rimmed with gold. Some of the pieces have trompe l'oeil features, such as cup handles that look like flower stems. Commissioned in 1790 by the crown prince Frederik, the original set took 13 years to complete and is still part of the Danish royal collection today; pieces of that original set are on display at Copenhagen's Rosenborg Slot. You can also see examples – or if money is no obstacle, purchase your own reproduction set – at the Royal Copenhagen porcelain shop on Strøget in Copenhagen.

The other leader in Danish porcelain is Bing & Grøndahl, which was founded in 1853 to compete with Royal Copenhagen for the lucrative ceramics market. It too produces a variety of tableware, much of it decorated with finely painted floral designs. Bing & Grøndahl is perhaps most widely known for its annual Christmas plates, which have been issued for more than 100 years. These plates, which are cobalt blue and white with a traditional winter design, are collected by millions of people worldwide.

The trademark gentle curves of Danish design are also evident in industrial and other products ranging from plastic blocks created by Lego to avant-garde sound systems and televisions produced by Bang & Olufsen.

Left: Leading lights: Poul Henningsen's series of PH lamps is globally renowned.

Literature

The first half of the 19th century has been characterised as the 'Golden Age' of Danish literature. The foremost writers of that period included Adam Oehlenschläger (1779-1850), a romantic lyric poet who also wrote short stories and plays; Steen Steensen Blicher (1782-1848), a writer of tragic short stories; Hans Christian Andersen (1805-75), whose fairy tales have been translated into more languages than any other book except the Bible; and philosopher Søren Kierkegaard (1813-55), who is considered the father of existentialism.

Around 1870 a trend towards realism emerged, focusing on contemporary issues

Hans Christian Andersen

Born on 2 April 1805 in Odense, Hans Christian Andersen was the son of a poor cobbler. At the age of 14 he ran away to Copenhagen 'to become famous' and the following year entered Det Kongelige Teater (The Royal Danish Theatre) as a student of dance and music. In 1822, on the recommendation of the theatre board, he was sent to a preparatory school in Helsingør and in 1828 he passed his university entrance exams.

The following year Andersen self-published his first book, *A Walk From Holmen's Canal to the Eastern Tip of Amager*. In 1831, after being jilted in a love affair with Riborg Voight of Faaborg, Andersen travelled to Germany and wrote the first of a number of stories about his travels abroad.

In 1835 he finally made a name for himself with the successful novel *The Improvisators*. He followed that with his first volume of fairy tales, *Tales, Told for Children*, which included such classics as 'The Tinderbox' and 'The Princess and the Pea'. Over the next few decades he continued writing novels and accounts of his travels, but it was his fairy tales that brought him worldwide fame.

Andersen had a superb talent for humanising animals, plants and inanimate objects without compromising their original character. In his stories the villains are not evil characters such as witches or trolls, but rather human weaknesses such as indifference and vanity, and his tales are imbued with moral realism instead of wishful fantasy. Some of his most famous fairy tales are 'The Little Mermaid', 'The Ugly Duckling', 'The Snow Queen', 'The Constant Tin Soldier', 'The Nightingale' and the satirical 'The Emperor's New Clothes'.

Besides his fairy tales and poems, Andersen wrote six novels, numerous travel books, many dramatic works and two autobiographies, of which the most highly regarded is *The Fairy Tale of My Life*. All in all, he published 156 stories and other works.

Andersen had a penchant for travel and over his lifetime made 29 journeys abroad, several of them lasting many months. On 4 August 1875, at the age of 70, he died of liver cancer at a villa outside Copenhagen. His grave is in the capital's Assistens Kirkegård.

Søren Kierkegaard

Denmark's most famous philosopher, Søren Kierkegaard was born into a prosperous Copenhagen family on 5 May 1813. When Søren was in his early 20s his father died, leaving him with an inheritance that freed him from the need to work. He studied theology and philosophy at Copenhagen University and devoted his entire life to studying and writing.

Kierkegaard was vehemently opposed to the philosophy of Georg Wilhelm Friedrich Hegel, which was prevalent in 19th century Europe and embraced by the Danish Lutheran Church. In contrast, Kierkegaard's writings challenged the individual to make choices entirely of his or her own among the alternatives that life offered. In his first great work, *Either/Or*, published in 1843, the alternative was between aesthetic pleasures or an ethical life. This work, like many that followed, was in part inspired by Kierkegaard's lifelong pain over breaking off an engagement to a young woman named Regine Olsen. He continued to wrestle with the implications of his broken engagement in subsequent writings, including *Fear and Trembling* (1843), which compares the biblical tale of Abraham's sacrifice of Isaac to Kierkegaard's own sacrifice.

Kierkegaard's greatest attack on Hegelianism, and his most philosophically important work, was *Concluding Unscientific Postscript to the Philosophical Fragments* (1846), which passionately expounded the tenets of existentialism.

Kierkegaard was considered by many members of the establishment to be a fanatic and his friends were few, even in the literary world. His works remained virtually unknown outside Denmark until the 20th century.

The last years of Kierkegaard's life were dominated by an acrimonious battle with the established Church. It slowly drained his health and he died of exhaustion in a Copenhagen hospital in 1855 at the age of 42. At the time of his death, Kierkegaard felt his works had largely fallen upon deaf ears, but his writings posthumously formed the vanguard of the work of existentialist philosophers worldwide.

---

of the day. A writer of this genre, novelist Henrik Pontoppidan, won the Nobel Prize for Literature in 1917 shortly after publishing the epic *The Realm of the Dead*, which attacked materialism. Another Dane who won the Nobel Prize for Literature was Johannes Vilhelm Jensen (1873-1950), who wrote the six volume novel *The Long Journey*, and *The Fall of the King*, a story about Danes in Renaissance times. Better known outside Denmark is Martin Andersen Nexø (1869-1954), whose novels about the proletariat, the four volume *Pelle the Conqueror* and *Ditte, Child of Man*, helped to bring attention to the conditions of the poor and spurred widespread reform in Denmark.

The most famous Danish writer of the 20th century, Karen Blixen (1885-1962), started her career with *Seven Gothic Tales*,

Great Danes

Thirteen Danes have received the Nobel Prize since 1901, the year in which it was first awarded. They are as follows:

1903 Physiology/Medicine: Niels R Finsen, for his research including the introduction of light-radiation treatment for diseases such as lupus

1908 Peace: Fredrik Bajer, for his work as a peace activist and writer

1917 Literature: Karl A Gjellerup, for poetry inspired by lofty ideals, and Henrik Pontoppidan, for his insightful descriptions of everyday life in Denmark

1920 Physiology/Medicine: Auguste Krogh, for discovering the capillary motor-regulating mechanism

1922 Physics: Niels Bohr, one of the fathers of atomic power, for his investigation into radiation and the structure of atoms

1926 Physiology/Medicine: cancer researcher Johannes AG Fibiger, for his discovery of the Spiroptera carcinoma

1943 Physiology/Medicine: Henrik CP Dam (with Edward Doisy of the USA), for the discovery of Vitamin K

1944 Literature: Johannes V Jensen, for the strength of his poetic imagination

1975 Physics: Aage Bohr and Ben Mottelson (with James Rainwater of the USA), for the discovery of the link between collective motion and particle motion in atomic nuclei and the development of the theory of the structure of the atomic nucleus

1984 Physiology/Medicine: Niels K Jerne (with Georges JF Koehler of Germany and Cesar Milstein of the UK), for theories on the development and control of the immune system and the discovery of the principle of monoclonal antibody production

1997 Chemistry: Jens C Skou (with John Walker of the UK and Paul Boyer of the USA), for discovering aspects of how the body's cells store and use energy

---

which was published in New York under the pen name Isak Dinesen. She is best known for *Out of Africa*, the memoirs of her farm life in Kenya, which she wrote in 1937. Other works include *Winter's Tales* (1942), *The Angelic Avengers* (1944), *Last Tales* (1957), *Anecdotes of Destiny* (1958) and *Shadows on the Grass* (1960). See the boxed text under Rungsted in the Øresund Coast section of the North Zealand chapter for more details of her life.

Denmark's foremost contemporary novelist is Peter Høeg who in 1992 wrote the international bestseller *Miss Smilla's Feeling For Snow* (published in the USA as *Smilla's Sense of Snow*), a suspense mystery set in Copenhagen and Greenland that touches upon Danish colonialism and the struggle for Greenlandic cultural identity. Since then, three other Høeg novels have been published in English: *The History of Danish Dreams*, a narrative that sweeps through many generations of a Danish family; *Borderliners*, which deals with social issues surrounding private schooling in Denmark; and *The Woman and the Ape*, the main character of which saves a rare primate from the clutches of scientists. All of Høeg's works focus on nonconformist characters on the margins of Danish society.

Theatre & Dance

Det Kongelige Teater (The Royal Theatre) in Copenhagen first opened in 1748 as a court theatre, performing the plays of Denmark's most famous playwright,

Ludvig Holberg (1684-1754). Today its repertoire encompasses international works, including Shakespearian plays as well as classical and contemporary Danish plays.

In the mid-19th century, Den Kongelige Ballet (The Royal Danish Ballet), which also performs at Det Kongelige Teater, took its present form under the leadership of the French choreographer and ballet master August Bournonville (1805-79). Today Den Kongelige Ballet, which has a troupe of nearly 100 dancers, still performs a number of Bournonville's romantic ballets, such as *La Sylphide* and *Napoli*, along with more contemporary works. Considered the finest ballet company in northern Europe, it is currently directed by Peter Schaufuss, who started his career in Denmark as a dancer and previously directed the English National Ballet and the Berlin Ballet.

Also based in Det Kongelige Teater is Den Kongelige Opera (The Royal Danish Opera), which has an ensemble of 32 singers and a renowned 60 member opera chorus. It performs about 16 operas each season.

Det Kongelige Kapel (The Royal Danish Orchestra) was founded in 1448, giving it claim to be the oldest orchestra in the world; it accompanies the ballet and opera performances at Det Kongelige Teater.

Cinema

The best-known Danish director of the early 20th century was Carl Theodor Dreyer (1889-1968), who directed numerous films including the 1928 French masterpiece *La Passion de Jeanne d'Arc*, which was acclaimed for its rich visual textures and innovative use of close-ups. In the midst of WWII, Dreyer boldly filmed *Vredens Dag* (Day of Wrath), which made so many allusions to the tyranny of Nazi occupation that he was forced to flee to Sweden.

It wasn't until the 1980s that Danish directors attracted a more widespread international audience. In 1988 *Babette's Feast*, directed by Gabriel Axel, won the Academy Award for Best Foreign Film. *Babette's Feast* was an adaptation of a story

written by Karen Blixen, whose novel *Out of Africa* had been turned into an Oscar-winning Hollywood movie just three years earlier.

In 1989 Danish director Bille August won the Academy Award for Best Foreign Film as well the Cannes Film Festival's Palme d'Or award for *Pelle the Conqueror*, a film adapted from Martin Andersen Nexø's book about the harsh reality of life as an immigrant in 19th century Denmark. August also directed *Smilla's Sense of Snow* (1997), based on the bestseller by Peter Høeg, which starred Julia Ormond and Gabriel Byrne, and *Les Miserables* (1998), an accessible adaptation of Victor Hugo's classic tale of good and evil, starring Liam Neeson and Geoffrey Rush.

Up-and-coming Danish directors include Lars von Trier, whose best-known film to date is *Breaking the Waves* (1996), and Thomas Vinterberg, whose film *Festen* (The Celebration) won the jury prize at the 1998 Cannes Film Festival. Both directors are known for their minimalist approach, which involves using only hand-held cameras, shooting on location with natural light and an absence of superficial action or music.

SOCIETY & CONDUCT

Danes pride themselves on being thoroughly modern, and the wearing of folk costumes, the celebration of traditional festivals and the tendency to cling to old-fashioned customs is less prevalent in Denmark than in most other European countries. There are, of course, traditional aspects of the Danish lifestyle that aren't apparent at first glance.

Perhaps nothing captures the Danish perspective more than the concept of *hygge* which, roughly translated, means cosy and snug. It implies shutting out the turmoil and troubles of the outside world and striving instead for a warm intimate mood. Hygge affects how Danes approach many aspects of their personal lives, from the design of their homes to their fondness for small cafés and pubs. There's no greater compliment

Christmas Celebrations

By far the most eagerly awaited holiday in Denmark is *jul* (Christmas). Celebrations begin on 1 December with the lighting of candles, the placing of wreaths in windows and the opening of advent calendars. Every day from 1 December to 23 December children unwrap a small gift. A couple of weeks before the holiday a Christmas tree is brought in and decorated with candles, heart-shaped ornaments and strings of miniature Danish flags.

The main celebration takes place on 24 December, when Danes have their traditional Christmas dinner. This usually features apple-stuffed roast goose or duck, sweet and sour red cabbage, liver pâté, caramelised potatoes and an abundance of sweets, including *brune kager* (gingerbread), *klejner* (fried knotted dough) and *pebernødder* (spiced cookies). After the meal, the family joins hands and circles around the tree, singing traditional Christmas songs; the unwrapping of presents follows. On 25 December most Danes have a Christmas lunch featuring a hearty cold table with plenty of leftovers from the day before.

that a Dane can give their host than to thank them for a cosy evening.

One thing visitors will notice is how prevalently Danes display their national flag, called the Dannebrog. Red with a white cross, the flag can be seen hanging pennant-style in shopping streets, as graphics in magazine ads and flying high on the flagpoles that stand beside virtually every home in the countryside. To Danes, displaying the Dannebrog is an equal measure of colourful adornment and national pride. For more information on the history and etiquette connected with the Dannebrog, see the boxed text in the History section earlier in this chapter.

Visitors will find Danes to be relaxed, casual and not given to extremes. They are tolerant of different lifestyles; indeed, in 1989 Denmark became the first European country to legalise same-sex marriages and to offer gay partners the same rights as heterosexual couples (see the boxed text 'Gay Marriages' in the Facts for the Visitor chapter for more details).

RELIGION

More than 90% of all Danes officially belong to Folkekirken (Danish People's Church) an Evangelical Lutheran denomination which is the state-supported national church; however, fewer than 5% are regular churchgoers.

Although Folkekirken is connected with the state, Danes enjoy freedom of religion and in most larger cities there are also places of worship for Catholics, Anglicans and Jews.

LANGUAGE

The national language is Danish; English and German are widely spoken. For more information on Danish, including a guide to pronunciation and a list of useful words and phrases, see the language chapter at the back of this book. For a more comprehensive guide to the language, as well as those of the surrounding countries and Iceland, get a copy of Lonely Planet's *Scandinavian Europe phrasebook*.

Facts for the Visitor

SUGGESTED ITINERARIES

Depending on the length of your stay and your interests, you might like to see and do the following:

Two Days
Buy a Copenhagen Card and explore the capital's palaces, museums, parks and gardens.

One Week
Visit Copenhagen and then head for North Zealand's castles and beaches, Roskilde, Trelleborg and perhaps other sights in southern Zealand such as historic Køge, Ringsted or the hamlet of Vallø.

Two Weeks
Having covered the areas listed previously, continue to Funen, stopping off at Odense and Ærø, then onwards to Århus, Skagen, Ribe and other places of interest in Jutland.

One Month
Extend your range to include Bornholm, southern Funen (including the islands of Tåsinge and Langeland), Møn and Falster.

Two Months
Take the opportunity to visit the main places of interest at a more leisurely pace; cycle between sights to experience the gentle charms of the Danish countryside.

Highlights

Be sure to jump in and absorb some of what's quintessentially Danish: pass a sunny afternoon in an outdoor café over a plate of herring and a glass of Carlsberg, see the country from a cyclist's perspective or spend a night on the town sampling the music scene.

Viking Sites

Denmark is rich with Viking sites, including circular ring fortresses dating back to around 980 AD. The best preserved are the Trelleborg fortress in Zealand and the Fyrkat fortress in Jutland; both have reconstructed Viking houses and summer activities.

For maritime history, visit the Vikingeskibshallen (Viking ship museum) in Roskilde, Bangsbomuseet in Frederikshavn and Ladbyskibet outside Kerteminde. Also well worth a visit is Lindholm Høje outside Aalborg, containing the largest plot of Viking and Iron Age graves in Scandinavia.

In the summer, several Danish towns hold open-air Viking plays. The most atmospherically set is held at the Fyrkat fortress outside Hobro, but there are also plays at Lindholm Høje and Jels, both in Jutland, and in Frederikssund in North Zealand.

Museums

The most impressive open-air museum is Den Gamle By in Århus, set up as a provincial town, while Den Fynske Landsby folk museum in Odense has the most engaging natural setting.

The best preserved bog people – intact Iron Age bodies found preserved in peat bogs – are in the Silkeborg Museum in Silkeborg and Forhistorisk Museum Moesgård (Moesgård Prehistoric Museum) in Århus. In Zealand, the best art museums are Ny Carlsberg Glyptotek in Copenhagen and Louisiana in Humlebæk. Copenhagen's Nationalmuseet has a superb collection of Danish historical artefacts, including Viking weaponry and rune stones.

PLANNING
When to Go

Considering its northerly latitude, Denmark has a fairly mild climate year-round; still, the winter months – cold and with short daylight hours – are certainly the least hospitable. Many tourist destinations are mothballed in the winter and don't come alive until late April, when the weather begins to warm up and the daylight hours start to increase; by October they become sleepers again.

May and June can be delightful months in which to visit: the land is a rich green accented with fields of yellow rapeseed flowers, the weather is generally warm and comfortable and you'll beat the rush of tourists. Although autumn can also be pleasant, it's not nearly as scenic because the rural landscape has by then largely turned brown.

The peak tourist season (July and August) is the time for open-air concerts, lots of street activity and basking on the beach. Other bonuses for travellers during the high season are longer hours at museums and other sightseeing attractions and potential savings on accommodation, as some hotels drop their rates. Of course you won't be the only tourist during summer because many Danes and other Europeans travel during their summer holidays and celebrate midsummer with gusto. The Danish school year is back into full swing by mid-August, so the last half of August can be a particularly attractive time to travel –

Highlights

Castles
The most strikingly set castle is Egeskov Slot in Funen, surrounded by a moat and formal gardens. Frederiksborg Slot in Hillerød boasts the most elaborately decorated Renaissance interior. In Copenhagen, the king of castles is Rosenborg Slot, housing the dazzling crown jewels.

Historic Towns
Half-timbered houses, cobblestone streets and ancient churches are thick on the ground in Denmark, but a few places are unique. Ribe, the oldest town in Denmark, has an exquisite historic centre encircling a 12th century cathedral.

The tiny fortress island of Christiansø, off Bornholm, retains its ramparts and 17th century buildings, with almost no trace of the 20th century. And Ærøskøbing on Ærø has a town centre of 18th century houses that's arguably the most picturesque in Denmark.

Sports & Concerts
Bornholm and Funen are popular destinations for cyclists or you can traverse the regional and national cycling routes that crisscross the country.

Windsurfers will find ideal conditions on Jutland's western coast at Hvide Sande, Klitmøller and Rømø. Favourite beaches include Marielyst on Falster, Hornbæk and Tisvildeleje in North Zealand, and Skagen on the northern tip of Jutland. The Lake District is a centre for canoeing and walking; the Rebild Bakker area is also a good place for hiking.

Denmark hosts some grand concerts. Each summer Roskilde stages the largest rock festival in northern Europe, while Copenhagen sponsors the region's largest jazz festival and Tønder holds a noteworthy folk festival.

there's still summer weather but fewer crowds.

Some sightseeing spots and businesses use the terms 'high season' and 'low season' to define periods when they have different opening hours or prices. These are somewhat elastic terms, depending on the business, but generally the high season (when opening hours are longer and some prices are higher) coincides with the school summer holiday, from about mid-June to mid-August. The low season is generally taken to mean any time outside that period, but some businesses also have further variations during a 'shoulder season' that typically covers a period of a few weeks to a month immediately before and after the high season.

Before planning a trip, check more detailed information in the Climate section in the Facts about Denmark chapter; details of festivals can be found in the Public Holidays & Special Events section later in this chapter.

Maps

There are excellent maps of Denmark's larger cities, such as Copenhagen, Århus, Aalborg and Odense, that can be picked up free from tourist offices. Staff at tourist offices in smaller cities and towns can generally provide simpler maps that are suitable for local sightseeing.

The *Map of Denmark – ferry guide & attractions*, a quality foldout, four-colour road map, can be obtained free from Denmark's overseas tourist offices.

If you're renting a car, you can usually obtain good Denmark road maps free from the rental agency when you pick up your car.

Although the aforementioned maps will suit most travellers' needs, if you enjoy exploring backroads, nooks and crannies you may also want to pick up the detailed road map of Denmark published by Kort-og Matrikelstyrelsen in a handy atlas format and labelled *Færdselskort 1:200,000 Danmark*. It's sold in Danish bookshops and costs 100 kr.

What to Bring

Travelling light is always the best policy. It's very easy to find almost anything you need along the way; however, keep in mind that, because of the value-added tax (VAT) and the overall high price of goods, most people won't want to be stocking up excessively in Denmark.

Travelpacks, a combination of backpack and shoulder bag, are very popular for carrying gear. The backpack straps zip away inside the pack when not needed so you almost have the best of both worlds – a smart-looking soft bag for checking in at hotels, and a suitable backpack for walking. Some packs have sophisticated shoulder-strap adjustment systems so you can use them comfortably even on long hikes. Travelpacks can be reasonably thief-proofed with small padlocks.

The secret of successful packing is using plastic carrier bags inside your travelpack: they keep things organised, and also keep things dry if the bag gets soaked.

Airlines do lose luggage occasionally, but you've got a better chance of it being retrieved if it's tagged with your name and address *inside* as well as outside. Outside tags can always fall off or be removed.

As for clothing, the season you travel in will have a major bearing on what you should bring along. However, even during the warmest months, it's good to carry at least a light jacket, as cool weather can sweep across Denmark at any time.

A minimum packing list could include:

- underwear, socks and swimming gear
- a pair of jeans or trousers
- a pair of shorts or a skirt
- a few T-shirts and shirts
- a warm sweater
- a comfortable pair of shoes
- sandals or thongs (flip-flops) for shared showers
- a coat or jacket
- a raincoat, umbrella, or waterproof jacket
- a medical kit and sewing kit
- a combination padlock
- a Swiss Army knife
- soap and towel
- toothpaste, toothbrush and toiletries
- a small daypack

Bringing a tent and a sleeping bag is vital if you're camping. A sleeping sheet with a pillow cover is necessary if you plan to stay in hostels – you'll have to hire or purchase one if you don't bring your own. You can make one of these sleeping sheets yourself out of old sheets or buy one from your hostel association. A bath towel is also necessary if you stay in hostels.

A Swiss Army knife is useful for all sorts of things (any pocket knife is fine, so long as it includes a bottle opener and a strong corkscrew). Note that in Denmark an anti-gang law makes it illegal in most cases to carry a knife with a blade more than 7cm long.

A small daypack will prove convenient for city sightseeing. Other items might include a compass, a torch (flashlight), an alarm clock or a watch with an alarm function, an adapter plug for electrical appliances, a pair of sunglasses and an elastic clothesline.

If you're travelling to Denmark in the summer, when daylight hours are long, you'll find an eye mask helpful to fall asleep while it's still light and to avoid being awoken by an early dawn.

TOURIST OFFICES

More than 100 tourist offices are found throughout Denmark, and staff can be amazingly helpful, providing you with information on virtually anything from what's happening at the concert hall to the location of the nearest coin laundry or bicycle rental shop. Of course they can also help you to book accommodation or find a certain type of restaurant as well as providing specific advice on local sightseeing.

Most offices have multilingual staff who can handle inquiries in English, German and Danish.

Local Tourist Offices

Virtually every good-sized town in Denmark has a tourist office, most often found in the *rådhus* (town hall) or elsewhere on *torvet* (the central square).

Telephone and fax numbers and address details of local tourist offices are listed under individual towns throughout this book. You can pick up general visitor literature at these offices once you arrive or, upon request, staff at most offices will mail out a package of tourist brochures specific to their area.

If you want to stock up on materials before heading off to the countryside, brochures and booklets about all parts of Denmark are available to walk-in visitors at Copenhagen Information on Bernstorffsgade 1, opposite Central Station. Although the Copenhagen office is the best-stocked tourist office in Denmark, other major city offices, such as those in Odense, Århus and Aalborg, can also pile visitors high with a good range of brochures pertaining to all parts of Denmark.

The administrative headquarters for the national tourist organisation is: Danish Tourist Board (☎ 33 11 14 15, fax 33 93 14 16), Vesterbrogade 6D, 1620 Copenhagen V; its Web site is at www.dt.dk.

Tourist Offices Abroad

You can receive general information on travel in Denmark, including a road map and an annually updated hotel guide, from Danish tourist offices abroad.

Overseas representatives of the Danish Tourist Board include:

Finland
    Tanskan Matkailutoimisto
    (☎ 90 644 255, fax 90 644 267,
    email dt@dt.dk)
    Yrjörikatu 30, 2kerros, 00100 Helsinki
France
    Le Conseil du Tourisme de Danemark
    (☎ 01 53 43 26 26, fax 01 53 43 26 23,
    email dt@dt.dk)
    18 boulevard Malesherbes, 75008 Paris
Germany
    Dänisches Fremdenverkehrsamt
    (☎ 040-32 0210, fax 33 021111,
    email daninfo@dt.dk)
    Postfach 101329, 20008 Hamburg
Italy
    Ente Danese per il Turismo
    (☎ 02-87 48 03, fax 86 07 12,
    email edanese@tin.it)
    Via Cappuccio 11, 20 123 Milan

Japan
   Scandinavian Tourist Board
   (☎ 03-35 80 50 30, fax 35 03 44 57,
   email stbjapan@twics.com)
   Sanno Grand Bldg, Room 912,
   2-14-2 Nagata-cho, Chiyoda-ku, 100 Tokyo
Netherlands
   Deens Verkeersburo Benelux
   (☎ 0715-233 283, fax 211 794,
   email denemarken@dt.dk)
   Postbus 266, 2300 AG Leiden
Norway
   Danmarks Turistkontor
   (☎ 22 00 76 46, fax 22 41 38 02,
   email danmark@dt.dk)
   Tollbugaten 27, Postboks 406 Sentrum,
   0103 Oslo
Sweden
   Danska Turistbyrån
   (☎ 86 11 72 22, fax 86 11 72 35,
   email info@dtab.se)
   Biblioteksgatan 25, Box 5524,
   114 85 Stockholm
UK
   Danish Tourist Board
   (☎ 020-7259 5959, fax 7259 5955,
   email dtb.london@dt.dk)
   55 Sloane St, London SW1X 9SR
USA
   Danish Tourist Board
   (☎ 212-885 9700, fax 885 9710,
   email info@goscandinavia.com)
   PO Box 4649, Grand Central Station,
   New York, NY 10163

VISAS & DOCUMENTS
Passport

Your most important travel document is a passport, which should remain valid until well after your trip. If it's about to expire, renew it before you go; this may not be easy to do overseas.

Applying for or renewing a passport can take anything from a few days to several months, so don't leave it until the last minute. First check what is required: passport photos, birth certificate, exact payment in cash, whatever.

Australian citizens can apply at a post office, or at the passport office in their state capital; Britons can apply at major post offices; Canadians can apply at regional passport offices; New Zealanders can apply at any district office of the Department of Internal Affairs; and US citizens must apply in person (but may usually renew by mail) at a US Passport Agency office or at some courthouses and post offices.

Citizens of many European countries don't always need a valid passport for travel within Europe; a national identity card may be sufficient. An EU citizen travelling to another EU country will generally face the least problems. Check with a travel agency, airline or embassy before starting your trip.

Once you start travelling, carry your passport (or national identity card) at all times and guard it carefully. It's a good idea to also carry a photocopy of it in a separate place.

Visas

A visa is a stamp in your passport permitting you to enter the country in question and stay for a specified period of time. There's a wide variety, including tourist, transit and business visas. Visa regulations are always subject to change, so it's advisable to check the situation with the Danish embassy or consulate before leaving home. Although most travellers won't need a visa to visit Denmark, those going on to other countries nearby, such as Russia, may need one for travel there.

Citizens of the USA, Canada, Australia and New Zealand need a valid passport to enter Denmark, but they don't need a visa for stays of less than three months.

In addition, no entry visa is required for citizens of most other countries, including those of the EU and Scandinavia.

Travel Insurance

A travel insurance policy to cover theft, loss and medical problems is a good idea. There is a wide variety of policies available, so check the small print.

Some policies specifically exclude 'dangerous activities', which can include scuba diving, motorcycling, even trekking. A locally acquired motorcycle licence is not valid under some policies.

You may prefer a policy that pays doctors or hospitals directly rather than you having to pay on the spot and claim later. If you have to claim later make sure you keep all documentation. Some policies ask you to call back (reverse charges) to a centre in your home country where an immediate assessment of your problem is made.

Check that the policy covers ambulances or an emergency flight home.

Driving Licence & Permits

Bring your home driving licence: Denmark accepts many foreign driving licences without restriction, including those issued in the USA, Canada, the UK and other EU countries. If you don't hold a European driving licence and plan to drive elsewhere in the region, it's a good idea to obtain an International Driving Permit (IDP) from your local automobile association before you leave – you'll need a passport photo and a valid licence. IDPs are usually inexpensive and valid for one year only.

Also, if you're an automobile association member, take your association card. This may entitle you to services offered by affiliated organisations in Denmark.

If you're planning to drive your own car into Denmark, see also under Paperwork & Preparations in the Car & Motorcycle section of the Getting There & Away chapter.

Hostel Cards

If you have an international hostel card be sure to bring it. In Denmark, if you don't have an international card you must either buy a one night Hostelling International guest card for 25 kr or an annual card for 125 kr; both are available on the spot at hostels.

Another advantage of hostel cards is that they'll get you discounts at some museums and sightseeing spots. A complete list of the discounts available are found in the free Danish hostelling booklet *Danhostel Danmarks Vandrerhjem*. See under Hostels in the Accommodation section later in this chapter for more details about this card.

Student & Youth Cards

The most useful of these is the International Student Identity Card (ISIC), a plastic ID-style card carrying your photograph, which confers discounts on many forms of transport and cheap or free admission to some museums and sights.

There is a worldwide industry in fake student cards, and many places now stipulate a maximum age for student discounts or, more simply, they've substituted a 'youth discount' for a 'student discount'. If you're aged 25 or younger but you're not a student, you can apply for the Federation of International Youth Travel Organisations (FIYTO) card, called GO25, which allows much the same discounts for holders as an ISIC.

Both types of card are issued by student unions, hostelling organisations and student travel agencies. They don't automatically entitle you to discounts, but you won't find out until you flash the card.

International Health Card

You need to carry proof of your vaccinations only if you're coming into the region from areas, such as parts of Africa and South America, where diseases like yellow fever are prevalent.

Camping Card

In many countries local automobile associations issue a Camping Card International (CCI) which is basically a camping ground ID. CCI cards are also issued by local camping federations and sometimes on the spot at camping grounds. These passes incorporate third-party insurance for any damage you may cause. In Denmark your CCI will be accepted if it holds the current year's stamp. If you arrive in Denmark without a CCI, you can buy a Danish camping pass instead; see under Camping in the Accommodation section later in this chapter for more details of camping cards.

Photocopies

All important documents (passport, credit cards, travel insurance policy, air/bus/train tickets, driving licence etc) should be photocopied before you leave home. Leave one copy with someone at home and keep another with you, but separate from the originals.

EMBASSIES & CONSULATES
Danish Embassies & Consulates

Danish embassies and consulates abroad include:

Australia
(☎ 02-6273 2195, 6273 3864)
15 Hunter St, Yarralumla, ACT 2600
There's also a consulate in Sydney.

Canada
(☎ 613-562-1811, fax 234-7368)
47 Clarence St, Suite 450, Ottawa,
Ontario K1N 9K1
There's also a consulate in Toronto.

Finland
(☎ 90-17 15 11, fax 17 17 41)
Centralgatan 1 (PB 1042),
00101 Helsinki

France
(☎ 01 44 31 21 21, fax 01 44 31 21 88)
77 ave Marceau, 75116 Paris
There's also a consulate in Marseille.

Germany
(☎ 0228-729 910, fax 729 9131)
Pfälzer Strasse 14 (Postfach 180220),
53032 Bonn
There are also consulates in Berlin, Dresden, Düsseldorf, Flensburg, Frankfurt, Hamburg and Munich.

Iceland
(☎ 56 21 230, fax 56 23 316)
Hverfisgata 29 (Postboks 1540),
121 Reykjavík

Ireland
(☎ 01-475 6404, fax 478 4536)
121 St Stephen's Green, Dublin 2

Italy
(☎ 06-3200 441, fax 3610 290)
Via dei Monti Parioli 50, 00197 Rome
There's also a consulate in Milan.

Japan
(☎ 03-34 96 30 01, fax 34 96 34 40)
29 6 Sarugaku-cho, Shibuya-ku, Tokyo 150

Netherlands
(☎ 070-365 5830, fax 360 2150)
Koninginnegracht 30 (Postbus 85654),
2508 CJ Den Haag

New Zealand
Contact the embassy in Australia.

Norway
(☎ 22 54 08 00, fax 22 55 46 34)
Olav Kyrres Gate 7, 0244 Oslo

Poland
(☎ 022-490 056, fax 487 580)
Ul Rakowiecka 19, 02-517 Warsaw

Russia
(☎ 095-238 6930, fax 230 2072)
Korovy Val 7, 2nd Floor, 117049 Moscow
There's also a consulate in St Petersburg.

Sweden
(☎ 84 06 75 00, fax 791 72 20)
Jakobs Torg 1 (Box 1638),
11186 Stockholm

UK
(☎ 020-7333 0200, fax 7333 0270)
55 Sloane St, London SW1X 9SR

USA
(☎ 202-234 4300, fax 328 1470)
3200 Whitehaven St NW,
Washington DC 20008
There are also consulates in Los Angeles, Chicago and New York.

Embassies & Consulates in Denmark

As a tourist, it's important to realise what your own embassy – the embassy of the country of which you are a citizen – can and can't do.

Generally speaking, your embassy won't be much help in emergencies if the trouble you're in is your own fault. Remember that you are bound by the laws of the country you are in. In most cases, your embassy is not likely to be terribly sympathetic if you end up in jail after committing a crime locally, even if such actions are legal in your own country. Some embassies do send representatives to visit citizens arrested abroad, however, so don't hesitate to contact them.

In genuine emergencies you might get some assistance, but only if all other channels have been exhausted. For example, if you need to get home urgently, a free ticket home is exceedingly unlikely – the embassy would expect you to have insurance. If you have all your money and documents stolen, its assistance will probably be limited to providing you with a new passport.

The following foreign diplomatic representatives are in Copenhagen:

Australia (honorary consulate)
 (☎ 39 29 20 77) Strandboulevarden 122
Canada
 (☎ 33 12 22 99) Kristen Bernikowsgade 1
Finland
 (☎ 33 13 42 14) Sankt Annæ Plads 24
France
 (☎ 33 15 51 22) Kongens Nytorv 4
Germany
 (☎ 35 26 16 22) Stockholmsgade 57
Iceland
 (☎ 33 15 96 04) Dantes Plads 3
Ireland
 (☎ 35 42 32 33) Østbanegade 21
Italy
 (☎ 39 62 68 77) Gammel Vartov Vej 7,
 Hellerup
Japan
 (☎ 33 11 33 44) Pilestræde 61
Netherlands
 (☎ 33 15 62 93) Toldbodgade 33
New Zealand
 Contact the UK embassy.
Norway
 (☎ 33 14 01 24) Amaliegade 39
Poland
 (☎ 39 62 72 45) Richelius Allé 12,
 Hellerup
Russia
 (☎ 35 42 55 85) Kristianiagade 5
Sweden
 (☎ 33 36 03 70) Sankt Annæ Plads 15A
UK
 (☎ 35 44 52 00) Kastelsvej 40
USA
 (☎ 35 55 31 44) Dag Hammarskjölds Allé 24

CUSTOMS

Check out the duty-free regulations in the EU before you arrive in Denmark. From non-EU countries the following items can be brought into Denmark duty-free: 1L of hard liquor or 2L of fortified or sparkling wine, as well as 2L of table wine, 200 cigarettes and general items of a personal nature.

When you arrive in Denmark, there will be two customs channels. You must use the red channel if you're bringing in more than the usual allowance of duty-free goods or any restricted items (such as guns or drugs). Use the green channel – which is generally a quick exit – if you have nothing to declare.

MONEY
Currency

The Danish *krone* is most often written DKK in international money markets, Dkr in northern Europe and kr within Denmark.

The krone is divided into 100 *øre* (pronounced ore-a). There are 25 øre, 50 øre, one krone, two kroner, five kroner, 10 kroner and 20 kroner coins. Notes come in denominations of 50, 100, 200, 500 and 1000 kroner.

Exchange Rates

The following currencies convert at these approximate rates:

country	unit		krone
Australia	A$1	=	4.30 Dkr
Canada	C$1	=	4.43 Dkr
euro	€1	=	7.45 Dkr
France	1FF	=	1.13 Dkr
Germany	DM1	=	3.81 Dkr
Japan	¥100	=	5.84 Dkr
New Zealand	NZ$1	=	3.65 Dkr
Norway	10 Nkr	=	8.62 Dkr
Sweden	10 Skr	=	8.40 Dkr
UK	UK£1	=	10.69 Dkr
USA	US$1	=	6.60 Dkr

Exchanging Money

It's convenient to have Danish currency on hand when you arrive. Fortunately the Copenhagen airport bank is open to meet most incoming flights. If you're on an international ferry to Denmark, they'll not only exchange US dollars and local currencies to Danish kroner on board but, if you buy a meal or use the duty-free shops, regardless of the currency you pay in, many will give you change in Danish kroner upon request.

Because of its international acceptance, the US dollar is generally the handiest foreign currency to bring, particularly if you're travelling farther afield than Denmark. However, Danish banks will convert a wide range of currencies including the US dollar, Canadian dollar, UK pound, German Deutschmark, French franc, Japanese yen,

Introducing the euro

On 1 January 1999 a new currency, the euro, was introduced in Europe. It's all part of the harmonisation of the European Union (EU) countries. Along with national border controls, the currencies of various EU members are being phased out. Denmark is one of the EU countries (along with Greece, Sweden and the UK) which have rejected or postponed participation in the initial wave of change; some or all of these countries may adopt the new currency within the next few years. The 11 countries which have participated from the beginning of the process are Austria, Belgium, Finland, France, Germany, Ireland, Italy, Luxembourg, the Netherlands, Portugal and Spain, so travellers to Denmark who pass through nearby countries are likely to be affected by the introduction of the euro.

The timetable for the introduction of the euro runs as follows:

• On 1 January 1999 the exchange rates of the participating countries were irrevocably fixed to the euro. The euro came into force for 'paper' accounting and prices could be displayed in local currency and in euros.

• On 1 January 2002 euro banknotes and coins will be introduced. This ushers in a period of dual use of euros and existing local notes and coins (which will, in effect, simply be temporary denominations of the euro).

• By July 2002 local currencies in the 11 countries will be withdrawn. Only euro notes and coins will remain in circulation and prices will be displayed in euros only.

The same euro notes and coins will be used in all participating countries. One of the main benefits will be that you will be able to easily compare prices in the 11 countries, avoiding all those tedious calculations. Also, once euro notes and coins are issued in 2002, you won't need to change money at all when travelling to other single-currency members. Banks may still charge a handling fee (yet to be decided) for travellers cheques but they won't be able to profit by buying the currency from you at one rate and selling it back to you at another, as they do at the moment. However, even EU countries not participating may price goods in euros and accept euros over shop counters.

There are many Web sites dealing with the introduction of the euro but most are devoted to the legal implications and the processes by which businesses may adapt to the single currency and are not particularly interesting or informative for the traveller. The Lonely Planet Web site at www.lonelyplanet.com has a link to a currency converter and up-to-date news on the integration process.

Dutch guilder, Swiss franc, Austrian schilling, Italian lira, Finnish markka and kroner from Norway, Sweden and Iceland. Foreign coins are seldom accepted by banks, so it's best to try to offload those before arriving in Denmark.

Exchange Fees All common travellers cheques are accepted at major banks in Denmark. It's a good idea to bring travellers cheques in higher denominations because bank fees for changing money are a hefty 20 kr per cheque, and there's a 40 kr minimum. Cash transactions usually incur a 25 kr fee however much you change; that doesn't necessarily make cash more favourable however, because travellers cheques command about a 1% better exchange rate.

Post offices also exchange foreign currency at comparable rates – the main benefit of this for travellers being that Danish post offices open on Saturday morning.

Travellers Cheques The main benefit of travellers cheques is that they can provide protection from the effects of theft. Large companies such as American Express and Thomas Cook generally offer efficient replacement policies.

Keeping a record of the cheque numbers and those you have used is vital when it comes to replacing lost cheques. You should keep this information separate from the cheques themselves.

Eurocheques Taking guaranteed personal cheques is another way of carrying money or obtaining cash. The most popular type of these is the Eurocheque, which requires the holder to have a European bank account in their name.

Throughout Europe, when paying for something in a shop or withdrawing cash from a bank or post office, you write out a Eurocheque (up to its maximum limit; otherwise simply write out two or more cheques) and show the accompanying guarantee card with your signature and registration number.

The card can double as an ATM card and should be kept separate from the cheques for safety.

ATMs Most banks in Denmark have automatic teller machines (ATMs), many of them accessible outside normal banking hours; they give cash advances on Visa and MasterCard credit cards as well as Cirrus and Plus bank cards. A few banks, especially in Copenhagen, have also installed 24-hour cash-exchange machines that change major foreign currencies, such as the US dollar and the British pound, into Danish kroner.

Credit & Debit Cards If you're not familiar with the options, ask your bank to explain the workings and relative merits of credit, debit, charge and cash cards.

Plastic cards are ideal travelling companions – not only can you make purchases without carrying a wad of money but you can also use them to withdraw cash from

banks and ATMs. However, to use a credit card with an ATM you will need to have established a PIN number, so be sure to do that before you travel.

Cash cards, which you use to withdraw money directly from your bank account, have become increasingly linked internationally. Both the Cirrus and Plus network are now used at ATMs throughout Denmark. However, seek advice from your home bank before you travel because some accounts can be accessed internationally, while others can't.

Credit cards such as Visa and Master-Card (also known as Access or Eurocard) are widely accepted in Denmark. Charge cards such as American Express and Diners Club are also accepted in Denmark, but not in as many places as credit cards. On the plus side, charge cards have a reputation for quick replacement, often within 24 hours of reporting the card lost.

The best advice is to not put all your eggs in one basket. If you want to rely heavily on bits of plastic, bring at least two different cards. Better still is a combination of plastic cards and travellers cheques so you have something to fall back on if an ATM swallows your card or the bank fails to recognise your account.

International Transfers The transfer of money from your home bank will be easier if you've authorised someone back home to access your account. Specify the city, the bank and the branch to which you want your money directed or ask your home bank to tell you where there's a suitable one and make sure you get the details right. If you have the choice, find a large bank and ask for the international division.

Costs

By anything other than Scandinavian standards, Denmark is an expensive country. One reason for this is the 25% VAT, called *moms* in Danish, which is included in every price – from hotel rooms and restaurant meals to car rentals and shop purchases.

Still, your costs will depend on how you travel and it's possible to see Denmark without spending a fortune. If you're travelling on a budget, one way to cut down on expenses is to take advantage of Denmark's extensive network of camping grounds and hostels. The latter are widely used by all age groups and are usually set up more like small hotels than cavernous drop-in centres.

In terms of basic expenses, if you camp or stay in hostels and prepare your own meals you might get by on 175 kr a day. If you stay in modest hotels and eat at inexpensive restaurants, you can expect to spend about 400 kr a day if you're doubling up, 500 kr if you're travelling alone. Interestingly, top-end hotels, which commonly have good weekend and holiday rates, often cost only about 30% more than budget hotels.

On top of the amounts given above you'll need to budget for local transport (about 12 kr a ride), admission fees to museums and other attractions, entertainment and incidentals. Long-distance public transport is reasonably priced and it helps that Denmark is small – the most expensive train ticket between two points in Denmark costs just 272 kr.

If you're travelling by car, it's going to be more expensive. Petrol costs around 6.5 kr a litre, car ferries are reasonable but the charges can add up, and if you opt to hire a car in Denmark the costs range from expensive to exorbitant. Expect to pay 650 kr a day for car hire, although the daily rate on week-long rentals can average about half that – in either case this is for the cheapest economy car! One advantage of travelling by car is that you can often find economical accommodation options outside the city centre, so you should save a bit on hotel bills.

Of course there are always ways to circumvent some of the high costs. For instance if you're willing to enter Denmark via Germany you can pick up a rental car there for about one-third of the Danish car-hire fees and then drive north into Denmark.

Tipping & Bargaining

Restaurant bills and taxi fares include service charges in the quoted prices. Further tipping is unnecessary, although rounding up the bill is not uncommon when the service has been especially good. Bargaining is not a common practice in Denmark.

Taxes & Refunds

Visitors from countries outside the EU who buy goods in Denmark can claim a refund of the 25% VAT, less a handling fee, if they spend at least 300 kr at any retail outlet that participates in the Tax-Free plan; this includes most shops catering to tourists. The 300 kr can cover a single item or several items, as long as they're purchased from the same shop.

Be sure to obtain the tax-refund 'cheque' from the store when you make the purchase; it should include the date, both the buyer's and seller's name and address, the number and type of goods, the selling price and the VAT amount.

Contact the VAT refund bureau at your point of departure from Denmark to claim the refund, and allow extra time in case there's a queue at the booth. At Copenhagen airport you'll find a booth in the departure hall; if you're leaving by international train, inform the conductor when you board; if you depart by ship, inquire at the port. If you have questions about VAT refunds call ☎ 32 52 55 66, or pick up a brochure on the programme from participating shops.

POST & COMMUNICATIONS
Post

Most post offices are open either from 9 am to 5.30 pm or from 10 am to 5 pm on weekdays, and until noon on Saturday. You can receive mail c/o poste restante at any post office in Denmark, but it's usually held for only two weeks.

It costs 4.50 kr to airmail a postcard or letter weighing up to 20g to Scandinavia or Western Europe, 5.50 kr to other countries. Heavier letters weighing up to 50g cost 5 kr within Denmark, 6.50 kr to other Scandinavian countries, 9.75 kr to Western Europe and 12.25 kr to other countries. International mail sent from Copenhagen is generally out of the country within 24 hours.

Telephone

Denmark has an efficient phone system.

If you're going to be making many calls, consider using a debit phonecard (*telekort*), sold in denominations of 30, 50 and 100 kr. These cards can be used for making both local and international calls and are more convenient than pumping in coins. Cards can be bought at post offices and many kiosks, especially those at train stations.

Cardphones are found in busy public places side by side with coin phones. Cardphones work out slightly cheaper than coin phones because you pay for the exact amount of time you speak; an LCD screen keeps you posted on how much time is left on the card. It's possible to replace an expiring card with a new card without breaking the call. Cardphones are posted with information in English detailing their use as well as the location of the nearest place that sells phonecards.

Domestic Calls All telephone numbers in Denmark have eight numbers. There are no area codes; all eight numbers must be dialled, even when making calls within the same city.

It generally costs a minimum of 2 kr to make a local call at coin phones. Local calls are timed and you get twice as much calling time for your money on domestic calls made between 7.30 pm and 8 am. For directory assistance dial ☎ 118 but be aware it costs a hefty 5 kr per minute.

International Calls to Denmark The country code for Denmark is 45. To call Denmark from another country, dial the international-access code for the country you're in followed by 45 and the local eight digit number.

International Calls from Denmark The international-access code in Denmark is 00. To make direct international calls from Denmark dial 00 followed by the country code for the country you're calling, the area code, then the local number.

For assistance, including information on rates for international calls, ☎ 141. Although the 141 call is toll free, if you do decide to place your international call you're better off hanging up and then dialling direct rather than having the operator connect you through, as there's a 40 kr service charge for operator-assisted calls.

Fax

Faxes can be sent from hotels and larger post offices.

Email & Internet Access

Travelling with a portable computer is a great way to stay in touch with home but, unless you know what you're doing, it's fraught with potential problems. If the power supply voltage in the countries you plan to visit varies from that at home, bring a universal AC adapter, which will enable you to plug it in without frying the innards. You may also need a plug adapter, which is often easiest to buy before you leave home.

Also, your PC-card modem may not work once you leave your home country – but you won't know for sure until you try. The safest option is to buy a 'global' modem before you leave home. Keep in mind that the telephone socket may be different from that at home as well, so ensure that you have at least a US RJ-11 telephone adapter that works with your modem. You can almost always find an adapter that will convert from RJ-11 to the local variety. For more information on travelling with a portable computer, visit the Web sites www.teleadapt.com and www.warrior.com.

Major Internet service providers (ISPs) such as AOL (www.aol.com), CompuServe (www.compuserve.com) and IBM Net (www.ibm.net) have dial-in nodes throughout Europe; it's best to download a list of the dial-in numbers before you leave home. If you access your Internet email at home through a smaller ISP, your best option is either to open an account with a global ISP, such as those mentioned above, or to rely on public access points to collect your mail.

To use public access points to get your email, you'll need to know your incoming (POP or IMAP) mail server name, your account name and your password. A final option for collecting mail through public access points is to open a free Web-based email account such as HotMail (www .hotmail.com) or Yahoo! Mail (mail.yahoo .com). You can then access your mail from anywhere in the world from any Internet-connected machine running a standard Web browser.

A growing number of hotels in Denmark are adding modem hookups in guest rooms, so if you intend to use your own computer, you should inquire when making reservations.

Many public libraries in Denmark have computers with Internet access, though access policies vary; sometimes you need to book in advance. Larger post offices usually have Internet computers in the lobby that can be accessed with a phonecard (see Telephone earlier in this section). As most families in Denmark have their own computers, cybercafés are not terribly abundant and tend to be short-lived.

INTERNET RESOURCES

The World Wide Web is a rich resource for travellers. You can research your trip, hunt down bargain air fares, book hotels, check on weather conditions or chat with locals and other travellers about the places to visit (or avoid!).

There's no better place to start your Web explorations than the Lonely Planet Web site (www.lonelyplanet.com). Here you'll find succinct summaries of travel in most places on earth, postcards from other travellers and the Thorn Tree bulletin board, where you can ask questions before you go or dispense advice when you get back. You can also find travel news and updates to many of our most popular guidebooks, and the subWWWay section links you to the most useful travel resources elsewhere on the Web.

In addition, the Danish foreign ministry site at www.denmark.org has a wealth of information, including updated weather and exchange rates, plus links to many other Danish sites. Addresses of other Web sites are provided throughout this book, listed under specific topics.

BOOKS
Lonely Planet

If your travels will include other parts of Scandinavia or Baltic Europe, you'll find these destinations covered in Lonely Planet's *Scandinavian & Baltic Europe* guide. A good companion to help you to communicate with people along the way is Lonely Planet's *Scandinavian Europe phrasebook*.

History

Numerous books about Viking-era culture and history are available. *The Viking World*, by James Graham-Campbell, is a book with handsome photos that outlines the history of the Vikings by detailing excavated Viking sites and artefacts. *The Viking*, by Bertil Almgren, is an authoritative book tracing Viking history in both the Old and New Worlds.

The hardback *Denmark: A Modern History*, by W Glyn Jones, is one of the more comprehensive and insightful accounts of contemporary Danish society.

Women in Denmark, Yesterday and Today, by Inga Dahlsgård, traces Danish history from a woman's perspective.

General

Danmark, by John Roth Andersen, is an attractive hardback, four-colour, coffee-table-style pictorial of the country with multilingual commentary.

Discover Denmark – on Denmark and the Danes; Past, Present and Future, by the Danish Cultural Institute, provides a comprehensive overview of Danish society, covering topics such as history, politics, arts, culture and social issues.

Philosopher Søren Kierkegaard produced volumes of works, including *The Concept of Dread* (1844), which is considered by many to be the first work of depth psychology ever written, and *Concluding Unscientific Postscript to the Philosophical Fragments* (1846), in which Kierkegaard passionately expounded the tenets of the school of thought that would become existentialism. *A Kierkegaard Anthology*, by Robert Bretall, comprises a broad cross section of his major works.

There's an avalanche of books by and about Hans Christian Andersen as well as numerous biographies of the author, including the definitive *Hans Christian Andersen* by Elias Bredsdorff.

The Golden Age of Danish Art, by Hans Edvard Norregard-Nielsen, takes a look at the art and artists of the early 19th century; it includes 115 colour illustrations.

Camping Danmark, published annually by Campingrådet (Danish Camping Board), includes detailed information on all approved camping grounds in Denmark.

NEWSPAPERS & MAGAZINES
Denmark has about 50 daily newspapers, of which *Jyllandsposten* and *Politiken* have the largest circulations.

Although none of the dailies are in English, the *Copenhagen Post* is a quality weekly newspaper that publishes an interesting mix of Danish news, events and entertainment information in English.

Foreign English-language magazines and newspapers are readily available at train-station kiosks in larger towns. Among the more common English-language newspapers sold in Denmark are the *International Herald Tribune, USA Today,* the *Wall Street Journal,* the *European* and the *Guardian.* In the news magazine category, *Time* and the *Economist* are widely available.

RADIO & TV
You can hear a five minute news brief in English at 8.30 am Monday to Friday on Danmarks Radio channel 3 (93.8 FM in Copenhagen, 91.7 FM in Århus). The BBC World Service is broadcast on short wave at 6195 and 9410kHz.

British and US network programmes are common on Danish TV and are often presented in English with Danish subtitles. Many hotels have live CNN news, BBC World Service and other English-language cable and satellite TV programming.

VIDEO SYSTEMS
If you purchase videos in Denmark, make sure they're compatible with your home system. Denmark uses PAL, which is incompatible with the North American NTSC system.

PHOTOGRAPHY & VIDEO
Print and slide film is readily available in major cities and towns. A 24 exposure roll of Kodacolor Gold 100 will cost about 50 kr to buy and 100 kr to develop and print. A 36 exposure roll of Kodak slide film costs about 65 kr.

In many larger cities you can find photo centres that offer a range of photo-processing options. The cost to develop and print a roll of 24 exposure film is around 125 kr for one hour photo processing, 100 kr for same-day service and 75 kr for three day service.

In Denmark, photo stores sell P-5 videotape; a 90 minute tape costs around 80 kr.

TIME
Time in Denmark is normally one hour ahead of GMT/UTC, the same as in neighbouring European countries. When it's noon in Denmark, it's 11 am in London, 6 am in New York and Toronto, 3 am in San Francisco, 9 pm in Sydney and 11 pm in Auckland.

Clocks are moved forward one hour for daylight-saving time from the last Sunday in March to the last Sunday in October. Denmark uses the 24 hour clock system and all timetables and business hours are posted accordingly. Klokken, which means o'clock, is abbreviated kl (kl 19.30 is 7.30 pm).

Dates are written with the day followed by the month, thus 3/6 means 3 June and 6/3 means 6 March.

Daylight Hours

Throughout the summer, visitors to Denmark can enjoy long lingering hours of daylight. The longest days are in late June, when the sun rises at around 4.30 am and sets at around 10 pm, providing nearly 17½ daylight hours.

month	sunrise	sunset
1 January	8.40 am	3.48 pm
1 February	8.08 am	4.39 pm
1 March	7.06 am	5.40 pm
1 April	6.36 am	7.51 pm
1 May	5.29 am	8.46 pm
1 June	4.36 am	9.40 pm
1 July	4.33 am	9.54 pm
1 August	5.17 am	9.23 pm
1 September	6.16 am	8.02 pm
1 October	7.14 am	6.43 pm
1 November	7.15 am	4.31 pm
1 December	8.23 am	3.37 pm

ELECTRICITY
Voltages & Cycles

Denmark, like most of Europe, runs on 220V (volts), 50Hz (cycles) AC.

Check the voltage and cycle (usually 50Hz) used in your home country. Most appliances that are set up for 240V (such as those used in the UK) will handle 220V without modifications and vice versa. It's always preferable to adjust your appliance to the exact voltage if you can – a few items, such as some electric razors and radios, will do this automatically. If your appliance doesn't have a built-in transformer, don't plug a 110/125V appliance (the kind used in the USA and Canada) into a Danish outlet without using a separate transformer.

Plugs & Sockets

Denmark uses the 'europlug' with two round pins. Many europlugs and some sockets don't have provision for earth wiring because most local home appliances are double-insulated; when provided, earth usually consists of two contact points along the edge.

If your plugs are of a different design, you'll need an adapter. These are usually available in shops specialising in travel needs; get one before you leave, because the adapters available in Denmark usually go the other way.

WEIGHTS & MEASURES

Denmark uses the metric system. Petrol and beverages are sold by the litre, meats and vegetables are weighed in kilograms, distance is measured in kilometres or metres and speed limits are posted in kilometres per hour (km/h).

Fruit is often sold by the piece (*stykke*), abbreviated 'stk'. Decimals are indicated by commas and thousands by points.

For those unaccustomed to the metric system, there's a conversion chart on the inside back cover of this book.

LAUNDRY

Møntvaskeri (coin laundries) are relatively easy to find in cities and towns; hostels and camping grounds usually have coin or token-operated machines as well. The cost to wash and dry a load of clothes is generally around 40 kr.

TOILETS

Toilets in Denmark are western-style. Public ones are generally free and easy to find at such places as train stations, town squares and ferry harbours.

HEALTH

Denmark is a healthy place and travellers shouldn't need to take any unusual health precautions.

Visitors whose countries have reciprocal agreements with Denmark are covered by the Danish national health-insurance programme.

All visitors, however, receive free hospital treatment in the event of an accident or sudden illness, provided the patient has not come to Denmark for the purpose of obtaining the treatment and is too ill to return home.

In Denmark, controlled medicine is only available from a pharmacy with a prescription that is issued by a Danish or other Scandinavian doctor. Although most pharmacies have the same opening hours as other shops, in major population centres there's usually at least one *apotek* (pharmacy) open 24 hours; an additional charge is levied for using the pharmacy outside normal opening hours. When a pharmacy is closed, it's required to display the address of a nearby outlet that's open.

In medical emergencies dial ☎ 112; the call can be made without coins from public phones.

Predeparture Planning

Health Insurance Ensure that you have adequate health insurance. Before leaving home, ask your insurance company what your coverage is when you're abroad and consider buying additional travel insurance if it's not sufficient.

Citizens of EU countries are covered by public health insurance based on existing agreements between their home country and Denmark. In most cases you'll need to present EU form E111; inquire at your national health service or travel agency before leaving home. Similar reciprocal arrangements exist between the Nordic countries. However, travel insurance may still be advisable because of the flexibility it offers in where and how you're treated, as well as covering expenses for an emergency flight home.

See also under Travel Insurance in the Visas & Documents section earlier in this chapter.

Health Preparations Make sure you're healthy before you start travelling. If you are going on a long trip make sure your teeth are OK. If you wear glasses take a spare pair and your prescription. Pharmacies in Denmark stock all of the items you

Medical Kit Check List

Following is a list of items you should consider including in your medical kit – consult your pharmacist for brands available in your country.

☐ **Aspirin** or **paracetamol** (acetaminophen in the US) – for pain or fever.

☐ **Antihistamine** – for allergies, eg hay fever; to ease the itch from insect bites or stings; and to prevent motion sickness.

☐ **Antibiotics** – consider including these if you're travelling well off the beaten track; see your doctor, as they must be prescribed, and carry the prescription with you.

☐ **Loperamide** or **diphenoxylate** – 'blockers' for diarrhoea; **prochlorperazine** or **metaclopramide** for nausea and vomiting.

☐ **Rehydration mixture** – to prevent dehydration, eg due to severe diarrhoea; particularly important when travelling with children.

☐ **Insect repellent, sunscreen, lip balm** and **eye drops**.

☐ **Calamine lotion, sting relief spray** or **aloe vera** – to ease irritation from sunburn and insect bites or stings.

☐ **Antifungal cream** or **powder** – for fungal skin infections and thrush.

☐ **Antiseptic** (such as povidone-iodine) – for cuts and grazes.

☐ **Bandages, Band-Aids (plasters)** and other wound dressings.

☐ **Water purification tablets** or **iodine**.

☐ **Scissors, tweezers** and a **thermometer** (note that mercury thermometers are prohibited by airlines).

☐ **Syringes** and **needles** – in case you need injections in a country with medical hygiene problems. Ask your doctor for a note explaining why you have them.

☐ **Cold** and **flu tablets, throat lozenges** and **nasal decongestant**.

☐ **Multivitamins** – consider for long trips, when dietary vitamin intake may be inadequate.

are likely to need, but it is a good idea to carry a basic medical kit.

If you require a particular medication take an adequate supply, as it may not be available locally. Take part of the packaging showing the generic name of the drug, rather than the brand, which will make getting replacements easier. It's a good idea to have a legible prescription or letter from your doctor to show that you legally use the medication in order to avoid any problems.

Immunisations Jabs are generally not necessary for Denmark or elsewhere in Europe; however, a yellow fever vaccination may be a requirement if you're coming from an affected area.

Basic Rules

Water & Food Tap water is safe to drink throughout Denmark.

Stomach upsets are a possibility anywhere you travel but in Denmark these are likely to be relatively minor.

As a general rule take care with fish and shellfish (for instance, cooked mussels that have not opened properly can be dangerous) and avoid undercooked meat.

Medical Problems & Treatment

Local pharmacies are good places to visit if you have a small medical problem and can explain what it is. Hospital casualty wards will help if it's more serious, and will tell you if it's not. Major hospitals and emergency numbers are mentioned in the text. Staff at tourist offices, pharmacies and hotels can put you in touch with a doctor or dentist.

Environmental Hazards

Sunburn You can get sunburnt surprisingly quickly, even through cloud. Use a sunscreen, hat and barrier cream for your nose and lips. Calamine lotion is good for mild sunburn. Protect your eyes with good quality sunglasses, particularly if you will be near water, sand or snow.

Cold If you are cycling or hiking in cool wet weather, be prepared.

It is surprisingly easy to progress from being very cold to dangerously cold due to a combination of wind, wet clothing, fatigue and hunger, even if the air temperature is above freezing. It is best to dress in layers; silk, wool and some of the new artificial fibres are all good insulating materials. A hat is important, as a lot of heat is lost through the head. A strong, waterproof outer layer is essential, as keeping dry is vital.

Motion Sickness Eating lightly before and during a trip will reduce the chances of motion sickness. If you are prone to motion sickness, try to find a place that minimises movement – near the wing on aircraft, close to midships on boats, near to the centre on buses. Fresh air usually helps; reading and cigarette smoke don't. Commercial motion-sickness preparations, which can cause drowsiness, have to be taken before the trip commences. Ginger (available in capsule form) and peppermint (including mint-flavoured sweets) are natural preventatives.

Jet Lag When we travel long distances rapidly, our bodies take time to adjust to the 'new time' of our destination, and we may experience fatigue, disorientation, insomnia, anxiety, impaired concentration and loss of appetite. These effects will usually be gone within three days of arrival, but there are ways of minimising the impact of jet lag:

- Rest for a couple of days prior to departure; try to avoid late nights and last-minute dashes for travellers cheques and the like.
- Try to select flight schedules that minimise sleep deprivation; arriving late in the day means you can go to sleep soon after you arrive. For very long flights, try to organise a stopover.
- Avoid excessive eating (which bloats the stomach) and alcohol (which causes dehydration) during the flight. Instead, drink plenty of noncarbonated, nonalcoholic drinks such as fruit juice or water.

- Avoid smoking, as this reduces the amount of oxygen in the plane cabin even further and causes greater fatigue.
- Make yourself comfortable by wearing loose-fitting clothes and perhaps bringing an eye mask and earplugs to help you sleep.

Infectious Diseases

Diarrhoea Simple things such as a change of water, food or climate can all cause a mild bout of diarrhoea, but making a few rushed toilet trips with no other symptoms is not indicative of a major problem.

Dehydration is the main danger with any diarrhoea, particularly in children or the elderly, as dehydration can occur quite quickly. Under all circumstances *fluid replacement* (at least equal to the volume being lost) is the most important thing to remember. Weak black tea with a little sugar, soda water or soft drinks allowed to go flat and diluted 50% with clean water are all good.

HIV & AIDS Infection with the human immunodeficiency virus (HIV) may lead to acquired immune deficiency syndrome (AIDS), which is a fatal disease. HIV is a major problem in many countries, including Denmark. Any exposure to blood, blood products or body fluids may put the individual at risk. The disease is often transmitted through sexual contact or via dirty needles – vaccinations, acupuncture, tattooing and body piercing can be potentially as dangerous as intravenous drug use.

If you have any questions regarding AIDS while in Denmark, there's an AIDS Hotline (☎ 33 91 11 19) based in Copenhagen, open daily from 9 am to 8 pm.

Sexually Transmitted Diseases Gonorrhoea, herpes and syphilis are among these diseases; sores, blisters or rashes around the genitals, discharges or pain when urinating are common symptoms. In some STDs, such as wart virus or chlamydia, symptoms may be less marked or not observed at all, especially in women. Syphilis symptoms eventually disappear completely but the disease continues and can cause severe problems in later years. While abstinence from sexual contact is the only 100% effective prevention, using condoms is also effective. The treatment of gonorrhoea and syphilis is with antibiotics. The different sexually transmitted diseases each require specific antibiotics. There is no cure for herpes or AIDS.

Cuts, Bites & Stings

Insect Stings Bee and wasp stings are usually painful rather than dangerous; however, in people who are allergic to them severe breathing difficulties may occur and they may require urgent medical care. Calamine lotion will give relief and ice packs will reduce the pain and swelling.

Ticks You should always check all over your body after you have been walking through a potentially tick-infested area because ticks can cause skin infections and other more serious diseases (such as Lyme disease). If a tick is found attached, press down around the tick's head with tweezers, grab the head and gently pull upwards. Avoid pulling the rear of the body as this may squeeze the tick's gut contents through the attached mouth parts into the skin, increasing the risk of infection and disease. Smearing chemicals on the tick will not make it let go and is not recommended.

Snakes To minimise your chances of being bitten always wear boots, socks and long trousers when walking through undergrowth where snakes may be present. Don't put your hands into holes and crevices, and be careful when collecting firewood.

Snake bites do not cause instantaneous death and antivenenes are usually available. Immediately wrap the bitten limb tightly, as you would for a sprained ankle, and then attach a splint to immobilise it. Keep the victim still and seek medical help, if possible with the dead snake for identification. Don't attempt to catch the snake if there is a possibility of being bitten again. Tourniquets and sucking out the poison are now comprehensively discredited.

WOMEN TRAVELLERS

Although women travellers are less likely to encounter problems in Denmark than in most other countries, the usual common-sense precautions apply when it comes to potentially dangerous situations such as hitchhiking and walking alone in cities at night.

KVINFO, Center for Information om Kvinde-og Kønsforskning (Danish Centre for Information on Women and Gender; ☎ 33 13 50 88, email kvinfo@kvinfo.dk), Christians Brygge 3, Copenhagen, is a good place to study and get involved in feminist issues. Kvindehuset (☎ 33 14 28 04), Gothersgade 37, Copenhagen, is a help centre and meeting place for women. In Århus, a good place to contact regarding women's issues is Kvindemuseet (☎ 86 13 61 44), Domkirkeplads 5, which has a café and a women's museum.

Dial ☎ 112 for rape crisis assistance or in other emergencies.

GAY & LESBIAN TRAVELLERS

Denmark is a popular destination for gay and lesbian travellers. Copenhagen in particular has an active, open gay community and lots of nightlife options, but you'll find gay and lesbian venues in other cities as well.

The *Spartacus International Gay Guide*, by Bruno Gmünder (Berlin), is a good directory of gay men's entertainment venues in Europe. It's best used in conjunction with listings in local papers. *Inn Places: Worldwide Gay & Lesbian Accommodations Guide* by the Ferrari international publishing staff focuses on the best places to stay for both gay men and lesbians. Another good book to pick up is *Are You Two ... Together? A Gay and Lesbian Travel Guide to Europe*, by Lindsy Van Gelder & Pamela Robin Brandt, which has a particularly enjoyable chapter on Copenhagen.

Landsforeningen for Bøsser og Lesbiske (LBL; ☎ 33 13 19 48, email lbl@lbl.dk), the national organisation for gay men and lesbians, is at Teglgårdstræde 13 in Copenhagen. It has a library, bookshop, café, various gay and lesbian support groups, religious services and counselling. There's also a telephone information line (☎ 33 36 00 86) that operates from 8 to 11 pm on Monday, Thursday and Sunday. LBL has branches in Århus (☎ 86 13 19 48) and Aalborg (☎ 98 16 45 07).

LBL is also behind the main gay magazine in Denmark, *PAN-bladet for bøsser og lesbiske*, which covers gay-related issues, upcoming events and entertainment, with an emphasis on what's happening

---

Gay Marriages

In October 1989 the Danish Law of Registered Partnership took effect, allowing people of the same sex to tie the knot. During the first decade some 3500 couples have taken advantage of the law and registered their partnership with city hall. One-third of the partnerships are lesbian women and two-thirds are gay men, though in recent years the numbers have tended to even out.

So, how do gay marriages hold up? Approximately 500 partnerships have broken up, with more women going their separate ways than men.

Those interested in being joined in a same-sex marriage can have the ceremony performed at the city hall in Copenhagen by applying to: Bryllupskontoret (☎ 33 66 23 34), Rådhuset, Room 803, 1599 Copenhagen V. The waiting list to book the ceremony is generally two to three weeks long and the processing fees for tourists are about 500 kr.

If you're interested in the background to the current situation, visit the Web site at users.cybercity.dk/~dko12530/, produced by the first gay couple to be 'married' in Denmark.

in Copenhagen. There's an annual English-language version, called *ExPANsion – Your Homo-guide to Denmark*, published each June. For more information contact PAN-Bladet (☎ 33 36 00 82, email lbl-pan blad@lbl.dk), PO Box 1023, 1007 Copenhagen K, or cruise the LBL Web site at www.lbl.dk.

Denmark's Radio Rosa (91.4MHz) has gay and lesbian programmes from 9.30 to 11.30 pm daily, but it's mainly of interest to those who understand Danish.

A useful Web site in English that covers gay and lesbian happenings is at hjem.get2 net.dk/cphgayinfo/.

DISABLED TRAVELLERS

If you have a physical disability, get in touch with your national support organisation (preferably the 'travel officer' if there is one). They often have libraries devoted to travel and can put you in touch with travel agents who specialise in tours for disabled travellers.

For instance, the UK-based Royal Association for Disability & Rehabilitation (RADAR) publishes a useful guide called *Holidays and Travel Abroad: A Guide for Disabled People*, which gives a good overview of the facilities available in Europe. The book is available by post (UK£5) from RADAR (☎ 020-7250 3222), 12 City Forum, 250 City Rd, London EC1V 8AF.

Most Danish tourist literature, such as the Danish Tourist Board's hotel guide, the camping association listings and the hostel booklet, indicate which places have rooms and facilities accessible to people in wheelchairs.

In addition the Danish Tourist Board, in association with the Committee for Housing, Transportation and Technical Aids, produces a useful English-language publication: *Access in Denmark – a Travel Guide for the Disabled*. The book contains practical information for disabled travellers, including a list of accommodation with suitable access, information on using public transport and the accessibility of museums and sights to people in wheelchairs. It's available from larger Danish tourist offices and costs 60 kr.

Once in Denmark, two places that can sometimes help disabled travellers with specific questions are the Dansk Handicap Forbund (☎ 39 29 35 55), Kollektivhuset, Hans Knudsens Plads 1A, 2100 Copenhagen, and Invalideorganisationernes Brugerservice (Disabled People's User Service; ☎ 36 75 17 93), Kløverprisvej 10B, 2650 Hvidovre, Copenhagen.

SENIOR TRAVELLERS

Many discounts are available for things like public transport and museum admission fees, with proof of age. The minimum qualifying age is generally between 60 and 65. One example is the discount system on Danske Statsbaner (DSB; Danish State Railways), which offers reductions of from 25 to 50% to seniors aged 65 and older for travel on most days; see the Getting Around chapter for more information.

Some private companies also offer discounts: the SAS hotel chain, for example, gives guests aged 65 and older a 50% reduction off the standard published rates. The basic rule is to always inquire about the availability of senior discounts whenever you're booking transport or accommodation, or even just visiting a museum or other attraction.

In your home country, people of lower ages may be entitled to all sorts of interesting travel packages and discounts (on car rental, for instance) through organisations and travel agencies that cater for senior travellers.

TRAVEL WITH CHILDREN

Denmark is a family-oriented place, with plenty of activities geared for children. Even stuffy history museums often have a hands-on section for the kids; camping grounds commonly have playgrounds; in cities you'll find duck ponds and gardens that invite picnics; and amusement parks abound throughout the country. Staff at local tourist offices are happy to point visitors towards sights and activities of interest to children and they can sometimes provide information on babysitting services.

Successful travel with young children requires planning and effort. Try not to overdo things; even for adults, packing too much into the time available can cause problems. And make sure the activities include the kids as well – balance that day of museum-hopping with a day at Legoland. Include children in the planning of the trip; if they've helped to work out where you will be going, they will be much more interested when they get there. A good book to pick up is Lonely Planet's *Travel with Children* by Maureen Wheeler, which is loaded with tips and information.

USEFUL ORGANISATIONS
Danish Cultural Institute

The Danish Cultural Institute (Det Danske Kulturinstitut; ☎ 33 13 54 48, fax 33 15 10 91, email dancult@cultur.dk), Kultorvet 2, 1175 Copenhagen K, arranges cultural events and exchanges, sponsors Danish language classes and distributes information on various aspects of Danish culture. Its Web site is at www.dancult.demon.co.uk. It has branches in the following countries:

Belgium
  Deens Cultureel Instituut/
  Institut Culturel Danois:
  (☎ 02-230 7326, fax 230 5565,
  email d-k-i@innet.be/d-k-i@club.innet.be)
  rue du Comet/Hoomstraat 22, 1040
  Brussels
Estonia
  Taani Kultuuriinstituut
  (☎/fax 6-466 373, email dki@uninet.ee)
  Vene 14, 0001 Tallinn
Germany
  Dänisches Kulturinstitut
  (☎ 0511-6965 005, fax 6965 008,
  email d-k-i@t-online.de)
  Pelikanstrasse 7, 30177 Hannover
Hungary
  Dán Kulturális Intezét
  (☎ 76-481 554, fax 323 923,
  email d-k-i@mail.datanet.hu)
  Zimay L u 4, 6000 Kecskemét

Latvia
  Danijas Kulturas Instituts
  (☎/fax 7-289 994,
  email d-k-i@mail.bkc.lv)
  Marijas iela 13, k3, 2sal, 1050 Riga
Lithuania
  Danijos Kulturos Institutas
  (☎ 2-222 607, fax 222 412,
  email d-k-i@post.omnitel.net)
  Vilniaus 39/6, Room 208, 2001 Vilnius
Poland
  Dunski Instytut Kultury
  (☎ 58-661 5553, fax 661 5469,
  email d-k-i@rubikon.net.pl)
  ul Kilinskiego 16, 81 393 Gdynia
UK
  Danish Cultural Institute
  (☎ 0131-225 7189, fax 220 6162,
  email dci.dancult@dancult.demon.co.uk)
  3 Doune Terrace, Edinburgh EH3 6DY

American-Scandinavian Foundation

In the USA, the American-Scandinavian Foundation (☎ 212-879-9779, fax 249-3444), 725 Park Ave, New York, NY 10021, arranges cultural exchanges, publishes an English-language magazine and also presents a wide range of cultural programmes. It covers not only Denmark but all of Scandinavia. In addition, members are entitled to discounted air fares between the USA and Scandinavia, which sometimes work out to be good deals. Membership costs US$35 per year (seniors and students US$25).

DANGERS & ANNOYANCES

Denmark is by and large a very safe country and travelling presents no unusual dangers. Travellers should nevertheless be careful with their belongings, particularly in busy places, for example Copenhagen's Central Station.

In cities, you'll need to quickly become accustomed to the busy cycle lanes that run beside roads between the vehicle lanes and the pedestrian pavement, as these cycle lanes (and fast-moving cyclists) are easy to veer into accidentally.

Throughout Denmark, ☎ 112 for emergency police, fire or ambulance services.

Theft

As a traveller you're often fairly vulnerable and when you do lose things it can be a real hassle. The most important things to guard are your passport, important papers, tickets and money. It's best to always carry these next to your skin or in a sturdy leather pouch on your belt.

Carry your own padlock for hostel lockers. Be careful even in hotels; don't leave valuables lying around in your room.

Never leave your valuables unattended in parked cars. If you must leave your luggage in a vehicle, be sure that your car has a covered area that keeps bags out of sight and carry the most important items with you in a daypack. Remove all luggage overnight, even if the car is left in a garage.

Precautions

The hassles created by losing your passport can be considerably reduced if you have a record of its number and issue date or, even better, photocopies of the relevant data pages. A photocopy of your birth certificate can also be useful.

In addition keep a record of the serial numbers of your travellers cheques and photocopies of your credit cards, airline tickets and other travel documents. Keep all of this emergency material separate from your passport, cheques and cash and leave extra copies with someone you can rely on back home. Add some emergency money, say US$50, to this separate stash as well. If you do lose your passport, notify the police immediately to get a statement, then contact your nearest embassy or consulate.

LEGAL MATTERS

The authorities are very strict about drink-driving. It's illegal to drive with a blood-alcohol concentration of 0.05% or greater and drivers under the influence of alcohol are liable to stiff penalties and a possible prison sentence.

Always treat drugs with a great deal of caution. There is a fair bit of marijuana and hashish available in the region, sometimes quite openly, but note that in Denmark

(unlike in the Netherlands) all forms of cannabis are officially illegal.

If you are arrested for any punishable offence in Denmark, you can be held for up to 24 hours before appearing in court. You have a right to know the charges against you and a right to a lawyer, and you are not obliged to answer police questions before speaking to the lawyer. If you don't know of a lawyer, the police will provide a list. You don't have a legal right to a phone call but if you're cooperative they'll usually allow you one or make the contact for you.

You can get free legal advice on your rights from EU Legal Aid (☎ 33 14 41 40) or Emergency Legal Aid (☎ 35 37 68 13), both in Copenhagen.

BUSINESS HOURS

Office hours are generally from 9 am to 4 pm Monday to Friday. Most banks are open from 9.30 am to 4 pm Monday to Friday (to 6 pm on Thursday), although banks at international ports and at Copenhagen's Central Station are open longer hours and at weekends.

Most shops are open from 9.30 am to 5.30 pm on weekdays (to 2 pm on Saturday), although the trend in larger cities, such as Copenhagen, is towards longer opening hours.

PUBLIC HOLIDAYS & SPECIAL EVENTS

Summer holidays for schoolchildren begin around 20 June and end around 10 August. Schools also take a break for a week in mid-October and during the Christmas and New Year period. Many Danes take their main work holiday during the first three weeks of July.

Banks and most businesses are closed on public holidays, and transport schedules are commonly reduced as well. Public holidays observed in Denmark are:

New Year's Day (Nytårsdag)
    1 January
Maundy Thursday (Skærtorsdag)
    Thursday before Easter

Good Friday (Langfredag)
Friday before Easter
Easter Day (Påskedag)
Easter Monday (2.påskedag)
day after Easter
Common Prayer Day (Stor Bededag)
fourth Friday after Easter
Ascension Day (Kristi Himmelfartsdag)
fifth Thursday after Easter
Whitsunday (Pinsedag)
seventh Sunday after Easter
Whitmonday (2.pinsedag)
eighth Monday after Easter
Constitution Day (Grundlovsdag)
5 June
Christmas Eve
24 December (from noon)
Christmas Day (Juledag)
25 December
Boxing Day (2.juledag)
26 December

There are lots of small local festivals, agricultural shows, regattas and fairs all around Denmark that can be fun to attend if chanced upon. In addition, most towns of any size have a weekly market in the town square on either Wednesday or Saturday.

Following is a list of some of Denmark's larger annual events. Since the dates and venues can change a bit from year to year, check with tourist offices for current schedule information. Handy to pick up is the English-language *Coming Events* booklet, published by the Danish Tourist Board and containing updated schedules and details for all events nationwide.

January
New Year Concerts
Classical music performed in major cities in early January by the Zealand, Århus, Odense, Aalborg and West Jutland symphony orchestras.

February & March
Despite a paucity of major festivals in winter, there are concerts by local musicians, changing museum exhibitions and full programmes by the royal ballet and opera companies.
Night Film Festival
Held in Copenhagen; features 140 international films shown in their original languages over a nine day period between late February and early March.

Bakken
An amusement park outside Copenhagen that opens for the season at the end of March; celebrations are kicked off by a parade of some 5000 motorcyclists.

April
Queen Margrethe's Birthday
Celebrated on 16 April at Amalienborg in Copenhagen, with the royal guards in full ceremonial dress and the queen waving from the palace balcony at noon.
Tivoli and Legoland Openings
Tivoli in Copenhagen and Legoland in Billund, Denmark's two major amusement parks, open for the season in April.

May
Viking Market
Held in Ribe during the first weekend in May. A Viking marketplace is re-created with costumed vendors, craft demonstrations, riding and archery.
Tulip Festival
Held in Ribe in late May. Highlights are a parade, music and entertainment.
Wonderful Copenhagen Marathon
A 42km race through the streets of Copenhagen, held on a Sunday in mid-May and open to both amateur and professional runners.
Fyrkatspillet
A Viking play presented for two weeks from late May to early June at the Viking-era Fyrkat ring fortress outside Hobro.
Copenhagen Carnival
A three day event in the heart of the capital on Whitsunday weekend (usually in late May). Highlights include an offbeat parade, samba dancing in the streets and various carnival activities. During the day there are special events for children.

June
Riverboat Jazz Festival
Held in Silkeborg in mid-June; attracts about 25,000 jazz enthusiasts for numerous performances. Many concerts are free; there's a fee for events that take place on boats.
Midsummer Eve
Evening bonfires at beaches all around Denmark on 23 June.
Danish Derby
Denmark's most important horse race, held in late June at Klampenborg near Copenhagen.
Skagen Festival
Held in late June at various indoor venues.

Folk and world music is performed by Danish and international artists.

Round Zealand Boat Race
One of Europe's largest yacht races, held over three days in late June, starting and ending in Helsingør.

Roskilde Festival
Northern Europe's largest rock music festival, held over four days in late June or early July. Some 150 bands, including big-name international performers, attract 80,000 concert-goers.

Viking Festival
Held in Frederikssund over a two week period in late June and early July. Costumed 'Vikings' present an open-air drama, followed by a banquet with Viking food and entertainment.

Viking Play at Lindholm Høje
Held north of Aalborg over a two week period in late June and early July.

Jels Viking Play
Held next to the lake Jels Sø near Rødding in southern Jutland. A local troupe re-creates the Viking Age in an open-air play. It takes place over two weeks in late June and early July.

July
Tilting Festival
Held in Aabenraa for five days in early July and one of the largest festivals of its kind in Europe. About 500 uniformed tilters (jousters) parade on horseback and there's a big fair and fireworks.

Midtfyns Festival
Held in Ringe over five days in early July; features international rock, pop, world, folk and jazz musicians in scores of concerts.

Fourth of July Celebrations
Held to commemorate US Independence Day each 4 July in Rebild Bakker. Thousands of Danes and Danish-Americans attend.

Fannikerdage
Held in Nordby on Fanø during a weekend in early July. This event features islanders wearing traditional costumes and performing folk dances.

Copenhagen Jazz Festival
Held for 10 days in early July. This is one of the world's major jazz festivals, with indoor and outdoor concerts all around the city.

Århus Jazz Festival
Held the week following the Copenhagen Jazz Festival. Modern and traditional jazz is performed in venues all around Århus.

Maribo Jazz Festival
Held in Maribo for four days in mid-July. Traditional New Orleans jazz and big bands are featured.

Viking plays and festivals are popular events throughout Denmark in the summer months.

Copenhagen Summer Festival
Held in Copenhagen over two weeks from late July. Features chamber and classical music concerts.

Viking Moot
Held for two days in late July at the Forhistorisk Museum Moesgård in Århus, it features a Viking-style market with crafts, food and equestrian events.

August
Odense Film Festival
An international film festival in Odense that runs for six days in early August.

SCC Country Music Festival
Held in Silkeborg for three days in early August. Features country bands and soloists.

Danmarks Smukkeste Festival
Held in Skanderborg over three days in early August. Performers include Danish and international rock and folk bands.

Ballet Festival
Held for 14 days in August in Copenhagen. Features top solo dancers from Den Kongelige Ballet (Royal Danish Ballet) as well as

visiting performers from international ballet companies.

Randers Week

Held in Randers for 10 days in mid-August. Music, dance, theatre, a bicycle race and other sports events.

Tønder Festival

One of northern Europe's largest folk festivals, held in Tønder for four days in late August and featuring numerous indoor and outdoor performances.

Ny Musik i Suså

Held over a weekend in mid-August. Danish classical music is performed at the Suså school in Skelby, between Sorø and Næstved.

Danish Trotting Derby

Denmark's major trotting event, held in late August at the Charlottenlund Travbane near Copenhagen.

September

Århus Festuge (Århus Festival)

Held the first week in September and lasting for 10 days. Århus is turned into a stage for nonstop revelry featuring jazz, rock, classical music, drama and dance. As one of Scandinavia's largest cultural festivals, it encompasses hundreds of events, including street theatre, concert-hall performances and a popular road race.

Music Festivals

More than 175 music festivals are held each year in Denmark. Concerts run the gamut from hard rock music to classical, Nordic ballads to techno, gospel to jazz, and everything in-between. The festivals are spread out between May and November, with the vast majority held in July and August.

Denmark's largest rock event is the Roskilde Festival, followed by the Midtfyns Festival in Ringe. Both are large Woodstock-like events that take place in early summer, last four to five days, include more than 100 performances and attract tens of thousands of rock fans from throughout Europe. Both festivals bring in big-name international musicians: headliners at the Roskilde Festival have included the Beastie Boys, Bob Dylan and UB40, while the Midtfyns Festival has featured the likes of Aerosmith, Miles Davis and Joe Cocker.

For jazz fans the major attraction is the 10 day Copenhagen Jazz Festival held in early July. It's a total immersion jazz scene, with more than 450 concerts, some held in indoor music halls but most held in cafés, pubs and outdoor venues such as parks, squares and pedestrian streets. It's followed the next week by the smaller but still significant Århus Jazz Festival.

The village of Tønder boasts one of northern Europe's largest folk festivals. It's held over four days in late August and features both Danish and international musicians. In addition to traditional folk music there's also bluegrass, cajun and blues. About half of the performers come from the UK, the USA or Canada and typically include folk icons such as Arlo Guthrie or The Chieftains.

In some festivals all concerts are staged indoors in music halls and clubs, whereas others mix it up, with both indoor and outdoor venues. Admission charges vary according to the festival. At some events you pay for an individual performance, while at others there's a single price for the entire festival. The outdoor Roskilde Festival, for instance, costs around 800 kr and includes all concerts as well as space to pitch a tent.

In Denmark most concerts can be booked in advance through BilletNet (☎ 38 88 70 22), the national on-line ticket system, which can be found at larger post offices.

A free pamphlet with an updated listing of all music festivals, including exact dates, featured performers and admission fees, is available from Danish tourist offices or the Dansk Musik Informations Center (☎ 33 11 20 66, fax 33 32 20 16, email mic@mic.dk), Gråbrødretorv 16, 1154 Copenhagen K. Information is also available at www.mic.dk on the Web.

Golden Days Festival
  Held in Copenhagen throughout September. Features art exhibits, poetry readings, theatre, ballet and concerts that focus on Denmark's 'Golden Age' (1800-50).

Kite Flying Festival
  Held over three days in early September on Lakolk beach on Rømø.

Tour de Gudenå
  One of the world's longest kayak and canoe races; takes place in early September on the Gudenå river from Skanderborg to Randers via Ry and Silkeborg.

Amager Musikfestival
  Held from mid-September to early October. Features music performances by Danish and international soloists and ensembles at several churches in Amager; admission to all concerts is free.

October

Cultural Night in Copenhagen
  Held on the first night of the autumn school holidays (typically the second Friday in October). Museums, theatres, galleries and even Rosenborg Slot open their doors free of charge between 6 pm and midnight. There are musical events, backstage tours and fireworks.

November

Copenhagen Irish Festival
  Held in Copenhagen for four days in early November. Features traditional Irish folk music.

Musikhøst (Music Harvest)
  Held in Odense for five days in early November. Classical music and jazz is performed by musicians from Denmark and abroad. Soloists, ensembles and orchestras perform at Odense Koncerthus and other city venues.

December

Tivoli Reopening
  Reopening of Tivoli gates in Copenhagen from mid-November to a few days before Christmas with a holiday market and fair. There's ice-skating on the pond and some Tivoli restaurants offer menus with hot mulled wine and traditional holiday meals.

Christmas Fairs
  Held all around Denmark throughout December. Fairs feature food booths, arts and crafts stalls, and sometimes parades. Particularly atmospheric is the Christmas fair held for two days in early December at Den Gamle By in Århus.

ACTIVITIES

Walking

Although Denmark does not have substantial forests, there are numerous small tracts of woodland crisscrossed by a few kilometres of walking trails. Skov og Naturstyrelsen (Forest & Nature Bureau) produces brochures with sketch maps showing trails in nearly 200 such areas. These brochures can be picked up free of charge at public libraries and tourist offices.

There's public access to the coast in Denmark whether the land is publicly or privately owned, and in many areas there are walking tracks along the shoreline. Access is also granted for walkers to virtually all forests; in publicly owned areas you can walk about freely, while in privately owned woodland you must stick to the established trails. Brief walks are described under the relevant areas in the text of this book.

Swimming

Denmark is well endowed with beaches. There are attractive sandy strands all around the country, from the southern shores of Bornholm to Skagen at the northernmost tip of Jutland.

Although topless sunbathing is common on all beaches, nude sunbathing is more restricted and is generally practised only on the more private and remote sections of beaches. Unless the beach is specifically set aside for nude bathing, follow local custom.

Don't expect tropical conditions. Even in July, water temperatures in the seas around Denmark average just 16°C (61°F) in the north and 17.3°C (63°F) in the south, so most beach-goers are Germans and Scandinavians rather than visitors from warmer climes.

If you find the waters chilly, most larger towns and cities have heated public swimming pools (svømmehal) that are open to all for a modest fee. Additionally, there are numerous 'water world' parks around the country with pools and water slides that are geared to children.

CYCLING IN DENMARK

Denmark prides itself on being a bicycle-friendly country. With a gentle terrain that peaks at a mere 173m, in Central Jutland's Lake District, cycling routes are well suited to recreational cyclists, including families with children. The country is crossed by thousands of kilometres of established cycling routes, some running parallel to lightly trafficked roads and others passing through nature reserves and woods.

Denmark is a country of cyclists. Fully half of its citizens ride bicycles on a regular basis, businesspeople unabashedly cycle into their corporate parking spaces and one of the prime minister's first acts in the international arena was leading cyclists on an anti-nuclear protest to France.

Danish cyclists have rights that in many other countries are reserved for motorists. There are bicycle lanes along major city roads and through central areas, road signs are posted for bicycle traffic and bicycle racks can be found outside grocery shops, museums and many other public places.

For more details of cycling as a mode of transport, see under Bicycle in the Getting Around chapter.

Rules of the Road

Just as cyclists' rights are taken seriously in Denmark, so too are their responsibilities. Here are some of the traffic regulations geared to cyclists.

- All traffic in Denmark, both bicycle and motor vehicle, drives on the right-hand side of the road.
- Cyclists are obliged to obey traffic lights, pedestrian rights-of-way and most other road rules that apply to motor vehicles.
- When making a left turn at crossings, a large left turn is mandatory; that is, you must cycle straight across the intersecting road, staying on the right, before turning left into the right-hand lane of the new road. Do not cross diagonally.
- Use hand signals to indicate turns: your left arm should be outstretched prior to a left turn, and your right arm outstretched before a right turn.
- When entering a roundabout (traffic circle), yield to vehicles already in the roundabout.
- If you're transporting children, the bicycle must have two independent brakes. A maximum of two children under the age of six can be carried on the bicycle or in an attached trailer.

Inset: Well-signposted cycling routes and smooth, level countryside make Denmark an ideal place for family cycling trips (photograph by Ned Friary).

National Cycling Routes

Over the past decade Denmark has established a mind-boggling network of regional and national cycling routes. For distance cyclists the 10 national cycling routes, which collectively cover some 3500km, offer a wide range of options that can take you from one end of the country to the other.

1. The West Coast Route (Vestkystruten)

This route runs 550km from Rudbøl on the German border to Skagen at the northernmost tip of Denmark. Along the way it passes Denmark's longest unbroken stretch of sand and sea – bear in mind though that the coast is also windswept. You'll keep more of the wind at your back if you take this route when heading from south to north. You won't need to trudge across sand but there are many gravel sections, so it's best suited to a sturdy mountain bike.

2. Copenhagen to Hanstholm

Covering some 350km, this route takes you from the bustling capital Copenhagen across quiet North Zealand and onward by ferry to Ebeltoft, which provides a charming introduction to Jutland. From there it goes to the summer resort of Grenaa and slices west across central Jutland, taking in lots of farmland and fjords before terminating at the country's newest port town, Hanstholm. There are some gravel stretches, but most of the route is on asphalt roads.

3. The Old Military Road (Hærvejen)

Established as Denmark's first national cycling route in 1989, this route actually dates back more than a millennium, having been travelled by nomadic hunters and Viking armies. It runs 450km from Padborg to Skagen along Jutland's central ridge, which minimises the need to cross rivers and fjords. With its lengthy history, it's not surprising that cyclists pass numerous rune stones, ancient barrows and centuries-old churches along the way.

4. Copenhagen to Søndervig

This 300km route out of the capital heads west via Roskilde with its Viking ships and royal tombs and on to a ferry crossing from Kalundborg to Århus. From there you'll get a chance to switch gears as the route takes you through the Lake District and Denmark's most hilly country before depositing you at Søndervig, where you could trade in your bike for windsurfing gear. This route runs mostly along municipal roads.

NATIONAL CYCLE ROUTES

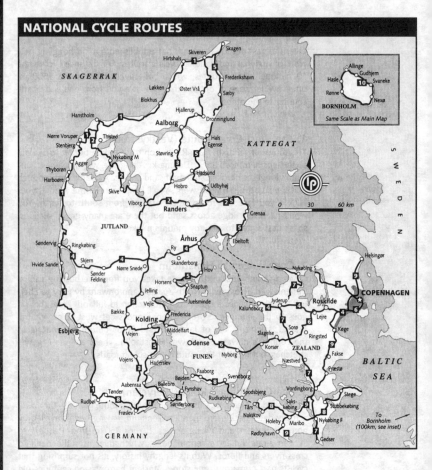

5. The East Coast Route (Østkystruten)

From Sønderborg in southern Jutland to Skagen at the northern tip of Jutland, this route meanders its way along the east coast, winding around so many peninsulas, spits and harbours that it traverses some 625km – making it the longest of all of the national cycling routes. As the east coast tends to be more protected than the west, you'll encounter far less wind, not to mention a fine variety of coastal scenery. There are also some fun places to stop along the way, such as Århus, which comes up around the halfway mark.

6. Copenhagen to Esbjerg

Funen has lovely countryside and rolling hills; this route takes in some of them, as well as circling past the fairy-tale sights of Odense. In all it covers 325km from Copenhagen to Esbjerg, Jutland's second city and Denmark's main port of entry for sea passengers from the UK. This route is particularly attractive in late spring, when much of the country-side is ablaze with a brilliant yellow carpet of flowering rapeseed.

7. Gedser to Sjællands Odde

This 230km route follows a more regional track, running from Gedser at the southern tip of Falster to Sjællands Odde in the north-west of Zealand. Falster is a straight and level section, whereas the journey though Zealand is a bit more varied, passing by the old city of Næst-ved and some lovely wooded countryside near Sorø. If you want to lengthen the journey it's possible to take a ferry from Sjællands Odde to Ebeltoft and pick up cycle route No 5 from there.

8. Rudbøl to Møn

After hugging virtually the entire Danish-German border, where most historical sites are dedicated to land struggles and battlefields, this 325km route winds through the agreeable coastal cities of Sønderborg, Faaborg, Svendborg and Rudkøbing. It then crosses Lolland and Fal-ster, with their abundant agricultural fields, before taking in Møn's medieval sites and ending at the white cliffs of Møns Klint, where you can enjoy one of Denmark's most stunning coastal vistas.

9. Rødby to Helsingør

This relatively short route covers just 230km from Rødby in sleepy Lolland to Helsingør, the busy port city that's home to Kronborg Slot, the castle made famous in Shakespeare's *Hamlet*. In-between there's rural countryside, the seaside village of Præstø, the historic town of Køge, Bakken amusement park and museums at Rungsted and Humle-bæk. All in all, a good route for those who want to mix cycling with stops at some of eastern Zealand's sightseeing attractions.

10. Around Bornholm

There are hundreds of kilometres of sea between Bornholm and the rest of Denmark, so this is strictly a one-island national cycling route – but it doesn't disappoint. Bornholm, with its granite-based geology, offers scenery not found elsewhere in Denmark, as well as unique medieval round churches and picturesque coastal villages. The Born-holm route winds along an enjoyable 115km network of cycling paths utilising former railway lines and forest trails.

Cycling Maps

There are excellent maps available for every corner of Denmark that show not only the cycling routes but also the camping grounds, hostels and sights along the way. These maps also indicate which of Denmark's vehicle roads have cycle paths and which vehicle roads prohibit bicycles altogether.

When buying maps, be sure to request an English-language version; some maps are produced in separate Danish, English and German versions, while others combine all three languages on the same map.

The best all-Denmark map for cyclists is *Cykelferiekort*, a 1:500,000 scale map published by Dansk Cyklist Forbund, the main Danish cycling organisation. It costs 49 kr.

There are separate detailed cycling maps covering each of the 14 *amt* (counties) in Denmark. Most of these are based on maps from Kort-og Matrikelstyrelsen, the company that makes Denmark's best road maps. The county maps provide greater detail than the all-Denmark map, showing such things as grocery shops, cycle repair shops and topography.

NED FRIARY

Left: Once you've stopped off for a refreshing beer in an attractive seaside village such as Præstø, it's hard to get back in the saddle.

The maps are as follows:

- Bornholms Amt (island of Bornholm), 1:50,000; 40 kr
- Frederiksborg Amt (most of North Zealand), 1:100,000; 50 kr
- Fyns Amt (Funen county, including Langeland and Ærø), 1:100,000; 75 kr
- Københavns Amt (greater Copenhagen area), 1:50,000; 20 kr
- Nordjyllands Amt (northernmost part of Jutland), 1:100,000; 55 kr
- Ribe Amt (includes Ribe and Esbjerg area), 1:100,000; 50 kr
- Ringkjøbing Amt (central part of Jutland's west coast), 1:100,000; 50 kr
- Roskilde Amt (Zealand west and south of Copenhagen), 1:100,000; 50 kr
- Storstrøms Amt (southernmost part of Zealand, plus Møn, Falster and Lolland), 1:100,000; 50 kr
- Sønderjyllands Amt (southernmost part of Jutland), 1:100,000; 50 kr
- Vejle Amt (south-east-central Jutland), 1:100,000; 50 kr
- Vestsjællands Amt (western Zealand), 1:100,000; 40 kr
- Viborg Amt (north-west-central Jutland), 1:100,000; 60 kr
- Århus Amt (greater Århus area), 1:100,000; 80 kr

Purchasing Maps

All of the maps listed here can be ordered from Dansk Cyklist Forbund (see under Resources below for details). Once in Denmark, the county maps are readily available at larger tourist offices and the whole series of maps can be bought at quality bookshops throughout the country.

Resources

The main office of the Dansk Cyklist Forbund (Danish Cyclists' Federation; ☎ 33 32 31 21, fax 33 32 76 83) is at Rømersgade 7, 1362 Copenhagen K. Maps can be ordered from there; contact the office for details of maps and postage fees. Its useful Web site is at www.dcf.dk.

CykelGuide, a brochure summarising (in Danish) the national and regional cycle routes of Denmark, is available from the national road directorate: Vejdirektoratet (☎ 70 10 10 40), Trafikantservice, Postboks 1569, Niels Juels Gade 13, 1020 Copenhagen K. This brochure can also be picked up free at tourist offices in Denmark.

There are two free regional cycling publications in English, Cycling Holidays in West Jutland and Funen and the Isles – a bike's eye view, both 32 page booklets that list suggested routes with details of things to see and do, as well as accommodation options along the way. They are available from tourist offices in Denmark. Cycling Holidays in West Jutland can also be ordered from Turistgruppen Vestjylland (fax 75 28 86 76, email tgv@tgv.dk), Torvet 5, Nørre Nebel, or from its

Web site at www.tgv.dk. *Funen and the Isles* can also be ordered from Cykelnetværk Fyn (☎ 66 13 13 37, fax 66 13 13 38, email bikefunen @fyntour.dk), Svendborgvej 83-85, Postboks 499, 5260 Odense S, or from its Web site at www.fyntour.dk.

Overnighting along the Way

As distances between villages and towns are not great in Denmark, you'll seldom be very far from one of Denmark's 525 camping grounds or one of its 100 hostels. Indeed there are some places, such as the Kongskilde Friluftsgård hostel in Sorø in southern Zealand, that are right on a cycling route.

Many camping grounds, particularly those close to cycling routes, have special areas set aside for cyclists and as a general rule they can often make space for cycling campers, even after the camping ground has been closed to motorists. All camping grounds with a four star or five star rating have bicycle racks and a covered bicycle repair area where tools can be borrowed; some of the camping grounds with fewer than four stars have these facilities as well.

In addition to conventional camping grounds, some 750 farmers throughout Denmark allow cyclists to pitch a tent on their property. It's primitive camping, but the cost is just 15 kr or less per night. The booklet *Overnatning i det fri*, which is published by Dansk Cyklist Forbund and costs 80 kr, lists the locations of the farms.

Cycling Tours

Denmark's cycling maps make it easy to plan your own tour because they show places to stay and all sorts of sightseeing spots, such as castles, museums and historic sights.

However, if you're interested in joining an organised cycling tour, the Dansk Cyklist Forbund (see under Resources) arranges tours, as do the following companies:

BikeDenmark (☎ 35 36 41 00, fax 35 36 42 00), Åboulevard 1, 1635 Copenhagen V

Cykelferie i Danmark (☎ 58 19 45 15, fax 58 19 01 15), c/o Hotel Kobæk Strand, 4230 Skælskør

Sydfyns Turistbureau (☎ 62 21 09 80, fax 62 22 05 33), Centrumpladsen 4, 5700 Svendborg

Prices will vary by tour, depending in part on what kind of accommodation is provided. With BikeDenmark, for example, seven-day tours of southern Funen, western Jutland or northern Zealand cost around 5000 kr, based on double occupancy stays in small hotels or inns.

Windsurfing

Denmark has excellent conditions for windsurfing (often called 'surfing' in Danish), varying from open seas favoured by pros to inland fjords and sheltered coastal areas with calm waters that are ideal for beginners. If you want to hire equipment or take lessons, you can do so at a number of windsurfing shops around Denmark. Most are in Jutland, the west coast of which has some of the country's top wind and wave conditions, but you'll also find a few along the Zealand coast within easy reach of the capital.

Hiring a board and rig typically costs between 250 and 350 kr per day, with the lower prices for beginners' gear. You can get a three hour introductory lesson for about 400 kr or a more substantial lesson for double that price, which includes use of the equipment.

The largest windsurfing organisation, Surf & Ski, publishes the Danish-language magazine *Surf News*, which lists the locations of windsurfing shops, gives dates and details of windsurfing tournaments and advertises equipment. It can be picked up at windsurfing shops around the country or by contacting Surf & Ski (☎ 75 22 02 11, fax 75 22 51 37, email intsurf@web4u.dk), Håndværkervej 10a, 6800 Varde.

Sailing

With more than 7300km of coastline and hundreds of islands, Denmark offers some excellent sailing possibilities. There are lots of calm-water fjords and protected seas such as Smålandsfarvandet (the area nestled between Zealand and Lolland) and the popular island-dotted waters to the south of Funen.

Although most sailors in Danish waters are Scandinavians and Germans with their own boats, it's also possible to hire boats in Denmark, with or without crew. The Maritime Center Danmark (☎ 62 80 02 16, fax 62 80 02 15), Havnepladsen 2, 5700 Svendborg, can arrange cruises and charters, including some on historic wooden sailing ships. It is also a good source of general information for yachters and can

help to arrange maritime school camp stays and trips on Viking-style square-rigged vessels.

Fishing

Denmark abounds with streams and lakes, many of which are stocked with pike, perch and trout. In addition, with so much shoreline the saltwater fishing possibilities are nearly endless; the most common saltwater fish are cod, mackerel, plaice and sea trout.

Anglers between the ages of 18 and 67 must buy a fishing licence, which costs 25 kr per day or 75 kr per week and can be purchased at tourist offices and post offices. There are also a number of privately run 'put and take' fishing holes that allow you to fish for an established fee (no licence required).

Golf

In Denmark you are seldom far from a golf course – there are about 120 scattered around the Danish countryside. By Danish standards, green fees are reasonable: about 175 kr on weekdays, 250 kr at the weekend. Some of the courses are private clubs, so if you have a membership card from a golf club at home bring it along as it'll sometimes get you temporary membership at Danish golf clubs. You can obtain more information on golf courses from Danish tourist offices.

COURSES

Scandinavia's unique *folkehøjskole*, literally 'folk high school' (the 'high' meaning institute of higher learning), provides a liberal education within a communal living environment. Folk high schools were first established in Denmark, inspired by philosopher NFS Grundtvig's concept of 'enlightenment for life'. The curriculum varies between schools but includes such things as drama, Danish culture, peace studies and organic farming. People aged 19 and older can enrol and there are no entrance exams and no degrees. For more information, including a catalogue of the nearly 100 schools, contact Højskolernes Sekretariat

Tracing Your Danish Roots

Many visitors of Danish descent take advantage of their trip to Denmark to trace their roots and seek out the birthplace of their ancestors. If your family hasn't kept in touch with relatives still living in Denmark, establishing your genealogy will generally require some careful investigation.

The best place to begin your research is at home before you go. People generally hold on to their naturalisation papers; these and other official forms can indicate such vital information as an immigrant's birth date and place of birth. Any old letters from Denmark that have been stowed away may also reveal important clues, including the return addresses of relatives. Other possible sources of immigration records are the national archives in your home country.

Once you've determined the birthplace or last Danish address of your ancestors, Udvandrerarkiv Det Danske (Danish Emigration Archives), which maintains the history of Danish emigrants and their offspring, can help you to establish your genealogy and make contact with distant relatives. Its address is: Udvandrerarkiv Det Danske (☎ 99 31 42 20), Postboks 1731, Ved Vor Frue Kirke, 9000 Aalborg; its Web site is at www.cybercity.dk/users/ccc13656.

Among the resources maintained by Udvandrerarkiv Det Danske are copies of the old emigration lists compiled by the police and numerous manuscripts and periodicals relating to emigration. If you contact them in advance of your trip, they can help you to place ads in local newspapers in an effort to make contact with distant relatives. Once in Denmark, you can use their library and research facilities to learn more about your family history.

In addition, Rigsarkivet (National Archives) in Copenhagen keeps various records. The most important for genealogical research are census forms and military draft registers, which date back as far as 1787; note, however, that only people of the peasantry had to register for the draft prior to 1849. The address is: Rigsarkivet, 9 Rigsdagsgården, 1218 Copenhagen K.

There are also four provincial archives that keep birth, death and marriage certificates and other similar records. They are: Landsarkivet for Sjælland (Zealand), 10 Jagtvej, 2200 Copenhagen N; Landsarkivet for Fyn (Funen county), 36 Jernbanegade, 5000 Odense; Landsarkivet for Nørrejylland (northern Jutland), 5 Lille Sankt Hansgade, 8800 Viborg; and Landsarkivet for de Sønderjyske Landsdele (southern Jutland), 45 Haderslevvej, 6200 Aabenraa.

(☎ 33 13 98 22, email hs@grundtvig.dk), Nytorv 7, 1450 Copenhagen K, or visit the Web site at www.folkehojskoler.dk.

While most folk high schools teach in Danish only, at the International People's College (☎ 49 21 33 61), Montebello Allé 1, 3000 Helsingør, students and teachers come from around the world, instruction is in English and foreigners are welcome to enrol in short-term courses, typically lasting from two to eight weeks. The cost of an eight week course is 10,900 kr, including meals accommodation, tuition and outings. The Web site is at www.ipc.dk.

Language

Contact the Danish Cultural Institute (see under Useful Organisations earlier in this chapter) for information on Danish language courses that might be offered in your home country.

In Denmark there are several schools set up to teach Danish to foreigners, but most focus on teaching immigrants or other long-term residents. Studieskolen, however, currently offers a six week course that has a more open enrolment than most programmes; lessons are twice weekly and the course costs 1675 kr.

Three schools in Copenhagen that offer Danish language courses to foreigners are:

AOF
(☎ 39 16 82 00) Lersø Park Allé 44, 2100 Copenhagen Ø
KISS
(☎ 33 11 44 77) Nørregade 20, 1165 Copenhagen K
Studieskolen
(☎ 33 14 43 22) Antonigade 6, 1106 Copenhagen K

WORK

Denmark has a significant level of unemployment and the job situation is not very promising for non-Danes, and much less so for those who don't speak Danish.

In terms of qualifying to work in Denmark, foreigners are divided into three categories: Scandinavian citizens, citizens of EU countries and other foreigners. Essentially, other Scandinavian citizens have the easiest go of it because they can reside and work legally in Denmark without restrictions.

Although there can be snarls, EU citizens are entitled to look for work in Denmark and it's fairly straightforward to get a residency permit once a job is established. The main prerequisite is that your job provides an income that's high enough to cover your living expenses.

Citizens of other countries are required to obtain a work permit before entering Denmark. You must first secure a job offer and then apply for a work and residency permit at a Danish embassy or consulate while still in your home country (or the country where you've had legal residency for the last six months). You can enter Denmark only after the permit has been granted. Currently these permits are rarely given to anyone without a specialised skill.

If you do decide to look for work in Denmark, the AF Arbejdsmarkedsservice (☎ 33 55 10 20), a public job centre at Kultorvet 17, 1019 Copenhagen K, helps link up the unemployed with employers looking for workers. The newspapers with the best jobs-wanted columns are the Sunday issues of *Politiken* and *Berlingske Tidende*. If you

don't mind being a waiter, kitchen helper or cleaner, restaurants and hotels are two types of businesses that are reasonably likely to offer jobs to foreigners, so you might try inquiring directly.

Regulations regarding street musicians and other buskers are determined by each municipality and are subject to change, so if you're interested in performing, check first at the local police station.

In Copenhagen, for example, rules in force at the time of research allowed unobtrusive individuals, duos and trios to perform acoustic (nonamplified) music from 4 to 8 pm Monday to Thursday, 3 to 8 pm on Friday, 10 am to 5 pm on Saturday and noon to 5pm on Sunday in city squares. Jugglers, magicians and other street performers, as well as any musical group consisting of more than three people, must apply at the police station for permission before performing.

ACCOMMODATION

Denmark has a wide range of accommodation options and your budget will be greatly affected by which types you select. Although truly cheap hotels are virtually unknown in Denmark, there are some good alternatives. If you're on a tight budget, you'll save money by camping, staying in hostels or booking rooms in private homes.

If you do opt to stay in hotels there are some schemes, especially in the summer and at weekends, that can bring hotel rates down to a more reasonable level. You may find it works out best to combine different types of accommodation to suit your travelling needs. For example, with a moderate budget, on weekdays you could stay in hostels (most have private rooms available for couples or families) and then end the week in comfortable chain hotels that offer discounted weekend rates. Self-catering flats and cottages may be worth considering if you're with a group and are planning to stay in one place for a while.

Staff at local tourist offices are generally very helpful and can provide lists of in-town and nearby accommodation options.

Sometimes they can also call round and do the actual booking for you, for which there may be a nominal fee.

During the high season accommodation can be hard to find and it's advisable to book ahead. Even camping grounds can fill up, especially popular ones in big cities. Because most people travel in Denmark with advance reservations, in this book you'll find the phone number, fax number and postal address listed for each hostel, camping ground and hotel.

Accommodation rates quoted in Denmark, including those listed in this book, include all taxes and service charges.

Camping

Camping is very popular in Denmark and there were, at last count, 525 camping grounds spread around the country. No matter where you're travelling you'll seldom be far from one. In resort areas camping grounds are commonly found right in the thick of it all, whereas in cities and large towns they tend to be on the outskirts of the municipality. For this reason camping is most popular for people with their own vehicles. If you're on foot the money you save by camping can quickly be outweighed by the money you spend commuting to and from a town centre. Of course you'll also need a tent, sleeping bag, cooking equipment and other bits and pieces – easier to cart around if you have a vehicle.

Although most camping grounds are seasonal, about 100 places stay open year-round. The rest vary quite a bit in their opening season; some, particularly those in seaside resort areas, are open only in the summer months, while others operate from spring to autumn. Many of those that have a longer season offer discounted rates outside the summer high season.

Although other factors come into play, prices are largely dependent upon the camping ground's rating (see under Ratings later in this section), and rise by roughly 10% with each additional star. The per-night charge to pitch a tent or park a caravan typically ranges from 45 to 55 kr for each

---

Danish Camping Terms

Here are some common Danish words that campers are apt to come across on camping signs and price lists:

voksne	adult
børn	child
hund	dog
campingvogn	caravan, house trailer
campingbil	motorised caravan
hytte	cabin, hut
udlejning	rental
strøm	electricity charge
handicapvenligt	an area accessible by wheelchair
dag/uge	day/week

Danish camping logo

---

adult and about half that for each child. In the summer, some places also tack on a surcharge of 15 to 30 kr per tent/caravan.

A camping pass is required for stays at all camping grounds. If you don't have a valid Camping Card International, then you can purchase a Danish carnet at the first camping ground you visit or from tourist offices. The cost for an annual pass is 30 kr for an individual or 60 kr for a family. See under Camping Card in the earlier Visas & Documents section of this chapter.

Camping is regulated in Denmark and is only allowed in established camping grounds or on private land with the owner's permission. Although it may seem tempting, camping in a car or caravan at the beach, in a car park or along the street is prohibited and can result in an immediate fine.

If you're camping with a car or caravan, particularly in the high season, it's wise to make reservations. If you're backpacking or travelling by bicycle, note that even if a camping ground is signposted as fully booked to motorists, it's worth stopping to talk to the warden, as they will often be able to find a site for a camper who is travelling light.

Most road maps of Denmark show camping grounds but the handiest is the free fold-out map distributed by the Danish Tourist Board that lists the addresses of camping grounds throughout Denmark.

If you're camping your way around Denmark, a useful book is the annually updated *Camping Danmark*, published by Camping-rådet (Danish Camping Board), which lists all approved camping grounds in Denmark and gives details on their exact facilities, ratings and opening dates. It can be bought in most bookshops and in some tourist offices, and costs 95 kr.

Alternately, DK-Camp (☎ 75 82 49 55), the largest camping association in Denmark, publishes the annual book *DK Camping Danmark* listing details of its 320 member camping grounds; the publication is available free at larger tourist offices and affiliated camping grounds. Its Web site is at www.dk-camp.dk.

Cabins & Caravans Many Danish camping grounds also rent cabins (and/or on-site caravans) sleeping four to six people and costing from about 200 to 450 kr per night in the summer high season, a bit less in the low season. Although cabins often have cooking facilities, bed linen and blankets are rarely provided so it's best to bring your own sleeping bag. Toilet and shower facilities are not in the cabins but shared with other campers.

Most camping grounds in Denmark gear their facilities to people touring by caravan

– in fact, many Danish camping grounds look more like car parks than nature reserves. All sites classified two star or higher are equipped to accommodate caravans, with facilities for emptying toilets, replenishing drinking water and cleaning tanks.

Ratings Camping grounds in Denmark are rated by the Danish Camping Board using a star system: the number of stars relates to the facilities. That rating is displayed at the camping ground, as well as in literature that lists camping areas. Throughout this book we give the star rating, as it indicates both the level of facilities and the relative price.

One-star camping grounds fulfil minimum standards, providing running water, toilets, at least one shower and at least one electricity outlet for shavers.

Two-star places have a minimum of one shower for every 25 sites, a kitchen with hot tap water and hotplates, as well as a playground for children. To qualify for a two star rating, the site must also be within 2km of a grocery shop.

Camping grounds with three stars, the most common rating, have more elaborate facilities, including hot water in the washbasins, a communal lounge, a larger play area for children, nursing rooms for babies, and sinks or washing machines for laundry. They must also be within 1km of a grocery shop.

In recent years the system was expanded to make way for four and five-star ratings. The higher standards required to earn the additional stars are mostly creature comforts, but these higher ratings also require that there be a separate pitch area for tents and an equipped bicycle repair area. Currently only a few camping grounds have received the new top ratings but it has provided an incentive for many three-star places to upgrade their facilities, so camping – already of a high standard in Denmark – should become an increasingly comfortable option each year.

When selecting a camping ground keep in mind that, although the stars give a good indication of what to expect, they don't tell the whole story. For example, if a place meets all of the qualifications for a three star rating but is more than 1km from a grocery shop, it still can't be rated higher than two stars.

Hostels

Denmark's 100 hostels (*vandrerhjem*) are members of the Hostelling International (HI) organisation, which in recent years has changed its name from International Youth Hostel Federation (IYHF) in order to attract a wider clientele and move away from the emphasis on youth. Some countries have been slow in making the switch to HI, so if your home hostel card says IYHF, HI or YHA, it's all the same thing.

Most of Denmark's hostels have private rooms in addition to dormitory rooms, which makes them a good-value alternative to hotels. Danish hostels appeal to a wide range of guests in all age categories and are oriented as much towards families and groups as they are to backpackers, students and other budget travellers.

Facilities in hostels vary but most newer hostels have two and four-bed rooms and are thus well suited for use by couples and small groups. Most hostels list rates for singles and doubles, although during the busier periods some are loathe to rent private rooms to individuals or couples unless you're willing to pay for all of the beds in that room.

Hostels are categorised by a star system, with ratings ranging from one to five stars. One-star hostels meet the basic requirements, whereas two-star hostels add on luggage storage facilities and a small shop; three-star hostels also have a TV lounge. Four and five-star hostels have more fancy facilities and a minimum of 75% of their rooms have a shower and toilet.

Depending on the hostel category, dorm beds cost from 65 to 90 kr, while private rooms range from 140 to 265 kr for singles and 150 to 300 kr for doubles, plus about 40 to 60 kr for each additional person.

With few exceptions, Danish hostels have single bunk-style beds with comfort-able foam mattresses. Blankets and pillows are provided at all hostels but if you don't bring your own sheets you'll have to hire them; they cost around 35 kr per stay. Sleeping bags are not allowed. A handy, lightweight pouch-style sleeping sheet with an attached pillow cover can be purchased at many hostels worldwide and will save you a bundle on sheet-rental charges.

Travellers who don't have an international hostel card can buy one once they arrive in Denmark for 125 kr (annual fee) or pay 25 kr extra for each night's stay. If you're not sure whether you'll be staying at hostels often enough to make it worth buying an annual card, ask for a sticker each time you pay the 25 kr per-night fee; if you accumulate six stickers you'll earn yourself an annual hostel card.

In the summer and other holiday periods many hostels get fully booked, so it's always a good idea to make advance reservations, which can be done by telephone, fax or letter (and, at some hostels, by email). Outside Copenhagen, you can generally check in between 4 and 9 pm, but in a few places reception closes as early as 6 pm. In most hostels the reception office is closed – and the phone not answered – between noon and 4 pm.

In the spring and autumn, hostels can get crowded with children on school outings; many hostels require reservations from individual travellers between 1 September and 15 May. Most Danish hostels close in the winter for a period ranging from a few weeks to several months.

You can pick up the handy 185 page *Danhostel Danmarks Vandrerhjem* guide free from hostels or tourist offices; it provides information on individual hostels, including a breakdown of each hostel's facilities and a simple sketch map showing its location.

All Danish hostels provide an all-you-can-eat breakfast costing 40 kr or less and many also provide dinner (65 kr maximum). Most hostels also have guest kitchens with pots and pans where you can cook your own food.

The Danish hostelling association is Danhostel (☎ 33 31 36 12, fax 33 31 36 26, email ldv@danhostel.dk), Vesterbrogade 39, 1620 Copenhagen V. The association's Web site is at www.danhostel.dk. A growing number of individual hostels also have Web sites; these can often be accessed by adding the individual hostel name to the end of the association address; hence the Web site for the Ribe hostel is www.danhostel.dk/ribe.

To join HI before you leave, ask at your nearest hostel or contact your national hostelling association. National offices include:

Australia
Australian Youth Hostel Association
(☎ 02-9565 1699) Level 3, 10 Mallett St, Camperdown, NSW 2050
Canada
Hostelling International – Canada
(☎ 613-237-7884) 205 Catherine St, Suite 400, Ottawa, Ontario K2P 1C3
England & Wales
Youth Hostels Association
(☎ 01727-855215) Trevelyan House, 8 St Stephen's Hill, St Albans, Herts AL1 2DY
Ireland
An Oige, Irish Youth Hostel Association
(☎ 01-8304555) 61 Mountjoy St, Dublin 7
New Zealand
Youth Hostels Association of New Zealand
(☎ 03-379 9970) PO Box 436, 173 Gloucester St, Christchurch 1
Northern Ireland
Youth Hostel Association of Northern Ireland
(☎ 028-9032 4733) 22 Donegall Rd, Belfast BT12 5JN
Scotland
Scottish Youth Hostels Association
(☎ 01786-891400) 7 Glebe Crescent, Stirling FK8 2JA
USA
Hostelling International – American Youth Hostels
(☎ 202-783-6161) 733 15th St NW, Suite 840, Washington, DC 20005

Rooms in Private Homes
Staff at many tourist offices can book rooms in private homes in their region for a small fee or can provide a free list of the rooms so travellers can phone for themselves. Rates vary widely but average about 150/250 kr for singles/doubles. In most cases, breakfast is available, costing an additional 30 to 40 kr per person. This is not only a cheaper accommodation option than the hotels, but can also be a good opportunity to meet local families.

In addition, Dansk Bed & Breakfast (☎ 39 61 04 05), Postbox 53, 2900 Hellerup, publishes the free booklet *Bed & Breakfast in Denmark*, which lists 500 homes throughout Denmark offering private rooms at similar rates. Its Web site is at www.bbdk.dk.

There's an excellent B&B association in Funen; see the boxed text in the Funen chapter.

Farm Stays
If you'd like to be in the country, Danish Farmhouse Holidays (☎ 75 60 21 20, fax 75 60 21 90), Søndergade 26, 8700 Horsens, books stays on 50 farms throughout Denmark. There's an interesting variety of farmhouses, ranging from modern homes to traditional straw-roofed timber-framed places. The cost, including breakfast, averages 200 kr per person per day (half-price for children under 12 years old). They also book self-contained flats and small houses that can accommodate up to six people, costing around 3000 kr per week. Upon request, the organisation will mail you a booklet containing a colour photo and brief description of each place as well as booking details. You can also visit the Web site at www.countryside-holidays.dk.

Landsforeningen for Landboturisme (☎ 86 37 39 00, fax 86 37 35 50), Lerbakken 7, Følle, 8410 Rønde, produces a similar picture booklet listing farmhouses around Denmark that welcome holiday visitors. The main difference is that this booklet has mailing addresses for each farm so you can book directly.

Although it's wise to make plans in advance, if you're cycling or driving around Denmark on your own you're also likely to come across farmhouses displaying *værelse* (room) signs.

Manor Houses

Danske Slotte & Herregaarde (☎ 86 60 38 44, fax 86 60 38 31), Fælledvej 1B, 8800 Viborg, books rooms in two dozen manor houses and small castles around Denmark. The cost ranges from 495 to 1100 kr for singles and 695 to 1590 kr for doubles, including breakfast. Brochures can be obtained by mail in advance or picked up at some of the larger tourist offices once you arrive in Denmark.

Hotels

Hotels can be found in the centre of all major Danish cities and towns. Prices at the budget end average around 375/500 kr for singles/doubles. Although the cheapest places tend to be spartan, Danish hotels are rarely seedy or unsafe. Interestingly, while budget hotels tend to be pricey for what you get, the difference in rates between categories is relatively small. Standard top-end hotels generally cost only about a third more than budget hotels, particularly if you use weekend rates or other hotel schemes.

Kro, a name that implies a country inn but is more commonly the Danish version of a motel, is a type of accommodation typically found along major motorways near the outskirts of town. A kro is generally cheaper than a hotel but the rooms are usually simpler and the walls may well be thin. As a rule, they're not a practical option unless you have your own transport.

Both hotels and kros usually include an all-you-can-eat breakfast, which can vary from a simple meal of bread, cheese and coffee to a generous full-table buffet.

Hotel Schemes There are a number of hotel schemes that can pare down room costs in Danish hotels and inns. The main programmes, outlined below, cover many of Denmark's mid-range and top-end hotels, so if you plan to use hotels as your main accommodation, these schemes are well worth considering.

Dansk Kroferie This organisation (☎ 75 64 87 00, fax 75 64 87 20), Vejlevej 16, 8700 Horsens, operates a system of 'Inn Cheques' valid at the 84 inns that belong to its association. The cheques can be purchased at Danish tourist offices and travel agencies, and cost 595 kr for a double room, 675 kr for a family of three and 775 kr for a family of four. Each cheque covers breakfast and a room with bath. Although most of the association's hotels and inns accept the cheques at face value, some add on a surcharge ranging from 125 to 175 kr. The association publishes a 50 page booklet

---

Danish Hotel Terms

Here are some words you'll come across in hotel brochures:

værelse	room
enkeltværelse	single room
dobbeltværelse	double room
eget bad og toilet	with shower and toilet
bad og toilet på gangen	shower and toilet in the hallway
morgenmad inkl i prisen	breakfast included in the price
senge; køjsenge	beds; bunk beds
med opredning	with extra bed
lejlighed	flat, apartment
adgang til køkken	access to kitchen
vaskemaskine og tørretumbler	washing machine and tumbler drier

providing a brief description of member hotels and noting which add the surcharge; its Web site is at www.dansk-kroferie.dk.

Scandic Hotels The Scandic Holiday Card, which costs 100 kr and is valid for one year, can be used at 15 Scandic hotels (listed on the Web site at www.scandic-hotels.com) in Denmark to obtain one night's accommodation at a cost of 625 kr per room, breakfast included. The rooms are in top-end hotels and have bath, TV and minibar. The price covers two adults and up to two children. The card can be used at Scandic hotels at weekends year-round and on any day during Danish school holidays, including the summer high season. The cards can be purchased on the spot at any Scandic hotel and from some tourist offices, and come with a voucher valid for a 100 kr discount at the hotel restaurant.

Best Western Hotels The Best Western group, which runs 35 hotels in Denmark, has a straightforward weekend and holiday discount that doesn't require vouchers or advance payment. Under this plan, a room sleeping up to two adults and two children costs 695 kr per night including breakfast. The rate is effective at weekends year-round and on weekdays during school holiday periods, including from mid-June to early August. It's best to book as far in advance as possible as the offer is valid on a limited number of rooms, but you can sometimes benefit from the deal on a walk-in basis. The Best Western Web site is at www.bestwestern.com.

Seaside Cottages & Flats

In many seaside resort areas, cottages and flats account for a significant slice of the accommodation options. They are suited mostly to visitors who are planning to holiday at one specific location, as they are generally booked by the week and require reservations. Rates vary greatly, depending upon the type of accommodation and the season, but generally work out cheaper than hotels.

The Green Key

Ecology-minded Denmark has instituted a new system known as Den Grønne Nøgle (The Green Key) to acknowledge environmentally friendly hotels and hostels.

Numerous criteria must be fulfilled for a place to be awarded Den Grønne Nøgle. These include limiting water consumption by fitting water-saving shower heads, using low-energy light bulbs and ecologically friendly detergents, recycling waste, having smokefree rooms and serving at least two organic products at breakfast.

Places that qualify for Den Grønne Nøgle display a special logo that looks like a smiling green key standing on end.

DanCenter (☎ 70 13 16 16, fax 33 33 75 94), Søtorvet 5, 1371 Copenhagen K, handles cottage bookings on a nationwide basis and publishes a free catalogue with a colour photo of each place available to rent. Many tourist offices can also help make reservations or you can visit DanCenter's Web site at www.dancenter.dk.

FOOD

Nothing epitomises Danish food more than *smørrebrød* (literally 'buttered bread'), an open sandwich that ranges from very basic fare to elaborate sculpture-like creations. Typically it's a slice of rye bread topped with either roast beef, tiny shrimps, roast pork or fish fillet and finished off with a variety of garnishes. Although smørrebrød is served in most restaurants at lunchtime, it's cheapest in bakeries or specialised smørrebrød takeaway shops found near train stations and office buildings.

Also distinctively Danish is the *koldt bord* (literally 'cold table'), a buffet-style spread of cold foods, including cold cuts, smoked fish, cheeses, vegetables, salads, condiments, breads and crackers, plus usually a few hot dishes such as meatballs and fried fish. The cornerstone of the koldt bord is herring, which comes in pickled, marinated and salted versions. Generally a serving of herring with raw onions is treated as a starter, because it's thought to prime the stomach for the meal. The pickled herring is almost invariably washed down with cold *akvavit* (schnapps), a type of spirit.

Apart from Danish food, plenty of other international cuisines are available, including some expensive French fare, moderately priced Indian, Turkish and Chinese food, and generic American fast food such as McDonald's and Burger King. Some of the cheapest and most common places to eat are Italian restaurants, all of which offer the standard pizza and pasta menu. Simple Greek eateries serving inexpensive *shawarma*, a filling pitta-bread sandwich of shaved meat, are also common in larger towns and cities. You can find a cheap, if not particularly healthy, snack at one of the ubiquitous *pølsemandens*, the wheeled carts that sell a variety of hot dogs and sausages.

The rich pastry known elsewhere in the world as 'Danish' is called *wienerbrød* in Denmark and nearly every second street corner has a bakery with mouthwatering varieties. Less universal in appeal is the salty liquorice *lakrids* that's a favourite among Danes; one popular type is *piratos*, which comes in a flat coin shape.

Dagens ret, which means daily special, is usually the best deal on the menu, while the *børnemenu* is for children.

Although strictly vegetarian restaurants are rare, vegetarians should be able to get by fairly comfortably in Denmark. Danish cafés commonly serve a variety of salads and vegetarians can often find something suitable at the smørrebrød counter. In addition there are a growing number of Middle Eastern restaurants with buffets that include vegetarian dishes, and if cheese is acceptable to you there are scores of pizzerias throughout Denmark.

A comprehensive glossary of Danish food and drink terms can be found in the Language chapter at the back of this book.

Danish Cuisine

Danish cuisine relies heavily on fish, meat and potatoes. The following are some typical Danish dishes:

Flæskesteg – roast pork, usually with crackling, served with potatoes and cabbage

Frikadeller – fried ground-pork meatballs, commonly served with boiled potatoes and red cabbage

Fyldt hvidkålshoved – ground beef wrapped in cabbage leaves

Gravad laks – cured or salted salmon marinated in dill and served with a sweet mustard sauce

Hakkebøf – a ground-beef burger, usually covered with fried onions and served with boiled potatoes, brown sauce and beets

Hvid labskovs – Danish stew made from square cuts of beef boiled with potatoes, bay leaves and pepper

Kogt torsk – poached cod, usually in a mustard sauce and served with boiled potatoes

Mørbradbøf – small pork fillets, commonly in a mushroom sauce

Stegt flæsk – crisp-fried pork slices, generally served with potatoes and a parsley sauce

Stegt rødspætte – fried, breaded plaice, usually served with parsley potatoes

Æggekage – a rich Funen omelette served with dark bread

DRINKS

Denmark's Carlsberg and Tuborg breweries both produce excellent beers. Beer (*øl*) can be ordered as *fadøl* (draught beer), *pilsner* (lager), *lyst øl* (light beer), *lagerøl* (dark lager) or *porter* (stout).

The most popular spirit in Denmark is the Aalborg-produced *akvavit* (aquavit). There are several dozen types, the most common of which is spiced with caraway seeds. In Denmark akvavit is not sipped but is swallowed straight down as a shot, usually followed by a chaser of beer. A popular Danish liqueur made from cherries is Peter Heering, which is good sipped straight or served over vanilla ice cream.

Common wine terms include *hvidvin* (white wine), *rødvin* (red wine), *mousserende vin* (sparkling wine) and *husets vin* (house wine). *Gløgg* is a mulled wine that's a favourite speciality during the Christmas season.

Danish Beer

Danes are great producers and drinkers of beer. Denmark's United Breweries, an amalgamation of Carlsberg and Tuborg breweries, is the largest exporter of beer in Europe. Not all of the brew makes its way out of Denmark, however: Danes down some seven million hectolitres (roughly two billion bottles) of brew a year, ranking them sixth among the greatest beer drinkers worldwide.

The bestselling beers in Denmark are pilsners, lagers with an alcohol content of 4.6%, but there are scores of other beers to choose from as well. These range from light beers with an alcohol content of 1.7% to hearty stouts that kick in at 8%. You'll find the percentage of alcohol listed on the bottle label and Danish beers are classified with ascending numbers according to the amount of alcohol they contain, with *klasse 1* referring to the common pilsners and *klasse 4* to the strongest stouts.

Beer, wine and spirits are served in most restaurants and cafés. They can be purchased at grocery shops during normal shopping hours and prices are quite reasonable compared with those in other Scandinavian countries. The minimum legal age for purchasing alcoholic beverages is 18 years.

ENTERTAINMENT

Denmark's cities have some of the most active nightlife in Europe, with live music wafting through numerous side-street cafés, especially in the university cities of Copenhagen, Århus and Odense. You'll find a wide range of music, including current alternative trends, rock, folk, jazz and blues. Not much begins before 10 pm or ends before 3 am.

Den Kongelige Ballet is one of the most highly regarded in Europe. The larger Danish cities have concert halls with their own symphony orchestras; these halls also double as venues for big-name Danish and international musicians of all genres, including classical music, pop and jazz.

Most towns have cinemas showing first-run English-language films. Foreign films are not dubbed – movies are shown in their original language with Danish subtitles.

Casino gambling has been introduced and casinos can now be found in the following locations: SAS Scandinavia Hotel in Copenhagen, Hotel Marienlyst in Helsingør, SAS HC Andersen Hotel in Odense, Hotel Royal in Århus, Hotel Munkebjerg in Vejle and Limfjordshotellet in Aalborg.

SPECTATOR SPORTS

The national sport is football (soccer). See the boxed text 'Danish Football Teams' on the following page for details of teams and venues.

Cycling, rowing and sailing are popular; there are numerous regional competitions throughout Denmark during the relevant seasons.

Despite the country's small size, over the years Denmark has won Olympic gold

Danish Football Teams

Denmark's national football team has fared fairly well in recent years and is usually rated in the top 20 teams worldwide. Denmark won the Euro '92 championship, beating Germany 2-0 in the final after a late withdrawal by Yugoslavia led to their inclusion in the competition. In the 1998 World Cup, Denmark made it to the quarter-finals, losing to top-ranked Brazil. Danish players can be found in teams worldwide; the Laudrup brothers, Michael and Brian, and goalkeeper Peter Schmeichel are easily recognised by football fans abroad. If you're keen to watch an international match, games are played at Parken, Denmark's national stadium in Copenhagen.

The national leagues or *Serie* are headed by the *Superliga*, the top division containing 12 teams who slug it out through the season (late July to late May, with a break from early December to early March) for the league title. Prominent are teams from Copenhagen such as Brøndby and the more recently formed FC København, although Århus has two teams in the Superliga and other main cities are also represented. You can usually see a game for less than 100 kr; the home grounds and contact details of the main Superliga clubs are listed below.

AB (Akademisk Boldklub)
Gladsaxe Idrætspark
(☎ 44 98 75 33) Skovdiget 1, 2880 Bagsværd

Aalborg Boldspiklub
Aalborg Stadion
(☎ 98 15 72 22) Hornevej 2,
9220 Aalborg Øst

Aarhus Fremad
Riisvangen Stadion
(☎ 86 16 41 00) Hans Egedesvej 21,
8200 Århus

AGF
Århus Stadion
(☎ 86 11 27 33) Terp Skovvej 16-18,
8260 Viby J

B93
Østerbro Stadion
(☎ 39 27 18 90) Ved Sporsløfjem 10,
2100 København

Brøndby IF
Brøndby Stadion
(☎ 43 63 08 10) Brøndbyvester Boulevard 8,
2605 Brøndby

FC København
Parken
(☎ 35 43 74 00) Øster Allé 50,
2100 København

Herfølge Boldklub
Herfølge Stadion
(☎ 56 27 42 30) Vordingborgvej 124,
4681 Herfølge

Lyngby FC
Lyngby Stadion
(☎ 45 88 40 60) Lundtoftevej 61,
2800 Lyngby

Silkeborg IF
Silkeborg Stadion
(☎ 86 80 44 77) Ansvej 10, 8600 Silkeborg

Vejle Boldklub
Vejle Stadion
(☎ 75 72 75 00) Helligkildevej 2,
postboks 444, 7100 Vejle

Viborg FF
Viborg Stadion
(☎ 86 60 10 66) Kirkebækvej 94,
postboks 214, 8800 Viborg

medals in cycling and in water sports such as sailing, kayaking, swimming and platform diving. In 1996 Denmark won four gold medals, for women's team handball, women's yachting, men's badminton and men's rowing. In the same year cyclist Bjarne Riis was paraded as a national hero through the streets of Copenhagen after creating a surprise upset in capturing the Tour de France.

Denmark is the adopted home of runner Wilson Kipketer, a native Kenyan who moved to Denmark in 1990. In 1997 he captured the world 800m record and received the IAAF Athlete of the Year award.

SHOPPING

Because prices tend to be high, few people come to Denmark to go on shopping sprees; however, there are some distinctively Danish products that can make fine items to bring home. Danish amber, which washes up on Jutland's west coast beaches, makes lovely jewellery and prices are relatively reasonable.

Other popular purchases are silverwork, ceramics and hand-blown glass – all in the sleek style that typifies Danish design. Georg Jensen silverworks, Royal Copenhagen Porcelain and Holmegaard Glass & Crystal are the biggest names in their fields. You can find their products, as well as scores of others, along Strøget, Copenhagen's famed shopping street. In addition to speciality shops, Denmark has large department stores (Magasin du Nord, Illum and Salling) that stock virtually everything you can think of, from souvenir picture books to Scandinavian-designed furniture and fluffy continental quilts (goose-down comforters). For more information on top Danish products to look out for on a shopping trip, see the Danish Modern Design section under Arts in the Facts about Denmark chapter.

Getting There & Away

The information in this chapter details the various ways of getting directly to Denmark – by air, land and sea.

As Copenhagen is one of northern Europe's main gateway cities, you'll find a multitude of international flights to Denmark. However, depending on the particular airline deals available at the time of travel, overseas visitors might sometimes find that it's cheaper to fly to another city in Europe first and then travel onward to Denmark by boat, train, bus or car. This is particularly true of travellers who are including Denmark as just one destination in a larger European trip, but even those travellers who are interested solely in Denmark might want to compare prices of air fares to Copenhagen with the cost of flying to, say, Frankfurt and using a rail pass or renting a car from there.

AIR
Airports & Airlines
The vast majority of overseas flights to Denmark arrive at Copenhagen international airport, which is conveniently located on the outskirts of Copenhagen, just a 12 minute train ride south of the city centre.

A few international flights, mostly those coming from other Scandinavian countries or the UK, land at small regional airports in Århus, Aalborg, Esbjerg and Billund.

Scandinavian Airlines (SAS) is the carrier with most services to Denmark. Other scheduled international carriers flying into Copenhagen include Aer Lingus, Aeroflot, Air France, Alitalia, Austrian Airlines, British Airways, British Midland, Delta Air Lines, EgyptAir, El Al Israel Airlines, Finnair, Iberia, Icelandair, Kenya Airways, KLM Royal Dutch Airlines, LOT Polish Airlines, Lufthansa Airlines, Maersk Air, Olympic Airways, Pakistan International Airlines, Sabena, South African Airways, Swissair, TAP Air Portugal, Thai Airways International, Turkish Airlines and Varig.

Buying Tickets
World aviation has never been so competitive, making air travel better value than ever, but you have to research the options carefully to make sure you get the best deal.

The Internet is a useful source for checking air fares: many travel agencies and airlines have a Web site.

Some airlines now sell discounted tickets direct to the customer, and it's worth contacting airlines anyway for information on routes and timetables. Sometimes there is nothing to be gained by going direct to the airline – specialist discount agencies often offer fares that are lower and/or carry fewer conditions than the airline's published prices. You can expect to be offered a wider range of options than a single airline would provide and, at worst, you will just end up paying the official airline fare.

The exception to this rule is the new breed of 'no-frills' carriers, which mostly sell direct. At the time of writing only Go of the UK and Virgin Express of Belgium had established links to Denmark, but Copenhagen is sure to be on the wish-lists of some of the other leading players (easyJet of the UK and Ryanair of Ireland).

Unlike the 'full-service' airlines, the no-frills carriers often make one-way tickets available at around half the return fare, meaning that it is easy to stitch together an open jaw itinerary. Regular airlines may also offer open jaws, particularly if you are flying in from outside Europe.

Round-the-World (RTW) tickets are another possibility, and are comparable in price to an ordinary return long-haul ticket. RTWs start at about UK£800, A$1800 or US$1300, vary depending on the season, and can be valid for up to a year. Special conditions might be attached to such tickets (such as you can't backtrack on a route). Also beware of cancellation penalties for these and other tickets.

Courier fares, whereby you get cheap passage in return for accompanying an urgent package through customs, offer very low prices but there are usually special restrictions attached; in addition, demand for couriers is decreasing in this electronic age.

You may find that the cheapest flights are being advertised by obscure agencies. Most such firms are honest and solvent, but there are some rogue fly-by-night outfits around. Paying by credit card generally offers protection since most card issuers will provide refunds if you don't get what you've paid for. Similar protection can be obtained by buying a ticket from a bonded agent, such as one covered by the Air Transport Operators Licence (ATOL) scheme in the UK. If you feel suspicious about a firm it's best to steer clear, or only pay a deposit before you get your ticket, then ring the airline to confirm that you are actually booked on the flight before you pay the balance. Established outfits such as those mentioned in this book offer more security and are about as competitive as you can get.

The cheapest deals are only available at certain times of the year or on weekdays, and fares are particularly subject to change. Always ask about the route: the cheapest tickets may involve an inconvenient stopover. Don't take schedules for granted, either: airlines usually change their schedules twice a year, at the end of March and the end of October.

Ticketless travel, whereby your reservation details are contained within an airline computer, is becoming more common. On simple return trips the absence of a ticket can be a benefit – it's one less thing to worry about; however, if you are planning a complicated itinerary which you may wish to amend en route, there is no substitute for the good old paper version.

Air Passes

This section will be of interest mainly to those who plan to visit other European countries in conjunction with their trip to Denmark.

Visitors who fly SAS to Scandinavia from continental Europe, North America or Asia can purchase Visit Scandinavia Air Pass tickets that allow one-way travel on direct flights between any two Scandinavian cities served by SAS for US$85 (some long-distance flights add a US$60 surcharge). You can buy up to six tickets; they must be purchased before arriving in Scandinavia and in conjunction with a return SAS international air ticket.

A similar deal applies with the SAS Visit Europe and SAS Visit Baltic Air Passes. You can buy from three to eight Visit Europe Air Pass tickets, valid for a one-way flight on a number of routes within Europe, for US$180 each. You can also buy from two to four Visit Baltic Air Pass tickets, valid for a one-way flight between Denmark and the Baltic countries, for US$115 each.

A handy new pass gives access to an expansive network of air routes within Scandinavia and the Baltic States. Called the Nordic Air Pass, it's a collaboration between Denmark's Maersk Air, Norway's Braathens, Sweden's Transwede Airways, Finland's Finnair and the Baltics' Estonian Air and Lithuanian Airlines. A book of four coupons costs US$360; each coupon is valid for a direct flight on any of the aforementioned airlines. There's no surcharge for long-distance flights but if your journey requires a connecting flight it will take two coupons – so be sure you're booking the most direct route possible. The Nordic Air Pass is valid from 1 May to 30 September.

US and Canadian citizens can use the Eurairpass; holders can fly between designated European cities for US$90. At the time of publication Copenhagen was served by Spanair flights from Madrid and Barcelona, and Virgin Express flights from Brussels. A minimum of three tickets must be bought before leaving North America. For details, see the Web site at www.eurairpass.com.

International offices of the participating airlines, as well as travel agencies specialising in Scandinavian and Baltic travel, sell the above air passes.

Air Travel Glossary

Baggage Allowance This will be written on your ticket and usually includes one 20kg item to go in the hold, plus one item of hand luggage.

Bucket Shops These are unbonded travel agencies specialising in discounted airline tickets.

Bumped Just because you have a confirmed seat doesn't mean you're going to get on the plane (see Overbooking).

Cancellation Penalties If you have to cancel or change a discounted ticket, there are often heavy penalties involved; insurance can sometimes be taken out against these penalties. Some airlines impose penalties on regular tickets as well, particularly against 'no-show' passengers.

Check-In Airlines ask you to check in a certain time ahead of the flight departure (usually one to two hours on international flights). If you fail to check in on time and the flight is overbooked, the airline can cancel your booking and give your seat to somebody else.

Confirmation Having a ticket written out with the flight and date you want doesn't mean you have a seat until the agent has checked with the airline that your status is 'OK' or confirmed. Meanwhile you could just be 'on request'.

Courier Fares Businesses often need to send urgent documents or freight securely and quickly. Courier companies hire people to accompany the package through customs and, in return, offer a discount ticket which is sometimes a phenomenal bargain. In effect, what the companies do is ship their freight as your luggage on regular commercial flights. This is a legitimate operation, but there are two shortcomings – the short turnaround time of the ticket (usually not longer than a month) and the limitation on your luggage allowance. You may have to surrender all your allowance and take only carry-on luggage.

Full Fares Airlines traditionally offer 1st class (coded F), business class (coded J) and economy class (coded Y) tickets. These days there are so many promotional and discounted fares available that few passengers pay full economy fare.

ITX An ITX, or 'independent inclusive tour excursion', is often available on tickets to popular holiday destinations. Officially it's a package deal combined with hotel accommodation, but many agents will sell you one of these for the flight only and give you phoney hotel vouchers in the unlikely event that you're challenged at the airport.

Lost Tickets If you lose your airline ticket an airline will usually treat it like a travellers cheque and, after inquiries, issue you with another one. Legally, however, an airline is entitled to treat it like cash and if you lose it then it's gone forever. Take good care of your tickets.

MCO An MCO, or 'miscellaneous charge order', is a voucher that looks like an airline ticket but carries no destination or date. It can be exchanged through any International Association of Travel Agents (IATA) airline for a ticket on a specific flight. It's a useful alternative to an onward ticket in those countries that demand one, and is more flexible than an ordinary ticket if you're unsure of your route.

No-Shows No-shows are passengers who fail to show up for their flight. Full-fare passengers who fail to turn up are sometimes entitled to travel on a later flight. The rest are penalised (see Cancellation Penalties).

On Request This is an unconfirmed booking for a flight.

Air Travel Glossary

Onward Tickets An entry requirement for many countries is that you have a ticket out of the country. If you're unsure of your next move, the easiest solution is to buy the cheapest onward ticket to a neighbouring country or a ticket from a reliable airline which can later be refunded if you do not use it.

Open Jaw Tickets These are return tickets where you fly out to one place but return from another. If available, this can save you backtracking to your arrival point.

Overbooking Airlines hate to fly empty seats and since every flight has some passengers who fail to show up, airlines often book more passengers than they have seats. Usually excess passengers make up for the no-shows, but occasionally somebody gets bumped. Guess who it is most likely to be? The passengers who check in late.

Point-to-Point Tickets These are discount tickets that can be bought on some routes in return for passengers waiving their rights to a stopover.

Promotional Fares These are officially discounted fares, available from travel agencies or direct from the airline.

Reconfirmation At least 72 hours prior to departure time of an onward or return flight, you must contact the airline and 'reconfirm' that you intend to be on the flight. If you don't do this the airline can delete your name from the passenger list and you could lose your seat.

Restrictions Discounted tickets often have various restrictions on them – such as needing to be paid for in advance and incurring a penalty to be altered. Others are restrictions on the minimum and maximum period you must be away, such as a minimum of 14 days or a maximum of one year.

Round-the-World Tickets RTW tickets give you a limited period (usually a year) in which to circumnavigate the globe. You can go anywhere the carrying airlines go, as long as you don't backtrack. The number of stopovers or total number of separate flights is decided before you set off and they usually cost a bit more than a basic return flight.

Stand-by This is a discounted ticket where you only fly if there is a seat free at the last moment. Stand-by fares are usually available only on domestic routes.

Transferred Tickets Airline tickets cannot be transferred from one person to another. Travellers sometimes try to sell the return half of their ticket, but officials can ask you to prove that you are the person named on the ticket. This is less likely to happen on domestic flights, but on an international flight tickets are compared with passports.

Travel Agencies Travel agencies vary widely and you should choose one that suits your needs. Some simply handle tours, while full-services agencies handle everything from tours and tickets to car rental and hotel bookings. If all you want is a ticket at the lowest possible price, then go to an agency specialising in discounted tickets.

Travel Periods Ticket prices vary with the time of year. There is a low (off-peak) season and a high (peak) season, and often a low-shoulder season and a high-shoulder season as well. Usually the fare depends on your outward flight – if you depart in the high season and return in the low season, you pay the high-season fare.

Travellers with Special Needs

If you have special needs of any sort – you require a vegetarian diet, are taking a baby or have a medical condition that warrants special consideration – you should let the airline know as soon as possible so that they can make arrangements accordingly. Remind them when you reconfirm your booking and again when you check in at the airport. It may also be worth ringing around the airlines before you make your booking to find out how each of them can handle your particular needs.

Most international airports will provide an escorted cart or wheelchair from check-in desk to plane where needed, although some airlines levy a charge for this service. There should be ramps, lifts, accessible toilets and reachable phones. Aircraft toilets, on the other hand, are likely to present a problem for some disabled passengers; travellers should discuss this with the airline at an early stage and, if necessary, with their doctor.

As a general rule, children under two years old travel for 10% of the standard fare (or free on some airlines) as long as they don't occupy a seat. They don't get a baggage allowance either. 'Skycots', baby food and nappies should be provided by the airline if requested in advance. Children aged between two and 12 can usually occupy a seat for half to two-thirds of the full fare, and do get a baggage allowance.

Departure Tax

There are no departure taxes to pay when leaving Denmark.

See the Money section in the Facts for the Visitor chapter for details on how to reclaim value-added tax (VAT) when you depart.

The UK

London is the major centre for discounted fares in the UK. Among the agencies specialising in discount travel are: Trailfinders (☎ 020-7937 5400), 215 Kensington High St, London W8 6BD, which upon request will send you a free copy of its magazine that includes air fare details; Usit Campus Travel (☎ 020-7730 3402), 52 Grosvenor Gardens; and STA Travel (☎ 020-7361 6262), 117 Euston Rd. Trailfinders' Web site is at www.trailfinders .co.uk, the Usit Campus Web site is at www.usitcampus.co.uk, and STA Travel information can be found at www.statravel .co.uk.

The listings magazine *Time Out*, the weekend papers and *Exchange & Mart* all carry ads for cheap fares. Also look out for the free magazines (such as *TNT*) and newspapers widely available in London; they're easy to find in busy public areas such as main train stations.

There are many scheduled commercial flights between Denmark and the UK. At the time of research the cheapest flights were with Go (☎ 0845-60 54 321) and Virgin Express (☎ 020-7744 0004). Go flies daily to Copenhagen from London Stansted; the fare is around UK£65/100 one way/return year-round. Virgin Express also flies daily via Brussels; fares are about UK£45/100 one way/return in the low season, UK£70/180 in the high season.

SAS (☎ 0845-60 727 727) operates six daily flights between London and Copenhagen; the unrestricted one-way fare is around UK£250, but you can get a non-refundable 30 day return fare for as little as UK£139. SAS also operates a daily flight between London and Århus for the same price as its Copenhagen flights. The two other main carriers on the London-Copenhagen route, British Airways (☎ 0345-222111) and Maersk Air (☎ 020-7333 0066), also offer multiple daily flights at similar fares.

Although the London-Copenhagen route is the busiest, there are numerous other flight options. Business Air (☎ 01382-593 000 in Scotland, ☎ 75 16 07 77 in Esbjerg) operates a fleet of 31-passenger SAAB 340 turboprops, flying to Esbjerg from Aberdeen and Manchester. However, the fares for this trip are generally higher than those charged on the more competitive London-Copenhagen route.

Continental Europe

While the cheapest way to travel between Denmark and the rest of continental Europe is usually by land, cheap discount flights are often available to travellers aged under 26. Sample fares to Copenhagen include f278 from Amsterdam, DM188 from Berlin, DM270 from Frankfurt and 800FF from Paris.

There are many travel agencies throughout Europe where you can purchase both discounted tickets and youth identity cards (see Student & Youth Cards in the Facts for the Visitor chapter). These include: NBBS Travelshop (☎ 020-62 40 989), Rokin 38, Amsterdam; Council Travel Services (☎ 01 44 55 55 50), 22 rue des Pyramides, Paris; STA Travel (☎ 069-703 035), Bockenheimer Landstrasse 133, Frankfurt; STA Travel (☎ 030-311 0950), Goethestrasse 73, Berlin; International Student and Youth Travel Service (☎ 01-322 1267), Nikis 11, Athens; and CTS (☎ 06-467 9271), Via Genova 16, Rome.

The USA

The North Atlantic is the world's busiest long-haul air corridor and the flight options can be bewildering. Larger newspapers such as the *New York Times*, the *Chicago Tribune*, the *San Francisco Chronicle* and the *Los Angeles Times* produce weekly travel sections in which you'll find any number of travel agencies' ads for air fares to Europe.

You should be able to fly return to Copenhagen from major east coast cities such as New York, Washington DC or Boston for around US$500 in the low season and around US$750 in the high season. Add about US$100 for flights from the midwest and about US$200 from the west coast. You might be able to get better rates if the airlines are battling for passengers with promotional fares or you could end up with a higher fare if all the cheapest fares are booked out on the day you want to leave. Most budget fares between the USA and Denmark are valid for either a 30 day or a 60 day stay.

With many tickets you can travel open jaw even with the cheaper fares, allowing you to land in one city (Copenhagen for example) and return from another (either a Danish city such as Rønne or Aalborg, or another Scandinavian city such as Oslo or Stockholm) at no extra cost.

An interesting alternative to a direct flight is offered by Icelandair (☎ 800-223 5500), which allows a free stopover in Iceland's capital, Reykjavík. Its prices are similar to the direct east coast-Copenhagen fares offered by other airlines and it flies from New York, Baltimore-Washington, Boston, Fort Lauderdale, Minneapolis and Orlando.

There are other, less orthodox, ways of getting to Europe, including purchasing tickets through an agency that specialises in discount fares. For example, Airhitch (☎ 800-326 2009 in New York, ☎ 310-394 0550 in Los Angeles) specialises in standby tickets to Europe for US$159/239 one way from the east coast/west coast, but the destinations are by region (not a specific city or country).

You can find out about courier flights from the USA from Now Voyager (☎ 212-431 1616) or Halbart (☎ 718-656 5000) in New York and IBC in Los Angeles (☎ 310-665 1760). They all work slightly differently: Now Voyager charges a US$50 annual registration fee and a deposit cheque of US$100 (which is torn up on your arrival), after which most flights to Europe (including Copenhagen) cost about US$300 return and allow a stay of seven days.

The *Travel Unlimited* newsletter, available from PO Box 1058, Allston, MA 02134, publishes details of the cheapest air fares and courier possibilities for destinations all over the world. A single monthly issue costs US$5 and a year's subscription costs US$25 (US$35 abroad). The new Travel Unlimited Web site is at www.travel unlimited.org.

Canada

For scheduled commercial flights to Copenhagen, you'll generally have to fly first to

New York or Chicago and pick up a connecting flight from there.

However, Icelandair (☎ 800-223 5500) offers a twice weekly direct flight from Halifax to Reykjavík (Iceland) with connections to Copenhagen. Fares vary with the season but tend to be significantly higher than Icelandair fares from the USA, so it may still work out cheaper to fly from Boston or New York. At the time of research the return fare to Copenhagen was C$1025 from Halifax compared with C$615 from New York.

Travel CUTS is one agency that offers low air fares and has offices in major cities, including Toronto (☎ 416-979 2406), at 187 College St, and Vancouver (☎ 604-681 9136), at 567 Seymour St. Also, scan the budget travel agencies' ads in major newspapers such as the National Post, Toronto's *Globe & Mail* and the *Vancouver Sun*.

For more general information on courier flights, see the previous USA section.

Australia

One place to check for cheap air fares is STA Travel, which has branches in larger cities. You can call ☎ 131 7766 from anywhere in Australia for the locations of all STA offices. The main Sydney branch (☎ 02-9212 1255) is at 855 George St, Ultimo, and the main Melbourne office (☎ 03-9349 2411) is at 222 Faraday St, Carlton. Check the travel agencies' ads in the Yellow Pages and phone around.

The weekend travel sections of major newspapers have many ads offering cheap fares to Europe, but don't be surprised if they happen to be sold out when you contact the agencies: they're often low-season fares on obscure airlines with conditions attached.

Discounted return fares on mainstream airlines through a reputable agency generally cost between A$1600 (low season) and A$2800 (high season).

New Zealand

Depending on which airline you choose, you may fly across Asia to Europe, with possible stopovers in India, Bangkok or Singapore, or across the USA, with possible stopovers in Honolulu, Australia or one of the Pacific islands. Worth considering is a RTW ticket, which can be around the same price as, or cheaper than, an advance-purchase return ticket. In the low season RTW fares start at around NZ$2299. Two places specialising in discounted tickets are STA Travel (☎ 09-309 9995), 10 High St, Auckland, and Suntravel (☎ 09-525 3074), Penrose, Auckland.

Africa

Kenya Airways is the only airline to fly direct from Africa to Copenhagen, leaving Nairobi every Friday. There are regular connections from South Africa with Lufthansa and Turkish Airlines (both offer a student discount) and British Airways, flying from both Johannesburg and Cape Town. These flights involve a change of flight in a European city.

Good places to look for cheap tickets are STA Travel (☎ 021-418 6570), 31 Riebeck St, Cape Town; there are also two offices in Johannesburg at (☎ 011-447 5551) 34 Mutual Gardens, Oxford Rd and 12c Seven St, Melville.

Asia

Although most Asian countries are now offering fairly competitive air fare deals, Bangkok, Singapore and Hong Kong are still the best places to shop around for discount tickets. Hong Kong's travel market can be unpredictable but some excellent bargains are available if you are lucky.

Discount ticket agencies in the region include: Sincerity Travel (☎ 2736 3392), 112 Argyle Centre, 688 Nathan Rd, Kowloon, Hong Kong; STA Travel (☎ 737 7188), Orchard Parade Hotel, 1 Tanglin Rd, Singapore; STA Travel (☎ 02-236 0262), Wall St Tower Bldg, 33/70 Surawong Road, Bangkok; and STA Travel (☎ 03-5391 2922), Nukariya Bldg, 1-16-20 Minami-Ikebukuro, Toshima-ku, Tokyo.

From India and Pakistan the cheapest flights tend to be with Eastern European carriers, but the national carriers, Air India and Pakistan International Airlines (PIA), can also offer bargains. Although you can get cheap tickets in Mumbai (Bombay) and Calcutta, Delhi is where the real wheeling and dealing goes on. In Delhi there are a number of discount travel agencies around Connaught Place but, as always, be careful before handing over your cash. If you use one of these discount agencies, double check with the airline to make sure that the booking has been made. Try STIC Travel (☎ 011-576 8492), New Rajinder Nagar, New Delhi.

LAND

The final link between Western Europe and Scandinavia is due to be sealed in 2000, when the Øresundsforbindelsen (a bridge-and-tunnel road and rail route between Copenhagen and Malmö in southern Sweden) is completed. This should lead to a sharp improvement in links with Denmark.

Bus

If you're coming from elsewhere in Europe and you don't already have a rail pass, it's often cheaper to get to Denmark by bus than it is by train or plane. Long bus rides can be tedious, so bring along a good book. On the plus side, some of the coaches are quite luxurious with a WC, air-con, stewards and a snack bar.

Small bus companies with discount rates come along from time to time but most of them don't remain in business for more than a year or two. Ask around at student and discount travel agencies for the latest information.

Eurolines One of the biggest and most well-established express-bus services is Eurolines, connecting Denmark with the rest of Europe. Most of the buses operate daily (or near-daily) in summer and between two and five times a week in winter.

Sample one-way Eurolines fares from Copenhagen are 395 kr to Stockholm, 405 kr to Amsterdam, 595 kr to Berlin or

Frankfurt, 645 kr to Paris and 675 kr to London. There's a discount of about 10% for those aged under 26 or over 60. Return fares are about 15% less than two one-way fares.

There's also a Eurolines pass that covers unlimited travel between 30 cities in 16 European countries, including the Danish cities of Copenhagen and Aalborg. Cities included in the pass are as far flung as Dublin, London, Paris, Madrid, Stockholm, Warsaw and Rome. A youth pass for travellers aged under 26 costs US$309/389 for 30/60 days from 15 June to 30 September, US$239/299 during the rest of the year. Travellers aged over 60 can get a senior pass at the same rates. The adult pass costs US$359/439 in the high season, US$299/ 379 in the low season.

Offices in Denmark are:

Copenhagen
  (☎ 33 25 12 44) Reventlowsgade 8,
  1651 Copenhagen V
Århus
  (☎ 86 12 36 11) Rådhuspladsen 3,
  8000 Århus C
Aalborg
  (☎ 99 34 44 88) JF Kennedys Plads 1,
  9000 Aalborg
Odense
  (☎ 66 14 21 00) Kongensgade 53,
  5000 Odense C

Eurolines' representatives elsewhere in Europe include:

Belgium
  (☎ 02-203 07 07) CCN-Gare du Nord,
  1000 Brussels
Czech Republic
  (☎ 02-74 69 63) Konevova 126,
  130 00 Prague 3
France
  (☎ 01 49 72 51 51) Paris Gare Routière Int,
  Avenue du Général de Gaulle,
  93170 Bagnolet
Germany
  (☎ 040-24 71 06) ZOB Adenauerallee 78,
  20097 Hamburg
  Deutsche Touring
  (☎ 069-79 03 53)
  Am Römerhof 17, 60486 Frankfurt am Main

Netherlands
(☎ 020-62 75 151) Rokin 10,
Amsterdam
Norway
Nor-Way Bussekspress
(☎ 81 54 44 44) Bussterminalen Galleriet,
Schweigaardsgata 8-10, 0154 Oslo
Sweden
(☎ 31 10 02 40) Kyrkogatan 40,
411 15 Gothenburg
UK
(☎ 01582-40 45 11) 52 Grosvenor Gardens,
London SW1W 0AU

These offices may also have information on other bus companies and deals. Advance reservations may be necessary on international buses; either call the bus companies directly or inquire at a travel agency.

Busabout This UK-based budget alternative to Eurolines is aimed at younger travellers, but has no upper age limit. During the winter its routes are divided into two zones, 'North' and 'South', which don't include Denmark. During the summer season (mid-April until 31 October) a much more extensive coverage is offered, visiting over 60 European cities, including cities in Denmark. During the summer a two week pass costs UK£199/249 with/without a student card, a three week pass costs UK£275/345, a one month pass costs UK £325/425, a two month pass is UK£485/595 and a ticket valid for unlimited travel during the season costs UK£720/895.

You can buy Busabout tickets directly from the company (☎ 020-8784 2816) or from suppliers such as Usit Campus and STA Travel. The Eurobus company, which used to offer a similar service, went out of business in 1998. The Busabout Web site is at www.busabout.com.

Train

Trains are a popular way of getting around; they are good meeting places and in northern Europe they are generally comfortable, frequent and reliable.

If you plan to travel extensively around Europe by train, it might be worth getting hold of the *Thomas Cook European Time-*

table, which gives a complete listing of train schedules and indicates where supplements apply or where reservations are necessary. It is updated monthly, costs UK£9/US$20 and is available from Thomas Cook outlets worldwide.

In the discussion of rail passes that follows, keep in mind that Denmark is a small country so domestic fares are quite moderate. Squeezing your money's worth out of a rail pass that is used solely in Denmark can be a real challenge (for more details on Denmark's domestic fares, see the Train section in the Getting Around chapter). On the other hand, if you will also be making excursions to neighbouring countries then that will certainly boost the value of a rail pass.

For comparison purposes, standard 2nd class train fares from Copenhagen are 1010 kr to Frankfurt, 735 kr to Oslo, 370 kr to Gothenburg and 760 kr to Stockholm. For passengers aged under 26, these fares are discounted to 765 kr to Frankfurt, 530 kr to Oslo, 265 kr to Gothenburg and 540 kr to Stockholm.

Rail Passes A multitude of rail passes is available for travel in Europe and it's important to find a travel agency which is familiar with the various options.

Two agencies in the USA that specialise in selling rail passes are Budget Europe Travel Service (☎ 800-441 2387), 2557 Meade Court, Ann Arbor, MI 47105, and Europe Through the Back Door (☎ 206-771 8303), 120 Fourth Ave N, PO Box 2009, Edmonds, WA 98020.

Among the agencies selling rail passes in the UK are Wasteels Travel (☎ 020-7834 7066), Victoria train station, London, and Usit Campus (☎ 020-7730 3402), 52 Grosvenor Gardens, London SW1W 0AU. In continental Europe, rail passes can be purchased at larger train stations and travel agencies.

If you buy a rail pass, read the small print. There are certain rules for validation and the pass cannot be transferred. Lost or stolen Eurailpasses can be reissued only in

No refunds; store credit on books ONLY.

The Complete Traveller

COMPLETE TRAVELLER
199 MADISON AVE
NEW YORK, NY 10016

TIME 11:29 AM   DATE 05/18/00
TERM# 08463539   MER# 000035203891996
TRAN TYPE SALE
#5463696000083760
CARD TYPE MASTERCARD
EXP DATE 08/01   SEQ #   003
TICKET # 005406
AUTH CODE 035900

$10.95

TOTAL $57.21

$17.95

SIGN X _____
     KAREN H OZTEMEL

$23.95

I AGREE TO PAY ABOVE TOTAL AMOUNT
ACCORDING TO CARD ISSUER AGREEMENT

$52.85
$4.36

$57.21

Discount: $0.00
Total Tendered: $57.21
Change Due: $0.00

Payment Via:
  VISA/MC/DINERS $57.21

Don't leave home without us!!

No refunds; Store credit on books ONLY.

The Complete Traveller
199 MADISON AVENUE

CORNER E 35 ST
NEW YORK, NY 10016
(212) 685-9007

18-May-00 11:34 AM
Clerk: Admin Register # 2

Trans. #6848
- Non Taxable Items

3259011455 1 $10.95 $10.95
MAP-DENMARK
0864426097 1 $17.95 $17.95

LP DENMARK
088729460X 1 $23.95 $23.95
INSIGHT DENMARK
Total Items: 3

Sub-Total: $52.85
Tax: $4.36

Total: $57.21
Discount: $0.00
Total Tendered: $57.21
Change Due: $0.00

Payment Via:
VISA/MC/DINERS $57.21

Don't leave home without us!

Denmark offers abundant opportunities for sporting activities; its sweeping beaches and clear waters are ideal for swimming, canoeing and windsurfing, and its bike tracks and country lanes attract cyclists.

As a country of islands and peninsulas, Denmark's ties with the sea are strong.

certain circumstances and with the correct supporting documents. For Scanrail passes, refunds can be made only if the card is returned unused before the first day of validity – there are no refunds for theft, loss or partial usage.

Keep in mind that rail passes do not cover seat reservation costs and fees for supplements such as sleepers. Also, if you are taking a high speed train or a business class train, there is sometimes an extra supplement.

Pass holders must always carry proper identification, such as a passport or national identity card. Overnight journeys commencing after 7 pm generally count as the following day's travel.

The traveller must fill out in ink the relevant box in the calendar before starting a day's travel. Be sure to get the date right, as tampering with the pass (which includes erasing) or failing to validate it runs the risk of fines and possible forfeiture of the pass. We've had reports of Danish train conductors being extremely scrupulous in their checks, even examining passes with a magnifying glass.

Eurail For travel within Scandinavia, the Scanrail pass (detailed later) is generally a better deal than the Eurailpass, so the following Eurailpass information will be of greatest interest to travellers visiting other parts of Europe as well as Denmark. One plus for Eurailpasses is that they often include supplements for high speed trains that aren't covered by regional and national passes.

Eurailpasses are valid for unlimited travel on national railways (and some private lines) in Austria, Belgium, Denmark, Finland, France, Germany, Greece, Hungary, Ireland, Italy, Luxembourg, the Netherlands, Norway, Portugal, Spain, Sweden and Switzerland. The passes do *not* cover the UK.

Eurailpasses are also valid for free travel on some ferries, including those between Italy and Greece, and from Sweden to Denmark, Finland and Germany. In addi-

tion, discounts are given on some other ferry routes.

There are two Eurailpasses for travellers aged under 26. The Eurail Youthpass is valid for unlimited 2nd class travel for 15 days (US$388), 21 days (US$499), one month (US$623), two months (US$882) or three months (US$1089). The Eurail Youth Flexipass, also covering 2nd class travel, is valid for freely chosen days within a two month period: 10 days for US$458 or 15 days for US$599.

For those aged over 26, a Eurail Flexipass (available for 1st class travel only) costs US$654 or US$862 for 10 or 15 freely chosen days within two months. The standard Eurailpass has five versions, all for unlimited travel in 1st class: US$554 for 15 days, US$718 for 21 days, US$890 for one month, US$1260 for two months and US$1558 for three months.

Two or more people travelling together can get a 15% discount by buying a Eurail Saverpass or Eurail Saver Flexipass, which work like the standard Eurailpass and Eurail Flexipass.

Eurailpasses for children are also available: half fare for those aged under 12, free for those under four. There's also a Euraildrive Pass for travellers who want to combine rental car and train travel.

Eurailpasses can only be bought by residents of non-European countries, and are supposed to be purchased before arriving in Europe. They can actually be purchased within Europe as long as your passport proves you've been there for less than six months, but will be more expensive than those purchased outside Europe and the outlets where you can buy them are limited. Copenhagen's Central Station is the only place in Denmark where you can buy a Eurailpass.

If you've lived in Europe for more than six months, you are eligible for an Inter-Rail pass instead.

Inter-Rail These passes are available to residents of European countries. To purchase this pass you will be expected to show proof of European residency covering a minimum of six months.

The Inter-Rail pass is split into zones, with the fare depending upon how many zones you plan to travel within. Zone A comprises Great Britain and Ireland; B is Finland, Norway and Sweden; C is Austria, Denmark, Germany and Switzerland; D is Croatia, the Czech Republic, Hungary, Poland and Slovakia; E is Belgium, France, Luxembourg and the Netherlands; F is Morocco, Portugal and Spain; G is Italy, Greece, Slovenia and Turkey; and H is Bulgaria, Macedonia, Romania and Yugoslavia. The price for 22 days travel in any one zone is UK£159 for travellers aged under 26 and UK£229 for adults. Multizone passes are valid for one month: a two zone pass costs UK£209/279 for travellers aged under 26/adults, three zones UK£229/309 and all zones UK£259/349.

Terms and conditions vary slightly from country to country, but for travel in the country of origin expect only limited discounts – if you're departing from the UK, for instance, the pass covers the channel crossing but no domestic travel.

The pass also gives free travel on shipping routes from the Italian port of Brindisi to Patras in Greece, as well as 30 to 50% discounts on numerous other ferry routes (more than are covered by Eurailpass). Brochures containing details of Inter-Rail passes can be picked up at the international counter in larger train stations throughout Europe.

Scanrail These rail passes cover travel in Denmark, Norway, Sweden and Finland.

Flexible and consecutive-day passes are available. For travel on any five days within a 15 day period, the pass costs US$249/187 in 1st/2nd class (US$187/140 for travellers aged under 26). Travel on any 10 days within a one month period costs US$400/301 for 1st/2nd class (US$300/226 for those aged under 26).

For 21 consecutive days of unlimited travel, the pass costs US$452/348 for 1st/2nd class (US$339/261 for people aged under 26). For one month of unlimited travel, the cost is US$532/426 for 1st/2nd class (US$399/320 for those aged under 26). The cost for children aged under 12 is half the adult fare; children aged under four travel free.

If you're 55 years old (60 if the pass is purchased in Europe) or over, then you're eligible for a senior pass, which is valid for 1st/2nd class travel over five days in a 15 day period for US$222/166, 10 days in a one month period for US$356/268 and 21 consecutive days for US$402/310.

To get Scanrail passes at these prices, they must be purchased before you arrive in Scandinavia. Scanrail passes purchased in Scandinavia will usually cost a bit more, but of course prices depend upon exchange rates.

Scanrail passes are valid on trains run by state railways in Denmark (Danske Statsbaner or DSB), Finland (VR), Norway (NSB) and Sweden (SJ), except on the Stockholm Local (SL).

The pass includes free travel on DSB domestic ferry lines in Denmark and on boats between Helsingør and Helsingborg (Sweden) and between Rødbyhavn and Puttgarden (Germany).

There's a 50% discount if you're travelling on the following services:

Esbjerg-Harwich (DFDS Scandinavian Seaways)
Copenhagen-Rønne (Bornholmstrafikken)
Rønne-Ystad (Bornholmstrafikken)
Copenhagen-Oslo (DFDS Scandinavian Seaways)
Hjørring-Hirtshals (train)
Frederikshavn-Oslo (Stena Line)
Frederikshavn-Gothenburg (Stena Line)
Frederikshavn-Larvik (Color Line)
Frederikshavn-Skagen (train)
Hirtshals-Kristiansand (Color Line)
Stockholm-Helsinki (Viking or Silja Line)

There are a few other boat lines operating between Scandinavian ports outside Denmark that also offer a 50% discount, as well as some buses in northern Norway. A few other services, including Flyvebådene between Copenhagen and Malmö, offer a discount of 25% to holders of Scanrail passes.

Other Discounts There are numerous other discount schemes for train travel across Europe, so always ask about off-peak travel, family plans and special promotions. Many routes also have discounted return fares; if you purchase your tickets a couple of days in advance you can sometimes get a return ticket for just a bit more than the one-way fare.

For a small fee, European residents aged over 60 can get a Rail Europe Senior Card as an add-on to their national senior rail pass. It entitles the holder to reduced European fares; the percentage saved varies according to the route.

Car & Motorcycle

Denmark's only land border is with Germany. The E45, part of the European motorway network, is the main route between Germany and the Jutland peninsula, although there are several smaller border crossings as well.

Until 1998 it was necessary to take a car ferry to get to Copenhagen (on the island of Zealand) from anywhere outside Denmark, but now Storebælts-forbindelsen (the Store Bælt Bridge) connects Zealand with the Jutland peninsula and the rest of the European mainland. After the year 2000, when the lengthy new bridge and tunnel under construction between Zealand and Sweden are due to open, Denmark will also be connected by road to the rest of Scandinavia (see the boxed text 'Bridge to Sweden' for details).

For information on car ferry services to Denmark, see the Sea section later in this chapter. For information on travelling around Denmark by private vehicle, see the Car & Motorcycle section in the Getting Around chapter.

Paperwork & Preparations Proof of vehicle ownership (such as a Vehicle Registration Document for British-registered cars) should always be carried when driving in Europe. Also carry your national driving licence, as well as an International Driving Permit (IDP) if appropriate (see under Visas & Documents in the Facts for the Visitor chapter).

Third-party motor insurance is a minimum requirement in most of Europe. Most UK motor insurance policies automatically provide third-party cover valid in EU countries and some others. Get your insurer to issue a Green Card (it may cost extra), which is internationally recognised as proof of insurance, and check that it lists all of the countries you intend to visit. You'll need this in the event of an accident outside the country where the vehicle is insured. Also ask your insurer for a European Accident Statement form, which can simplify things. Never sign statements you can't read or understand – insist on a translation and sign that only if it's acceptable.

It's advisable to have a European breakdown assistance policy, such as the RAC Eurocover Motoring Assistance plan. Ask

---

Bridge to Sweden

An ambitious new bridge and tunnel project, called Øresundsforbindelsen (the Øresund Fixed Link), aims to connect Denmark and Sweden by both road and rail by the year 2000, with a tentative opening date of 1 July.

The bridge will stretch nearly 16km across the sound from Kastrup, near Copenhagen airport, to Malmö in Sweden. An artificial island, some 4km wide, had to be constructed halfway across the Øresund to provide a point where the 3.5km-long immersed motorway and railway tunnel could connect with the 8km-long two-level bridge.

The total project is expected to cost more than US$3.6 billion and is one of the largest international civil engineering projects to have been undertaken since the Channel Tunnel was constructed between the UK and France. You can follow its progress online at the Web site www.ore sundskonsortiet.com.

your motoring organisation for details about free and reciprocal services offered by affiliated organisations in countries you'll be visiting.

Every vehicle travelling across an international border should display a nationality plate of its country of registration. A warning triangle, to be used in the event of breakdown, is compulsory almost everywhere. Recommended accessories are a first-aid kit, a spare bulb kit and a fire extinguisher.

Road Rules Vehicles drive on the right in all northern European countries. Vehicles brought over from the UK or Ireland should have their headlights adjusted to avoid blinding oncoming traffic at night (a simple solution on older headlight lenses is to cover up the triangular section of the lens with tape). Priority is usually given to traffic approaching from the right in countries that drive on the right-hand side. The British RAC publishes an annual *European Motoring Guide*, which gives an excellent summary of regulations in each country, including parking rules. Motoring organisations in other countries produce similar publications.

Take care with speed limits as they vary significantly from country to country. You may be surprised at the apparent disregard of traffic regulations in some places but as a visitor it is always best to err on the side of caution. In Denmark and a number of other European countries, many driving infringements are subject to on-the-spot fines. Always ask for a receipt if you're fined.

All Scandinavian countries are particularly strict on drink-driving regulations, with permitted blood-alcohol concentration limits ranging from 0.05 to 0.02%. For practical purposes, such low limits allow for little more than a margin of error, so don't drive at all after drinking.

For road rules specific to Denmark, see under Road Rules in the Car & Motorcycle section of the following Getting Around chapter.

Camper Van Travelling in a camper van can be a surprisingly economical option for budget travellers, as it can take care of eating, sleeping and travelling in one convenient package. London is a good place to buy: look in *TNT* magazine and *Loot* newspaper, or go to the van market on Market Rd, London N7. Expect to spend at least UK£2000 (US$3200).

The most common camper van is the VW based on the 1600cc or 2000cc Transporter, and spare parts are widely available in Europe. Note that although discreet free camping, such as in motorway rest areas, is rarely a problem in much of Europe (and is actually permitted in most places in Austria, Germany and Switzerland), it is illegal in Denmark.

A drawback with camper vans is that they're expensive to buy in spring and hard to sell in autumn. A car and tent might do just as well instead.

Bicycle

A bicycle can make a great travelling companion in cycle-friendly Denmark. If you're flying to Denmark you should be able to take your bicycle along with you on the plane relatively easily. You can dismantle the bicycle and put the pieces in a bike bag or box, but it's easier to simply wheel your bike to the check-in desk, where it should be treated as a piece of baggage. You may have to remove the pedals and turn the handlebars sideways so that it takes up less space in the aircraft's hold. Check all this with the airline well in advance, preferably before you pay for your ticket.

It's also possible to send bicycles between Denmark and most other European countries via train as international luggage. The bicycle must be easy to handle; it cannot be locked and anything bulky, such as baskets and panniers, must be removed. The transport time can take as much as three days to other stations in Scandinavia and five days to elsewhere in Europe.

Still, if you have an option, the easiest and cheapest way is to take an international ferry to Denmark. You'll get to travel on the same boat as your bike, and the additional fee is usually minimal.

Touring northern Europe by bike may seem a daunting prospect; one organisation in the UK that can help with your planning is the Cyclists' Touring Club (☎ 01483-417 217), 69 Meadrow, Godalming, Surrey GU7 3HS. It can supply information to members on cycling conditions in Europe, as well as detailed routes, itineraries, maps and cheap specialised insurance. Membership costs UK£25 per annum, UK£15 for people aged under 26 or over 65.

A primary consideration on a cycling tour is to travel light, but you should take a few tools and spare parts, including a puncture repair kit and an extra inner tube. Panniers are essential to balance your possessions on either side of the bike frame. A bike helmet is also a must. Take a good lock and always use it when you leave your bike unattended.

Seasoned cyclists can average 80km a day, but there's no point in overdoing it. The slower you travel, the more local people you are likely to meet.

Once in Denmark, you'll find that many trains and buses are specially equipped to carry bicycles at a nominal fee. Information on travelling around Denmark by bicycle can be found in the Bicycle section of the Getting Around chapter, and also in the special section 'Cycling in Denmark' in the Activities section of the Facts for the Visitor chapter.

SEA

Ferry travel can be an economical way of getting to Denmark because it often includes overnight accommodation. It's also a pleasant way to travel as the boats are generally of a high standard. The long-distance boats usually have duty-free shops, lounges, nightclubs and both cafeterias and formal restaurants. Many of the boats between Denmark and other Scandinavian countries have floating casinos and small grocery shops on board as well.

The fares in this section are for one-way travel unless otherwise noted. There are often discounts on return tickets, particularly for people travelling by car, and occasionally there are some very good excursion deals – always ask about special promotions. If you're carrying a rail pass or a student card, be sure to flash it when you purchase a ticket, as it may entitle you to a substantial discount. A child's fare is usually half of the adult fare, and there are sometimes senior discounts as well.

Keep in mind that the same ferry company can have a whole host of different prices for the same route, depending upon the day of the week you travel and on the season. Note that cabin fares are quoted on a per-person (not a per-cabin) basis. Car fares given in this section are for a standard car (generally up to 6m in length and 2m in height); most fares inch up as the vehicle increases in size, and fares for camper vans are higher still.

Particularly if you're bringing along a vehicle, you should always make reservations well in advance – this is doubly true in summer and at weekends. During busy periods you'll also get the best cabin selection by booking in advance.

Ferry Companies

Following are the reservation numbers for the largest ferry companies operating international routes to and from Denmark.

DFDS Scandinavian Seaways This company runs ferries from Copenhagen to Oslo via Helsingborg (Sweden) and from Esbjerg to Harwich (UK). Its Web site is at www.scansea.com.

Booking agencies include:

Denmark
  DFDS Scandinavian Seaways
  (☎ 33 42 30 00, fax 33 42 30 11)
  Sankt Annæ Plads 30, 1295 Copenhagen
  DFDS Scandinavian Seaways
  (☎ 79 17 79 17, fax 79 17 79 18)
  Englandskajen, 6700 Esbjerg
Germany
  DFDS Scandinavian Seaways
  (☎ 040-38903 71, fax 38903 141)
  DFDS Gmbh, Van-der-Smissen-Strasse 4,
  22 767 Hamburg

Netherlands
DFDS Scandinavian Seaways
(☎ 02550-34546, fax 35349)
Felison Terminal, Sluisplein 33,
1975 AG IJmuiden
Norway
DFDS Scandinavian Seaways
(☎ 22 41 90 90, fax 22 41 38 38)
Utstikker II Vippetangen, Oslo
Sweden
DFDS Scandinavian Seaways
(☎ 31 65 06 00, fax 31 53 51 37)
Skandiahamnen, PO Box 8895,
402 72 Gothenburg
(☎ 42 24 10 00, fax 42 24 24 77)
Sundsterminalen, Oceangatan,
252 25 Helsingborg
UK
DFDS Scandinavian Seaways
(☎ 020-7616 1414, fax 7616 1450)
28A Queensway, London W2 3RX
DFDS Scandinavian Seaways
(☎ 0990-333 111, fax 01255-244 370)
Scandinavia House, Parkeston Quay
Harwich, Essex CO12 4QG
DFDS Scandinavian Seaways
(☎ 0191-293 6262, fax 293 6223)
Royal Quays, North Shields, Tyne & Wear,
Newcastle NE29 6EE
USA
DFDS Scandinavian Seaways
(☎ 800-533 3755)
Cypress Creek Business Park,
6555 NW 9th Ave, Suite 207,
Fort Lauderdale, FL 33309

Color Line Ferries between Hirtshals and the Norwegian cities of Kristiansand, Oslo and Moss, and from Frederikshavn and Skagen to Larvik (Norway), are operated by Color Line. Its Web site is at www.color line.no. Booking agencies include:

Denmark
Color Line
(☎ 99 56 19 77, fax 99 56 20 20)
Fergeterminalen, 9850 Hirtshals
France
Color Line
(☎ 01 42 85 60 80, fax 01 42 85 62 70)
c/o Scanditours, 140 rue du Faubourg,
Saint Honoré, 75008 Paris
Germany
Color Line
(☎ 0431-7300 300, fax 7300 400)
Postfach 2646, 24025 Kiel

Norway
Color Line
(☎ 81 00 08 11, fax 22 83 04 30)
Postboks 1422 Vika, 0115 Oslo
(☎ 38 07 88 00)
Fergeterminalen, Postboks 82,
4601 Kristiansand
(☎ 33 12 28 00)
Ferjeterminalen, Postboks 2002, 3255 Larvik
(☎ 69 24 56 20)
Værlebrygga, 1531 Moss
USA & Canada
Bergen Line
(☎ 800-323 7436, fax 212-319 1390)
405 Park Ave, New York, NY 10022

Stena Line This company operates ferries from Frederikshavn to Oslo in Norway and to Gothenburg in Sweden, as well as from the Danish port of Grenaa to Varberg and Halmstad in Sweden. Booking agencies include:

Denmark
Stena Line
(☎ 96 20 02 00, fax 96 20 02 81)
Stenaterminalen, 9900 Frederikshavn
Germany
Stena Line
(☎ 0211-905 50)
Hildebrandtstrasse 40, 40 215 Düsseldorf
Norway
Stena Line
(☎ 23 17 90 00)
Utstikker II Vippetangen, Oslo
Sweden
Stena Line
(☎ 31 85 80 00)
405 19 Gothenburg
UK
Stena Line
(☎ 01233-647022)
Charter House, Park St, Ashford,
Kent TN24 8EX

Germany
Rødbyhavn to Puttgarden The busy train, car and passenger ferry between Puttgarden in Germany and Rødbyhavn in Denmark (the quickest way to Copenhagen) goes nearly every 30 minutes, 24 hours a day; it takes 45 minutes. If you're travelling by train, the cost of the ferry will be included in your ticket. Otherwise the cost is

160 kr for a motorcycle with two riders and 315 kr for a car with up to five passengers. For reservations contact Scandlines (☎ 33 15 15 15) in Denmark, DFO (☎ 04371-86 51 61) in Germany. The relevant Web sites are at www.scandlines.dk and www.dfo.de.

Gedser to Rostock The ferry service between Rostock (Germany) and Gedser (Denmark) runs an average of three times a day. There are two boats: a slow one that takes two hours and an express that takes 1¼ hours. For a car with up to five people, the base fare is from 325 to 445 kr, depending on the season and day of the week. If you opt for the express boat, there's a surcharge of 75 to 225 kr. For reservations call Scandlines (☎ 33 15 15 15) in Denmark, DFO (☎ 0381-673 12 17) in Germany.

Bagenkop to Kiel The Langeland-Kiel Linien (☎ 62 56 14 00 in Bagenkop, ☎ 0431-97 41 50 in Kiel) operates a car ferry between Kiel in Germany and Bagenkop on the Danish island of Langeland two or three times a day. The passenger fare is 30 kr (36 kr in July). A motorcycle costs 95 kr, a car from 95 to 145 kr; vehicle drivers are included in the price year-round, and in the low season up to three passengers can also travel free with a car. The trip takes 2½ hours.

Marstal to Kiel The passenger ferry *Fair Lady* (☎ 62 53 10 74 in Marstal, ☎ 04351-5531 in Kiel) runs twice daily between Kiel and Marstal (on the Danish island of Ærø) from mid-May to the end of August. The boat leaves Kiel at 8.30 am and 2.30 pm, and departs from Marstal 2½ hours later. The fare is 70 kr.

Rømø to Sylt The Rømø-Sylt Linie (☎ 73 75 53 03 in Rømø, ☎ 4651-87 0475 in Sylt) operates car ferries between Havneby on the Danish island of Rømø and List on the German island of Sylt numerous times each day. The trip takes one hour and costs 31 kr for a passenger, 97 kr for a motorcycle and rider and 231 kr for a car and passengers.

Bornholm Ferries For information on ferries between Rønne on the Danish island of Bornholm and Sassnitz-Mukran in Germany, see under Getting There & Away in the Bornholm chapter.

Poland

Polferries operates a year-round ferry service between Swinoujscie (☎ 9132-16140) and Copenhagen (☎ 33 11 46 45); the Web site is at www.polferries.com.pl. The trip takes 10 hours. Ferries depart from Copenhagen at 10 pm on Monday, Wednesday, Thursday and Friday and at 10.30 am on Sunday. From Swinoujscie, ferries depart at 10.30 am on Thursday and Friday and at 10.30 pm on Tuesday, Saturday and Sunday. The fare is 315 kr for a passenger, 460 kr for a car with driver or 760 kr for a car with up to five passengers. Motorcycles and bicycles are carried free of charge. There are good discounts on return fares.

For information on the summertime ferry between Swinoujscie and Rønne, see the Getting There & Away section of the Bornholm chapter.

Sweden

Note that once Øresundsforbindelsen (the Øresund Fixed Link) – the new tunnel and bridge across the Øresund channel (see the boxed text 'Bridge to Sweden' earlier in this chapter) – is completed, it will provide a direct vehicle link between Denmark and Sweden. Consequently, some of the following boat services will undoubtedly be scaled back, and the car ferry from Dragør will probably be eliminated completely.

Helsingør to Helsingborg The cheapest ferry route between Denmark and Sweden is the shuttle between Helsingør and Helsingborg, which takes 20 minutes and costs just 15 kr; if you're travelling by train it's included in your train fare. Ferries leave from opposite Helsingør train station every 20 minutes during the day and once an hour through the night. The fare for a motorcycle and up to two riders is 100 kr, while a car with up to five passengers costs about

250 kr. There are various car discounts, and you can often get a return ticket for the same price as a one-way ticket. Both HH-Ferries (☎ 49 26 01 55 in Helsingør, ☎ 42 19 80 00 in Helsingborg) and Scandlines (☎ 33 15 15 15 in Helsingør, ☎ 42 18 61 00 in Helsingborg) ply this route.

There's also a frequent passenger-only hydrofoil service offered by Sundbusserne (☎ 49 21 35 45) that shaves a few minutes off the travel time but costs about twice as much.

Dragør to Limhamn Scandlines (☎ 32 53 15 85 in Dragør, ☎ 40 36 20 41 in Limhamn) operates between Dragør (Denmark) and Limhamn (Sweden) about a dozen times a day. The trip takes 55 minutes and costs 45 kr for passengers, 175 kr for a motorcycle with up to two riders and 445 kr for a car with up to five passengers.

Copenhagen to Malmö There are a couple of companies running hydrofoils from Copenhagen to Malmö. Pilen (☎ 33 32 12 60 in Copenhagen, ☎ 40 23 44 11 in Malmö) has the most frequent service, operating hourly, except on Sunday when it leaves every other hour. The standard fare is 90 kr but because of price wars it's not uncommon to find a fare for half that. The crossing takes only 45 minutes. Pilen's Web site is at www.pilen.dk.

Frederikshavn to Gothenburg Stena Line operates car ferries six to 10 times a day between Frederikshavn and Gothenburg, charging 100 kr for a passenger, 300 kr for a motorcycle with up to two riders and 400 kr for a car with up to five passengers. The trip takes 3¼ hours. In summer, a few of the journeys are made by a high-speed catamaran that cuts the journey to two hours and costs an extra 15 kr for passengers, 75 kr for vehicles.

Another company operating on this route is SeaCat (☎ 96 20 32 00 in Frederikshavn, ☎ 31 72 00 800 in Gothenburg), which offers only catamaran services; its Web site is www.seacat.se. Depending on the day

and season, it charges from 70 to 100 kr for passengers, from 180 to 300 kr for a motorcycle with up to two riders and from 450 to 720 kr for a car with up to five passengers. The boat operates four times a day in summer, three times a day during the rest of the year.

Grenaa to Varberg & Halmstad Stena Line (☎ 87 58 75 00 in Grenaa, ☎ 31 85 80 00 in Sweden) operates daily year-round between Grenaa and the Swedish ports of Varberg and Halmstad. The crossing takes 4½ hours. For either route, the fare is 100 kr for a passenger, 300 kr for a motorcycle and driver and from 400 to 1200 kr for a car with up to five people.

Bornholm Ferries For information on ferries from Ystad in Sweden to Rønne, see the Getting There & Away section in the Bornholm chapter.

Norway

Copenhagen to Oslo DFDS Scandinavian Seaways runs daily overnight ferries between Oslo and Copenhagen, with the cheapest cabin fare costing from 400 kr in the low season to 760 kr in summer. Cabin fares are half-price for people aged under 25. A car costs an additional 240 kr, a motorcycle 160 kr. This is a great way to travel between these two Scandinavian capitals – the cabins in all categories are quite pleasant and you can linger over a splendid buffet dinner (199 kr). The departure in either direction is at 5 pm, with arrival at 9 am.

The same boats can also be booked as a mini-cruise; this allows you to spend the day in Oslo, leaving your luggage in the cabin, returning to Copenhagen the next night.

Frederikshavn to Larvik Color Line operates a daily year-round ferry between Frederikshavn (Denmark) and Larvik (Norway). The schedule varies with the day of the week and the season, and it can be either a day ferry (6¼ hours) or an overnight ferry

(10½ hours). The fare for passengers is 144/190 kr on weekdays/weekends in winter, 190/230 kr in spring and autumn and 316/352 kr from mid-June to mid-August. A car costs an additional 180/240 kr on weekdays/weekends in winter, 240/304 kr in spring and autumn and 380/505 kr in summer. A motorcycle costs from 135 to 260 kr. There are 50% discounts for senior travellers and for children aged between four and 15. Sleeperettes (reclining chairs) are free of charge. Cabin prices begin at an additional 114 kr in a four berth cabin and 210 kr in a two berth cabin during the summer.

Skagen to Larvik Color Line also operates a high-speed catamaran between Skagen (Denmark) and Larvik from April to September. The travel time is three hours. The boat runs twice a day, departing from Larvik at 8.30 am (9 am in summer) and 4.30 pm (5 pm in summer), and departing from Skagen four hours later. Reservation numbers and fares are exactly the same as those listed earlier for the Frederikshavn-Larvik route.

Frederikshavn to Oslo Stena Line operates ferries between Oslo and Frederikshavn daily during the summer, slightly less frequently the rest of the year. The ferries leave Oslo at 8 pm, arriving in Frederikshavn at 7.30 am. In the opposite direction they operate as a day ferry, leaving Frederikshavn at 10.30 am and arriving at 7 pm. In the low season, departure times from Frederikshavn vary a bit but from Oslo the service remains an overnight ferry on all runs. Standard passenger fares range from 250 to 450 kr, with discounts for return fares, children and those aged over 67. Cabins, which are mandatory on overnight sailings, cost an additional fee, ranging from 100 kr for a lower-deck four person cabin that can be booked as a dorm to 1000 kr for a luxury cabin with a sea view. A motorcycle with up to two riders costs from 550 to 950 kr, a car and driver from 600 to 1000 kr.

Hirtshals to Kristiansand, Oslo & Moss
Color Line runs two to five ferries daily between Hirtshals (Denmark) and Kristiansand (Norway), the busiest ferry connection between the two countries. The schedule varies with the day of the week and the season. The trip takes 4¼ hours.

There's also a daily ferry between Hirtshals and Oslo. The boat from Oslo operates as an overnight ferry, departing at 7.30 pm; the boat from Hirtshals leaves at 10 am and arrives in Oslo at 6.30 pm.

Color Line has a third ferry line between Hirtshals and Moss. The schedule varies with the day of the week and the season but there's at least one ferry a day. The trip takes from eight to 11 hours, depending on whether it's overnight.

Color Line reservation numbers and fares on all three routes from Hirtshals are exactly the same as on the Frederikshavn-Larvik route listed earlier.

Hanstholm to Egersund & Bergen
Fjord Line (☎ 97 96 14 01 in Hanstholm, ☎ 51 49 49 00 in Egersund, ☎ 55 54 88 00 in Bergen) operates a year-round ferry to Egersund and Bergen from Hanstholm on Tuesday, Thursday, Saturday and Sunday. The boats depart from Hanstholm in the afternoon (exact times vary with the day), arriving in Egersund seven hours later and in Bergen the next morning (except for the Saturday boat, which terminates in Egersund). From Norway, departure times vary with both the day of the week and the season. Fares depend on the day of the week and the season, ranging from 190 to 356 kr to Egersund and from 247 to 627 kr to Bergen. Add another 152 to 276 kr for the cheapest four berth cabin, 223 to 323 kr for the cheapest two berth cabin. To Egersund a car costs from 228 to 456 kr, a motorcycle from 119 to 223 kr.

The UK

DFDS Scandinavian Seaways operates car ferries between Esbjerg and Harwich.

From June to September, one boat sets sail in each direction every second day;

during the rest of the year boats leave Esbjerg on Monday, Wednesday and Friday and Harwich on Tuesday, Thursday and Saturday. Throughout the year the boats depart from Harwich at 5 pm, except on Saturday when they sail at 8 pm, and depart from Esbjerg at 6 pm. The crossing takes 19 hours.

These are pleasant boats with full amenities, and all cabins have a shower and toilet. Fares vary according to the season and the day of week, ranging from 420 to 980 kr for a reclining chair, from 630 to 1305 kr for a bed in a four berth cabin and from 840 to 1520 kr for a bed in a two berth cabin. You can save between 10 and 30% by travelling between Sunday and Wednesday.

It costs an additional 415 kr to take a car, 210 kr for a motorcycle and 45 kr for a bicycle. There are discounts on return tickets and for senior travellers, students and children.

Iceland & the Faroe Islands

Smyril Line (☎ 33 16 40 04) operates a weekly ferry service from Hanstholm to Tórshavn (Faroe Islands) and Seyðisfjörður (Iceland) between late May and the end of August.

The boat leaves Hanstholm at 8 pm on Saturday, arriving in Tórshavn at 6 am on Monday. Visitors then have a two day stopover in the Faroe Islands (while the boat makes a run to Bergen, Norway), departing from Tórshavn at 6 pm on Wednesday and arriving in Seyðisfjörður at 9 am on Thursday. The return boat departs from Seyðisfjörður at noon on Thursday, arriving in Tórshavn at 6 am on Friday and in Hanstholm at 4 pm on Saturday.

The cheapest fares are for a couchette, which costs 1300 kr to Tórshavn and 2040 kr to Seyðisfjörður. There's a 25% discount for students aged under 26. You can take a bicycle along for an extra 80 kr, a motorcycle for about 500 kr and a car for about 85% of the couchette fare. Prices are a bit cheaper for the first and last few sailings of the season.

ORGANISED TOURS

If time is limited, there are various package tours that include transport to Denmark, hotel accommodation and, in most cases, sightseeing. Standard tours can be arranged through your travel agency or SAS.

An array of package tours that include hotels can also be arranged through the large ferry companies, such as Stena Line and DFDS Scandinavian Seaways, the addresses of which are listed under Ferry Companies earlier in this chapter.

The American-Scandinavian Foundation and the Danish Cultural Institute arrange study tours to Denmark. Contact addresses are listed under Useful Organisations in the Facts for the Visitor chapter.

Cruise Ships

In recent years, Copenhagen has grown in popularity as a cruise ship stopover, usually as part of a larger Scandinavian, Baltic or Western European tour.

Between mid-May and mid-September some 200 cruise ships call at Copenhagen's Langelinie harbour, just north of the Little Mermaid.

Companies operating cruises stopping in Copenhagen include Costa Cruises, Crystal Cruises, Cunard Line, EuroCruises, the Fred Olsen Line, Princess Cruises and Renaissance Cruises.

There are numerous different itineraries. The Fred Olsen Line offers a 12 day cruise from Dover (UK) that includes Bergen, Oslo, Copenhagen, Kaliningrad, Bornholm, Kiel, Hotlenau and Brunsbattel, costing from US$2400. Princess Cruises puts together a 14 day sail that includes London, Paris, Dublin, Edinburgh, Oslo, Copenhagen, Kiel Canal, Amsterdam and Brussels, but it's much pricier at US$4300.

Travel agencies, particularly those specialising in cruises, can detail all the possibilities and pile you high with brochures. They can also give you the lowdown on special promotions and discounts, such as those for early booking, which can cut as much as 25 to 40% off the standard fares.

WARNING

The information in this chapter is particularly vulnerable to change: prices for international travel are volatile, schedules change, special deals come and go, routes are introduced and cancelled, and rules and visa requirements are amended. Airlines and governments seem to take a perverse pleasure in making price structures and regulations as complicated as possible. You should check directly with the airline or a travel agency to make sure you understand how a fare (and ticket you may buy) works. In addition, the travel industry is highly competitive and there are many lurks and perks.

The upshot of this is that you should get opinions, quotes and advice from as many airlines and travel agencies as possible before you part with your hard-earned cash. The details given in this chapter should be regarded as pointers and are not a substitute for your own careful, up-to-date research.

Getting Around

AIR

Many of Denmark's domestic air routes are operated by Maersk Air (☎ 32 31 45 45), which connects Copenhagen with Billund, Esbjerg and Rønne. The regular one-way fares from Copenhagen are 590 kr to Rønne, 700 kr to Billund and 710 kr to Esbjerg. The regular listed return fare is double the single fare, but a number of discounts are available. Discounted return fares to each destination range from 400 to 870 kr, depending on special conditions and availability.

Other discounts include a one-way youth fare of 290 kr for people aged 21 or under, and various deals for families travelling together. Children under the age of two travel free. Maersk's English-language Web site is at www.maersk-air.com.

Scandinavian Airlines (SAS; ☎ 70 10 30 00) flies from Copenhagen to Århus and Aalborg numerous times per day. The one-way/return fare is 818/900 kr to Århus and 710/869 kr to Aalborg. SAS offers a few discounts, including a youth stand-by fare of 268 kr one way for people aged from 12 to 25, and a weekend return fare of about 500 kr for people of any age, plus other periodic offers (see the Århus and Aalborg Getting There & Away sections for details).

In addition, Cimber Air (☎ 74 42 22 77) flies from Copenhagen to Sønderborg for 779 kr one way, and upwards of 894 kr return. If you're aged under 26 or over 60 you can fly the route on a stand-by basis for just 242 kr one way. Cimber Air also flies from Copenhagen to Århus and Aalborg at fares comparable to SAS prices.

If your travel plans include an international flight to and from Copenhagen you can often work in a free domestic flight by getting an 'open jaw' ticket. This would allow you, at either the start of your trip or on the return flight, to add a connecting flight between Copenhagen and another Danish city at no extra cost. Buying an 'open jaw' ticket into Copenhagen and out of Aalborg, for example, would allow you to rent a car in Copenhagen, self-tour one way, and drop the car at Aalborg airport on the last day of your stay.

BUS

All large cities and towns have a local bus system and most places are also served by countywide regional buses. More often than not, the central bus stop is beside the train station and in many cases regional buses conveniently time their services to dovetail with train schedules.

Stiff competition from trains has left the long-distance bus a very secondary mode of transport in Denmark. There are, however, a handful of cross-country bus routes that can work out about 25% cheaper than train fares.

Daily express buses include a run between Copenhagen and Århus that takes 3½ hours and costs 190 kr, and another from Copenhagen to Aalborg that takes six hours and costs 190 kr. There's also an express-bus service running a couple of times a day between the Jutland port cities of Frederiks-havn and Esbjerg (190 kr, five hours).

See the Getting Around sections of the relevant destinations for more details.

TRAIN

Denmark has a good, reliable train system with reasonable fares and frequent services. Most long-distance trains, such as those on the busy Copenhagen-Aalborg route, operate at least hourly throughout the day. With the exception of a few short private lines, Danske Statsbaner (Danish State Railways; DSB) runs all train services in Denmark. Rail passes such as Scanrail and Eurailpass (see under Train in the Getting There & Away chapter) are valid on DSB trains but cannot be used on the private lines.

RAILWAYS

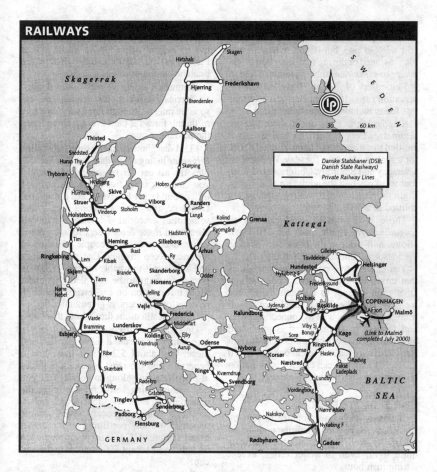

Map legend:
Danske Statsbaner (DSB); Danish State Railways
Private Railway Lines

0   30   60 km

DSB essentially operates two types of standard long-distance train; ticket prices are the same on both. The sleek InterCity (IC) trains have ultramodern comforts. The carriage layout resembles a more spacious version of a plane interior, complete with cushioned seats, overhead reading lights and individual music headphones. IC trains also have play areas for children and roomy WCs with nappy-changing facilities. Reservations are generally required for travel on IC trains.

In addition to the standard IC trains there are also Business IC trains (designated as InterCityLyn on schedules) on certain routes, such as Copenhagen to Esbjerg, Århus and Aalborg. These are geared to business travellers, go marginally faster than standard IC trains, are a bit more posh and offer free drinks and snacks. For the pampering you'll pay a 50% surcharge over the standard train fares.

Interregional (IR) trains are older, a bit slower and more basic, but are comfortable in all respects. Reservations are optional on IR trains and in most cases you can find a seat without one, but if you're travelling a long distance or during rush hour you might prefer to make one to be guaranteed a seat.

Regardless of distance travelled, the reservation fee is 15 kr; on Business IC trains this fee is included in the ticket price.

Standard fares work out at about 1 kr per kilometre. People aged 65 and over are entitled to a discount of approximately 50% for travel on Monday, Tuesday, Wednesday, Thursday and Saturday. Children aged from four to 14 pay half the adult fare at all times. Eight or more adults travelling together are entitled to a 30% discount.

Those aged from 15 to 25 can buy an *Ungdomskort* (youth card) for 150 kr; it allows half-price train fares on Tuesday, Wednesday, Thursday and Saturday.

You can get free pocket-sized schedules that cover the main railway lines at any DSB train station. In addition there's the weighty *DSB Køreplan* which covers all train schedules (as well as connecting buses and ferries) in Denmark; it is published biannually, costs 30 kr and is sold at train stations. There's also a telephone line (☎ 70 13 14 15) that you can call for information on train travel throughout Denmark.

CAR & MOTORCYCLE

Denmark is a pleasant country to tour by car. Roads are in good condition and almost invariably well signposted, and traffic is quite light, even in major cities, except during rush hours.

Motorway signs are colour coded. Blue signs indicate exits and green signs show places that are reached by continuing along the motorway. Petrol stations, with toilets, nappy-changing facilities and minimarkets, are at 50km intervals on all motorways.

Access to and from Danish motorways is straightforward: roads leading out of city and town centres are named after the main city that they lead to. For instance, the road heading out of Odense to Faaborg is called Faaborgvej, the road leading to Nyborg is called Nyborgvej, and so on.

Denmark's main motoring organisation, Forenede Danske Motorejere, or FDM, has its central office (☎ 45 93 08 00) at Firskovvej 32, 2800 Lyngby. There are branches in major towns and cities.

Denmark's extensive network of domestic ferries carries motor vehicles at reasonable rates. Although fares vary, as a rule of thumb fares for cars average three times the passenger rate.

FDM distributes a handy timetable called *Bilfærger* listing up-to-date fares and schedules for all car ferries serving Denmark; you can pick it up free of charge at FDM offices and larger tourist offices throughout Denmark. It's always a good idea – and sometimes essential – for drivers to call ahead and make ferry reservations, even if you can only do so a couple of hours in advance. Keep in mind that on weekends and holidays it's possible for every ferry on prime crossings to be completely booked. More information on car ferries, including reservation numbers, is given under the appropriate destinations throughout this book.

Unleaded petrol costs about 6.4 kr per litre, super petrol about 6.7 kr per litre and diesel fuel about 5.2 kr per litre. You'll generally find the most competitive prices at petrol stations along motorways. If you don't mind using self-service pumps, the unstaffed OK Benzin stations, which are adjacent to Brugsen grocery shops, charge about 25 øre less per litre than the name-brand stations. OK Benzin pumps are open 24 hours and accept 100 kr notes and credit cards.

The Danish Road Directorate (☎ 70 10 10 40) offers a helpful 24 hour telephone service that can provide traffic forecasts and nationwide information on roadworks, detours, passes that are closed in winter and ferry cancellations; information is available in English. It can also tell you approximately how long your journey should take.

Road Rules

In Denmark vehicles are driven on the right-hand side of the road. Cars and motorcycles must have dipped headlights on at all times and drivers are required to carry a warning triangle.

Seat belt use is mandatory. Children aged under three must be secured in a child seat or other approved child restraint appropriate to the child's age, size and weight. Children aged from three to six may use a child seat or booster seat instead of seat belts. Motorcycle riders must wear helmets.

Speed limits are generally 50km/h in towns and built-up areas, 80km/h on major roads and 110km/h on motorways. However, if you're towing a trailer the maximum speed you can travel on major roads and motorways is 70km/h.

Speeding fines, which can be collected on the spot, vary with the offence. As an example, driving just 10km over the speed limit in a 50km/h zone warrants a 400 kr fine, while going 20km/h over that limit increases the fine to 1100 kr. On motorways

the fine is 600 kr for driving 10km over the speed limit, 2900 kr for going 175km/h and 6800 kr for going twice as fast as the speed limit. Although the latter occurrence may be a rare case of madness, Danish drivers do commonly exceed speed limits by a good 10 to 20km/h, so don't rely upon the flow of traffic as an indication of whether your speed is within legal limits.

The authorities are very strict about driving under the influence of alcohol. It's illegal to drive with a blood-alcohol concentration of 0.05% or greater; driving under the influence will render drivers liable to stiff penalties and a possible prison sentence.

Emergencies

Motorways have emergency telephones at 2km intervals; an arrow on marker posts along the shoulder indicates the direction

Road Distances (km)

Note: Distances between Jutland & Zealand are via Funen.

	Aalborg	Copenhagen	Esbjerg	Frederikshavn	Grenaa	Helsingør	Kalundborg	Kolding	Næstved	Nyborg	Odense	Ringkøbing	Rødby	Skagen	Thisted	Tønder	Viborg	Århus
Aalborg	---																	
Copenhagen	384	---																
Esbjerg	216	280	---															
Frederikshavn	65	447	278	---														
Grenaa	136	349	216	193	---													
Helsingør	425	47	321	488	390	---												
Kalundborg	327	103	223	390	292	139	---											
Kolding	199	212	72	261	164	253	155	---										
Næstved	324	85	220	387	289	125	71	152	---									
Nyborg	274	110	170	337	239	151	53	102	50	---								
Odense	243	147	139	306	208	188	90	71	87	37	---							
Ringkøbing	174	318	81	236	188	359	261	115	258	208	177	---						
Rødby	410	163	306	473	375	203	158	238	87	136	173	344	---					
Skagen	105	487	319	41	233	528	430	302	427	377	346	277	513	---				
Thisted	90	381	185	138	186	422	324	196	321	271	240	123	407	172	---			
Tønder	284	297	77	347	249	338	240	86	237	187	156	148	323	387	252	---		
Viborg	80	305	136	142	100	346	248	119	245	195	164	94	331	183	87	205	---	
Århus	112	286	153	171	63	327	ferry	101	226	176	145	127	312	212	153	186	66	---

The Marguerite Route

A special network of scenic routes recommended for people touring by car and motorcycle has been designated and signposted throughout Denmark. Known as the Marguerite Route, it is not a single route that can be taken from end to end but rather a series of routes comprising 3500km of roads in all. Some roads have been chosen for their rural appeal, others have been selected because they pass tourist attractions.

Most of the Marguerite Route is along secondary highways and minor country roads and, consequently, it usually makes an enjoyable alternative to a mundane zip along the main motorways.

The route is marked by a road sign consisting of a white daisy set against a brown backdrop. Virtually all Danish highway maps show the route, either with heavy green dots or solid green outlines. While it's fun to include sections of the Marguerite Route in any self-drive itinerary, at times you'll find alternative country roads parallel to the route to be just as scenic.

The Marguerite Route is not intended for cars pulling trailers, as some of the roads are narrow and cross small bridges. For more details on the route and sights along the way, pick up the small self-touring book *The Marguerite Route*, which is published in English, Danish and German by the Danish Tourist Board. The book can be purchased in larger tourist offices and at many Statoil petrol stations.

Symbol marking the
Marguerite Route

of the nearest phone. From ordinary payphones, dial ☎ 112 for emergencies.

Parking

To park on the street in city centres, you usually have to buy a ticket from a kerbside machine, labelled *billetautomat*. These have LCD screens showing the current time. Put in money until the screen displays the time until which you intend to stay and then push the button to eject the ticket from the machine. Place the ticket, which shows the exact time that you can stay until, face up inside the car windscreen. The cost is generally from 5 to 20 kr an hour. Unless otherwise posted, street parking is usually free from 6 pm to 8 am, after 2 pm on Saturday and all day on Sunday.

The billetautomat only charges for hours when a ticket is required, so if you were to park your car at 5 pm and leave it overnight in a space where tickets are required from

8 am to 6 pm, and put in sufficient coins for two hours, the ticket would be valid until 9 am the next morning.

In smaller towns, which are delightfully free of coin-hungry billetautomats, street parking is free within the time limits posted. These parking spaces will be marked by a blue sign with the letter 'P'; beneath it will be the time limit for free parking (*1 time* is one hour, *2 timer* is two hours). You will, however, need to use a windscreen parking disk. This is a flat plastic card with a clock face and a movable hour hand which must be set to show the time you parked the car. Parking disks can be picked up for a nominal fee from tourist offices and petrol stations.

Parkering forbudt means 'no parking' and is generally accompanied by a round sign with a red diagonal slash. You can, however, stop for up to three minutes to unload bags and passengers. A round sign with a red 'X', or a sign saying *Stopforbud*, means that no stopping at all is allowed.

Rental

Rental cars are expensive in Denmark – you could easily pay as much to hire a car for just one day in Denmark as it would cost to hire one for a week across the border in Germany.

This is one area where it certainly can save you a bundle to do a little research in advance. You'll generally get the best deal on a car rental by booking through an international rental agency before you arrive in Denmark. Be sure to ask about promotional rates, pre-pay schemes and the like, then compare the options. Otherwise if you just show up at the counter at Copenhagen airport you're likely to find the rates for the cheapest cars (including VAT, insurance and unlimited kilometres) beginning at about 650 kr per day, or 470 kr per day for rentals of two days or more.

One of the better car rental deals that doesn't require booking before you arrive in Denmark is the weekend rate offered by some companies. This allows you to keep the car from Friday afternoon to Monday morning, including VAT and insurance, for around 1000 kr. Request a plan that includes unlimited kilometres, as some plans begin tacking on an extra fee after 250km.

Avis, Europcar and Hertz are among the largest operators in Denmark, with offices in major cities, airports and other ports of entry. See the Getting Around sections in regional chapters for details of offices and local operators.

BICYCLE

Cycling is both a practical and an immensely popular way to get around Denmark. There are extensive cycling routes linking towns throughout the country, as well as bike lanes along the streets of most city centres.

Three out of four Danes own bicycles, and half use them on a regular basis. Postal workers are more likely to deliver mail by bicycle than by motor vehicle, and it's not uncommon to see executives beating the rush hour by cycling through city traffic. It's easy to travel with a bike, even when you're not riding it, as bicycles can readily be taken on ferries and most trains. On shorter ferry routes it'll generally cost about 20 kr to bring along your bike, while the longest routes, such as the one between Copenhagen and Bornholm, charge around 50 kr. On DSB trains, carrying a bicycle costs between 20 and 80 kr, depending on the distance; reservations should be made at least three hours prior to departure because bikes generally travel in a different section of the train from passengers. The DSB pamphlet *Cykler i tog*, available at larger train stations, gives details.

In Denmark, most long-distance buses and domestic flights will also carry bicycles for a modest fee, but you'll need to make advance arrangements because the capacity is often limited to a few bikes.

If you prefer to leave your bike at home, it's easy to hire bikes throughout Denmark. Prices average around 50/250 kr per day/week, although if you want a fancy multispeed bike it'll cost more. You might want to bring your own bike helmet, as helmets are not included with most hired bicycles.

Always be careful locking up your bike, especially if you're travelling with an expensive model, as bike theft is common in Denmark, particularly in larger cities such as Copenhagen and Århus.

For more information on cycling, including cycle routes and maps, see the special section 'Cycling in Denmark' in the Facts for the Visitor chapter.

HITCHING

Hitching is never entirely safe in any country in the world, and we don't recommend it. Travellers who decide to hitch should understand that they are taking a small but potentially serious risk. People who do choose to hitch will be safer if they travel in pairs and let someone know where they are planning to go.

At any rate, hitching in Denmark is uncommon and usually not rewarding, although we have heard from a couple of people who've had luck at it. Keep in mind that hitchhiking is illegal on motorways. Most Danes who hitch usually only do so when they are travelling outside their own country.

BOAT

An extensive network of ferries links Denmark's many populated islands; important routes include Copenhagen to Bornholm, Århus to Kalundborg, Ebeltoft to Sjællands Odde, Tårs to Spodsbjerg, and Svendborg to Ærøskøbing. For ferry information see the Getting There & Away sections of relevant destinations throughout this book.

LOCAL TRANSPORT

All cities and towns of any size in Denmark are served by a local bus system. As a general rule, the main terminal for local buses is adjacent to the train station or ferry depot. Copenhagen also has a local train system called the S-train.

For more details, see the relevant destination sections.

Taxi

Taxis are readily available throughout Denmark in city centres, at train stations and around major shopping centres. If you see a

taxi with a lit *fri* sign, you can wave it down, but you can always phone for a taxi as well. See the Getting Around sections of individual cities for phone numbers of taxi companies.

The fare is typically from 20 to 25 kr at flagfall and from 8 to 10 kr per kilometre, with the higher rates prevailing at night and on weekends. There's no need for tipping because a service charge is built into the fare.

ORGANISED TOURS

Denmark is so small and public transport systems are so extensive that organised tours are not all that common.

The national rail company, DSB (☎ 33 12 80 88), packages a couple of self-guided tours, the most interesting being a circular boat-train tour around the Øresund (129 kr), from Copenhagen to Malmö (Sweden), north to Helsingborg (Sweden) and back to Copenhagen via North Zealand.

Within Denmark, the main tour destination is Legoland; day-long packages that cover transport and admission fees are available from several Danish cities.

Some Danish tourist offices offer walking tours of their towns, and occasionally provide more extensive city tours. For information on sightseeing tours within a specific city, see the relevant destination section.

Copenhagen

Copenhagen (København) is Scandinavia's largest and liveliest city, home to a quarter of all Danes.

Despite a population of nearly 1.5 million, Copenhagen is an appealing and still largely low-rise city comprised of block after block of period six-storey buildings. Church steeples add a nice punctuation to the skyline and only a couple of modern hotels burst up to mar the scene.

Capital of Denmark since the early 15th century, Copenhagen grew by gradually radiating out from its centre; consequently most of the city's foremost historical and cultural sites remain concentrated in a relatively small area. Parks, gardens, water fountains, squares and green areas lace the city centre. Along the waterfront you'll find the scenic row (terraced) houses that line Nyhavn, the famed statue of the Little Mermaid and the canal-cut district of Christianshavn.

For a big city, Copenhagen is surprisingly easy to get around. It's a particularly pleasant place for walking, as many of the sightseeing areas and shopping districts in the city centre are reserved for pedestrians. For those who prefer to move at a faster pace, there are bicycle lanes on Copenhagen's main roads as well as an excellent metropolitan bus and train system.

A cosmopolitan city, Copenhagen boasts a plethora of sightseeing and entertainment possibilities. For music lovers and other revellers there's an active nightlife scene which buzzes into the early hours of the morning, and for sightseers the city has a treasure-trove of old churches, museums and castles to explore.

No trip to Copenhagen is complete without a visit to Tivoli and a stroll down Strøget. Another area you shouldn't miss is scenic Nyhavn, from where you can catch a canal tour for a glimpse of the city's historic waterfront sights.

The most outstanding of Copenhagen's numerous museums are the Ny Carlsberg

Highlights

- Have fun at Tivoli, the famed amusement park in the city centre
- Visit some of Copenhagen's world-class museums, most notably Nationalmuseet and Ny Carlsberg Glyptotek
- Enjoy shopping and street entertainment on Strøget, the world's longest pedestrian mall
- Board a canal boat for a guided tour of the historic waterfront
- Peer down on the city from the rooftops of the Rundetårn and Vor Frelsers Kirke
- Soak up the ambience in an al fresco café on scenic Nyhavn canal
- Club-hop your way through the city's spirited nightlife scene
- Walk or cycle along the quiet paths of Dyrehaven (Klampenborg)

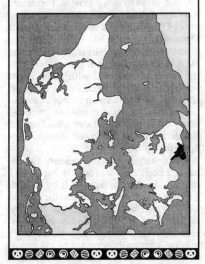

Glyptotek and Nationalmuseet. Of special interest among churches are Vor Frue Kirke, the city's cathedral with its famed statues by Bertel Thorvaldsen, and Christianshavn's Vor Frelsers Kirke, which has an elaborate Baroque altar and a spiral tower with a magnificent city view.

HISTORY

The city of Copenhagen was founded in 1167 by Bishop Absalon, who constructed a fortress on Slotsholmen Island, fortifying a small and previously unprotected harbourside village. The bishop had been granted the land by King Valdemar I, who wanted to put an end to the free movement of marauding Wends who were staging frequent raids along the East Zealand coast.

After the fortification was constructed, the harbourside village grew in importance and took on the name Kømandshavn (Merchant's Port), which over time was condensed to København. Absalon's fortress stood until 1369, when it was destroyed in an attack on the town by the powerful Hanseatic states.

In 1376 construction began on a new Slotsholmen fortification, Copenhagen Castle, and in 1416 King Erik of Pomerania took up residence there, marking the beginning of Copenhagen's role as the capital of Denmark.

Still, it wasn't until the reign of Christian IV, in the first half of the 17th century, that the city was endowed with much of its splendour. A lofty Renaissance designer, Christian IV began an ambitious construction scheme, building two new castles and many other grand edifices including the Rundetårn observatory and Børsen, Europe's first stock exchange.

By the turn of the 18th century Copenhagen's population was 60,000, but in 1711 the bubonic plague reduced it by a third. Later two fires, one in 1728 and the other in 1795, wiped out large tracts of the city, including most of its timber buildings. However, the worst scourge in the city's history is generally regarded as the unprovoked British bombardment of Copenhagen in 1807, during the Napoleonic Wars. The attack targeted the heart of the city, inflicting numerous civilian casualties and setting hundreds of homes, churches and public buildings on fire. In the mêlée that followed, British admiral Horatio Nelson captured the Danish fleet and took it as war booty, ostensibly to prevent it from falling into the hands of Napoleon, who had been pressuring a neutral Denmark to close its ports to the English.

Copenhagen flourished in the 19th and 20th centuries, expanding beyond its old city walls and establishing a reputation as a centre for culture and the arts.

ORIENTATION

The main train station, Central Station (also called Hovedbanegården or København H), is flanked to the west by the main hotel zone and to the east by Tivoli amusement park. Opposite the northern corner of Tivoli is Rådhuspladsen, the central city square and the main terminus for buses around the city.

The world's longest pedestrian mall, Strøget, runs through Copenhagen's city centre between Rådhuspladsen and Kongens Nytorv, the square at the head of the Nyhavn canal. Strøget, which abounds with shopping, dining and entertainment possibilities, is made up of five continuous streets: Frederiksberggade, Nygade, Vimmelskaftet, Amagertorv and Østergade. Pedestrian walkways run north from Strøget into the triangle of streets forming the Latin Quarter.

Maps

Both Copenhagen Information and Use It (see under Tourist Offices) produce free, detailed, four-colour maps of Copenhagen with street indexes and keys for major attractions. Although there's not much that these free tourist maps don't show, you can also buy inexpensive commercial maps at bookshops that are slightly larger and have more complete indexes; one of the best is *København Kort & Godt*, produced by Stadskonduktørembedet.

INFORMATION
Tourist Offices

Copenhagen Information, the city tourist office (☎ 33 11 13 25, fax 33 93 49 69, email woco@inet.uni-c.dk), Bernstorffs-gade 1, 1577 Copenhagen V, is just north of Central Station. Its information desk distributes the useful booklet *Copenhagen This Week*, as well as free maps and bro-chures covering destinations throughout Denmark; there's also a room and hotel booking service on site. Copenhagen Infor-mation is open from 9 am to 9 pm daily between 1 May and 15 September; during the rest of the year it's open from 9 am to 4.30 pm on weekdays and from 9 am to 1.30 pm on Saturday.

Use It (☎ 33 73 06 20, fax 33 73 06 49, email useit@ui.dk), Rådhusstræde 13, 1466 Copenhagen K, is a terrific alternative in-formation centre catering to young budget travellers but open to all; it books rooms, stores luggage, holds mail, provides infor-mation on everything from hitching to nightlife and produces a useful general magazine-style guide, *Playtime* – all free of charge. It's open from 9 am to 7 pm daily between mid-June and mid-September, and from 11 am to 4 pm on weekdays (to 2 pm on Friday) at other times.

Money

American Express (Amex; ☎ 33 12 23 01), Nørregade 7A, on the 3rd floor of an in-conspicuous office building, cashes Amex travellers cheques free of commission (al-though not always at the best exchange rate) and other travellers cheques at a cost of 15 kr per transaction. It's open from 9 am to 5 pm on weekdays.

Banks, all of which charge transaction fees, are plentiful along Strøget and can

---

Copenhagen Card

The Copenhagen Card, a tourist pass, allows unlimited travel on buses and trains in Copen-hagen and throughout North Zealand, as well as free admission to most of the region's museums and attractions.

Copenhagen attractions offering free admission to cardholders include Tivoli, Ny Carlsberg Glyptotek, Nationalmuseet, Statens Museum for Kunst, Rosenborg Slot, Amalienborg Slot exhibits, Rundetårn, Vor Frelsers Kirke, Arken, Zoologisk Have, Den Hirschsprungske Samling, Orlogsmuseet, Jens Olsen's clock, Kunstindustrimuseet, Musikhistorisk Museum, Arbejder-museet, Guinness World of Records Museum, Ripley's Believe It or Not!, Louis Tussaud's Wax Museum and all of the Slotsholmen sights except De Kongelige Repræsentationslokaler.

The card also confers free admission to the Vikingeskibshallen (Viking Ship Museum) and domkirke (cathedral) in Roskilde, Frederiksborg Slot in Hillerød, Karen Blixen Museet in Rungsted, Louisiana in Humlebæk, Frilandsmuseet in Lyngby, Danmarks Akvarium in Char-lottenlund and the museums in Køge.

In addition, the card offers discounts on a few other sights, such as the Eksperimentarium and the Omnimax cinema at Tycho Brahe Planetarium, as well as 20% off car rentals and canal tours.

An adult card costs 140/255/320 kr for one/two/three days; it's half-price for children aged from five to 11 years. Cards can be purchased at Central Station, at tourist offices and in some hotels.

If you want to run through a lot of sightseeing in a few days, the Copenhagen Card can be a real bargain. However, for a more leisurely exploration of select places it may work out cheaper to pay individual admission charges and use one of the transport passes (see the Getting Around section later in this chapter for details).

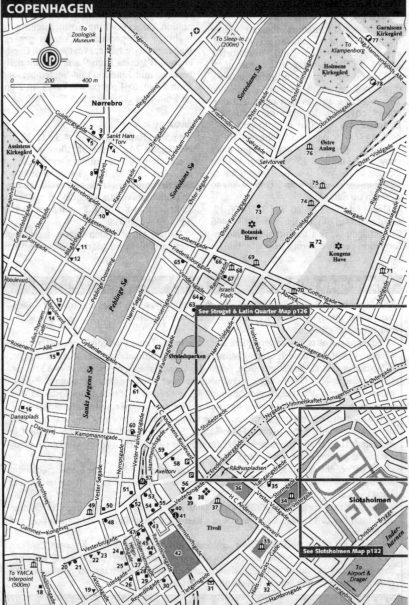

COPENHAGEN

To Zoologisk Museum

0 200 400 m

Nørrebro

Assistens Kirkegård

Sankt Hans Torv

Garnisons Kirkegård

Holmens Kirkegård

Østre Anlæg

Østre Kirkegård

Sortedams Sø

Botanisk Have

Kongens Have

See Strøget & Latin Quarter Map p126

Ørstedsparken

Sankt Jørgens Sø

Peblinge Sø

Danasplads

Axeltorv

Rådhuspladsen

Tivoli

Slotsholmen

See Slotsholmen Map p132

Inderhavnen

To YMCA Interpoint (500m)

To Airport & Dragør

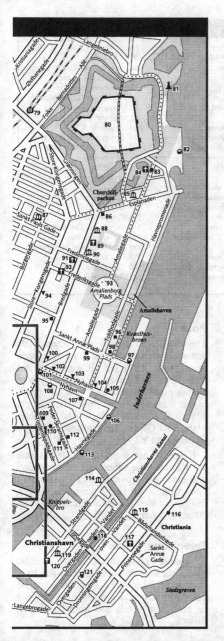

COPENHAGEN

PLACES TO STAY
9 Sleep-In Green
14 Hotel Sankt Jørgen
15 Cab-Inn Scandinavia
16 Cab-Inn Copenhagen
18 City Public Hostel
24 Hotel Hebron
25 Selandia Hotel
26 Hotel Centrum
27 Hotel du Nord
28 Absalon Hotel
29 Saga Hotel
30 Turisthotellet
44 Missionshotellet Nebo
46 Grand Hotel
50 Scandic Hotel Copenhagen
51 Hotel Imperial
55 Radisson SAS Royal Hotel
58 Ascot Hotel
64 Hotel Jørgensen
67 Hotel Windsor
86 Hotel Esplanaden
95 Phoenix
96 Copenhagen Admiral Hotel
98 Sophie Amalie Hotel
99 Neptun Hotel
105 71 Nyhavn Hotel
107 Sømandshjemmet Bethel
109 Hotel Opera
111 Hotel City
112 Hotel Maritime

PLACES TO EAT
3 Sebastopol
4 Picnic
5 Quattro Fontane
6 Indian Corner
7 Naturbutik
11 Floras Kaffe Bar
12 Solsikken
13 Mexicali
19 Restaurant Shezan
20 Merhaba
22 Alanya
23 Restaurant Koh-I-Noor
40 Hard Rock Café
43 Astor Pizza
56 Scala; Matahari; Streckers
66 Govindas
94 Ida Davidsen
100 Els
102 Nyhavns Færgekro
103 Cap Horn
104 Pizzabageren

OTHER
1 Rigshospitalet (Hospital)

continued ...

COPENHAGEN

2 Rust	54 Steno Apotek	84 St Alban's Church
8 Barcelona	57 Vesterport S-Train Station	85 Frihedsmuseet
10 Bananrepublikken	59 Pumpehuset	87 Nyboders Mindestuer
17 Københavns Bymuseum	60 Petrol Station	88 Kunstindustrimuseet
21 Danhostel Office	61 Peugeot	89 Sankt Ansgars Kirke
31 Main Post Office	62 Café Babooshka	90 Medicinsk-Historisk Museum
32 Main Police Station	63 Dansk Cyklist Forbund	91 Alexander Newsky Kirke
33 Ny Carlsberg Glypotek	65 Babel	92 Marmorkirken
34 Nationalmuseet	68 Arbejdermuseet	93 Amalienborg Slot
35 Mojo	69 Botanisk Museum	97 Ferries to Oslo & Bornholm
36 Rådhus	70 Musikhistorisk Museum	101 Canal Tours Copenhagen
37 Louis Tussaud's	71 Davids Samling	106 Flyvebådene
Wax Museum	72 Rosenborg Slot	(Hydrofoil to Bornholm)
38 Rådhusarkadan	73 Palmehus	108 Netto-Bådene
39 Tivoli Main Entrance	74 Geologisk Museum	110 Coin Laundry
41 Copenhagen Information	75 Statens Museum for Kunst	113 Pilen (Hydrofoil to Malmö)
(Tourist Office)	76 Den Hirschsprungske Samling	114 Gammel Dok
42 Central Station	77 US Embassy	115 Orlogsmuseet
45 Eurolines Ticket Office	78 German Embassy	116 Entrance to Christiania
47 Danwheel	79 Østerport S-Train Station	117 Vor Frelsers Kirke
48 Europcar/Interrent	80 Kastellet	118 Christianshavns Bådudlejning
49 Tycho Brahe Planetarium	81 The Little Mermaid	119 B & W Museum
52 Budget/Pitzner	82 Ferry to Swinoujscie (Poland)	120 Christians Kirke
53 Hertz	83 Gefionspringvandet	121 Sofies Kælder

also be found on nearly every second corner elsewhere in the city centre. Most are open from 9.30 am to 4 pm on weekdays (to 6 pm on Thursday); many also have ATMs outside their entrances that can be accessed with credit and bank cards after business hours. There are also private exchange booths along Strøget, but commissions can run as high as 10%.

Den Danske Bank in Central Station is open from 7 am (8 am in winter) to 8 pm daily, although higher commissions are charged outside normal banking hours. The Forex exchange booth in Central Station opens longer hours (from 8 am to 9 pm daily) and has lower commission fees and sometimes better rates as well.

There are 24-hour cash-exchange machines that change major foreign currencies (bills only) into Danish kroner, minus a 25 kr fee, at a number of locations, including Den Danske Bank in Central Station, Unibank on Axeltorv and Jyske Bank at Vesterbrogade 9 near the Grand Hotel.

Post

The main post office, on Tietgensgade just south-east of Central Station, is open from 11 am to 6 pm on weekdays and from 10 am to 1 pm on Saturday. If you're having poste restante mail sent to Copenhagen, it can be picked up there; have letters addressed to: addressee, Poste Restante, Main Post Office, Tietgensgade 37, 1500 Copenhagen V.

If you're not using the poste restante service, the post office in Central Station will generally prove more convenient. It's open from 8 am to 10 pm on weekdays, from 9 am to 4 pm on Saturday and from 10 am to 5 pm on Sunday.

Telephone & Fax

Payphones can readily be found in public places such as shopping arcades and train stations. You can make international phone calls from any public payphone. Faxes can be sent from hotels and from larger post offices.

Email & Internet Access

At Babel (☎ 33 33 93 38, email postmaster @babel.dk), a cybercafé at Frederiksborggade 33, Internet access costs 16 kr per half-hour. If you just want to check your email, both Use It and the Telia phone company, on Strøget at Amagertorv 18, offer free Internet access.

Internet Resources

Three good Web sites that will link you to a wealth of information in English are www.woco.dk (run by Wonderful Copenhagen, the tourism office), www.kbhbase .copenhagencity.dk (run by the city of Copenhagen) and www.useit.dk (run by Use It, the youth information centre). Other sites are listed in the text under specific topics.

Gay & Lesbian Travellers

The national organisation for gays and lesbians, called Landsforeningen for Bøsser og Lesbiske (LBL; ☎ 33 13 19 48, email lbl @lbl.dk), has its headquarters at Teglgårdsstræde 13 in central Copenhagen. The site has a café and a library that are open on weekday evenings. Copenhagen Gay Life is a network of gay and gay-friendly businesses in Copenhagen. The Web site, which includes useful tourist information and listings, is at www.copen hagen-gay-life.dk.

See the Gay & Lesbian Travellers section in the Facts for the Visitor chapter for other helpful organisations.

Travel Agencies

Kilroy Travels (☎ 33 11 00 44), Skindergade 28, and Wasteels (☎ 33 14 46 33), Skoubogade 6, specialise in student and budget travel; both are north of Strøget and just a minute's walk apart.

General travel agencies include Inter-Travel (☎ 33 15 00 77), opposite the Use It office at Frederiksholms Kanai 2, and the Amex office (see under Money earlier in this section).

Bookshops

Substantial bookshops stocking good selections of English-language books, travel guides and maps include GAD, on Strøget at Vimmelskaftet 32, Politiken Boghallen at Rådhuspladsen 37, and Arnold Busck at Købmagergade 49 in the Latin Quarter.

If you're looking specifically for international travel guidebooks, try Kupeen, at Kilroy Travels (see under Travel Agencies), which has a comprehensive selection. Nordisk Korthandel, Studiestræde 26, sells an extensive range of guidebooks as well as cycling and hiking trail maps of Denmark. Libraire Française, south of Strøget at Badstuestræde 6, sells French-language books.

Interkiosk, a newsstand in Central Station, sells international newspapers, including the *Guardian,* the *Telegraph, Le Monde,* the *International Herald Tribune,* the *Wall Street Journal* and *USA Today.* You can also buy foreign newspapers at most international hotels and at some of the larger newspaper kiosks, such as those on Rådhuspladsen. Look too for the *Copenhagen Post,* a weekly newspaper that publishes Danish news and events in English.

Library

Hovedbiblioteket, the central library at Krystalgade 15, has international magazines and newspapers in English that visitors are free to browse. It's open from 10 am to 7 pm on weekdays and from 10 am to 2 pm on Saturday.

Laundry

Coin laundries (look for the word *møntvask)* are not terribly difficult to find around the city. There's one at Holbergsgade 9 near Nyhavn, open from 6 am to 10 pm daily.

Medical Services

Several city hospitals have 24-hour emergency wards. The most central are Rigshospitalet (☎ 35 45 35 45), Blegdamsvej 9, which is in the Østerbro area north of the city centre, and Frederiksberg Hospital (☎ 38 34 77 11), west of the city centre at Norde Fasanvej 57.

Private doctor visits (☎ 33 93 63 00 for referrals) usually cost around 350 kr.

There are numerous pharmacies around the city; look for the sign *apotek*. Steno Apotek (☎ 33 14 82 66), at Vesterbrogade 6 opposite Central Station, is open 24 hours. Like all Danish pharmacies it sells both nonprescription and prescription medications; you'll need a local doctor's order for the latter.

Emergency

Dial ☎ 112 for police, ambulance or fire services; the call can be made without coins from public phones.

There's a small police office (☎ 33 15 38 01) in Central Station and a major police station (☎ 33 14 14 48) at Polititorvet, a couple of blocks south-east of the main post office.

WALKING TOUR

Taking a half-day's walk from rådhus (city hall) to the *Little Mermaid* is a good way to get oriented in Copenhagen and to take in many of the city's central sights. As you stroll the narrow streets, be sure to look up now and then to appreciate the gargoyles and other ornamentations that decorate many of the older buildings.

Major sights are marked with an asterisk (*) and described in greater detail under separate headings at the end of this Walking Tour section.

Before heading off, you might want to take a closer look at the red-brick **rådhus**. The building was completed in 1905 and displays elements of 19th century national Romanticism, medieval Danish design and northern Italian architecture, the latter most notably in the central courtyard. You can see the theatre-like interior for free or, for 10 kr, walk to the top of the 105m tower on weekdays at 10 am, noon and 2 pm.

Rådhuspladsen, the large central square fronting the city hall, is the main terminus for city buses. At the south-western side of the plaza you'll find a **statue** of Hans Christian Andersen and a **water fountain** with spouting dragons, while on the eastern side, as you face the Palace Hotel, there's a note-

Jens Olsen's Clock

This elaborate clock, designed by Danish astro-mechanic Jens Olsen (1872-1945) and built at a cost of one million kroner, is of special note to chronometer buffs. The clock displays not only the local time but also solar time, sidereal time, sunrises and sunsets, firmament and celestial pole migration, planet revolutions, the Gregorian calendar and even changing holidays such as Easter. Of its numerous wheels, the fastest turns once every 10 seconds, while the slowest will finish its first revolution after 25,753 years.

The clock was first put into motion in 1955 and its weights are wound weekly. It can be viewed in a side room off the foyer of rådhus (city hall) on weekdays from 10 am to 4 pm and on Saturday from 10 am to 1 pm. Admission costs 10 kr (children 5 kr).

worthy column capped with a pair of bronze **Vikings** blowing *lurs* (horns).

Rådhuspladsen also offers a good view of the Unibank building on the north-western corner of Vesterbrogade and HC Andersens Blvd. The building is topped with a unique **barometer** that displays a girl on her bicycle when the weather is fair or with an umbrella when rain is predicted. This bronze sculpture was created in 1936 by the Danish artist E Utzon-Frank.

From Rådhuspladsen walk down **Strøget** which, after a couple of blocks, cuts between two spirited pedestrian squares, **Gammel Torv** and **Nytorv**. A popular summertime gathering spot in Gammel Torv is the gilded **Caritas Fountain**, erected in 1608 by Christian IV and marking what was once the old city's central market. As in days past, pedlars still sell jewellery, flowers and fruit on the square. At the south-western corner of Nytorv is **Domhuset**, an imposing neoclassical building that once served as the city hall and now houses the city's law courts.

Continuing down Strøget, you'll pass **Helligåndskirken** (the Church of the Holy Ghost), one wing of which dates from medieval times. The church interior, most of which was rebuilt after a fire in 1732, is sometimes open for viewing on weekday afternoons. Also along the Amagertorv section of Strøget are some of the city's finest speciality shops, including **Royal Copenhagen Porcelain** and **Georg Jensen**; this latter houses a small free museum featuring early 20th century silverwork. The WØ Larsen pipe shop, diagonally opposite Georg Jensen at Amagertorv 9, boasts another little free speciality exhibition, the **Tobaksmuseet** (Tobacco Museum), which displays hand-carved pipes.

The adjacent square, **Højbro Plads**, marked by a water fountain with bronze storks, is a popular venue for street musicians. At the southern end of this elongated square is a **statue** of city founder Bishop Absalon on horseback; behind it, the appropriate backdrop is Slotsholmen, where the bishop erected Copenhagen's first fortress. If you look due east from Højbro Plads you'll see the steeple of **Nikolaj Kirke**. The tower of this church dates from the 16th century, although most of the church was rebuilt in 1915. No longer consecrated, the church is now owned by the municipality and is used for contemporary art exhibits, open free to the public each afternoon.

At the end of Strøget you'll reach **Kongens Nytorv**, a square boasting an equestrian statue of its designer, Christian V, and circled by gracious old buildings. Notable from Christian V's era are *Charlottenborg, a 17th century Dutch Baroque palace that houses Det Kongelige Kunstakademi (The Royal Academy of Fine Arts), and the 1685 **Thott's Palæ** (Thott's Mansion), which now houses the French embassy. There are also some 100-year-old buildings, including the department store **Magasin du Nord**, with its ornate cupola, and **Det Kongelige Teater** (the Royal Theatre), which is fronted by statues of the playwrights Adam Oehlenschläger and Ludvig Holberg. The theatre, home to Den Kongelige Ballet (the Royal

Danish Ballet) and Den Kongelige Opera (the Royal Danish Opera), has two stages, one on either side of Tordenskjoldsgade. An **archway** with a mosaic depicting Danish poets and artists spans the road connecting the two stages.

To the east of Kongens Nytorv is the picturesque **Nyhavn** canal, dug 300 years ago to allow traders to bring their wares into the heart of the city. Long a haunt for sailors and writers (including Hans Christian Andersen, who lived in the house at No 67 for nearly two decades), Nyhavn today is half salty and half gentrified, with a line of trendy pavement cafés and restored gabled townhouses. It makes an invitingly atmospheric place to break for lunch or an afternoon beer. At the head of the canal is a huge frigate **anchor** that commemorates the Danish seamen who died in WWII serving with the Allied merchant marines.

From the northern side of Nyhavn, head north along Toldbodgade, turn right onto Sankt Annæ Plads, left onto Havnepromenade and continue walking north along the waterfront. You'll pass a couple of **18th century warehouses** that have been converted for modern use. One of them is now the Copenhagen Admiral Hotel (see under Places to Stay for details); its lobby is worth a peek.

When you reach the fountain that graces **Amaliehaven** (Amalie Gardens), turn inland to get to *Amalienborg Slot, home of the royal family since 1794. The palace's four nearly identical rococo mansions, designed by architect Nicolai Eigtved, surround a central cobblestone square and an immense **statue** of Frederik V (1746-66) on horseback sculpted by JFJ Saly. Looking west from the square you'll get a head-on view of the imposing *Marmorkirken (Marble Church), which was designed in conjunction with the Amalienborg complex as part of an ambitious plan by Frederik to extend the city northward by creating a new district geared to the affluent.

From here you could make a detour along *Bredgade, where there are a couple of churches and small museums. Otherwise,

The Headless Mermaid

In January 1998 the Little Mermaid (Den Lille Havfrue) – Denmark's famous tourist icon – lost her head.

It seems that, in the middle of the night, someone took a saw and decapitated the bronze statue. The next day, CNN and other international news services spread the gory scene around the world, as divers searched the waters around the statue for clues – to no avail. Three days later the severed head mysteriously turned up in a box outside a Copenhagen TV station – and it was speedily reattached.

This isn't the first time the gentle lady has been the subject of undesired attention. In 1967 the original head was lopped off and in 1983 an arm was sawn off – neither were ever found again and both appendages had to be recast and welded back on.

The famous statue of Hans Christian Andersen's heroine, with all appendages intact

continue north on Amaliegade to **Churchill-parken**, where you'll pass *****Frihedsmuseet**, a museum dedicated to the Danish resistance movement of WWII, followed by the attractive Gothic **St Alban's Church**, which serves the city's English-speaking Anglican community. The church's location, in the midst of a public park, may seem a bit curious – the site was provided by Christian IX following the marriage of his daughter to the Prince of Wales, who later ascended the British throne as King Edward VII.

Beside the church sits the immense **Gefionspringvandet** (Gefion Fountain), a monument to yet another overseas relationship. According to Scandinavian mythology, when the Swedish king offered the goddess Gefion as much land as she could plough in one night, Gefion turned her four sons into powerful oxen and ploughed the entire area that now comprises the is-

land of Zealand. The bronze statue in the fountain depicts the goddess and her oxen at work.

A 10 minute walk through the park past the fountain and along the waterfront will lead you to the statue of the **Little Mermaid** (Den Lille Havfrue), which was designed by Edvard Eriksen in 1913. Inspired by Hans Christian Andersen's fairy tale, the statue depicts a mermaid who had fallen in love with a prince but had to wait for 300 years to become human. This much-photographed bronze figure, perched on a rock at the water's edge, has a certain grace, but don't expect a monument – the mermaid is indeed little, and sports a rather drab industrial harbour backdrop.

From the Little Mermaid continue on the road inland. After just a few minutes you'll reach steps leading down to a wooden bridge that crosses a moat into **Kastellet**, a citadel built by Frederik III in the 1660s. The fortress is still surrounded by some of the city's original ramparts. Although the fortress buildings remain in use by the Danish military, the park-like grounds are open to the public from 6 am to sunset daily. Walk south through Kastellet and you'll go past its main row of historic buildings before reaching a second bridge that spans the moat and leads back into Churchillparken.

Back at the park entrance, turn right onto Esplanaden to Store Kongensgade; from there you can catch bus No 6 back to Rådhuspladsen or No 1 to Central Station.

Charlottenborg

Fronting Kongens Nytorv, south-west of Nyhavn, is Charlottenborg, which was built in 1683 as a palace for the royal family. Since 1754 Charlottenborg has housed Det Kongelige Kunstakademi. The Kunstakademi's exhibition hall, on the eastern side of the central courtyard, features changing exhibitions of modern art, design and architecture by Danish and international artists. It's open daily from 10 am to 5 pm (to 7 pm on Wednesday). Admission usually costs 20 kr but varies according to the current exhibition.

Amalienborg Slot

Although most of the palace is not open to the public, visitors can enter one wing that features exhibits of the royal apartments used by three generations of the monarchy from 1863 to 1947.

The rooms, faithfully reconstructed in the styles of the period, are decorated with heavy oak furnishings, gilt-leather tapestries, family photographs and old knick-knacks. They include the study and drawing room of Christian IX (1863-1906) and Queen Louise, whose six children wedded into nearly as many royal families – one eventually ascending the throne in Greece and another marrying Russian tsar Alexander III. Also displayed is the study of Frederik VIII (1906-12), who decorated it in a lavish neo-Renaissance style, and the study of Christian X (1912-47), the grandfather of the present queen Margrethe II.

The wing is open daily from 10 am to 4 pm in summer and from 11 am to 4 pm during the rest of the year; it's closed on Monday in winter. Admission costs 35 kr (children 5 kr).

Marmorkirken

The Marble Church, also known as Frederikskirken, is a stately neo-Baroque church

Changing of the Guard

When the queen is in residence at Amalienborg Slot, mainly from December to April, a colourful changing of the guard takes place in the palace square at noon. The ceremony begins with a procession from Rosenborg Slot by the Royal Guard, bedecked in full regalia and marching to the sound of fifes and drums. The guard contingent leaves the Rosenborg Slot gardens at 11.30 am and marches to Amalienborg on a curving route that takes them to Kultorvet in the Latin Quarter, south on Købmagergade and then east along Østergade to Kongens Nytorv. From there they continue to Amalienborg Slot along Bredgade, Sankt Annæ Plads and Amaliegade.

Upon reaching the square, the old guard are ceremoniously relieved of their duties by their fresh replacements, who take up sentry posts in front of the palace. The relieved guards then join the marching band and return to their barracks at Rosenborg Slot, on a route that takes them along Frederiksgade, Store Kongensgade and Gothersgade.

In spring and early summer, when the queen takes up residence at her summer palace in Fredensborg, a version of the changing of the guard occurs there.

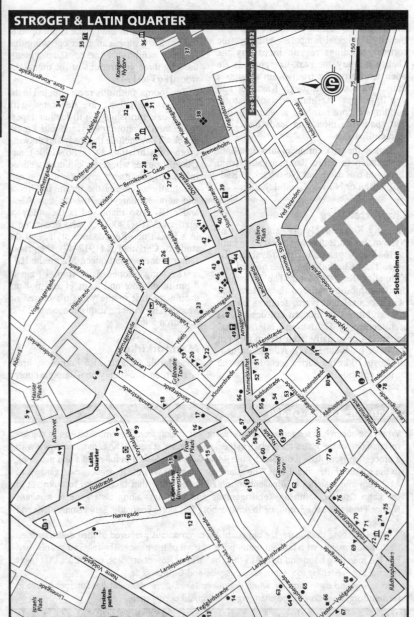

STRØGET & LATIN QUARTER

STRØGET & LATIN QUARTER

PLACES TO STAY
32 Hotel d'Angleterre
66 Hotel Kong Frederik
74 Palace Hotel

PLACES TO EAT
3   Hellas
4   Klaptræet
5   St Gertruds Kloster
8   Ankara
16 Ristorante Italiano
18 Det Lille Apotek
19 Tacos Cantina
20 Peder Oxe
21 Jensen's Bøfhus
22 Pasta Basta
25 Café Sommersko
28 Netto Supermarket
29 Reinh van Hauen
33 Kommandanten
40 Croissant'en
42 McDonald's
51 Trianon Konditori
52 Café de Paris; Restaurant
    Eastern; Café Size
53 Café Sorgenfri
58 La Glace
60 McGrails
62 Huset med det Grønne Træ
67 Coxx Café
69 Shawarma Grill House

70 Reinh van Hauen
71 McDonald's; Burger King
75 Peppe's Pizza
80 RizRaz

OTHER
1   Nørreport S-Train Station;
    ARTE Kiosk
2   Crazy Daisy
6   Rundetårn
7   Arnold Busck Bookshop
9   Hovedbibliotek
    (Public Library)
10 Synagogen
11 University Library
12 Sankt Petri Kirke
13 Landsforeningen for
    Bøsser og Lesbiske (LBL)
14 Kul-Kaféen
15 Vor Frue Kirke
17 Kilroy Travels
23 Copenhagen Jazz House
24 Post Office
26 Museum Erotica
27 Canadian Embassy
30 Guinness World of Records
    Museum
31 Bang & Olufsen
34 Jyske Bank
35 Thott's Palæ; French Embassy
36 Charlottenborg

37 Det Kongelige Teater
38 Magasin du Nord
39 Nikolaj Kirke
41 Illum
43 Georg Jensen Shop &
    Museum
44 The Dubliner
45 Tobaksmuseet; WØ Larsen
    Pipe Shop; Pizza Hut
46 Royal Copenhagen Porcelain
47 Illums Bolighus
48 Telia
49 Helligåndskirken
50 Sebastian
54 Pan Disco
55 Libraire Française
56 GAD Bookshop
57 Wasteels
59 Unibank
61 American Express
63 Cosy Bar
64 Nordisk Korthandel
65 Masken
68 Politiken Boghallen
72 Ripley's Believe It or Not!
73 Viking Statue
76 Sweater Market
77 Domhuset
78 Inter-Travel
79 Use It
81 La Fontaine

on Frederiksgade, a block west of Amalienborg Slot. The church's massive dome, which was inspired by St Peter's in Rome and which measures more than 30m in diameter, is one of Copenhagen's most dominant skyline features.

The original plans for the church were ordered by Frederik V and drawn up by Nicolai Eigtved as part of a grand design that included the Amalienborg mansions. Although church construction began in 1749, it encountered problems as costs overran, due in part to the prohibitively high price of Norwegian marble, and the project was soon shelved.

It wasn't until Denmark's wealthiest 19th century financier, CF Tietgen, bankrolled the project's revival that it was finally taken to completion. It was consecrated as a church in 1894.

The church's soot-blackened exterior is ringed by statues of Danish theologians and saints. The interior, with its immense circular nave, can be viewed free on weekdays from 11 am to 2 pm, on Saturday from 11 am to 4 pm and on Sunday from noon to 4 pm.

On Saturday at 11 am and Sunday at noon in winter, and on weekdays only at 11 am and 12.45 pm in summer, you can tour the dome itself (20 kr) and catch a broad view of the city from its rim.

Bredgade Sights

There are a cluster of sights between Marmorkirken and Churchillparken.

Heading north, first up is **Alexander Newsky Kirke**, at Bredgade 53, which was built in Russian Byzantine style in 1883 by

Tsar Alexander III. The church is usually open only for services.

Next to the north is **Medicinsk-Historisk Museum**, Bredgade 62, which is housed in a former surgical academy dating from circa 1786 and deals with the history of medicine, pharmacy and dentistry over the past three centuries. It's open only for guided tours, which are offered at 11 am and 1 pm on Wednesday, Thursday, Friday and Sunday; in July and August, the 1 pm tours are conducted in English. Admission is free.

At 64 Bredgade is **Sankt Ansgars Kirke**, Copenhagen's Roman Catholic cathedral, which has a colourfully painted apse and a small museum on the history of Danish Catholicism. Admission is free and it's usually open for viewing on weekday afternoons.

Kunstindustrimuseet (Museum of Decorative Art) is at Bredgade 68. Housed in the former Frederiks Hospital (circa 1752), the museum highlights innovations in Danish design and crafts during the 20th century, with displays of furniture, ceramics, silver and textiles. It's open from 10 am to 4 pm Tuesday to Saturday and from 1 to 4 pm on Sunday. Admission costs 35 kr (children free). Its Web site is at www .mus-kim.dk.

Frihedsmuseet

This museum (☎ 33 13 77 14), in Churchillparken, features exhibits on the Danish resistance movement from the time of the German occupation in 1940 to liberation in 1945. There are displays on the Danish underground press, the clandestine radio operations that maintained links with England, and the smuggling operations that saved Danish Jews from capture by the Nazis.

Admission to the museum is free. Between May and mid-September it's open from 10 am to 4 pm Tuesday to Saturday and from 10 am to 5 pm on Sunday. During the rest of the year it's open from 11 am to 3 pm Tuesday to Saturday and from 11 am to 4 pm on Sunday.

LATIN QUARTER

With its cafés and second-hand bookshops, the area north of Strøget that surrounds the old campus of Københavns Universitet (Copenhagen University) is a good place for ambling around. The university, which was founded in 1479, has largely outgrown its original quarters and moved to a new campus on Amager, but parts of the old campus, including the law department, remain here.

At the north of the Latin Quarter is **Kultorvet**, a lively pedestrian plaza and summertime gathering place with beer gardens, flower stalls and produce stands. On sunny days you'll almost always find impromptu entertainment here, which can range from Andean flute playing to local street theatre and dancing.

Ascend the stairs of the **university library** (enter from Fiolstræde) to see one quirky remnant of the 1807 British bombardment of Copenhagen: a glass case containing a cannonball in five fragments and the target it hit, a book entitled *Defensor Pacis* (Defender of Peace). The library is open from 9 am to 6 pm on weekdays.

Opposite the university is **Vor Frue Kirke**, Copenhagen's cathedral, which was founded in 1191 and rebuilt on three occasions after devastating fires. The current structure dates from 1829 and was designed in neoclassical style by CF Hansen. With its high vaulted ceilings and columns, Vor Frue Kirke seems as much museum as church – quite apropos because it's also the showcase for sculptor Bertel Thorvaldsen's statues of Christ and the 12 apostles, his most acclaimed works. Thorvaldsen's depiction of Christ, with comforting open arms, became the most popular worldwide model for statues of Christ and remains so today. Admission to the cathedral is free; it's open from 9 am to 5 pm Monday to Saturday and from noon to 4 pm on Sunday.

Two other handsome places of worship in the Latin Quarter are **Sankt Petri Kirke**, on the corner of Nørregade and Sankt Pedersstræde, a German church that dates from the 15th century and is currently

Copenhagen's maritime traditions are still alive.

Majestic ships continue to grace Christianshavn.

The Tivoli version of the Royal Guard.

Hans Christian Andersen surveys Rådhuspladsen.

The capital's free bikes are great for sightseeing.

Stately Amalienborg Slot is the Copenhagen home of Denmark's royal family.

Café life on Strøget.

Terraced houses line picturesque Nyhavn canal.

The steeple of Vor Frelsers Kirke offers fine views.

undergoing renovations, and **Synagogen**, the Jewish synagogue, two blocks to the east at Krystalgade 12, which was built in 1831 in neoclassical style. Both places can be viewed from the exterior but are not generally open to the public.

Rundetårn

The Rundetårn (Round Tower), Købmagergade 52, is the best vantage point from which to admire the old city's red-tiled rooftops and abundant church spires. This vaulted brick tower, 35m high, was built by Christian IV in 1642 and used as an astronomical observatory in conjunction with the nearby university. Although the university erected a newer structure in 1861, amateur astronomers have continued to use the Rundetårn each winter, which gives credence to its claim to be the oldest functioning observatory in Europe.

A 209m spiral walkway winds up the tower around a hollow core; about halfway up is a small exhibition hall housing changing displays of art and culture that is worth a visit.

The Rundetårn (☎ 33 73 03 73) is open during the summer from 10 am to 8 pm daily (from noon on Sunday). Between September and May it's open from 10 am to 5 pm daily (from noon on Sunday). Admission costs 15 kr (children 5 kr). The Web site is at www.rundetaarn.dk.

Winter visitors who'd like to view the night sky from the 3m-long telescope that's mounted within the rooftop dome should make inquiries at the ticket booth. The observatory is generally open on Tuesday and Wednesday nights.

ROSENBORG SLOT

This early 17th century castle, with its moat and garden setting, was built in Dutch Renaissance style by King Christian IV to serve as his summer home. A century later King Frederik IV, who felt cramped at Rosenborg, built a roomier palace north of the city in the town of Fredensborg. In the years that followed, Rosenborg was used mainly for official functions and as

a place in which to safeguard the monarchy's heirlooms.

In the 1830s the royal family decided to open the castle to visitors as a museum, while still using it as a treasury for royal regalia and jewels. It continues to serve both functions today.

The 24 rooms in the castle's upper levels are chronologically arranged, housing the furnishings and portraits of each monarch from Christian IV to Frederik VII; however, it's the lower level, where the treasury remains, that's the main attraction, with its dazzling collection of crown jewels. These include Christian IV's ornately designed crown, the jewel-studded sword of Christian III and Queen Margrethe II's emeralds and pearls; the latter are displayed here when the queen is not wearing them to official functions.

Rosenborg Slot is open from 10 am to 4 pm daily between 1 June and 31 August, and from 11 am to 3 pm daily in spring and autumn; winter hours are more restricted. Admission costs 40 kr (children 10 kr).

The entrance to the castle is off Øster Voldgade. There is no entry from Kongens Have, the adjacent gardens. For details of access, see the following Gardens section.

GARDENS

The green stretch of gardens along Øster Voldgade offers a quiet refuge from city traffic. The following gardens are conveniently located opposite each other, so visits to them can be combined in a lengthy stroll. There are no admission charges.

Kongens Have (King's Gardens), the expansive green space behind Rosenborg Slot, is the city's oldest public park. It has manicured box hedges, lovely rose beds and plenty of shaded areas. Kongens Have is a popular picnic spot and the site of a free marionette theatre, performing on summer afternoons. If you time your trip well, you can include a visit to **Davids Samling**, just east of Kongens Have at Kronprinsessegade 30, housing Scandinavia's largest collection of Islamic art. It's open from 1 to 4 pm daily except Monday; admission is free.

In the 10 hectare **Botanisk Have** (Botanical Garden), to the west of Rosenborg Slot, you can wander along fragrant paths amid arbours, terraces, rock gardens and ponds. It's open from 8.30 am to 6 pm daily between April and October, from 8.30 am to 4 pm daily during the rest of the year. Within the Botanisk Have is the **Palmehus** (Palm House), a large walk-through glasshouse containing a lush collection of tropical plants, open from 10 am to 3 pm daily year-round. There's also a cactus house and an orchid greenhouse, open only from 1 to 3 pm on Saturday and Sunday. The modest **Botanisk Museum** (Botanical Museum), at the southern corner of the garden, features plants from Denmark and Greenland, but is open only on summer afternoons. One entrance to the Botanisk Have is at the intersection of Gothersgade and Øster Voldgade, the other is off Øster Farimagsgade.

The **Geologisk Museum**, at Øster Voldgade 5 at the eastern corner of the Botanisk Have, is Denmark's foremost geological museum. You'll find the usual exhibits of fossils, minerals, crystals and rocks, including one from the moon. In addition it houses some interesting Danish displays, such as a huge 4.5kg chunk of amber, and some quite notable finds from Greenland; a highlight is the world's sixth-largest iron meteorite, which weighs in at 20 tonnes. The museum is open from 1 to 4 pm daily except Monday year-round; admission is free.

You can get to the gardens and Rosenborg Slot by taking the S-train to Nørreport station and walking north for two blocks, or via numerous buses including Nos 14, 16, 31, 42 and 43.

STATENS MUSEUM FOR KUNST

Denmark's national gallery, Statens Museum for Kunst (Royal Museum of Fine Arts; ☎ 33 74 84 94), Sølvgade 48, was founded in 1824 to house art collections belonging to the royal family. Originally sited at Christiansborg Slot, the museum opened in its current location in 1896.

As might be expected, the museum contains a good collection of fine art, including works by Danish artists such as Jens Juel, CW Eckersberg, Christen Købke and PS Krøyer. There's also an interesting collection of old masters by Dutch and Flemish artists, including Rubens and Frans Hals, as well as more contemporary European paintings by Matisse, Picasso and Munch.

The museum is open Tuesday to Sunday year-round from 10 am to 5 pm (to 8 pm on Wednesday). Admission costs 30 kr for adults (except during special exhibitions, when it can be as much as 50 kr), free for children. Bus Nos 10, 14, 40, 42 and 43 run there.

DEN HIRSCHSPRUNGSKE SAMLING

This museum (☎ 35 42 03 36), dedicated to Danish art of the 19th and early 20th century, is at Stockholmensgade 20, a 10 minute walk from the Statens Museum for Kunst. Originally the private holdings of tobacco magnate Heinrich Hirschsprung, the collection contains works by painters of Denmark's Golden Age such as Christen Købke and CW Eckersberg, a notable selection by Skagen painters PS Krøyer and Anna and Michael Ancher, and works by the Danish symbolists and the Funen painters. The museum is open year-round from 11 am to 4 pm, except on Tuesday when it's closed and on Wednesday when it's open from 11 am to 9 pm. Admission costs 25 kr (free on Wednesday). Bus Nos 10, 14, 40, 42 and 43 run to Den Hirschsprungske Samling.

NATIONALMUSEET

If you want to learn more about Danish history and culture, don't miss the National Museum (☎ 33 13 44 11) at Ny Vestergade 10, opposite the western entrance to Slotsholmen.

This quality museum boasts the country's most extensive collection of Danish historical artefacts, dating from the Upper Palaeolithic period to the 1840s and including Stone Age tools, Viking weaponry and impressive Bronze Age, Iron Age and rune-stone collections. Don't miss the exhibit of bronze lurs, some of which date back 3000 years and are still capable of blowing a tune, and the finely crafted 3500-year-old Sun Chariot, unearthed in a Zealand field a century ago.

There are sections on the Norsemen and Inuit of Greenland, collections of 18th century Danish furniture, a 'Please Touch' exhibition for sight-impaired visitors and a special children's wing.

The museum also boasts a noteworthy coin collection containing Greek, Roman and medieval coins and a Classical Antiquities section complete with Egyptian mummies. There's a café and a gift shop inside the museum, and ramps and lifts provide access for disabled visitors. Interpretive signs are in English as well as Danish.

The museum is open from 10 am to 5 pm Tuesday to Sunday year-round. On Wednesday admission is free to all; on other days it costs 30 kr (children free).

SLOTSHOLMEN

Slotsholmen is the seat of Denmark's national government and a repository of historical sites. Located on a small island separated from the city centre by a moat-like canal, Slotsholmen's centrepiece is **Christiansborg Slot**, a large rambling palace that now contains government offices.

Several short bridges link Slotsholmen to the rest of Copenhagen. If you walk into Slotsholmen from Ny Vestergade, you'll cross the western part of the canal and enter Christiansborg's large main courtyard, which was once used as a royal riding grounds. The courtyard still maintains a distinctively equestrian character, overseen by a **statue** of Christian IX (1863-1906) on horseback and flanked to the north by stables and to the south by carriage buildings.

The stables and buildings surrounding the main courtyard date back to the original Christiansborg palace, which was built in the 1730s by Christian VI to replace the more modest Copenhagen Castle that previously stood there. The grander west wing of Christian VI's palace went up in flames in 1794, was rebuilt in the early 19th century and was once again destroyed by fire in 1884. In 1907 the cornerstone for the third (and current) Christiansborg palace was laid by Frederik VIII and, upon completion, the national parliament and the Supreme Court moved into new chambers there.

In addition to the sights listed here, visitors are also free to enter **Slotskirke**, the castle's domed church, which was set ablaze by stray fireworks in 1996 and has since been painstakingly restored.

Folketinget

The parliamentary chamber, called Folketinget, can be visited on Sunday year-round as well as on weekdays in summer; tours run on the hour from 10 am to 4 pm (except at noon). The tours, which are free and conducted in Danish, visit the chamber where the 179 members of Parliament meet to debate national legislation. The tour also takes in Wanderer's Hall, which contains the original copy of the Constitution of the Kingdom of Denmark.

De Kongelige Repræsentationslokaler

The grandest part of Christiansborg is De Kongelige Repræsentationslokaler (Royal Reception Chambers), an ornate Renaissance hall where the queen holds royal banquets and entertains heads of state. The chambers are closed to the public when in use and also on Monday year-round. Tours with commentary in English are conducted at 11 am and 3 pm Tuesday to Sunday from May to September (also at 1 pm from June to August) and at 11 am and 3 pm on Tuesday, Thursday, Saturday and Sunday during the rest of the year. Admission costs 37 kr (children 10 kr).

Kongelige Stalde & Kareter

In the Royal Stables & Coaches buildings, visitors can view a collection of antique

SLOTSHOLMEN

0   60   120 m

1 Slotskælderen hos Gitte Kik
2 Statue of Bishop Absalon
3 Krogs Fiskerestaurant
4 Canal Tours Copenhagen
5 Slotskirke
6 Thorvaldsens Museum
7 De Kongelige Repræsentationslokaler
8 Ruins under Christiansborg
9 Statue of Frederik VII
10 Netto-Bådene
11 Holmens Kirke
12 Børsen
13 Folketinget
14 Statue of Christian IX
15 Kongelige Stalde & Kareter
16 Teatermuseet
17 Tøjhusmuseet
18 Kongelige Bibliotek

coaches, uniforms and riding paraphernalia, some of which are still used for royal receptions. You can also see the royal family's carriage and saddle horses. However, the collection is only open at weekends between 2 and 4 pm. Admission costs 10 kr (children 5 kr).

Ruins under Christiansborg

A walk through the crypt-like bowels of Slotsholmen offers a unique perspective on Copenhagen's lengthy history. In the basement of the current palace, beneath the tower, are the remains of two earlier castles. The most notable are the ruins of Absalon's fortress, Slotsholmen's original castle, built by Bishop Absalon in 1167. The excavated foundations, which consist largely of low limestone sections of wall, date back to the founding of the city.

Absalon's fortress was demolished by Hanseatic invaders in 1369. Its foundations, as well as those of Copenhagen Castle that replaced it and stood for more than three

Free Museums

In egalitarian Denmark some of the finest things in life are free – on at least one day a week – so you might want to plan your museum browsing accordingly.

Every Wednesday the Statens Museum for Kunst, Nationalmuseet, Den Hirschsprungske Samling, Tøjhusmuseet and Ny Carlsberg Glyptotek all turn off their cash registers and open their doors gratis to all. Ny Carlsberg Glyptotek is also free on Sunday.

In addition, there are a handful of Copenhagen museums that never charge for admission: Thorvaldsens Museum, Frihedsmuseet, Bymuseet, Davids Samling, Geologisk Museum, Georg Jensen Museum, B & W Museum and Medicinsk-Historisk Museum.

centuries, were excavated when the current tower was built in the early 20th century.

The ruins can be explored daily from 9.30 am to 3.30 pm in summer and every day except Saturday and Monday from October to April. Admission costs 20 kr for adults (children 5 kr).

Teatermuseet

This museum occupies the Hofteater (Old Court Theatre), which dates from 1767 and drips with historic character. Performances over the years have ranged from Italian opera and pantomime to shows by local ballet troupes, one of which included fledgling ballet student Hans Christian Andersen. The theatre, which took on its current appearance in 1842, drew its final curtain in 1881 but was reopened as a museum in 1922. The stage, boxes and dressing rooms can be examined, along with displays of set models, drawings, costumes and period posters tracing the history of Danish theatre. It's open year-round from 2 to 4 pm on Wednesday and from noon to 4 pm on Saturday and Sunday. Admission costs 20 kr (children 5 kr).

Thorvaldsens Museum

This museum exhibits the works of the famed Danish sculptor Bertel Thorvaldsen (1770-1844), who was heavily influenced by Greek and Roman mythology. After four decades in Rome, Thorvaldsen returned to his native Copenhagen and donated his private collection to the Danish public. In return the royal family provided this site for the construction of a museum to house Thorvaldsen's drawings, plaster moulds and statues. The museum also contains antique art from the Mediterranean region that Thorvaldsen collected during his lifetime. Admission is free; the museum is open from 10 am to 5 pm Tuesday to Sunday year-round. The entrance is on Vindebrogade.

Tøjhusmuseet

Accessed from Tøjhusgade is Tøjhusmuseet (Royal Arsenal Museum), which contains an impressive collection of historic cannons, hand weapons and armour. The 163m-long building that houses the arsenal was constructed by King Christian IV in 1600 and boasts Europe's longest vaulted Renaissance hall. It's open from noon to 4 pm Tuesday to Sunday year-round. Admission costs 20 kr (children 5 kr; free on Wednesday).

Kongelige Bibliotek

The Royal Library, which dates from the 17th century, is the largest library in Scandinavia. Its main collection is housed in a suitably classical building with arched doorways, columned halls, chandeliers and high-ceilinged reading rooms. The library not only serves as a research centre for scholars and university students, but also doubles as a repository for rare books, manuscripts, prints and maps. As Denmark's national library it contains a complete collection of all Danish printed works produced since 1482.

The library, which is backed by lovely flower gardens containing a fishpond and a statue of Søren Kierkegaard, can be entered from Rigsdagsgården, just west of Tøjhusmuseet. Hours vary with the season, but it's

An Author's Burden

In 1834 Hans Christian Andersen applied for work at the Kongelige Bibliotek (Royal Library) in Copenhagen 'to be freed from the heavy burden of having to write in order to live'. Apparently the library administrators weren't too impressed with his résumé – he was turned down. Ironically, Andersen's unsuccessful application is now preserved as part of the library's valued archives, along with many of his original manuscripts. They can be viewed on weekdays, provided advance notice is given.

typically open to the public from 9 am to 6 pm Monday to Saturday. Admission is free.

Børsen

Another striking Renaissance building is Børsen, the stock exchange, at the eastern corner of Slotsholmen on Børsgade. Constructed in the 1620s, it's of note particularly for its ornate spire, formed from the entwined tails of four dragons, and for its richly embellished gables. This still-functioning stock exchange, which first opened during the bustling reign of Christian IV, is the oldest in Europe.

Holmens Kirke

Just across the canal to the north-east of Slotsholmen is Holmens Kirke (Church of the Royal Navy). This historic brick structure, with a nave that was originally built in 1562 to be used as an anchor forge, was converted into a church for the Royal Navy in 1619. Most of the present structure, which is predominantly in Dutch Renaissance style, dates from 1641. The church's burial chapel contains the remains of some important naval figures, including Admiral Niels Juel, who beat back the Swedes in the crucial 1677 Battle of Køge Bay.

It was at Holmens Kirke that Queen Margrethe II took her marriage vows in 1967.

The interior of the church, which has an intricately carved 17th century oak altarpiece and pulpit, can be viewed daily except Sunday from 9 am to 2 pm (to noon on Saturday) between mid-May and mid-September, and from 9 am to noon during the rest of the year. Admission is free.

CHRISTIANSHAVN

Christianshavn, on the eastern flank of Copenhagen, was established by Christian IV in the early 17th century as a commercial centre and a military buffer for the expanding city. It's cut with a network of canals, modelled after those in Holland, which leads Christianshavn to occasionally be dubbed 'Little Amsterdam'.

Still surrounded by its old ramparts, Christianshavn today is a hotchpotch of newer apartment complexes and renovated period warehouses that have found second lives as upmarket housing and restored government offices. The neighbourhood attracts an interesting mix of artists, yuppies and dropouts. Christianshavn is also home to a sizeable Greenlandic community and was the setting of the public housing complex in the popular novel and movie *Miss Smilla's Feeling for Snow*.

To get to Christianshavn, you can walk over the Knippelsbro bridge from the northeastern part of Slotsholmen, take the canal Water Bus or catch bus No 8 or 2 from Rådhuspladsen. If you're going to Christiania first, bus No 8 is the best, as it stops near the gate.

Christiania

In 1971 an abandoned 41 hectare military camp on the eastern side of Christianshavn was taken over by squatters who proclaimed it the 'free state' of Christiania, subject to their own laws. The police tried to clear the area but it was the height of the 'hippie revolution' and an increasing number of alternative folk from throughout Denmark continued to pour in, attracted by the concept of communal living and the prospect of reclaiming military land for peaceful purposes.

The momentum became too much for the government to hold back and, bowing to public pressure, the community was allowed to continue as a 'social experiment'. About 1000 people settled into Christiania, turning the old barracks into schools and housing, and starting their own collective businesses, workshops and recycling programmes.

As well as hosting progressive happenings, Christiania also became a magnet for runaways and junkies. Although Christiania residents felt that the conventional press played up an image of decadence and criminality – as opposed to portraying Christiania as a self-governing, ecology-oriented and tolerant community – they did, in time, find it necessary to modify their free-law approach. A new policy was established that outlawed hard drugs in Christiania, and the heroin and cocaine pushers were expelled.

Still, Christiania remains controversial. Some Danes resent the community's rent-free, tax-free situation and more than a few Christianshavn neighbours would like to see sections of Christiania turned into public parks and school grounds.

Although the police don't regularly patrol Christiania, they have staged numerous organised raids on the community and it's not unknown for police training to include a tactical sweep along Pusherstreet.

Visitors are welcome to stroll or cycle through car-free Christiania, though large dogs may intimidate some free spirits. Photography is frowned upon, and outright forbidden on Pusherstreet, where marijuana joints and hashish are openly (though not legally) sold and smoked.

Christiania has a small market where pipes and jewellery are sold, a few craft shops, a bakery and a couple of simple café-like places where you can get coffee and light eats. There's also a sit-down restaurant, Loppen (see the Entertainment section towards the end of this chapter for details), which serves good organic food at moderate prices, and a few entertainment spots.

The main entrance into Christiania is on Prinsessegade, 200m north-east of its intersection with Bådsmandsstræde. Pusherstreet and most of the shops are within a few minutes walk of the entrance.

If you want to learn more about Christiania, informative guided tours (25 kr; meet inside the main entrance) are conducted daily at 3 pm in summer.

Vor Frelsers Kirke

A few minutes south-west of Christiania is the 17th century Vor Frelsers Kirke (Our Saviour's Church), Sankt Annæ Gade 29. The church, which once benefited from close ties with the Danish monarchy, has a grand interior that includes an elaborately carved pipe organ dating from 1698 and an ornate Baroque altar with marble cherubs and angels.

For a panoramic city view, make the dizzying 400-step ascent of the church's 95m spiral tower – the last 160 steps run along the outside rim of the tower, narrowing to the point where they literally disappear at the top. This colourful spire was added to the church in 1752 by Lauritz de Thurah, who took his inspiration from Boromini's tower of St Ivo in Rome.

Admission to the church is free. It costs 20 kr to climb the tower, which recently reopened after a lengthy renovation. It's open daily from 9 am to 4.30 pm in summer, from 9 am to 3.30 pm in spring and autumn and from 10 am to 2 pm in winter.

Orlogsmuseet

The Royal Danish Naval Museum occupies a former naval hospital at Overgaden oven Vandet 58 on Christianshavn Kanal. This museum houses more than 300 model ships, many dating from the 16th to the 19th century. Some were built by naval engineers to serve as design prototypes for the construction of new ships; consequently the models take many forms, from cross-sectional ones detailing frame proportions to full-dressed models with working sails.

The museum also displays a collection of figureheads, navigational instruments, ship lanterns, a Fresnel lens from a lighthouse and the propeller from the German U-boat that sank the *Lusitania*. It's open from noon to 4 pm Tuesday to Sunday year-round. Admission costs 30 kr (children 20 kr).

Other Christianshavn Sights

At Strandgade 1 is **Christians Kirke**, designed by Danish architect Nicolai Eigtved and completed in 1759. This church once served the local German congregation and has an expansive, theatre-like rococo interior. It's open from 8 am to 6 pm (to 5 pm in winter) daily year-round, except during church services. Admission is free.

Nearby at Strandgade 4 is the **B & W Museum**, which displays the history of Burmeister & Wein, the shipbuilding company that in 1912 pioneered the use of diesel engines in ocean-going ships. In January 1943 Burmeister & Wein became the target of the first Allied air raid on Copenhagen, when British bombers levelled the company's Christianshavn factory to put an end to its production of German U-boat engines. The museum is open from 10 am to 1 pm Monday to Friday (and on the first Sunday of the month) year-round. Admission is free.

The architectural museum **Gammel Dok**, Strandgade 27B, features changing exhibitions of Danish and international architecture, design and industrial art. It's open from 10 am to 5 pm daily year-round. Admission costs 30 kr (children free).

TIVOLI

Situated right in the heart of the city, Tivoli is a tantalising combination of flower gardens, food pavilions, amusement rides, carnival games and open-air stage shows. This genteel entertainment park, which dates from 1843, is delightfully varied. Visitors can ride the roller coaster, take aim at the shooting gallery, enjoy the pantomime of Commedia dell'Arte or simply sit and watch the crowds stroll by.

During the day children flock to Tivoli's ferris wheel, carousel, bumper cars and other rides. In the evening Tivoli takes on a more romantic aura as the lights come on and the cultural activities unfold, with one stage hosting traditional folk dancing as another prepares a theatrical performance.

Each of Tivoli's numerous entertainment venues has a different character. Perhaps best known is the open-air Peacock Theatre, which features mime and ballet and was built in 1874 by Vilhelm Dahlerup, the renowned Copenhagen architect who also designed Det Kongelige Teater. Tivoli also has an indoor cabaret theatre and a large concert hall featuring performances by international symphony orchestras and ballet troupes.

Between all the neon and action, Tivoli makes for a fun place to stroll around, and if you feel like a splurge there are some good restaurants that enjoy stage views and make for a memorable dining experience (see under Tivoli in the Places to Eat section later in this chapter).

Wednesday and Saturday are the best nights to visit as they include a fireworks display shot off shortly before the clock strikes midnight.

Tivoli (☎ 33 93 18 81) is open daily from 11 am to midnight (to 1 am from Thursday to Saturday) between late April and mid-September. Admission costs 39 kr for adults (35 kr for entry before 1 pm) and 20 kr for children. Amusement ride tickets cost 9 kr (many rides require two tickets), but there are multiticket schemes and passes as well. The numerous open-air performances are free of charge, but there's usually an admission fee for the indoor performances. For more information, see under Entertainment later in this chapter, or visit the Web site at www.tivoligardens.com.

Tivoli also opens for a few weeks prior to Christmas for holiday festivities, a Christmas market and ice-skating on the lake. Some of Tivoli's restaurants reopen for that period, serving traditional Danish Christmas fare.

NØRREBRO

The Nørrebro quarter of the city developed in the mid-19th century as a working-class neighbourhood. In more recent times it's attracted a large immigrant community and has become a haunt for students, musicians and artists. It consequently boasts lots of interesting Middle Eastern and Asian restaurants and some of Copenhagen's hottest night spots. There are a number of second-hand clothing shops in the streets radiating out from Sankt Hans Torv, antique shops along Ravnsborggade, and a Saturday morning flea market a few blocks to the west on Nørrebrogade along the wall of the Assistens Kirkegård.

Assistens Kirkegård

This cemetery in the heart of Nørrebro is the burial place of some of Denmark's most celebrated citizens, including philosopher Søren Kierkegaard, physicist Niels Bohr, authors Hans Christian Andersen and Martin Andersen Nexø, and artists Jens Juel, Christen Købke and CW Eckersberg. It's an interesting place to wander around – as much a park and garden as it is a graveyard.

The city publishes an informative English brochure that maps out famous grave sites; ask for it at Copenhagen Information. In addition, tours (20 kr) are conducted on Sunday at 1 pm; these are sponsored by the Assistens Kirkegårds Formidlingscenter (☎ 35 37 19 17), a cultural group based at Kapelvej 2 (whose motto is 'Meet the Danes – both the living and the dead!').

The cemetery is open from 8 am to 8 pm between May and August, with shorter winter hours; admission is free. Bus Nos 5 and 16 stop nearby.

Zoologisk Museum

This modern zoological museum, 1km north of Assistens Kirkegård on the corner of Jaglvej and Universitetsparken, displays all sorts of stuffed animals, from North Zealand deer to Greenlandic polar bears. There are also interesting dioramas, recorded animal sounds, a whale skeleton and insect displays. It's open Tuesday to Sunday from 11 am to 5 pm. Admission costs 20 kr (children 10 kr). Bus Nos 18, 42, 43 and 184 run to the museum.

NY CARLSBERG GLYPTOTEK

This exceptional museum, on HC Andersens Blvd near Tivoli, houses an excellent collection of Greek, Egyptian, Etruscan and Roman sculpture and art. It was built a century ago by beer baron Carl Jacobsen, who was an ardent collector of classical art. The museum's main building, designed by architect Vilhelm Dahlerup, is centred around a glass-domed conservatory replete with palm trees and Mediterranean greenery, creating an atmospheric complement to the collection.

Although Ny Carlsberg Glyptotek was originally – and primarily remains – dedicated to classical art, a gift of more than 20 paintings by Paul Gauguin led to the formation of an impressive 19th century French and Danish art collection. The Gauguin works, now numbering 50, are displayed alongside pieces by Cézanne, Van Gogh, Pissarro, Monet, Renoir and Degas in a new wing of the museum that opened in 1996. This 'French Wing' also boasts one of only three complete series of Degas bronzes.

Ny Carlsberg Glyptotek (☎ 33 41 81 41) is open daily except Monday from 10 am to 4 pm. Admission costs 15 kr (children free) but it's free to all on Wednesday and Sunday. Call the museum (☎ 33 41 81 41) for information on chamber concerts presented on Sunday from October to March.

VESTERBRO

The Vesterbro district has a varied character that's readily observed by walking along its best-known street, Istedgade, which runs west from Central Station. The first few blocks are lined with rows of respectable hotels that soon give way to the city's main red-light area. When Denmark became the first country to legalise pornography in the 1970s, Vesterbro's porn shops and seedy nightclubs became a magnet for tourists and voyeurs. Although it's not necessarily any tamer these days, liberalisation elsewhere has made the area less of a novelty.

About halfway down Istedgade the red-light district recedes and the neighbourhood becomes increasingly multiethnic, with a mix of Pakistani and Turkish businesses. Vesterbro, together with the adjacent district of Nørrebro, is home to much of the city's immigrant community and abounds with good restaurants serving international cuisine, as well as interesting shops.

Københavns Bymuseum

The Copenhagen City Museum (☎ 33 21 07 72), at Vesterbrogade 59 in the Vesterbro district, features – not surprisingly – diplays about the history and development of Copenhagen, mainly paintings and scale models of the old city. Of particular interest is the small exhibit dedicated to the religious philosopher Søren Kierkegaard, who was born in Copenhagen in 1813 and died in the city in 1855. The museum is open daily except Monday from 10 am to 4 pm between May and September and from 1 to 4 pm between October and April. Admission is free.

OTHER ATTRACTIONS
Musikhistorisk Museum

The Music History Museum (☎ 33 11 27 26), housed in an 18th century building at Åbenrå 30 just north of Kultorvet in the Latin Quarter, contains a quality collection of musical instruments dating from 1000 to 1900 AD. The exhibits are grouped according to theme and accompanied by musical recordings. Special emphasis is placed on the history of music as a social phenomenon, especially its effect on Danish culture. The museum is open from 1 to 3.30 pm Friday to Wednesday between May and September, and on Monday, Wednesday, Saturday and Sunday during the rest of the year. Admission costs 20 kr (children 5 kr). There are occasional concerts and special presentations.

Arbejdermuseet

The Workers' Museum, at Rømersgade 22, pays homage to the working class with exhibits portraying the lives of Danish labourers in the 1880s, 1930s and 1950s. It's open from 10 am to 4 pm daily, except on Monday in winter. Admission costs 30 kr (children 15 kr). You can get there by taking the S-train to Nørreport station and walking west on Frederiksborggade or by catching bus No 5, 14 or 16.

Nyboders Mindestuer

This museum, south-west of Kastellet at Sankt Paulsgade 20, stands in the midst of the old residential quarter laid out in 1630 by Christian IV to provide housing for his naval staff. Although the museum is in one of the original buildings, most of the neighbourhood housing – block after block of long ochre-coloured row (terraced) houses with red-tiled roofs – was built in later years. The museum contains period furnishings and is open from noon to 2 pm on Wednesday and from noon to 4 pm on Sunday. Admission costs 10 kr.

Guinness World of Records Museum

This touristy attraction, on Strøget at Østergade 16, uses displays, photos and film to depict the world's superlatives – the tallest, fastest, oddest and so on. It's open daily from 10 am to 10 pm in summer and from 10 am to 6 pm during the rest of the year. Admission costs 58 kr (children 25 kr).

Ripley's Believe It or Not!

This clichéd museum, at Rådhuspladsen 57, displays the expected collection of unexpected oddities from around the world (such as a six-legged calf) replicated in wax figures and tableaus. It's open daily from 10 am to 10 pm. Admission costs 58 kr for adults, 25 kr for children aged between five and 11, and 38 kr for children aged 12 to 15.

Louis Tussaud's Wax Museum

At this wax museum, located on the northern edge of Tivoli at HC Andersens Blvd 22, celebrities such as Elvis and Frankenstein can be found in the company of

Danish notables, including the royal family, Søren Kierkegaard and Hans Christian Andersen. Kids will enjoy the scenes from Andersen's 'Snow Queen' and the exhibits are spruced up with a few interesting holograms. Admission costs 58 kr (children 25 kr). It's open daily from 10 am to 11 pm in summer and from 10 am to 6 pm in winter.

Museum Erotica
A cross between a museum and a peepshow, Museum Erotica, two blocks north of Strøget at Købmagergade 24, is full of erotic paintings, posters, photographs, statues and sex toys. These range from hand-coloured daguerreotype photographs from the 1850s to a multiscreen video room playing modern-day porn movies. It's open daily from 10 am to 11 pm between May and September, and from 11 am to 8 pm between October and April. Admission costs 59 kr.

Eksperimentarium
This extensive hands-on technology and natural science centre is housed in a former bottling hall of Tuborg Breweries at Tuborg Havnevej 7 in Hellerup, north of the city. The centre contains some 300 hands-on exhibits.

It's a fun place for kids, featuring time-honoured standards such as the hall of mirrors, as well as computer-enhanced activities that make it possible to compose water music, stand on the moon or ride an inverted bicycle. In summer it's open daily from 10 am to 5 pm; during the rest of the year it's open from 9 am to 5 pm on Monday, Wednesday and Friday, from 9 am to 9 pm on Tuesday and from 11 am to 5 pm on weekends. Admission costs 69 kr (children 49 kr). To get there catch bus No 6 from central Copenhagen.

Tycho Brahe Planetarium
This planetarium (☎ 33 12 12 24) has a domed space theatre that offers shows of the night sky using state-of-the-art equipment capable of projecting more than 7500 stars, planets and galaxies. The planetarium's 1000 sq metre screen also screens Omnimax natural science films on subjects ranging from astronauts aboard the space shuttle to divers exploring tropical reefs.

The planetarium was named after the famed Danish astronomer Tycho Brahe (1546-1601), whose creation of precision astronomical instruments allowed him to make more exact observations of planets and stars and paved the way for the discoveries made by later astronomers.

The planetarium is at Gammel Kongevej 10, about 750m north-west of Central Station. It's open from 10.30 am to 9 pm daily. It costs 68 kr (children 50 kr) to see either the planetarium show or an Omnimax film. There are also general astronomy exhibits (15 kr) but unlike the audiovisual shows these are not translated into English.

Zoologisk Have
Copenhagen Zoo, at Roskildevej 32 in the Frederiksberg district, has the standard collection of caged creatures, including elephants, lions, zebras, hippos, gorillas and polar bears. Special sections include the Tropical Zoo, Children's Zoo, Ape Jungle, African Savannah and South American Pampas. It's open daily, from 9 am to 6 pm between June and August, from 9 am to 5 pm in spring and autumn, and from 9 am to 4 pm in winter. Admission costs 60 kr (children 30 kr). Bus No 28 from Rådhuspladsen stops outside the gate.

SWIMMING
Beaches
If brisk water doesn't deter you, the greater Copenhagen area has a number of bathing beaches. The water is tested regularly, and if sewage spills or other serious pollution occurs the beaches affected are closed and signposted.

A popular beach south of Copenhagen is Amager Strandpark (take bus No 9, 12 or 13). Playground facilities and shallow waters make it ideal for children. Deeper waters can be reached by walking out along the jetties. There's another beach,

Sydstranden, in Amager along the southern side of Dragør; take bus No 33 or 34.

Easily accessible to the north of Copenhagen are beaches at Charlottenlund and Klampenborg; for details see the Around Copenhagen section at the end of this chapter.

Pools & Saunas

Copenhagen has a handful of public saunas and swimming pools that visitors can use, costing from 20 to 25 kr. The following are two of the more central ones.

Øbro Hallen (☎ 35 42 30 65), Gunnar Nu Hansens Plads 3, near the national stadium in Østerbro, is open from 7 am until at least 4 pm on weekdays, from 8 am to 3 pm on Saturday and from 10 am to 3 pm on Sunday.

Vesterbro Svømmehal (☎ 33 22 05 00), Angelgade 4, is open from 9 am to 8.30 pm on Monday, from 7 am to 7 pm on other weekdays and from 9 am to 2 pm on Saturday and Sunday.

BOATING

You can hire rowboats from Christianshavns Bådudlejning (☎ 32 96 53 53) on the canal at Overgaden neden Vandet 29 in Christianshavn; they cost 30 kr for half an hour or 50 kr for an hour, and are available daily from 9 am to sunset between May and mid-September. There's also an atmospheric outdoor café right on the water where you can linger over cakes and drinks after your outing.

For details of boating in the Lyngby area, see under Lyngby in the Around Copenhagen section at the end of this chapter.

CYCLING

Cycle lanes are found along many city streets and virtually all of Copenhagen can be toured by bicycle, except for pedestrian-only streets such as Strøget. Bicycles are allowed to cross Strøget at Gammel Torv and Kongens Nytorv.

When touring the city, cyclists should be cautious of bus passengers who commonly step off the bus into the cycle lanes, and

of pedestrians (particularly tourists) who sometimes absentmindedly step off the kerb and into the path of oncoming cyclists. This is particularly a problem on roads such as Nørregade, where cyclists are allowed to ride against the one-way traffic.

Use It provides a useful free *Copenhagen By Bike* brochure that maps out some suggested cycling routes. For information on bicycle hire, see under Bicycle in the Getting Around section later in this chapter.

Cycle Tour

The most popular self-guided cycling tour in the Copenhagen area is the 12km ride north to Dyrehaven. There's a cycle path the entire way, much of it skirting the Øresund coast.

To begin, take Østerbrogade north from the city. After passing the S-train station Svanemøllen, the road continues as Strandvejen, passing through the busy suburb of Hellerup, where the intersections have blue-marked crossings to indicate cyclist rights-of-way, and then up through the quiet coastal village of Charlottenlund. Here the cycle lane widens and there's a beach, an old fort and an aquarium that can make for interesting diversions (see the Around Copenhagen section at the end of this chapter). Once you reach Klampenborg station, a bike path leads into Dyrehaven, a woodland crossed by a network of trails, and a perfect place to break out a picnic lunch; for more details see under Klampenborg in the Around Copenhagen section at the end of this chapter. Alternatively, if you want to continue farther north, an off-road cycling path runs parallel to the coastal road to Rungsted.

Either way, you have the choice of returning on the same route, taking an alternative route such as the inland road Bernstorffsvej, or putting your bike on the S-train and making it a one-way tour.

ORGANISED TOURS
Carlsberg Brewery

Carlsberg gives tours of its brewery at 11 am and 2 pm on weekdays. The guides at 9, 10 and 11 am and 1 and 2 pm. The factory has been on this site since 1884, though Royal Copenhagen has been making porcelain in Denmark since 1775. The adjacent shop is open from 9 am to 5.30 pm on weekdays and from 9 am to 2 pm on Saturday. Take bus No 1 or 14 from Rådhuspladsen.

Bus Tours

Copenhagen is so easy to get around that there's little need to consider a sightseeing bus tour. However, Copenhagen Excursions (☎ 32 54 06 06) does offer various guided tours of the city in splashy pink-and-yellow double-decker buses, starting at 100 kr. In addition, they run one-day tours from Copenhagen to North Zealand castles (335 kr), Odense (480 kr) and Legoland (450 kr).

There's also a red double-decker bus labelled 'Grand Tour of Wonderful Copenhagen' that runs along a circuit past the main sightseeing spots from mid-April to late September. You can get on and off as often as you like at sights such as Tivoli, Slotsholmen, Nationalmuseet, the Little Mermaid and Rosenborg Slot. In the summer high season it runs every 15 minutes from 9 am to 8 pm; in the shoulder season it runs once or twice an hour between 10 am and 5 pm. One-day tickets cost 100 kr and can be purchased at Copenhagen Information.

Canal Tours

For a different angle on the city, hop on to one of the boat tours that wind through Copenhagen's canals. Although most of the passengers are usually Danes, multilingual guides give a lively commentary in English as well. All the tours follow a similar loop route, passing by Slotsholmen, Christianshavn and the Little Mermaid. All tour rates are half-price for children.

The biggest company, Canal Tours Copenhagen (☎ 33 13 31 05), operates from April to mid-October. Boats leave twice an hour from two locations – one at the head

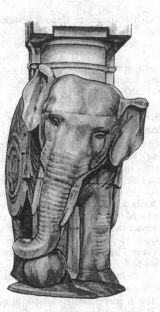

The impressive elephants at the Carlsberg Brewery gate guard the precious stocks of beer.

speak both English and Danish. There's no fee, but it's a good idea to call (☎ 33 27 13 14) to make sure there's space available before jumping on a bus. After learning a bit about Carlsberg's 150 year history and seeing how barley turns to beer, you get to sample a variety of the final products. The brewery is to the west of the city centre at the intersection of Valby Langgade and Ny Carlsbergvej. Although the operation is ultramodern, much of the architecture is attractively traditional. Take special note of the Elephant Gate, two elephant pillars at the entrance designed by architect Vilhelm Dahlerup. To get to the brewery, take bus No 6 westbound from Rådhuspladsen.

Royal Copenhagen

One-hour multilingual guided tours (25 kr) of the Royal Copenhagen porcelain factory (☎ 33 13 71 81), at Smallegade 45 in the Frederiksberg area, are given on weekdays of Nyhavn and the other on Gammel Strand, north of Slotsholmen. Tours, which last 50 minutes, run from 10 am to 5 pm, except in July and August when the Nyhavn departures extend to 7.30 pm; the cost is 42 kr.

A better deal is with Netto-Bådene (☎ 32 54 41 02), which charges just 20 kr and operates from late April to mid-September. Its cruises, which last an hour, leave from near Holmens Kirke, opposite Børsen, as well as from Nyhavn, between two and four times an hour from 10 am to 5 pm, with the greatest frequency in the summer high season.

Canal boats can also be a fine traffic-free way of getting to some of Copenhagen's famous waterfront sites. Canal Tours Copenhagen charges 40 kr for a one-day pass on its green-route Vandbussen (Water Bus), which runs along a route similar to its guided tours but has no commentary. These boats leave Nyhavn every 30 minutes daily from 10.15 am to 4.45 pm between mid-May and mid-September, and make 10 stops, including Christiansborg Slot, Christianshavn and the Little Mermaid, allowing you to get on and off as often as you like. You can also ride just one way from one stop to another for 25 kr.

Night Watchman Tours

From late May to mid-September a 'night watchman' dressed in period clothing and carrying a lantern and spiked mace makes his rounds of the older quarters of the city, with sightseers in tow. The one hour tour is conducted in English on Thursday and Saturday, and in German on Friday. Yes, it's touristy, but it's colourful and free. Meet at 9 pm at Gråbrødre Torv, the small square fronting Peder Oxe restaurant.

PLACES TO STAY

Copenhagen is a popular convention city and if you happen to arrive when one is taking place, finding a room could be a challenge. At most other times a visit to the Copenhagen Information accommodation counter or a stroll through the main hotel district (adjacent to Central Station) can land you a room without advance reservations. Still, if you have a particular place in mind it's a good idea to book in advance – rooms in many of the most popular mid-range hotels fill quickly, particularly during the high season.

Booking Services & Private Rooms

The accommodation counter (*værelseanvisning*) at Copenhagen Information books rooms in private homes; singles/doubles cost 185/285 kr. It also books unfilled hotel rooms, commonly at around 25% less than published rates. These discounts, however, are based on supply and demand and are not always available during busy periods. The counter is open from 9 am to 9 pm daily between 1 May and 15 September, and from 9 am to 4.30 pm on weekdays and 9 am to 1.30 pm on Saturday the rest of the year. There's a 35 kr fee per booking.

The airport information desk in the arrival area, outside customs, also books unfilled Copenhagen hotel rooms at similarly discounted rates for a 35 kr booking fee. It's open from 6 am to 11 pm daily.

Use It books rooms in private homes, costing from 150 to 250 kr for singles and from 225 to 300 kr for doubles; there's no booking fee. It also keeps tabs on which hostel beds are available, and is a good source of information on subletting student housing and other long-term accommodation. For more information see under Tourist Offices in the Information section earlier in this chapter.

The annual *Bed & Breakfast in Denmark* guide, which can be picked up free at Copenhagen Information, lists a couple of dozen homes in the greater Copenhagen area that each have a room or two for rent. Rates are similar to those offered through Use It and the accommodation counter.

If you're looking for a long-term rental, BoligButikken (☎ 33 32 80 11, fax 33 32 90 11, email lejeboliger@boligbutikken-forht.dk), in Central Station above the post office, is a search service that books rooms and flats in the Copenhagen area; rents range from 1200 to 7000 kr per month.

PLACES TO STAY – BUDGET
Camping

Bellahøj Camping (☎ 38 10 11 50, fax 38 10 13 32, Hvidkildevej 66, 2400 Copenhagen NV), close to the middle of the city near the Bellahøj Vandrerhjem (hostel), is a simple one star camping ground open from 1 June to 31 August. It costs 50 kr per person. Showers and cooking facilities are available. To get there, take bus No 11 from Rådhuspladsen.

The two star *Absalon Camping* (☎ 36 41 06 00, fax 36 41 02 93, Korsdalsvej 132, 2610 Rødovre) is 9km west of the city centre in the Rødovre suburb, near Brøndbyøster station on S-train line B. There's a coin laundry, food kiosk, group kitchen and playground. In addition to camping sites, which cost 50 kr per person, caravans and five-person cabins can be rented from about 200 kr per day, plus the per-person camping fee. It's open year-round.

A delightful alternative is *Charlottenlund Strandpark* (☎ 39 62 36 88, fax 39 61 08 16, Strandvejen 144B, 2920 Charlottenlund), 8km north of central Copenhagen. This camping ground, on Charlottenlund beach, is appealingly set in the tree-lined grounds of an old moat-encircled coastal fortification. The cost is 60 kr per person but space is limited, advance bookings are recommended. There are showers and a coin laundry; a bakery and a small shop are just a few hundred metres away. The frequent bus No 6 connects the camping ground with Copenhagen city centre.

Hostels

HI Hostels There are two Copenhagen hostels run under the auspices of Hostelling International, each about 5km from the city centre. Bellahøj Vandrerhjem is open year-round except from 16 January to 28 February, while the Amager hostel is closed from 1 December to 14 January. Both hostels have laundry facilities and are accessible to people in wheelchairs, but only the Amager hostel has a guest kitchen. Breakfast (40 kr) and dinner (58 kr) are available at both. These hostels often fill early in summer so it's best to call ahead for reservations.

The conveniently located *Bellahøj Vandrerhjem* (☎ 38 28 97 15, fax 38 89 02 10, Herbergvejen 8, 2700 Brønshøj) has 250 dorm beds costing 80 kr and a limited number of four-bed family rooms. Reception is open 24 hours and lockers are available for 5 kr. From Rådhuspladsen take bus No 2-Brønshøj and get off at Fuglsangs Allé, or take night bus No 82N.

The newer, Orwellian *Copenhagen Amager Hostel* (☎ 32 52 29 08, fax 32 52 27 08, email cph_amag@postb.tele.dk, Vejlands Allé 200, 2300 Copenhagen S), just off the E20 in Amager, is one of Europe's largest hostels, with 528 beds in cell-like two and five-bed rooms. It costs 80 kr per person and it's usually easy to get a double room for 220 kr. Check-in time is from 1 pm. Bus No 46 runs directly to the hostel from Central Station on weekdays until about 6 pm; otherwise take the S-train to Sjælør station, then change to bus No 37 and get off at Vejlands Allé.

A third alternative, farther from the city, is the *Lyngby Vandrerhjem* (☎ 45 80 30 74, fax 45 80 30 32, Rådvad 1, 2800 Lyngby), in a small hamlet nestled in the woods on the northern side of Dyrehaven. The hostel occupies a manor-like house that can accommodate 94 people, mostly in rooms with four to six beds. Open to individuals from April to late October, it costs 85 kr for a dorm bed, 204 kr for a double; meals are available. The area is quite pretty, with swan-filled ponds, and it's within walking distance of the house where silversmith Georg Jensen was born in 1866; however, it's not a terribly practical place to make a base if your main focus is exploring central Copenhagen. Bus No 187 runs from Lyngby S-train station to the hostel, but it's an infrequent weekday-only bus, so check the schedule in advance. Otherwise it's a 2km walk between the hostel and the nearest regularly serviced bus stop in Hjortekær.

Other Hostels Even when the HI hostels are full you can almost always find a bed at one of the community-sponsored hostels. Although they tend to offer more of a crash-pad scene than the HI hostels, they're also more central and don't require hostel membership.

City Public Hostel (☎ 33 31 20 70, fax 33 23 51 75, Absalonsgade 8, Vesterbro, 1658 Copenhagen V) has 200 beds. There's one 68 bed dorm, but other rooms contain from six to 12 beds each. It's open from early May to late August, has 24 hour reception and costs 110 kr per person. You can use your own sleeping bag or rent bed sheets for 30 kr to use during the length of your stay. Breakfast is available (20 kr), there's a guest kitchen and you'll find some good restaurants within a few blocks of the hostel. To get to City Public Hostel from Central Station, walk west along Vesterbrogade for 10 minutes; it's less than 1km.

The city-run *Sleep-In* (☎ 35 26 50 59, fax 35 43 50 58, 132A Blegdamsvej, 2100 Copenhagen Ø), a few kilometres north of the city centre in the Østerbro district, is open from late June to 31 August. The 270 beds are in a badminton hall that has been partitioned into compartments, each containing two to six beds; there are no doors, but the compartments have curtains to offer a little privacy. A bed costs 75 kr; add another 30 kr if you want breakfast. This well-run facility has free lockers, a guest kitchen and a café. You can use your own sleeping bag or rent bed linen (30 kr). Reception is open 24 hours. From the city centre take bus No 1-Ordrup, 6-Klampenborg or 14, get off at Trianglen and then walk south-west on Blegdamsvej for a couple of minutes. You can also take night bus No 85N or 95N or take the S-train to Østerport station, from where the hostel is about a 15 minute walk (1km) to the north-west. There's a bakery, a grocery shop and a few eating and drinking places within easy walking distance.

Sleep-In Heaven (☎ 38 10 44 45, Peter Bangs Vej 30, 2000 Frederiksberg), near the zoo, is a friendly place with 76 beds in five dorms. The cost, including breakfast and bed sheets, is 80 kr (use your sleeping bag or rent blankets for 15 kr). There's a pool table, a lounge, a group kitchen and cheap beer and coffee; it's open from May to October. From Central Station take bus No 1; from Rådhuspladsen take bus No 14 or night bus No 85N.

Sleep-In Green (☎ 35 37 77 77, fax 35 35 56 40, Ravnsborggade 18) is in the Nørrebro area close to cafés and nightlife. Open from June to September, it has 68 dorm beds costing 70 kr. A breakfast of organic fare is available for 35 kr. Take bus No 5 or 16, or walk north-west on Frederiksborggade over the canal before turning right onto Ravnsborggade.

YMCA Interpoint (☎ 33 31 15 74, Valdemarsgade 15), in the Vesterbro district, is open from the end of June to mid-August and has separate dormitories for men and women. Because there are only 28 dorm beds, it fills up early, so call ahead for reservations. It costs 65 kr for the bed and another 20 kr to rent sheets; breakfast is available for 29 kr and there are good restaurants within walking distance. Reception hours are from 8.30 to 11.30 am, 3.30 to 5.30 pm and 8 pm to 12.30 am. It's about a 15 minute walk from Central Station (take Vesterbrogade 1km west to Valdemarsgade, then turn left), or take bus No 6 or 16.

Also see *Hotel Jørgensen*, which offers dorm beds year-round, in the following hotel section.

PLACES TO STAY – MID-RANGE

Copenhagen's main hotel quarter (and red-light district) is along the western side of Central Station, where rows of six-storey, early 20th century buildings house one hotel after the other. Despite the porn shops and streetwalkers, the area is neither unpleasant nor notably dangerous, at least not by the standards of large cities elsewhere in Europe. In addition, its central location makes it a convenient spot in which to be based.

Although this Central Station area is jammed with mid-range hotels, Copenhagen has very few hotels that are priced affordably enough to really warrant the term 'budget'. If you're on a tight budget, the cheapest hotel rooms are those with shared bath and toilets off the hall.

By and large, the months from May to September comprise the summer season, while October to April constitutes the winter season. Many hotels lower their rates by 10 to 20% in winter. The hotel rates given in this section include service charge, the 25% value-added tax (VAT) and, except where noted, a complimentary buffet-style breakfast.

Around Central Station

The area's cheapest place, *Turisthotellet* (✆ *33 22 98 39, Reverdilsgade 5, 1701 Copenhagen V*), is very basic with a handful of small, shabby rooms. Despite the term 'hotel' there's no front desk or hotel amenities – it's more like a run-down boarding house. The rates posted in the window are 200/300 kr for singles/doubles with shared bath but the quoted rates are often 50 kr higher.

The *Saga Hotel* (✆ *33 24 49 44, fax 33 24 60 33, Colbjørnsensgade 18-20, 1652 Copenhagen V*) has 76 rooms, most of which have been renovated. There's no lift and it's multistorey, so you will probably have to climb some stairs. The standard rooms are straightforward, but some also have a TV. Singles/doubles start at 350/ 450 kr with shared bath, 495/600 kr with private bath.

The 88 room *Hotel du Nord* (✆ *33 31 77 50, fax 33 31 33 99, Colbjørnsensgade 14, 1652 Copenhagen V*) is a small, tidy hotel with comfortable rooms, most with a desk, a TV and a phone. It's best to request one of the courtyard rooms, which are larger and quieter than those overlooking the street. In summer singles/doubles with shared bath cost 525/650 kr if it's busy, a bit less otherwise. Winter rates can be as low as 375/450 kr.

Missionshotellet Nebo (✆ *33 21 12 17, fax 33 23 47 74, Istedgade 6, 1650 Copenhagen V*) is very convenient, a mere stone's throw from Central Station. The 96 rooms are small with rather dull décor but each is perfectly adequate, with a sink, TV and phone, and the common areas include a front parlour, large, clean showers and toilets, and a bright, cheery breakfast room. In summer singles/doubles cost 380/580 kr with shared bath, 690/790 kr with private bath; winter rates are about 15% lower.

The *Selandia Hotel* (✆ *33 31 46 10, fax 33 31 46 09, Helgolandsgade 12, 1653 Copenhagen V*) has 84 rooms, each with a desk, sink and TV. Cheapest are the 27 rooms with shared bath costing 390/540 kr year-round, though the shower facilities are uncomfortably cramped. Rooms with bath start at 700/850 kr in summer, slightly less in winter.

The 81 room *Hotel Centrum* (✆ *33 31 31 11, fax 33 23 32 51, Helgolandsgade 14, 1653 Copenhagen V*) has straightforward singles/doubles with a sink, phone and shared bath costing 395/600 kr. There are also larger rooms with TV and bath costing 630/800 kr. Prices are about 15% cheaper in winter. When the hotel's not busy, the management is willing to negotiate a bit on rates, so it can be a good place to start if you're looking for a last-minute bargain.

At the 253 room *Absalon Hotel* (✆ *33 24 22 11, fax 33 24 34 11, Helgolandsgade 15, 1653 Copenhagen V*), the cheaper rooms are straightforward, have shared baths and cost 525/650 kr for singles/doubles in summer. Although not special, these rooms are commonly available at discounted rates from Copenhagen Information's accommodation counter – when they can be a good deal. Rooms with bath start at 630/720 kr.

The 100 room *Hotel Hebron* (✆ *33 31 69 06, fax 33 31 90 67, Helgolandsgade 4, 1653 Copenhagen V*) is a quiet hotel with pleasant renovated rooms with a desk, a TV and a phone. Singles/doubles with bath cost 730/980 kr in summer, 625/830 kr in winter. The hotel also has a handful of rooms with shared bath but, because renting them would lower its classification in the new nationwide hotel rating system, they are generally left vacant.

Nyhavn & Around

A good budget option is **Sømandshjemmet Bethel** (☎ 33 13 03 70, fax 33 15 85 70, Nyhavn 22, 1051 Copenhagen K), which calls itself a seamen's hotel but is open to all. This cosy little place has a nice location right on Nyhavn canal, a lift to all floors, and two dozen good-sized rooms with an eclectic variety of furnishings. Many also have unbeatable views of Nyhavn – for the best, ask for a corner room. Singles/doubles cost 295/450 kr with shared bath and start at 440/595 kr with private bath.

Hotel Maritime (☎ 33 13 48 82, fax 33 15 03 45, email hotel@maritime.dk, Peder Skrumsgade 19, 1054 Copenhagen K) has 64 renovated rooms that are small but inviting. Each has a TV, a phone and a bath. Rates fluctuate with demand and can begin anywhere from 545 to 775 kr for singles and 675 to 950 kr for doubles. The location, just a few minutes walk from the hydrofoil docks, is convenient for those travelling by boat.

Elsewhere in Copenhagen

Hotel Jørgensen (☎ 33 13 81 86, fax 33 15 51 05, Rømersgade 11, 1362 Copenhagen K), conveniently near Nørreport station, is popular with gay travellers but accommodates plenty of straight guests as well. The rooms are simple but have some pleasant touches. Singles/doubles cost 400/500 kr with shared bath, 100 kr more with private bath. The hotel also has 140 dorm beds, spread across 15 rooms, that cost 115 kr including a good breakfast. There are lockers for dorm guests and a laundrette is just metres away.

One block to the east is **Hotel Windsor** (☎ 33 11 08 30, fax 33 11 63 87, email hotelwindsor@inet.uni-c.dk, Frederiksborggade 30, 1360 Copenhagen K), an exclusively gay and lesbian hotel in an older building opposite Israels Plads. The 25 rooms are straightforward but all have TV and most have refrigerators. Rooms start at 400/600 kr.

Hotel Sankt Jørgen (☎ 35 37 15 11, fax 35 37 11 97, email st.jørgen@teliamail.dk, Julius Thomsens Gade 22, 1632 Copenhagen V) is family-run and pleasantly old-fashioned. There are 17 comfortable and spacious doubles costing 500 kr and two rather cramped singles for 400 kr. If space is available, single travellers are usually given a double room for the price of a single. Most rooms have three to six beds, so they can easily accommodate families (add 125 kr for each person beyond two). All bathrooms are shared. It's about a 20 minute walk from the centre.

The modern **Cab-Inn Scandinavia** (☎ 35 36 11 11, fax 35 36 11 14, Vodroffsvej 55, 1900 Frederiksberg C) has 201 sleekly compact rooms that resemble cabins in a cruise ship, complete with upper and lower bunks. Although small, the rooms are quite comfortable and have cable TV, phone, complimentary instant coffee and bathroom. Singles/doubles cost 410/520 kr and basement parking costs 30 kr per day. It's a popular place, especially in summer, so reservations are recommended. Unlike in most other Copenhagen hotels, breakfast is not included in the room rate here but it is available in the hotel café for an extra 40 kr.

A few blocks to the south-west is the 86 room **Cab-Inn Copenhagen** (☎ 33 21 04 00, fax 33 21 74 09, Danasvej 32, 1900 Frederiksberg C), which has the same type of rooms and the same rates as Cab-Inn Scandinavia. Both hotels have rooms that are accessible to people in wheelchairs and are about a 20 minute walk (1.5km) from Rådhuspladsen.

The 117 room **Hotel Esplanaden** (☎ 33 91 32 00, fax 33 91 32 39, Bredgade 78, 1260 Copenhagen K), a Best Western affiliate, is a sister hotel to the upmarket Neptun Hotel. Located opposite Churchillparken, it's a nice choice for those who want to be near green space. The hotel is a pleasant, older place offering modernised rooms with bath, TV, minibar and phone. Rooms cost 880/1040 kr but there's a special 695 kr rate that covers weekends and most of the summer and includes up to two adults and two children.

PLACES TO STAY – TOP END
Around Central Station

The *Grand Hotel* (☎ 33 31 36 00, fax 33 31 33 50, Vesterbrogade 9, 1620 Copenhagen V) is conveniently located just north of Central Station. This pleasant 100-year-old hotel has 151 renovated rooms, each with bath, desk, minibar, TV and phone. Non-smoking rooms are available. Standard rates start at 995/1295 kr but there are various discount schemes, including a 15% weekend reduction and a 'summer special' for 695/895 kr. There's a bar and restaurant on site.

Despite its rather nondescript façade, *Hotel Imperial* (☎ 33 12 80 00, fax 33 93 80 31, email imperial@imperialhotel.dk, Vester Farimagsgade 9, 1606 Copenhagen V), opposite Vesterport S-train station, has one of the best reputations for service among Copenhagen's top-end hotels. Each of the 163 rooms has modern décor with a desk, a phone, cable TV, a minibar and a deep Japanese-style bathtub. Rates start at 1240/1625 kr.

The 465 room *Scandic Hotel Copenhagen* (☎ 33 14 35 35, fax 33 32 12 23, Vester Søgade 6, 1601 Copenhagen V), near the Tycho Brahe Planetarium, is a well-regarded chain hotel with all the expected facilities, including a health club, a concierge and secretarial services. Weekday rates begin at 995/1545 kr for singles/doubles; weekend and summer rates start at 850/950 kr.

The *Radisson SAS Royal Hotel* (☎ 33 42 60 00, fax 33 42 61 00, Hammerichsgade 1, 1611 Copenhagen V) is a centrally located, 265 room, multistorey hotel. Rooms are modern with full amenities. The hotel has a centre for business travellers, restaurants, a nightclub and a fitness centre. Singles/doubles cost 1395/1895 kr, but cheaper promotions are often available; for details, see the listings for other SAS hotels later in this section.

Rådhuspladsen & Around

The *Ascot Hotel* (☎ 33 12 60 00, fax 33 14 60 40, Studiestræde 61, 1554 Copenhagen V) occupies a former bathhouse erected 100 years ago by the same architect who designed Copenhagen's rådhus. The lobby boasts some interesting bas reliefs depicting scenes from the bathhouse days. Most rooms are large, each has a bath, TV and phone, and some have a kitchen. Singles/doubles start at 950/1090 kr. Free parking is provided for guests.

Hotel Kong Frederik (☎ 33 12 59 02, fax 33 93 59 01, email anglehot@remmen.dk, Vester Voldgade 25, 1552 Copenhagen V) is a classic hotel with historic character, dark woods, antique furnishings and paintings of Danish royalty. The 110 rooms are poshly comfortable and each has a TV, phone, minibar and hairdryer. Singles/doubles start at 1150/1450 kr; breakfast is optional and costs 100 kr extra per person.

The *Palace Hotel* (☎ 33 14 40 50, fax 33 14 52 79, Rådhuspladsen 57, 1550 Copenhagen) is in an interesting period building and has recently undergone a lengthy renovation. The 162 rooms are spacious, each with a TV, phone, room safe, minibar and desk. The décor is old-fashioned, with upholstered chairs, heavy curtains and brass lamps. The cheapest rooms face the rear and are without views, but they are also the quietest. It'd be a pleasant place to stay if the price was right, and when things are slow the rate can be discounted by as much as 50% for last-minute customers. The regular rates for singles/doubles begin at 1325/1525 kr. The front rooms, which are fancier and overlook Rådhuspladsen, cost 200 kr more.

Nyhavn & Around

Hotel City (☎ 33 13 06 66, fax 33 13 06 67, Peder Skramsgade 24, 1054 Copenhagen K) is a smaller hotel with 81 standard 1st class rooms, each with bath, cable TV, phone and trouser press. Most contain two single beds, placed side by side. Regular rates for singles/doubles start at 825/995 kr year-round. The hotel, which is a Best Western affiliate, also has a more tempting weekend rate of 695 kr but it's only available in winter. About a five minute walk from the hydrofoil docks, it's convenient for visitors travelling by boat to Malmö in Sweden or to Bornholm.

Hotel Opera (☎ 33 12 15 19, fax 33 32 12 82, Tordenskjoldsgade 15, 1055 Copenhagen K), just south of Det Kongelige Teater, has an old-world character befitting its theatre district location. Although it's not as fancy as other top-end period hotels, the rates are a bit lower. All 87 rooms have bath, phone and TV. Singles/doubles begin at 890/1090 kr; weekend rates are 750/925 kr.

For nautical atmosphere, it's hard to beat the waterfront *Copenhagen Admiral Hotel (☎ 33 11 82 82, fax 33 32 55 42, email admiral@euroconnect.dk, Toldbodgade 24-28, 1253 Copenhagen K)*, located between Nyhavn and Amalienborg Slot. The hotel occupies a renovated 18th century granary and is replete with brick archways and sturdy old beams of Pomeranian pine. Each of the 366 rooms has a nice blend of period charm and modern conveniences, including a TV, a desk, a couch and a bathroom with bidet. The junior suites are split level, with a queen-size bed in the loft and a sitting area with a sofa bed below. The hotel has a sauna, a solarium and a restaurant. Regular singles/doubles cost 920/1120 kr. Junior suites cost 1295 kr for one or two people, 1490 kr for four people. Breakfast costs an extra 95 kr.

The 82 room *71 Nyhavn Hotel (☎ 33 11 85 85, fax 33 93 15 85, Nyhavn 71, 1051 Copenhagen K)* is another hotel in a renovated 200-year-old harbourside warehouse. It too has incorporated some of the building's period features, such as its exposed wooden beams. Standard singles/doubles cost 1050/1350 kr, superior rooms with views cost 1200/1550 kr and waterfront corner suites with great views of both the harbour and Nyhavn canal cost 2695 kr. There's a weekend rate of 695/995 kr (minimum stay two nights).

The *Sophie Amalie Hotel (☎ 33 13 34 00, fax 33 11 77 07, email anglehot@rem men.dk, Sankt Annæ Plads 21, 1250 Copenhagen K)* is popular with business travellers. The 134 rooms are modern and each has the standard amenities, including a desk, a minibar and cable TV. Regular singles/doubles cost 895/1080 kr. Much more interesting are the 6th floor split level suites with a harbour view; there's a living room with a sofa bed on the lower level and a loft bedroom above. The suites cost 1230 kr for two people, 65 kr more for a third or fourth person. Breakfast costs an extra 90 kr. The hotel offers a 10% discount for payment by cash or travellers cheque.

The *Neptun Hotel (☎ 33 13 89 00, fax 33 14 12 50, Sankt Annæ Plads 14, 1250 Copenhagen K)* is a well-regarded 1st class hotel a block north of Nyhavn. The most refined Copenhagen hotel affiliated with the Best Western chain, it has 122 rooms and 12 suites. Every room has a TV, a phone, an electronic room safe, a minibar, a trouser press and other facilities. Regular rates start at 1270/1360 kr but there's a weekend and summer special: 995 kr covers a room sleeping up to two adults and two children.

The *Phoenix (☎ 33 95 95 00, fax 33 33 98 33, Bredgade 37, 1260 Copenhagen K)*, a block north of Nyhavn, is one of the city's more popular deluxe hotels. It has 212 plush rooms with heavy carpets, upholstered chairs, chandeliers and the like. There's a restaurant and pub on site. Rates start at 1120/1490 kr.

Visiting celebrities generally opt for the exclusive *Hotel d'Angleterre (☎ 33 12 00 95, fax 33 12 11 18, Kongens Nytorv 34, 1050 Copenhagen K)*, which has chandeliers, marble floors and a history dating back to the 17th century. It also has Copenhagen's highest rates, starting at 1875/2075 kr for singles/doubles. Despite its lengthy history, the hotel has changed ownership a number of times in recent years and it no longer enjoys the solidly preeminent reputation it once had among Copenhagen's top hotels.

Elsewhere in Copenhagen

Copenhagen's four SAS hotels offer discounts of at least 25% to seniors (aged 65 or older) and to any visitor travelling in conjunction with an SAS or Lufthansa flight. Under these schemes a double room at any of Copenhagen's SAS hotels typically costs between 795 and 1295 kr. In addition, SAS offers other promotions, open to anyone, whenever demand is slack, so you can almost always beat the published rates listed below. You can get details of the latest deals by calling any Radisson Hotels reservations office worldwide.

All of the following SAS hotels have modern rooms with TVs, phones, minibars, hairdryers, trouser presses and the like, and all offer nonsmoking rooms.

The 542 room *SAS Scandinavia Hotel* (☎ *33 96 50 00, fax 33 96 55 00, Amager Blvd 70, 2300 Copenhagen S*) is a high-rise hotel south of Christianshavn. The hotel has free parking, services for business travellers, a pool and fitness centre, squash courts, several restaurants, a bar and Copenhagen's only casino. Singles/doubles cost 1095/1545 kr.

The 166 room *SAS Falconer Hotel* (☎ *38 19 80 01, fax 38 87 11 91, Falconer Allé 9, 2000 Frederiksberg, Copenhagen*) is west of central Copenhagen near Frederiksberg S-train station. The hotel, which is a popular convention spot, has a large banquet hall, a health club, a restaurant and a bar. Some rooms have been specially adapted for disabled people. Singles/doubles cost 1195/1540 kr.

About 2km north of the airport is the 197 room *SAS Globetrotter Hotel* (☎ *32 87 02 02, fax 32 87 02 20, 171 Engvej, 2300 Copenhagen S*). There are services for business travellers, a restaurant and bar, an indoor swimming pool, a fitness centre and a free airport shuttle service on weekdays. Singles/doubles cost 1095/1460 kr.

PLACES TO EAT
Central Station

Central Station has a *McDonald's*, a *Subway* sandwich shop, a small *fruit stand* and a *supermarket* open from 8 am to midnight daily. The *Kringlen* bakery, in the northeastern corner of the station, serves good

breads and pastries; it's open from 6.30 am (7 am on Sunday) to 6 pm daily.

Spise Hjørnet, a DSB cafeteria open from 6.30 am to 10 pm, offers a daily hot special costing 37 kr on weekdays, 47 kr at weekends. These are filling but unexciting meals. You can also make your own single-serving salad from a limited salad bar for 22 kr including bread.

Around Central Station

For an all-you-can-eat deal there's *Astor Pizza*, just north of Central Station on Reventlowsgade, which has a reasonable pizza-and-salad bar for 39 kr from 11 am to 5 pm, 49 kr after 5 pm.

The *Hard Rock Cafe* (☎ *33 12 43 33, Vesterbrogade 3*), beside the tourist office, features burgers and other American-style fare, has a happy hour from 5.30 pm, and of course sells its logo T-shirts.

Scala, on Vesterbrogade opposite Tivoli, is a multistorey building full of fast-food eateries, though few are notable. The best bets include *Matahari*, offering wok-cooked East Asian dishes for around 50 kr, and *Strecker's*, where chilli con carne, cheeseburgers and chicken cost 35 kr.

Restaurant Shezan (☎ *33 24 78 88*), on the corner of Viktoriagade and Istedgade, serves authentic Pakistani food daily from 11 am to 11 pm. Vegetarian dishes such as *dhal turka* (spiced lentils) or *chana* (chickpea) curry cost 40 kr, while a range of chicken and lamb dishes cost from 50 to 65 kr.

Restaurant Koh-I-Noor (☎ *33 24 64 17, Vesterbrogade 33*) offers candlelight dining and a tasty Indian buffet that includes curried lamb, beef and chicken dishes, naan bread, soup and salad for 79 kr, served nightly from 5 to 10 pm. There's also an à la carte menu, which includes vegetarian dishes, priced from 65 to 100 kr. The kitchen stays open until midnight, later at weekends.

Merhaba (☎ *33 25 10 10, Vesterbrogade 39*) is a popular Turkish restaurant with good food, a pleasant décor and honest prices. It offers a three course meal costing

69 kr that includes a choice of starter, main dish and dessert, or a 10 course meal for 99 kr. Either way there are a wide variety of Mediterranean dishes to select from. Open from 11.30 am to midnight, it's candlelit in the evening and makes for a pleasant night out that's easy on the wallet. On Friday and Saturday there's belly dancing.

Another nearby Turkish restaurant that attracts a crowd is *Alanya* (☎ 33 31 92 33, *Vesterbrogade 35*), which offers a good-value dinner buffet of 20 cold and 14 hot traditional Middle Eastern dishes, including calamari, chicken, lamb and salads, costing 59 kr and served daily from 4 pm to midnight. A smaller but still substantial lunch buffet (39 kr) is served from noon to 4 pm.

Rådhusarkaden, an indoor shopping centre on Vesterbrogade near Rådhuspladsen, houses an *Irma* grocery shop and the *Conditori Hans Christian Andersen*, which offers good sandwiches, pastries and coffee.

Tivoli

Tivoli boasts nearly 30 places to eat. These range from simple self-service cafés offering typical amusement-park fare to some of the city's more respected eating establishments. You'll need to pay Tivoli admission (or have a valid Copenhagen Card) to eat at these places – and they're only open during the Tivoli season. Depending upon the restaurant, the kitchen generally stays open until around 11 pm; the restaurants close when Tivoli does.

A fun spot with relatively moderate prices is *Hercegovina* (☎ 33 15 63 63), which specialises in Bosnian and Hercegovinian food and often has roaming musicians performing ethnic music. In the evenings there's a nice buffet of meats and fish costing 149 kr. Wine is usually included if you eat between 5 and 6 pm or after 9 pm. Dine on the balcony and you'll be able to watch Tivoli's pantomime ballet perform below.

Another good, moderately priced restaurant is *Promenaden* (☎ 33 14 68 16), which enjoys a view of the open-air stage and

serves spareribs, steaks and other beef dishes.

Also popular is *Grøften* (☎ 33 12 11 25); the speciality here is a type of smørrebrød with tiny fjord shrimps spiced with lime and fresh pepper.

If money is not an issue, *Divan 2* (☎ 33 12 51 51) is widely considered to be Tivoli's finest restaurant for both food and service. In operation since Tivoli opened in 1843, this restaurant serves gourmet French food and has a vintage wine collection. Its sister restaurant, *Divan 1* (☎ 33 11 42 42), has a similar history and garden setting and also enjoys a reputation for good food but with a menu emphasising Danish and international fare. A meal at either Divan could easily set you back at least 500 kr.

Strøget & Around

Strøget has an abundance of cheap eateries, including ice-cream, hamburger and hot-dog stands as well as numerous hole-in-the-wall kebab joints selling felafel for around 25 kr.

For a cheap treat try *Shawarma Grill House* at the western end of Strøget, a two minute walk from Rådhuspladsen. This bustling, unpretentious eatery serves an excellent *shawarma* (27 kr), a pitta-bread sandwich of shaved beef and lamb topped with a yoghurt dressing. Inexpensive felafel and kebabs are also served. It's open daily from 11 am to midnight (to 5 am at weekends) and has a sit-down counter on the ground floor and a dining room upstairs. More mundane options in the same price range can be found at the nearby *Burger King* and *McDonald's*.

The best of the area's numerous pizzerias is *Peppe's Pizza* (☎ 33 32 59 59, *Rådhuspladsen 57*), which offers an all-you-can-eat pizza and salad buffet from noon to 4 pm costing 49 kr. This popular Norwegian chain pizzeria has a nice setting in the basement of an old building with open brick and timber posts. Pizzas cost 100 kr for a small and 135 kr for a large one: the latter is big enough for three people. It's open until at least 11 pm daily. If you prefer

Cultured Cafés

As you make your way around the sights of the city, you'll find inviting lunch options in some of Copenhagen's top exhibition venues.

Ny Carlsberg Glyptotek, on HC Andersens Blvd, has a pleasant atrium café, overlooking the museum's palm garden, which serves tempting cakes and fruit tarts. Expect a crowd at weekends.

Nationalmuseet, Ny Vestergade 10, has a stylish 2nd floor café that offers a nice soup-and-bread combination as well as sandwiches, salads and desserts costing from 30 to 70 kr – or you can just relax over a glass of wine.

The exhibition hall at *Charlottenborg*, near Kongens Nytorv, has an arty café with a changing chalkboard menu of creative light eats costing a reasonable 40 to 50 kr.

Caféen Nikolaj, at the rear of the Nikolaj Kirke, near Højbro Plads, serves salads, sandwiches and other light food such as goat cheese carpaccio, costing from 50 to 100 kr.

American chain pizza, the *Pizza Hut* on Amagertorv beside the Tobacco Museum has similar prices and a relatively good salad bar.

For a bargain, try the little *Café de Paris* pizzeria in the arcade at Vimmelskaftet 39, which offers a reasonable pizza and salad buffet for just 35 kr. At *Restaurant Eastern*, in the same arcade, a buffet of Indian and Pakistani dishes, served from 11 am to 4 pm, costs 49 kr, and a three course dinner costs 98 kr.

La Glace (Skoubogade 3) is a classic *konditori* (bakery-café) that has been serving tea and fancy cakes to socialites for more than a century. It's open from 8 am to 5.30 pm on weekdays, with somewhat shorter weekend hours.

Huset med det Grønne Træ (☎ 33 12 87 86) is at the north-western corner of Gammel Torv and beside the linden tree from which it takes its name. This little lunch café, housed in a period building dating from 1796, offers quintessential Danish fare, with smørrebrød sandwiches, draught beer and a dozen brands of schnapps. Sandwiches cost 35 kr, a lunch dish 100 kr. It's open from 11 am to 3 pm Monday to Friday.

Also abundant in local character is *Café Sorgenfri* (☎ 33 11 58 80, Brolæggerstræde 8), a corner pub serving good Danish food. Traditional cold dishes such as smørrebrød

and pickled herring cost around 45 kr. Hot dishes, including tasty roast pork, are a few kroner more; or you can jump in and sample it all with a variety plate (103 kr) that includes herring, roast pork and meatballs with beets, cheese and other items. The kitchen is open from noon to 8.30 pm daily.

One of our favourite Copenhagen lunch spots is *RizRaz* (☎ 33 15 05 75, Kompagnistræde 20), just south of Strøget and conveniently located around the corner from Use It. At this pleasant café you can feast on a superb Mediterranean-style vegetarian buffet (49 kr), including felafel, pizza, hummus and salads, served daily from 11.30 am to 5 pm (weekends to 4 pm). At dinner, served from 5 to 11 pm, the buffet costs 59 kr. You can also order from the menu: lamb kebabs, grilled fish or fried calamari cost 94 kr, including a helping from the buffet.

The arty new *Coxx Café* (☎ 33 14 13 30, Vester Voldgade 10), opposite the Hotel Kong Frederik, attracts a predominately gay and lesbian crowd. It has excellent food and a changing menu of innovative dishes; most cost around 100 kr, but there's also a daily special for 70 kr. The café is open for dinner from 5 pm daily.

The *Brasserie on the Square* (☎ 33 14 40 50, Rådhuspladsen 57), in the lobby of the

Palace Hotel, offers a Danish buffet, including herring dishes, salmon pâté and salads, from noon to 3 pm daily. Although it's not an elaborate affair, it has a pleasant upmarket setting and is a reasonable deal, costing 98 kr.

Slotskælderen hos Gitte Kik (☎ 33 11 15 37, Fortunstræde 4), a few minutes walk from Folketinget, is a compact smørrebrød lunch spot where you can literally rub shoulders with Danish members of parliament. A drawback is that it can be quite smoky. Open on weekdays until 5 pm, it serves a variety of sandwiches costing from 33 to 70 kr.

A good option for fine dining is *Krogs Fiskerestaurant* (☎ 33 15 89 15, Gammel Strand 38), north of Slotsholmen Kanal. It specialises in fresh fish served with organic produce. The three course meal of the day costs 198 kr at lunchtime and 385 kr at dinner.

Kommandanten (☎ 33 12 09 90, Ny Adelgade 7), just west of Kongens Nytorv, has received numerous accolades, including the Michelin Guides' highest rating among Copenhagen's restaurants. Its French chef, Francis Cardenau, prepares à la carte main courses such as rack of lamb or duck in cabernet sauce (around 250 kr), and there is a changing five course menu costing 580 kr. It's open from 5.30 to 10 pm daily except Sunday.

A superb bakery is *Reinh van Hauen*, which uses mainly organic ingredients and has branches at the western end of Strøget near McDonald's and at the eastern end at Østergade 22. There's another good bakery, *Trianon Konditori*, at Vimmelskaftet 37. For food with a French influence, try *Croissant'en* (Østergade 59), which has tempting takeaway quiches and sandwiches.

Netto supermarket, near the eastern end of Strøget, has relatively cheap grocery prices. For a more upmarket selection try the bakery and grocery shop on the 1st floor of *Magasin du Nord* department store, a block south of Østergade at the eastern end of Strøget. *McGrails*, a small health-food shop on the north-eastern corner of Gammel Torv, sells tofu, snacks, vitamins and organic wines.

If you just want to kick back and have a beer, *The Dubliner*, on the western side of Højbro Plads, is a trendy pub serving both Danish and Irish brews.

Gråbrødre Torv

Greyfriars' Square, between Strøget and the Latin Quarter, has a handful of popular restaurants grouped around a cobblestone plaza.

For a pleasant dinner treat, consider *Peder Oxe* (☎ 33 11 00 77), which fronts the square and offers affordable fine dining with a cosy Danish country ambience. It's open from 11.30 am to 10.30 pm and specialises in hearty meat dishes, served with a salad buffet, costing from 95 to 160 kr. Copenhagen's oldest monastery was built on this site in 1238 and the restaurant's wine cellar retains part of the old stone foundations.

There's also a nice atmosphere at *Jensen's Bøfhus* (☎ 33 32 78 00), one of a Danish chain of steak restaurants, nearby in another period house fronting Gråbrødre Torv. Although the food is just average, the prices are cheap. For lunch, served from 11.30 am to 4 pm, you can get a steak and baked potato for 39 kr. In the evening there's a good chicken dish with a reasonable salad buffet costing 79 kr. Dinner steaks average 130 kr but there's usually a 180g 'whiskey steak' special for 88 kr.

If you prefer Mexican or Italian fare, *Tacos Cantina* on the eastern side of Gråbrødre Torv offers enchilada-and-rice or pizza-and-salad specials for 39 kr, served from 11.30 am to 5 pm. Dinners are pricier.

The mainstay at *Pasta Basta* (☎ 33 11 21 31, Valkendorfsgade 22), immediately south of Gråbrødre Torv, is a self-service buffet of various cold pasta and salad dishes costing 69 kr. You can also order from the main menu, which includes hot pasta dishes served with the likes of mussels, red snapper or lamb; most cost from 60 to 115 kr. The restaurant is open from 11.30 am to 3 am on weekdays, to 5 am on weekends, and it's a popular spot with night owls looking for a late meal or drink.

Latin Quarter & Around

Hellas (☎ *33 14 05 00, Fiolstræde 21*) has an authentic Greek atmosphere and a hard-to-beat lunch buffet of Greek salads and hot dishes costing 32 kr, served from noon to 4 pm. From 5 to 11 pm you can eat a more elaborate dinner buffet for 78 kr or a three course moussaka meal costing 88 kr. You can also order from the menu, with main dishes costing around 75 kr. It's open daily except Sunday.

The 2nd floor café *Klaptræet* (☎ *33 13 31 48, Kultorvet 11*) is a student haunt serving burgers, chilli con carne and salads for less than 50 kr. There's also a daily home-made soup with bread (28 kr). It's open from 10 am until at least midnight daily. Kultorvet itself becomes a popular beer garden in summer, when some of the nearby businesses, including Klaptræet, set up tables in the square and sell beer on tap.

Ankara (☎ *33 15 19 15, Krystalgade 8*), a pleasant Turkish restaurant, offers a good buffet of salads, hummus, rice and various hot and cold dishes; it costs a reasonable 39 kr until 4 pm, 59 kr from 4 pm to midnight.

An old favourite for traditional Danish food at moderate prices is *Det Lille Apotek* (☎ *33 12 56 06, Store Kannikestræde 15*), tucked in a basement. Meals that include pickled herring, fish fillet and smørrebrød cost from 75 to 100 kr at lunch and a three course dinner costs 158 kr. It's open from 11 am (noon on Sunday) until at least midnight daily.

Ristorante Italiano (☎ *33 11 12 95, Fiolstræde 2*), at the back of Vor Frue Kirke, has authentic Italian food and décor. Lunch specials, including lasagne or calamari, cost 49 kr, and prices on the dinner menu range from 54 kr for pizzas to 139 kr for scampi. In summer the outdoor café tables are an agreeable sunny-day option.

Café Sommersko (☎ *33 14 81 89, Kronprinsensgade 6*), open from 9 am to 2 am daily, draws a high-energy university crowd

and serves a wide variety of drinks, including 50 different brands of beer. The menu offers the likes of satay with jasmine rice or *laks* (salmon) and pasta for around 75 kr. The café also serves cakes, desserts and light breakfast items at moderate prices.

You can eat good vegetarian food at *Govindas* (☎ *33 33 74 44, Nørre Farimagsgade 82*), south of the Botanisk Have, where Hare Krishna devotees serve up an all-you-can-eat meal costing 45 kr. It's open from 12.30 to 8.30 pm Monday to Saturday.

St Gertruds Kloster (☎ *33 14 66 30, Hauser Plads 32*), just off Kultorvet, is an elegant restaurant in a former medieval monastery, sections of which date from the 14th century. The most popular of the four dining rooms is the one occupying the cellar, which has arched brick walls and is lit by 1500 candles. The restaurant specialises in Danish-French cuisine. Starters, including smoked salmon, lobster and escargot, are priced from 140 to 230 kr, while main dishes begin at 230 kr; there's also a fixed-price, three course 'business dinner' costing 405 kr. The kitchen is open from 5 to 11.30 pm nightly; reservations are requested.

The city's main *produce market* is at Israels Plads, a few minutes walk west of Nørreport station. Stalls are set up until 5 pm Monday to Friday and until 2 pm on Saturday, when it doubles as a flea market.

Nørrebrogade

The Nørrebrogade area, with its mix of students and immigrants, has a nice variety of cafés, restaurants serving various cuisines, fruit stands and health-food stores.

Floras Kaffe Bar (☎ *35 39 00 18, Blågårdsgade 27*) is a relaxed place offering a full range of coffees, good pastries and reasonably priced soups, sandwiches and salads. There are usually a couple of hot dinner specials as well and some of the fare is organic. In summer you can sit outside and soak up the sunshine. It's open from 10 am until at least midnight daily.

Indian Corner (☎ *35 39 28 02, Nørrebrogade 59*) is a pleasant little restaurant serving good Indian food at moderate prices. Vegetarian dishes cost around 50 kr, meat curries are a few kroner more and tandoori or tikka chicken costs 72 kr; add another 20 kr for rice. It's open from 4 to 11 pm daily except Tuesday.

Sebastopol (☎ *35 36 30 02, Sankt Hans Torv*) is a trendy café offering baguette sandwiches, Greek salads, nachos and other light eats at moderate prices. It's open from 9 am until at least 1 am daily.

The nearby *Picnic* (☎ *35 39 09 53, Fælledvej 22*) is a cosy café where healthy dishes, such as organic Greek salad with tzatziki and rice, cost around 60 kr. It's open from 11 am (noon at weekends) to 10 pm daily.

At *Quattro Fontane* (☎ *35 39 39 31, Guldbergsgade 3*), just west of Sankt Hans Torv, good pizza and pasta dishes cost around 50 kr and a few meat and fish dishes are double that price; there's also a 22 kr children's menu. It's open from 4 to 11.30 pm daily.

Mexicali (☎ *35 39 47 04, Åboulevard 12*) offers Mexican vegetarian dishes such as cheese burrito or enchilada with rice for between 75 and 80 kr; meat dishes cost a bit more. Open from 5 pm to midnight daily, it's just over 1km north-west of Rådhuspladsen on the way to Nørrebro.

Health-food shops include *Naturbutik* (*Nørrebrogade 57*), which stocks an array of bulk and prepackaged foods, teas and vitamins, and *Solsikken* (*Blågårdsgade 33*), which sells the usual health-food products and has produce, wine and crystal sections.

Nyhavn & Around

In the summer season the restaurants that run along the northern side of the scenic Nyhavn canal set tables outside, turning the street into a line of pavement cafés. On sunny days this is a favourite spot for Copenhageners to sit with friends and linger over a cold beer.

Apart from the *hot-dog wagon* that customarily sets up by the inner canal, the cheapest eats on Nyhavn can be found at *Pizzabageren*, a fast-food joint on the cor-

ner of Nyhavn and Toldbodgade, which serves pitta-bread sandwiches, burgers and chips – nothing notable, but you can quiet your stomach for 30 kr or so.

For a thoroughly Danish experience, don't miss the herring buffet at *Nyhavns Færgekro* (☎ *33 15 15 88, Nyhavn 5*), an atmospheric restaurant right on the canal. The herring is prepared in 10 different ways, including baking, marinading and pickling, with condiments to sprinkle on top and bread and boiled potatoes to round off the meal. The all-you-can-eat buffet costs 78 kr and is available daily from 11.30 am to 5 pm. If you're not a herring lover, there's also a variety of smørrebrød costing around 50 kr. Dinner, served from 5 to 11.30 pm, betrays French influences and is pricier.

Also on the canal is *Cap Horn* (☎ *33 12 85 04, Nyhavn 21*), where creative organic fare, such as chicken tandoori salad or risotto with asparagus, costs around 100 kr. It's open daily for lunch from 11.30 am to 5.30 pm and for dinner until the crowds die down, which is usually late.

If you're up for formal dining, *Els* (☎ *33 14 13 41, Store Strandstræde 3*) offers very good food in a classic upmarket Danish setting. Although the décor is 19th century, the menu blends French and contemporary Danish influences. A two course lunch, served from noon to 3 pm, will set you back 168 kr; a three course dinner, available from 5.30 to 10 pm, costs 300 kr.

A few minutes walk north of Nyhavn is *Ida Davidsen* (☎ *33 91 36 55, Store Kongensgade 70*). Considered the top smørrebrød restaurant in Denmark, it has a nearly limitless variety of open sandwiches. Prices average 50 kr but more exotic versions can cost up to 150 kr each. It's open from 11.30 am to 4 pm on weekdays only.

ENTERTAINMENT

Copenhagen is a 24 hour party city. For free entertainment simply stroll along Strøget, especially between Nytorv and Højbro Plads, which in the late afternoon and evening is a bit like an impromptu three-ring circus with musicians, magicians, jugglers and other street performers.

There are scores of backstreet cafés and clubs with live music. As a general rule, entry is free on weeknights, while there's usually a cover charge at weekends or any time someone special is playing. Danes tend to be late-nighters and many places don't really start to get going until 11 pm or midnight.

The free publications *Nat & Dag* and *Musik Kalenderen* list concerts and entertainment schedules in detail; they're available from Use It, Copenhagen Information and various clubs.

See also the Public Holidays & Special Events section in the Facts for the Visitor chapter for details of festivals.

Music & Dance Clubs

Copenhagen Jazz House (☎ 33 15 26 00, *Niels Hemmingsensgade 10*) is the city's leading jazz spot, featuring top Danish musicians and occasional international performers. The music runs the gamut from bebop to fusion jazz, and there's a large dance floor. The main nights are Thursday, Friday and Saturday but there can be performances on other nights as well.

La Fontaine (☎ 33 11 60 98, *Kompagnistræde 11*) is a casual late-night venue for swing and mainstream jazz musicians, including visiting artists who sometimes end up jamming together.

Sofies Kælder (☎ 32 54 29 45, *Sofiegade 1*), in Christianshavn, is popular for its long tradition of Sunday afternoon jazz concerts.

The Nørrebro area has a number of hot entertainment spots. *Rust* (☎ 35 24 52 00, *Guldbergsgade 8*) attracts a mixed-age crowd with disco on some nights and live bands on others; there's techno on Wednesday. *Stengade 30* (☎ 35 36 09 38, *Stengade 18*) has a lively alternative scene with a college-age crowd, while *Barcelona* (☎ 35 35 76 11, *Fælledvej 21*) is heavily into funk and soul and serves relatively cheap beer. *Bananrepublikken* (☎ 35 36 08 30, *Nørrebrogade 13*) is a friendly café that appeals to a mixed bunch of various ages. It stays

open until 5 am on the busiest nights: Thursday, when there's live music, typically funk, rap or jam, and Friday and Saturday, when disco usually dominates.

Closer to the centre is *Pumpehuset* (☎ 33 93 14 32, *Studiestræde 52*), which features top Danish and international rock, soul and blues groups. *Mojo* (☎ 33 11 64 53, *Løngangstræde 21*) is a hot spot for blues, with live entertainment nightly.

Crazy Daisy (☎ 33 13 67 88, *Nørregade 41*), a trendy club that attracts a young crowd, is open from Thursday to Saturday. For an inexpensive taste of the student scene, *Klaptræet* (see the Places to Eat section for details) has a free club night featuring British pop on Thursday and 10 kr standard club nights at weekends.

Loppen (☎ 32 57 84 22) in Christiania is a popular Christianshavn spot with live music ranging from techno-rock to acid jazz. It's open from Wednesday to Saturday.

Kul-Kaféen (☎ 33 32 17 77, *Teglgårdsstræde 5*), dubbed a 'culture information café' and geared to a youthful crowd, is an interesting place to stop for a beer or coffee.

Ballet, Opera & Theatre

Den Kongelige Ballet and Den Kongelige Opera perform at *Det Kongelige Teater* at Kongens Nytorv. The season runs from mid-August to late May, skipping the main summer months.

An English-language brochure with the season schedule is available from Copenhagen Information, or write to The Royal Theatre, Box Office, PO Boks 2185, 1017 Copenhagen K. If booking from abroad, you can charge the tickets to a credit card and have them mailed to you. For bookings and information call ☎ 33 69 69 69 from Monday to Saturday between 1 and 7 pm, or fax 33 69 69 30. Tickets cost from 50 to 300 kr.

There are also a few smaller *theatres* in Copenhagen that stage performances of popular plays and musicals; programmes are published in the daily newspapers and in *Copenhagen This Week*.

Of special interest for children are the **marionette shows** performed during the months of June, July and August at the eastern side of Kongens Have, the public gardens near Rosenborg Slot. The shows last about half an hour and begin at 2 and 3 pm daily except Monday. There's no admission charge for the show or the gardens.

Tivoli The *Concert Hall* is the venue for symphony orchestra, string quartet and other classical music performances by Danish and international musicians. There's a ballet festival each season featuring top international troupes, as well as cabaret performances. Tickets are sold on weekdays at Tivoli Billetcenter (☎ 33 15 10 12), Vesterbrogade 3, near the main Tivoli entrance.

Tivoli also hosts numerous free performances free (you have to pay the general Tivoli admission fee), including the Italian-influenced *Commedia Dell'Arte*, a pantomime that plays twice nightly, except on Sunday and rainy days, at the open-air theatre near the Vesterbrogade entrance.

Booking Offices ARTE (☎ 38 88 22 22, fax 38 88 22 23), Hvidkildevej 64, sells tickets for theatre performances and concerts throughout Denmark; it's open from 10 am to 4 pm Monday to Friday.

The ARTE kiosk, on the corner of Fiolstræde and Nørre Voldgade, sells half-price theatre and concert tickets for same-day Copenhagen performances; it's open from noon to 7 pm Monday to Friday and from noon to 3 pm on Saturday.

Gay & Lesbian Venues

Copenhagen has one of the liveliest gay and lesbian scenes in Europe.

Two of the most popular meeting places are the *Cosy Bar* (☎ 33 12 74 27, Studiestræde 24), a busy late-night place that attracts mostly men and is open from 11 pm to 6 am daily, and *Café Babooshka* (☎ 33 15 05 36, Turensensgade 6), a lesbian hangout that's open from 4 pm until at least 1 am daily except Sunday, serves light meals, and has a disco on Friday and Saturday.

Sebastian (☎ 33 32 22 79, Hyskenstræde 10) is a pleasant bar and café that attracts a mixed gay and lesbian crowd; it's open from noon until at least 1 am daily. *Masken* (☎ 33 91 09 37, Studiestræde 33), open from 4 pm to 2 am daily, offers a mellow atmosphere and serves cheap beer and good sandwiches.

The favourite mixed gay and lesbian dance spot is *Pan Disco* (☎ 33 11 37 84, Knabrostræde 3), open from 10 pm until at least 4 am daily. Also in the Strøget area, mostly frequented by gay men, is the new *Café Size* (☎ 33 13 20 02, Vimmelskaftet 41), in an alley just east of Café de Paris; it has a couple of bars and a game room.

Copenhagen has about two dozen other gay bars, clubs and cafés, nearly half of them concentrated along Studiestræde in the two blocks between Vester Voldgade and Nørregade. For a complete list pick up a copy of *PAN-bladet for bøsser og lesbiske*, which is available at gay businesses, including the aforementioned clubs. This monthly gay newspaper also has information on gay organisations, saunas, cinemas and other places of interest. An English-language version is published each June.

Ørsteds Parken, a couple of blocks northwest of Studiestræde, is popular as a gay cruising site, but note that anti-gay gangs occasionally come through the park as well.

Also of interest is Bøssehuset (☎ 32 95 98 72) in Christiania, which organises theatre and other events for gay men.

For information on gay-friendly hotels, see Hotel Jørgensen and Hotel Windsor in the earlier Places to Stay section. For information on Coxx Café, a splendid gay-oriented restaurant, see Places to Eat under Strøget & Around.

Open-Air Concerts

Throughout the summer numerous concerts are held in city parks and squares; most are free, though some charge small fees.

The favourite venue is Fælledparken, a large, open park in the Østerbro district to the north of the city centre, which stages free weekend concerts all summer long.

Copenhagen Jazz Festival

The Copenhagen Jazz Festival is the biggest entertainment event of the year, with 10 days of music beginning on the first Friday in July. The festival features a range of Danish and international jazz, blues and fusion music. It's a cornucopia of more than 450 indoor and outdoor concerts, with music wafting out of practically every public square, park, pub and café from Strøget to Tivoli.

'Great Jazz' concerts, which in recent years have featured performers such as trumpeter Wynton Marsalis and saxophonist Sonny Rollins, cost from 150 to 300 kr, while the cover charge in small clubs is typically around 50 kr. Many of the outdoor concerts are free; get hold of a festival programme and you can plan your own jazz tour. For schedules, prices and ticket information, contact Copenhagen Jazz Festival (☎ 33 93 20 13, fax 33 93 20 24), Nytorv 3, 1450 Copenhagen K, or check out the Web site at www.cjf.dk.

Just a few minutes walk from Sleep-In (see Places to Stay), it can easily be reached from the city centre by taking bus No 1, 6 or 14.

The biggest open-air concerts are those sponsored by the city breweries and held on Saturday or Sunday afternoons from early June to mid-August at Femøren park on the coast of Amager. Admission fees average 40 kr, but depend upon the group. The music is rock or jazz, usually by top Danish groups, and each summer there's at least one concert featuring a well-known international name such as Joe Cocker or Van Halen. Femøren (☎ 32 59 79 33) can be reached via bus No 12 or 13. Its Web site is at www.5-oeren.dk.

Cinema

There are about 20 screens showing first-release movies in the group of cinemas along Vesterbrogade between Rådhuspladsen and Central Station. Tickets for movies generally cost from 50 to 60 kr, though the price can be as low as 30 kr for weekday off-peak shows. As elsewhere in Denmark, movies are generally shown in their original language with Danish subtitles.

Casino

If you want to try your hand with the high rollers, the *Casino Copenhagen* (☎ 33 96 59 65), at the SAS Scandinavia Hotel in Amager, has slot machines, stud poker, blackjack tables and both American and French roulette. It's open from 2 pm to 4 am daily; admission is restricted to those aged 18 and over, and costs 80 kr.

SHOPPING

Along Copenhagen's main shopping street, Strøget, you can find numerous speciality shops selling everything from clothing to Danish porcelain and electronics.

Danish amber can be purchased at reasonable prices from one of the many jewellery shops along Strøget; your best bet is to do a little window shopping before you buy.

The Sweater Market, at Frederiksberggade 15 on Strøget, sells quality Scandinavian sweaters, mostly costing upwards of 1000 kr.

For sleek, top-priced audio equipment, there's a Bang & Olufsen shop at Østergade 3, at the eastern end of Strøget.

China & Silver

Denmark's best-known porcelain and silver are made under the umbrella of Royal Copenhagen Ltd. The two shops listed here are side by side on Strøget and have museum-quality displays that are worth a look whether you're a shopper or not.

Royal Copenhagen Porcelain, which is famous for its Flora Danica pattern, is at

Amagertorv 6, in an imposing Renaissance house (circa 1616) near Højbro Plads.

The Georg Jensen shop, Amagertorv 4, features fine silverwork, including cutlery, candleholders, jewellery and designer art pieces.

Books & Stamps

Book lovers and collectors will find good browsing in the antique bookshops along Fiolstræde in the block running between Krystalgade and Nørre Voldgade.

For information on shops that sell new English-language books, see under Bookshops in the Information section earlier in this chapter.

Stamp collectors can buy commemorative stamps from the Postens Frimærke Center, Vesterbrogade 67; it's open on weekdays from 10 am to 3.30 pm (to 6 pm Thursday).

Department Stores

Copenhagen's largest department store, Magasin du Nord, covers an entire block on the south-western side of Kongens Nytorv and contains everything from clothing and luggage to a bookshop and a grocery shop. Illum, another large department store, on Strøget at Østergade 52, has a 3rd floor crafts and antique market selling items ranging from toys to paintings and furniture.

Illums Bolighus, at Amagertorv 10 on Strøget, stocks stylish Danish-designed furniture, continental quilts, ceramics, silverware and glass, but is also a good place to look for simple gifts such as a quality toy or a stainless steel cheese-slicer.

Airport Shops

Copenhagen international airport has a few dozen tax-free shops selling a wide range of products, including men's and women's clothing, continental quilts, Royal Copenhagen porcelain, Georg Jensen silverware, jewellery, photographic and audio equipment, watches, travel bags, skin creams, lingerie, chocolates and, of course, alcohol.

Most of the shops are open from 6 am to 11 pm daily.

GETTING THERE & AWAY
Air

Copenhagen airport is Scandinavia's busiest hub, serving more than 16 million passengers a year with flights to nearly 150 destinations. There are daily direct flights to Copenhagen from numerous cities in Europe, Asia and North America, as well as a handful of Danish cities. More detailed information on flying to and from Copenhagen can be found in the introductory Getting There & Away and Getting Around chapters.

Copenhagen Airport The modern international airport is in Kastrup, 9km southeast of Copenhagen city centre. It has a large shopping area as well as numerous eateries and bars, most located in the transfer area. There's also a simple minihotel (☎ 32 31 32 31) for transfer passengers, with showers, saunas and 'slumber cabins' where you can nap; you pay by the hour.

You'll find a full-service Den Danske Bank on the 2nd floor of the departure hall, open from 9.30 am to 4 pm on weekdays, as well as foreign exchange booths in the departure, arrival and transit halls that are open from 6.30 am (7.30 am in the departure hall) to 10 pm daily. The VAT refund bureau is on the 2nd floor of the departure hall next to the bank.

There's a post office in the international terminal between the arrival and departure halls, open from 10 am to 5 pm Monday to Friday.

It's a sprawling airport, so when you get off the plane grab one of the free and ubiquitous baggage trolleys to cart your luggage around.

There's a left-luggage room between the departure and arrival halls on the ground floor where you can store luggage for 25 kr per piece per day. Lockers (20 kr for 24 hours) can be found nearby.

If you're waiting for a flight, note that this is a 'silent' airport and there are no boarding calls, although there are numerous monitor screens throughout the terminal.

Airline Offices Most airline offices are north of Central Station near the intersection of Vester Farimagsgade and Vesterbrogade. The SAS/Lufthansa ticket office, in the Radisson SAS Royal Hotel (see the Places to Stay section), is open from 9 am to 5.30 pm on weekdays. Cimber Air flights can be booked through SAS.

The following are the office locations and reservation numbers of airlines serving Copenhagen:

Aer Lingus
(☎ 33 12 60 55) Jernbanegade 4
Aeroflot
(☎ 33 12 63 38) Vester Farimagsgade 1
Air France
(☎ 33 12 76 76) Ved Vesterport 6
Air India
(☎ 33 15 70 70) Vester Farimagsgade 1
Alitalia
(☎ 33 36 93 69) Vesterbrogade 6D
Austrian Airlines
(☎ 33 12 80 90) Vester Farimagsgade 6
British Airways
(☎ 33 14 60 00) Rådhuspladsen 16
British Midland
(☎ 70 10 20 00) Hammerichsgade 1
EgyptAir
(☎ 33 32 90 60) Jernbanegade 7
El Al Israel Airlines
(☎ 33 14 64 17) Vesterbrogade 6
Estonian Air
(☎ 32 31 45 40) Vester Farimagsgade 7
Finnair
(☎ 33 36 45 45) Nyropsgade 47
Iberia
(☎ 33 12 22 22) Jernbanegade 4
Icelandair
(☎ 33 12 33 88) Vester Farimagsgade 1
Kenya Airways
(☎ 33 23 01 00) Trommesalen 5
KLM-Royal Dutch Airlines
(☎ 32 51 26 26) Copenhagen Airport
Lithuanian Airlines
(☎ 32 52 81 50) Copenhagen Airport
LOT Polish Airlines
(☎ 33 14 58 11) Vester Farimagsgade 21
Lufthansa Airlines
(☎ 33 37 73 33) Radisson SAS Royal Hotel, Hammerichsgade 1

Maersk Air
(☎ 32 31 45 45) Vester Farimagsgade 7
Olympic Airways
(☎ 33 12 61 00) Vester Farimagsgade 9
Pakistan International Airlines (PIA)
(☎ 33 14 18 33) Vester Farimagsgade 4
Sabena
(☎ 33 33 08 00) Nyropsgade 47
Scandinavian Airlines (SAS)
(☎ 32 54 17 01) Radisson SAS Royal Hotel, Hammerichsgade 1
Singapore Airlines
(☎ 33 14 34 56) Nyropsgade 47
South African Airways
(☎ 33 14 30 31) Vester Farimagsgade 1
Swissair
(☎ 33 12 80 90) Vester Farimagsgade 6
TAP Air Portugal
(☎ 33 91 29 26) Vesterbrogade 6
Thai Airways International
(☎ 33 75 01 20) Rådhuspladsen 16
Turkish Airlines
(☎ 33 14 51 90) Ved Vesterport 6
Varig
(☎ 33 11 91 22) Vester Farimagsgade 1

Bus

Buses to Bornholm and to Ystad (☎ 44 68 44 00) and Malmö (☎ 44 68 09 99) in Sweden leave from Bernstorffsgade in front of Central Station. Eurolines buses to Prague and numerous other European cities, including Paris, Frankfurt and Amsterdam, also leave from Central Station; the Eurolines ticket office (☎ 33 25 12 44) is at Reventlowsgade 8. Busabout buses depart from City Public Hostel on Absalonsgade. There are buses to the Swedish cities of Halmstad, Helsingborg and Malmö from Copenhagen airport in Kastrup; call ☎ 32 52 66 31 for details. More information is in the Getting There & Away chapter.

Daily buses to Århus (☎ 86 78 48 88) leave from Valby station; the fare for the 3½ hour trip is 190 kr. Buses to Aalborg (☎ 70 10 00 30) leave from Central Station daily and take six hours (190 kr).

Train

See the relevant Getting There & Away sections for details of individual journeys; for information, call ☎ 33 14 17 01. All long-distance trains arrive at and depart from

Central Station, a huge complex housing eateries and numerous services including currency exchange, a post office and a supermarket. There are lockers (25 kr per 24 hours) on the lower level near the Reventlowsgade exit and showers (15 kr) at the underground toilets opposite the police office.

Car & Motorcycle

The main highways into Copenhagen are the E20 from Jutland and Funen and the E47 from Helsingør and Sweden. If you're coming from the north on the E47, exit onto Lyngbyvej (route 19) and continue south to reach the heart of the city.

Hitching

Although hitching is not a very good option and we don't recommend it, if you want to try your luck it's best to start outside the city centre. For rides north, take bus No 1 to Vibenhus Runddel, at the north-western corner of Fælledparken in the Østerbro area. If you're heading towards Funen, take S-train line A to Ellebjerg station, at the south-western outskirts of the city. Keep in mind that it's illegal to hitch on motorways throughout Denmark.

Use It has a free message board that attempts to link up drivers and riders, though there's usually far more of the latter than the former.

Boat

The Oslo ferry departs from Copenhagen daily at 5 pm and the Bornholm ferry departs nightly at 11.30 pm (further details are in the Getting There & Away section of the Bornholm chapter). Both services leave from Kvæsthusbroen, north of Nyhavn. Hydrofoils to Malmö and Bornholm leave from Havnegade, south of Nyhavn. Ferries to Swinoujscie in Poland leave from Nordre Toldbod, east of Kastellet. Cruise ships use Langelinie harbour, just north of the Little Mermaid. Details of international ferry routes can be found in the Sea section of the Getting There & Away chapter.

GETTING AROUND
To/From the Airport

The airport is 15 minutes (about 125 kr) from the city centre by taxi.

A new rail system links the airport with Central Station. Trains runs every 20 minutes until midnight from 4.55 am on weekdays, 5.35 am on Saturday and 6.35 am on Sunday. The trip takes just 12 minutes and costs 16.50 kr. The train from the airport goes on to Helsingør in North Zealand and, beginning in summer 2000, trains from the airport will also serve Malmö in Sweden.

If your baggage is light, you could take local bus No 250S, which runs between the airport and Rådhuspladsen (and Central Station) every 10 to 20 minutes, but it takes about 35 minutes; the fare is 16.50 kr.

There's also a direct SAS airport bus (35 kr) that makes regular runs to the airport from Central Station and the SAS hotels.

Bus & Train

Copenhagen has an extensive public transit system consisting of a metro rail network called S-train, with 10 lines passing through Central Station (København H), and a vast bus system called HT (Hovedstadsområdets Trafikselskab), the main terminus of which is at Rådhuspladsen, a couple of blocks to the north-east.

Buses and trains use a common fare system based on the number of zones you pass through. The basic fare of 11 kr for up to two zones covers most city runs and allows transfers between buses and trains on a single ticket as long as they're made within an hour. Third and subsequent zones cost 5.50 kr more, with a maximum fare of 38.50 kr for travel throughout North Zealand. Danske Statsbaner (DSB; Danish State Railway) lines are also included in the common fare system as far north as Helsingør, west to Roskilde and south to Køge.

On buses, you board at the front and pay the fare to the driver (or stamp your clip card in the machine next to the driver). On S-trains, tickets are purchased at the station and then punched in the yellow time clock on the platform before boarding the train.

S-TRAIN

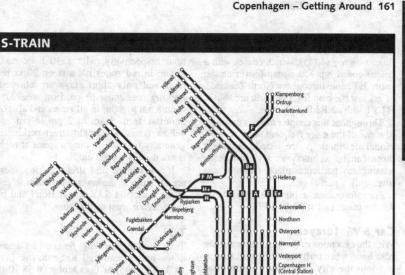

NOTE
Lines labelled '+' are extra Monday to Saturday
daytime trains, while lines labelled 'x' run only
during weekday rush hours.

Instead of buying a single destination ticket, you can buy a *klippekort* (clip card) which is valid for 10 rides in two zones (70 kr) or three zones (100 kr), or you can get a 24 hour ticket valid for unlimited travel in all zones (70 kr). Passengers who are stopped and found to be without a stamped ticket are liable to a fine of 500 kr.

Children aged under seven travel free, while those aged from seven to 14 travel half-price.

All rides on Copenhagen's regional buses and trains are free for visitors holding a valid Copenhagen Card.

Trains and buses run from about 5 am (6 am on Sunday) to around 12.30 am, though buses continue to run through the night (charging double the usual fare) on a few main routes.

The free Copenhagen city maps distributed by Copenhagen Information show bus routes (with numbers) and are very useful for finding your way around the city. If you plan to use buses extensively, you might want to buy HT's hefty timetable book *Busser og tog* (40 kr), which comes with a colour-coded bus route map (covering the entire HT route throughout North Zealand), or get just the map for 5 kr. Both are sold at HT's booth on Rådhuspladsen.

Throughout this chapter the bus numbers of some of the more frequent buses to individual destinations are listed, but since there can be as many as a dozen buses passing any particular place, our listing is often only a partial one.

For information on buses call ☎ 36 45 45 45; for trains call ☎ 33 14 17 01.

Car & Motorcycle

With the exception of the weekday-morning rush hour, when traffic can bottleneck coming into the city (and vice versa around 5 pm), traffic in Copenhagen is usually manageable. Getting around by car is not problematic, excepting the usual challenge of finding an empty parking space in the most popular places.

To explore sights in the centre of the city, you're best off on foot or using public transport, but a car is quite convenient for reaching suburban sights.

Rental The following car hire companies have booths at the airport in the international terminal. Each also has an office in central Copenhagen:

Avis
   (☎ 33 15 22 99) Kampmannsgade 1
Budget/Pitzner
   (☎ 33 11 12 34) Trommesalen 4
Europcar/Interrent
   (☎ 33 55 99 00) Gammel Kongevej 13
Hertz
   (☎ 33 17 90 21) Ved Vesterport 3

Peugeot (☎ 33 13 55 35), Gyldenløvesgade 17, hires out motor scooters for between 250 and 400 kr per day.

Parking For street parking, buy a ticket from a kerbside *billetautomat* (automated ticket machine) and place it inside the windscreen. Search out a blue, green or yellow zone where parking costs 5, 9 or 12 kr per hour respectively, with a 10 hour maximum; in red zones it's a steep 20 kr per hour and only short stays are allowed. Parking fees must be paid on weekdays from 8 am to 8 pm in all zones and also on Saturday from 8 am to 2 pm in red and yellow zones. Overnight street parking is generally free and finding a space at night is not usually a problem.

If you cannot find street parking, there are car parks at the main department stores, at the Radisson SAS Royal Hotel and on Jerbanegade, east of Axeltorv.

Taxi

Taxis with signs saying *fri* can be flagged down or you can call Københavns Taxa (☎ 35 35 35 35) or Taxa Motor (☎ 38 10 10 10). The cost is 22 kr at flagfall, plus about 8 kr per kilometre (10 kr at night and at weekends). Most taxis accept credit cards. A service charge is included in the fare, so tips are not expected.

Bicycle

Despite the motor traffic Copenhagen, with all its cycle paths, is a great city for getting around by bicycle. If you're travelling with a bike be careful: expensive bikes are hot targets for thieves on Copenhagen streets.

If you don't have a bike, there are several places around Copenhagen where they can be hired. In addition to rental rates, expect to pay a refundable deposit of between 200 and 300 kr for a regular bike, 1000 kr for a mountain bike or tandem.

One of the most convenient rental places is Københavns Cykler (☎ 33 33 86 13), just outside Central Station on Reventlowsgade. It's open from 8 am to 6 pm on weekdays and from 10 am to 1 pm on Saturday, and also from 10 am to 1 pm on Sunday in summer. The cost is 50/225 kr per day/week for a three speed bike, 200/900 kr for a tandem or mountain bike. A sister operation, Østerport Cykler (☎ 33 33 85 13) at Østerport S-train station near track 13, has

Free Copenhagen Bikes

The city of Copenhagen operates a generous scheme, called Bycykler (City Bikes), by which anyone can borrow a bicycle for free. It's motivated in part by an effort to control motor-vehicle traffic in the heart of the city. Sponsors, who paint the bikes with their logos, include private businesses, the local tourism office and the city council. In all there are some 2000 bikes available each summer.

Although the bicycles are not streamlined and are certainly not practical for long-distance cycling, that's part of the plan – use of the cycles is limited to the city centre. To deter theft and minimise maintenance, the bicycles have a distinctive design that includes solid spokeless wheels with puncture-resistant tyres. The bikes can be found at 150 widely scattered street stands in public places, including S-train stations.

If you're able to find a free bicycle, you deposit a 20 kr coin in the stand to release the bike. When you're done using the bicycle you can return it to any stand and get your 20 kr coin back.

the same rates and hours as Københavns Cykler, except that it's closed on Sunday year-round.

For a cheaper deal without going too far out of the way, Danwheel (☎ 33 21 22 27), Colbjørnsensgade 3, a couple of blocks north-west of Central Station, hires older bikes for 35 kr per day, 85 kr for three days. Danwheel is open from 10 am to 5.30 pm on weekdays, to 2 pm at weekends.

Except during weekday rush hours (from 7 to 8.30 am and from 3.30 to 5 pm), you can carry bikes on the S-trains (buy the 10 kr ticket from the red machine). You can load your bicycle in any carriage that has a cycle symbol and you must stay with the bike at all times. On the DSB route between Hillerød and Helsingør there are no rush-hour restrictions.

For more information on cycling, see the special section 'Cycling in Denmark' in the Facts for the Visitor chapter.

Boat

For information on getting around Copenhagen's waterfront by boat, see under Canal Tours in the Organised Tours section earlier in this chapter.

Around Copenhagen

Many places in the greater Copenhagen area make for quick and easy excursions from the city. The following destinations offer a good variety of outings to woodlands, lakes, beaches and historic areas. For other day-trip possibilities a bit farther afield, see the North Zealand chapter.

ARKEN

This large new contemporary art museum is on the coast at Skovvej 100 in Ishøj, 17km south of central Copenhagen. The stark modernistic building (the Ark) rises above the beach and is as much a work of art as the exhibits inside. The Arken collection features the works of leading Danish artists since 1945, with an emphasis on photo-based art, sculpture and installations. There are other changing exhibits such as works by the artists from the regional COBRA (COpenhagen-BRussels-Amsterdam) movement and by French artists Marc Chagall and Christian Boltanski. Arken (☎ 43 54 02 22) is open from 10 am to 5 pm Tuesday to Sunday (to 9 pm on Wednesday). Admission costs 40 kr (children 15 kr). You can get to Arken by taking the S-train to Ishøj station and boarding bus No 128 there.

DRAGØR

If Copenhagen begins to feel crowded, consider an afternoon excursion to Dragør, a maritime town on the island of Amager, a few kilometres south of the airport. In the early 1550s Christian II allowed Dutch farmers to settle in Amager to provide his court with flowers and produce, and the town of Dragør still retains a bit of Dutch flavour.

Along the waterfront are fish shops, smokehouses, a sizeable fishing fleet and the **Dragør Museum**, a half-timbered house featuring model ships and period furnishings. The museum is open from Tuesday to Sunday, afternoons only, and admission costs 20 kr.

A fun way to spend time is to simply wander the narrow, winding cobblestone streets leading up from the harbour, which are lined with the thatch-roofed, mustard-coloured houses comprising the **old town**. One interesting little ramble is to take Strandgade, a pedestrian alley that begins opposite the museum, and continue up to Badstuevælen, an old square lined with some attractive houses dating from the 1790s (houses No 9 and 12).

There are a few restaurants near the waterfront, including an open-air café in the historic *Dragør Strandhotel* that serves smørrebrød, fish and chips and other light fare at moderate prices.

To get to Dragør take bus No 30, 33 or 350S (16.50 kr) from central Copenhagen, a 35 minute ride.

CHARLOTTENLUND

Charlottenlund is a well-to-do coastal suburb just beyond the northern outskirts of Copenhagen. Despite being so close to the city, it has a decent **sandy beach**, although the smokestacks of Hellerup to the south are part of the backdrop.

Just inland from the beach is the moat-encircled **Charlottenlund Fort**, which now harbours a camping ground (see under Camping in the Copenhagen Places to Stay section) and an expensive seaview restaurant. There's not much left of the old fort other than some cannons, but it's still a pleasant place, with wading ducks and lots of birdsong.

Danmarks Akvarium, an aquarium at Kavalergården 1, is 500m north of the beach on the inland side of the road. By Scandinavian standards it's a fairly large

aquarium and the well-presented collection includes cold-water fish, tropical fish, live corals, nurse sharks, sea turtles, crocodiles and piranhas. It's open from 10 am to 6 pm daily (to 4 or 5 pm in the low season). Admission costs 55 kr (children 30 kr). There's a cafeteria.

From the aquarium car park a path leads 200m west to **Charlottenlund Slotshave**, an attractive three storey manor house that's now been converted to offices. Walkways lead around the park-like grounds, making for an enjoyable stroll if you're already in the area.

If you're interested in horse races, Charlottenlund's other attraction is **Charlottenlund Travbane**, a trotting (harness racing) track.

Bus No 6 from central Copenhagen runs by the beach, aquarium and trotting track.

KLAMPENBORG

Klampenborg, being only 20 minutes from Central Station on S-train line C, is a favourite spot for Copenhageners on family outings.

A few hundred metres east of Klampenborg station is **Bellevue beach**, a sandy stretch that gets packed with sunbathers in summer.

A 10 minute walk west from Klampenborg station is the 400-year-old **Bakken**, the world's oldest amusement park. A blue-collar version of Tivoli, it's a honky-tonk carnival of bumper cars, roller coasters, slot machines and beer halls. It's open from 2 pm to midnight daily between late March and late August; admission is free. Children's rides cost around 10 kr, adult rides about double that, and there are discounted multi-use passes.

Bakken is at the southern edge of **Dyrehaven** (more formally called Jægersborg Dyrehave), an expansive 1000 hectare area of beech trees and meadows crisscrossed by an alluring network of walking and cycling trails. Dyrehaven was established as a royal hunting ground in 1669 and has evolved into the capital's most popular picnicking area. Dyrehaven also contains the

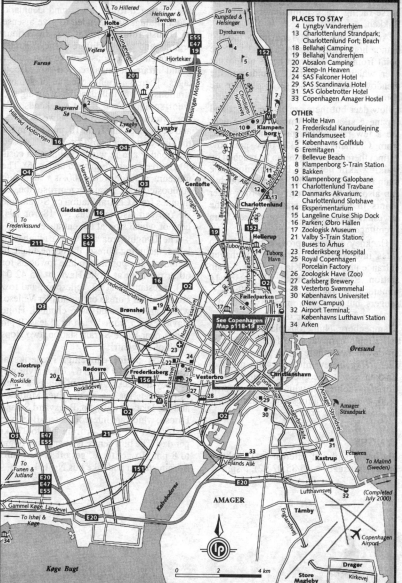

AROUND COPENHAGEN

PLACES TO STAY
4 Lyngby Vandrerhjem
13 Charlottenlund Strandpark;
   Charlottenlund Fort; Beach
18 Bellahøj Camping
19 Bellahøj Vandrerhjem
20 Absalon Camping
22 Sleep-In Heaven
24 SAS Falconer Hotel
29 SAS Scandinavia Hotel
31 SAS Globetrotter Hotel
33 Copenhagen Amager Hostel

OTHER
1 Holte Havn
2 Frederiksdal Kanoudlejning
3 Frilandsmuseet
5 Københavns Golfklub
6 Eremitagen
7 Bellevue Beach
8 Klampenborg S-Train Station
9 Bakken
10 Klampenborg Galopbane
11 Charlottenlund Travbane
12 Danmarks Akvarium;
   Charlottenlund Slotshave
14 Eksperimentarium
15 Langeline Cruise Ship Dock
16 Parken; Øbro Hallen
17 Zoologisk Museum
21 Valby S-Train Station;
   Buses to Århus
23 Frederiksberg Hospital
25 Royal Copenhagen
   Porcelain Factory
26 Zoologisk Have (Zoo)
27 Carlsberg Brewery
28 Vesterbro Svømmehal
30 Københavns Universitet
   (New Campus)
32 Airport Terminal;
   Københavns Lufthavn Station
34 Arken

Københavns Golfklub, an 18 hole golf course, and **Klampenborg Galopbane**, a horse-racing track immediately south of Bakken.

At the centre of Dyrehaven is the old manor house **Eremitagen**, a good vantage point from which to spot herds of grazing deer, which are especially abundant in the meadows west of the house. In all, there are about 2000 deer in the park; they're mostly fallow deer but there are also red deer and Japanese sika deer. Among the red deer are a few rare white specimens imported from Germany in 1737; they are now extinct there. Eremitagen can be reached by walking 2km north of Bakken along the main route, Christiansholmsvej, although it can also be reached from numerous other points in the park because most of the largest trails radiate out like spokes from Eremitagen.

Hackney carriages provide horse-drawn rides into the park from the Dyrehaven entrance just north of Klampenborg S-train station. Rides cost about 100 kr for 15 minutes; the coaches carry up to five passengers, but it's most romantic with two!

There are a number of places to eat in Klampenborg. Numerous places in Bakken sell simple carnival-style fare. For a nice sit-down meal there's the popular *Peter Lieps Hus*, a few minutes walk north of Bakken near the corner of Fortunvej and Christiansholmsvej, which serves smørrebrød, game specialities and other Danish food at moderate prices.

LYNGBY

The main sight of interest in Lyngby is **Frilandsmuseet** (☎ 45 85 02 92), a sprawling open-air museum of old countryside dwellings, workshops and barns that have been gathered from sites around Denmark. The buildings are intended to give a sense of Danish rural life as it was in various regions and across different social strata; consequently, the houses range from rather grand affairs to meagre, sod-roofed cottages. There's a light schedule of demonstrations such as folk dancing, weaving and wool spinning, mostly at weekends. It's open from 10 am to 5 pm between Easter and September and from 10 am to 4 pm for the first three weeks of October; it's closed on Monday and in winter. Admission costs 30 kr (free for children aged under 16). The museum, at Kongevejen 100, is a 10 minute signposted walk from Sorgenfri station, 25 minutes from Central Station on S-train line B. You can also take bus No 184 or 194, both of which stop at the entrance.

The Lyngby area also has a number of **lakes**, including Furesø, the deepest lake in Denmark. It's possible to hire rowboats for 60 kr per hour at Holte Havn (☎ 45 42 04 49), a restaurant at 22 Vejlesøvej, and row around either Furesø or the smaller Vejlesø, which are connected by a channel. Holte Havn is open from 10 am to at least 9 pm and is near Holte S-train station, two stops north of Sorgenfri.

If you prefer canoeing, Frederiksdal Kanoudlejning (☎ 45 85 67 70) at Nybrovej 520 (by the locks) hires out canoes as well as rowboats for use on the river Mølleåen and the lakes Lyngby Sø, Bagsværd Sø and Furesø, which are interconnected. Boat hire costs 60 kr per hour, or from 220 to 270 kr per day. The hire centre is open from 10 am to 8 pm. To get there, get off at Sorgenfri S-train station and take bus No 191.

North Zealand

Considering its proximity to Copenhagen, the northern part of Zealand is surprisingly rural, with small farms, wheat fields and beech woodlands. It also boasts fine beaches and some notable historic sights.

One of the most popular day trips from Copenhagen is a loop tour taking in Frederiksborg Slot in Hillerød and Kronborg Slot in Helsingør, with a stop at Fredensborg Slot in-between. With an early start you might even have time to continue on to one of the north shore beaches or visit Louisiana, the modern art museum in Humlebæk, on the way back to the city.

If you're not tight for time, however, North Zealand has a number of destinations that invite a longer stay. You could even hop on a ferry in Helsingør and skip over to Sweden for about the same price as a bottle of beer!

When planning your tour, keep in mind that the Copenhagen Card allows free access to trains, buses and most sightseeing attractions throughout North Zealand; for details see the boxed text under Information in the Copenhagen chapter.

If you're driving between Helsingør and Copenhagen ignore the motorway and take the coastal road, Strandvej (route 152), which is far more scenic.

Information on Charlottenlund, Lyngby and Klampenborg, just north of Copenhagen, is in the Around Copenhagen section at the end of the Copenhagen chapter.

Inland Towns

The inland area of North Zealand, sometimes referred to as the heartland, has two towns of special interest to visitors, Hillerød and Fredensborg.

HILLERØD
Hillerød, 30km north of Copenhagen, is a small town centred around a grand lakeside castle, Frederiksborg Slot.

Highlights

- Marvel at the lakeside Frederiksborg Slot with its magnificent interior (Hillerød)

- Browse Denmark's most renowned modern art collection at Louisiana (Humlebæk)

- Rock at the summertime Roskilde Festival, northern Europe's largest rock music event

- Stand in awe next to the bones of 37 Danish kings and queens in Roskilde Domkirke

- Stroll through history at Kronborg Slot, the setting for Shakespeare's *Hamlet* (Helsingør)

- Unwind in the unhurried fishing hamlets such as Gilleleje along the north coast

- Soak up the rays on the broad sandy beaches at Hornbæk and Tisvildeleje

An administrative centre and transport hub for North Zealand, Hillerød isn't notably quaint in itself but the castle and the surrounding gardens are lovely. You can enjoy picturesque views of the castle by following the path that skirts the castle lake. If you feel like taking a longer stroll, paths run through the newly restored Slotshaven, an expansive Baroque-style privet garden immediately north of the castle and lake. The paths leading through Slotshaven connect with trails in the adjacent woodlands of Lille Dyrehave and Indelukket which, taken together, could easily make a pleasant one or two hour outing.

Orientation

If you arrive at Hillerød by bus or train, follow the signs to the central square, Torvet. The main route through town, Slotsgade, leads directly from Torvet to the gate of Frederiksborg Slot, 500m to the north-west.

Information

The Hillerød Turistbureau (☎ 48 26 28 52), Slangerupgade 2, 3400 Hillerød, is 50m

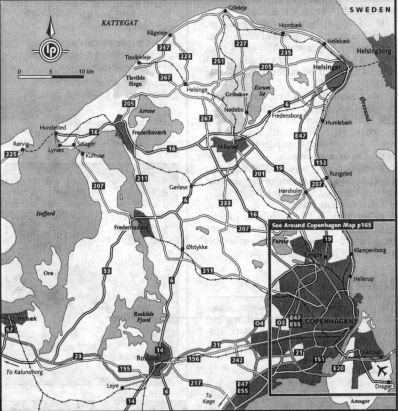

NORTH ZEALAND

KATTEGAT

SWEDEN

Gilleleje

Rågeleje

Hornbæk

Hellebæk

Helsingborg

Tisvildeleje

Helsingør

Tisvilde Hegn

Helsinge

Gribskov

Esrum Sø

Nødebo

Fredensborg

Humlebæk

Arresø

Frederiksværk

Hillerød

Øresund

Hundested

Rørvig

Sølager

Lynæs

Kulhuse

Rungsted

Gørløse

Hørsholm

Isefjord

Frederikssund

Ølstykke

See Around Copenhagen Map p165

Furesø

Lyngby

Klampenborg

Orø

Hellerup

Roskilde Fjord

Hojbæk

COPENHAGEN

Roskilde

Kastrup

To Kalundborg

Lejre

To Køge

Dragør

Amager

south of the castle entrance. It's open from 10 am to 4 pm on weekdays and 10 am to 1 pm on Saturday, except between mid-June and August when it's open from 9 am to 6 pm on weekdays and 10 am to 5 pm on Saturday.

Frederiksborg Slot

This impressive Dutch Renaissance castle spreads across three islets at the eastern side of the castle lake, Slotsø. The oldest part of Frederiksborg Slot dates from the reign of Frederik II, after whom the castle is named, but most of the present structure was built in the early 17th century by Frederik II's more extravagant son, King Christian IV.

As you enter the main gate you'll pass old stable buildings dating from the 1560s and then cross over a moat to the second islet, where you'll enter an expansive central courtyard with a grandly ornate **Neptune fountain**. The relatively modest wings that flank the fountain once served as residences for court officers and government officials. A second bridge crosses to the northernmost islet, the site of the main body of the castle which served as the home of Danish royalty for more than a century.

Frederiksborg Slot was ravaged by a fire in 1859. The royal family, unable to undertake the costly repairs, decided to give up the property. Carlsberg beer baron JC Jacobsen then stepped onto the scene and spearheaded a drive to restore the castle as a national museum, a function it still serves today.

The sprawling castle has a magnificent interior boasting gilded ceilings, wall-sized tapestries, fine paintings, memorabilia and antiques, with exhibits occupying 70 of its rooms. The richly embellished **Riddershalen** (Knights Hall) and **Slotskirken** (Coronation Chapel), where Danish monarchs were crowned from 1671 to 1840, are alone worth the admission fee. The chapel, incidentally, was spared serious fire damage and retains the original interior commissioned by Christian IV, including a lavish

hand-carved altar and pulpit created by Mores of Hamburg in 1606 and a priceless Compenius organ built in 1610. The organ is played each Thursday between 1.30 and 2 pm.

Frederiksborg Slot is open daily from 10 am to 5 pm between May and September, from 10 am to 4 pm in April and October, and from 11 am to 3 pm during the rest of the year. Admission costs 40 kr (children 10 kr). Outside opening hours visitors are still free to stroll around the grounds and enter the castle courtyard.

If you arrive at the castle by car, there's free parking off Frederikværksgade, west of the castle.

Places to Stay

Hillerød Camping (☎/fax 48 26 48 54, email hillcamp@post8.tele.dk, Dyrskuepladsen, 3400 Hillerød) is a three star camping ground about a 20 minute walk directly south of the castle along Slangerupgade. It's open between May and mid-September. There are cooking facilities and a coin laundry, and cabins are available to rent.

Hotel Hillerød (☎ 48 24 08 00, fax 48 24 08 74, Milnersvej 41, 3400 Hillerød), about 2km south of the castle, has an atrium filled with flowering plants and 62 modern rooms with bath, TV and kitchenette. Normal rates for singles/doubles are 625/800 kr but from July to mid-August there's a summer reduction to 525/600 kr.

Places to Eat

There are a number of inexpensive places to eat a few minutes walk from the castle on Slotsgade. At No 38 is a *McDonald's*, 200m farther east is an *Irma* grocery shop and just beyond that at No 27D is *Gonzales Cantina*, which serves the best pizza in town. Gonzales also offers good-value 29 kr lunch specials (from 11 am to 4 pm) including spaghetti, pizza, fish or beef, while at other times steak or chicken dishes with salad and chips cost around 50 kr and pitta-bread sandwiches cost 25 kr. For drinks or a snack try *Hennessy's* (*Slotsgade*

52), an Irish pub that serves up afternoon apple cake and tea (25 kr) on a verandah overlooking the castle.

Getting There & Away

The S-train (A & E lines) runs every 10 minutes between Copenhagen and Hillerød (38.50 kr), a 40 minute ride. Trains from Hillerød run east to Helsingør (33 kr, 30 minutes), north to Gilleleje (27.50 kr, 31 minutes) and west to Tisvildeleje (27.50 kr, 31 minutes); all services operate at least hourly.

Buses also link Hillerød with North Zealand towns. Bus No 305 runs to Gilleleje, Nos 306, 336 and 339 go to Hornbæk, and Nos 336 and 339 go to Fredensborg. Hillerød's bus terminal is immediately north of its train station.

Getting Around

Buses No 701 and 702 (11 kr) depart frequently from the train station and can drop you near the castle gate.

The little ferry *Frederiksborg* sails across the castle lake about every 30 minutes daily from June to August, and on weekends in May and September, landing at three small piers: one just north of Torvet, another near the castle entrance and the third north of the castle on the road to Slotshaven. The fare is 15 kr (children 5 kr) for any journey.

FREDENSBORG

Fredensborg is a quiet town with a royal palace, a lakeside location and some pleasant walking tracks.

Information

Fredensborg Turistinformation (☎ 48 48 21 00, fax 48 48 04 65), just outside the palace at Slotsgade 2, is open from 10 am to 4 pm Monday to Friday and from 11 am to 2 pm on Saturday.

There are a couple of banks in the centre of town, including Den Danske Bank at Jernbanegade 5.

The post office is at Helsingørvej 2 at the intersection with Jernbanegade.

Fredensborg Slot

Fredensborg Palace, the royal family's residence during most of the summer, was built in 1720 by Frederik IV. It was named Fredensborg, which means Peace Palace, to commemorate the peace that Denmark had recently achieved with its Scandinavian neighbours. The palace certainly reflects the more tranquil mood of that era and is largely in the style of a country manor house, an abrupt contrast with the moat-encircled fortresses of Kronborg and Frederiksborg that preceded it.

The main mansion was designed by the leading Danish architect of the day, JC Krieger, and is in Italian Baroque style with marble floors and a large central cupola. It's fronted by an expansive octagonal courtyard framed by two-storey buildings.

Partly because of its spread-out design, the palace is not as impressive as other Danish royal palaces in North Zealand. Fredensborg's interior can only be visited during July, when the royal family holidays elsewhere; guided tours cost 25 kr and run every 30 minutes between 1 and 5 pm.

At other times in the summer, when the queen is in residence, you might want to time your arrival to catch the changing of the guard that takes place just before noon.

The palace is backed by 120 hectares of **wooded parkland**, crisscrossed by trails and open to the public year-round. Take a stroll through **Normandsdalen**, west of the palace, to a circular amphitheatre with 70 life-sized sandstone statues of Norwegian folk characters – fisherfolk, farmers and so on – in traditional dress. If you continue walking a few minutes west from there you'll reach Esrum Sø, a lake skirted by another trail. To get to Fredensborg Slot from the train station, turn left onto Stationsvej and then turn right onto Jernbanegade, which merges with Slotsgade near the palace gate; the whole walk takes about 10 minutes.

Other Attractions

The south-eastern shore of **Esrum Sø**, Denmark's second-largest lake, borders Fredensborg and offers swimming, boating and fishing. Along the shore you can sometimes spot ospreys and cormorants, and the surrounding woods are the habitat of roe deer.

It's a 10 minute walk west from the palace gate along Skipperallé to **Skipperhuset** (☎ 48 48 01 07), a lakeside restaurant where there's a summer ferry service and rowboats for hire. The main beach is nearby. The ferry can take you to **Gribskov**, a forested area with trails and picnic grounds that borders the western side of Esrum Sø.

Slotsgade, the road that terminates at the palace gate, has a number of historic buildings, including **Hotel Store Kro** at No 6. **Villa Bournonville**, the former home of the 19th century ballet master Auguste Bournonville at Slotsgade 9, is now an art gallery; **Havremagasinet**, Slotsgade 11, once served as horse stables. **Kunstnegården**, an art and crafts gallery a bit farther south at Slotsgade 17, was originally an inn built in 1722.

Places to Stay

The hostel, *Fredensborg Vandrerhjem* (☎ 48 48 03 15, fax 48 48 16 56, Østrupvej 3, 3480 Fredensborg), has a prime location just 300m south of the castle; it's open year-round. Most of the 88 beds are in double rooms; some have toilets but all showers are off the hall. There's a TV room, a playroom with a dartboard, and a guest kitchen. The cost, for either dorm beds or double rooms, is 93 kr per person; private rooms for individual travellers cost 170 kr. To get there turn west off Slotsgade at Hotel Store Kro and continue for about 50m.

Staff at the tourist office can book *rooms* in private homes; doubles cost around 350 kr including breakfast. There's a 25 kr booking fee.

At *Endruplund Country House* (☎ 48 48 02 38, Holmeskovvej 5, 3480 Fredensborg), a former farmhouse about 1km north of the train station (off Helsingørsvej), singles/doubles cost 240/340 kr with shared bath, 260/380 kr with bath. Breakfast is optional and costs 40 kr more.

Just outside the palace gate is *Hotel Store Kro* (☎ 48 48 00 47, fax 48 48 45 61, Slotsgade 6, 3480 Fredensborg), a classic inn; the earliest sections were built by Frederik IV in 1723 to accommodate palace guests. No two rooms are alike but all have traditional décor as well as a bathroom, a TV, a phone and a minibar. Singles/doubles cost 850/1150 kr.

For an upmarket rural getaway, try *Pension Bondehuset* (☎ 48 48 01 12, fax 48 48 03 01, Sørupvej 14, Box 6, 3480 Fredensborg), which also dates from the early 18th century. It's by the lake on the western outskirts of Fredensborg, and boasts classic manor house furnishings and rowboats for guests to use. Rooms with bath cost 465/755 kr for singles/doubles including breakfast, or 650/1125 kr with full board.

Places to Eat

There's a good *fruit stand* and a *bakery* at Jernbanegade 20, next to a *Netto* grocery shop, about halfway between the train station and Fredensborg Slot. *Ciao*, a pleasant Italian café near the Netto grocery shop, serves good pizza and pasta costing 39 kr between 11 am and 4 pm, as well as pricier dinners.

For ice cream, sandwiches and coffee, the café *Under Kronen* (*Jernbanegade 1*) is conveniently located just outside the palace gate.

At the top end, *Hotel Store Kro* offers engaging old-world charm and a three course Danish dinner (335 kr) with a menu that changes nightly.

Getting There & Away

Fredensborg is midway on the railway line between Hillerød (11 kr, 12 minutes) and Helsingør (27.50 kr, 20 minutes). Trains run about twice hourly from early morning to around midnight.

Buses No 336 and 339 run hourly between Fredensborg train station and Hillerød (11 kr, 20 minutes), stopping en route near Fredensborg Slot.

NORTH ZEALAND

Øresund Coast

The Øresund Coast, the eastern shore of North Zealand, extends north from Copenhagen to the Helsingør area and is largely a run of small seaside suburbs and yachting harbours. It is the Øresund (Sound) that connects the Baltic Sea to the south with the Kattegat to the north and separates Denmark from Sweden. On clear days you can look across the sound and see southern Sweden on the opposite shore.

Partly because of the exclusive homes along the waterfront, the local tourist authorities sometimes rather grandly refer to this area as the Danish Riviera. In reality its main appeal to visitors lies not in its beaches but in two museums, one dedicated to author Karen Blixen, the other to modern art.

RUNGSTED

The coastal town of Rungsted is the site of Rungstedlund, the estate that houses the Karen Blixen museum.

Rungstedlund was originally built in around 1500 as an inn. King Karl XII of Sweden stayed there in around 1700 and the Danish lyric poet Johannes Ewald, who wrote Denmark's national anthem, was a boarder from 1773 to 1776. The property was later turned into a private residence and in 1879 was purchased by Karen Blixen's father, Wilhelm Dinesen. Blixen was born at Rungstedlund in 1885 and lived there off-and-on until her death in 1962.

There's a tourist office in a small kiosk at the intersection of Rungstedvej and Rungsted Strandvej.

Karen Blixen Museet

Karen Blixen's former home, now a museum, is furnished in much the way she left it and contains photographs, paintings, Masai spears and shields and other mementoes of her time in Africa, such as the gramophone given to Blixen by her lover Denys Finch-Hatton. On the desk in her study, beside a photograph of Denys, is the old Corona typewriter that Blixen used to write her novels.

One wing of the museum, a converted carriage house and stables, houses a library of Blixen's books in many languages, a café and a bookshop; there's also an audio-visual presentation on Blixen's life. The grounds contain gardens and a wood, part of which has been set aside as a bird sanctuary. Blixen lies buried in a little clearing shaded by a sprawling beech tree, her grave marked by a simple stone slab inscribed with just her name.

Between May and September the museum is open from 10 am to 5 pm daily. Between October and April it's open from 1 to 4 pm on Wednesday, Thursday and Friday, and from 11 am to 4 pm on Saturday and Sunday. Admission costs 30 kr (children free).

The museum is at Rungsted Strandvej 111, opposite the yacht harbour and 1.25km from the train station. To get there, walk north from the train station up Stationvej, turn right at the lights onto Rungstedvej and then at its intersection with Rungsted Strandvej walk south about 300m and you'll come to the museum; the whole walk takes about 15 minutes.

Getting There & Away

Copenhagen-Helsingør trains stop at Rungsted. The fare is 27.50 kr from Helsingør, 38.50 kr from Copenhagen.

HUMLEBÆK

The coastal town of Humlebæk has a couple of harbours and bathing beaches and some wooded areas, but the main focus for visitors is the modern art museum Louisiana.

Louisiana

Louisiana, Denmark's most renowned modern art museum, is on a seaside knoll in a strikingly modernistic complex with sculpture-laden grounds. The sculptures on the lawns, which include works by Henry Moore, Alexander Calder and Max Ernst, create an engaging interplay between art, architecture and landscape. Louisiana is a

Karen Blixen

Karen Blixen was born Karen Christenze Dinesen on 17 April 1885 in Rungsted, a well-to-do community north of Copenhagen. She studied art in Copenhagen, Rome and Paris. In 1914, when she was 28 and eager to escape from the confines of her bourgeois family, she married her second cousin Baron Bror von Blixen-Finecke, after having a failed love affair with his twin brother Hans. It was a marriage of convenience – she wanted his title and he needed her money.

The couple moved to Kenya and started a coffee plantation, which Karen was left to manage. The baron, who had several extramarital affairs, eventually infected Karen with syphilis. She came home to Denmark for medical treatment, but subsequently returned to Africa and divorced the baron in 1925.

In 1932, after her coffee plantation had failed and the great love of her life, Englishman Denys Finch-Hatton, had died in a tragic plane crash, Karen Blixen left Africa and returned to the family estate in Rungsted, where she began to write. Danes were slow to take to Blixen's writings, in part because she consistently wrote about the aristocracy in approving terms and used an old-fashioned idiomatic style that some thought arrogant. Her insistence on being called 'Baroness' also took its toll on her popularity in a Denmark bent on minimising class disparity.

Following rejection by publishers in Denmark and England, her first book, *Seven Gothic Tales*, a compilation of short stories set in the 19th century, was published in New York in 1934 (under the pseudonym Isak Dinesen) and was so well received that it was chosen as a Book-of-the-Month selection. It was only after her success in the USA that Danish publishers took a serious interest in her works.

In 1937 Blixen's landmark *Out of Africa*, the memoirs of her life in Kenya, was published in both Danish and English. This was followed by *Winter's Tales* in 1942, *The Angelic Avengers* in 1944, *Last Tales* in 1957, *Anecdotes of Destiny* in 1958 and *Shadows on the Grass* in 1960. Three of Blixen's books were published after her death: *Daguerreotypes and Other Essays*, *Carnival: Entertainments and Posthumous Tales* and *Letters from Africa 1914-1931*. Two of Blixen's works were turned into the Oscar-winning films *Out of Africa* and *Babette's Feast*.

A few years before her death, Blixen arranged for her estate to be turned over to the private Rungstedlund Foundation. For years the foundation had only enough money to maintain the grounds as a bird sanctuary, but the posthumous book sales that were spurred by the success of the films made it possible to turn her former home into a museum in 1991.

Karen Blixen achieved fame by writing about her life on a Kenyan coffee plantation.

fascinating place to visit even for those not passionate about modern art.

Items from the museum's permanent collection, mainly paintings and graphic art from the postwar era, are creatively displayed and grouped. There are sections on constructivism, COBRA (COpenhagen-BRussels-Amsterdam)-movement artists, abstract expressionism, minimal art, pop art and staged photography. Some of the more prominent Danish artists represented are Asger Jorn, Robert Jacobsen and Richard Mortensen.

The museum also has top-notch temporary exhibitions, which over the years have had such diverse themes as an Andy Warhol retrospective, Toulouse-Lautrec & Paris, Claude Monet, and the English painter Francis Bacon. The museum also presents concerts and films and has a shop and café.

Louisiana is 1km from Humlebæk train station, a 10 minute signposted walk along Gammel Strandvej. It's open from 10 am to 5 pm (to 10 pm on Wednesday) daily year-round. Admission costs 53 kr (children 15 kr).

Places to Eat

There are a number of simple eating options along Gammel Strandvej just outside Humlebæk train station. To the south of the station is *Slagter Bagger*, a deli offering tempting smørrebrød sandwiches as well as cheeses and meats sold by weight. Adjacent is a good *fruit stand* and right around the corner is a small *grocery shop* and a *bakery*.

If you're looking for a place to have a picnic lunch, immediately east of Louisiana there's a bench on the cliffs and steps leading down to a rocky beach.

Getting There & Away

Danske Statsbaner (DSB; Danish State Railways) trains leave Copenhagen a few times each hour for Humlebæk, a ride that takes about 40 minutes and costs 38.50 kr. DSB also offers a Louisiana excursion ticket for 96 kr that includes the museum admission price and the return train fare from Copenhagen. The train from Hels-

ingør takes 12 minutes and costs 16.50 kr. Though it's a bit slower, you could also take bus No 388, which runs between Copenhagen (38.50 kr) and Helsingør (16.50 kr).

HELSINGØR

Helsingør (Elsinore), at the narrowest point of the Øresund, has long been a busy port town. Indeed, with ferries shuttling to and from Sweden 24 hours a day, this is the world's busiest shipping channel, a virtual water highway bustling with ships carrying everything from passengers and cargo to tour buses and railway cars.

Although Swedish shoppers hopping over on day trips comprise many of Helsingør's visitors (which accounts for the plethora of liquor shops near the harbour), the town offers enough sightseeing possibilities to make for an enjoyable half-day of touring.

Helsingør has maintained some of its historic quarters, including a block of old homes and warehouses known as Sund-toldkarreen (Sound Dues Square) at the north-eastern end of Strangade. Helsingør's top sight, perched across the harbour on the northern side of town, is the imposing Kronborg Slot, made famous as Elsinore Castle in Shakespeare's *Hamlet*.

Information

Tourist Office The Helsingør Turistbureau (☎ 49 21 13 33, fax 49 21 15 77), Havnepladsen 3, 3000 Helsingør, is opposite the train station. Appropriately, being in a port of entry, it offers a wide range of services, including booking accommodation and selling Camping Card International passes, Hostelling International cards and phonecards. Between late June and 31 August it's open from 9 am to 6 pm Monday to Friday and from 9 am to 4 pm on Saturday, and during the rest of the year it's open from 9 am to 4 pm on weekdays and from 10 am to 1 pm on Saturday.

Money Den Danske Bank, Stengade 55, is open from 9.30 am to 4 pm Monday to Friday (to 6 pm on Thursday).

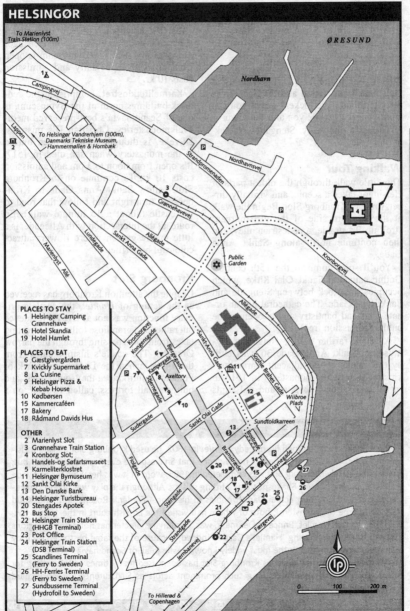

HELSINGØR

ØRESUND

Nordhavn

To Marienlyst
Train Station (100m)

Campingvej

Lappen

To Helsingør Vandrerhjem (300m),
Danmarks Tekniske Museum,
Hammermøllen & Hornbæk

Strandpromenaden

Nordhavnsvej

Grønnehavevej

Allégade

Marienlyst Allé

Lundegade

Sankt Anna Gade

Public
Garden

Kronborgvej

Allégade

Kongensgade

Kronborgvej

Bjergegade

Kampergade

Stjernegade

Axeltorv

Sankt Anna Gade

Sophie Brahes Gade

Wiibroe
Plads

Suddergade

Sankt Olai Gade

Sundtoldkarreen

Fiolgade

Bramstræde

Havnegade

Stengade

Brostræde

Strandgade

Jernbanevej

Færgevej

To Hillerød &
Copenhagen

NORTH ZEALAND

PLACES TO STAY
1 Helsingør Camping
   Grønnehave
16 Hotel Skandia
19 Hotel Hamlet

PLACES TO EAT
6 Gæstgivergården
7 Kvickly Supermarket
8 La Cuisine
9 Helsingør Pizza &
   Kebab House
10 Kødbørsen
15 Kammercaféen
17 Bakery
18 Rådmand Davids Hus

OTHER
2 Marienlyst Slot
3 Grønnehave Train Station
4 Kronborg Slot;
   Handels-og Søfartsmuseet
5 Karmeliterklostret
11 Helsingør Bymuseum
12 Sankt Olai Kirke
13 Den Danske Bank
14 Helsingør Turistbureau
20 Stengades Apotek
21 Bus Stop
22 Helsingør Train Station
   (HHGB Terminal)
23 Post Office
24 Helsingør Train Station
   (DSB Terminal)
25 Scandlines Terminal
   (Ferry to Sweden)
26 HH-Ferries Terminal
   (Ferry to Sweden)
27 Sundbusserne Terminal
   (Hydrofoil to Sweden)

0   100   200 m

Post The post office, south-west of the DSB terminus at the train station, is open from 9.30 am to 5 pm on weekdays (to 5.30 pm on Thursday) and from 10 am to 1 pm on Saturday.

Other Facilities The DSB terminus at Helsingør train station and the Scandlines ferry terminal have lockers where you can store your bags while you tour the town.

There's a pharmacy, Stengades Apotek, at Stengade 46.

Walking Tour

This little walk through the oldest parts of Helsingør takes a scenic, and virtually direct, route to Kronborg Slot. Begin the walk at the northern side of the turistbureau; stroll up Brostræde, a pedestrian alley, and then continue north along Sankt Anna Gade.

You'll soon come to the 15th century Gothic cathedral **Sankt Olai Kirke**, which occupies the block between Stengade and Sankt Olai Gade. The cathedral has an ornate altar and baptistry and is open to the public (admission free).

A block farther north, **Helsingør Bymuseum**, Sankt Anna Gade 36, was built by the monks of the adjacent Karmeliterklostret (Carmelite monastery) in 1516 to serve as a sailors' hospital and did stints as a poorhouse and a town library before being converted to a history museum in 1973. The hotchpotch of exhibits includes about 200 dolls and a model of Helsingør as it was in 1801. The Bymuseum is open from noon to 4 pm daily and admission costs 10 kr.

Karmeliterklostret, comprising the redbrick buildings north of the Bymuseum, is one of Scandinavia's best-preserved medieval monasteries. Christian II's mistress, Dyveke, is thought to have been buried at the monastery when she died in 1517. It's open from noon to 3 pm and admission costs 10 kr. To continue on to Kronborg Slot, follow Sankt Anna Gade to Kronborgvej, turn right and follow that road to the castle (about a 15 minute walk). En route, at the intersection with Allégade, is a little public garden where flowers attract colourful butterflies.

Kronborg Slot

Despite the attention Kronborg has received as the setting of *Hamlet*, the castle's primary function was not as a royal residence but rather as a grandiose tollhouse, wresting taxes from ships passing through the narrow Øresund. The castle's history dates from the 1420s, when the Danish king Erik of Pomerania introduced the 'sound dues' and built a small fortress, called Krogen, on a

---

To Be or Not To Be

When Shakespeare penned his tragedy *Hamlet* in 1602, he used Kronborg Slot (calling it Elsinore Castle) as its setting. There is no evidence that Shakespeare ever visited Helsingør but, when the stately Kronborg Slot was completed in 1585, word of it was heralded far and wide and it apparently struck Shakespeare as a fitting setting. Although the play was fiction, Shakespeare did include two actual Danish nobles in his plot – Frederik Rosenkrantz and Knud Gyldenstierne (Guildenstern), both of whom had visited the English court in the 1590s.

The fact that Hamlet, Prince of Denmark, was a fictional character has not deterred legions of sightseers from visiting 'Hamlet's Castle'. Indeed, because of the fame bestowed on it by Shakespeare, Kronborg is the most widely known castle in all of Scandinavia.

During the past few decades Kronborg Slot has been used many times as the setting for performances of *Hamlet*, featuring such prominent actors as Sir Laurence Olivier, Richard Burton and Michael Redgrave.

promontory at the narrowest part of the sound.

Financed by the generous revenue from shipping tolls, the original medieval fortress was rebuilt and enlarged by Frederik II between 1574 and 1585 to form the present Kronborg Slot. Much of Kronborg was ravaged by fire in 1629, but Christian IV rebuilt it, preserving the castle's earlier Renaissance style. In 1658, during the war with Sweden, the Swedes occupied Kronborg and removed practically everything of value, leaving the interior in shambles. After that, Danish royalty rarely visited the castle, although the sound dues continued to be collected for another 200 years. In 1785 Kronborg was converted into barracks; that remained its chief function until 1922. Since then the castle has been thoroughly restored and is now open to the public as a museum.

Some of the castle's more interesting quarters include the king's and queen's chambers, which have marble fireplaces and detailed ceiling paintings; the small chamber, which boasts royal tapestries; and the great hall, one of the longest Renaissance halls in Scandinavia. The chapel is one of the best-preserved parts of the castle and has some choice wood carvings, while the gloomy dungeons make for more unusual touring.

In the dungeon you'll pass the resting statue of the legendary Viking chief Holger Danske (Ogier the Dane) who is said to watch over Denmark, ever-ready to come to her aid should the hour of need arise. The low-ceilinged dungeon includes areas that once served as soldiers' quarters and storerooms for salted fish, which these days are homes for nesting bats!

Also housed in the castle is **Handels-og Søfartsmuseet** (Danish Maritime Museum), a collection of model ships, paintings, nautical instruments and sea charts illustrating the history of Danish shipping and trade. Model ship enthusiasts will find it interesting. The remains of the original Krogen fortress can be seen in the masonry of the museum's showrooms No 21 and 22.

Both Kronborg Slot and Handels-og Søfartsmuseet are open from 10.30 am to 5 pm between May and September, from 11 am to 4 pm in April and October and from 11 am to 3 pm between November and March; they're closed on Monday between October and April.

You can cross the moat and walk around the castle courtyard free of charge, tour the chapel, dungeon and royal quarters for 30 kr (children 10 kr), or buy a combined ticket costing 45 kr (children 15 kr) that includes admission to the maritime museum. If you have a Copenhagen Card, it provides free entry to the latter (admission 25 kr) but doesn't cover the other Kronborg sights.

Kronborg is 1km from Helsingør train station (see the earlier Walking Tour for a suggested route) but you can also take the Hornbæk-bound train to Grønnehave station and walk east for a few minutes to the castle.

Outskirts of Town

About 1.5km north-west of the town centre is **Marienlyst Slot**, a three storey manor house. It was built in 1763 in the Louis Seize neoclassical style by French architect NH Jardin and encompasses parts of an early summer house constructed by Frederik II. The interior exhibits include local paintings and silverwork. Admission costs 20 kr (children free); it's open to the public from noon to 5 pm daily. The Hornbæk-bound train stops at Marienlyst station, just north of the manor house.

If you'd like to examine technological inventions from the late 19th and early 20th centuries, the **Danmarks Tekniske Museum** at Nordre Strandvej 23, opposite the hostel, displays early gramophones, radios, motor vehicles and a 1906 Danish-built aeroplane that's claimed to be the first plane flown in Europe (it stayed airborne for 11 seconds!). The museum is open from 10 am to 5 pm Tuesday to Sunday; admission costs 30 kr (children 15 kr). It's a short walk east from Højstrup train station, or you can take bus No 340.

Hammermøllen, 5km west of Helsingør town centre in the village of Hellebæk, is an old smithy that was founded by Christian IV and used to make muskets for the Kronborg arsenal. The current building, which dates from 1765, has also functioned as a water wheel-operated copper mill and textile mill. It's open from 10 am to 5 pm Tuesday to Sunday. Admission costs 10 kr (children 5 kr). Hammermøllen is a five minute walk south of Hellebæk train station.

Places to Stay

The two star *Helsingør Camping Grønnehave* (☎/fax 49 21 58 56, Campingvej 1, 3000 Helsingør) is on the beach about 1.5km north-west of the town centre. Open all year round, it has 120 sites, a kiosk, cooking facilities and a coin laundry. To get there take the Hornbæk-bound train or bus No 340 from Helsingør station then get off at Marienlyst train station and walk east to Campingvej.

Helsingør Vandrerhjem (☎ 49 21 16 40, fax 49 21 13 99, email helsingoer@danhostel.dk, Nordre Strandvej 24, 3000 Helsingør) is 2km north-west of the town centre in a renovated coastal manor house. This 200 bed hostel is open year-round except during the months of December and January. Most of the rooms have baths and just two to six beds, and many are equipped for disabled visitors. Dorm beds cost 80 kr, doubles from 170 to 255 kr. There's a beach nearby. From Helsingør train station catch bus No 340 or take the Hornbæk-bound train and walk north-west from Marienlyst station.

Staff at the turistbureau can book *rooms* in private homes for you; singles/doubles cost 150/280 kr, plus a 25 kr booking fee.

The cheapest hotel in town is the 40 room *Hotel Skandia* (☎ 49 21 09 02, fax 49 26 54 90, Bramstræde 1, 3000 Helsingør). This family-run place offers large, clean singles/doubles costing 340/540 kr with shared bath, or 425/680 kr with private bath, including breakfast. If you request one of the north-facing top-storey rooms

(No 48 is a good choice) there's a view of Kronborg Slot.

The other central option is the 36 room *Hotel Hamlet* (☎ 49 21 05 91, fax 49 26 01 30, Bramstræde 5, 3000 Helsingør), but the rooms are much pricier at 625/825 kr for singles/doubles.

Places to Eat

The DSB railway terminal and the adjacent ferry terminals have food kiosks and places serving inexpensive eats. If you're on your way to Sweden, the Scandlines ferry has an on-board restaurant serving good food at moderate prices.

Kammercaféen, in the old customs house behind the turistbureau, offers reasonably priced sandwiches, drinks and live entertainment. A block to the south-west is *Rådmand Davids Hus* (Strandgade 70), a popular café housed in a 300-year-old half-timbered building. The special is the 'shopping lunch' (58 kr), a big plate of traditional Danish foods, typically salmon pâté, salad and slices of lamb, cheese and bread, served Monday to Saturday from 10 am to 4 pm.

You'll find the main cluster of eateries around Axeltorv, four blocks north-west of Helsingør train station; there are a dozen places to eat as well as beer gardens selling Helsingør's own Wiibroe pilsner.

Kødbørsen, a butcher shop on the southern side of Axeltorv, makes good takeaway smørrebrød costing just 8 kr a piece. The nearby *Helsingør Pizza & Kebab House* offers 29 kr pizza or lasagne specials until 4 pm and cheap kebab or felafel sandwiches all day. Two more upmarket options, both on the northern side of the square, are *La Cuisine*, with a French à la carte menu, and *Gæstgivergården*, a candlelit, pub-like place serving traditional Danish fare.

There's a *bakery* opposite Helsingør train station and another in the *Kvickly* supermarket (Stjernegade 25), a block west of Axeltorv.

Getting There & Away

Bus Bus No 340 runs to/from Hornbæk (16.50 kr, 25 minutes) and Gilleleje (33 kr,

50 minutes) twice hourly. Bus No 388 runs to Humlebæk (16.50 kr) and Copenhagen (38.50 kr, 75 minutes).

Train Helsingør train station has two adjacent terminals: the main DSB terminal for national trains and the Helsingør-Hornbæk-Gilleleje Banen (HHGB) terminal for the private railway that runs along the north coast. DSB trains to and from Copenhagen run about three times hourly from early morning to around midnight (38.50 kr, 55 minutes). DSB trains to and from Hillerød (33 kr, 30 minutes) run at least once hourly until around midnight. The HHGB train from Helsingør to Gilleleje via Hornbæk runs an average of twice hourly (33 kr, 40 minutes), with the last train pulling out of Helsingør at 10.54 pm.

Car & Motorcycle Helsingør is 64km north of Copenhagen and 24km north-east of Hillerød. There's free parking through out the city, including at car parks northeast of the turistbureau, to the west of the Kvickly supermarket and outside Kronborg Slot.

Boat For information on the frequent ferries to Helsingborg in Sweden (15 kr, 20 minutes), see the Getting There & Away chapter in the front of this book. Visitors arriving by train can make a beeline to the Scandlines ferry office by walking through the back exit of the DSB railway terminal.

North Coast

The north coast of Zealand, also known as the Kattegat coast, is a pleasant mix of dunes, heathlands and coastal woodlands. Development is limited to a handful of small fishing towns that dates back to the 1500s, their backstreets bordered by half-timbered thatch-roofed houses with their tidy flower gardens. Although the towns have only a few thousand residents in winter, the population swells with throngs of beachgoers in summer.

HORNBÆK
Hornbæk has the best beach on the north coast, a vast expanse of soft white sands that runs the entire length of the town. It's backed by sand dunes with beach grass and thickets of *Rosa rugosa*, a wild pink seaside rose that blooms all summer. Even though it borders the town the beach is pleasantly undeveloped, with all of the commercial facilities on the inland side of the dunes.

Poet Holger Drachmann, who died in Hornbæk in 1908, is memorialised by a harbourside monument. These days the salty fisherfolk, about whom Drachmann often wrote, share their harbour with scores of sailing boats and yachts.

Orientation
From the train station it's a five minute walk directly north along Havnevej to the harbour. Climb the dunes to the left and you're on the beach.

Information
Tourist Office The Hornbæk Turistbureau is inside the library (☎ 49 70 47 47, fax 49 70 41 42, email hornbaek@inet.uni2.dk), Vester Stejlebakke 2A, 3100 Hornbæk; to get there take the walkway at the side of Den Danske Bank. The turistbureau is open from 2 to 7 pm on Monday, Tuesday and Thursday, from 10 am to 4 pm on Wednesday and Friday, and from 10 am to 2 pm on Saturday.

Other Facilities The post office is opposite the train station. There are public toilets and showers at the harbour. Den Danske Bank is in the town centre at Nordre Strandvej 350.

Things to See & Do
The **beach** is without a doubt Hornbæk's main attraction and offers good swimming conditions and plenty of space for sunbathing. If you're interested in **windsurfing**, contact Hornbæk Surfudlejning (☎ 49 70 33 75), Drejervej 19. To charter a boat to go **fishing**, contact the turistbureau or the

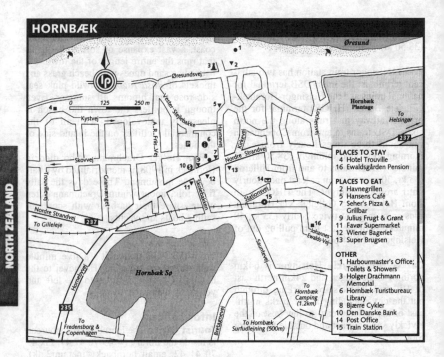

HORNBÆK

Øresund

Øresundsvej

Hornbæk
Plantage

To
Helsingør

0   125   250 m

Kystvej

A. R. Friis Vej

Vester Stejlebakke

Havnevej

Kirkevej

Lochersvej

Skovvej

Nordre Strandvej

Granvænget

Trouillevej

Hornbævej

Bretagnevej

Stationsvej

Sauntevej

Johannes
Ewalds Vej

PLACES TO STAY
4   Hotel Trouville
16 Ewaldsgården Pension

PLACES TO EAT
2   Havnegrillen
5   Hansens Café
7   Seher's Pizza & Grillbar
9   Julius Frugt & Grønt
11 Favør Supermarket
12 Wiener Bageriet
13 Super Brugsen

OTHER
1   Harbourmaster's Office; Toilets & Showers
3   Holger Drachmann Memorial
6   Hornbæk Turistbureau; Library
8   Bjærre Cykler
10 Den Danske Bank
14 Post Office
15 Train Station

Hornbæk Sø

Nordre Strandvej
237
To Gilleleje

235

To
Fredensborg &
Copenhagen

To
Hornbæk
Camping
(1.2km)

To Hornbæk
Surfudlejning (500m)

---

harbourmaster's office at the southern side of the harbour. You can rent **bicycles** at Bjærre Cykler (☎ 49 70 32 82), Nordre Strandvej 338.

If you're up to an enjoyable nature stroll, **Hornbæk Plantage**, a public woodland that extends 3.5km along the coast east from Hornbæk, has numerous interconnecting trails branching out either side of route 237. There are wild roses along the coast and pine trees and flowering Scotch broom inland. One trail follows the coast from Lochersvej in Hornbæk to the eastern end of the plantage. Other trails go inland, including one path that leads to Hornbæk Camping. There are several areas along Nordre Strandvej (route 237) where you can park a car and start your wanderings. A free forestry map, *Vandreture i Statsskovene, Hornbæk Plantage*, shows all the trails and is available from the turistbureau.

Places to Stay

There's a three star camping ground, *Hornbæk Camping* (☎ 49 70 02 23, fax 49 70 23 91, Planetvej 4, 3100 Hornbæk), on the outskirts of town off Sauntevej, about 1.5km south-east of the centre. Open from late March to late September, it has a coin laundry, a group kitchen and heated cabins for hire.

Ewaldsgården Pension (☎/fax 49 70 00 82, Johannes Ewalds Vej 5, 3100 Hornbæk), south-east of the train station and about a 10 minute walk from the harbour, occupies an early 18th century country house. The interior is light and airy with a cosy mix of antiques and cottage-style furnishings. All 12 rooms have a washbasin; shared showers and toilets are off the hall. There's a guest kitchen for simple preparations such as sandwiches and coffee, and lounge areas where guests can relax.

Singles/doubles cost 350/495 kr including breakfast.

Hornbæk's biggest hotel is the 50 room *Hotel Trouville* (☎ 49 70 22 00, fax 49 70 18 27, email info@trouville.dk, Kystvej 20, 3100 Hornbæk), just inland of the dunes on the western side of town. Singles/doubles with bath, TV, phone and balcony cost 670/815 kr including breakfast. The hotel has facilities including an indoor swimming pool, a sauna, a solarium, a bar and an expensive restaurant. It's part of the Best Western chain.

If you're interested in renting a *summer house* by the week, the main local agency is Hornbæk Sommerhusudlejning (☎ 49 70 20 20, fax 49 70 20 98), Hornebyvej 62E, 3100 Hornbæk.

Places to Eat

Eating opportunities down at the harbour include a little shop, a fish market and *Havnegrillen*, a fast-food stand selling hot dogs, burgers, fish sandwiches and Underground ice cream.

Seher's Pizza & Grillbar (Nordre Strandvej 336) serves pizza and pasta that costs 30 kr at lunchtime, a bit more at other times.

Hansens Café (Havnevej 19) is in the town's oldest house, a sod-roofed half-timbered building with a pleasant pub-like atmosphere. The handwritten menu changes daily but you can expect to find good Danish food at moderate prices.

You can pick up groceries at the *Super Brugsen* or at the nearby *Favør* supermarket at Nordre Strandvej 349. There's a bakery, *Wiener Bageriet*, midway between the two and a good fruit stand, *Julius Frugt & Grønt*, next to Den Danske Bank.

Getting There & Away

Trains between Helsingør and Hornbæk (25 minutes) run about twice hourly every day, while bus No 340 (28 minutes) does the same run hourly. Either way the fare is 16.50 kr. Bus No 340 also runs to Gilleleje (22 kr, 20 minutes) and buses No 306, 336 and 339 go to Hillerød.

An Inspiring Rescue

In 1774, Hornbæk fishermen came to the rescue of British captain Thomas Brauwn, whose ship was being battered by a raging storm. These unhesitant Danes, braving treacherous seas, so inspired their countryfolk that a popular play, *Fiskerne*, was written about them by the lyricist poet Johannes Ewald. A song taken from the play became Denmark's national anthem. The rescue was also immortalised by the painter CW Eckersberg, who used it as a theme in a number of his paintings.

GILLELEJE

Zealand's northernmost town, Gilleleje has lots of attractive straw-roofed houses as well as the island's largest fishing harbour. Despite its size, the harbour has an appealing character, filled as it is with colourful wooden-hulled fishing boats.

Many of the attractions the town has to offer to visitors are in one way or another connected with fishing, including smokehouses along the harbour and a little dockside fish auction that can be viewed by early-risers.

It's a five minute walk north from the train station to the harbour. Although they are not on a par with those at Hornbæk or Tisvildeleje, there are public beaches on either side of town.

Information

The Gilleleje Turistbureau (☎ 48 30 01 74, fax 48 30 34 74) is in the town centre at Hovedgade 6, 3250 Gilleleje, 200m east of the train station. It's open from 10 am to 5 pm (to 6 pm in the summer high season) Monday to Saturday between May and August, and from 9 am to 4 pm on weekdays and 9 am to noon on Saturday during the rest of the year.

Den Danske Bank is in the centre of town at Vesterbrogade 6. The post office is at Stationsvej 6, just north of the train station.

Things to See & Do

The local museum of fishing, **Det Gamle Fiskerhus/Skibshallen** at Hovedgade 49, about 400m east of the tourist office, features a fisherman's house dating from 1850 and displays about the lives of fisherfolk from the Middle Ages onward.

Midway between the turistbureau and Det Gamle Fiskerhus/Skibshallen, on the northern side of Hovedgade, is **Gilleleje Kirke**, originally built from timbers salvaged from shipwrecks in the early 16th century to minister to seamen. The church boasts a 17th century hand-carved pulpit and a painted altar dating from 1834. In 1943 Danish Jews waiting to be rowed across to neutral Sweden took refuge in the church attic; a displayed Medal of Merit from the Jewish community honours the local efforts.

The **Gilleleje Museum**, on the western side of town at Vesterbrogade 56, is dedicated to the history of the town, from the Middle Ages to the advent of summer tourism.

There are **coastal trails** heading in both directions from the town centre. The trail to the west, which starts near the intersection of Nordre Strandvej and Vesterbrogade, leads about 1.75km to a stone **memorial** dedicated to the Danish philosopher Søren Kierkegaard, who used to make visits to this coast.

The trail to the east, which begins off Hovedgade at the eastern side of the fishing museum, leads 2.5km to the site where two lighthouses with coal-burning beacons were erected run 1772. In 1899 the western lighthouse was modernised with rotating lenses and the eastern one, no longer needed, was abandoned. In 1980 the eastern lighthouse, **Nakkehoved Østre Fyr**, was restored as a museum. You can get to this lighthouse on the coastal footpath or by turning north off route 237 onto Fyrvejen. The two museums in town and the lighthouse are open from 1 to 4 pm daily except Tuesday between mid-June and mid-September; a single ticket costing 20 kr (free for children) covers all three sights.

Places to Stay

There's an inland camping ground, *Gilleleje Camping* (☎ 49 71 97 55, *Bregnerødvej 21, 3250 Gilleleje*), 3km south-east of the town centre.

Staff at the Gilleleje tourist office can book double *rooms* in private homes, costing from 240 to 400 kr.

The 25 room *Hotel Strand* (☎ 48 30 05 12, email hotelstr@post.7.tele.dk, *Vesterbrogade 4, 3250 Gilleleje*) is in the centre of town, a short walk west from the harbour. There are three rooms that are a tad small but have showers (toilets are off the hall) and cost 360/550 kr for singles/doubles. Other rooms are larger and more modern with bath, balcony, TV and phone and cost 410/680 kr. Rates include breakfast.

Places to Eat

Rogeriet Bornholm, a smokehouse on the harbour, sells smoked fish by the piece; a herring makes a tasty snack and costs about 10 kr. At the nearby *Adamsen's Fisk* you can buy affordable deli items such as fish cakes, rollmops and shrimp salad to take away.

Hos Karen & Marie (*Nordre Havnevej 3*) is an excellent little seafood restaurant in a period building overlooking the harbour. At lunchtime there's a great sampler plate that includes pickled herring, butter-fried plaice, salmon, pork tenderloin and brie; it costs 129 kr. Dinner is more expensive. It's open from noon to 4.30 pm for lunch and from 6 to 10 pm for dinner.

Getting There & Away

Trains run betwen Hillerød and Gilleleje (27.50 kr, 31 minutes) about twice hourly on weekdays, hourly at weekends, and between Helsingør and Gilleleje (33 kr, 40 minutes) about twice hourly every day.

There's no rail link between Gilleleje and Tisvildeleje but all of the north coast towns are linked by bus. Bus No 340 connects Gilleleje with Hornbæk (22 kr, 20 minutes) and Helsingør (33 kr, 50 minutes). Bus No 363 connects Gilleleje with Tisvildeleje, but it's a roundabout hour-long ride (16.50 kr).

Gilleleje's bus and train stations are adjacent to each other.

TISVILDELEJE

Tisvildeleje is a pleasant little seaside village with an invitingly slow pace, a comfortable hostel and fine nature walks. It's bordered by a broad stretch of sandy beach that's backed by low dunes; the nearest beach is just a short walk from the train station but the most glorious sweep is at the end of Hovedgaden, 1km west of the village centre. That beach has a large car park, a changing room, toilets and an ice-cream kiosk.

Inland of the beach is Tisvilde Hegn, a windswept forest of twisted trees and heather-covered hills that extends southwest from Tisvildeleje for more than 8km. Much of this enchanting forest was planted in the 18th century to stabilise the sand drifts that were threatening to turn the area into desert.

Information

Both the post office and the seasonal tourist office (☎ 48 70 74 51), Banevej 8, are in Tisvilde train station. The tourist office is open from 10 am to 5 pm Monday to Saturday between 1 June and 31 August.

Walks in Tisvilde Hegn

From the beach parking area at the end of Hovedgaden you can walk, either along the beach or on a dirt path through the woods, about 3km south to **Troldeskoven** (Witch Wood), an area of ancient trees that have been sculpted by the wind into haunting shapes. On the way make a short detour east at Brantebjerg for a nice hill-top view.

Tisvilde Hegn has many other trails, including one to **Asserbo Slotsruin**, the moat-encircled ruins of a former manor house and a 12th century monastery, which are near the southern boundary of the forest. The south-western part of Tisvilde Hegn merges with **Asserbo Plantage**, a wooded area that borders lake Arresø. Trail maps are available free from the tourist office.

Places to Stay

The cheery 272 bed hostel, **Tisvildeleje Vandrerhjem** (☎ 48 70 98 50, fax 48 70 98 97, email shc@helene.dk, Bygmarken 30, 3220 Tisvildeleje), is 1km east of the town centre and within walking distance of a sandy beach that's shallow and safe for children. This hostel is the centrepiece of the Sankt Helene complex, which runs nature courses and thematic holidays for schoolchildren and other groups. Its 12-hectare grounds have jogging paths, walking trails, tennis courts, sports fields and playgrounds. Most of the complex is accessible to people in wheelchairs.

Hostel accommodation is provided in modern rooms, each with four beds, a little sitting area and a bathroom. Rates are 90 kr for a dorm bed or 300/360 kr to use a room as a single/double. There are also cabins containing up to five beds (360 kr) and apartments accommodating from four to six people that are rented by the week and cost from 1950 to 5200 kr, depending on the season. Campers can pitch a tent in the field adjacent to the reception office for 25 kr, including use of the showers and kitchen.

The hostel is open year-round but reservations are often essential from May to mid-September. There's a food kiosk on site and a reasonably priced restaurant serving three meals a day. If you're arriving by train, get off at Godhavns station, one stop before Tisvilde station; the hostel is just north of the tracks. If arriving by car, turn north on Godhavnsvej.

The tourist office maintains a list of half a dozen families that rent **rooms** costing from 200 to 450 kr for doubles, 50 kr less for singles; staff at the tourist office can also book summer cottages.

The 29 room **Tisvildeleje Strand Hotel** (☎ 48 70 71 19, fax 48 70 71 77, Hovedgaden 75, 3220 Tisvildeleje) is in the centre of town and within walking distance of the beach. Singles/doubles with shared bath cost 350/550 kr while rooms with private bath are 425/700 kr, all rates including breakfast.

Places to Eat

There's a small cluster of eateries in the town centre on Hovedgaden, including a good bakery, *Tisvildeleje Bageri*, at No 60, a little *grocery shop* on the opposite side of the street and *Tisvildeleje Caféen* at No 55, which serves good, moderately priced fare.

The trendiest place in town is the *Bio Bistro (Hovedgaden 38)*, a café at the cinema offering good food and occasional live music. Two-course dinners cost around 235 kr but there's usually a daily special costing half that price.

Getting There & Away

Bus No 363 runs between Gilleleje and Tisvildeleje (16.50 kr, one hour) but it takes a circuitous route. Trains run between Hillerød and Tisvildeleje (31 minutes, 27.50 kr) once an hour; there are a few extra trains in the early morning and the late afternoon.

Getting Around

Bicycles can be hired both at the hostel and in the town centre from the Hydro petrol station, Hovedgaden 53, a few minutes walk west of the train station. Both places charge 50/200 kr per day/week.

Fjord Towns

North Zealand has two interlinking fjords, the Isefjord and the Roskilde Fjord, that connect with the Kattegat at the town of Hundested. The largest towns in the region, Frederiksværk and Frederikssund, border the Roskilde Fjord and are along the main Tisvildeleje-Roskilde road route.

HUNDESTED

The main attraction in Hundested, a small town at the mouth of the Isefjord, is the home built by Knud Rasmussen (1879-1933), Denmark's most famous arctic explorer. Located near the lighthouse, at Knud Rasmussensvej 9, the home has been turned into a museum, **Knud Rasmussens Hus**. It contains Rasmussen's original furnishings, although the thousands of archaeological artefacts that he collected on his expeditions are kept in Nationalmuseet in Copenhagen. It's open from 11 am to 4 pm daily between mid-April and mid-October; admission costs 10 kr.

The Lynæs area, a few kilometres south of Hundested, is a **windsurfing** mecca with good wind conditions as well as shallow-water areas suitable for beginners. Lynæs Surfcenter (☎ 47 98 01 00) on Lynæs Havnevej has windsurfing gear for hire and offers lessons. There's a frequent train between Hundested and Hillerød (38.50 kr, 45 minutes) that runs about twice an hour.

FREDERIKSVÆRK

Frederiksværk, at the north of the Roskilde Fjord, is Denmark's oldest industrial town, founded in 1756 by order of King Frederik V, from whom the town takes its name. At that time a canal was dug between the Roskilde Fjord and Arresø lake to provide water power for mills, a gunpowder factory and a cannon foundry.

The tourist office (☎ 47 72 30 01) is in Gjethuset, a former cannon foundry on Torvet that has been converted into a **cultural centre** with changing art exhibits.

Fittingly, Frederiksværk's two museums, both near the canal in the centre of town, are dedicated to the town's industrial history. **Frederiksværk Bymuseum** near Torvet features artefacts and displays on Frederiksværk's early industries, while the open-air **Krudtværksmuseum** (Gunpowder Factory Museum) on Krudtværksalleén consists of period buildings equipped with the original machinery and a working water mill. Both are open from noon to 4 pm Tuesday to Sunday and admission to each costs 10 kr.

The town sits on the western shore of Arresø which, at 41 sq km, is Denmark's largest lake. Leisurely **boat excursions** (☎ 47 72 30 01; 50 kr) cruise the lake on summer afternoons.

If you need to spend the night here, Frederiksværk has a convenient combination hostel and camping ground, *Frederiksværk Vandrerhjem & Campingplads (☎ 47 77*

07 25, Strandgade 30), right by the canal in the centre of town; dorm beds cost 80 kr, singles/doubles cost 160/210 kr.

Frederiksværk is on the rail line between Hundested (18 minutes) and Hillerød (28 minutes).

FREDERIKSSUND

Frederikssund, at the narrowest part of the Roskilde Fjord, is best known to visitors for the **Viking play** performed from mid-June to early July by a troupe of 200 local actors. The performance takes place in a large open-air theatre on the fjord, a 10 minute walk south of the train station. Admission costs 90 kr, or 130 kr if you want to join the feast that follows the play. For information or bookings call ☎ 47 31 06 85.

Also in town is the **JF Willumsens Museum**, at Jenriksvej 4, which contains paintings, sculpture and drawings by Jens Ferdinand Willumsen (1863-1958), one of Denmark's leading symbolists. The mu-seum also displays some works by other artists which belonged to Willumsen's private collection. It's open from 10 am to 4 pm daily and admission costs 20 kr.

Frederikssund is at the end of the S-train H line, a 45 minute (38.50 kr) ride from Copenhagen.

Roskilde

Roskilde, Denmark's first capital, was a thriving trade centre throughout the Middle Ages. It was also the site of Zealand's first Christian church, built by Viking king Harald Bluetooth in 980 AD.

In 1026 Canute I, in a fit of anger over a chess match, had his brother-in-law Ulf Jarl assassinated in that church. Ulf's widow, Canute's sister Estrid, insisted on having the wooden stave church in which her husband was ambushed torn down, and then donated property for the construction of a new stone church. The foundations of that early stone church are beneath the floor of

---

Roskilde Festival

Northern Europe's largest music festival rocks Roskilde for four consecutive days each summer on either the last weekend in June or the first weekend in July.

More than 150 rock, techno and world music bands play on seven stages. In 1998, the festival's 28th year, the line-up included Black Sabbath, the Beastie Boys, Bob Dylan, Iggy Pop, Marilyn Manson, Tori Amos, Portishead and The Verve. Over the years the promoters have also been particularly astute at presenting new trends in rock and at booking lesser-known groups (such as UB40 and Talking Heads) who have later gone on to stardom.

The Roskilde Festival is more than just music – it's a huge spirited bash with lots of drinking and partying. The average age of the festival-goers is 24 and about half come from other countries, particularly Germany, Sweden, Finland, the Netherlands, Norway and Belgium. There are stalls selling everything from tattoos to fast food but you may want to bring some food supplies of your own as prices are high.

The profits from the Roskilde Festival are distributed to charitable causes both at home and abroad. Festival tickets cost around 800 kr, including camping at the site, and can be purchased in Denmark through BilletNet (☎ 38 88 70 22). Tickets can also be obtained by calling ☎ 020 623 73 21 in Amsterdam, ☎ 03-233 5669 in Antwerp, ☎ 01787-222233 in Essex, UK, or ☎ 09-694 1166 in Helsinki. Tickets are limited to 80,000 and advance sales start in December. It's also possible to buy a ticket at the gate for just the last day of the festival. More information can be obtained by calling ☎ 70 10 17 17 in Denmark or by visiting the Web site at www.roskildefestival.dk.

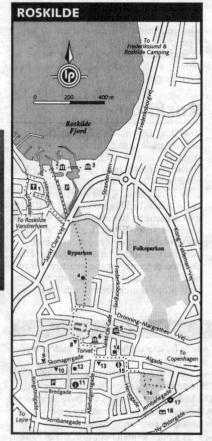

ROSKILDE

PLACES TO STAY
14 Hotel Prindsen

PLACES TO EAT
8 Raadhus-Kælderen
9 Jensens Bøfhus
10 Strandberg Supermarket
13 Den Gamle Bagergård

OTHER
1 Sankt Jørgensbjerg Kirke
2 Museumsø
3 Vikingeskibshallen
4 Site of Medieval Town
5 Roskilde Museum
6 Palæet; Museet for
   Samtidskunst; Palæsamlingerne
7 Roskilde Domkirke
11 Roskilde Turistbureau
12 JAS Cykler
15 Bank
16 Old Churchyard
17 Train Station
18 Post Office

the present-day Roskilde Domkirke (cathedral). Estrid and her son Svend Estridsen are among the multitude of Danish royals buried in the cathedral.

As the centre of Danish Catholicism, medieval Roskilde had not only a cathedral but also nearly 20 churches and monasteries. After the Reformation swept Denmark in 1536 the monasteries and most of the churches were demolished. Consequently the town, which had been in decline since the capital moved to Copenhagen in the early 15th century, saw its population shrink radically.

Today Roskilde is a likeable, low-profile town with 52,000 inhabitants. Only 30km west of Copenhagen, it is on Denmark's main east-west train route.

Information

Tourist Office The Roskilde Turistbureau (☎ 46 35 27 00, fax 46 35 14 74) is at Gullandsstræde 15, Postboks 637, 4000 Roskilde; its Web site is at www.destination-roskilde.dk. In July and August it's open from 9 am to 6 pm Monday to Friday, from 9 am to 3 pm on Saturday and from 10 am to 2 pm on Sunday. During the rest of the year it's open from 9 am to 5 pm on weekdays (to 4 pm on Friday in autumn and winter) and from 10 am to 1 pm on Saturday.

Money There are a couple of banks along Algade just east of Torvet.

Post The post office is at Jernbanegade 3, to the south-west of the train station.

Walking Tour

Roskilde's most notable sights are within walking distance of each other. **Roskilde Domkirke** is on Torvet, a 10 minute walk north-west from the train station: cut diagonally across the old churchyard and go left along Algade.

From the cathedral, you can take a 15 minute walk through the extensive green belt of Byparken on the way down to **Vikingeskibshallen**, the Viking ship museum. The route begins at the northern side of the cathedral and crosses a field where wildflowers blanket the unexcavated remains of Roskilde's original **medieval town**. The rectangular depression at this site marks the spot where the 12th century church Sankt Hans Kirke was torn down during the Reformation.

After visiting Vikingeskibshallen, a five minute walk west along the harbour will bring you to the **Sankt Jørgensbjerg quarter**, where the cobbled walkway Kirkegade leads through a neighbourhood of old thatched-roofed houses and into the courtyard of the hill-top **Sankt Jørgensbjerg Kirke**. This church, the nave of which dates from the 11th century, is one of the oldest in Denmark.

Roskilde Domkirke

Although most of Roskilde's medieval buildings have vanished in fires over the centuries, this imposing cathedral still dominates the city centre. Started in 1170 by Bishop Absalon, Roskilde Domkirke has been rebuilt and added to so many times that it represents a millennium of Danish architectural styles.

Roskilde Domkirke boasts tall spires, a splendid interior and the crypts of 37 Danish kings and queens. Some of the crypts are

NORTH ZEALAND

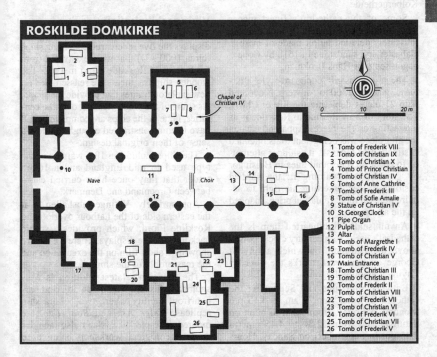

ROSKILDE DOMKIRKE

Chapel of Christian IV

Nave

Choir

0 10 20 m

1 Tomb of Frederik VIII
2 Tomb of Christian IX
3 Tomb of Christian X
4 Tomb of Prince Christian
5 Tomb of Christian IV
6 Tomb of Anne Cathrine
7 Tomb of Frederik III
8 Tomb of Sofie Amalie
9 Statue of Christian IV
10 St George Clock
11 Pipe Organ
12 Pulpit
13 Altar
14 Tomb of Margrethe I
15 Tomb of Frederik IV
16 Tomb of Christian V
17 Main Entrance
18 Tomb of Christian III
19 Tomb of Christian I
20 Tomb of Frederik II
21 Tomb of Christian VIII
22 Tomb of Frederik VII
23 Tomb of Christian VI
24 Tomb of Frederik VI
25 Tomb of Christian VII
26 Tomb of Frederik V

spectacularly embellished and guarded by marble statues of knights and women in mourning, while others are simple unadorned stone coffins. There's something quite awesome about being able to stand next to the bones of so many of Scandinavia's most powerful historical figures.

Of particular interest is the chapel of King Christian IV, off the northern side of the cathedral. It contains the coffin of Christian flanked by his young son, Prince Christian, and his wife, Anne Cathrine, as well as the brass coffins of his successor, Frederik III, and his wife, Queen Sofie Amalie. The bronze statue of Christian IV beside the entranceway is the work of Bertel Thorvaldsen, while the huge wall-sized paintings, encased in trompe l'oeil frames, were created by Wilhelm Marstrand and include a classic scene depicting Christian IV rallying the troops aboard the warship *Trinity* during the 1644 battle of Kolbergerheide.

Some of the cathedral's finest pieces were installed by Christian IV, including the intricately detailed pulpit made of marble, alabaster and sandstone in 1610 by Copenhagen sculptor Hans Brokman.

The enormous gilt 'cupboard-style' altarpiece, made in 1560 in Antwerp, is adorned with 21 plates depicting the life of Christ. The story of how it came to Roskilde is as interesting as the piece. Apparently when the altarpiece was being sent to its intended destination of Gdansk, its shipper attempted to cheat on the sound dues in Helsingør by grossly undervaluing it; the shrewd customs officer, asserting his right to acquire items at their valuation price, snapped up the altarpiece.

An unusually lighthearted item is the cathedral's early 16th century clock, poised above the entrance, on which a tiny St George on horseback marks the hour by slaying a yelping dragon.

Between mid-June and September the cathedral is open from 9 am to 4.45 pm Monday to Friday, from 9 am to noon on Saturday and from 12.30 to 4.45 pm (to 3.45 pm in September) on Sunday. Hours

are the same in spring except that it's closed on Monday. Between October and March it's open from 10 am to 3.45 pm Tuesday to Friday, from 11.30 am to 3.45 pm on Saturday and from 12.30 to 3.45 pm on Sunday.

It's not unusual for the cathedral to be closed on Saturday for weddings and occasionally on other days for funerals. You can check in advance whether it's open by calling the turistbureau.

Admission costs 12 kr (children 6 kr). In summer, tours are conducted by multilingual guides on weekdays at 11.30 am and 1.30 pm, Saturday at 11 am and Sunday at 1.30 pm; tours cost 25 kr.

Free concerts given on the splendid 16th century Baroque pipe organ are held at 8 pm on Thursday in June, July and August.

Roskilde Domkirke is one of Denmark's UNESCO-designated World Heritage Sites.

Vikingeskibshallen

This well-presented Viking ship museum displays the five reconstructed Viking ships (circa 1000 AD) that were excavated from the bottom of Roskilde Fjord in 1962. The wooden ship fragments are reassembled on new skeleton frames that provide the shape. As some of the wood was lost over the centuries, none of the ships are complete but all have been reconstructed enough to allow a sense of their original design.

The ships include an 18m warship of the type used to raid England and a 16.5m trader that may once have carried cargo between Greenland and Denmark.

Appropriately, Vikingeskibshallen is at the eastern side of the harbour overlooking Roskilde Fjord, which provides a scenic backdrop for the displays. There's a theatre showing a short film on the excavation and the reassembly of the ships.

The museum's latest addition is **Museumsø** (Museum Island), an adjacent harbourfront facility where two Viking ship replicas, *Helge Ask* and *Roar Ege*, are moored. The pier-like island also includes an archaeological workshop being used

Excavating the Fjord

Towards the end of the Viking era, the narrower necks of Roskilde Fjord were purposely blocked to prevent raids by Norwegian fleets. The five Viking ships that are now displayed at Vikingeskibshallen in Roskilde were thought to have been deliberately sunk in one such channel and then piled with rocks to make a reinforced barrier similar to an underwater stone wall. Although people had long suspected that there was a ship beneath the ridge of stones, folklore had led them to believe it was a single ship sunk by Queen Margrethe in the 15th century.

It wasn't until researchers from the national museum made a series of exploratory dives in the late 1950s that it was discovered that there were several ships at the site and that they dated from the Viking period. Excavations began in 1962 when a cofferdam was built around the ships in the middle of the fjord and pumps were used to drain sea water from the site. Within just four months archaeologists were able to take apart the mound of stones and excavate the ships, whose wooden hulks were now in thousands of pieces. The ship fragments were then reassembled within the purpose-built museum that opened on the harbourfront in Roskilde in 1969.

In the mid-1990s, with the deepening of the harbour and the construction of a new artificial island west of the museum, nine more ships were discovered, seven dating from the Middle Ages and two from the Viking period. The largest is a warship estimated to be 38m long and nearly 1000 years old.

to reconstruct excavated ships, a boatyard where more Viking ship replicas are being built, workshops where schoolchildren can try their hand at sailmaking and other maritime crafts, and a cafeteria.

Vikingeskibshallen is open daily from 9 am to 5 pm April to October and daily from 10 am to 4 pm November to March. Admission costs 40 kr (children 25 kr, family admission 85 kr). In summer the museum also sponsors daily hour-long fjord sailing trips; call ☎ 46 30 02 00 for more information.

Other City Museums
Palæet (the Palace), an attractive 18th century building fronting Torvet, is a former bishops' residence that now houses **Museet for Samtidskunst** (Museum of Contemporary Art), a small museum with changing exhibits, and **Palæsamlingerne** (Palace Collections), containing 18th and 19th century paintings that once belonged to wealthy Roskilde merchants. Museet for Samtidskunst is open from 11 am to 5 pm Tuesday

to Friday and from noon to 4 pm at weekends; admission costs 10 kr (children free). Palæsamlingerne are open from 11 am to 4 pm daily between mid-May and mid-September, and from 1 to 3 pm on Saturday and Sunday during the rest of the year; admission costs 5 kr (children 2 kr).

In addition the **Roskilde Museum**, Sankt Olsgade 18, covers Roskilde's history in displays ranging from the Stone Age up to the contemporary 'rock age' of the Roskilde Festival. It's open from 11 am to 4 pm daily. Admission costs 20 kr (children free).

Cycling Tours
If you want to do some serious exploring of the region by bicycle, consider picking up a copy of *Cykelruter og udflugter i Roskilde Amt* (Bicycle Routes and Excursions in the County of Roskilde), a good detailed cycling map of Roskilde county published by Dansk Cyklist Forbund. This map, which is printed in both English and Danish-language versions, suggests tours into the countryside and gives brief descriptions of

the places you'll encounter along the way. It costs 50 kr and can be purchased at the Roskilde Turistbureau and in bookshops. Bicycles can be rented from JAS Cykler (☎ 46 35 04 20), Gullandsstræde 3.

Places to Stay

Most travellers visit Roskilde on a day trip but, should you want to stay overnight, there are a few options.

The three star **Roskilde Camping** (☎ 46 75 79 96, Baunehøjvej 7, Veddelev) is by a sandy beach right on Roskilde Fjord, 3km north of Vikingeskibshallen. It's open from early April to mid-September and is served by bus No 603 from the train station.

The 92 bed hostel, **Roskilde Vandrerhjem** (☎ 46 35 21 84, fax 46 32 66 90, Hørhusene 61, 4000 Roskilde), is 3km west of the city centre, served by bus No 601 or 604. Dorm beds cost 90 kr, while family rooms sleeping one to four people cost from 180 to 360 kr. It's open between 1 May and 1 October. A new hostel, to be built adjacent to Vikingeskibshallen, is being planned.

Staff at the turistbureau can book *rooms* in private homes; singles/doubles cost from 125/250 kr, plus a 25 kr booking fee; breakfast is optional and costs 40 kr per person. Rooms can be booked in town, in the suburbs and on farms.

In the city centre is **Hotel Prindsen** (☎ 46 35 80 10, fax 46 35 81 10, Algade 13, 4000 Roskilde), Denmark's oldest continuously operating hotel. First opened in 1695, its guest list reads like a who's who of great Danes, from King Frederik VII to Hans Christian Andersen. As befits an old hotel, the rooms are different sizes and have varied décor, but all have a bath, a phone, a TV and a minibar. Singles/doubles cost 825/915 kr on weekdays and 685/735 kr at weekends. Between mid-June and mid-August there's a special 695 kr summer rate that covers a room sleeping up to two adults and two children. Rates include breakfast. There's a restaurant, a bar and a sauna. The hotel is a member of the Best Western chain.

Places to Eat

On Skomagergade, the pedestrian street that runs west from Torvet, there are numerous places to eat. The **Strandberg** supermarket (*Skomagergade 11*), a large grocery shop with a good wine section, has a rooftop cafeteria with an interesting city view and a varied menu, including a 29 kr daily special. For a few kroner more, you can get a simple steak lunch at the nearby **Jensen's Bøfhus** (*Skomagergade 38*).

Den Gamle Bagergård (*Algade 6*) is a good bakery with pastries and takeaway sandwiches. On Wednesday and Saturday mornings there's a **market** on Torvet selling fresh produce as well as handicrafts and flowers.

For a treat, the atmospheric **Raadhus-Kælderen**, in the cellar of the old town hall (circa 1430), just south of the cathedral, offers tempting 68 kr lunch deals, including fish fillet with shrimp and asparagus, from 11 am to 5 pm. Evening meals are more expensive (around 150 kr) and feature the likes of duck in orange sauce or filet mignon.

Getting There & Away

Trains from Copenhagen to Roskilde are frequent (25 minutes, 38.50 kr). Trains also run between Roskilde and Køge (33 kr, 25 minutes) and Næstved (43 kr, 42 minutes). There are lockers at the train station.

If you're coming from Copenhagen by car, route 21 leads to Roskilde. Upon approaching the city, exit onto route 156, which leads into the centre. There are car parks south of Strandberg Supermarket and down by the Viking ship museum.

LEJRE

The countryside on the outskirts of Lejre, a village 8km south-west of Roskilde, has two sightseeing attractions that could be combined in an afternoon outing.

Lejre Forsøgscenter

This 'archaeological experimental centre' contains a reconstructed Iron Age village where Danish families can volunteer to spend their summer holidays as 'prehistoric families', using technology and dressed in clothing from that period. The reconstructed houses they live in and the tools they use are modelled on finds from archaeological excavations around Denmark.

The centre, which is a popular destination for school outings, also has craft demonstrations and a small cottage-farm area where the lives of 19th century Danish farmers are re-enacted. In summer children can paddle dugout canoes and partake in a few other hands-on activities such as grinding flour. Although the centre is open between 1 May and mid-September from 10 am to 5 pm daily, the majority of the activities take place in the summer high season when the 'prehistoric families' are present.

Admission to Lejre Forsøgscenter (☎ 46 48 08 78) costs 50 kr (children 30 kr).

Ledreborg Slot

This grand manor house, set on a knoll overlooking 80 hectares of lawns and woods, was built by Count Johan Ludvig Holstein in 1739 and has been home to the Holstein-Ledreborg family ever since. The interior has hardly changed since the house was originally decorated and consequently it's considered one of the finest period manor houses in Denmark.

Visitors are required to put on booties at the entrance to prevent damage to the marble and parquet floors. The house is chock-full of antique furniture, gilded mirrors, chandeliers, oil paintings and wall tapestries. One of the most superb rooms is the banquet room, which was designed by architect Nicolai Eigtved, the creator of Copenhagen's Amalienborg Slot. Also in the house is a chapel, constructed by JC Krieger in 1745, which served as the parish church until 1899.

Ledreborg (☎ 46 48 00 38) is open to visitors from 11 am to 5 pm daily between mid-June and August, and from 11 am to 5 pm on Sunday in May, early June and September. Admission costs 45 kr (children 20 kr).

Getting There & Away

From Roskilde it's a short train ride to Lejre station, where the seasonal bus No 233 (10 kr) continues to both Ledreborg Slot and Lejre Forsøgscenter.

If you have your own transport, from Roskilde take Ringstedvej (route 14), turn right on route 155 and then almost immediately turn left onto Ledreborg Allé. Follow the signs to Ledreborg, 6km away, where a long drive lined by old elm trees leads to the entrance. Lejre Forsøgscenter is 2km farther along the same road.

Southern Zealand

Steeped in history, southern Zealand has played an important role in the shaping of Denmark since the Viking era. It was a stomping ground in medieval times of significant historical characters such as Bishop Absalon and the royal Valdemar family. In the 17th century the area was the stage for some of the most important battles of the lengthy wars between Denmark and Sweden. The most pivotal defeat in Danish history was played out here in 1658 when the Swedish king Gustave marched across southern Zealand en route to Copenhagen, where he forced a treaty that nearly cost Denmark its sovereignty.

Today the region contains a mix of peaceful towns, rural villages and patchwork farmland. Highlights of southern Zealand include: two notably engaging towns, Køge and Sorø; one of Denmark's most impressive Viking sites, the 1000-year-old ring fortress at Trelleborg; and some interesting medieval churches.

If you're travelling across the region between Køge and Korsør using your own transport, the rural route 150 makes a fine alternative to zipping along on the E20 motorway. Not only is it a slower, greener route but it will take you right into the most interesting towns and villages.

KØGE

Køge has a rich history stretching back to 1288, when it was granted its municipal charter by King Erik VI. With its large natural harbour, Køge quickly developed into a thriving fishing and trade centre.

In 1677 one of the most important naval engagements of the Danish-Swedish wars was fought in the waters off Køge. Known as the Battle of Køge Bay, it made a legend of Danish admiral Niels Juel, who resoundingly defeated the attacking Swedish navy and thwarted their attempted invasion.

Today the harbour still plays an important role in Køge's economy, having been

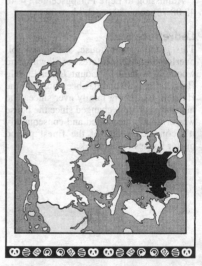

Highlights

- Wander around Sorø, a charming town with a rich cultural background
- Explore the Viking past at the fascinating ring fortress at Trelleborg
- Stroll through the well-preserved historic quarter of the ancient town of Køge
- Poke around the rural hamlet of Vallø, with its castle and woodland
- Enjoy centuries-old frescoes at Sankt Bendts Kirke, Ringsted's medieval church

developed into a modern commercial facility. Although parts of the city have been industrialised, the authorities in Køge have done a superb job of retaining the period character of its central historic quarter. The narrow streets that radiate from Torvet, the town square, are lined with old buildings, some having survived a sweeping fire in

The interior of Frederiksborg Slot, Hillerød's Renaissance castle, matches its magnificent exterior.

NED FRIARY

NED FRIARY

DAMIEN SIMONIS

NED FRIARY

North Zealand's historic towns showcase the country's vernacular architecture.

NED FRIARY

Danish families volunteer to live in the reconstructed Iron Age village at Lejre Forsøgscenter.

A fine beach is one reason not to pass by the attractions offered by the port town of Korsør.

Trelleborg's archaeological sites offer clues to the true nature of everyday Viking life.

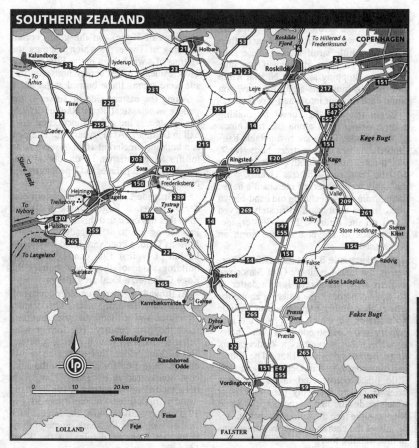

SOUTHERN ZEALAND

1633, and many others built in the construction boom spawned by that blaze.

Information

Tourist Office Køge Turistbureau (☎ 56 65 58 00, fax 56 65 59 84), near Torvet at Vestergade 1, 4600 Køge, distributes a free 70 page booklet, with English and German translations, describing the town's sights. The turistbureau is open from 9 am to 5 pm on weekdays year-round. Saturday opening hours are from 9 am to 3 pm between June and August, from 10 am to 1 pm the rest of the year.

Money The Unibank on the eastern side of Torvet has a 24 hour ATM that accepts international bank and credit cards.

Post The post office is at Jernstøbervænget 2, west of Torvet. It's open from 10 am to 5 pm on weekdays (to 5.30 pm on Thursday) and from 10 am to 12.30 pm on Saturday.

Walking Tour

Most of Køge's finest historic sites are within easy walking distance of each other. A pleasant little stroll visiting these sites lasts about an hour, although if you take your time, stopping at Sankt Nicolai Kirke and the two museums along the way, you could easily turn it into a half-day outing.

Begin the walk at Torvet by making a short detour west along the first block of **Vestergade**. There are two notable half-timbered houses on this street: house **No 7**, which dates from the 16th century, and **No 16** (the restaurant Richters Gaard), a remarkably well-preserved merchant's house dating from 1644, featuring old hand-blown glass in the doors and intricately carved detail on the timbers. From Vestergade, return back to Torvet and head north on Kirkestræde.

At **Kirkestræde 3**, just metres from Torvet, is the house built by Oluf Sandersen and his wife Margareta Jørgensdatter in 1638, as is noted in the lettering above the gate. Other timber-framed houses include **Kirkestræde 13**, which dates from the 16th century, and Kirkestræde 10, a 17th century house that has served as a kindergarten, **Køge Børneasyl**, since 1856. The oldest half-timbered house in Denmark, a modest little place constructed in 1527 with a brick front and a steeply tiled roof, is at **Kirkestræde 20**. Just to the north is **Sankt Nicolai Kirke** (see the following sections for details of the church and the two museums in this walking tour).

Turn right onto Katekismusgade and you'll immediately come to the art museum **Køge Skitsesamling**. In the grounds near the museum is a bronze sculpture by Svend Rathsack, of a young boy with scurrying lizards.

Immediately north of the museum, at Nørregade 31, is an attractive red timbered house built in 1612 that now holds a **goldsmith shop**. Continuing south on Nørregade, you'll pass more houses built in the early 17th century: No 5, which now houses the **Arnold Busck bookshop**, and No 4, home to the **Køge Museum**.

Look for the marble plaque marked **Kiøge Huskors** (Kiøge and Kjøge are old spellings of Køge), on the green corner building at Torvet 2, which honours the victims of a witch-hunt in the 17th century. Two residents of an earlier house on this site were among those burned at the stake.

Along the eastern side of Torvet is the yellow neoclassical **Køge Rådhus** which, it's boasted, is the oldest functioning town hall in Denmark. At the rear of this complex is a building erected in 1600 to serve as an inn for King Christian IV on journeys between his royal palaces in Copenhagen and Nykøbing.

At Brogade 1, by the south-eastern corner of Torvet, is **Køge Apotek**, a chemist shop that has occupied this site since 1660. Proceeding south, at Brogade 7 is **Oluf I Jensens Gård**, a courtyard lined with a collection of typical 19th century merchant buildings; one of these now houses the **Køge Galleriet**, a local art gallery.

At Brogade 19 there's an older courtyard, **Hugos Gård**, featuring some 17th century structures and a medieval brick building from the 14th century. The former wine cellar of the latter now houses a wine bar, Hugos Vinkjælder, that makes an enjoyable place to stop for a break. In the adjacent courtyard, at Brogade 17, workers unearthed a buried treasure in 1987 – an old wooden trunk filled with more than 30kg of 17th century silver coins, the largest such find ever made in Denmark. Some of these coins are now on display in the Køge Museum.

The building at **Brogade 23** (circa 1638) is decorated with cherubs carved by the famed 17th century artist Abel Schrøder. If you cross the street and return back to Torvet along the western side of Brogade, you'll pass Køge's longest timber-framed house at **Brogade 16**, a yellow-brick structure erected in 1636 by the town mayor.

Sankt Nicolai Kirke

This church on Kirkestræde, two blocks north of Torvet, is named after St Nicholas,

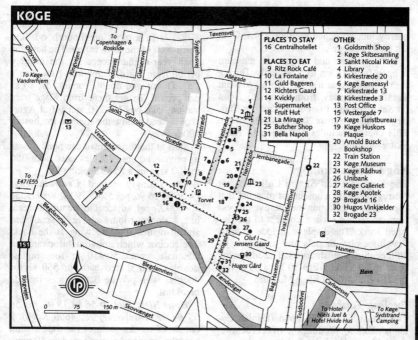

KØGE

PLACES TO STAY	OTHER
16 Centralhotellet	1 Goldsmith Shop
	2 Køge Skitsesamling
PLACES TO EAT	3 Sankt Nicolai Kirke
9 Ritz Rock Café	4 Library
10 La Fontaine	5 Kirkestræde 20
11 Guld Bageren	6 Køge Børneasyl
12 Richters Gaard	7 Kirkestræde 13
14 Kvickly	8 Kirkestræde 3
Supermarket	13 Post Office
18 Fruit Hut	15 Vestergade 7
21 La Mirage	17 Køge Turistbureau
25 Butcher Shop	19 Kiøge Huskors
31 Bella Napoli	Plaque
	20 Arnold Busck
	Bookshop
	22 Train Station
	23 Køge Museum
	24 Køge Rådhus
	26 Unibank
	27 Køge Galleriet
	28 Køge Apotek
	29 Brogade 16
	30 Hugos Vinkjælder
	32 Brogade 23

the patron saint of mariners. At the upper eastern end of the church tower there's a little brick projection called the Lygten, which for centuries was used to hang a burning lantern on as a guide for sailors returning to the harbour. It was from the top of the church tower that Christian IV kept watch on his naval fleet as it successfully defended the town from Swedish invaders during the Battle of Køge Bay.

The church dates from 1324 but was largely rebuilt in the 15th century. Most of the ornately carved works that adorn the interior were added later, including the altar and pulpit, which date from the 17th century. Between mid-June and late August, Sankt Nicolai Kirke is open from 10 am to 4 pm on weekdays and from 10 am to noon on Saturday. During the rest of the year it's open on weekdays only from 10 am to noon. In summer you can climb the tower

at 11 am, noon and 1 pm. Admission costs 5 kr.

Køge Museum

The Køge Museum, Nørregade 4, occupies a lovely building dating from 1619 that was once a wealthy merchant's home and store. A few dozen of its rooms now feature exhibits illustrating the cultural history of the town and surrounding region. As well as the expected period furnishings and artefacts, there's an interesting hotchpotch of displays ranging from a Mesolithic-era grave to hundreds of recently discovered silver coins, including those discovered in the courtyard at Brogade 17, part of a huge stash thought to have been hidden during the Swedish wars of the late 17th century. The museum also contains a desk used by Danish philosopher NFS Grundtvig, who lived on the outskirts of Køge, and a windowpane onto which Hans Christian Andersen, during an apparently stressed-out stay at a nearby inn, scratched the words 'Oh God, Oh God in Kjøge'.

Between June and August the museum is open from 11 am to 5 pm daily. During the rest of the year it's open from 1 to 5 pm Tuesday to Friday, from 11 am to 3 pm on Saturday and from 1 to 5 pm on Sunday. Admission costs 20 kr (children 10 kr). This charge includes admission to Køge Skitsesamling.

Køge Skitsesamling

The Køge Art and Sketch Collection, at Nørregade 29, is a unique art museum that specialises in outlining the creative process from an artist's earliest concept to the finished work. The displays include original drawings, clay models and mock-ups by 20th century Danish artists. The admission price of 20 kr (children 10 kr) also covers the aforementioned Køge Museum.

Cycling Tours

The Dansk Cyklist Forbund (Danish Cyclists' Union) produces a free brochure, available in English at the turistbureau, detailing five suggested cycling tours of the greater Køge area. These range in length from a 6km route, passing NFS Grundtvig's grave, to a 40km tour that includes Vallø Slot. In addition the turistbureau sells highly detailed cycling maps.

De Unges Hus (☎ 46 15 12 76) hires out bicycles (50/250 kr per day/week); it requires one day's advance notice. You can arrange to have the bike delivered to the turistbureau or the hostel. Mountain bike tours can also be arranged.

Places to Stay

The closest camping ground to the town centre is *Køge Sydstrand Camping* (☎ 56 65 07 69, fax 56 65 59 84, Søndre Badevej, 4600 Køge), south of the harbour. A two star facility, sited on a beach with an industrial backdrop, it's about a 20 minute walk south from the train station via Toldbodvej, Carlsensvej and Strandpromenaden.

The 80 bed *Køge Vandrerhjem* (☎ 56 65 14 74, fax 56 66 08 69, Vamdrupvej 1, 4600 Køge) is in a quiet neighbourhood 2km north-west of the town centre. The hostel is open year-round except for the holiday period from mid-December to New Year's Day. Dorms and double rooms cost 80 kr per person. To get there from Køge train station, take bus No 210, get off at Agerskovvej and follow the signs to the hostel, 400m away.

Staff at the turistbureau can book *rooms* in private homes; doubles cost from 350 to 400 kr, plus a 25 kr booking fee.

The fittingly named *Centralhotellet* (☎ 56 65 06 96, fax 56 65 59 84, Vestergade 3, 4600 Køge), adjacent to the turistbureau, has a dozen rooms above a small bar and also in a separate wing at the back. The rooms, which are straightforward but adequate, cost 250/450 kr for singles/doubles with shared bath, or 550 kr for doubles with private bath; prices include breakfast.

Hotel Niels Juel (☎ 56 63 18 00, fax 56 63 04 92, Toldbodvej 20, 4600 Køge), a couple of blocks south of the train station near the inner harbour, is a modern 50 room hotel affiliated with the Best Western chain. Singles/doubles with bath, TV, phone and minibar cost 815/1015 kr.

There's a second Best Western, *Hotel Hvide Hus* (☎ 56 65 36 90, fax 56 66 33 14, Strandvejen 111, 4600 Køge), near the beach at the less developed end of town to the south. It has 126 modern rooms costing 715/915 kr for singles/doubles. In addition to the standard rates, both Best Western hotels offer a special discounted weekend and summer rate of 695 kr that covers up to two adults and two children. All rates include breakfast.

Places to Eat

For good value you can't beat *Guld Bageren*, a combination bakery and self-service café on the north-western side of Torvet, which serves good breads, fresh salads, mouth-watering fruit tarts and sandwiches. Enjoy it all in the 2nd floor dining area

SOUTHERN ZEALAND

overlooking the square. It's open from 5.30 am daily.

The adjacent *La Fontaine (Torvet 28)* is a smoky pub that sells not only beer but also coffee, cappuccino and light eats. It's open until at least midnight daily.

Ritz Rock Café (Torvet 22) is a Tex-Mex nachos and steak place that doubles as a weekend disco. Prices are reasonable and hours are long.

Bella Napoli (Brogade 21), a popular and somewhat upmarket Italian restaurant, serves pizza and pasta dishes starting at around 40 kr at lunchtime, 60 kr for dinner. It's open from noon to 11 pm. Cheaper pizza (32 kr) as well as inexpensive chicken and chips can be found at *La Mirage (Nørregade 9)*, which does mainly takeaway business but has a couple of tables and is open until late.

Richters Gaard (Vestergade 16), a fine-dining restaurant in a half-timbered building dating from 1644, offers two-course meals, including dishes such as steak or salmon, for 99 kr at lunchtime, 198 kr for dinner. It also has a casual open-air courtyard, pleasant in summer.

On the eastern side of Torvet you'll find a *fruit hut* and a *butcher shop* offering takeaway smørrebrød sandwiches. There's a produce, cheese and flower *market* at Torvet, held on Wednesday and Saturday mornings, and a *Kvickly* supermarket on Vestergade.

Entertainment

A nice place for a drink is *Hugos Vinkjælder*, in Hugos Gård at Brogade 19. This cosy little wine bar, in the cellar of a medieval brick building dating from the 14th century, sells half a bottle of wine for just 58 kr and also serves inexpensive beer. It's open from 10 am to 11 pm on weekdays, to 1 am on Friday and Saturday. Live jazz bands play in the courtyard on summer Saturdays from 10.30 am to 1.30 pm.

Getting There & Away

Train Køge is at the end of the E (and A+) lines, the southernmost station on greater Copenhagen's S-train network. Trains from Copenhagen run three to six times an hour, take 38 minutes and cost 38.50 kr. Køge is also on the rail line between Roskilde (33 kr, 25 minutes) and Næstved (43 kr, 34 minutes).

Car & Motorcycle Køge is 42km southwest of Copenhagen and 25km south-east of Roskilde. If you're coming by road take the E47/E55 from Copenhagen or route 6 from Roskilde and then pick up route 151 south into the centre of Køge. There's free parking on Torvet with a one hour limit during business hours and less-restricted parking off Havnen, north of the harbour.

VALLØ

Vallø is a charming little hamlet with cobblestone streets, a dozen mustard-yellow houses and an attractive moat-encircled Renaissance castle, Vallø Slot. Situated in the countryside about 7km south of Køge, Vallø makes an enjoyable little excursion for those looking to get off the beaten path. If old-world character and mildly eccentric surroundings appeal, it could also be a fun place to spend the evening.

Vallø Slot

The red-brick Vallø Slot dates from 1586 and retains most of its original style, even though much of it was rebuilt following a fire in 1893.

The castle has a rather unusual history. On her birthday in 1737 Queen Sophie Magdalene, who owned the estate, established a foundation that turned Vallø Slot into a home for 'spinsters of noble birth'. Until a few decades ago unmarried daughters of Danish royalty who hadn't the means to live in their own castles or manor houses were allowed to take up residence at Vallø, supported by the foundation and government social programmes.

In the 1970s, bowing to changing sentiments that had previously spared this anachronistic niche of the Zealand countryside, the foundation amended its charter to gradually make the estate more accessible to the

SOUTHERN ZEALAND

general public. For now, the castle remains home solely to a handful of ageing blue-blooded women who had taken up residence prior to 1976.

Vallø Slot is surrounded by 2800 hectares of woods and ponds and 1300 hectares of fields and arable land reaching clear down to the coast. Although the main castle buildings are not yet open to the public, visitors are free to walk in the gardens and the adjacent woods.

Hestestalden, the stables at Vallø Slot, feature an exhibition on the history of the castle, open between early May and August from 11 am to 4 pm daily. Admission costs 10 kr, free if you have a Køge Museum ticket for the same day.

Places to Stay & Eat

Vallø Slotskro (☎ 56 26 70 20, *Slotsgade 1, 4600 Køge*), a 200-year-old inn, sits just outside the castle gate. The 11 pleasantly decorated rooms start at 500/625 kr for singles/doubles and have bath, TV and phone; there's also a suite with a jacuzzi, costing 1200 kr.

The inn's restaurant serves traditional Danish cuisine with a French accent. From 11.30 am to 3 pm, it serves reasonably priced lunches (around 75 kr), including steak with chips or fresh fish with prawns and dill. A fixed-price three course dinner costs 195 kr and typically includes the likes of smoked salmon and venison fillet.

Getting There & Away

Take the train to Vallø station, two stops south of Køge, and from there it's a pleasant 1.25km stroll east down a tree-lined country road to the castle.

If travelling by road take route 209 south from Køge, turn right onto Billesborgvej and then left (south) onto Valløvej, which leads to Slotsgade.

There's a signposted cycle route from Køge that leads into Valløvej.

RINGSTED

Situated at a crossroads in central Zealand, Ringsted was an important market town during the Middle Ages and also served as the site of the *landsting*, a regional governing assembly. The town grew up around Sankt Bendts Kirke, which was built during the reign of Valdemar I (1157-82). This historic church still marks the town centre and is Ringsted's most interesting sight.

Immediately east of the church is Torvet, the central square, which features a statue of Valdemar I, sculpted by Johannes Bjerg in the 1930s, as well as three sitting stones that were used centuries ago by the landsting members.

Ringsted's town centre is a 10 minute walk north from the train station.

Information

The Ringsted Turistbureau (☎ 57 61 34 00, fax 57 61 64 50) is at Sankt Bendtsgade 10, 4100 Ringsted, to the north of Sankt Bendts Kirke; the Web site is at www.ringsted .dk/turist. Between May and August it's open from 9 am to 5 pm on weekdays and from 9 am to 2 pm on Saturday; in winter it's open from 9 am to 2 pm Monday to Friday.

Sankt Bendts Kirke

This imposing church was erected in 1170 by Valdemar I, partly to serve as a burial sanctuary for his murdered father, Knud Lavard (who had recently been canonised by the Pope), and partly as a calculated move to shore up the rule of the Valdemar dynasty and intertwine the influences of the Crown and the Catholic Church.

Although Sankt Bendts Kirke was substantially restored in the 1900s, it retains much of its original medieval style and still incorporates travertine blocks from an 11th century abbey church that had earlier occupied the same site.

The nave is adorned with magnificent frescoes, including a series depicting Erik IV (known as Erik Ploughpenny, for the despised tax he levied on ploughs), which were painted in about 1300 in a failed campaign to get the assassinated king canonised. These frescoes show Queen Agnes

The Dagmar Cross

Queen Dagmar, the first wife of Valdemar II, was born a princess in Bohemia. Although she lived in Denmark for only a few years before her premature death in 1212, she was much beloved by the Danes and is revered in several ballads as a kind, good-hearted woman.

In 1683, as Queen Dagmar's tomb was being removed from Sankt Bendts Kirke in Ringsted, a small gold cross with finely detailed enamel work was found at the site. Now known as the Dagmar Cross, it is thought to date from 1000 AD. One side shows Christ with arms outstretched on the cross and the other side depicts him with the Virgin Mary, John the Baptist, St John and St Basil.

This perfectly preserved cross of Byzantine design is now in Nationalmuseet in Copenhagen. It has been widely replicated as a pendant by Ringsted jewellery shops and is popularly worn as a necklace by brides who marry in Sankt Bendts Kirke.

---

seated on a throne; on her left is a scene of Ploughpenny's murderers stabbing the king with a spear, while the right-hand scene depicts the king's corpse being retrieved from the sea by fishermen.

Sankt Bendts Kirke was a burial place for the royal family for 150 years. In the aisle floor beneath the nave are flat stones marking the tombs of (in order from the font) Valdemar III and his queen, Eleonora; Valdemar II, flanked by his queens Dagmar and Bengærd; Knud VI; Valdemar I, flanked by his queen, Sofia, and his son Christopher; and Knud Lavard. Also buried in the church are Erik VI (Menved) and Queen Ingeborg, whose remains lie in an ornate tomb in the chancel, and King Birger of Sweden and his queen Margarete, who occupy the former tomb of Erik Ploughpenny.

Some of the tombs, including the empty one that once held Queen Dagmar, have been disturbed over the centuries to make room for later burials. A few of the grave relics removed from these tombs can be found in the church's museum chapel, along with a copy of the Dagmar Cross (see the boxed text above).

The church also has some interesting carved works, including pews from 1591 (note the dragons on the seats near the altar), an elaborate altarpiece from 1699 and a pulpit from 1609. The oldest item in the church is the 12th century baptismal font which, despite its historical significance, once served a stint as a flower bowl in a local garden.

The church is open from 10 am to noon and 1 to 5 pm daily between May and mid-September, and from 1 to 3 pm during the rest of the year. Note that the church is closed whenever there are weddings, a particularly common occurrence on Saturdays in spring.

Ringsted Museum

This small museum of local cultural history, which includes a restored 1814 Dutch windmill, is on the eastern side of town at Køgevej 37, within walking distance of Torvet and the train station. It's open from 11 am to 4 pm Tuesday to Sunday; admission costs 20 kr.

Places to Stay

The 78 bed hostel, *Ringsted Vandrerhjem* (☎ *57 61 15 26, fax 57 61 34 26, Sankt Bendtsgade 18, 4100 Ringsted)*, has an ideal location opposite Sankt Bendts Kirke. Dorm beds cost 90 kr; private rooms cost 220/270 kr for singles/doubles. Each room has a bathroom. The hostel is closed from 20 December to 10 January.

Staff at the turistbureau can help you to book *rooms* in private homes; rooms cost from 125 to 150 kr per person, which sometimes including breakfast; there's no booking fee.

Places to Eat

Raadhuskroen (Sankt Bendtsgade 8), next to the turistbureau, is a pub-style restaurant specialising in steaks served with salad, costing around 100 kr at dinner, a bit less at lunchtime.

If you take the alley between the turistbureau and Raadhuskroen you'll reach a *Netto* grocery shop. A two minute walk north-east from Netto is *La Coruna (Nørregade 31)*, where specials such as lasagne, pizza or a chicken dish cost around 30 kr until 5 pm, 45 kr after that.

Getting There & Away

There are numerous trains throughout the day to Ringsted from Roskilde (28 kr, 18 minutes) and Næstved (28 kr, 20 minutes).

Ringsted is on route 150 and just off the E20 motorway, 27km west of Køge and 16km east of Sorø. Roskilde is 30km to the north via route 14.

Getting Around

Mountain bikes can be hired from Cykelsporten (☎ 57 61 82 82), Sankt Hansgade 22, for 100 kr per day.

SORØ

Bordered by lakes and woodlands, Sorø is a delightful little town steeped in history. Bishop Absalon established a Cistercian monastery here in 1161, six years before he founded Copenhagen. The bishop and four Danish monarchs lie buried in Sorø Kirke, the church that Absalon erected in the monastery grounds.

After the Reformation, when Catholicism was banned and Church properties were turned over to the Crown, Frederik II set aside the monastery grounds to be used as a school. His successor, Christian IV, developed it into the Sorø Academy of Knights, an elite school dedicated to the education of the sons of the nobility.

The great Danish playwright Ludvig Holberg (1684-1754), a summer resident of Sorø and a patron of the academy, helped to revive the school during faltering times by bequeathing it his substantial estate. Other significant men of letters had connections

---

Bishops & Bricks

Shortly after the end of the Viking era, two things happened that had a significant and lasting impact on church architecture in Denmark. First, Sweyn II (1047-74) found himself deep in a power struggle with the Archbishop of Bremen, the leader of the Danish Church. To weaken the influence of the archbishop, the king divided Denmark into eight separate dioceses, which set the stage for a flurry of church and cathedral building.

In the 12th century the art of brick-making was introduced to Denmark from northern Italy and Germany. Before then, most churches were constructed from wood or calcareous tufa and rough stone. The use of bricks allowed construction on a much larger scale and within a few decades grand churches were being built all around Denmark. Some of the buildings from that era still stand today, including stalwart churches in Sorø and Ringsted, and the cathedrals in Roskilde and Århus.

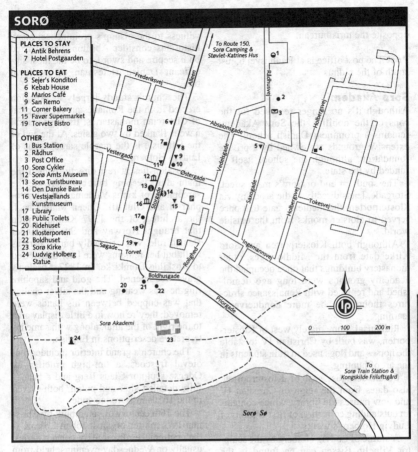

SORØ

PLACES TO STAY
4 Antik Behrens
7 Hotel Postgaarden

PLACES TO EAT
5 Sejer's Konditori
6 Kebab House
8 Marios Café
9 San Remo
11 Corner Bakery
15 Favør Supermarket
19 Torvets Bistro

OTHER
1 Bus Station
2 Rådhus
3 Post Office
10 Sorø Cykler
12 Sorø Amts Museum
13 Sorø Turistbureau
14 Den Danske Bank
16 Vestsjællands Kunstmuseum
17 Library
18 Public Toilets
20 Ridehuset
21 Klosterporten
22 Boldhuset
23 Sorø Kirke
24 Ludvig Holberg Statue

To Route 150,
Sorø Camping &
Støvlet-Katrines Hus

Frederiksvej

Alleen

Rådhusvej

Holbergsvej

Absalonsgade

Vestergade

Vedildgade

Saxogade

Holbergsvej

Tokesvej

Østergade

Storgade

Ingemannsvej

Søgade

Torvet

Rolighed

Boldhusgade

Priorgade

Sorø Akademi

Sorø Sø

To
Sorø Train Station &
Kongskilde Friluftsgård

0   100   200 m

SOUTHERN ZEALAND

with the academy, including the poet and novelist Bernhard Severin Ingemann (1789-1862), who taught literature here for three decades from 1822.

During Denmark's 'Golden Age' of national romanticism (1800-50), Sorø became a haunt for some of the country's most prominent cultural figures, including Bertel Thorvaldsen, NFS Grundtvig and Adam Oehlenschläger.

Sorø is a pleasant destination with an interesting air of culture and history. The streets of the town centre are thick with old timber-framed houses, and the academy grounds and surrounding lakeside park are open to the public.

Information

Tourist Office The Sorø Turistbureau (☎ 57 82 10 12, fax 57 82 10 13) is in the town centre at Storgade 15, 4180 Sorø. It's open from 9 am to 5 pm Monday to Friday and from 9 am to 3 pm on Saturday (to noon on Saturday between September and May).

Money There are several banks in town including Den Danske Bank at Storgade 28, opposite the turistbureau.

Post The post office is at Rådhusvej 6, just south of the rådhus.

Sorø Akademi

Although it's no longer reserved for the sons of the nobility, the Sorø Akademi remains a prominent Danish school. The extensive grounds are owned by a private foundation, although the school itself is funded by the state.

The southern end of Sorø's main street, Storgade, leads directly to the academy via **Klosterporten**, the medieval gate that once served to cloister monks from the outside world.

Although both Klosterporten and Sorø Kirke date from the Middle Ages, other monastery buildings that once occupied the academy grounds were long ago demolished and replaced with Renaissance structures thought to be more conducive to learning.

Ridehuset, immediately west of Klosterporten, was built by Christian IV to stable the horses and dogs used to train students in the art of hunting.

Boldhuset, just east of Klosterporten, also dates from the reign of Christian IV and now houses the library, which contains an outstanding collection of first editions of Ludvig Holberg's works.

A **statue** of Ludvig Holberg by the sculptor Vilhelm Bissen can be found in the garden area in the western part of the grounds. If you're up to a stroll, walking **trails** lead west from the statue down to the lake, Sorø Sø.

Sorø Kirke

The 12th century Sorø church, in the centre of the academy grounds, is one of Denmark's oldest brick structures and the country's largest monastery church. It was built to serve as a sepulchral church for Bishop Absalon and his prestigious family, the Hvides, whose landholdings included the Sorø region. The fact that five monarchs opted to be buried next to Absalon bears witness to the bishop's prominence; many historians consider Absalon, who carried both sceptre and sword, to be the most significant Danish statesman of medieval times.

The church stands largely as Absalon erected it, in the Romanesque style typical of Cistercian monasteries. Its huge central nave is flanked by two aisles. At the end of the left aisle is the marble sarcophagus of Ludvig Holberg.

Absalon lies at rest directly behind the main altar; keeping him company are the sarcophagi of kings Valdemar IV, Christopher II and Oluf III. Queen Margrethe I, the architect of the 1397 Kalmar Union that brought Norway and Sweden under Danish rule, was originally buried here as well, but her remains were later transferred to Roskilde Domkirke. In 1827 Absalon's grave was opened. The gold and sapphire ring he was wearing and the silver chalice that was cupped between his hands were removed; they're now in a little display area to the right of the altar, along with some interpretive descriptions in English.

The church's grand interior includes medieval frescoes, a 6m-high crucifix by Odense sculptor Claus Berg and a beautifully detailed altar and pulpit, both carved in the 1650s in Baroque style.

The 16th century organ, rebuilt by Christian IV's master organist Johan Lorenz, is the centrepiece of a weekly concert series, usually on Wednesday evenings, held from late June to early September; schedule information and advance tickets (80 kr) are available from the turistbureau.

Between mid-May and early September the church is open to visitors from 10 am (noon on Sunday) to 4 pm daily; hours are limited in the low season. Admission is free.

Sorø Amts Museum

This regional cultural museum at Storgade 17 is housed in a handsome half-timbered building dating from 1625.

It contains rooms with period furnishings, ranging from a peasant's simple quarters to the stylish living room of an aristocrat. There's also a room furnished with the personal belongings of the romanticist poet BS Ingemann, a grocery shop from 1880 and displays of vintage costumes, old bottles and archaeological finds. Sorø Amts Museum is open from 1 to 4 pm Tuesday to Sunday; admission costs 20 kr (children free).

Vestsjællands Kunstmuseum
Another worthwhile stop is the Art Museum of West Zealand, housed in a period building at Storgade 9. Its varied collection of regional art runs the gamut from medieval church pieces and stodgy portraits by CW Eckersberg to wildly expressionist modern art. It's open from 10 am to 4 pm between mid-May and mid-August, and from 1 to 4 pm during the rest of the year; it's closed on Monday year-round. Admission is free.

Other Attractions
Inside the courtyard at Storgade 7 is an attractive timber-framed Renaissance building, constructed by King Christian IV, that now comprises a wing of the town library.

From Torvet, consider taking a walk down Søgade, an inviting street of leaning half-timbered mustard-yellow houses with red tiled roofs. You can follow this street 400m down to the lake and its garden-like setting, where there are trails in both directions.

Places to Stay
Sorø Camping (☎ 57 83 02 02, fax 57 82 11 02, Udbyhøjvej 10, 4180 Sorø) borders the lake Pedersborg Sø to the north-west of town, about 150m north of Slagelsevej. This three star camping ground is accessible to visitors in wheelchairs and has a coin laundry, kitchen and cabins for rent. Open year-round, the camping ground is a 20 minute walk from town along a lakeside trail; bus No 234 stops nearby.

Antik Behrens (☎/fax 57 83 53 52, Absalonsgade 19, 4180 Sorø), a 10 minute walk east of the town centre, is a private home with four comfortable rooms costing 225/350 kr for singles/doubles, including breakfast. The friendly owners are former antiques dealers and the breakfast room is so laden with period paintings and furniture that it resembles a museum.

Hotel Postgaarden (☎ 57 83 22 22, fax 57 82 01 58, Storgade 25, 4180 Sorø), an inn-style hotel with a 300 year history, sits right in the town centre. The 23 rooms are pleasantly simple with bath, desk and phone; TVs are available. Singles/doubles cost 495/695 kr, including breakfast.

Kongskilde Friluftsgård (☎ 57 84 92 00, fax 57 84 92 01), Skælskørvej 34, 4180 Sorø), 7km south-west of town on route 157, is an appealing lakeside inn that's recently been converted into a hostel. In the midst of a nature reserve, it's a popular respite for both hikers and cyclists – two national cycle routes, Nos 6 and 7, cross right at the inn, and there are nature trails leading from the front door. Bus No 83 connects it with Sorø train station hourly on weekdays but only twice daily at weekends. Dorm rooms cost 85 kr. Singles/doubles cost 240/280 kr with shared bath, 265/310 kr with private bath. Breakfast is available for 40 kr, while an excellent two course dinner of organic fare costs 165 kr. It's open year-round and is accessible to people in wheelchairs.

Places to Eat
There are a few places to get inexpensive eats along Storgade near Hotel Postgaarden. To the north is *Kebab House*, which serves not only kebabs but also chicken and chips. Opposite the hotel is *Marios Café*, a hole-in-the-wall place selling cheap pizza, lasagne and chicken. Just to the south of it is *San Remo* (Storegade 38), a more standard pizzeria where pizza starts at 35 kr and pasta costs around 55 kr. Across the street is the *Corner Bakery*, which offers good breads and pastries. There's another bakery, *Sejer's Konditori*, on Absalonsgade, and a

fast-food kiosk, **Torvets Bistro**, right on Torvet. You can pick up groceries at the **Favør** supermarket east of Storegade.

Støvlet-Katrines Hus (*Slagelsevej 65*), at the western edge of town, is an atmospheric restaurant that was originally built as a home for Christian VII's mistress. Today it serves good Danish food at moderate prices and is a favourite spot for a night out.

Getting There & Away
Sorø is 15km east of Slagelse and 16km west of Ringsted via route 150 or the E20. Trains run about hourly to Sorø from Slagelse (20 kr, 10 minutes) and Ringsted (20 kr, 8 minutes). Sorø train station is in Frederiksberg, 2km south of the town centre; buses No 806 and 807 run between Sorø centre and the train station at least hourly. There's also a bus service (No 234) between Sorø and Slagelse (25 kr, 24 minutes), which also runs to Ringsted and Roskilde. The bus station is on Rådhusvej between Absalonsgade and Fægangen.

Getting Around
Sorø Cykler (☎ 57 83 42 01), on the corner of Storgade and Østergade, hires out bicycles for 50 kr per day.

SLAGELSE
Slagelse is best known to visitors as the starting point for outings to the nearby Viking fortress of Trelleborg. Although Slagelse doesn't have any particular allure, there are a couple of local sights you could take in if time permits and it's an agreeable place to stay if you need to break for the night.

The town centre is dominated by Sankt Mikkels Kirke, a Gothic church built of brick in the early 14th century. To the east of the church is Nytorv, the main commercial square.

Information on Trelleborg is in the section that follows Slagelse.

Information
Tourist Office The Slagelse Turistbureau (☎ 58 52 22 06, fax 58 52 86 87), Løvegade 7, 4200 Slagelse, is a 10 minute walk south of the train station and a few hundred metres west of Nytorv. Between mid-June and August it's open from 9 am to 5 pm on weekdays and to 3 pm on Saturday; during the rest of the year it's open from 10 am to 5 pm on weekdays and to 1 pm on Saturday.

Money & Post There are several banks around town, including Den Danske Bank at Nytorv 1. The post office is immediately east of the train station.

Slagelse Museum
This local museum, at Bredegade 11, is a short walk south-west from Nytorv. It displays the craft and industrial history of Slagelse, featuring the old tools and workshops of a grocer, barber, butcher, blacksmith and so on, as well as rooms of period furniture. It's open year-round from 2 to 5 pm on Saturday, and also from noon to 4 pm on weekdays in summer. Admission costs 20 kr.

Ruins of Antvorskov
The brick ruins of Antvorskov, a medieval monastery founded by Valdemar I in 1164, are about 2km south of the town centre. Antvorskov's most significant role in history is its connection with Hans Tausen, the renegade monk who took his monastic training here. Hans was vexed by the excessive privilege he found at Antvorskov, which was one of the wealthiest monasteries in Denmark and open only to the sons of the nobility. After a study tour abroad, during which he heard Martin Luther preaching in Wittenburg, Germany, Hans returned to Antvorskov, where on Maundy Thursday in 1525 he delivered a fiery speech that helped to spark the Danish Reformation.

Following the Reformation, Antvorskov was confiscated by the Crown and became a favourite hunting manor of King Frederik II, who died here in 1588. Eventually it was sold off and the buildings, including the old monastery church, were demolished.

About half of the former monastery grounds are now buried under the E20 motorway, but some of the brick remains of the original foundations can still be seen. A couple of interpretive plaques at the site detail the ruins. Although historically significant, the ruins aren't overwhelmingly interesting in themselves and are out of the way if you don't have your own transport. You can get there by taking Slotsalléen from the town centre to its end, then turning right and proceeding about 200m to the car park opposite Munkebakken.

Places to Stay

Slagelse Campingplads and *Slagelse Vandrerhjem* (☎ 58 52 25 28, fax 58 52 25 40, Bjergbygade 78, 4200 Slagelse) are run by the same management and are next to each other, 2km south of the train station. The one star camping ground is open from 1 May to 1 September and charges 46 kr per person. Hostel dorm beds cost 90 kr, while family rooms sleeping one to six people cost from 190 to 540 kr. The hostel is closed between mid-December and mid-January. There's a coin laundry. You can take bus No 303 (10 kr) or a taxi (about 40 kr) from the train station.

Staff at the turistbureau can book *rooms* in private homes for you; these start at 200 kr per room, plus a 10 kr booking fee.

At *Hotel Slagelse* (☎ 58 52 01 72, Sondre Stationsvej 19, 4200 Slagelse), an older 35 room hotel near the train station, straightforward singles/doubles with bath cost 350/595 kr, including breakfast.

Hotel Frederik den II (☎ 58 53 03 22, fax 58 53 46 22, Idagårdsvej 3, 4200 Slagelse) is a modern Best Western hotel near the intersection of route 22 and the E20, to the south of town. The rooms are comfortable, with bath, TV, phone and coffee maker. There's a pleasant little sauna and a good breakfast is included in the price. The standard rates for singles/doubles are a hefty 785/1040 kr, but there's a 695 kr rate in summer and at weekends year-round. The hotel is adjacent to a large shopping complex called Bilka.

Places to Eat

There are a number of places to eat around Sankt Mikkels Kirke and Nytorv, including a *bakery (Nytorv 6)*; *Paradiso Kebab (Nytorv 8)*, serving inexpensive kebabs and burgers; *Nat Toget (Gammel Torv 8)*, a pleasant pub-style place offering reasonably priced pizza, pasta and beef dishes; and the more upmarket *Nytorv 2*, where Danish meat and fish dishes cost around 150 kr.

Getting There & Away

Slagelse is at the intersections of routes 150 and 22 and by the E20 motorway. It's 37km south-east of Kalundborg and 19km northeast of Korsør.

Slagelse is on the main east-west rail line between Copenhagen and Jutland and has frequent rail services. From Slagelse, it's 33 minutes (49 kr) to Roskilde, 12 minutes (20 kr) to Korsør and 10 minutes (20 kr) to Sorø.

Getting Around

Bicycle hire can be arranged at HJ Cykler (☎ 58 52 28 57), Løvegade 46 near the turistbureau, for 35 kr per day.

TRELLEBORG

Trelleborg, in the countryside 7km west of Slagelse, is the best preserved of the four Viking ring fortresses in Denmark.

At the entrance to Trelleborg is a reconstructed Viking house built in Viking stave style using rough oak timbers erected above mud floors. The inside features earthen benches of the type used by warriors for sleeping on and a central hearth with a simple opening in the roof for venting smoke.

There's a museum exhibiting pottery and other items excavated from the fortress grounds; it also shows a 20 minute video on Trelleborg's history, with commentary in Danish, English and German. There are usually a few costumed interpreters, chopping wood for a fire or giving archery demonstrations to Danish schoolchildren, but the highlight is just strolling around the grounds.

Trelleborg's Precise Design

Trelleborg's military origins are visible in its precise mathematical layout and use of the Roman foot (29.33cm) as a unit of measure.

The Trelleborg compound consists of two wards that encompass about 7 hectares in all. The inner ward is embraced by a circular earthen rampart 6m high and 17m thick at its base. Four gates, one at each point of the compass, cut through the rampart. The ward is crossed by two streets, one east-west, the other north-south, which has the effect of dividing it into four symmetrical quadrants. In Viking times, each quadrant contained four long elliptical buildings surrounding a courtyard. Each of the 16 buildings was exactly 100 Roman feet long and contained a central hall and two smaller rooms.

Following the arc along the exterior of the inner rampart was an 18m-wide ditch; two bridges spanned the ditch, crossing over to the outer ward. This outer ward contained a cemetery holding about 150 graves and 15 houses, each of which was 90 Roman feet long and lined up radially with its gable pointing towards the inner rampart. A second earthen ward separated the outer ward from the surrounding countryside.

You can walk up onto the grassy circular rampart and readily grasp the geometric design of the fortress. From on top of the rampart, Trelleborg appears strikingly symmetrical and precise; cement blocks have been laid to show the outlines of the elliptical house foundations. Grazing sheep wandering in from the surrounding farmland imbue the scene with a timeless aura. A few interpretive plaques in English describe burial mounds and other features along the way.

Trelleborg (☎ 58 54 95 06) is on Trelleborg Allé and is open from 10 am to 5 pm daily. It's a fairly compact site and you could easily take it all in during an hour-long visit. Admission costs 35 kr. There's a café and gift shop at the site.

Getting There & Away

Bus No 312 goes from Slagelse to Trelleborg (10 kr, 12 minutes) but it's infrequent and the schedule can vary a bit each year. Currently, between June and August a bus leaves Slagelse bus station hourly from 10.06 am to 3.06 pm on weekdays, once only at 12.41 pm on Saturday and not at all on Sunday. During the school year the bus follows school schedules, leaving earlier and returning later.

To get to Trelleborg from Slagelse using your own transport, take Strandvejen to its end at the village of Hejninge (where there's an attractive church with early 15th century frescoes) and then follow the signs to Trelleborg, 1km farther on. A taxi to the site costs around 90 kr.

A good alternative to relying on the bus is to cycle your way across the rural countryside between Slagelse and Trelleborg (see the Slagelse Getting Around section for details of bike hire).

KORSØR

Situated at the narrowest point of the Store Bælt (Great Belt), the channel that separates Zealand from Funen, Korsør takes much of its character from its strategic location. The town boomed in the 1850s with the construction of the Zealand railway and until recently all vehicles – trains and cars alike – had to board ferries in Korsør to continue across the channel to Funen. In 1998 all that changed with the opening of Storebælts-forbindelsen (the Great Belt Fixed Link), which now connects Zealand and Funen via 18km of bridges and tunnels providing a 'land link' between the two islands.

With the new link and Korsør's new train station both situated 3km north of the town centre, Korsør is now largely bypassed by most travellers. If you have extra time there are a couple of local sights in town that could be visited, but if time is tight Nyborg,

A Record-Setting Bridge

The largest engineering scheme ever undertaken in Denmark was Storebælts-forbindelsen (the Great Belt Fixed Link), an 18km bridge and tunnel project across the narrowest point of the Store Bælt, the body of water that separates Zealand from Funen. A decade in the making, Storebælts-forbindelsen opened to traffic in June 1998.

There are two bridges, the Østbro (East Bridge) and the Vestbro (West Bridge), linking at the little island of Sprogø near the centre of the Store Bælt.

The Østbro, which has a total length of 6790m, has a free span above the fairway of 1624m. That span was set to become the world's longest suspension bridge, but the Japanese stole the Danes' thunder with the early opening, in April 1998, of the Akashi Kaikyo suspension bridge, which boasts a 2000m free span. Prior to 1998 the Humber Bridge in Britain was the world's longest suspension span, at 1410m.

The Østbro's two towers, which reach a height of 254m, are the highest structures ever erected in Scandinavia. The cables supporting the suspended span are 3km long and 85cm thick, and consist of enough coiled wire to circle the globe three times.

Beneath the Østbro, trains travel through an 8km-long undersea twin tunnel which at its deepest point is nearly 80m below sea level.

On the Vestbro, both cars and trains cross above the water. Measuring 6.6km in length the Vestbro, with its four lane motorway and double-track railway, is currently Europe's longest combined road and railway bridge.

This being Denmark, aesthetics were budgeted into the cost and the Danes' renowned flair for design was incorporated into the project. Despite its record-setting dimensions, the bridge has a gentle geometric appeal.

By eliminating a fleet of ferries that used to leisurely shuttle both cars and trains across the Store Bælt, the project has effectively made little Denmark an even smaller country, reducing travel time across the channel from one hour to just 10 minutes.

Those looking for even more nitty-gritty on the construction can stop at Storebælt Udstillingscenter, an exhibition centre in Korsør to the south of the E20 just east of the Store Bælt crossing.

on the other side of the channel, holds far more allure.

Information

The Korsør Turistbureau (☎ 58 35 02 11, fax 58 35 02 66), at Nygade 7, 4220 Korsør, is open from 10 am to 5 pm Monday to Friday and from 10 am to 1 pm on Saturday.

Things to See

The **Fæstning** (Fortress) tower, near the town centre on the southern side of the harbour, is one of Denmark's few remaining medieval towers. About 24m high and 9m wide, the tower was built using monkstone,

a type of oversized brick. It is owned by the adjacent **Korsør By-og Overfartsmuseum** (Korsør Town & Ferry Service Museum), which features ship models and other displays portraying the history of the ferries and icebreakers that have crossed the Store Bælt over the past two centuries. Opening hours are from 11 am to 4 pm Tuesday to Sunday; admission costs 15 kr (children 5 kr).

Kongegården, in the town centre at Algade 25, is a small art museum that has one floor dedicated to the works of Harald Isenstein, a Jewish sculptor who fled Nazi Germany in the 1930s. There are also temporary exhibitions of regional work. It's open daily from 10 am to 4 pm (to 8 pm on Wednesday), and admission is free. Konge-gården is in a neighbourhood of interesting 18th century buildings.

Places to Stay
Halskov Camping (☎ 58 37 50 80, Revvej 175, 4220 Korsør) is on the waterfront just south of the E20. This two star facility has a kitchen, a coin laundry and a small beach. It's open from 1 April to 1 October.

Korsør Vandrerhjem (☎ 58 37 10 22, fax 58 35 68 70, Tovesvej 30F, 4220 Korsør) is on the eastern outskirts of town, midway between the train station and the city centre. This modern hostel has 20 four-bed rooms, each with a shower and toilet. It's open year-round except from mid-December to mid-January. Dorm beds cost 90 kr; private rooms cost 270 kr for up to three people, 360 kr for four people. It's accessible to people in wheelchairs.

South of the fortress is the *Jens Bagge-sen Hotel* (☎ 58 35 10 00, fax 58 35 10 01, Batterivej 3, 4220 Korsør), a 40 room hotel in a converted period warehouse. Singles/doubles with bath, phone and TV cost 595/830 kr on weekdays, 525/750 kr at weekends; all prices include breakfast.

Places to Eat
In the town centre, near the intersection of Nygade and the pedestrian walkway Algade, you'll find two *bakeries*, a *super-market*, a *pizzeria* serving lunches costing 30 kr and a couple of *cafés* serving drinks and light meals.

Getting There & Away
Train As Korsør is on the main rail line between Zealand and Funen, there are fre-quent train services to Copenhagen (84 kr, one hour) and Odense (92 kr, 28 minutes), and the places in-between.

Car & Motorcycle At the northern out-skirts of Korsør the E20 crosses the Store Bælt channel to Nyborg on Funen; the car toll for the 18km bridge is 210 kr.

Boat The only ferry still running from Korsør goes to Langeland; see the Lange-land section in the Funen chapter for details.

Getting Around
Bus Buses No 501 and 502 connect the town centre with the train station.

Bicycle Bicycles can be hired for 50 kr per day from Svend Eriks Cykler & Symaskiner (☎ 58 37 04 29), in the centre of town at Algade 35.

KALUNDBORG
For those heading directly to Århus from Zealand, Kalundborg makes a convenient jumping-off point. The railway line ends at the central harbour, so you can walk off the train and right onto the boat.

If you have time to spare before catching a ferry, consider a stroll over to Vor Frue Kirke, an intriguing medieval church and Kalundborg's main site of interest.

Things to See
Vor Frue Kirke was erected in the late 12th century and, with its five towers, is one of the most unique medieval churches in Denmark. It was built as a castle church by Esbern Snare, Bishop Absalon's brother, using a Byzantine-like design based upon the Greek cross. The cross shape takes the form of a square central tower connected by cross appendages to four equidistant octag-onal towers. The church was originally part of an extensive fortress but in 1658 the townspeople tore down the fortress walls to minimise the risk of an attack by the Swedes. The church is on Adelgade, just west of Torvet and a short walk north-west from the harbour. The site of Snare's castle is in **Ruinparken**, a few minutes farther west, but there's little left to decipher among the ruins.

If you make a loop around Vor Frue Kirke via Præstegade and Adelgade you'll pass through the oldest part of town, where there are cobbled streets and 16th cen-tury homes; the one at Adelgade 23 houses the **Kalundborg-og Omegns Museum**, the local history museum. The museum is open from 11 am to 4 pm Tuesday to Sunday between May and August, at weekends only during the rest of the year; admission costs 20 kr.

Places to Stay & Eat

The modern 118 bed hostel, *Kalundborg Vandrerhjem (☎ 59 56 13 66, fax 59 56 46 26, Stadion Allé 5, 4400 Kalundborg)*, is just north-west of Ruinparken, within walking distance of the train station and the boats to Århus. Dorm beds cost 85 kr and there are also family rooms sleeping up to six people (300 kr). It's open year-round.

There are restaurants in the town centre and snack bars on the ferries. For a sit-down meal, *Restaurant Bispegården (Adelgade 6)*, near Vor Frue Kirke, serves everything from sandwiches to fish dinners.

Getting There & Away

Train Services between Copenhagen and Kalundborg operate at least hourly throughout the day. The journey takes 1¾ hours and costs 84 kr.

Car & Motorcycle Kalundborg is at the terminus of routes 22 and 23, some 51km north of Korsør and 69km west of Roskilde.

Boat The fastest way to zip over to Århus is by Scandlines (☎ 35 15 15 15) Cat-Link, a sleek catamaran ferry that takes just 95 minutes. The fare is 170 kr for adults, 85 kr for children, 435 kr for a car with up to four passengers, 210 kr for a motorcycle with up to two riders and 25 kr for a bicycle. It leaves Kalundborg nearly a dozen times a day between 8.30 am and 10.30 pm (8.30 pm on Saturday). From Århus, the first sailing is at 6.30 am (8.30 am on Sunday) and the last is at 8.30 pm Monday to Friday, 6.30 pm on Saturday and 9.30 pm on Sunday.

Slower and less frequent is the Scand-lines car ferry, which takes 3¼ hours and costs 290 kr for a car with up to three pas-sengers, 160 kr for a motorcycle and driver. It leaves Kalundborg at 1.30 and 11.45 am and 5 and 8.30 pm Monday to Friday, and at 1.30 am on Saturday. It leaves Århus at 12.45 am and 12.45, 5.15 and 9.15 pm Monday to Friday and at 9.15 pm on Sunday.

NÆSTVED

Located at the mouth of the Suså river, the town of Næstved has been an important trading centre since medieval times. Industry grew following the introduction of the railway in the 19th century and with the later dredging of a new commercial harbour.

With nearly 45,000 residents, Næstved is the largest town in southern Zealand. The town centre has a few interesting historic buildings, including two medieval Gothic churches, all within easy walking distance of each other.

Orientation

The bus and train station are close together on Farimagsvej, opposite its intersection with Jernbanegade. To get to Axeltorv (also spelt Akseltorv), the central square, take Jernbanegade west to Sankt Mortens Kirke and then continue west on Torvestræde; it's a walk of about five minutes in all. All of the town's sights are within a few minutes walk of Axeltorv.

Information

Tourist Office The Næstved Turistbureau (☎ 55 72 11 22, fax 55 72 16 67) is a few blocks south of Axeltorv at Det Gule Pakhus, Havnegade 1, 4700 Næstved; its Web site is at www.naestvednet.dk/turist /dk. Between mid-June and 31 August it's open from 9 am to 5 pm Monday to Friday and from 9 am to 2 pm on Saturday; in the low season it closes at 4 pm on weekdays and at noon on Saturday.

Money There are a few banks in the town centre including a Jyske Bank opposite Sankt Mortens Kirke at Østergade 2 and a Unibank on Axeltorv.

SOUTHERN ZEALAND

Post The post office is to the south of the train station on Farimagsvej.

Sankt Peders Kirke

This large Gothic brick church dominates the square Sankt Peders Kirkeplads. Just south of Axeltorv, the church features notable 14th century frescoes, including one depicting King Valdemar IV and Queen Helvig kneeling before God. The Latin inscription to the left of the king reads 'In 1375, the day before the feast of St Crispin, King Valdemar died, do not forget it'. Sankt Peder's Kirke is open from 10 am to noon Tuesday to Friday year-round; between May and August it's also open in the afternoon from 2 to 4 pm. Admission is free.

Sankt Mortens Kirke

Also built of brick, this smaller church, midway between the train station and Axeltorv, has a strikingly similar design to Sankt Peders Kirke. The interior has period frescoes and a 6m-high altar created by the master Næstved carver Abel Schrøder in 1667. The pulpit, which dates from the early 17th century, is thought to have been carved by Schrøder's father. The church is open from 9 to 11 am Monday to Friday year-round and also from 2 to 5 pm between mid-June and mid-September. Admission is free.

Næstved Museum

The Næstved Museum has two sections. Fittingly, the local history section is in Næstved's oldest building, the 14th century Helligåndshuset (House of the Holy Ghost) at Ringstedgade 4, just north of Axeltorv. It contains 13th and 14th century church carvings and exhibits of farm, trade and peasant life from Næstved's past.

The museum's second section, Boderne, on Sankt Peders Kirkeplads, displays Næstved silverwork, Holmegaard glass and locally made pottery. Both are open from 10 am to 4 pm Tuesday to Sunday; a combination ticket costs 20 kr for adults (children free).

Other Central Sights

Constructed in 1493, **Kompagnihuset** on Kompagnistræde, just south-east of Sankt Peders Kirke, is said to be the only medieval guildhall remaining in Denmark. This timber-framed building was recently restored and can be appreciated from the outside, but the interior is not open to the public.

Apostelhuset, a half-timbered medieval building at Riddergade 5 just south of Sankt Mortens Kirke, takes its name from the 13 wooden exterior braces that separate the windows, each carved with the figure of Christ or one of the 12 apostles. Dating from about 1510, they are some of the oldest and best preserved timber-frame carvings in Denmark.

Also with roots in the medieval period is the old town hall, **Rådhuskirken**, the brick and half-timbered building at the northern side of Sankt Peders Kirke.

The town's most novel curiosity is Denmark's smallest equestrian **statue**, a tiny bronze atop a tall brick pedestal depicting Næstved's founder, Peder Bodilsen. It's located at Hjultorv, a small square just north of Axeltorv.

Holmegaards Glasværker

If you have your own transport you might want to drive out to Fensmark, about 8km north-east of Næstved, to visit the Holmegaard Glassworks. Founded in 1825, this is Denmark's principal producer of quality glass. Visitors can view the process of glass being blown by hand; there's also a shop and a little museum. It's open from 9.30 am to 1 pm Monday to Thursday and from 9.30 am to noon on Friday, as well as on summer weekends from 11 am to 4 pm. Admission is free.

Canoeing

The Suså river, which has calm waters that make for good canoeing, runs through the western part of town. You can rent canoes for 50 kr per hour (plus a 20 kr registration fee) from Suså Kanoudlejning (☎ 57 64 61 44) at Slusehuset at the southern end of

Rådmanshave, a large park north of the town centre.

Places to Stay

Næstved Vandrerhjem & Camping (☎ 55 72 20 91, fax 55 72 56 45, email nstvh @post4.tele.dk, Frejasvej 8, 4700 Næstved) is a combined hostel and one star camping ground. At the 85 bed hostel, which is open to individuals from mid-March to mid-November, dorm beds cost 70 kr and family rooms sleeping between one and six people cost from 130 to 420 kr. It's a 15 minute walk from the train station and town centre; to get there, walk south from the station and then continue east on Præstøvej.

The turistbureau maintains a list of private *rooms* available in the greater Næstved area.

Hotel Vinhuset (☎ 55 72 08 07, fax 55 72 03 35, email vinhuset@post4.tele.dk, Sankt Peders Kirkeplads 4, 4700 Næstved) is an 18th century hotel with modern renovated rooms and a prime location on the square opposite Sankt Peders Kirke. Singles/doubles with bath, phone, TV and minibar start at 615/770 kr.

Places to Eat

The *DSB Restaurant* at the train station offers moderately priced food. *Sesam Burger (Jernbanegade 13)*, a few minutes walk west of the train station, serves burgers and pitta-bread sandwiches (20 kr).

There's a *Kvickly* grocery shop about 50m farther west on Jernbanegade and a *Greek restaurant* with a moderately priced buffet at the intersection of Jernbanegade and Kattebjerg.

The central square, Axeltorv, has a *Netto* grocery shop and an outdoor *café* offering sandwiches and beer. For something more upmarket you can try one of the two restaurants at *Hotel Vinhuset*.

Getting There & Away

Næstved is 25km south of Ringsted and 28km north of Vordingborg, at the crossroads of routes 14, 22, 54 and 265. Trains run about hourly from Copenhagen (71 kr, one hour), Roskilde (43 kr, 42 minutes) and Ringsted (28 kr, 20 minutes). There are also services to Vordingborg (28 kr, 20 minutes) and Køge (43 kr, 34 minutes).

PRÆSTØ

This seaside village, on the southern coast of the Præstø Fjord, largely retains the look of a sleepy 19th century provincial town. It has a small centre with older homes and handsome buildings that can make for a pleasant hour or so of wandering; however, the main activity is at the yacht harbour, which spreads across the northern side of the town centre. Although foreign tourists are few, Præstø attracts plenty of Danish visitors, particularly sailors with their own boats.

Information

The Præstø Turistbureau (☎ 55 99 11 90), Jernbanevej 22, 4720 Præstø, is open from 9 am to 4 pm on weekdays year-round and from 9 am to 2 pm on Saturday in summer as well.

There's a Unibank at Adelgade 72 and a Den Danske Bank at Adelgade 92. The post office is north of the tourist office on Jernbanevej.

Things to See & Do

Just south of Hotel Frederiksminde on Klosternakken is **Præstø Kirke**, a church with a north nave dating from the 13th century. Before the Reformation it was an

SOUTHERN ZEALAND

Off With His Head

The old rådhus building in Præstø's cobbled town square, Torvet, once served not only as the town hall but also as a combined jail and courthouse.

It was here that a notorious criminal, Balle-Lars, was held in 1860 before his sentence was carried out; his head was chopped off in what turned out to be Denmark's last execution by decapitation.

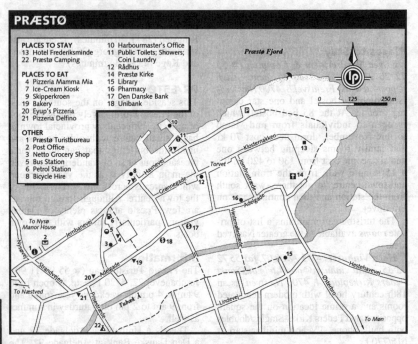

PRÆSTØ

PLACES TO STAY
13 Hotel Frederiksminde
22 Præstø Camping

PLACES TO EAT
4 Pizzeria Mamma Mia
7 Ice-Cream Kiosk
9 Skipperkroen
19 Bakery
20 Eyup's Pizzeria
21 Pizzeria Delfino

OTHER
1 Præstø Turistbureau
2 Post Office
3 Netto Grocery Shop
5 Bus Station
6 Petrol Station
8 Bicycle Hire

10 Harbourmaster's Office
11 Public Toilets; Showers;
     Coin Laundry
12 Rådhus
14 Præstø Kirke
15 Library
16 Pharmacy
17 Den Danske Bank
18 Unibank

Præstø Fjord

0   125   250 m

To Nysø
Manor House

To Næstved

To Møn

abbey church for monks of the order of St Anthony. Each of its two naves has an altar; most notable is the detailed altarpiece in the south nave, which was created by Abel Schrøder in 1657. The religious philosopher NFS Grundtvig was the parish rector here from 1821 to 1822.

A kilometre north-west of town is **Nysø**, a private manor house built in the 1670s. Although it's a low-key site, it has an interesting history. Baroness Christine Stampe, who owned Nysø in the mid-19th century, opened it as a retreat for many Danish writers and artists, including sculptor Bertel Thorvaldsen who set up a studio here. The manor isn't open to the public but a building in the grounds contains **Thorvaldsen-samlingen** (admission 15 kr), a collection of Thorvaldsen's works; it's open from 11 am to 5 pm at weekends between May

and August and daily except Monday in the summer high season.

The waters around Præstø are mostly shallow – a challenge for yachters but quite suitable for waders. There's a public **beach** good for children below Hotel Frederiksminde at the north-east of the peninsula.

Places to Stay

Præstø Camping (☎ 55 99 11 48, Spangen 2, 4720 Præstø), a simple one star facility, is 300m south of the centre of town. Cabin rentals can be arranged. It's open from mid-April to mid-September.

Hotel Frederiksminde (☎ 55 99 10 42, fax 55 99 17 65, Klosternakken 8, 4720 Præstø), built in 1868, is set on a seaside knoll. Singles/doubles cost 450/575 kr including breakfast. The two dozen rooms are all different, some quite spacious, some with ocean views, others with balcony.

Places to Eat

At *Pizzeria Mamma Mia (Adelgade 45)*, in a quaint courtyard off Jernbanevej, good pizzas start at 46 kr and lasagne and other pasta dishes cost from around 60 kr. It's open from 4 to 10 pm on Sunday and from noon to 11 pm on other days. There are two more pizzerias, *Eyup's Pizzeria* and *Pizzeria Delfino*, at the western end of Adelgade, and a fast-food *grill* at the bus station.

Down at the harbour in the attractive old customs house is *Skipperkroen*, which offers good fish dishes and an engaging atmosphere. A light lunch will cost about 75 kr, a full lunch 150 kr and dinner a bit more. It's open from noon to 8 pm daily.

Getting There & Away

Route 265 passes Præstø on its way between Næstved (25km) and Møn (26km). Bus No 79 connects Præstø with Næstved (28 kr, 40 minutes) hourly, and bus No 256 connects Præstø with Møn (28 kr, 40 minutes) every two or three hours. There are no train services to Præstø.

VORDINGBORG

Strategically located on the strait between Zealand and Falster, Vordingborg played an important role in Denmark's medieval history. It was the royal residence of Valdemar I, whose ascension to the throne in 1157 marked the end of a contentious period of rebellion and served to reunite the Danish kingdom, and it continued to be a favoured residence of other kings of the Valdemar dynasty. With its large natural harbour, Vordingborg also served as the staging area for Bishop Absalon's late-12th century military campaigns against the Wends of eastern Germany.

During the 15th century Vordingborg slipped from prominence, in part because the Kalmar Union had so greatly expanded Danish rule elsewhere in Scandinavia that the royal family now took little interest in it.

Vordingborg is now a quiet town (population 10,000) built around the ruins of the old castle and fortress. It's also the

---

The Jutland Code

The Jutland Code, which codified traditional law and was thus one of the most important doctrines of the Middle Ages, was sanctioned by Valdemar II in Vordingborg in 1241. Today virtually every schoolchild in Denmark can recite the code's preamble 'Mæth logh skal land byggiæs' (With law shall a land be built).

---

jumping-off point for trips to Møn if you're travelling by public transport.

Information

The Vordingborg Turistbureau (☎ 55 34 11 11, fax 55 34 03 08) at Algade 96, 4760 Vordingborg, just east of Gåsetårnet, is open from 9 am to 4 pm Monday to Friday and from 9 am to noon on Saturday. In summer it stays open to 5 pm on weekdays and to 2 pm on Saturday. Its Web site is at www.vordingborg.dk/bibliotek/turisti .htm.

There are several banks on Algade, including a Jyske Bank at Algade 57 and a Unibank at Algade 78.

The post office is just north of the train station at Årsleffsgade 1.

Things to See & Do

The 14th century **Gåsetårnet** (Goose Tower), once part of a huge royal castle and fortress, is Scandinavia's best-preserved medieval tower and the only intact structure remaining from the Valdemar era. The name stems from 1368, when Valdemar IV placed a golden goose on top of the tower to express his scorn for the German Hanseatic League's declaration of war (Valdemar referred to the league as 'cackling geese'). The rest of the fortress, including seven other towers, has been demolished over the centuries but the 36m-high Gåsetårnet was spared because of its function as a navigational landmark. The tower's 101 steps can be climbed for a good view of the surrounding area.

The fortress grounds, which have been turned into a pleasant park with walking paths, also contain various brick and stone **foundation ruins** and an attractive little **botanical garden** (admission free).

In addition, the grounds hold the **Sydsjællands Museum**, southern Zealand's regional history museum, which has a Stone Age collection as well as sections on the Middle Ages and the Renaissance, including trade and craft exhibits, church decorations and textiles.

Both the museum and Gåsetårnet are open from 10 am to 5 pm daily between June and August, and from 10 am to 4 pm Tuesday to Sunday during the rest of the year. The admission fee, 20 kr for adults and 5 kr for children, covers both sights. To get there from the train station, walk north to the nearby post office and then turn south-east onto Algade, which leads directly to the fortress grounds.

A few minutes walk to the west at Kirketorvet is **Vor Frue Kirke**, which has a nave dating from the mid-15th century, frescoes and a Baroque altarpiece carved by Abel Schrøder in 1642. It's open to the public from 10 am to noon daily (admission free).

Walking Track If you have your own transport and are up to a walk, **Knudshoved Odde**, the narrow 18km-long peninsula west of Vordingborg, offers some hiking opportunities in an area known for its 'Bronze Age landscape'. The peninsula also has a small herd of American buffalo brought in by the Rosenfeldt family who own Knudshoved Odde. There's a car park (10 kr) about halfway down the peninsula, where the trail begins.

Places to Stay

At the **Vordingborg Vandrerhjem** (☎ 55 36 08 00, fax 55 36 08 01, email vandrerhjem @videnscentret.dk, Præstedgårdsvej 14, 4760 Vordingborg), in the countryside about 2km north of town, dorm beds cost 90 kr and singles/doubles cost 180/270 kr. It's open year-round except from mid-December to early January.

The 65 room **Hotel Kong Valdemar** (☎ 55 34 30 95, fax 55 34 04 95, Algade 101, 4760 Vordingborg) is in the town centre opposite Gåsetårnet. Singles/doubles with bath, phone, TV and minibar cost 575/750 kr, but there are also a few simple rooms with shared bath costing 375/500 kr. The hotel has a restaurant, a bar and a sauna.

Places to Eat

There are numerous cafés and restaurants on Algade, the town's main commercial street. These include **Vagns Konditori** (Algade 31), which is both a bakery and a café; two inexpensive pizzerias, **Milas Pizza-Bar** (Algade 16) and **Pizzeria Roma** (Algade 80); and **Restaurant Konya** (Algade 69), which blends Turkish and Chinese cuisines.

Getting There & Away

Vordingborg is 28km south of Næstved via route 22 and 13km from Møn via route 59. By train, Vordingborg is 80 minutes (84 kr) from Copenhagen and 20 minutes (28 kr) from Næstved. If you're en route to Møn, you'll need to switch from the train to the bus at Vordingborg train station; see the Getting There & Away section of the Møn chapter for more details.

Møn, Falster & Lolland

The three main islands south of Zealand – Møn, Falster and Lolland – are all connected with Zealand by bridges. Møn is known for its unique chalk seacliffs and Falster has fine white-sand beaches. Lolland, the largest of the three islands, has a handful of scattered sights that are only practical to explore if you have your own transport. All three islands are predominantly rural and, except for Møn's rolling hills, the terrain is largely flat and monotonous.

Møn

Although its main allure is the spectacular white cliffs of Møns Klint on the east coast, Møn is a thoroughly appealing island. The scenery is rustic and the pace slow; the entire island has only 11,000 residents. There are good beaches, prehistoric passage graves and medieval churches with outstanding frescoes.

Møn's interior is largely given over to fields of rapeseed, grain and sugar beet, although agriculture has been in decline since the island's only sugar refinery closed in the early 1990s. Møn's rich clay soil has given rise to numerous pottery shops, and *keramik* signs are commonplace along its country roads.

Travellers using public transport should note that the island lacks a train system and the bus service is sketchy. Still, for those with time to explore, Møn offers a generous dose of what Danes call 'lovely nature'.

GETTING THERE & AWAY

Route 59 connects southern Zealand with Møn.

As there's no rail service to Møn, visitors travelling on the train need to take the Copenhagen-Nykøbing F line to Vordingborg in southern Zealand and switch to a bus there. Trains from Copenhagen to Vordingborg (84 kr, 80 minutes) leave about

Highlights

- Hike around the gleaming white chalk cliffs at Møns Klint
- Tour Møn's medieval churches, admiring their splendid frescoes
- Join the holiday-makers at Marielyst, Falster's premier summer beach resort
- Visit Maribo, a peaceful town with lakeside walking trails (Lolland)
- Drive through Knuthenborg Safari Park with its free-roaming animals (Lolland)

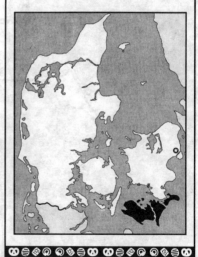

hourly from early morning until around midnight.

Bus No 62 from Vordingborg to Stege (28 kr, 45 minutes) connects with train arrivals, leaving Vordingborg about once an hour; as with the train, there's a somewhat fuller service during weekday rush hours and a lighter service at weekends. Bus No

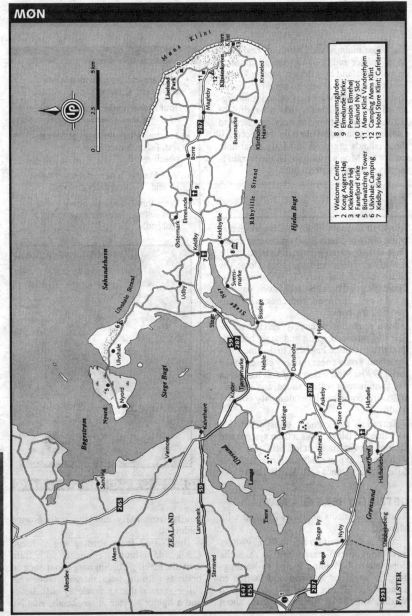

MØN

Møn Klint
Liselund Park
10
11
112
Klinteskoven
Store Klint
13
Kraneled
Magleby
287
Busemarke
Borre
Klintholm Havn
Råbylille Strand
Østermark
9
Elmelunde
Keldby
Keldbylille
7
Hjelm Bugt
Sehundehavn
8
Svens-marke
Ulvshale Strand
Udby
Bissinge
Stege Nor
Ulvshale
6
Stege
Hjelm
5
59
287
Nyord
Neble
Damsholte
Stege Bugt
Koster
Tømmerække
287
Askeby
Store Damme
Hårbølle
4
Bøgestrøm
Kalvehave
Røddinge
Toftenæs
Sandvig
Vemose
Ulvsund
Raddinge
2
Hårbøllebo
Mem
Langebæk
59
Langø
Tærø
Fanefjord
Grønsund
Stubbekøbing
265
Stensved
Bøge By
Nyby
Allerslev
ZEALAND
Bøge
293
E47
E55
287
1
FALSTER

1 Welcome Centre
2 Kong Asgers Høj
3 Klekkende Høj
4 Fanefjord Kirke
5 Birdwatching Tower
6 Ulvshale Camping
7 Keldby Kirke
8 Museumsgården
9 Elmelunde Kirke;
   Pension Elmehøj
10 Liselund Ny Slot
11 Møns Klint Vandrerhjem
12 Camping Møns Klint
13 Hotel Store Klint; Cafeteria

0   2.5   5 km

50 runs between Stege and Nykøbing F about once every two hours; the trip costs 28 kr and takes 55 minutes.

GETTING AROUND

Møn's main road is route 287, which cuts across the centre of the island from east to west. There are lots of narrow rural roads branching off route 287 that can be slow-going but fun to explore.

Bus

Møn's bus station is in Stege, the departure point for all bus routes. Fares depend on the number of zones you travel in, with the highest fare between any two points on Møn being 20 kr, although most buses cost only 8 kr if you don't need to transfer, 12 kr if you do. Frequency of service varies with the day of the week and the season.

The most frequent service is bus No 62, which goes from Stege to Klintholm Havn via Elmelunde and Magleby about hourly on weekdays and every couple of hours at weekends. Magleby is the most easterly town with a year-round bus service but from late June to mid-August the seasonal bus No 54 runs from Stege to Møns Klint three times each day. Bus No 63 runs from Stege to Ulvshale and No 64 runs from Stege to Bogø.

Bicycle

There's a signposted cycle path running between Stege and Møns Klint, and another from Stege to Bogø. Møns Turistbureau distributes a free Danish-language pamphlet called *Cykelture på Møn* that maps out six suggested cycling tours of the island, collectively taking in all of the island's major sights.

Bicycles can be rented in Stege at Møn Cykler (☎ 55 81 02 67), Storegade 60, and at Møns Dæk Service (☎ 55 81 42 49), Storegade 91.

STEGE

Stege is the main town and commercial centre of the island of Møn. Most visitors to Møn will pass through Stege, as it contains the bus terminal, the tourist office and other central facilities. It also boasts the island's best selection of places to eat, most of which can be found along Storegade, the main shopping street.

During the Middle Ages, Stege was one of Denmark's wealthiest provincial towns, thanks to its position as a central market for the lucrative herring fishing business. The entire town was once surrounded by fortress walls; remnants of the ramparts can still be found, including a section near Stege Camping.

In the mid-19th century a large sugar mill was erected on the western side of town but, with the demise of the sugar beet industry, the mill has been converted into a fledgling business zone where a handful of small enterprises, including an eel farm, are being encouraged.

Information

Tourist Office Møns Turistbureau (☎ 55 81 44 11, fax 55 81 48 46), Storegade 2, 4780 Stege, adjacent to the bus station, has information on the entire island. Staff there can book beach cottages and rooms in island farmhouses for you. The turistbureau also sells a few inexpensive publications on local topics such as Møn's passage graves. Between mid-June and 31 August it's open from 10 am to 6 pm Monday to Saturday and from 10 am to noon on Sunday; during the rest of the year it's open from 10 am to 5 pm Monday to Friday and from 9 am to noon on Saturday. Its Web site is at www.moen-tourist bureau.dk.

Money There are three banks in Stege centre, including a Unibank at Storegade 23 that has an ATM. All banks are open from 9.30 am to 4 pm Monday to Friday (to 6 pm on Thursday).

Post The post office, opposite the turistbureau, is open from 10 am to 5 pm Monday to Friday and from 10 am to noon on Saturday.

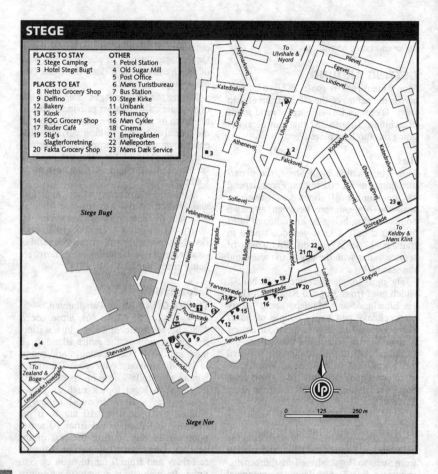

STEGE

PLACES TO STAY
2 Stege Camping
3 Hotel Stege Bugt

PLACES TO EAT
8 Netto Grocery Shop
9 Delfino
12 Bakery
13 Kiosk
14 FOG Grocery Shop
17 Ruder Café
19 Stig's
   Slagterforretning
20 Fakta Grocery Shop

OTHER
1 Petrol Station
4 Old Sugar Mill
5 Post Office
6 Møns Turistbureau
7 Bus Station
10 Stege Kirke
11 Unibank
15 Pharmacy
16 Møn Cykler
18 Cinema
21 Empiregården
22 Mølleporten
23 Møns Dæk Service

Stege Kirke

The oldest part of the Stege church was built in Romanesque style in the early 13th century by Møn's ruler, Jakob Sunesen, a member of the powerful Hvide family that controlled much of southern Zealand. In the late 15th century this 60m-long church was expanded to its present dimensions; the main nave is flanked by two smaller naves, each of which boasts high vaulted ceilings and pointed arch windows.

Noteworthy are the primitive-style ceiling frescoes, some with whimsical jester-like characters, including one depicting a hunter with a pack of dogs chasing a fox and hare. The frescoes, which were white-washed over centuries ago, were exposed and restored in 1892 (see the boxed text 'Church Frescoes' on page 221). The church also has a splendidly carved pulpit dating from 1630, featuring reliefs of biblical scenes. Each relief is separated by a narrow vertical panel depicting virtues such as hope and truth, and below each of those is a grotesque little caricature mask to serve as a reminder of the horrors that await the unvirtuous.

The church, on Provstestræde, is open to the public from 9 am to 5 pm daily, except on Monday and during church services.

Empiregården

The Møn Museum has two sections, one in Stege and the other near Keldbylille village. The Stege section, called Empiregården, is at Storegade 75 and covers local cultural history. There are fossilised sea urchins, archaeological finds dating from the Stone Age to the Middle Ages, old coins, pottery and displays of 19th century house interiors. It's open from 10 am to 4 pm Tuesday to Sunday. Admission costs 25 kr (children free).

Mølleporten

Of the three medieval gates that once allowed entry into the town, Mølleporten (Mill Gate) on Storegade is the only one still standing and is considered one of the best-preserved town gates in the whole of Denmark. It bears a resemblance to the Stege Kirke tower; both are made of red brick and are distinctively lined with horizontal strips of white chalk from Møns Klint.

Places to Stay

The town-owned *Stege Camping* (☎ 55 81 84 04, Falcksvej 5, 4780 Stege) is a pleasant little camping ground just 500m north of the town centre. It's open from 1 May to 15 September.

Hotel Stege Bugt (☎ 55 81 54 54, fax 55 81 58 90, Langelinie 48, 4780 Stege), a small, modern, three storey motel-style place, is 600m north of the turistbureau. Each of the 27 rooms has a bath, TV, phone and minibar, and many have balconies with sea views. Singles/doubles cost 500/650 kr.

Places to Eat

There's a good *bakery* at Storegade 36 and three *grocery shops* elsewhere along Store-gade. On Torvet you'll find a *kiosk* selling inexpensive hot dogs and ice cream.

Ruder Café (Storegade 68) is an appealing café serving reasonably priced light eats such as salads, sandwiches and ice cream.

Stig's Slagterforretning, a butcher shop at Storegade 59, sells takeaway smørrebrød sandwiches and is open until at least 5 pm on weekdays and 1 pm on Saturday.

Delfino (Storegade 10) is a popular Italian restaurant where pizza starts at 33 kr and pasta dishes cost from around 55 kr. It's open from noon to 10 pm daily, but try to avoid peak hours as service can grind to a virtual halt when it's busy.

ULVSHALE & NYORD

The north-eastern side of the Ulvshale peninsula, 6km north of Stege, boasts one of Møn's best beaches and a primeval forest that's one of the few virgin woods left in Denmark. The main road, Ulvshalevej, runs right along the beach, called Ulvshale Strand. If you're travelling by car, there's a car park just south of Ulvshale Camping, but you can also park along the road. The forest, which is crisscrossed by a network of walking trails, begins north-west of Ulvshale Camping and extends to the end of the peninsula, where there's a bridge to the island of Nyord.

Nyord has been connected to the Møn mainland for just a decade. Its former isolation served to safeguard the island from development; now its little one-lane bridge boasts Møn's only traffic light! Its sole village, also named Nyord, is a characteristic 19th century hamlet of old houses with well-tended gardens. There's a yacht harbour, a small octagonal church (built circa 1846) and a little red-brick hut called Møllestangen where villagers once kept watch over the sound to make sure no boats came through without first stopping to hire a Nyord pilot.

Much of the island, particularly the eastern side, is given over to marshland and offers excellent **birdwatching** opportunities. There's a birdwatching tower on the northern side of the road about 1km west of the

MØN, FALSTER & LOLLAND

bridge. The bridge itself is also a good bird-watching site, as is the marsh on the Ulvshale side.

Birds spotted in the area include osprey, kestrel, rough-legged hawk, snow bunting, ruff, avocet, swan, black-tailed godwit, arctic tern, curlew and various ducks.

Places to Stay & Eat
Ulvshale Camping (☎ 55 81 53 25, *Ulvshalevej 236, 4780 Stege*), a two star town-owned camping ground, is right by the beach and on the main road through Ulvshale. There's a shop selling bread, pastries and limited groceries, and bikes are available for hire. The camping ground is open from April to September.

Fætter Fiks (Ulvshalevej 151), opposite Ulvshale Strand, is a popular place offering reasonably priced food. It serves burgers, ice cream and more substantial fare such as half a chicken with chips (54 kr).

On Nyord, *Lolles Gård* is a pleasant little lunch spot in the village centre that specialises in fried eels (125 kr) but also serves omelettes and other light eats for half that price.

KELDBY
The Keldby area, about 5km east of Stege, is noted mainly for its roadside church, but there's also a small farm museum 3km south of route 287.

Keldby Kirke
Keldby's brick church, the nave of which dates back to the early 13th century, has a splendid collection of fresco paintings splashed across its walls, arches and ceiling. The frescoes were painted over a period of two centuries, with the oldest (1275) decorating the chancel walls and depicting scenes from the book of Genesis. Scores of other expressionistic scenes, from the vivid sacrifice of Cain and Abel to a large mural of doomsday, make this one of the most intriguing collection of church frescoes in Denmark. The church pulpit was carved in 1586. You'll find an interesting tombstone at the northern side of the chancel that dates

back to 1347 and shows three nobles in period dress.

The church is open from 7 am to 5 pm between April and October and from 8 am to 4 pm during the winter.

Museumsgården
This low-key museum, in a four-winged farmhouse at Skullebjergvej 15, south of Keldbylille, depicts life on a small Møn farm in the 19th century. Essentially it's an old farmstead that remained in the same family for generations and was turned over to the Møns Museum after its bachelor owner, Hans Hansen, died in 1964. The drive to it takes you, appropriately, through fields of sugar beet and wheat. The museum is open from 10 am to 4 pm Tuesday to Sunday between May and October. Admission costs 25 kr (children free).

ELMELUNDE
Elmelunde is a small, rural hamlet with an appealing guesthouse and an ancient church, both on the main road between Stege and Møns Klint. Bus No 62 stops right in front of the church.

Elmelunde Kirke
Elmelunde Kirke is one of Denmark's oldest stone churches; the section around the choir dates back to 1080. The nave was lengthened during the Romanesque period and the lower section of the tower was added in around 1300. The church features wonderful frescoes ranging in subject from Adam and Eve's expulsion from Eden at the rear of the church to heavenly scenes above the altar. The altar, from 1646, is intricately carved and painted, while the pulpit, its weight carried by a figure of the apostle Peter, dates back to 1649. The three-pointed vaults over the nave were added in 1460 and painted by the Elmelunde master (see the boxed text 'Church Frescoes'). Elmelunde Kirke is open from 7 am to 5 pm.

Places to Stay & Eat
Pension Elmehøj (☎ 55 81 35 35, fax 55 81 32 67, Kirkebakken 39, 4780 Stege), right

Church Frescoes

Møn's churches are enlivened with some of the best-preserved frescoes in Denmark. A vivid form of peasant art, the paintings are so splendid that the churches can be likened to medieval art galleries. The frescoes, which served as a means of describing the Bible to illiterate peasants, run the gamut from light-hearted scenes from Genesis to depictions of grotesque demons and the fires of hell.

Frescoes are created by painting with watercolours on newly plastered, still-wet walls or ceilings, which allows the colours to penetrate deep into the plaster before it dries. The frescoes in Stege Kirke were painted solely in black and ochre-red, whereas those in the other Møn churches employ a fuller range of colour.

Møn's frescoes were whitewashed over in the 17th century by Lutheran ministers who thought they too closely represented Catholic themes of the pre-Reformation days. In many cases a protective layer of dust separated the frescoes from the whitewash. Ironically, the whitewashing served to preserve this medieval art from soiling and fading, rather than obliterating it. The whitewash wasn't removed from most of the churches until the 20th century, at which time the frescoes were restored by artists under the auspices of Denmark's national museum.

When you visit Møn's churches you may notice a similar style in many of the frescoes. This is because most of those dating from the 15th century were painted by the same artist, whose exact identity is a mystery but who has come to be known over the centuries as Elmelundemesteren (the Elmelunde master). This artist used distinctive warm earth tones: russet, mustard, sienna, brick red, chestnut brown, soft grey and pale aqua.

---

next door to Elmelunde Kirke, makes a convenient base because it's equidistant from Stege, Klintholm Havn and Møns Klint. Møn-born Brit and her Australian husband, Jonathan Olifent, have taken a former home for the elderly and turned it into an inviting, good-value guesthouse. There are 23 pleasant rooms, all with shared toilets and showers. Singles/doubles cost 230/390 kr including breakfast. Guests have access to a shared kitchen and a TV lounge. Pension Elmehøj is accessible to people in wheelchairs and has a lift.

With advance notice, you can eat a two course dinner for 90 kr at the guesthouse, and a simple inexpensive lunch is usually available as well.

The nearest restaurant is *Kaj Kok (Klintevej 151)*, on the main road 2km west of the pension. Kaj Kok serves good but pricey steaks and schnitzels as well as light eats such as chicken and chips (55 kr).

MØNS KLINT & KLINTESKOVEN

The chalk cliffs at Møns Klint were created 5000 years ago when the calcareous deposits from aeons-worth of seashells were lifted from the ocean floor. The gleaming white cliffs rise sharply 128m above an azure sea, presenting one of the most striking landscapes in Denmark. The cliffs are a repository for fossilised Cretaceous-period shells, many of them from creatures long extinct.

Møns Klint is a popular destination for Danish tourists. The main visitor area, Store Klint, has a cafeteria, a small hotel, souvenir shops, a car park (parking costs 25 kr) and picnic grounds. Still, none of this detracts from the natural beauty of the cliffs themselves.

You can walk down the cliffs to the beach and directly back up again in about 30 minutes; alternatively, you can head along the shoreline in either direction and then loop back up through a thick forest of wind-gnarled beech trees for a harder walk lasting about 1½ hours. Either way, start on the steps directly below the cafeteria – it's a quick route to the most scenic stretch of the cliffs.

You needn't limit your hiking to the coast. Klinteskoven (Klinte Forest), the woodland that extends 3km inland from the cliffs, is crisscrossed by an extensive network of footpaths and horse trails. Although most people start their hikes from the cliffs, if you're staying at Camping Møns Klint (see the Places to Stay & Eat section), there's a trail from there as well. One interesting track leads 1km west from Store Klint to Timmesø Bjerg, a hilltop that is the site of castle ruins dating back to around 1100 AD. Other trails lead to lakes, marshes, ancient barrows and old-growth forests where deer run free.

Rent A Horse (☎ 55 81 25 25) at Lange-bjergvej 1, near Møns Klint Vandrerhjem, offers 1½ hour guided horse-riding tours of the Møns Klint area costing 150 kr.

Places to Stay & Eat

Camping Møns Klint (☎ 55 81 20 25, fax 55 81 27 97, Klintevej 544, 4791 Borre) borders Klinteskoven. This two star camping ground has a 25m swimming pool, a guest kitchen, a coin laundry, bicycles for hire and a shop selling bread, beer and other basics. It's open from 1 April to 31 October.

Møns Klint Vandrerhjem (☎ 55 81 20 30, fax 55 81 28 18, Langebjergvej 1, 4791 Borre) is in a former hotel 3km north-west of Møns Klint, opposite Camping Møns Klint. It has a pleasant location, right on a lake, with lots of shady trees and scurrying hares. The 29 rooms contain 105 beds in all; dorm beds cost 80 kr, singles/doubles cost 175/220 kr. Breakfast is available and there's a guest kitchen. It's open from 1 May to 1 October. From late-June to mid-August you can take the Møns Klint bus No 54 from Stege, but during the rest of the year the nearest stop is in Magleby, 2.75km west of the hostel, where bus No 62 drops off.

Møns Klint's Unusual Flora

The unique ecosystem at Møns Klint is the result of its unusual soil. The beech trees along this coast keep their fresh spring-green hue throughout the summer thanks to the soil's high chalk content, which inhibits their intake of iron and magnesium, the elements that cause leaves to darken.

The calcareous soil also provides ideal conditions for orchids. Klinteskoven, the wood that backs the cliffs, is the habitat of 20 species of orchid, the greatest variety anywhere in Denmark. The flowering season is from May to August. The grassy hills in the Mandemarke area in the southern part of the woods are particularly abundant with wild orchids.

Two of the more beautiful flowers are the pyramidal orchid (*Anacamptis pyramidalis*), which has a mounded, multiblossomed pink head, and the dark red helleborine (*Epipactis atrorubens*), which has an oval leaf and a tall stem with numerous crimson flowers. Look but don't touch, as many of the orchids are rare and all are protected.

pyramidal orchid
(*Anacamptis pyramidalis*)

The 18 room *Hotel Store Klint* (☎ 55 81 90 08, Stengårdsvej 6, 4791 Borre) offers the only accommodation right at Møns Klint. This three storey hotel is perched above the cliffs a stone's throw from the cafeteria, where you check in. Singles cost 350 kr, doubles from 475 to 550 kr, depending on the room and view. The bathrooms are shared. Breakfast is included in the price.

The *cafeteria* at Møns Klint, which is open from 10.30 am to 6 pm, offers simple food such as soup and bread (35 kr) and chicken or fish with chips (55 kr). There's a little *kiosk* below the cafeteria where you can buy ice cream.

If you'd like to stay in a small manorhouse hotel, *Liselund Ny Slot* (☎ 55 81 20 81, fax 55 81 21 91, Langebjergvej 6, 4791 Borre) occupies an upmarket 19th century home in the midst of an expansive estate that's been turned into a park of lawns, duck ponds and gardens. There are 15 rooms with bath, costing 720/1030 kr for singles/doubles including breakfast. There's also an expensive fine-dining restaurant. Liselund is near the coast, 2km north of Møns Klint Vandrerhjem.

KLINTHOLM HAVN

Klintholm Havn is a pleasant little harbourside village with a long sandy beach. Half touristy, half local, it has one harbour filled with working fishing boats and an adjacent harbour given over to yachts, many belonging to German tourists.

This one-road village has a bank that's open for two hours in the morning, a grocery shop, a handful of eateries, a large harbourside resort and a little seaside inn.

Beyond that, it's mostly beach, which extends in both directions from the two harbours. The section that runs east is particularly appealing and pristine, with light grey sand backed by low dunes; it can be a fun place to stroll along and also has the best surf. The safest swimming is found along the western section. There are public toilets and showers near the end of the road by the western part of the beach.

Places to Stay

Klintholm Søbad (☎ 55 81 91 23, Thyravej 19, 4791 Borre) is a small *kro* (inn) comprising half a dozen cottages with kitchens and TV; each can accommodate a small family and costs 550 kr. There are also a couple of rooms with shared bath in the main building that cost 300/400 kr for singles/doubles.

Danland/Feriehotel Østersøen (☎ 55 81 90 55, fax 55 81 90 56, 4791 Borre) is a large apartment resort spread across an artificial peninsula separating the two harbours. It's modern and has a pool, sauna, restaurant, coin laundry and other conveniences. Each of the 79 units has two bedrooms, a bathroom, a kitchen and a TV. The complex rate system varies with the season, with the highest prices in summer when the cheapest rooms (those without sea views) cost 2000 kr for a three night stay.

Places to Eat

There are half a dozen restaurants along the waterfront road, ranging from a beachside hot dog and burger joint to seafood restaurants.

For a typically Danish experience, try *Klintholm Søbad*, which has a dining room with a sea view and fresh fish dishes costing around 100 kr at dinner; at lunchtime there are specials costing around 40 kr.

More touristy is *Hyttefadet*, a lively eatery opposite the fishing harbour, offering a daily meal for 75 kr; it's open from noon to 10 pm daily.

For the best value in the area, take the coastal road 250m east of the fishing harbour to *Klintholm Røgeri*, where you can buy smoked and fried fish by the piece, enjoy an inexpensive beer and sit down to feast at picnic tables. It's open from 10 am to 6 pm daily.

WESTERN MØN

The western end of Møn is largely farmland crisscrossed by narrow country roads. This part of the island has a few worthwhile historic sights but you'll need your own transport to visit them, as the public bus system primarily serves route 287.

Passage Graves

Møn's two best-known Stone Age passage graves, Kong Asgers Høj and Klekkende Høj, are not far from each other on the western side of the island. Both are about 2km from the village of Røddinge and are signposted.

Kong Asgers Høj is in a farmer's field north-west of Røddinge on Kong Asgers Vej; you can see the mound clearly from the road. This is Denmark's largest passage grave, with a burial chamber 10m long and more than 2m wide. Bring a torch (flashlight) and watch your head!

Klekkende Høj, south-east of Røddinge, is the only double passage grave mound on Møn. It has two entrances side by side, each leading to a 7m-long chamber.

Fanefjord Kirke

Fanefjord Kirke, overlooking the Fanefjord, was built in around 1250 in the early Gothic style. The current church still incorporates parts of the original structure but there have been a number of additions over the centuries. The church is adorned with superb frescoes; the oldest, which date back to 1350 and can be seen at the rood arch, depict St Christopher carrying Christ across a ford. Most of the other frescoes date from around 1450 and were created by the Elmelunde master, whose mark (which resembles a stick man with rabbit ears) can be seen on an altar-facing rib in the north-eastern vault. The church is open from 8 am to 6 pm (from 9.30 am on Sunday).

BOGØ

The island of Bogø, west of Møn, is connected to Møn by a causeway and to Zealand and Falster via the impressive Farø bridges.

Bogø chocolate, well known throughout Denmark, hails from the island, which also has a Dutch windmill built in 1852 and a Gothic church. A car ferry, dating back to the days when Bogø had no causeways or bridges, still shuttles between the southern side of the island and Stubbekøbing in Falster. Bicycles are not allowed on the Farø bridges so cyclists will need to take the ferry (60 kr) which runs once an hour.

Near the ramp to the Farø bridges is a **welcome centre** housing a cafeteria, toilets, money exchange and the Bogø chocolate production centre, which can be toured for 25 kr. There's also a tourist office where you can load up with brochures from 9 am to 5 pm daily (to 8 pm in summer).

Falster

The island of Falster is almost entirely given over to agriculture and its roads literally slice across farmers' fields. Although the scenery of the interior can become repetitious, Falster's south-eastern coast is a summer haven, lined with lovely white-sand beaches that are a magnet for German and Danish holiday-makers.

If you're poking around Falster, the island's rural hamlets and small towns contain a few sights, including a **tractor museum** in Eskilstrup, a **motorcycle and radio museum** in Stubbekøbing, a restored **windmill** in Gedesby and **frescoes** by the Elmelunde master at the church in Nørre Alslev.

The E55 highway runs the length of the island; for those travelling by bicycle there are cycle lanes along the motorway in both directions.

NYKØBING F

With a population of 25,000, Nykøbing F is Falster's only large town. The F, incidentally, stands for Falster and is used to differentiate the town from Denmark's two other Nykøbings, located in Zealand and Jutland.

The grand medieval castle of Nykøbing F was torn down in the 18th century (you can see a model of it in the local history museum) and with few exceptions the town has a predominantly modern façade. Still, if you need to stay overnight there's a hostel, a moderately priced hotel and some sights to fill the day.

The striking chalk cliffs of Møns Klint.

Half-timbered house in Maribo on Lolland.

Colourful medieval frescoes in Fanefjord Kirke.

Passage grave, Møn.

The ceiling of Elmelunde Kirke is adorned with fine frescoes.

Østerlars Rundkirke is the most impressive of Bornholm's fortified round churches.

Svaneke has a well-preserved historic character.

Tiny Christiansø is a charming fortress island.

Torvet, the town centre, is a 10 minute walk west of the train station.

Information

Nykøbing F Turistinformation (☎ 54 85 13 03, fax 54 85 10 05) is just south of Torvet at Østergågade 7, 4800 Nykøbing F. It's open from 10 am to 5 pm Monday to Thursday, from 10 am to 7 pm on Friday and from 10 am to 1 pm on Saturday.

The post office is to the north of the train station.

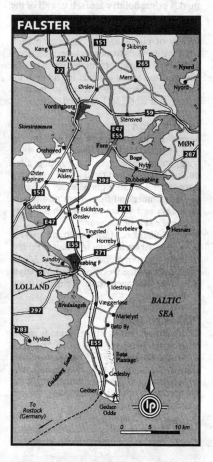

Things to See & Do

Climb the old **water tower** off Østergågade, just south of Nykøbing F Turistinformation, for a bird's-eye view of the town. It's open from 10 am to 4 pm on weekdays (to 1 pm on Saturday). Admission costs 20 kr.

Museet Falsters Minder, the local history museum, is in one of Nykøbing F's oldest houses, a half-timbered building dating back to around 1700. The house itself is referred to as Czarens Hus because the Russian tsar Peter the Great stayed here en route to Copenhagen in 1716. It's on the corner of Langgade and Færgestræde, on the western side of Torvet. Between May and mid-September it's open from 11 am to 5 pm Tuesday to Friday, from 11 am to 3 pm on Saturday and from 2 to 4 pm on Sunday; during the rest of the year it's open in the afternoon only. Admission costs 20 kr.

Brandmuseum (a fire engine museum), Vendersgade 6, is open from 10 am to 3 pm Monday to Friday and from 10 am to noon on Saturday. Admission costs 12 kr (children 6 kr).

There's a children's **zoo** at Østre Allé 97, 1km east of the train station, featuring flamingos, goats, deer, monkeys and llamas. It's open from 9 am to 8 pm daily in summer from 9 am to 4 pm in winter; admission is free.

The area's most popular sight is **Middelaldercentret** (Medieval Centre; ☎ 54 86 19 34) on the outskirts of town, which recreates a medieval village with costumed interpreters demonstrating crafts and games, falconry and the like. There's a large wooden catapult, a smithy and a number of buildings constructed as they would have been in the Middle Ages. The latest project is the construction of a medieval-style ship. A good time to visit is during one of the jousting tournaments, which typically occur daily in July and on Sunday in other months. Middelaldercentret is open from 10 am to 4 pm daily between 1 May and 30 September. Admission costs 60 kr (children 30 kr). It is located across the bridge in Lolland, at Ved Hamborgskoven 2 in

MØN, FALSTER & LOLLAND

Sundby; take bus No 2 (No 12 at weekends) from Nykøbing F train station.

Places to Stay

The two star *Nykøbing F Camping* (☎ *54 85 45 45, fax 54 82 32 42, Østre Allé 112, 4800 Nykøbing F)* is open from May to mid-September.

Falster's only hostel is the 94 bed *Nykøbing Falster Vandrerhjem* (☎ *54 85 66 99, fax 54 82 32 42, Østre Allé 110, 4800 Nykøbing F)*, 1km east of the train station and opposite the zoo. Dorm beds cost 85 kr and singles/doubles cost 200/250 kr; it's open from mid-January to mid-December. Bus No 42 (8 kr) from Nykøbing F station stops in front.

Nykøbing F Turistinformation keeps a list of *rooms* available in private homes; prices start at around 100 kr per person.

Teaterhotellet (☎ *54 85 32 77, fax 54 85 22 40, Torvet 3, 4800 Nykøbing F)*, a small central hotel, has 38 straightforward rooms that cost 290/425 kr for singles/doubles with shared bath, 335/460 kr with bath, including breakfast.

Places to Eat

Nykøbing F train station has a *kiosk* selling fresh fruit, a *snack bar* offering drinks, ice cream and sandwiches and a full *DSB Restaurant*. There's a *McDonald's* opposite the station.

You can find half a dozen simple places to eat on Torvet where the specials of the day are priced between 40 and 55 kr. On the pedestrian street Jernbanegade, about midway between the train station and Torvet, you'll find *Sanchos*, which serves inexpensive pizza and Mexican food, a *Kvickly* grocery shop and a *bakery*.

Getting There & Away

Trains leave Copenhagen hourly for Nykøbing F (102 kr, two hours).

The bus stop is to the south of the train station. Bus Nos 40, 41 and 42 run to Marielyst (20 kr, 25 minutes) frequently, particularly on weekdays. Bus No 39 runs

to Gedser (20 kr, 35 minutes) about hourly throughout the day.

Nykøbing F is 128km south-west of Copenhagen and 24km north of Gedser. The north-south E55 highway goes directly through Nykøbing F, while route 9 connects Nykøbing F with Lolland via the Frederik IX bridge.

MARIELYST

The most glorious stretch of beach in Falster is at Marielyst which, with 6000 summer cottages, ranks as one of Denmark's prime holiday areas. It has all of the expected beach resort facilities including numerous places to eat and drink and a variety of places to stay in, ranging from camping grounds to a chain hotel. Although Marielyst draws lots of visitors in the summer, the beach extends for many kilometres and there's easy access to its entire length so it won't feel crowded.

Information

Marielyst Turistbureau (☎ 54 13 62 98, fax 54 13 62 99), Marielyst Strandpark 3, 4873 Væggerløse, is next to the bowling alley on the north-western outskirts of town. It's open from 9 am to 5 pm Monday to Saturday in summer and from 9 am to 4 pm on weekdays and 10 am to 2 pm on Saturday during the rest of the year.

The Unibank at Marielyst Strandvej 54 is open from 10 am to 3 pm Monday to Friday.

There's a coin laundry, Marielyst Møntvask, towards the western end of Marielyst Strandvej; it's open from 7 am to 10 pm daily.

Places to Stay

There are several camping grounds in the area. *Smedegårdens* (☎ *54 13 66 17, fax 54 13 66 16, Bøtøvej 5, 4873 Væggerløse)* is a simple place, but it has cooking facilities and showers and is a two minute stroll from the beach. It's open from May to September and costs 50 kr per person.

Marielyst Camping (☎ *54 13 53 07, fax 54 13 53 06, Marielyst Strandvej 36, 4873 Væggerløse)* has a central location, friend-

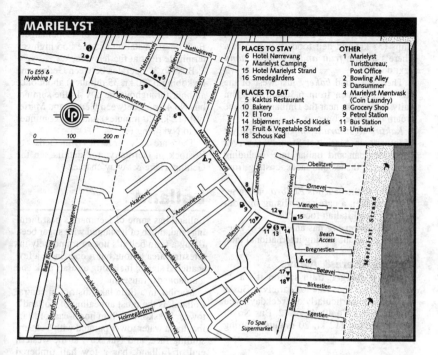

MARIELYST

To E55 &
Nykøbing F

0   100   200 m

PLACES TO STAY
6 Hotel Nørrevang
7 Marielyst Camping
15 Hotel Marielyst Strand
16 Smedegårdens

PLACES TO EAT
5 Kaktus Restaurant
10 Bakery
12 El Toro
14 Isbjørnen; Fast-Food Kiosks
17 Fruit & Vegetable Stand
18 Schous Kød

OTHER
1 Marielyst
   Turistbureau;
   Post Office
2 Bowling Alley
3 Dansummer
4 Marielyst Møntvask
   (Coin Laundry)
8 Grocery Shop
9 Petrol Station
11 Bus Station
13 Unibank

Obelitzvej
Ørnevej
Vænget
Beach
Access
Bregnestien
Bøtøvej
Birkestien
Egestien

Marielyst Strand

To Spar
Supermarket

ly managers and a young crowd. The tent sites are in a grassy field with hedges that offer some privacy. It's about 500m from the beach and is open from early April to late September; camping costs 48 kr per person.

The turistbureau has a list of *rooms* in private homes that cost about 150/250 kr for singles/doubles. Staff there can also help you to book small *apartments* costing around 2000 kr per week and *summer houses* ranging from 3000 to 15,000 kr per week. There are no booking fees.

You can also book *cottages* from Dansummer (☎ 54 13 66 22, fax 54 13 16 22), Marielyst Strandvej 26D.

At *Hotel Marielyst Strand* (☎ 54 13 68 88, Marielyst Strandvej 61, 4873 Væggerløse), a short stroll from the beach, straightforward doubles cost 375 kr with shared bath and 550 kr with bath.

Hotel Nørrevang (☎ 54 13 62 62, fax 54 13 62 72, Marielyst Strandvej 32, 4873 Væggerløse), part of the Best Western hotel chain, is Marielyst's most upmarket hotel and has some nice touches including a thatch-roofed reception building. There are 26 standard rooms with bath, phone and TV, as well as 57 bungalows and apartments that also have kitchens and balconies and can accommodate from two to six people. Singles/doubles start at 695/895 kr, but various package deals and discounts are available.

Places to Eat

Marielyst is thick with cafés and fast-food joints. On the corner of Bøtøvej and Marielyst Strandvej you'll find three *kiosks* selling pizzas, burgers, hot dogs and beer.

A good alternative to junk food is offered by *Schous Kød*, 200m south down Bøtøvej,

MØN, FALSTER & LOLLAND

which sells inexpensive cod cakes, fish and chips (25 kr), half a baked chicken with chips (35 kr) and deli foods to take away. There's a little *fruit and vegetable stand* next door.

There's a good *bakery* just west of the bus station, open from 6.30 am to 5 pm daily. *Isbjørnen*, near the Unibank, sells ice cream in waffle cones.

Kaktus Restaurant, next to Marielyst Møntvask on Marielyst Strandvej, serves good Mexican and Italian fare, including pizza, pasta dishes and tacos, costing from 50 to 75 kr.

Closer to the beach is *El Toro* on Marielyst Strandvej, a café specialising in moderately priced Italian food.

Hotel Nørrevang has an expensive fine-dining restaurant serving international fare.

Getting There & Away

From Nykøbing F train station it's a 25 minute (20 kr) bus ride to Marielyst. Buses are frequent, particularly on weekdays; you can catch bus No 40, 41 or 42. Bus No 45 runs to Gedser (12 kr, 20 minutes) during the summer.

Getting Around

Bicycles can be hired from Spar supermarket (☎ 54 13 61 04), 2km south of the centre at Lupinvej 1, for 35/200 kr per day/week.

GEDSER

Gedser, at the tip of Falster, is Denmark's southernmost point, but is otherwise little worthy of note and most visitors simply zip right through town on their way to a waiting ferry.

The tourist office (☎ 54 17 90 41), at Stationsvejen 7, is only open from 11 am to 1 pm on weekdays.

There is a nice stretch of beach, Gedesby Strand, a few kilometres east of Gedser but it's largely a residential and summer cottage community with none of the transient-visitor services found in Marielyst.

If you want to grab a meal, there are a couple of simple *cafés* in town on Langgade, north of the post office.

Getting There & Away

Gedser is 152km south of Copenhagen. Both the train station and the E55 highway terminate right at the ferry dock.

Bus No 39 operates between Gedser and Nykøbing F (20 kr, 35 minutes) about once an hour throughout the day. In the summer bus No 45 runs between Gedser and Marielyst (12 kr, 20 minutes) and also continues on to Nykøbing F.

There are daily car ferries from Gedser to Rostock in Germany; for details see the Getting There & Away chapter.

Lolland

Lolland has some of Denmark's best farming land, much of it planted with sugar beet. Being a farm belt it's not an immensely interesting area to tour but it does have a few scattered sights, including a safari park and a notable car museum.

Maribo, in a little lake district in central Lolland, is the most appealing of Lolland's towns. Sakskøbing, 9km north-east of Maribo, has a water tower painted with a cheery smiling face, and Nakskov, at the western end of Lolland, has a few half-timbered waterfront warehouses, a couple of local history museums and a U-359 Russian submarine that can be toured.

Rødbyhavn, a small harbourside town in the south, came into existence in the 1960s after a direct ferry service to Puttgarden, Germany, was introduced. That ferry service now provides the link in the inter-Europe E47 highway between Germany and Denmark.

GETTING THERE & AWAY
Bus & Train

There's a limited bus service on the island. The most useful route (No 47) connects Nykøbing F with Nakskov via Nysted and Rødby, and runs four times a day. For information on buses contact Storstrøms Trafikselskab (☎ 54 88 04 00).

There are two railway lines in Lolland. The main east-west route cuts across the centre of Lolland and is operated by the

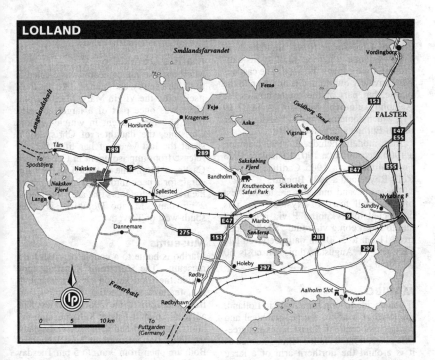

LOLLAND

private company Lollandsbanen. Its trains run between Nykøbing F and Nakskov, a trip lasting just 47 minutes, stopping en route in Sakskøbing and Maribo. Trains run about hourly during the week but less frequently at weekends. The fare between Nykøbing F and Nakskov is 44 kr; the fare to Maribo from either Nykøbing F or Nakskov is 28 kr.

The other rail line, from Rødby to Nykøbing F (23 minutes), is run by Danske Statsbaner (Danish State Railways; DSB). Trains leave Rødby several times a day in conjunction with the Puttgarden ferry service; in most cases the train continues from Nykøbing F on to Copenhagen.

Car & Motorcycle

Route 9 cuts across central Lolland from Nykøbing F in the east to Tårs in the west

(61km). There are no services at Tårs; it's simply a car-ferry terminal.

Boat

Scandlines operates the car ferry between Tårs and Spodsbjerg (in Langeland) about once every 30 minutes during the height of the day and hourly in the early morning and late evening. It costs 255 kr for a car carrying up to five people, 150 kr for a motorcycle with up to two riders. For reservations call ☎ 54 93 13 03 in Tårs and ☎ 62 50 10 22 in Spodsbjerg.

For information on the ferry from Rødbyhavn to Puttgarden, Germany, see the Getting There & Away chapter.

AALHOLM SLOT & AUTOMOBIL MUSEUM

Aalholm Slot, one of northern Europe's oldest inhabited castles, belonged to Danish royalty until 1725, when it was put up for auction. The estate dates back to the 12th century. Christopher II was imprisoned in his own dungeon here in 1332 by his half-brother, Count Johan the Mild. The castle is now privately owned and is not open to the public, but part of the estate houses the Aalholm Automobil Museum (☎ 54 87 19 11), which contains some 175 antique cars, one of Europe's largest collections.

Rare models include an 1899 Daimler, a 1900 Decauville, a 1902 Renault, a 1903 Ford Model A, a 1905 Cadillac, a 1911 Rolls Royce and a 1931 Bugatti.

The castle and museum are to the west of the small town of Nysted, which is connected to Nykøbing F via route 297 and to Sakskøbing via route 283. It's open from 11 am to 5.30 pm daily between late May and 31 August. Admission costs 60 (children 25 kr).

MARIBO

If you decide to stop for a night in Lolland, the town of Maribo, the geographical and commercial centre of the island, is an agreeable place. It has a choice setting, nestled as it is around the northern arm of a large inland lake, Søndersø. A historic cathedral sits on the eastern shore and Bangshave, a wood thick with beech trees, sits on the western shore.

The town centre, Torvet, is marked by Maribo's neoclassical 19th century rådhus (town hall), fronted by a water fountain and backed by a few 18th century timber-frame houses. Beyond that the main attraction is the lake and woods; there are trails along both sides of the lake beginning only minutes from the town centre.

The train/bus station is north of Torvet, about a five minute walk via Jernbanegade.

Information

Maribo Turistbureau (☎ 54 78 04 96), Rådhuset, Torvet, 4930 Maribo, is open from 9 am to 5 pm Monday to Friday and 10 am to noon (to 1 pm in summer) on Saturday.

There are a number of banks in the town centre including a Unibank at Vestergade 2,

diagonally opposite rådhus. The post office is at the western side of the train station.

Maribo Domkirke

Maribo's lakeside cathedral was erected in the 15th century and named, like the town itself, after the Virgin Mary. Maribo Domkirke was once part of a larger complex including the convent in which Leonora Christine, the daughter of Christian IV, spent the last years of her life after her release from imprisonment in Copenhagen Castle in 1685. She is buried in the cathedral; for a peek into her crypt join one of the free cathedral tours that are conducted at 2 pm daily. Maribo Domkirke is 200m south-west of Torvet.

Museums

Maribo is home to a couple of small local museums. The **Storstrøms Kunstmuseum**, beside the train station on Jernbanepladsen, features a collection of regional art from the 18th to the 20th centuries. The adjacent **Lolland-Falster Stiftsmuseum** exhibits church art and some social displays, including one on migrant farm labourers. Both are open from 9 am to 5 pm Tuesday to Sunday and admission to each costs 30 kr.

The **Frilandsmuseum** on Meinckesvej 5, in the Bangshave area 1km south-west of town, is an open-air museum with a wooden windmill and a few other period buildings. It's open from 10 am to 5 pm daily between May and September; admission costs 20 kr.

Museumsbanen

An antique steam-engined train known as Museumsbanen (☎ 54 78 85 45) makes a little jaunt north to Bandholm on Sunday mornings in June, July and August. The train leaves Maribo station at 10.05 am and the 90 minute return trip costs 40 kr (children 15 kr).

Places to Stay

Maribo Sø Camping (☎ 54 78 00 71, fax 54 78 47 71, Bangshavevej 25, 4930 Maribo), a three star camping ground right on Søndersø, is about a 20 minute walk south-west from the town centre. It has a kitchen, laundry facilities and a TV lounge and is accessible to people in wheelchairs. It's open from mid-March to the end of September.

The *Maribo Vandrerhjem* (☎ *54 78 33 14, fax 54 78 32 65, Søndre Boulevard 82B, 4930 Maribo*), about 2km south-east of Torvet, is a modern 96 bed hostel near Søndersø, open year-round. Dorm beds cost 75 kr, while rooms cost 225 kr for up to three people. There's a lakeside trail to the town centre.

Ebsens Hotel (☎ *54 78 10 44, Vestergade 32, 4930 Maribo*) is a small local hotel just a few minutes walk south-west from the train station. Although the rooms are straightforward, the hotel is pleasant and relatively cheap: singles/doubles with shared bath cost 275/425 kr.

Hotel Hvide Hus (☎ *54 78 10 11, fax 54 78 05 22, Vestergade 27, 4930 Maribo*) is a modern 63 room lakeside hotel 500m west of Torvet. A member of the Best Western chain, its rooms have bath, minibar, TV and lakeview balcony. Regular rates start at 715/845 kr for singles/doubles but there are cheaper weekend and summer deals.

Places to Eat
You'll find numerous places to eat on Vestergade, which runs west from Torvet.

There's a *grocery shop* and a *Chinese restaurant* a minute's walk from Torvet at Vestergade 4. Nearby *Café Maribo* (*Vestergade 6*) is a favourite spot for smørrebrød.

Omer's Pizza Bar (*Vestergade 13A*) sells pizza, pasta and shawarma sandwiches. *Ebsens Hotel* has a restaurant serving Danish dishes at moderate prices. There's a *bakery* just east of the hotel.

Popular for its lakeside setting is *Restaurant Bangs Have* on Bangshavevej, in an old manor house east of Maribo Sø Camping; it has a view of Maribo Domkirke across the water.

KNUTHENBORG SAFARI PARK
Knuthenborg Safari Park (☎ 54 78 80 88), 7km north of Maribo via route 289, is a large drive-through safari park with free-roaming zebras, antelopes, llamas, giraffes, rhinoceroses, camels and other exotic creatures. The park, which occupies the lawns of what was once Denmark's largest privately held estate, is enclosed by a 7km-long wall. In addition to the animals there are 500 varieties of trees and flowering bushes, an aviary, an enclosed tiger section and some simple amusement rides for young children. It's open from 9 am to 5 pm daily between May and September. Admission costs 76 kr (children 38 kr).

Bornholm

Bornholm (population 45,000) is a delightful slow-paced island that makes for a nice getaway. Lying 200km east of Copenhagen, it's connected to the capital by a daily ferry service but is actually closer to Germany and Sweden than it is to the rest of Denmark and sees more foreign tourists than Danes.

It's a pleasantly varied island. The centre of Bornholm is a mixture of wheat fields and forests, the coast is dotted with small fishing villages and there's a scattering of half-timbered houses across the island. The northern part of Bornholm has sea cliffs and a rocky shoreline, while the southern coast has long stretches of powdery white sand.

The island is easy to explore because there is a good island-wide bus system and an impressive network of bicycle paths.

In addition to its fortified *rundkirke* (round churches) and medieval fortress, Bornholm is renowned for its smokehouses. Be sure to try Bornholm's smoked herring, called *bornholmer*, and the spiced herring from the nearby island of Christiansø: it is considered the best in Denmark.

HISTORY

Bornholm's rich history, which goes back at least 5000 years, has been traced through Bronze Age burial mounds, rock engravings and monoliths. During the Iron Age Bornholm served as a trade centre for the Baltic region. Archaeological finds, including numerous Roman coins, indicate that trade between Bornholm and the rest of Europe was widespread.

In the Middle Ages Bornholm was administered by the Archbishop of Lund (Lund is now part of southern Sweden), who ruled from Hammershus, an expansive fortress on the island's northern coast.

During the wars between Sweden and Denmark in the mid-17th century, Bornholm fell into Swedish hands, along with Danish territories at the southern end of the Swedish mainland. In 1658, when it

Highlights

- Stop by one of Bornholm's unique 12th century *rundkirke*, its famous fortified round churches
- Cycle along some of the island's numerous bicycle trails
- Soak up history at the ruins of the 13th century fortress Hammershus Slot
- Explore Dueodde's fine white sand dunes and beach
- Saunter around the picturesque harbourside villages of Gudhjem and Svaneke
- Take a day visit to Christiansø, an offshore island with a well-preserved 17th century character

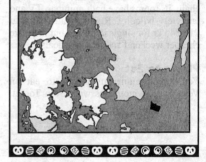

looked likely that the island might become a permanent part of Sweden, the Swedish commandant on Bornholm, Colonel Printzenskjöld, was murdered in an uprising. The rebels, led by Bornholm native Jens Kofoed, went on to expel the Swedish garrison from Bornholm and in 1660 returned the island to Danish rule. As a consequence, a defiant Bornholm managed to prevail as Denmark's easternmost province in a period when Denmark's borders were being substantially eroded by Swedish conquest.

The Soviet Occupation

At the end of WWII, when Germany surrendered to the Allies, Bornholm was occupied by a German garrison of about 20,000 soldiers. At that time the German naval commander in charge of Bornholm, Captain von Kamptz, fearful of Soviet reprisals, insisted on surrendering his troops only to the British. On 7 May 1945, when Soviet surveillance planes flew over the island, von Kamptz fired off a round from his anti-aircraft guns. Later that day the Soviets returned with a squadron of bombers, which released their loads onto the harbourfront towns of Nexø and Rønne. No warning was given to the islanders, who were still in the midst of celebrating the war's end, and 10 people died in the attack.

The Soviets gave the Germans until 10 am the next morning to surrender but von Kamptz held his ground, insisting once again on turning the island over to the British. He did, however, order a civilian evacuation of the two towns. The next morning, at 9.45 am, the Soviets attacked Nexø and Rønne again, this time using incendiary bombs that levelled one-third of the houses and damaged many of the rest. On 9 May the Germans finally capitulated and within a matter of days the Nazi soldiers had been repatriated from the island.

After the Germans had left, the Soviets built up their forces and continued to occupy the island instead of turning Bornholm over to the Danish government. For a while it looked as if Stalin, the Soviet leader, was going to wrap Bornholm within his Iron Curtain – but in March 1946 he abruptly announced plans to withdraw and within a month all the Soviet troops had left.

Peace in the 18th century brought prosperity to the island and to its merchants, who built timber-framed mansions along waterfront villages such as Svaneke and Rønne. Many of those harbourside homes still stand today.

Bornholm, like the rest of Denmark, was occupied by the Nazis during WWII. When Germany surrendered to the Allies on 4 May 1945, the German commander on Bornholm refused to step down and the Soviets bombed Rønne and Nexø, causing heavy damage. On 9 May the island was turned over to the Soviets, who occupied it until the spring of the following year (see the boxed text 'The Soviet Occupation' above).

GETTING THERE & AWAY

Bornholm can be reached by air, boat or a combination of bus and boat.

Air

Maersk Air (☎ 32 31 45 45 in Copenhagen, ☎ 56 95 11 11 in Bornholm) operates several flights a day between Copenhagen and Rønne. The one-way fare is 590 kr, but return fares as low as 520 kr are available if you book at least seven days in advance. For more information on air travel see the Getting Around chapter earlier in this book.

The domestic airport, Bornholms Lufthavn, is 5km south-east of Rønne, on the road to Dueodde. Bus No 7 stops on the main road in front of the airport.

Bus

Bornholmerbussen (☎ 44 68 44 00) runs a bus (No 866) between Copenhagen's Central Station and Ystad in Sweden, where it connects with a ferry to Rønne. The service runs twice daily, leaving Copenhagen at 8.30 am and 4.30 pm and Rønne at 8 am and 4 pm; it takes 5¼ hours and costs 190/95 kr for adults/children.

Boat

Copenhagen Bornholmstrafikken (☎ 33 13 18 66 in Copenhagen, ☎ 56 95 18 66 in Rønne) operates an overnight ferry service between Copenhagen and Rønne. This can be a very economical way to get to Bornholm because it doubles as a night's accommodation. The ferries depart (in each direction) at 11.30 pm daily; the trip takes seven hours. The one-way fare is 189 kr for adults and 95 kr for children. Add 62 kr for a dorm bunk, 148/182 kr per person for a double inside/outside. Alternatively, you can spread out your sleeping bag in the TV lounge and sleep there free of charge. It costs 52 kr to take a bicycle, 192 kr for a motorcycle and 389 kr for a car. The boats have lockers and a restaurant, and there are lockers at both ferry terminals.

Between late June and mid-August Bornholmstrafikken also runs services departing daily (except Wednesday) at 8.30 am from Copenhagen and 3.30 pm from Rønne. There are also a few daytime departures at weekends in the shoulder season. They cost the same as the overnight boat.

Flyvebådene (☎ 33 12 80 88) operates high-speed hydrofoil connections between Copenhagen and Rønne costing 190 kr for adults and 95 kr for children. The trip takes 4¾ hours. The boats leave Copenhagen daily at 9 am and 5 pm and depart from Rønne at 8 am and 4 pm.

Sweden Bornholmstrafikken (☎ 56 95 18 66 in Rønne, ☎ 041-11 80 65 in Ystad) runs ferries daily between Rønne and Ystad. They leave Ystad at 11.15 am and 7.15 pm and Rønne at 8 am and 4 pm; in summer there are extra sailings on some days. The journey takes 2½ hours. The cost in summer is 122 kr for adults, 61 kr for children and 530 kr for a car and up to five people; these standard prices are about 10 to 20% less in the low season.

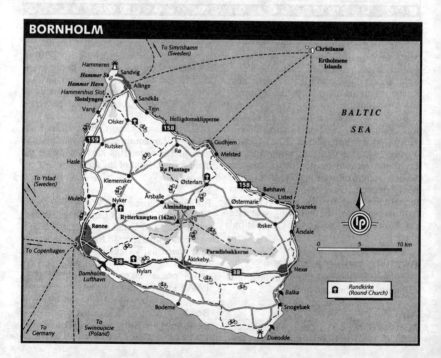

There can be some very cheap promotional discounts between Sweden and Rønne, especially during the winter, and the cost of a same-day return fare is equivalent to the one-way fare year-round; this is all designed to encourage Swedish shoppers.

DFO HansaFerry (☎ 56 48 00 01) also runs a ferry service between Ystad and Rønne. Between June and August it departs from Ystad daily and from Rønne Tuesday to Sunday. During the rest of the year sailings in both directions are on Tuesday and at the weekend. The trip takes 2½ hours. In summer it costs 110/55 kr for adults/children, at other times it costs 80/40 kr. The price for a car and up to five people ranges from 300 kr on winter weekdays to 530 kr on summer weekends. Departure times vary with the day and season.

There's also a seasonal boat service between Simrishamn (Sweden) and Allinge (Bornholm). The schedule varies a bit from year to year but ferries typically run three times a day from late June to August and twice daily in September. The trip takes one hour and costs 95 kr for adults, 55 kr for children. For details contact the Nordbornholms Turistbureau (☎ 56 48 00 01) in Bornholm or Bornholms Terminalen (☎ 041-41 43 45) in Simrishamn.

Germany There are a number of ferries to Bornholm from northern Germany.

The Sassnitz-Mukran to Rønne route, run by Bornholmstrafikken (☎ 56 95 18 66 in Bornholm, 038-39 23 52 26 in Sassnitz), operates six times a week in summer and less frequently during the rest of the year. The schedule varies with the day of the week; the trip takes 3¾ hours. The one-way fare and the same-day return fare is 100/50 kr for adults/children from June to August and 50/25 kr during the rest of the year. Depending on the day of the week and the season, it costs from 399 to 690 kr to take a car with up to five people.

DFO HansaFerry (☎ 56 48 00 01 in Bornholm, 038 39 26 41 80 in Sassnitz) departs from Sassnitz daily from 1 June to 31 August and from Rønne daily except

Friday. During the rest of the year there is an average of four sailings a week in both directions. Sailing times vary with the day of the week and season; the trip takes 3½ hours. From June to mid-September the one-way fare is 120/60 kr for adults/children, 80/40 kr during the rest of the year. The cost for a car (including up to five people) ranges from 425 kr midweek in winter to 695 kr on summer weekends.

Poland Polferries (☎ 09132-16140 in Swinoujscie, ☎ 56 95 10 69 in Rønne) runs a ferry between Poland and Bornholm on Saturday from late June to late August. The trip takes six hours, with the boat leaving Swinoujscie at 10 am and departing from Rønne at 5.30 pm. The one-way/return fare is 180/290 kr for adults, 110/160 kr for children, 360/580 kr for a car and driver and 600/960 kr for a car and five people. Motorcycles and bicycles travel free.

GETTING AROUND
Bus
Bornholms Amts Trafikselskab (BAT) runs a good, inexpensive bus service around the island. Fares, which are based on a 10 zone system, cost 7.50 kr per zone. You can save money by buying a bus pass (called RaBATkort) from the bus driver for 60 kr, which is valid for all 10 zones and can be used for multiple rides and by more than one person. There's also a one day pass (90 kr) and a weekly pass (330 kr); both allow unlimited travel. Children travel half-price. Buses operate year-round but services are less frequent in winter.

In summer bus No 7 leaves from the Rønne ferry terminal every two hours from 8 am to 6 pm and travels anticlockwise around the island, stopping at Dueodde and all major coastal villages before terminating at Hammershus Slot; the whole circuit takes two hours and 40 minutes. Other buses make direct runs from Rønne to Nexø, Svaneke, Gudhjem and Sandvig.

Standard fares on the main routes are: 21.50 kr from Rønne to Åkirkeby (bus No 5 or 6); 30 kr from Rønne to Sandvig (bus

No 1) or Gudhjem (bus No 3); and 37.50 kr from Rønne to Svaneke (bus No 4), Nexø (bus No 6) or Dueodde (bus No 7).

In midsummer BAT runs special sightseeing buses for pass-holders: Bondegårdsbussen services visit farms on Wednesday; Kunsthåndværkerbussen stops at craft studios on Tuesday and Thursday; Veteranbussen, an antique bus, visits 20th century historic sights on Wednesday; Middelalderbussen visits castle ruins and other sights relating to the Middle Ages on Thursday; and Havebussen visits five gardens on Friday. The tours leave Rønne at 10 am and last between five and six hours. You can use either the daily or weekly pass mentioned above; refreshments and admission fees (if applicable) are extra.

For details of buses and schedules contact the main bus office (☎ 56 95 21 21) or visit BAT's Web site at www.bat.dk.

Car & Motorcycle

Hiring a car is expensive on Bornholm. Even with advance reservations, expect to pay a good 600 kr per day for short-term rentals, although the rates can drop a bit if you keep the car for a longer period.

Avis is within walking distance of the Rønne ferry terminal at Rønne Autoudlejning ApS (☎ 56 95 22 08), Snellemark 19; you can drop off the car after hours. Europcar (☎ 56 95 43 00) has an office at Nørregade 6, Rønne; Hertz (☎ 56 91 00 12) is nearby at Nørregade 12. All three companies also serve the airport.

Europcar hires motorscooters for 225 kr per day.

The Q8 petrol station near the ferry terminal in Rønne is open from 6 am to midnight daily.

Bicycle

Cycling is a great way to get around because Bornholm is crisscrossed by more than 200km of bike trails. Some of the trails are built over former rail routes, some slice through forests and others run alongside main roads. Together they connect Bornholm's largest towns, cross a wide variety of landscapes and lead to most of the island's sightseeing attractions.

There are bike routes from Rønne to Allinge, to Helligdomsklipperne, through Åkirkeby to Nexø, through Dueodde to Nexø, and through Almindingen to Årsdale, and routes from Allinge to Åkirkeby, Helligdomsklipperne to Gudhjem, Gudhjem to Åkirkeby and Dueodde, Nexø to Svaneke and Svaneke to Gudhjem.

If you don't feel like pedalling the entire way, you can take your bike on public buses for an additional 19 kr.

The tourist office in Rønne (Bornholms Velkomstcenter) sells the handy 60 page English-language *Bicycle Routes on Bornholm* (40 kr), which maps out routes and describes sights along the way.

Rental Three-speed bicycles can be hired for about 50/200 kr per day/week; mountain bikes cost 60/350 kr. Two of the larger Rønne rental shops are Cykel-Centret (☎ 56 95 06 04) at Søndergade 7 and Bornholms Cykeludlejning (☎ 56 95 13 59), next to the tourist office at Nordre Kystvej 5. Elsewhere on the island most hostels and camping grounds hire out bicycles. Tourist offices and hotels can also arrange bicycle hire.

RØNNE

Rønne is Bornholm's administrative centre and largest town. It has 15,000 residents, one-third of the island's total population.

Spread around a large natural harbour, Rønne has been the island's commercial centre since the Middle Ages. Over the years the town has expanded and taken on a more suburban look, but there are still well-preserved quarters that provide some pleasant strolling, most notably the old neighbourhood west of Store Torv with its handsome period buildings and cobblestoned streets.

Rønne is seen more as a watering hole and shopping locale for Swedes on day trips than as a sightseeing destination but it can be an agreeable place to begin or end a longer tour of the island.

RØNNE

PLACES TO STAY
25 L'Oase Bed & Breakfast
27 Sverre's Small Hotel
35 Rønne Vandrerhjem
37 Galløkken Camping

PLACES TO EAT
1 Strøgets Spisehuz
12 Restaurant Perronen
13 Kvickly Supermarket & Bakery
18 Rothes Konditori
21 Netto Grocery Shop
23 Restaurant China

OTHER
2 Hertz
3 Rådhus
4 Library
5 Bornholms Museum
6 Europcar
7 Coin Laundry
8 Erichsens Gaard

9 Bornholms Cykeludlejning
10 Bornholms Velkomstcenter
11 Q8 Petrol Station
14 Avis
15 Amtmandsgården
16 Kommandantgården
17 Hjorths Fabrik
19 Unibank
20 Tinghus
22 Taxi Stand
24 Main Bus Stop
26 Toldboden
28 Bornholmstraffiken Ferry Terminal
29 Lighthouse
30 Sankt Nicolai Kirke
31 Rønne Theatre
32 Post Office
33 Cykel-Centret
34 Forsvarsmuseet; Kastellet
36 Bornholms Centralsygehus (Hospital)

Information

Tourist Office The helpful tourist office, Bornholms Velkomstcenter (☎ 56 95 95 00, fax 56 95 95 68), Nordre Kystvej 3, 3700 Rønne, a few minutes walk from the harbour, has information on the whole island; you can visit its Web site at www.bornholm info.dk. Between June and August it's open from 7 am to 6 pm Tuesday to Friday, from 7 am to 8 pm on Monday and Saturday and from 1 to 6 pm on Sunday. In May it's open from 9 am to 5 pm on weekdays, from

11 am to 3 pm on Saturday and from noon to 4 pm on Sunday. The rest of the year it's open from 9 am to 4 pm on weekdays and from 11.30 am to 2.30 pm on Saturday.

Other Facilities There's a Unibank just south of Store Torv. The post office is on the southern side of Lille Torv. There's a coin laundry, Rønne Møntvask, at Nørregade 7. The hospital, Bornholms Centralsygehus (☎ 56 95 11 65), is on Sygehusvej at the southern end of town.

Walking Tour

A good place to begin a walking tour of Rønne's older quarters is **Store Torv**, which once served as the military parade ground. Now the central commercial square, it's the site of a **public market** on Wednesday and Saturday mornings year-round. On the eastern side of the square, at Store Torv 1, is **Tinghus**, a neoclassical building dating from 1834. It used to house Rønne's city hall, courthouse and jail.

Continue up Store Torvegade and turn left on Laksegade, a picturesque cobblestoned street with a number of attractive houses built in the early 19th century. **Erichsens Gaard** at Laksegade 7, a merchant's house dating from 1806, has been turned into a museum complete with period furnishings; it's open from 10 am to 5 pm Tuesday to Saturday and admission costs 25 kr.

At the end of Laksegade turn left onto Storegade; at No 42 you'll find **Kommandantgården**, an imposing building built in 1846 as a residence for Bornholm's military commander.

If you enjoy arts and crafts, take a short detour to Krystalgade 5 for a visit to **Hjorths Fabrik**, a working ceramics museum open from 10 am to 5 pm Tuesday to Saturday; admission costs 25 kr.

Return to Storegade and proceed south to **Amtmandsgården**, a half-timbered 18th century structure at Storegade 36 that is now the Bornholm prefect's residence. Jens Kofoed, who liberated Bornholm from the Swedes in 1658, was born in a house that once stood on this site.

When you reach Rådhusstræde, turn right and you'll soon come to **Toldboden**, at Toldbodgade 1; this was constructed as a storehouse in 1684 and is one of the town's oldest timber-framed buildings. On the wall by the harbour-facing gable you can spot figurines of two menacing Dalmatians flanking a cloaked figure that is said to represent Satan.

Continue back down Rådhusstræde to Havnebakken, where you'll pass a quaint octagonal **lighthouse** (built in 1880) before reaching the attractive **Sankt Nicolai Kirke**, built in 1915. South of the church is **Bombehusene**, a neighbourhood that encompasses Kapelvej and Kirkestræde; this is one of the areas that was levelled by Soviet bombers in May 1945.

If you continue east from the church on Østergade, at the corner with Teaterstræde you'll pass the restored **Rønne Theatre**, which was built in 1823 and is one of the oldest functioning theatres in Denmark. Continue north onto Nellikegade and turn right at Tornegade to get back to Store Torv.

Bornholms Museum

This museum, at Sankt Mortensgade 29, has a hotchpotch local history collection that includes nature displays, antique toys, excavated Roman coins, pottery, paintings and an exhibition of *Bornholmerur*, a type of grandfather clock that's made on the island. From May to September it's open from 10 am to 5 pm Tuesday to Saturday; in winter it's open on Tuesday, Thursday, Saturday and Sunday afternoons only. Admission costs 25 kr.

Forsvarsmuseet

The Defence Museum is in the 17th century citadel called Kastellet, south of the town centre. It has the usual collection of armaments and military uniforms as well as displays on the bombing of Rønne and Nexø by the Soviets at the end of WWII and the subsequent Soviet occupation of the island. The museum is open between May and October from 10 am to 4 pm Tuesday to Saturday. Admission costs 20 kr.

Nylars Rundkirke

The attractive Nylars Rundkirke, built in 1150, is the most well-preserved and easily accessible round church in the Rønne area. Its central pillar is painted with 13th century frescoes, the oldest in Bornholm, depicting scenes from the Creation myth, including Adam and Eve's expulsion from the Garden of Eden. The cylindrical nave has three storeys, the top one of which has

Bornholm's Round Churches

Unique among Bornholm's sights are its four 12th century *rundkirke* (round churches), constructed with 2m-thick whitewashed walls and black conical roofs. The churches were built at a time when pirating Wends from eastern Germany were ravaging coastal areas throughout the Baltic Sea. They were designed not only as places of worship but also as refuges against enemy attacks – their upper storeys double as shooting galleries. Each church was built about 2km inland, and all four are sited high enough on knolls to offer a lookout to the sea. Fittingly, these bold churches have a stern, ponderous appearance, more typical of a fortress than of a place of worship.

Another unique architectural feature of each church is the detached belfry, made of stone and tarred timber. All four churches are still used for Sunday services and are open to visitors from Monday to Saturday.

a watchman's gallery that served as a defence lookout in medieval times.

Inside the church, the front door is flanked by two of Bornholm's 40 rune stones, carved memorial stones that date back to the Viking era.

Nylars Rundkirke is about 8km from Rønne, on the road to Åkirkeby. It's only a 15 minute ride from Rønne on bus No 6; alight at the bus stop near the Dagli Brugsen shop and turn north on Kirkevej for the 350m walk to the church. The cycle path between Rønne and Åkirkeby also goes past the church.

From May to September Nylars Rundkirke is open from 9 am to 5 pm Monday to Saturday; admission is free.

Places to Stay

Galløkken Camping (☎ 56 95 23 20, *Strandvejen 4, 3700 Rønne*) is a little over 1km south of the town centre in a pleasant setting on the bike trail along the southern coast. It's open from 1 May to 15 September. Bicycles can be hired for 50/195 kr per day/week.

The 148 bed *Rønne Vandrerhjem* (☎ 56 95 13 40, fax 56 95 01 32, rvh@post4.tele .dk, Arsenalvej 12, 3700 Rønne), just north of Galløkken Camping, is a 30 minute walk or a 45 kr taxi ride from the harbour. It's open from March to 1 November. Dorm beds cost 95 kr; family rooms range from 200 kr per person to 570 kr for six people.

Staff at Bornholms Velkomstcenter can book *rooms* in private homes costing 140 kr per person; there's no booking fee.

Sverre's Small Hotel (☎ 56 95 03 03, fax 56 95 03 92, Snellemark 2, 3700 Rønne) is centrally located. The friendly manager, 'Dr Jazz', is not only the island's top jazz trumpeter but runs a good budget hotel as well. There are 26 rooms at this site and seven above a nearby restaurant. They vary but are all clean and adequate. Singles/doubles with shared bath cost 290/460 kr from late June to mid-August, 240/360 kr from mid-September to May and 260/410 kr at other times. Rooms with bath and TV cost 120 kr more. Breakfast is included in the rates and there's a TV lounge.

L'Oase Bed & Breakfast (☎ 56 95 12 15, Snellemark 22, 3700 Rønne) consists of two rooms in the home of Edith Lærkesen. One room has a tiny balcony and a TV, the other is quite small but has a skylight. Depending on the room, the rates for single occupancy range from 280 to 350 kr in summer and 200 to 250 kr in winter, while the rates for double occupancy range from 420 to 560 kr in summer and 300 to 400 kr in winter. There's a shared refrigerator and coffee maker and guests are provided with bread and coffee to make their own breakfast.

Hotel Fredensborg (☎ 56 95 44 44, fax 56 95 03 14, Strandvejen 116, 3700 Rønne), the area's most upmarket hotel, is on a quiet knoll in a wooded coastal section at the southern end of Rønne. A modern hotel affiliated with the Best Western chain, it has 72 rooms with the standard amenities, including TV, minibar and trouser press. It also has a sauna, a pool and a tennis court. Singles/doubles cost 795/995 kr.

Places to Eat

For a quick breakfast, the ferry terminal has an upstairs *cafeteria* serving good pastries and coffee at reasonable prices. If you're sailing to or from Copenhagen overnight, the *ferry restaurant* offers a decent evening buffet, with a few hot dishes, salad items, cheeses and the requisite smoked herring, for 59 kr.

Kvickly supermarket, in Snellemark Centret opposite Bornholms Velkomstcenter, has a good, inexpensive bakery that opens at 6.30 am daily, although the supermarket itself doesn't open until 9 am.

Rothes Konditori (Snellemark 41), opposite the main bus stop, has good breads and pastries, sandwiches, coffee and minipizzas for 8 kr. It opens at 6 am from Monday to Saturday and there's both takeaway and sit-down service.

Store Torv has a number of *fast-food outlets* selling hamburgers, hot dogs and pizzas, as well as a *Netto* grocery shop.

Restaurant Perronen, south of Bornholms Velkomstcenter, has creative young owners serving good food at reasonable prices. At lunch there are pasta dishes and daily specials such as fresh fish and vegetables for around 50 kr. Dinner prices are about double that, but there's a vegetarian dish for 78 kr.

Strøgets Spisehuz (Store Torvegade 39) has a cosy atmosphere and hearty meat-and-potato dishes, including a 50 kr daily special and a selection of steaks costing around 100 kr. It's open for dinner only from Tuesday to Sunday.

Another dinner-only place is *Restaurant China (Tornegade 6)*, which offers the standard array of Chinese dishes at above average prices.

ÅKIRKEBY

Åkirkeby is an inland town with a mix of old half-timbered houses and newer, less characterful homes.

The tourist office and car park are at the eastern side of the church on Jernbanegade. The town square, post office and bank are 150m east of the tourist office.

The town takes its name from its main sight, the 12th century Romanesque stone church **Aa Kirke**, which is built on a knoll overlooking the surrounding farmland. The largest church on Bornholm, its crossroads location made it a convenient place of assembly for people from all over the island. Although it has been altered and renovated in recent centuries, the interior still houses a number of historic treasures, including a 13th century baptismal font of carved sandstone depicting scenes of Christ and featuring runic script. The ornate pulpit and altar date from around 1600 and are notable for their fine detail. For a 360° view of the town, climb the 22m-high bell tower, but watch your head on the low ceilings en route! Admission to Aa Kirke costs 6 kr. It's open from Monday to Saturday, from 10 am to 4 pm in spring and autumn and from 9.30 am to 5 pm in summer (closed in winter).

About 2km south of Åkirkeby centre, at Grammegaardsvej 1 on the road to Dueodde, is the **Bornholms Automobilmuseum**, a small museum featuring 1920s vintage cars and motorcycles. It's open from 10 am to 5 pm Monday to Saturday between May and October. Admission costs 25 kr.

There's a *grill* serving burgers and ice cream next to the tourist office and a *bakery* directly behind the tourist office.

INTERIOR WOODLANDS

Bornholm is the most wooded county in Denmark: one-fifth of the island is covered with woodland. Beech, fir, spruce, hemlock and oak are predominant. There are three main forested areas, each laid out with walking trails (you can pick up free maps at Bornholms Velkomstcenter). A single bicycle trail connects them all.

Almindingen, the largest forest (2412 hectares), is in the centre of the island and can be reached by heading north from Åkirkeby. It is the site of Bornholm's highest point, the 162m hill **Rytterknægten**, which has a lookout tower called Konge-mindet from which you can view the surrounding area.

Paradisbakkerne (Paradise Hills) is 2km north-west of Nexø and contains wild deer and a trail that passes an ancient monolithic gravestone. **Rø Plantage**, about 5km south-west of Gudhjem, has a terrain of heathered hills and woodlands.

DUEODDE

Dueodde, the southernmost point in Bornholm, is a vast stretch of beach backed by pine trees and expansive dunes. Its soft white sand is so fine-grained that it was once used in hourglasses and ink blotters.

There's no real village at Dueodde – the bus stops at the end of the road where there's a hotel, a restaurant, a couple of food kiosks and a footpath to the beach. Bicycles can be hired at the camping grounds and Dueodde Badehotel.

Dueodde is a true beach-bum hang-out. The only 'sight' is a **lighthouse**, on the western side of the dunes; you can climb the 197 stairs for a view of endless sand and sea.

The beach at Dueodde is a good place for children: the water is generally calm and is shallow up to about 100m out, after which it becomes deep enough for adults to swim.

Places to Stay

Møllers Dueodde Camping (☎ 56 48 81 49, fax 56 48 81 69, Duegårdsvej 2, 3730 Nexø) is open from 15 May to 20 September. This three star camping ground is in a wooded area 10 minutes walk north-east of the bus stop. Camping costs 48 kr per person, plus 20 kr per site. Cabins equipped with cooking facilities cost from 1820 to 2520 kr per week, depending on the season (high season lasts from mid-June to mid-August). There's a small shop on site.

The combined *Dueodde Vandrerhjem & Camp Ground* (☎ 56 48 81 19, fax 56 48 81 12, Skrokkegårdsvejen 17, 3730 Nexø)

borders the beach and is a 10 minute walk east of the bus stop. The hostel has simple rooms with private/shared bath costing 390/330 kr for one to four people from late June to early August. During the rest of the season, rates depend upon the number of people in the room: singles/doubles cost 160/230 kr with private bath or 150/200 kr with shared bath. There are level grassy tent sites shaded by pine trees; camping costs 40 kr per person plus 18 kr per tent. There's a coin laundry, a guest kitchen and a playground. It's open from April to mid-October.

Dueodde Badehotel (☎ 56 48 86 49, fax 56 48 89 59, Sirenevej 2, 3730 Nexø), right next to the bus stop, is a modern apartment-style hotel that rents units by the week; they cost from 3010 to 5880 kr, depending on the season. The one-bedroom units have TV, phone and sofa bed in the living room and can sleep up to five people. There's a coin laundry, a tennis court and a sauna.

Places to Eat

There are a few *kiosks* selling ice cream, hot dogs and snacks at the end of the road opposite the bus stop.

Also at the end of the road is *Granpavillonen*, where pizza costs around 60 kr and Danish and German dishes are about double that.

Dueodde Vandrerhjem has a cafeteria serving simple, inexpensive meals and a minimarket selling ice cream, fresh bread and a few basic supplies.

SNOGEBÆK

A quaint seaside village of older homes, Snogebæk makes a nice little detour if you're travelling by car or bike between Dueodde and Nexø. Down by the water, on Hovedgade, you'll find a shop selling quality hand-blown glass at reasonable prices. Immediately next to it is a good smokehouse where you can get smoked herring, mackerel and salmon as well as a few deli items and cold beer. The end of the road beyond the glassworks is a good site for spotting migratory ducks and other water birds. If you want to explore more, there's a coastal footpath leading north along the beach.

NEXØ

Nexø (also spelt Neksø) is Bornholm's second-largest town. It has a large modern harbour where both Danish and foreign fishing vessels unload their catch. The harbour, and much of the town, was reconstructed after being destroyed by Soviet bombings in WWII. Despite taking a back seat to more touristy towns such as Gudhjem and Svaneke, Nexø has its fair share of picturesque buildings.

Information

The Nexø-Dueodde Turistbureau (☎ 56 49 32 00, fax 56 49 43 10), Åsen 4, 3730 Nexø, in the centre of town two blocks inland of the harbour, has information on both Nexø and Dueodde.

There are a couple of banks on Torvet, the central square, just south of the turistbureau.

Things to See & Do

Nexø Museum is housed in a picturesque building constructed in 1796 from Nexø sandstone (once a major export of the town). Opposite the waterfront at Havnen 2, it features exhibits on the town's history with an emphasis on fishing and shipping, its main industries. Particularly notable are the reconstructions of fishers' houses. Nexø museum is open from 10 am to 4 pm Monday to Saturday between mid-May and mid-October; admission costs 10 kr.

The home where author Martin Andersen Nexø lived in his childhood is now a museum. It's on the corner of Andersen Nexøvej and Ferskeøstræde, in the southern part of town. Those interested in Nexø's life will find photos of the author, some of his letters and other memorabilia. It's open from noon to 4 pm Monday to Friday between mid-May and mid-October; admission costs 15 kr.

There's a butterfly farm, **Bornholms Sommerfuglepark & Tropeland**, on the western side of town at Gamle Rønnevej 14; you can walk among these colourful creatures which are at all stages of development, from foraging caterpillars to adults. It's open from 10 am to 6 pm daily between May and mid-October, and admission costs 40 kr.

Although Nexø's central waterfront is industrial, 2km south of town there's a popular seaside area called **Balka** with a gently curving white sand beach.

Places to Stay

Few people stay in Nexø proper because the beaches on the outskirts are much more appealing.

Hotel Balka Strand (☎ 56 49 49 49, fax 56 49 49 48, Boulevarden 9, 3730 Nexø), 200m from Balka's sandy beach, has double rooms as well as cheery apartments, all with modern décor. Rooms rates, which are per person and vary with the season, range from 435 to 545 kr including breakfast and dinner. Apartments cost 810 kr in midsummer, less at other times. There's a sauna, pool, tennis court, bar and restaurant.

Also in Balka is *Hotel Balka Søbad* (☎ 56 49 22 25, fax 56 49 22 33, Vester Strandvej 25, 3730 Nexø), an inviting hotel by the beach with 106 rooms in modern two-storey buildings. The rooms are large with at least two twin beds, a sofa bed and a balcony; some have a second bedroom. Rates vary with the season, costing from 405 to 570 kr per person, including breakfast and dinner. There's a sauna, a pool, a tennis court, a bar and a restaurant.

Places to Eat

If you want to pack a lunch for the beach, the large *Kvickly* supermarket (*Købmagerade 12*) near the bus stop in the town centre has a bakery, a deli and a good fruit and vegetable section.

Hotel Balka Strand offers a daily three course dinner menu for 158 kr. On Wednesday there's a cabaret dinner show costing 185 kr.

Hotel Balka Søbad's restaurant has a three course dinner and salad buffet for 135 kr.

SVANEKE

Svaneke is an appealing town of red-tiled 19th century buildings which has won international recognition for maintaining its historic character; in 1975 its efforts were rewarded with the prestigious Council of Europe's gold medal for town preservation for its efforts.

Information

Svaneke Turistbureau (☎ 56 49 63 50, fax 56 49 70 10), in the rådhus, Storegade 24, 3740 Svaneke, is open in summer from 9.30 am to 4.30 pm Monday to Friday and from 9 am to 2 pm on Saturday. In the low season it's open from 10 am to 4 pm Monday to Wednesday and from 11 am to 5 pm on Thursday and Friday.

There's a Unibank at Nansensgade 5 and the post office is at Postgade 2. Bicycles are available for hire at Boss Cykler,

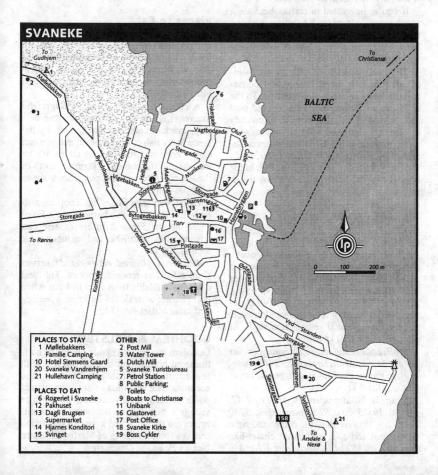

SVANEKE

PLACES TO STAY
1 Møllebakkens Familie Camping
10 Hotel Siemsens Gaard
20 Svaneke Vandrerhjem
21 Hullehavn Camping

PLACES TO EAT
6 Rogeriet i Svaneke
12 Pakhuset
13 Dagli Brugsen Supermarket
14 Hjarnes Konditori
15 Svinget

OTHER
2 Post Mill
3 Water Tower
4 Dutch Mill
5 Svaneke Turistbureau
7 Petrol Station
8 Public Parking; Toilets
9 Boats to Christiansø
11 Unibank
16 Glastorvet
17 Post Office
18 Svaneke Kirke
19 Boss Cykler

Søndergade 14; they cost 50/190 kr per day/week.

Things to See & Do

The **harbourfront** is lined with mustard-yellow half-timbered former merchants' houses, some of which have been turned into restaurants and hotels. There are also some interesting period buildings near **Svaneke Kirke**, a few minutes walk south of Torv (the town square). The church, which has a rune stone, dates from 1350, although it was largely rebuilt in the 1880s.

If you're interested in **crafts**, there are a number of pottery and handicraft shops dotted around town, and at **Glastorvet** in the town centre there's a workshop where you can watch glass being blown.

The easternmost town in Denmark, Svaneke is generally quite breezy and consequently has a number of **windmills**. To the north-west of town you'll find an old post mill (a type of mill that turns in its entirety to face the wind) and a Dutch mill, as well as an unusual three-sided water tower designed by architect Jørn Utzon in 1951. On the main road 3km south of Svaneke, in the hamlet of Årsdale, there's a working windmill where grains are ground and sold.

Places to Stay

Svaneke's two three-star camping grounds are open from mid-May to mid-September. Each is about 1km from the town centre and each has a coin laundry, a TV lounge, a playground, a food kiosk and caravans for rent. *Hullehavn Camping* (☎ 56 49 63 63, fax 56 49 63 90, Sydskovvej 9, 3740 Svaneke), 400m south of Svaneke Vandrerhjem, has the more natural setting. It costs 50 kr per person plus 10 kr per tent.

Møllebakkens Familie Camping (☎/fax 56 49 64 62, Møllebakken 8, 3740 Svaneke), to the north of town, charges 46 kr per person plus 8 kr per tent.

Svaneke Vandrerhjem (☎ 56 49 62 42, fax 56 49 73 83), Reberbanevej 9, 3740 Svaneke), 1km south of the centre and right on the bus route, is a pleasant chalet-like facility with 152 beds, open from 1 April to

1 October. Dorm beds cost 100 kr and doubles cost 300 kr. There's a coin laundry.

Staff at Svaneke Turistbureau can book single and double *rooms* in private homes costing 300 kr; there's no booking fee.

The 50 room *Hotel Siemsens Gaard* (☎ 56 49 61 49, fax 56 49 61 03, Havnebryggen 9, 3740 Svaneke) has a fine location opposite the harbour, pleasant rooms and a bit of old-world character. All rooms have bath, TV, phone and refrigerator. Singles/doubles cost 475/750 kr including breakfast.

Places to Eat

On Torv you'll find *Dagli Brugsen* supermarket and *Hjarnes Konditori*, serving bakery items, coffee and tea. Just south of Torv on Postgade, *Svinget* offers Underground natural ice cream, hot dogs and other fast food.

A cheap, fun place to eat is *Rogeriet i Svaneke*, where you can buy smoked herring, mackerel, shrimp and salmon by the piece; tasty fish cakes cost 8 kr, and you can chow down at outdoor picnic tables. It's by the water at the end of Fiskergade, north of the town centre, and is open from 9 am to 5.30 pm daily.

Hotel Siemsens Gaard has a popular outdoor dining spot with a harbour view. From 11.30 am to 5 pm it offers smørrebrød costing from 30 to 70 kr and set lunches for around 100 kr.

Pakhuset (*Brænderigænget 3*) serves simple food at moderate prices. The best deals are available from noon to 4 pm, when you can get a steak for 39 kr or a herring and salad buffet for 45 kr.

GUDHJEM & MELSTED

Gudhjem is a pretty seaside village of half-timbered houses and sloping streets. With fewer than 1000 inhabitants, it manages to accommodate an influx of summer visitors while maintaining its rustic character. The village's picturesque harbour is so well-preserved that it served as one of the period settings for the filming of Martin Andersen Nexø's *Pelle the Conqueror*.

Gudhjem would make a good base for exploring the rest of Bornholm; it has cycle paths, walking trails, convenient bus connections, reasonably priced places to stay and a boat service to Christiansø. It is also an enjoyable place in which to just wander about and soak up the harbourside atmosphere.

Information

Gudhjem Turistbureau (☎ 56 48 52 10, fax 56 48 52 74) is at Åbogade 9, 3760 Gudhjem, a block inland from the harbour. There's a Unibank at Brøddegade 6. The post office is inside the Favør grocery shop. The Christiansø boat ticket office at the harbour has a notice board listing community events. There are payphones, toilets and showers (5 kr) at the harbour.

Things to See & Do

At the dockside **Gudhjem Glasrøgeri**, Ejnar Mikkelsensvej 13A, which is open daily in the summer, you can watch top-quality Bornholm glass being hand blown.

The **Gudhjem Museum**, Stationsvej 1, in the handsome former train station in the southern part of town, features displays of local history, temporary art exhibits and outdoor sculptures. It's also the site of weekly summer concerts; check at the turistbureau for schedules. Gudhjem Museum is open from 10 am to 5 pm Monday to Saturday and from 2 to 5 pm on Sunday. Admission costs 15 kr.

The **Oluf Høst Museum**, Løkkegade 1, features the workshops and paintings of Oluf Høst (1884-1966), one of Bornholm's best-known artists; it occupies Norresân, where Oluf lived from 1929 until his death. It's open from 2 to at least 6 pm daily between mid-June and early September; admission costs 30 kr. You can visit the museum's Web site at www.ohmus.dk.

The five minute climb up the heather-covered hill **Bokul** gives great views over the town's red-tiled rooftops and out to sea.

If you walk up the hill at the south-eastern end of Gudhjem harbour you'll find a bench with a nice **harbour view**. You can also continue along this path, which runs above the shoreline, to Melsted, 2km to the south, where there's a little **sandy beach**. It's a delightful nature trail, with lots of swallows, nightingales and wildflowers. Gudhjem's beaches are rocky so if you want to see some sand, Melsted's your best bet.

Also in Melsted is **Landbrugsmuseet**, Melstedvej 25, an agricultural history museum in old farm buildings where costumed interpreters tend animals and demonstrate traditional techniques in activities such as farming and wool spinning. It's open from 10 am to 5 pm Tuesday to Sunday between mid-May and mid-October. Admission costs 25 kr.

In summer the boat *Thor* (☎ 58 48 51 65) makes regular sailings (at 10.30 am, 1.30 and 2.30 pm) along the rocky coastline from Gudhjem to Helligdomsklipperne; it costs 55 kr return.

Places to Stay

The nearest camping ground is the two star *Sletten Camping* (☎ 56 48 50 71, fax 56 48 52 56, email sletten@post10.tele.dk, Melsted Langgade 45, 3760 Gudhjem), a 15 minute walk south of Gudhjem harbour. Camping costs 45 kr per person plus 10 kr per tent; cabins and caravans can be rented for 300 kr and there are some cosy double rooms for 250 kr. It is open from mid-May to mid-September, has a shared kitchen, a coin laundry and a food kiosk, and is within walking distance of the Dagli Brugsen supermarket.

The central *Gudhjem Vandrerhjem* (☎ 56 48 50 35, fax 56 48 56 35, Ejnar Mikkelsensvej 14, 3760 Gudhjem) is in an attractive tile-roofed building opposite the harbourside bus stop. Dorm beds cost 95 kr. It also offers about 30 rooms in private homes; these cost 150/295 kr for singles/doubles. Breakfast and dinner are available for 40 kr each, and there's a coin laundry. Gudhjem Vandrerhjem, also known as Sct Jørgens Gaard, is open year-round. Reception is at a small grocery shop on Løkke-

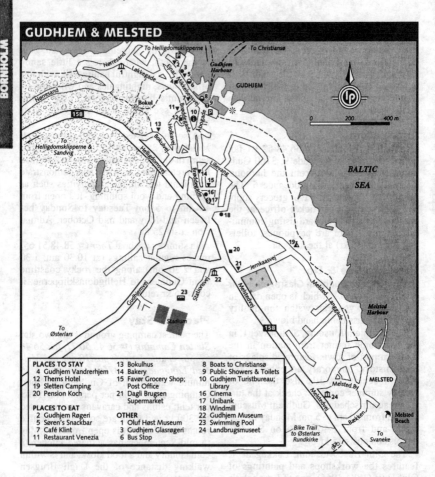

GUDHJEM & MELSTED

PLACES TO STAY	13 Bokulhus	8 Boats to Christiansø
4 Gudhjem Vandrerhjem	14 Bakery	9 Public Showers & Toilets
12 Therns Hotel	15 Favør Grocery Shop;	10 Gudhjem Turistbureau;
19 Sletten Camping	Post Office	Library
20 Pension Koch	21 Dagli Brugsen	16 Cinema
	Supermarket	17 Unibank
PLACES TO EAT		18 Windmill
2 Gudhjem Røgeri	OTHER	22 Gudhjem Museum
5 Søren's Snackbar	1 Oluf Høst Museum	23 Swimming Pool
7 Café Klint	3 Gudhjem Glasrøgeri	24 Landbrugsmuseet
11 Restaurant Venezia	6 Bus Stop	

gade, about 75m north-west of the hostel. Mountain bikes can be hired for 70 kr per day, tandem bikes 110 kr, with discounts for longer rentals.

Also managed by the Gudhjem Vandrerhjem is **Therns Hotel** (☎ 56 48 50 99, fax 56 48 56 35, Brøddegade 31, 3760 Gudhjem), a good-value hotel in the town centre. The 30 rooms vary but are all pleasant and clean. Most have a bath, a TV, a small refrigerator and an extra sofa bed; some also have kitchenettes. Singles cost

250 kr and doubles range from 450 to 700 kr including breakfast.

Pension Koch (☎ 56 48 50 72, fax 56 48 51 72, Melstedvej 15, 3760 Gudhjem) is a bright, cheery guesthouse in the southern part of Gudhjem, about a 10 minute walk from the centre. The 18 rooms are comfortably furnished, all with bath, TV, a coffee maker and a refrigerator. Rates from mid-June to mid-August are 450/560 kr for singles/doubles, including breakfast; low-season rates are 100 kr less. There are also double rooms with kitchenette for 60 kr more and apartments that can be rented by the week.

Places to Eat

Gudhjem Røgeri, a pleasant waterfront smokehouse on Ejnar Mikkelsensvej, sells deli-style fish and salads, offers an all-you-can-eat smoked fish buffet for 69 kr and has both indoor and outdoor dining areas. In summer it's open from 10 am to midnight, with live folk music nightly; in spring and autumn it closes at 5 pm.

Søren's Snackbar, adjacent to Gudhjem Glasrøgeri, serves up inexpensive chicken and chips, hot dogs and beer.

The popular *Restaurant Venezia (Brøddegade 33)* offers good Italian food, including pizzas and pastas costing from 50 to 70 kr, but is open for dinner only.

The *bakery* at Brøddegade 16 has a rooftop patio where you can have pastries and coffee. There's a *Favør* grocery shop around the corner to the south-east.

On a sunny day, the patio at *Café Klint*, opposite the harbour, is the spot for a leisurely cappuccino or beer.

Old-fashioned and a bit expensive, *Bokulhus (Bokulvej 4)* is nonetheless well regarded for its fish dishes. On weekday lunchtimes, from 11.30 am to 5 pm, you can get fish soup with bread for 65 kr, or a traditional fish dish costing 110 kr. There's a two course daily dinner menu that costs 150 kr.

ØSTERLARS RUNDKIRKE

The largest and most impressive of the island's round churches is Østerlars Rundkirke, which dates from 1150 and is set in the midst of wheat fields and half-timbered farmhouses. This fortress-like church has seven weighty buttresses and an upper-level shooting gallery. It's thought that the church roof was originally constructed with a flat top to serve as a battle platform, complete with a brick parapet. However, because of the extensive weight this exerted upon the church walls, the roof was eventually replaced with its present conical one.

The interior is largely whitewashed, although a swath of medieval frescoes has been uncovered and restored. There's a rune stone dating back to 1070 beside the church entrance and a sundial above it.

A cycle path to the church leads inland 4km south from Gudhjem. You can also reach it by taking a 10 minute ride from Gudhjem on bus No 9; Østerlars Rundkirke is a two minute walk from the bus stop. It's open from 9 am to 5 pm Monday to Saturday and admission costs 5 kr.

HELLIGDOMSKLIPPERNE

Perhaps because Denmark hasn't much in the way of hills or lofty rocks, those that it does have are almost revered. Such is the case with Helligdomsklipperne (Sanctuary Cliffs), where moderately high **coastal cliffs** of sharp granite rock formations attract sightseers. About 5km north of Gudhjem on the eastern side of the main coastal road, the Helligdomsklipperne area also has **nature trails** and an art museum.

Bornholms Kunstmuseum, a 100-year-old museum in a stylish modern building, exhibits paintings by artists from the Bornholm School, including Olaf Rude, Oluf Høst and Edvard Weie, who painted in the first half of the 20th century. There are also works by other Danish artists, including paintings of Bornholm by Skagen artist Michael Ancher. The museum is open from 10 am to 5 pm Tuesday to Sunday between May and October, and from 1 to 5 pm on Tuesday, Thursday and Saturday during the rest of the year. Admission costs 30 kr (children free). There's a café on site. Buses stop in front of the museum (bus No 2 from Rønne or Sandvig, or bus No 7 or 9 between Gudhjem and Sandvig).

For information about the sightseeing boat to Helligdomsklipperne, see under Things to See & Do in the Gudhjem section.

SANDVIG & ALLINGE

Sandvig is a quiet little seaside hamlet with attractive older homes, many fronted by rose bushes and tidy flower gardens. It's an easy place to stroll about on foot and it has a sandy beach and an indoor pool.

Three kilometres south-west of Sandvig is Bornholm's best-known sight, Hammershus Slot. There are enjoyable walking trails in the Hammeren area between Sandvig and Hammershus Slot. For details, see the Hammeren and Hammershus Slot sections later in this chapter.

Allinge, the larger and more developed half of the Allinge-Sandvig municipality, is 2km south-east of Sandvig. Although not as quaint as Sandvig, Allinge has the lion's share of commercial facilities, including banks, grocery shops and the area tourist office, Nordbornholms Turistbureau (☎ 56 48 00 01, fax 56 48 02 26, email mail @nbtbook.dk), Kirkegade 4, 3770 Allinge.

Seven kilometres south-east of Sandvig, in the small village of Olsker, is the slenderest of the island's four round churches. If you take the inland bus to Rønne, you can stop off en route to visit the rundkirke or just catch a passing glimpse of it as you ride by.

Places to Stay & Eat

Sandvig Familie Camping (☎ 56 48 04 47, *fax 56 48 04 57, Sandlinien 5, 3770 Allinge*), at the northern side of Sandvig, is backed by heathered hills and has an ideal location just minutes from the beach and nature trails. A three star camping ground, it has a coin laundry and is within walking distance of the bus stop. It's open from mid-May to mid-September.

Sandvig Vandrerhjem (☎ 56 48 03 62, *fax 56 48 18 62, Hammershusvej 94, 3770 Allinge*), open from 1 June to 1 October, has a pleasant rural location between Hammershus Slot and Sandvig. It's a 10 minute walk from the ruins, a bit farther from Sandvig; the public bus stops 100m from the hostel. Dorm beds cost 95 kr, singles/doubles cost 200/300 kr. Breakfast is available but other meals are not served.

Pension Lindesdal (☎ 56 48 17 50, *Hammersøvej 1, 3770 Allinge*) is at the western edge of Sandvig on the road to Hammershus Slot and 500m east of Sandvig Vandrer-

hjem. It has 14 good-value double rooms with private/shared bath that cost 390/320 kr including breakfast.

There are a number of other moderately priced *guesthouses* in Sandvig. For a full listing, contact the Nordbornholms Turistbureau (see the previous section).

There's a *snack bar* by the beach and a number of *restaurants* within easy walking distance of the camping ground, including *Ella's Konditori* (*Strandgade 42*), which has a pleasant garden setting and a varied menu with moderate prices.

HAMMERSHUS SLOT

The impressive 13th century castle ruins of Hammershus Slot, dramatically perched on top of a sea cliff, are the largest in Scandinavia. It is thought that construction was begun in around 1250 by the Archbishop of Lund, who wanted a fortress to protect his diocese against the Crown, which at that time was engaged in a power struggle with the Church. In the centuries that followed, the castle was enlarged, with the upper levels of the square tower added on during the mid-16th century.

Eventually, improvements in naval artillery left the fortress walls vulnerable to attack and in 1645 the castle temporarily fell to Swedish troops after a brief bombardment. Hammershus not only served as a military garrison but also as a prison; from 1660 to 1661 King Christian IV's daughter, Leonora Christine, was imprisoned here on treason charges along with her husband, Corfitz Ulfeldt.

In 1743 the Danish military abandoned Hammershus and many of the stones were carried away to be used as building materials elsewhere. Still, there's much to see – you shouldn't miss a stroll through these extensive fortress ruins. The grounds are always open and admission is free.

Looking north from the coastal sections of the ruins you can see Hammer Havn, a little harbour that was originally built to carry quarried rock to Germany but now shelters yachts, and Hammeren, the rocky jut of land in the background that's set aside as a nature reserve.

Getting There & Away

There's an hourly bus (No 7) from Sandvig to Hammershus Slot, but the most enjoyable way to get there is via footpaths through the hills of Hammeren – a wonderful hour's hike. The well-trodden trail begins by Sandvig Familie Camping and the route is signposted.

If you're coming from Rønne, bus No 1 makes the trip to Hammershus Slot about once an hour.

HAMMEREN

Hammeren, the hammerhead-shaped crag of granite at the northern tip of Bornholm, is crisscrossed by **walking trails** leading through hillsides thick with purple heather. Some of the trails are inland, while others run along the coast.

In addition to just wandering about, you can follow trails between Sandvig and Hammershus Slot. The shortest route to Hammershus goes along the inland side of Hammeren and passes **Hammer Sø**, Bornholm's largest lake, and **Opalsøen**, a deep lake at the bottom of an old quarry. A longer and more windswept route goes along the rocky outer rim of Hammeren, passes a **lighthouse** at Bornholm's northernmost point and continues south along the coast to a harbour, **Hammer Havn**.

From Hammershus Slot there are trails heading south through another heathered landscape, in a nature area called **Slotslyngen**, and east through public woodlands to **Moseløkke granite quarry**. Moseløkke is also the site of a small **museum** where you can see traditional rock-cutting techniques being demonstrated. It's open from 10 am to noon and 1 to 4 pm on weekdays in summer; admission costs 20 kr.

The whole area is a delight for people who enjoy nature walks. For a detailed map of the trails and terrain, pick up the free *Hammeren og Hammershus, Slotslyng* forestry brochure at one of the island's libraries or tourist offices.

CHRISTIANSØ

Tiny Christiansø is a charmingly preserved 17th century fortress island one hour's sail north-east of Bornholm. The largest of a cluster of small granite islands known collectively as Ertholmene, Christiansø has an intriguing history.

A seasonal fishing hamlet since the Middle Ages, Christiansø fell briefly into Swedish hands in 1658, after which Christian V decided to turn the island into an invincible naval fortress. Bastions and barracks were built; a church, a school and a hospital followed. Christiansø became the Danish Navy's forward position in the Baltic, serving to monitor Swedish trade routes and in less congenial times as a base for attacks on Sweden.

In 1808 the British Navy, keen on capturing Christiansø for its strategic significance, bombarded the island but withdrew after it was unable to make a landing. The island also played an infamous role in Danish history when a jail was built in 1825 for political prisoners, the most famous of whom was Dr Dampe, an insurgent who railed against the despotism of Frederik VI.

By the 1850s Christiansø was no longer needed as a base for defence from Sweden and the navy withdrew. Soldiers who wanted to stay on as fishermen were allowed to live as free tenants in the old cottages. Their offspring, and a few latter-day fisherfolk and artists, currently comprise Christiansø's 120 residents. The entire island is an unspoiled reserve – there are no cats or dogs, no cars and no modern buildings. Instead there are old stone-block fortifications and attractive yellow-washed houses.

Christiansø is connected to its smaller sister island, **Frederiksø**, by a footbridge.

Græsholm, the island to the north-west of Christiansø, is a wildlife refuge and an important breeding ground for razorbills, guillemots and other sea birds.

All of the Ertholmene islands, including Christiansø and Frederiksø, serve as spring breeding grounds for up to 2000 eider ducks. The ducks nest near coastal paths and visitors should take care not to scare the mothers away from their nests because predator gulls will quickly attack the unattended eggs. Also, conservation laws strictly forbid the removal of any plants from this unique ecosystem.

Things to See & Do

A leisurely walk around both Christiansø and Frederiksø exploring the sights takes a couple of hours, making this destination ideal for a day trip.

The two main sights are the two stone circular defence towers. The **Lille Tårn** (Little Tower) on Frederiksø dates from 1685 and is the site of the **local history museum**. The ground floor features fishing supplies, hand tools and iron works; upstairs there are cannons, period furnishings, models and a display of local flora and fauna. It's open afternoons daily during the tourist season. Admission costs 10 kr.

Christiansø's **Store Tårn** (Great Tower), built in 1684, is an impressive structure measuring a full 25m in diameter. The tower's 100-year-old **lighthouse** offers a splendid 360° view of the island; for 4 kr you can climb to the top.

The main activity on Christiansø is the walk along the fortified stone walls and cannon-lined batteries that surround the perimeter of the island. There are skerries (rocky islets) with nesting sea birds and a secluded **swimming cove** on Christiansø's eastern side.

Places to Stay & Eat

Camping (☎ 30 34 96 05) is allowed in summer in a small field called the Duchess Battery at the northern end of Christiansø

but because of the limited space it can be difficult to book.

Christiansø Gæstgiveriet (☎ 56 46 20 15, fax 56 46 20 86, 3740 Christiansø), built in 1730 as the naval commander's residence, is the island's only inn. It has half a dozen singles/doubles with shared bath costing 320/420 kr, including breakfast. It is open from 1 May to 1 October.

There's a moderately priced *restaurant* at the inn and a small *grocery shop* and *snack shop* nearby.

Getting There & Away

Christiansøfarten (☎ 56 48 51 76) operates passenger ferries to Christiansø from Allinge and Gudhjem in the high season, while the mail/passenger boat from Svaneke makes the trip year-round.

The boat leaves Gudhjem at 10.20 am daily from mid-May to late September and departs from Christiansø for the return trip at 2.20 pm. Between late June and 31 August there are additional sailings from Gudhjem at 9.40 am Monday to Saturday and at 12.15 pm daily.

The boat leaves Allinge at 1 pm from Monday to Saturday from mid-May to late September, departing from Christiansø at 4.20 pm.

From Svaneke, the boat leaves at 10 am on weekdays, departing from Christiansø at 2.30 pm (at 1.30 pm during the winter).

All boats charge 135 kr return for a day trip and 225 kr for an open return. Children aged from four to 11 pay 70/115 kr for a day trip/open return.

You can visit the company's Web site at www.christiansoefarten.dk.

Funen

Funen (Fyn) is the name of Denmark's second largest island as well as the name of the county (Fyn Amt) that includes Funen island and about 90 neighbouring

Highlights

- Admire Ærøskobing's leaning half-timbered houses
- Wander around the cobblestoned streets of Faaborg, an enjoyable coastal town
- Tour Egeskov Slot, a splendid moat-encircled Renaissance castle
- Explore the city of Odense with its interesting Gothic cathedral and museums
- Cycle through Funen's undulating countryside with its picturesque farms and villages
- Hop on a boat to one of the small islands off Funen's southern coast

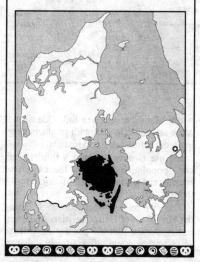

islands. While most of these neighbouring islands are small and privately owned, the largest three – Ærø, Langeland and Tåsinge – have appealing seaside towns and are fine destinations in themselves. All of Funen county has a bucolic character, with picturesque rural scenery and thatched farmhouses throughout.

The main railway line from Copenhagen runs straight through Odense, Funen's main city, and west to Jutland, but it would be a shame to zip through without stopping to explore more of Funen. Outside Odense, places of special merit include Egeskov Slot, the historic maritime town of Faaborg and the unspoiled island of Ærø.

BICYCLE ROUTES

Funen is an attractive place in which to cycle, with pleasant scenery and some gentle hills. In all, Funen county is crisscrossed by 1175km of marked cycle paths, some leading into the countryside and others running parallel with the main routes between major towns.

Cykelnetværk Fyn, in cooperation with the Funen county government, publishes an excellent cycling guide comprising a 50 page booklet and detailed 1:100,000 maps. The booklet describes 20 cycling routes around Funen, Langeland and Ærø, and includes distances, levels of difficulty and sightseeing spots along the way. It can be bought at local bookshops or tourist offices (75 kr). There are three versions: English, Danish and German. For more information on cycling, see the special section 'Cycling in Denmark' in the Getting Around chapter.

Odense

Odense, which translates as 'Odin's shrine', was named after the powerful Nordic god of war, poetry and wisdom. The city's history dates back to pre-Viking times, with the first known reference to Odense appearing

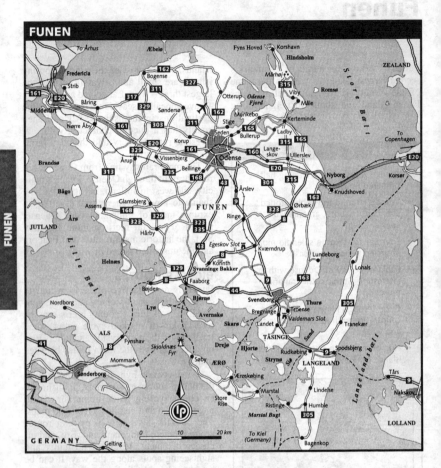

FUNEN

in a letter written by the German emperor Otto III in 988.

By the middle of the 18th century Odense was the largest provincial town in Denmark, with 5000 inhabitants, but it was the only major Danish town without a harbour and thus failed to benefit directly from the maritime trade that prospered in coastal towns such as Faaborg.

In 1800, in the largest construction project of that era, a canal was dug to connect Odense to the Odense Fjord, 5km to the north. With the new sea link Odense became an industrial city with products ranging from refined sugar to textiles.

Odense is now Denmark's third largest city (population 184,000), the capital of Funen county and a transportation hub for the region.

The city makes much ado about being the birthplace of Hans Christian Andersen, but Andersen himself got out of Odense as fast as he could, after a fairly unhappy childhood there (see the boxed text in the

Facts about Denmark chapter for more details of Andersen's life).

Whatever Andersen's experiences may have been, Odense today is an affable university city with lots of cycle paths and pedestrian streets, an interesting cathedral and a number of museums that are worth a visit. It's also relatively light on the wallet, with a pleasant hostel and some good-value hotels.

Orientation

The train station is in a large new complex called the Odense Banegård Center, which contains restaurants, shops, the public library and travel-related facilities. The tourist office (Odense Turistbureau), at rådhus, is a 10 minute walk south from the train station. The cathedral, Sankt Knuds Kirke, is on Klosterbakken, two minutes walk from the turistbureau, and most other sights are also within walking distance of each other in the city centre.

Information

Tourist Office The Odense Turistbureau (☎ 66 12 75 20, fax 66 12 75 86), Rådhuset, 5000 Odense C, is open from 9 am to 7 pm Monday to Saturday and from 11 am to 7 pm on Sunday from 15 June to 31 August. In the low season it's open from 9 am to 4.30 pm Monday to Friday and from 10 am to 1 pm on Saturday. This bustling office is well stocked with regional brochures and handles everything from currency exchange outside banking hours to sales of camping passes, hostel cards and the Odense Eventyrpas (see the boxed text for details). Its Web site is at www.odenseturist.dk.

Money There's a Sydbank at the northern end of Kongensgade and a number of banks on Vestergade, including a branch of Den Danske Bank opposite rådhus.

Post The main post office is north of the train station at Dannebrogsgade 2. There's also a branch in the centre at Gråbrødrestræde 1, open until at least 5 pm Monday to Friday and until 1 pm on Saturday, but it generally has longer queues.

Travel Agency Kilroy Travels (☎ 66 17 77 80), Pantheonsgade 7, specialises in youth and discount travel.

Bookshops The GAD Bookshop at Vestergade 37 and the Arnold Busck Bookshop at Vestergade 82 both have good selections of books in English. Antikvariatet, Kongensgade 13, is a good place to pick up second-hand paperback novels at reasonable prices.

Library The library, in the Odense Banegård Center, holds a few English-language foreign newspapers, including London's *Independent* and *Observer*. It's open from 10 am to 7 pm Monday to Thursday, from 10 am to 4 pm on Friday and from 10 am to 2 pm on Saturday. You can buy foreign newspapers at the kiosk on the 3rd floor of the same building.

Pharmacy There's a 24 hour chemist, Ørnen Apoteket (☎ 66 12 29 70), at Vestergade 80.

Odense Eventyrpas

The Odense Eventyrpas (Adventure Pass) gives a 75% discount on admission to most of the city sights, including Brandts Klædefabrik, Den Fynske Landsby, Fyns Kunstmuseum, the two Hans Christian Andersen museums and Møntergården. It gives a 50% reduction on Danmarks Jernbanemuseum and a 25% reduction on the zoo and the Odense Åfart riverboat. The pass also includes unlimited use of buses and trains within the city limits.

The pass is a bargain at 50 kr for one day or 90 kr for two days (half-price for children aged under 14). It can be purchased at the turistbureau, the train station, Odense Vandrerhjem and some hotels.

FUNEN

ODENSE

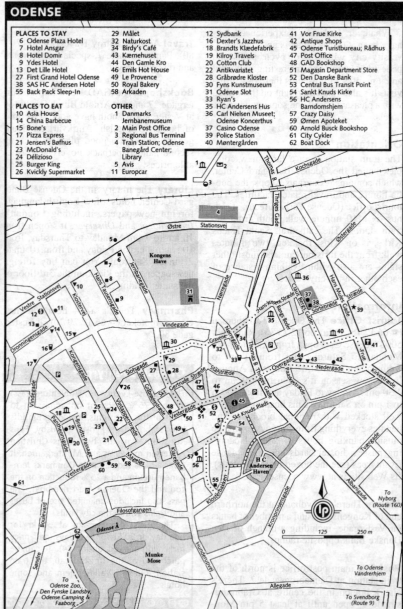

PLACES TO STAY
6 Odense Plaza Hotel
7 Hotel Ansgar
8 Hotel Domir
9 Ydes Hotel
13 Det Lille Hotel
27 First Grand Hotel Odense
38 SAS HC Andersen Hotel
55 Back Pack Sleep-In

PLACES TO EAT
10 Asia House
14 China Barbecue
15 Bone's
17 Pizza Express
21 Jensen's Bøfhus
23 McDonald's
24 Délizioso
25 Burger King
26 Kvickly Supermarket

29 Målet
32 Naturkost
34 Birdy's Café
43 Kærnehuset
44 Den Gamle Kro
46 Emils Hot House
49 Le Provence
50 Royal Bakery
58 Arkaden

OTHER
1 Danmarks
   Jernbanemuseum
2 Main Post Office
3 Regional Bus Terminal
4 Train Station; Odense
   Banegård Center;
   Library
5 Avis
11 Europcar

12 Sydbank
16 Dexter's Jazzhus
18 Brandts Klædefabrik
19 Kilroy Travels
20 Cotton Club
22 Antikvariatet
28 Gråbrødre Kloster
30 Fyns Kunstmuseum
31 Odense Slot
33 Ryan's
35 HC Andersens Hus
36 Carl Nielsen Museet;
   Odense Koncerthus
37 Casino Odense
39 Police Station
40 Møntergården

41 Vor Frue Kirke
42 Antique Shops
45 Odense Turistbureau; Rådhus
47 Post Office
48 GAD Bookshop
51 Magasin Department Store
52 Den Danske Bank
53 Central Bus Transit Point
54 Sankt Knuds Kirke
56 HC Andersens
   Barndomshjem
57 Crazy Daisy
59 Ørnen Apoteket
60 Arnold Busck Bookshop
61 City Cykler
62 Boat Dock

Meet the Danes Staff at the turistbureau can arrange for foreign travellers to meet with a Danish family at home for tea and conversation. Because they try to match people of similar ages and interests, you should request the 'Meet the Danes' programme at least a day in advance. There's no fee.

Walking Tour

The following route takes in many of the city's historic sights and museums. Although the walk itself takes only about an hour, if you stop at all the sights along the way it could easily take you the better part of a day to complete the tour. (The major sights listed in this walk are given more detail later in this section.)

Start at **rådhus**, the city hall, which is predominantly of 1950s vintage, although the west wing dates from the late 19th century. Hour-long tours of the city hall (10 kr) are conducted from Monday to Thursday at 2 pm in summer.

From rådhus head east on Overgade and then turn right onto **Nedergade**, a cobblestoned street with leaning half-timbered houses and antique shops.

At the end of Nedergade, a left turn onto Frue Kirkestræde will bring you to **Vor Frue Kirke**, erected in the 13th century. It has a rather plain, whitewashed interior, although there's an ornate Baroque pulpit that dates from the mid-17th century. It's open daily, except Sunday, from 10 am to 3 pm in summer and from 10 am to noon during the rest of the year.

From Vor Frue Kirke turn left back onto Overgade, where you'll soon reach **Møntergården**, the city museum, and then turn right onto Claus Bergs Gade, where you'll pass the city's only casino. Immediately to the north is the **Odense Koncerthus** (Concert Hall) and a museum dedicated to composer Carl Nielsen.

Just past the casino, turn left onto Ramsherred (which quickly changes into Hans Jensens Stræde) to reach **HC Andersens Hus**, the principal museum dedicated to Hans Christian Andersen. The museum is in a pleasant neighbourhood of narrow cobbled streets and old tile-roofed houses. If you desire some green space there's a little **park and duck pond** south of the museum.

Continue down Hans Jensens Stræde, cross Thomas B Thriges Gade and follow Gravene to Slotsgade: **Fyns Kunstmuseum**, Odense's notable fine arts museum, is on the corner of Slotsgade and Jernbanegade. Turn left and proceed down Jernbanegade to Vestergade. Along the way you'll pass the site of **Gråbrødre Kloster**, a medieval Franciscan monastery that has been converted into an old people's home.

When you reach Vestergade, turn east back to rådhus and then go south to **Sankt Knuds Kirke**, Odense's intriguing cathedral. Opposite the cathedral, turn onto Sankt Knuds Kirkestræde and then go south on Munkemøllestræde, where you'll pass **HC Andersens Barndomshjem**, the writer's childhood home.

Loop back around on Klosterbakken and take the path into the **HC Andersen Haven**, a riverside park with a prominent statue of the author. You can walk north through the park to get back to your starting point at rådhus.

Sankt Knuds Kirke

Odense's 12th century Gothic cathedral is one of the city's most interesting sights. It boasts an ornate gilded altar dating from 1520 that's considered the finest work of the master woodcrafter Claus Berg. An intricately detailed triptych, the altar stands 5m high and has nearly 300 carved figures, most depicting the life and death of Christ, although the bottom row also works in King Hans on the left and Queen Christine on the right. It was Christine, a friend of Berg's, who commissioned the work. Berg also created the large limestone sepulchral monument bearing the king's and queen's portraits in bas-relief.

The cathedral's most intriguing attraction lies in the basement beneath the altar, where you'll find a glass case containing the 900-year-old skeleton of King Canute

King Canute – the Unsaintly Saint

Canute (Knud) II reigned over Denmark from 1080 to his untimely death six years later. A ruthless tyrant, Canute led Viking raids abroad and instituted numerous taxes at home, often using brutal methods to collect them.

In 1086 Canute, trying to evade a crowd of angry farmers who had pursued him from Jutland, fled into Sankt Albans Kirke in Odense in an attempt to take sanctuary. There, while kneeling before the altar, he was killed by the mob.

Although less than saintly, in 1101 Canute II was canonised as Canute the Holy by the pope in a move to secure both the Crown and Church in Denmark. Despite being Denmark's first saint, Canute the Holy has never been widely popular and his name is still invoked as a term of abuse among farmers in Jutland.

(Knud) II and another displaying the skeleton of his younger brother Benedikt. An inconspicuous set of stairs leads from the right-hand side of the altar down to these basement treasures.

A few metres to the left of the coffins, steps lead down to the remains of Sankt Albans Kirke, which stood on this site before Sankt Knuds Kirke was built. It was at the altar of Sankt Albans Kirke that Canute II and Benedikt were killed during a tax revolt.

Between early May and mid-September Sankt Knuds Kirke is open from 10 am to 5 pm Monday to Saturday, and between June and August it's also open on Sunday from 11.30 am to 3.30 pm. During the rest of the year it's open from 10 am to 4 pm Monday to Saturday (to 2 pm on Saturday between October and March). Admission is free.

HC Andersens Hus

This museum, on a cobbled pedestrian-only street at Hans Jensens Stræde 39, tells Hans Christian Andersen's life story using a barrage of memorabilia. There's a room with slide presentations on Andersen's life, a reconstruction of his Nyhavn (in Copenhagen) study, displays of his fanciful silhouette-style paper cuttings and a voluminous selection of his books, which have been translated into some 80 languages ranging from Azerbaijani to Zulu.

HC Andersens Hus is open from 9.30 am to 7 pm daily between June and August, and from 10 am to 4 pm daily between September and May. Admission costs 40 kr (children 15 kr).

HC Andersens Barndomshjem

In the city centre, at Munkemøllestræde 3, HC Andersens Barndomshjem has a couple of rooms of exhibits in the small home where Andersen spent part of his childhood from 1807 to 1819. It's open from 10 am to 5 pm daily between June and August, and from 11 am to 3 pm daily between September and May. Admission costs 5 kr (children 2 kr).

Fyns Kunstmuseum

The Funen Art Museum, housed in a stately Graeco-Roman building at Jernbanegade 13, boasts a fine collection of Danish art, ranging from paintings by the old masters to abstract contemporary works. Among the museum's 2500 works of art are paintings by Jens Juel, PS Krøyer, Vilhelm Hammershøi, Asger Jorn and Richard Mortensen. A highlight is the collection of works by the local Fynboerne (Funen Group), which includes artists such as Fritz Syberg, Peter Hansen and Johannes Larsen.

Fyns Kunstmuseum is open from 10 am to 4 pm Tuesday to Sunday year-round. Admission costs 25 kr (children 10 kr).

Egeskov Slot, set in grand parkland with a moat and drawbridge, is Funen's finest Renaissance castle.

Viby's picturesque windmill, Hindsholm peninsula.

Cooling off at an ice cream shop in Ærøskøbing.

Historic smithy museum at Egeskov Slot.

Nyborg Slot, one of Denmark's oldest royal castles.

Step back in time at Den Fynske Landsby, Odense.

Carl Nielsen Museet

This museum, in the Odense Koncerthus at Claus Bergs Gade 11, details the career of Carl Nielsen (1865-1931), Denmark's best-known composer. Nielsen's music career began at the age of 14 when he became a trumpet player in Odense's military band. Four years later he moved to Copenhagen to undertake formal music studies and shortly afterwards, in 1888, his first orchestral work, *Suite for Strings*, was performed at Tivoli concert hall. It was critically acclaimed and has become a regular piece in the Danish concert repertory. Nielsen's music includes six symphonies, several operas and numerous hymn tunes and popular songs, some with patriotic themes.

The chronologically ordered exhibition details not only the life of Nielsen but also that of his wife, sculptor Anne Marie Brodersen. Displays include Brodersen's works and studio and Nielsen's study and piano.

It's open from 10 am to 4 pm Tuesday to Sunday year-round. Admission costs 15 kr (children 5 kr).

Møntergården

This city museum, at Overgade 48, has displays covering Odense's history dating back to the Viking Age, and a couple of 16th and 17th century half-timbered houses that you can walk through. There are numerous rooms with period furnishings, medieval exhibits, church carvings and local archaeological finds. It's open from 10 am to 4 pm Tuesday to Sunday. Admission costs 15 kr (children 5 kr).

Danmarks Jernbanemuseum

Train buffs shouldn't miss the 19th century locomotives at the Danish Railway Museum, just behind the train station. It has a replica of a period station and about two dozen engines and saloon cars, including a royal carriage that once belonged to Christian IX. There are also displays of model trains and ferries.

It's open from 10 am to 4 pm daily. Admission costs 20 kr (children 10 kr).

Brandts Klædefabrik

This former textile mill on Brandts Passage has been converted into a cultural centre with museums, an art academy and a cinema.

The **Danmarks Grafiske Museum/Dansk Pressemuseum** (Danish Museum of Printing/Danish Press Museum) traces the development of printing in Denmark over the last three centuries. One section of the museum covers old-fashioned lithography, engraving, bookbinding and papermaking, and the other concentrates on newspaper production. Former workers, now retired, re-enact the techniques they used in their working days (such as setting cold type), which have been made obsolete by computerised presses.

Museet for Fotokunst (Museum of Photographic Art) is Denmark's only museum dedicated solely to the art of photography. It has both a permanent collection and changing exhibitions by national and international photographers.

Kunsthallen, a modern art gallery, has four large halls with changing exhibitions largely dedicated to new trends in the visual arts. Displays include paintings, sculpture and installations as well as exhibits on Scandinavian design. There's also a videotheque with a library of art videos that can be viewed by visitors.

All three museums are open from 10 am to 5 pm Tuesday to Sunday, and also on Monday in July and August. Admission costs 25 kr to the art gallery and 20 kr each to the other museums. You can get a joint ticket to all three for 40 kr (children 10 kr).

Odense Slot

Kongens Have, the park directly opposite the train station, is the site of Odense Slot, a two storey castle with red-tiled roofs and a cobbled courtyard. Modest as castles go, it was erected in 1720 by Frederik IV to serve as a royal residence during his visits to Odense. The king died here in 1730, a victim of tuberculosis. Odense Slot was later converted into a governor's residence and now serves as administrative offices for

FUNEN

the local municipal and county governments. It's not open to visitors but you can stroll through the grounds.

Den Fynske Landsby

This is a delightful open-air museum with furnished period buildings laid out as they might have been in a small country village of the mid-19th century, complete with barnyard animals, a duck pond, apple trees and flower gardens. There are about two dozen thatched houses and farm buildings in all, including a windmill, a watermill and a smithy, which have been moved here from rural areas in Funen.

Den Fynske Landsby, in a green zone 4km south of the city centre, can be reached by bus No 42.

In summer you can also take the boat operated by Odense Åfart (see Boat under Getting Around later in this section) and get off at Erik Bøghs Sti, from where it's a refreshing 15 minute woodland walk south-east along the river to Den Fynske Landsby.

It's open from 9.30 am to 7 pm daily between June and August, and from 10 am to 5 pm daily except Monday in April, May and September. Admission costs 25 kr (children 10 kr). Activities ranging from beer brewing to crop harvesting take place at weekends and in midsummer.

Odense Zoo

This zoo, bordering the river Odense Å on Sondre Boulevard, is 2km south of the city centre. It's recently expanded from a relatively small operation to become Denmark's second largest zoo. Animals on display include tigers, lions, giraffes, zebras, camels and a collection of colourful African birds.

It's open daily, from 9 am to 7 pm in July, from 9 am to 6 pm in May, June and August, and from 9 am to 4 or 5 pm during the rest of the year. Admission costs 55 kr (children 27 kr). You can get there on bus No 31. Odense Åfart (see under Boat in the Odense Getting Around section) also stops at the zoo, or you could walk the entire way along

the wooded riverside path that begins at Munke Mose.

Places to Stay

Camping *Odense Camping* (☎ *66 11 47 02, fax 65 91 73 43, Odensevej 102, 5260 Odense S)* is a three star camping ground in a wooded area not far from Den Fynske Landsby, 3.5km south of the city centre. It has cooking and laundry facilities and cabins for hire. It's open year-round. You can get there on bus No 21, 22 or 23.

Hostels & Rooms *Odense Vandrerhjem* (☎ *66 13 04 25, fax 65 91 28 63, email odensehostel@mailhost.net, Kragsbjergvej 121, 5230 Odense M)* is in an exclusive suburb 2km south-east of the city centre. The hostel buildings, formerly a manor house, surround a cobbled courtyard and are half-timbered; the interior has been renovated and the rooms are modern. The 168 beds are mostly in four-bed rooms; dorm beds cost 85 kr. It's open from mid-February to the end of November. Bus No 61 or 62 can drop you 150m from the hostel; take the driveway lined with linden trees.

Back Pack Sleep-In (☎ *66 12 87 00, fax 66 17 87 12, Munkemøllestræde 2, 5000 Odense C)* is a small summer hostel in Studenterhus, a student centre in central Odense. Just a short walk south of Sankt Knuds Kirke, it has a simple mixed-sex dorm that can accommodate 20 people. There are showers, laundry facilities, a TV and a café selling sandwiches, coffee and beer. The price is a reasonable 75 kr, including sheets and breakfast. It's open in July and August only.

Staff at Odense Turistbureau can book *rooms* in private homes for 125 to 175 kr for singles and 250 kr for doubles, plus a 25 kr booking fee.

Hotels *Det Lille Hotel* (☎/fax 66 12 28 21, Dronningensgade 5, 5000 Odense C), a 10 minute walk west of the train station, is a guesthouse-like place with 14 rooms. Its straightforward singles/doubles, all with shared bath, cost 220/350 kr; rates include breakfast.

The recommended 38 room *Hotel Domir* (☎ *66 12 14 27, fax 66 12 17 82, Hans Tausensgade 19, 5000 Odense C*) has reasonable prices and a convenient location just minutes from the train station. The rooms are cheery with TV, phone, desk and bath; singles/doubles cost 360/480 kr. There are also a couple of very small rooms for 310/410 kr. Breakfast is included in these prices.

Also good value is Domir's nearby sister-operation, *Ydes Hotel* (☎ *66 12 11 31, fax 66 12 17 82, Hans Tausensgade 11, 5000 Odense C*). It has 29 compact but spotlessly clean and modern rooms with TV, desk and bath; singles/doubles cost 295/430 kr including breakfast.

Hotel Ansgar (☎ *66 11 96 93, fax 66 11 96 75, Østre Stationsvej 32, 5000 Odense C*) is central and has pleasantly renovated rooms with TV, minibar and bath. Overall the rooms are on a par with some of the city's top-end hotels but have relatively reasonable weekend and summer rates of 445/595 kr for singles/doubles.

Odense Plaza Hotel (☎ *66 11 77 45, fax 66 14 41 45, Østre Stationsvej 24, 5000 Odense C*) is a small period hotel southwest of the train station. A member of the Best Western chain, its rooms have minibars, trouser presses and TV. The staff are friendly and there's a pleasant sunroom where a better-than-average breakfast is served. The standard rates are 795/1095 kr for singles/doubles but there's a special 695 kr rate at weekends and in summer that covers up to two adults and two children, including breakfast.

The city's other historic hotel, the central *First Hotel Grand Odense* (☎ *66 11 71 71, fax 66 14 11 71, Jernbanegade 18, 5100 Odense C*), has a variety of rooms, some spiffier than others, most of them large and all with minibar, TV, phone and desk. Singles/doubles usually cost 895/1095 kr but there's a weekend rate of 700 kr for doubles.

SAS HC Andersen Hotel (☎ *66 14 78 00, fax 66 14 78 90, Claus Bergs Gade 7, 5000 Odense C*) is a modern four storey brick hotel. The rooms have modern amenities including TV, phone and minibar. There's a sauna, a solarium and a billiard table as well as a casino on site. The standard rate for singles/doubles is 995/1135 kr but there's a summer price of 675 kr. It's part of the Radisson chain.

Places to Eat

Budget Bakeries and cheap fast-food outlets are easy to find all around the city. *Royal Bakery*, on Vestergade opposite Jernbanegade, bakes good pastries; in summer it sets up a pavement stand selling organic ice cream.

On Wednesday and Saturday mornings there's a large *produce market* along Claus Bergs Gade, the pedestrian street that runs south from the Odense Koncerthus.

On the 3rd floor of the train station you'll find a good café-style *bakery* with both eat-in and takeaway items, and a *DSB Café* serving inexpensive meals.

Emils Hot House, opposite the turistbureau on Vestergade, has hot dogs and pizza by the slice. For good croissants and baguette sandwiches there's the French-influenced *Délizioso* on Kongensgade, opposite *McDonald's* and *Burger King*.

Café Biografen at Brandts Klædefabrik is a popular student haunt offering inexpensive pastries, coffees, light meals and beer. It's open from 11 am to at least midnight daily, although the kitchen closes at 9 pm.

Pizza Express (*Vindegade 73*) has 26 varieties of thin-crust takeaway pizza for 37 kr as well as 25 kr pitta-bread sandwiches. It's open daily except Monday from 3 to 11 pm (to 2 am Friday and Saturday).

For an alternative dining experience, try *Kærnehuset* (*Nedergade 6*); this vegetarian collective offers a 45 kr meal at 6 pm from Tuesday to Friday (daily in July) and welcomes visitors. You should help with the cooking or the cleaning up.

Kvickly, a central supermarket on Slotsgade, has a bakery and a large, inexpensive cafeteria where various full meals cost around 35 kr. At the eastern side of the train

FUNEN

station is a small **supermarket** that sells beer and wine and stays open daily until midnight. There's a well-stocked health-food shop, **Naturkost**, at Gravene 8; it's open from 9 am to 5.30 pm Monday to Friday and until 1 pm on Saturday.

Mid-Range There are numerous moderately priced restaurants and cafés along both Vestergade and Kongensgade, many of which chalk up daily specials. One cluster can be found at the **Arkaden** complex, at the southern end of Kongensgade on Vestergade, which contains Greek, Italian, Brazilian and a few other ethnic restaurants offering lunch specials for around 50 kr and full dinners for about 100 kr.

Jensen's Bøfhus (*Kongensgade 10*) offers grilled chicken and steaks costing from around 80 kr at dinner; the chain's usual lunch specials are about half that price. It's open until 11 pm daily. There's a second Jensen's Bøfhus at the train station. Trendier and of a higher quality is **Bone's** (*Vindegade 53*), which specialises in spareribs – generous servings together with a helping from the salad bar begin at around 100 kr. It's open from 5 to 10.30 pm daily.

Målet (*Jernbanegade 17*), a sports pub and restaurant, features 10 different kinds of schnitzel, all priced at 69 kr. It's open until 10 pm for food, 11 pm for drinks.

A popular student spot is **Birdy's Café** (*Nørregade 21*), where Mexican specialities such as enchiladas or fajitas cost around 75 kr. It's open from 4 pm to after midnight Monday to Saturday.

China Barbecue (*Kongensgade 66*) has a good-value Chinese buffet with six different dishes at lunch (49 kr) and 10 dishes at dinner (88 kr). Children under 12 years old eat for half price. It's open for lunch from noon to 3 pm Monday to Saturday and for dinner from 5.30 to at least 10 pm nightly.

Top End *Asia House*, on the corner of Vestre Stationsvej and Klostervej, serves good authentic Thai food. On Friday and Saturday nights there's a grand buffet spread

for 129 kr, on other nights à la carte main dishes cost around 90 kr. It's open from 5 pm nightly.

Le Provence (*Pogestræde 31*) is a pleasant French restaurant on a quiet back street in the city centre. It offers cosy candlelit dinners, with prices starting at 158 kr for a three course meal. It's open from 5.30 pm to midnight Monday to Saturday.

Den Gamle Kro (*Overgade 23*), in a historic building dating from 1683, offers traditional Danish fare. There are a few dining rooms, the most atmospheric in the brick-vaulted cellar. Expect lunch to cost about 125 kr and dinner nearly double that. It's open from 10 am to 10.30 pm daily (to 9.30 pm on Sunday).

Entertainment

University students hang out at *Ryan's*, a friendly Irish pub on Nørregade near rådhus. It has Guinness and Kilkenny on tap, stays open until around 3 am and offers live music, usually Irish folk, from Wednesday to Friday.

The most popular dance spot is *Crazy Daisy*, a nightclub on Sankt Knuds Kirkestræde, near Sankt Knuds Kirke; it's open from 9 pm to 5 am at the weekend.

The open-air amphitheatre at *Brandts Klædefabrik* is a venue for free summertime rock, jazz and blues concerts, particularly on Saturday. *Café Biografen*, also at Brandts Klædefabrik, screens first-run movies; tickets are cheaper than in cinemas.

Dexter's Jazzhus (*Vindegade 65*) is a good place to hear jazz; there's live music from Thursday to Saturday. *Cotton Club* (*Pantheonsgade 5*), which also has weekend jazz, tends to attract an older crowd.

The *outdoor cafés* on Vintapperstræde are good spots for a quiet evening drink.

On a splashier scale there's the *Casino Odense* (*Claus Bergs Gade 7*), at the SAS HC Andersen Hotel, where you can try your luck at blackjack, roulette and slot machines.

Symphony orchestra and other classical music performances are held at the *Odense Koncerthus* (*Claus Bergs Gade 9*); the programme commonly includes works by Carl Nielsen. The turistbureau can provide the current schedule.

Gay & Lesbian Venue The gay and lesbian organisation Lambda (☎ 66 17 76 92) hosts occasional events in the basement of Vindegade 100.

Shopping

You can find a variety of clothing and speciality shops in the city centre along Kongensgade and Vestergade. Magasin on Vestergade is the city's largest department store and stocks just about everything from food delicacies to cosmetics and clothing. For antiques, Kramboden at Nedergade 24 has an interesting hotchpotch of items including porcelain, toys, glass and pewter. Borsen Antikvardboghandel, next door at Nedergade 26, sells antique books.

Getting There & Away

Odense is 34km west of Nyborg, 44km north-west of Svendborg, 37km north-east of Faaborg and 50km east of the bridge to Jutland.

Bus Regional buses leave from the bus station at Dannebrogsgade 6, at the rear of the train station. There are bus services from Odense to all major towns on Funen (see under individual destinations for bus information).

Train Odense is on the main railway line between Copenhagen (170 kr, 1½ hours) and Århus (149 kr, 1¾ hours) via Nyborg (33 kr, 20 minutes); the service is frequent throughout the day. The only other train route in Funen is the hourly run between Odense and Svendborg (49 kr, one hour).

Car & Motorcycle Odense is to the north of the E20; you can exit the E20 and go into the city via route 9, 43 or 168. Odense is connected to Nyborg by route 160 and the E20, to Kerteminde by route 165, to Jutland by the E20, to Faaborg by route 43 and to Svendborg by route 9.

Rental The following companies have booths at the airport and in the city centre:

Avis
(☎ 66 14 39 99) Østre Stationsvej 31
Europcar
(☎ 66 14 15 44) Kongensgade 69
Hertz
(☎ 66 14 90 96) Odense Banegård Center

Getting Around

Bus The main transit point for city buses is in front of Sankt Knuds Kirke.

In Odense you board city buses at the back and pay the driver (10 kr) when you get off. It will generally work out cheaper to pick up a 24 hour bus pass, which costs just 25 kr and can be purchased at the turistbureau or the train station.

Car & Motorcycle Outside rush hour, driving in Odense is not difficult, but many of the central sights are on pedestrian streets and it's best to park your car and explore on foot.

Near the city centre, parking is largely metered, with a fee of 6 kr per hour on weekdays from 9 am to 5 pm and on Saturday to noon; outside those hours it's usually free. There's a large multistorey car park on the northern side of Filosofgangen and smaller car parks around Brandts Klædefabrik and at the northern side of the Carl Nielsen Museet.

Taxi Taxis are readily available at the train station, or you can order one by phoning Odense Taxa (☎ 66 15 44 15).

Bicycle You can hire bikes at City Cykler (☎ 66 13 97 83), Vesterbro 27, on weekdays from 9 am to 5.30 pm and weekends from 10 am to 4 pm. The cost is 45 kr per day for a three speed bike and 85 kr for a tandem.

Boat From 1 May to 15 August Odense Åfart (☎ 65 95 79 96) runs a little covered boat down the Odense Å to Erik Bøghs Sti, a landing in the woods at Fruens Bøge. The boat departs from Munke Mose, to the south-west of the city centre, at 10 and

11 am and 1, 2, 3 and 5 pm (and also at noon and 4 pm in midsummer). You can take it as a 70 minute return excursion in itself, or break your journey at the zoo or the woods. The cost is 26 kr one way, 40 kr return, 18/26 kr for children.

Around Funen Island

The island of Funen, nicknamed 'Denmark's garden island', is largely rural and green, with rolling woodlands, pastures, wheat fields and lots of old farmhouses. The terrain is gentler in the north, where it eventually levels out to marshland, and more hilly in the south. During May the landscape is ablaze with solid patches of yellow rapeseed flowers.

NYBORG

Nyborg is the easternmost town on Funen and the western terminus of Storebælts-forbindelsen (Store Bælt bridge). While most people pass right through the town without pause, seeing little more than its industrial harbourfront, for those with time to spare Nyborg can make an enjoyable stop.

The most appealing part of town is around Torvet, the main square, where there's an attractive brick rådhus, the remains of a medieval castle and some classic half-timbered houses. All are within a few hundred metres of each other and just a 10 minute walk west of the train station.

There are white-sand beaches alongside the Store Bælt on the eastern side of town, about 1.5km from the centre.

Tourist Office

The Nyborg Turistbureau (☎ 65 31 02 80, fax 65 31 03 80) is at Torvet 9, 5800 Nyborg. Between 15 June and 31 August it's open from 9 am to 5 pm Monday to Friday and from 9 am to 2 pm on Saturday. During the rest of the year it's open from 9 am to

Bed & Breakfast in Funen

Funen has a new countywide B&B association that encompasses nearly 100 homes. Some are modern places right in the city, others are centuries-old farmhouses in quiet countryside settings. Staying in one of these B&Bs is a great way to experience a slice of Denmark up close, to sit down at the breakfast table and rub shoulders with the Danes.

The association publishes an annually updated catalogue with a colour photo of each B&B along with a brief description that includes the number of guestrooms, the price, and information on facilities that may be available, such as a kitchen, a TV or a play area for children. The descriptions also note which foreign languages each host speaks – the majority speak English and German, but a number also speak French. Pictograms let you know which places have farm animals and which are close to good angling spots, hiking trails or beaches. The catalogue includes a detailed map of Funen county with the location of each B&B.

Prices, which include breakfast, bed linen and a towel, range from 150 to 200 kr per person based on double occupancy. The per-person charge runs a little higher for singles and a bit lower if there are more than two people to a room.

Advance reservations are advised, especially in the high season, and because many of the hosts work outside their homes it's wise to call at least an evening ahead to make arrangements at any time of the year. You can pick up the catalogue free at any tourist office in Funen. If you prefer, staff at tourist offices will call and find a place for you (25 kr booking fee) – they often know which B&Bs are likely to have vacancies so this can be a helpful service for last-minute bookings.

4 pm Monday to Friday and from 9 am to noon on Saturday.

Nyborg Slot

Nyborg Slot was one of half a dozen fortresses erected in strategic locations during the late 12th century to secure Denmark's coast. In 1282 Erik V, under pressure from nobles who wanted to limit royal power and safeguard individual rights, signed an important charter here that established an annual parliament known as the Danehof. The castle was used as a royal residence for centuries and was the birthplace of King Christian II.

The fortress once had an enclosing defence wall and four corner towers but only part of the original structure remains. Two of the towers fell victim to earlier modifications and in 1870 most of the ramparts were torn down to make room for the town's expansion.

Still, what remains is fun to explore. The **Danehof room**, where the Danehof met, has walls painted with an intriguing 16th century three-dimensional cube design that appears strikingly contemporary. Here and in other rooms you'll find old royal paintings, suits of armour, antique guns and swords. You can climb a spiral staircase to the loft and walk along the running boards past the machicolations through which boiling tar was once poured down onto attacking Swedes.

Nyborg Slot is open from 10 am to 4 pm daily between June and August, from 10 am to 3 pm Tuesday to Sunday in May, September and October, and at weekends only during the rest of the year. Admission costs 20 kr (children 10 kr).

Mads Lerches Gård

This engaging half-timbered merchant's house, built in 1601 at Slotsgade 11, just south of Nyborg Slot, puts on exhibitions of local cultural history. Some of its 30 rooms have period furnishings, others the usual assortment of old toys, model ships and antique tools. It's a seasonal operation that's open from 10 am to 4 pm daily in July and August and from 10 am to 3 pm Tuesday to Sunday in May, June and September. Admission costs 10 kr (children 5 kr).

Vor Frue Kirke

Vor Frue Kirke, Nyborg's central church, dates from 1388 but has been altered numerous times over the years, most extensively in 1870. Its beautifully detailed Baroque pulpit was carved in 1653 by Anders Mortensen of Odense. From left to right the pulpit sections depict the birth of John the Baptist, Christ's baptism, the Transfiguration, the Resurrection and the Ascension. There's also a wooden baptismal font dating from 1585. Vor Frue Kirke, which is on Gammel Torv, is open (via the southern door on Korsbrødregade) from 9 am to 6 pm in summer and from 9 am to 4 pm during the rest of the year.

Places to Stay

Nyborg Camping (☎ 65 31 02 56, fax 65 31 07 56, Hjejlevej 99, 5800 Nyborg) is a popular three star camping ground on a white sand beach about 2km east of the town centre. It offers access for people in wheelchairs, guest kitchens, a common room with TV, a minimarket, a handful of cabins and a view of the new Store Bælt bridge.

Nyborg Vandrerhjem (☎ 65 31 27 04, fax 65 30 26 04, Havnegade 28, 5800 Nyborg) is near the harbour, about a 10 minute walk south from the train station. It's a rather utilitarian facility with 88 beds in four-bed rooms, each with a toilet and shower. The hostel is accessible to people in wheelchairs, has laundry facilities and costs 90 kr per person. It's open from mid-January to mid-December.

The cheapest hotel in town is *Hotel Villa Gulle* (☎ 65 30 11 88, fax 65 30 11 33, Østervoldgade 44, 5800 Nyborg), which has 26 basic rooms. Singles/doubles with sink but without bath cost 280/430 kr, while those with bath cost 380/575 kr.

Hotel Hesselet (☎ 65 31 30 29, fax 65 31 29 58, Christianslundsvej 119, 5800 Nyborg), one of Funen's most exclusive hotels, has a pleasant location between the woods and the sea, 2km north-east of town. The 46 rooms have modern amenities and in most cases ocean views. There's an indoor swimming pool, billiards, a library and a lounge with an open fire. Singles/doubles begin at 890/1250 kr.

There is also a large and rather standard Best Western hotel, the *Hotel Nyborg Strand* (☎ *65 31 31 31, fax 65 31 37 01, Østerøvej 2, 5800 Nyborg*), north of Hotel Hesselet. Its 240 rooms cost 815/1015 kr for singles/doubles, but weekend and summer deals can lower the rate to 695 kr for a double.

Places to Eat

There are several places to eat in the streets south of Torvet. *Pomona Pizza (Kongegade 22)* offers pizza or chicken with chips for 40 kr, and cheaper sandwiches, burgers and salads. *Gertz Conditori (Kongegade 16)* sells pastries and sandwiches to eat-in or takeaway. You can get fish and chips for just 20 kr at *Fiskehallen (Korsgade 11)*.

Café Anthon (Mellemgade 25), a block north of Kongegade, is an inviting spot to relax over a beer or cappuccino.

An upmarket place is the atmospheric *Restaurant Østervemb (Mellemgade 18)*, which specialises in fresh fish and home-style Danish food. Expect a three course dinner to cost around 250 kr, lunch about half that.

Getting There & Away

Nyborg is on the E20, 34km east of Odense. Trains run an average of twice an hour between Nyborg and Odense (33 kr, 20 minutes). You can also take bus No 880 between Odense and Nyborg, but it's slower and costs 35 kr.

KERTEMINDE

Kerteminde is a seaside town with a pleasantly slow pace and a couple of minor sights. While it still has a few fishing boats, the town's waterfront has largely been given over to leisure craft, with yachters comprising the lion's share of Kerteminde's visitors.

Although Kerteminde is fronted by a harbour and a long marina, there are sandy beaches on both sides of the town: Nordstranden extends from the northern end of the marina, Sydstranden begins at the southern side of the harbour. A statue of Amanda the fishergirl, a town symbol of sorts, stands on the southern side of the Langebro, which crosses the Kerteminde Fjord and connects the northern and southern parts of Kerteminde.

Information

Tourist Office Kerteminde Turistbureau (☎ 65 32 11 21, fax 65 32 18 17, email ktb @kerteminde-turist.dk), at Strandgade 1B, 5300 Kerteminde, has a wide range of regional brochures. Between 15 June and 31 August it's open from 9 am to 5 pm Monday to Friday and from 9 am to 2 pm on Saturday; during the rest of the year it's open from 9 am to 4 pm on weekdays and from 9.30 am to 12.30 pm on Saturday.

Money There are a few banks in the town centre, including a BG Bank at Langegade 6 and a branch of Den Danske Bank at Langegade 31.

Post The post office is in the town centre on Strandvejen, immediately south of the bus station.

Museums

The local history museum **Farvergården**, at Langegade 8 in the town centre, is in a handsome half-timbered farm building built in 1630. Many of the rooms remain as they would have been in centuries past, with period furnishings, pottery and paintings, and there is a cellar full of dusty butter churns, washboards and candles. It's open from 10 am to 4 pm daily from March to October; admission costs 10 kr (children free).

Johannes Larsen Museet, Møllebakken 14, on the northern side of town, is in the artist's former home and retains its original furniture and décor. Larsen (1867-1961), one of the Fynboerne painters, is known for his paintings of wildlife and provincial Danish scenes. Also here is **Svanemøllen**, a windmill dating from 1853, and a modern 15 room exhibition centre with paintings by several dozen artists. It's open from 10 am to 5 pm daily between June and August, and from 10 am to 4 pm Tuesday to Sunday during the rest of the year. Admission costs 30 kr (children free). This museum has parking spaces for disabled people only; other travellers with cars should use the car park at the corner of Hindsholmvej and Marinavejen.

Romsø

For a quiet outing, consider a visit to the island of Romsø, a 30 minute boat ride from Kerteminde. The only residents are the boatman's family, a few hundred deer and numerous rabbits and birds. You can take a 3km coastal trail around the 109 hectare island, take the inland trails or just soak up the solitude. Bring a picnic lunch because there are no facilities.

The Romsø-Båden boat service (☎ 65 32 13 77) takes passengers to the island on Wednesday and Saturday, departing from Kerteminde at 9 am and from Romsø at 3.30 pm. Reservations are required. The return trip costs 75 kr for adults and 40 kr for children.

The same boat service also offers a 'fjord tour' (50 kr) of Kerteminde, Ladby and Munkebo on Tuesday.

Places to Stay

Kerteminde Camping (☎ 65 32 19 71, fax 65 32 23 27, Hindsholmvej 80, 5300 Kerteminde) is a three star camping ground opposite the beach and just 1.5km north of the town centre. There's a food kiosk, laundry facilities and cabins for hire. It's open from April to early September.

Kerteminde Vandrerhjem (☎ 65 32 39 29, fax 65 32 39 24, Skovvej 46, 5300 Kerteminde) is at the edge of a pleasant wooded area just five minutes walk from a sandy beach and 15 minutes south of the town

centre. The 30 rooms each have four beds, a shower and a toilet. The facilities include a guest kitchen, a laundry room and a TV room. The cost is 90 kr per person and it's open from early January to mid-December.

The turistbureau can provide a list of *rooms* in private homes, or for a 25 kr fee the staff will make the calls for you.

Tornøes Hotel (☎ 65 32 16 05, fax 65 32 48 40, Strandgade 2, 5300 Kerteminde), on the harbour in the town centre, has 27 basic rooms, each with a TV, phone and desk. Singles/doubles cost 395/495 kr with shared bath, 495/695 kr with private bath.

Places to Eat

There are a few places right in the centre where you can grab something inexpensive to eat. *Pizza Hot* (Langegade 9) is basically a takeaway joint but has a small counter where you can stand and eat; whole pizzas begin at 33 kr. A *polser wagon* selling hot dogs usually sets up on the square in front of Pizza Hot. *Clausens Konditori* (Langegade 39) has good bread and tempting pastries, and opens at 6.30 am daily. There's a *Super Brugsen* grocery shop, with a bakery and deli, on Hindsholmvej, opposite the rådhus.

For affordable waterfront dining, *Restaurant Sejlklub*, at the yacht marina on the northern side of town, offers meal specials, including a good steak dish, costing from 48 to 88 kr, and both indoor and patio seating. It's also a nice place to have a cold beer on a sunny afternoon.

At the top end is *Rudolf Mathis* (Dosseringen 13), a waterside restaurant on the southern side of Kerteminde harbour. Specialising in fresh fish, it is widely regarded as one of Funen's best restaurants and you should expect lunch to cost from around 250 kr, dinner from 400 kr.

Getting There & Away

Kerteminde is on route 165, 19km north-west of Nyborg and 21km north-east of Odense.

There are hourly bus services connecting Kerteminde with Odense (Nos 885 and 890)

FUNEN

and Nyborg (Nos 890 and 891); both routes take about 35 minutes and cost 25 kr.

Getting Around
Amanda Cykler (☎ 65 32 21 32), Hans Schacksvej 5, hires out bicycles for 50 kr per day, 300 kr per week.

LADBYSKIBET
The remains of a 22m-long Viking ship have been preserved in Ladby, at the site where it was excavated in 1935. The ship, which formed the tomb of a Viking chieftain, was buried in the 10th century and covered with an earthen mound. Although it was not uncommon for high-ranking Vikings to be buried in their wooden ships, along with supplies considered to be of use in the afterlife, Ladbyskibet (the Ladby ship) is the only Viking Age ship burial site uncovered in Denmark to date.

Unlike the spectacularly preserved Viking ships dug from clay burial sites in Norway and now on display in Oslo, all of the wooden planks from the Ladby ship, which was buried in turf, decayed long ago. What is preserved is the imprint of the hull moulded into the earth, along with iron nails, an anchor and the partial remains of the dogs and horses that were buried with their master.

An exhibition hall, which resembles a burial mound from the exterior, has been erected around the excavation. There's also a separate visitors' facility near the car park with a bit of background information; a full-scale copy of the Ladby ship is currently in the planning stages.

The exhibition hall is open from 10 am to 6 pm daily between mid-May and mid-September, 10 am to 4 pm daily between March and mid-May and mid-September to October, and 11 am to 3 pm Wednesday to Sunday in winter. Admission costs 20 kr (children free).

Getting There & Away
In the little village of Ladby, 4km southwest of Kerteminde via Odensevej, turn north onto Vikingevej, a one lane road that ends after 1.2km at the Ladbyskibet car park. From there it's a five minute walk along a dirt path to the mound, which is in a farmer's field.

Local bus No 482 makes the six minute trip from Kerteminde to the village of Ladby (10 kr) eight times a day from Monday to Friday, but don't leave too late as the last return bus is at 4.18 pm. Also, you'll have to walk the Vikingevej section.

HINDSHOLM
The Hindsholm peninsula, which stretches north from Kerteminde, is a rural area of small villages boasting 16th century churches and old half-timbered farmhouses. The most fetching village is **Viby**, which has a picturesque windmill and an early Gothic church with frescoes. Viby is at the southern end of the peninsula, only a 15 minute drive from Kerteminde.

Farther north, in Mårhøj, is Funen's largest single-chamber **passage grave**, which dates from 200 BC; it consists of a 10m-long chamber that visitors can enter, but it's only about 1m high so bring a torch and be prepared to crawl. The mound is easy to spot, in a farmer's field about five minutes walk from the road.

At the northernmost tip is **Fyns Hoved**, an island-like extension of the Hindsholm peninsula that's connected by a narrow causeway. You can walk to the edge of its 25m-high cliffs (high by Danish standards), from where there's a view of the northern Funen coast and, on a clear day, Jutland and Zealand as well.

Getting There & Away
Route 315 runs the length of the peninsula from south to north; villages and sightseeing spots along the way are signposted off route 315.

There are a couple of buses from Kerteminde to Hindsholm. Bus No 481 connects Kerteminde with Viby, while Nos 484 and 483 run up the peninsula to Korshavn, ending about 1km shy of Fyns Hoved. Both routes are covered about half a dozen times a day on weekdays only and cost 10 kr.

However, the best way to visit laid-back Hindsholm is by bicycle. There's a regional loop cycle route from Kerteminde to Fyns Hoved that makes a good day-long bike tour. You can get more information on cycling from the Kerteminde Turistbureau.

EGESKOV SLOT

Egeskov Slot is a splendid Renaissance castle complete with a moat and drawbridge. Egeskov, literally 'oak forest', was built in 1554 in the middle of a small lake on top of a foundation of thousands of upright oak trunks.

While it's most impressive from the outside, you can also tour the castle interior. It has antique furnishings, grand period paintings and an abundance of hunting trophies that include elephant tusks and the skins and heads of tigers, cheetahs and other rare and endangered creatures. Apparently the former owner, Count Gregers Ahlefeldt-Laurvig-Bille, was one of the more active hunters of African big game of his day.

The expansive 15 hectare park surrounding the castle was designed in the 18th century and includes 100-year-old privet hedges, topiary work, free-roaming peacocks and manicured English gardens.

However, not everything is formal – you can laugh your way through the bamboo grass labyrinth, dreamed up by the contemporary Danish poet-artist Piet Hein. A sign at the entrance of this 3m-high maze admonishes visitors 'Don't be afraid. We inspect the maze thoroughly each autumn', but most people make it through in about 15 minutes.

Also in the castle grounds is an antique vehicle museum that displays hundreds of period cars and motorcycles as well as some early aeroplane models. For children, there's a playground and a small petting zoo.

Egeskov (☎ 62 27 10 16) is open daily from May to October, from 10 am to at least 5 pm. In June and August the grounds and museum (but not the castle interior) stay open until 6 pm. In July the grounds and museum stay open until 8 pm, the castle interior until 7 pm. Admission to the grounds, the labyrinth and the museum costs 55 kr, while admission to the castle interior is an additional 50 kr. Children pay half-price. Its Web site is at www.egeskov.com.

Getting There & Away

Egeskov Slot is 2km west of Kværndrup on route 8. From Odense take the Svendborg-bound train to Kværndrup station (43 kr) and continue on foot or by taxi.

Alternatively, you could take bus No 801 from Odense to Kværndrup Bibliotek and there catch bus No 920, which stops in front of Egeskov Slot (it's a 700m walk to the entrance) on its way between Faaborg and Nyborg; be sure to ask for a through ticket (30 kr) from the bus driver in Odense.

FAABORG

In the 17th century Faaborg was a bustling harbour town with one of Denmark's largest fleets. Home to only 6000 people today, Faaborg retains many vestiges of that earlier era, and its picturesque cobbled streets lined with leaning half-timbered houses make for delightful walking. It has two notable museums, one dedicated to town history and the other to regional art. Faaborg also has reasonably priced places to stay, making it an appealing place to break your journey.

Information

Tourist Office Faaborg Turistbureau (☎ 62 61 07 07, fax 62 61 33 37), adjacent to the bus station at Banegårdspladsen 2A, 5600 Faaborg, has general brochures and sells cycling maps and telephone cards. Between May and September it's open from 9 am to 6 pm Monday to Saturday; between October and April it's open from 10 am to 6 pm Monday to Friday and from 10 am to 5 pm on Saturday.

Money There are a few banks in the town centre, including a Sparekassen on the northern side of Torvet and a Jyske Bank at Østergade 36.

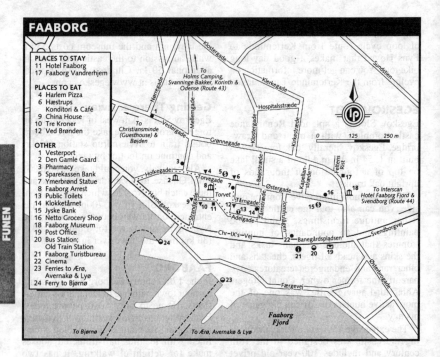

FAABORG

PLACES TO STAY
11 Hotel Faaborg
17 Faaborg Vandrerhjem

PLACES TO EAT
4 Harlem Pizza
6 Hæstrups Konditori & Café
9 China House
10 Tre Kroner
12 Ved Brønden

OTHER
1 Vesterport
2 Den Gamle Gaard
3 Pharmacy
5 Sparekassen Bank
7 Ymerbrønd Statue
8 Faaborg Arrest
13 Public Toilets
14 Klokketårnet
15 Jyske Bank
16 Netto Grocery Shop
18 Faaborg Museum
19 Post Office
20 Bus Station; Old Train Station
21 Faaborg Turistbureau
22 Cinema
23 Ferries to Ærø, Avernakø & Lyø
24 Ferry to Bjørnø

Post The post office is at Banegårdspladsen 4, just east of the bus station. It's open from 10 am to 5 pm Monday to Friday and from 10 am to noon on Saturday.

Walking Tour

You can explore Faaborg's older quarters by taking a short walking tour around the town centre. Begin at Torvet, where the prison in the old rådhus has been turned into **Faaborg Arrest**, a museum dedicated to prisons (admission 25 kr).

Walk west along Torvegade to Holkegade, a narrow and winding street of half-timbered houses that still looks much as it did in the 18th century. One of these period buildings, at Holkegade 1, has been turned into **Den Gamle Gaard** museum (described later in this section).

At the end of Holkegade, turn left onto Havnegade, where you'll pass the harbour

that once brimmed with merchant ships during Faaborg's heyday. Turn north onto Strandgade and then east at Torvet onto Adelgade, a street lined with restored 19th century homes. On the block between Adelgade and Tårngade is **Klokketårnet**, a belfry that was once part of a medieval church and which now serves as the town's clock tower; on summer afternoons you'll usually be able to find an elderly warden on site who'll let you climb the tower for 10 kr.

Proceed west on Tårngade, a cobbled lane lined with attractive period houses and hollyhock-trimmed doorways. On the eastern side of Torvet you'll find the **Ymerbrønd statue**; based on a Nordic creation myth, the controversial statue, which shows a man, a child and a cow entwined, created a minor uproar when it was unveiled in 1913.

Den Gamle Gaard

This well-presented museum, just west of Torvet at Holkegade 1, is in a timber-framed merchant's house that dates back to about 1725 and retains most of its original character. The 22 rooms are arranged to show how a wealthy merchant lived in around 1800; part of the house holds the family quarters and other sections contain workshops and storerooms. The museum is full of intriguing antiques, ranging from furniture, porcelain and toys to maritime objects and a hearse carriage. One room contains personal items that belonged to Riborg Voigt, a merchant's daughter with whom Hans Christian Andersen had a brief relationship and a lifelong infatuation. The mementoes include one of Andersen's business cards and a lock of his hair. Den Gamle Gaard is open daily between mid-May and mid-September from 10.30 am to 4.30 pm. Admission costs 25 kr (children free).

Faaborg Museum

In an attractive neoclassical building at Grønnegade 75, Faaborg Museum contains Denmark's best collection of Funen art, featuring works by Peter Hansen, Johannes Larsen, Poul Christensen and Fritz Syberg. Also on display is sculptor Kai Nielsen's original sandstone Ymerbrønd, the bronze copy of which stands on Torvet. The museum is open daily, from 10 am to 5 pm in summer, from 10 am to 4 pm in spring and autumn and from 11 am to 3 pm in winter. Admission costs 30 kr (children free).

Other Things to See & Do

Svanninge Bakker, the countryside north of Faaborg, has some pretty rolling hills, amusingly dubbed the Funen Alps by local tourism authorities. There are cycling and walking trails and a golf course.

Vesterport (West Gate), the brick town gate that was erected in the 15th century to allow entry into the city, still spans Vestergade, 500m north-west of Torvet. It's one of only a handful of such gates remaining in Denmark. The gate owes its existence primarily to Faaborg's economic decline in the 19th century, a time when many town gates elsewhere in Denmark were torn down to make room for wider roads and municipal expansion.

Between mid-June and late August a costumed night watchman winds his way through the old town, welcoming visitors to follow in his footsteps. He leaves from Klokketårnet at 9 pm from Thursday to Sunday.

On Sunday in summer, the antique train Syd Fyenske Veteranjernbane (☎ 63 63 36 96) makes three leisurely runs from the old Faaborg train station north to Korinth, departing at 10 am and 1 and 3 pm. The return trip lasts 80 minutes and costs 30 kr (children 15 kr). In July it also runs at 7 pm on Wednesday.

Places to Stay

There are half a dozen camping grounds within a 10km radius of Faaborg. *Holms Camping* (☎ 62 61 03 99, fax 62 61 33 63, *Odensevej 54, 5600 Faaborg*) is on route 43, just 1km north of the town centre. A two star facility, it's open from 1 May to 15 September.

The 74 bed hostel *Faaborg Vandrerhjem* (☎ 62 61 12 03, fax 62 61 35 08, *Grønnegade 71-72, 5600 Faaborg*) occupies two handsome historic buildings, one a former public bathhouse and the other a half-timbered house. Dorm beds cost 85 kr, doubles 250 kr. It's open from 1 April to 1 October and has a convenient location near the Faaborg Museum.

Christiansminde (☎ 62 61 90 18, fax 62 61 90 72, *Assensvej 66, 5600 Faaborg*), 1.5km west of Torvet, is an inviting guesthouse with four comfortable rooms in a 19th century home. Singles/doubles cost 185/270 kr. A large breakfast is available for an additional 55 kr, a smaller one for 35 kr. There's also a pleasant candlelit dining room where guests can opt for a home-made three course dinner costing 100 kr. Three flats are being added to the property, and when Christiansminde is full the hosts can often book rooms for you with a neighbour.

FUNEN

Hotel Faaborg (☎ 62 61 02 45, fax 62 61 08 45, Torvet 15, 5600 Faaborg), in a old brick building overlooking Torvet, has 10 renovated rooms, each with bath, TV and a small kitchenette with refrigerator and hotplate. There's a bar and a restaurant on the ground floor. Singles/doubles cost 425/550 kr; an optional breakfast costs an extra 50 kr.

Interscan Hotel Faaborg Fjord (☎ 62 61 10 10, fax 62 61 10 17, email faaborg fjord@get2net.dk, Svendborgvej 175, 5600 Faaborg), on the eastern outskirts of town, is a large hotel with standard tourist amenities. It has 131 modern rooms as well as a restaurant, a pool, a sauna and a billiards room. Standard rates are 795/995 kr for singles/doubles, but from June to August there's a summer rate of 595/695 kr.

Places to Eat

There are numerous places to eat in Faaborg, most of them within a few minutes walk of Torvet.

Early-risers can head for *Hæstrups Konditori & Café*, on Torvegade on the eastern side of Torvet; it opens at 6.30 am daily and offers good bakery items, juice and milk to take away or enjoy in the café at the side.

Harlem Pizza (Torvegade 10) cooks up good pizza with a wide range of toppings for between 30 and 50 kr, as well as reasonably priced pitta-bread sandwiches, lasagne and spaghetti. It stays open until 5 am on Friday and Saturday and until at least 10 pm on other days.

At *China House* (Strandgade 4), just south of Torvet, standard à la carte Chinese dishes cost from 65 to 85 kr.

Tre Kroner (Strandgade 1), a pub-style café with a charming old-world character, offers moderately priced Danish food such as smørrebrød, herring or æggekage, a rich Funen omelette served with dark bread.

The most popular dinner spot is *Ved Brønden* (Torvet 5), right on the square, which has classic décor and offers two-course fish or beef meals for around 150 kr. It also serves 55 kr lunch specials from 11.30 am to 2.30 pm.

Getting There & Away

Faaborg is 27km west of Svendborg and 37km south of Odense.

Bus Faaborg has no train service. Buses from Odense (No 960, 961 or 962) cost 45 kr, take 1¼ hours and operate at least hourly from sunrise to around 11 pm. Buses from Svendborg (No 930) are also frequent throughout the day, running at least hourly; the journey takes 40 minutes and costs 30 kr. Faaborg's bus station is on Banegårdspladsen, at the old train station on the southern side of town.

Car & Motorcycle Getting to Faaborg by car is straightforward: from the north, simply follow route 43, which is called Odensevej as it enters the town. From Svendborg, route 44 leads directly west into Faaborg, entering the town as Svendborgvej. Route 8 ends 10km west of Faaborg at Bøjden, from where a car ferry (☎ 33 15 15 15) runs half a dozen times a day (200 kr for a car with up to five people) to Fynshav on Als in Jutland.

Boat Ferries run to and from Faaborg daily to the island of Ærø; see under Getting There & Away in the Ærø section later in this chapter.

There are also ferries from Faaborg to the nearby offshore islands of Bjørnø, Lyø and Avernakø; see the following section for details.

Getting Around

Bicycles can be hired at Faaborg Turistbureau for 50 kr a day.

BJØRNØ, LYØ & AVERNAKØ

If you are looking for a quiet getaway while you're in the Faaborg area, consider a day trip to one of the three small offshore islands, Bjørnø, Lyø and Avernakø. All three islands are rural, unspoilt and connected by a daily ferry service to Faaborg. If you're interested in staying overnight, staff at the Faaborg Turistbureau can arrange B&B-style stays with local families.

The nearest and smallest island, Bjørnø, 3km south of Faaborg, is just 3km long and 1km wide. It has one small village with about 40 inhabitants. You can walk around the island but there are no real sights.

Lyø, about 10km south-west of Faaborg, is the most heavily populated of the islands – with all of 150 residents. Roughly 4km long and 2km wide, it has a small village perched in the middle of the island, with half-timbered houses, a school and a church with an unusual circular churchyard. It also has a few scattered sights, including a bell stone on the western side of the island, and enough narrow roads to make for an interesting day's cycling.

Avernakø, 6km south of Faaborg, is shaped a bit like a pair of spectacles, with two oval-shaped sides, both about 4km long, connected by a thin rim of land. There's a small village, Avernak, on the north-western side of the island and scattered farmsteads throughout. In all, about 120 people live on Avernakø.

Getting There & Away

The MS *Lillebjørn* (☎ 30 66 80 50), a little 20 passenger boat, makes six crossings between Faaborg and Bjørnø on weekdays, a few less at weekends. It takes about 20 minutes. The return trip costs 35 kr (children 17.50 kr). Bicycles cost an additional 12 kr.

The MF *Faaborg II* (☎ 62 61 23 07) carries 150 passengers and 12 cars and operates between Faaborg, Avernakø and Lyø at least six times daily. From Faaborg it takes between 30 and 70 minutes to get to your destination, depending on which island the boat pulls into first. It costs 70 kr return (children 45 kr), plus 20 kr for a bicycle, 60 kr for a motorcycle.

Because the roads are narrow, visitors are not encouraged to bring cars to Avernakø or Lyø; there's no car ferry to Bjørnø.

SVENDBORG

During the 19th century Svendborg was a busy harbour town with nearly two dozen shipyards producing almost half of all of the wooden-hulled ships built in Denmark. AP Møller, one of the world's largest shipping companies, formed in Svendborg during that period. With its excellent port facilities, Svendborg also became the site of foundries, tanneries, tobacco processing plants and mills.

Today Svendborg, southern Funen's largest municipality (population 40,000), remains an industrial city with commercial port facilities and two of Denmark's largest food processing companies. It also has a couple of shipyards that still build wooden ships and provide repair services to the scores of yachts that ply the waters off southern Funen.

Svendborg offers some nicely restored buildings and a comfortable hostel right in the city centre, so it can be a pleasant enough place to break your journey for the night; however, some of the less developed islands around Svendborg – such as Tåsinge, Langeland and Ærø – hold more allure.

Information

Tourist Office Sydfyns Turistbureau (☎ 62 21 09 80, fax 62 22 05 53, email sydfyntb@post7.tele.dk), Centrumpladsen, 5700 Svendborg, in the city centre, has information on all of southern Funen. Between 15 June and 31 August it's open from 9 am to 7 pm Monday to Friday and from 9 am to 3 pm on Saturday; during the rest of the year it's open from 9 am to 5 pm Monday to Friday and from 9.30 am to 12.30 pm on Saturday.

Money & Post There are several banks in the city centre, including a Unibank on Centrumpladsen, south of Sydfyns Turistbureau, and Den Danske Bank a few minutes walk from the train station on the corner of Brogade and Møllergade. The post office is to the south of the train station.

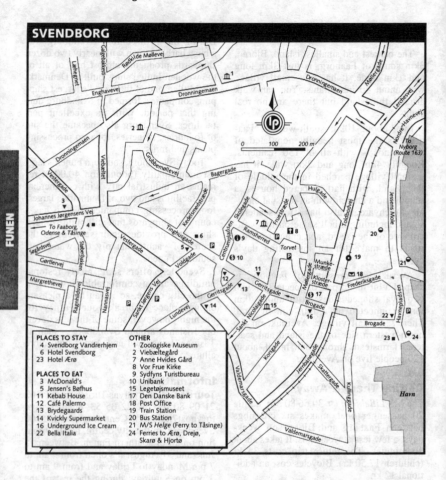

SVENDBORG

0   100   200 m

To Nyborg (Route 163)

To Faaborg, Odense & Tåsinge

Torvet

Havn

PLACES TO STAY
4 Svendborg Vandrerhjem
6 Hotel Svendborg
23 Hotel Ærø

PLACES TO EAT
3 McDonald's
5 Jensen's Bøfhus
11 Kebab House
12 Café Palermo
13 Brydegaards
14 Kvickly Supermarket
16 Underground Ice Cream
22 Bella Italia

OTHER
1 Zoologiske Museum
2 Viebæltegård
7 Anne Hvides Gård
8 Vor Frue Kirke
9 Sydfyns Turistbureau
10 Unibank
15 Legetøjsmuseet
17 Den Danske Bank
18 Post Office
19 Train Station
20 Bus Station
21 M/S Helge (Ferry to Tåsinge)
24 Ferries to Ærø, Drejø, Skarø & Hjortø

Things to See & Do

Near Torvet you'll find two attractive old structures. The handsome brick church, **Vor Frue Kirke**, was originally erected in the 13th century in Romanesque style, although subsequent alterations have given it a Gothic appearance. The church has a late-16th century pulpit and altar and is open from 8 am to 4 pm in summer, from 8 am to noon in winter. Just west of the church is the city's oldest secular building, **Anne Hvides Gård**, a large and lovely timber-framed

house that dates from 1560. It's now a local history museum displaying antiques, including locally made pottery, silverware and glass. It's open from 10 am to 5 pm in summer, with slightly shorter hours in the low season; admission costs 15 kr.

Viebæltegård, Grubbemøllevej 13, is a former poorhouse that exhibits its old workshops and displays some archaeological finds; admission costs 20 kr. **Legetøjs-museet** (admission 35 kr), a toy museum, is at Sankt Nicolaigade 18. The **Zoologiske**

Museum (admission 10 kr) at Dronninge-maen 30 displays the usual stuffed birds and mammals, as well as the skeleton of a baleen whale that beached on Tåsinge. All three museums are open from 10 am to 5 pm in summer, with slightly shorter hours in winter.

Places to Stay

The nearest camping grounds are on Tåsinge, on the southern side of the Svendborg sound; for details see the Tåsinge Places to Stay section.

Svendborg Vandrerhjem (☎ 62 21 66 99, fax 62 20 29 39, Vestergade 45, 5700 Svend-borg) is in a pleasantly renovated 19th century iron foundry in the city centre. The building, in which L Lange & Co produced kitchen stoves from 1850 to 1984, now also contains a small stove museum. This highly rated hostel has 34 double rooms, 28 three-bed rooms and 21 four-bed rooms, each with a shower and toilet. Dorm beds cost 88 kr, while private rooms cost 265 kr for one to three people. Open year-round except during the Christmas and New Year holidays, it has laundry facilities and conference rooms, and hires out bicycles.

Hotel Ærø (☎ 62 21 07 60, Brogade 1, 5700 Svendborg), opposite the Ærø ferry terminal, has 12 clean, basic rooms costing 250/400 kr for singles/doubles. Communal toilets and showers are off the hall.

Popular with businesspeople is *Hotel Svendborg* (☎ 62 21 17 00, fax 62 21 90 12, Centrumpladsen 1, 5700 Svendborg), a recently renovated medium-sized hotel in the city centre. Singles/doubles with bath, TV and phone cost 625/725 kr.

Places to Eat

There's a *DSB Restaurant* at the train station and a number of inexpensive restaurants within a five minute walk south-east from the train station along Brogade and Gerritsgade.

Underground Ice Cream (Brogade 37) sells natural ice cream in a variety of flavours. A few streets farther west, on the northern side of Gerritsgade, is *Kebab*

House, which offers inexpensive burgers, kebabs and pitta-bread sandwiches. About 100m farther west is *Brydegaards* (Gerritsgade 25), a bakery with café tables and simple eats. On the next block west is *Café Palermo*, which serves pizza, spaghetti and a few Greek dishes such as souvlaki for around 35 kr at lunch and 50 kr at dinner. *Jensen's Bøfhus*, in the complex opposite Hotel Svendborg, has a good salad bar and cheap lunch deals.

Hotel Ærø, opposite the ferry terminal, has an agreeable dining room which offers a hearty daily special, such as Danish beef and potatoes, for 68 kr. Otherwise most dishes are in the 95 to 150 kr price range at dinner.

At *Bella Italia* (Brogade 2), a pleasant Italian restaurant north of Hotel Ærø, pizza and spaghetti cost from 50 to 75 kr and there are more expensive meat and seafood dishes.

There's a *Kvickly* supermarket housing a bakery and a cafeteria-style restaurant at Vestergade 20, and a *McDonald's* on Johannes Jørgensens Vej near Svendborg Vandrerhjem.

Getting There & Away

For most travellers, Svendborg is the transit point between Odense and the southern Funen islands. It is 44km south-east of Odense on route 9, 33km south-west of Nyborg on route 163 and 27km east of Faaborg on route 44.

Bus & Train There are frequent bus services from Svendborg to Faaborg (No 930; 30 kr, 40 minutes) and other Funen towns including Rudkøbing on Ærø (25 kr, 25 minutes). Trains leave Odense for Svendborg about once an hour; the trip takes one hour and costs 49 kr. The bus and train stations are a few streets north of the ferry terminal.

Boat Ferries to Ærøskøbing depart five to six times a day; in summer the last boat leaves Svendborg at 10.30 pm. For more information see the Ærø Getting There & Away section in this chapter.

For information on the M/S *Helge*, which sails between Svendborg and Tåsinge, see under Getting There & Away in the Tåsinge section.

DREJØ, SKARØ & HJORTØ

Many of Svendborg's visitors are yachters who sail the protected waters along the southern Funen coast. Three popular local sailing spots are the small offshore islands of Drejø, Skarø and Hjortø, all 10 to 15km south-west of Svendborg.

Camping is allowed at designated sites on all three islands; Drejø has a restaurant and grocery shop, while Skarø has a small food shop and a snack bar serving beer, ice cream and simple grilled items.

Drejø, which has about 75 inhabitants, is the largest island, covering 412 hectares and extending about 5km in length. Its small central town, Drejø By, was devastated during a Midsummer Eve bonfire in 1942 when an ember landed on the vicarage's thatched roof – within minutes, 17 closely clustered half-timbered farmhouses had burned to the ground. Despite the fire, Drejø still has some attractive old houses and a community church that dates from 1535. The island is largely given over to moors and meadows (home to the endangered fire-bellied toad) and has a large protected harbour with good mooring facilities.

Skarø (population 21) is shaped a bit like a rabbit's head, covers 189 hectares and reaches an altitude of just 9m at its highest point. Part of the island's salt meadows are set aside as a bird sanctuary, home to about 50 species of breeding birds each summer. Skarø has mooring space for about 50 boats.

Hjortø (population 15) is the smallest of the three islands, measuring just 2km at its widest point. It's free from cars and motorcycles, attracts lots of sea birds and shore birds, and has some protected beaches. You can walk around the island in just a couple of hours. About 25 boats can moor in Hjortø's harbour.

Getting There & Away

If you don't have your own boat, it's possible to visit these islands on a day trip via small ferries that leave from Svendborg's harbour. The Hjortø ferry (☎ 62 54 15 18) generally sails twice daily, while the ferry to Drejø and Skarø (☎ 62 21 02 62) runs three to five times a day. The sailing time is 30 to 75 minutes, depending on the island and the route. The return trip costs 60 kr for adults, 40 kr for children, plus 20 kr for a bicycle. For more details, call the ferry company direct or pick up the current timetable at Sydfyns Turistbureau.

TÅSINGE

Tåsinge, the fourth largest island in Funen county, is connected by bridge to both Svendborg and Langeland. Most of the island is typically rural, a mix of woods and open fields.

The island's main road, route 9, cuts straight across Tåsinge, but it's well worth making a detour through the north-eastern quarter of the island, where you'll find Tåsinge's main sights: the old sea captains' village of Troense and the 17th century castle Valdemars Slot.

Troense is a well-to-do seaside village with lots of quaint thatched houses and a small yachting harbour. The main activity for visitors is just strolling around and admiring the old homes; two particularly interesting streets are Grønnegade and Bad stuen. There's also a small maritime museum, **Søfartssamlingerne i Troense** (admission 20 kr), at Strandgade 1, housed in the old village schoolhouse (dating from about 1790), which still has its rooftop belfry. The museum exhibits paintings, photos, model ships, figureheads and items from China brought back by local merchant ships in the 19th century.

From Troense the tree-lined Slotsalléen leads south-east to **Valdemars Slot** (Valdemar's Castle), constructed by Christian IV in 1639 for his son Valdemar. In 1677 the castle was transferred to the naval commander Niels Juel as part of the payment for his victory in the decisive Battle of Køge Bay; Juel's heirs still own the property today.

The main building, a brick manor house, is open to the public as a museum. About 20 of its rooms can be toured; they contain period furniture, wall tapestries, royal portraits and a few of Juel's personal belongings. It's open from 10 am to 5 pm daily between May and September, and on weekends in April and October. Admission costs 50 kr (children 25 kr).

The road from Troense passes right through the castle's two decorative gatehouses, which are open 24 hours. There's no admission charge to the castle grounds, which have a pond and a tea pavilion, or to the sandy beach just outside the castle's southern gate.

About 1km south-west of the castle, look for a grand oak tree in a field on the northern side of the road. Called **Ambrosius Egen** (Ambrosius' Oak), the tree, which is marked by a plaque, is named after Ambrosius Stub, a romantic poet who worked at Valdemars Slot in around 1700 and who composed many of his verses while relaxing beneath the shade of this tree. The oak tree is thought to be at least 600 years old and has a girth of nearly 7m.

The small village of **Bregninge**, on route 9, has a windmill with a restaurant inside and the **Bregninge Kirke**, a church that dates from medieval times. One of the church's three votive ships was built in 1727 as a replica of the battleship sailed by Niels Juel in the Battle of Køge Bay, but the main attraction is the panoramic view from the church tower (admission 5 kr), which at 72m is the highest point on the island. There's a local history museum, **Tåsinge Skipperkjem og Folkemindesamling** (admission 20 kr), nearby at Kirkebakken 1.

Landet, 3km south of Bregninge, also has a medieval church, most notable for the churchyard graves of the famous lovers Elvira Madigan and Sixten Sparre who died in a suicide pact in 1889.

Places to Stay

There are three camping grounds on Tåsinge. Closest to Svendborg is the seaside **Vindebyøre Camping** (☎ 62 22 54 25, fax 62 22 54 26, Vindebyørvej 52, Tåsinge, 5700 Svendborg), a three star facility with a coin laundry, a TV lounge and a guest kitchen. It costs 47 kr per person and is open from mid-April to mid-September. The local ferry, M/S Helge, docks out front and bicycles and boats can be hired.

A bit cheaper is **Tåsinge Camping** (☎ 62 54 13 27, Sundbrovej 130, Tåsinge, 5700 Svendborg), on route 9 on the south-eastern side of Tåsinge. It's a small friendly place open from May to September, with basic facilities and a snack bar. It costs 42 kr per person in a tent and there are a couple of cabins costing 200 kr plus the per-person fee.

Det Lille Hotel (☎ 62 22 53 41, email jeriksen@post8.tele.dk, Badstuen 15, 5700 Svendborg) is a half-timbered guesthouse in the village of Troense, with a coffee lounge, a quiet garden and bicycles for hire. It has eight rooms with shared baths starting at 300/450 kr for singles/doubles, including breakfast.

Also in the village of Troense is **Hotel Troense** (☎ 62 22 54 12, fax 62 22 78 12, Strandgade 5, Tåsinge, 5700 Svendborg), perched above the harbour 100m west of Søfartssamlingerne i Troense. Its 27 rooms each have bath, TV and phone and cost 460/665 kr for singles/doubles, including breakfast. The hotel is part of the Dansk Kroferie association and accepts its 'Inn Cheques' (see under Hotel Schemes in the Accommodation section of the Facts for the Visitor chapter for details).

Places to Eat

The restaurant at **Hotel Troense**, on the main road in the village of Troense, serves standard Danish fare at moderate prices. The village centre also has a **snack shop**, selling ice cream, hot dogs and burgers, plus a **bakery** and a **minimarket**.

At Valdemars Slot, the upmarket **Slotskælderen** in the basement of the main manor house has a changing menu with lunch dishes costing around 120 kr, dinner about double that. Also in the grounds is a cheaper snack-type restaurant and a picturesque seaside *tea pavilion* where you can get beverages and cakes.

Getting There & Away

Route 9 connects Tåsinge with Svendborg on Funen and with Rudkøbing on Langeland; there are cycle paths running the entire way.

The Svendborg city bus service operates between the city and Tåsinge, but the most enjoyable public transport option is the vintage ferry M/S *Helge* (☎ 62 50 25 00), which operates from early May to early September. From June to mid-August, the boat leaves Svendborg harbour at 9 and 11 am and 1.30, 3.30 and 5.30 pm. Ten minutes later it docks at Vindebyøre on the northern tip of Tåsinge and then crosses back across the sound to Christiansminde, a beach area to the east of Svendborg. The boat continues on to Troense and then to Valdemars Slot. Return departures from Valdemars Slot are at 9.55 and 11.55 am and 2.25, 4.25 and 6.25 pm. In May and late summer, the *Helge* operates the three middle sailings only. Fares range from 10 to 30 kr one way (children half price), depending on the distance. Bicycles are allowed on for an extra 15 kr provided space is available.

Langeland

Langeland is a long, narrow island with good beaches, a number of cycling paths and a wealth of bird life. It has an unhurried provincial character with small farming villages and a countryside dotted with windmills, both modern and vintage. There are ceramics shops and galleries selling local handicrafts scattered all around the island.

Langeland's only large town, Rudkøbing, has a handful of historic sights, but the island's most frequented visitor attraction is the medieval castle at Tranekær.

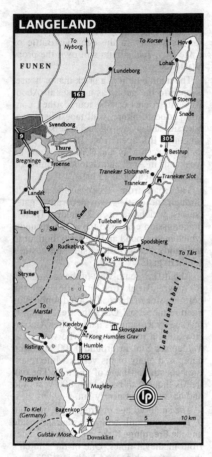

GETTING THERE & AWAY

Route 9, via the Langeland bridge, connects Langeland with Tåsinge and Svendborg.

Bus

Buses make the 25 minute, 20km run from Svendborg to Rudkøbing (25 kr) at least hourly.

Boat

Scandlines (☎ 33 15 15 15) operates a year-round car ferry a few times daily between

Korsør, in southern Zealand, and Lohals, in the far north of Langeland. A car and up to five people costs 295 kr; a motorcycle and rider costs 165 kr. The trip takes 75 minutes.

There are also daily ferries from Rudkøbing to Marstal on Ærø (see Getting There & Away in the Ærø section), from Spodsbjerg to Tårs on Lolland (see the Lolland Getting There & Away section), and from Bagenkop to Kiel in Germany (see the main Getting There & Away chapter earlier in this book).

GETTING AROUND
Route 305 runs from Lohals to Bagenkop, nearly the full north-south length of the island.

Bus
Buses that run the length of Langeland are all marked No 910, so you'll need to check the destination sign on the bus to see in which direction it's headed. Buses travel from Rudkøbing north to Lohals and south to Bagenkop at least once an hour (about half as often at weekends), connecting all of Langeland's major villages en route. The maximum one-way fare from Rudkøbing to anywhere else on Langeland is 30 kr, while the Lohals-Bagenkop fare is 50 kr; there's also a one day pass for 100 kr.

Within Rudkøbing there are special green buses that make a loop around the city outskirts, going as far east as Spodsbjerg harbour, about a dozen times a day from Monday to Friday. There are no charges to use these buses. The whole loop takes about an hour; hop on for an interesting little tour.

All buses leave from the Rudkøbing bus station on Ringvejen.

Bicycle
There are asphalt cycle paths running north from the Rudkøbing area to Lohals, east to Spodsbjerg and south to Bagenkop. The Langelands Turistforening (tourist office) in Rudkøbing sells a bicycle map of Langeland for 15 kr. In Rudkøbing you can hire bicycles at the cycle shop at Ørstedsgade 5;

elsewhere on the island they can be hired at camping grounds.

RUDKØBING
Rudkøbing is Langeland's commercial centre and main town, with a population of 5000. It's also the departure point for ferries to Ærø, which leave from the ferry harbour to the west of the town centre. North of the ferry harbour is a fishing harbour, followed by a 260 berth marina that attracts Germans in summer and Danes year-round.

Information
Tourist Office You can pick up information on the entire island from Langelands Turistforening (☎ 62 51 35 05, fax 62 51 43 35), Torvet 5, 5900 Rudkøbing. Between mid-June and 31 August it's open from 9 am to 5 pm Monday to Saturday; during the rest of the year it's open from 9.30 am to 4.30 pm Monday to Friday and from 9.30 am to 12.30 pm on Saturday.

Money There's a Unibank on Østergade 39, open from 9.30 am to 4 pm Monday to Friday (to 5.30 pm on Thursday).

Post The post office, at Brogade 13, is open from 10 am to 5 pm Monday to Friday and from 9.30 am to noon on Saturday.

Things to See & Do
Rudkøbing can appear rather nondescript from the ferry harbour, but it's well worth a closer look. Just east of Havnegade, the main harbour road, is a series of one-lane carriage roads that date from medieval times and are lined with old houses. Three of the most interesting streets – Ramsherred, Smedegade and Vinkældergade – can be combined in a pleasant 15 minute stroll between Havnegade and Brogade.

The town also has a few sights along its main street, which begins inland of the harbour as Brogade and changes to Østergade after Torvet. On Brogade, just east of Ramsherred, is a **statue of HC Ørsted**, the Danish physicist who was instrumental in the development of electromagnetic theory.

FUNEN

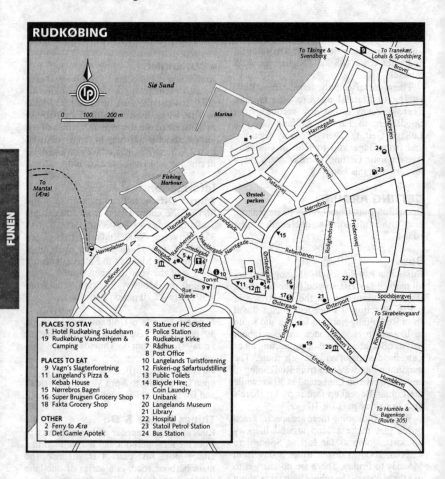

RUDKØBING

Si**ø** Sund

To Tåsinge &
Svendborg

To Tranekær,
Lohals & Spodsbjerg

Marina

To
Marstal
(Ærø)

Fishing
Harbour

Ørsted-
parken

Havnepladsen

Torvet

Rue
Stræde

Spodsbjergvej

To Skrøbelevgaard

To Humble &
Bagenkop
(Route 305)

PLACES TO STAY
1 Hotel Rudkøbing Skudehavn
19 Rudkøbing Vandrerhjem &
    Camping

PLACES TO EAT
9 Vagn's Slagterforetning
11 Langeland's Pizza &
    Kebab House
15 Nørrebros Bageri
16 Super Brugsen Grocery Shop
18 Fakta Grocery Shop

OTHER
2 Ferry to Ærø
3 Det Gamle Apotek

4 Statue of HC Ørsted
5 Police Station
6 Rudkøbing Kirke
7 Rådhus
8 Post Office
10 Langelands Turistforening
12 Fiskeri-og Søfartsudstilling
13 Public Toilets
14 Bicycle Hire;
    Coin Laundry
17 Unibank
20 Langelands Museum
21 Library
22 Hospital
23 Statoil Petrol Station
24 Bus Station

Across the street at Brogade 15 is the old
Rudkøbing Apotek, the site where Ørsted
was born. It now houses the small museum
Det Gamle Apotek, which contains two
replicas of the interiors of pharmacy shops,
one from the 18th century and the other
from the 19th century. It's open from 11 am
to 4 pm Monday to Friday between mid-
June and August. Admission costs 10 kr
(children free).

A block farther east on Torvet is the
19th century rådhus backed by the town

church, **Rudkøbing Kirke**. The church dates
from the early 12th century, although most
of the current building is from the post-
Reformation era.

At Østergade 25 there's **Fiskeri-og Søfartsudstilling**, a nautical museum featuring
fishing gear, dinghies and model ships. It's
open from 10 am to 4 pm Monday to Friday
and from 10 am to 1 pm on Saturday; admission is free.

Langelands Museum, about 500m farther east at Jens Winthers Vej 12, is the

region's history museum. It primarily displays archæological finds from Langeland and Ærø but also has a collection of 18th century glass, silver and furniture. It's open from 10 am to 4 pm Monday to Thursday, from 10 am to 1 pm on Friday and from 2 to 4 pm on Sunday; it's also open on Saturday afternoon in summer. Admission costs 15 kr (children free).

Places to Stay

Langeland's only hostel, *Rudkøbing Vandrerhjem & Camping* (☎/fax 62 51 18 30, *Engdraget 11, 5900 Rudkøbing*), has a convenient location a little over 1km east of the harbour and about a 10 minute walk from Torvet. Dorm beds cost 80 or 85 kr, depending upon whether the bathroom is off the room or in the hall, while private rooms for one or two people cost 260 kr. You can pitch a tent in the field at the side of the hostel for 40 kr per person. It's open from 15 March to 31 October; you can visit its Web site at www.danhostel.dk /rudkobing.

Langelands Turistforening maintains a list, with brief descriptions, of about 25 private homes with *rooms* for rent. Some are in villages, others on farms; a few are in Rudkøbing, the rest spread around the island. Doubles cost around 275 kr.

Hotel Rudkøbing Skudehavn (☎ 62 51 46 00, fax 62 51 49 40, Havnegade 21, 5900 Rudkøbing) is an apartment-style hotel fronting the marina. There are 33 two-storey buildings, each with a couple of units that can be rented as a two room apartment with a kitchen or as separate hotel rooms. All have a private bath and many also have harbourfront balconies with sunset views. Rooms with two twin beds, TV, phone and balcony cost 630/800 kr for single/double occupancy, while simpler rooms with a sofa bed cost 515/685 kr. Both rooms together as an apartment cost 1000 kr in summer (with a minimum two day stay) and from 500 to 800 kr during the rest of the year (no minimum stay). Breakfast is included in the hotel room rates. There's a large indoor pool.

If you enjoy historic settings and quiet countryside, a fine option is *Skrøbelevgaard* (☎ 62 51 45 31, Skrøbelev Hedevej 4, 5900 Rudkøbing), a cosy inn 4km east of Rudkøbing in the village of Ny Skrøbelev. Occupying a 17th century manor house, Skrøbelevgaard has 10 comfortable rooms ranging in price from 200 to 650 kr for singles, 350 to 650 kr for doubles. The inn has lovely gardens, a central courtyard, a summertime art gallery and friendly management. Breakfast or a light lunch is available for around 50 kr and a gourmet two course dinner can be arranged for 135 kr. The free city bus stops near the inn's gate on weekdays.

Places to Eat

There's a *Fakta* grocery shop on Engdraget, just a few minutes walk from Rudkøbing Vandrerhjem. The *Super Brugsen* grocery shop in the town centre has a good bakery and a café serving simple, cheap eats. You'll find another bakery, *Nørrebros Bageri*, a few streets away on Nørrebro.

Vagn's Slagterforetning, a butcher shop opposite Langelands Turistforening on Torvet, has a deli with inexpensive sandwiches and salads to take away.

Langeland's Pizza & Kebab House (Østergade 11) serves pizza and pitta-bread sandwiches starting at 30 kr, lasagne and salad for 40 kr. It stays open every day until at least 10 pm.

Hotel Rudkøbing Skudehavn, at the marina, has a restaurant with a nice harbour view. At lunch, salads and Danish dishes cost from 40 to 75 kr. At dinner, fish and meat main courses cost around 150 kr but there's usually a two course menu for a little less than that.

NORTHERN LANGELAND

Northern Langeland has a run of small villages separated by farmland. There's an occasional sign advertising organic produce for sale and a few roadside windmills, but the main sights are at Tranekær, a quiet village surrounding a lovely medieval castle.

You can continue travelling north from Tranekær to Lohals, a fair-sized village near the northern tip of Langeland. It and the neighbouring seaside area of Hov have a couple of camping grounds and hotels, but Lohals lacks the charm of Tranekær and its beaches are not as good as those in the south.

Tranekær

Tranekær has a quaint character and numerous timber-framed houses, but its dominant sight is the salmon-coloured **Tranekær Slot**; reflected in its swan pond, this looks like a fairytale castle.

The castle dates from around 1200 and was once the centrepiece of a royal estate that included more than half of Langeland. Although it's been altered several times, most recently in 1862, Tranekær Slot has been in the same family since 1659. Its current owner, Count Preben Ahlefeldt-Laurvig, still maintains it as a residence, so the castle interior cannot be toured, but parts of the grounds have been converted into a sculpture park called **Tickon** that's open to the public.

The park, the main path of which circles the castle pond, contains the environmental works of a dozen international artists who have used straw, stones and sticks to give their art a distinctively Nordic appearance. In addition, 70 different types of exotic trees, ranging from Norway spruce to California sequoia, are numbered and identified in a corresponding park brochure. It costs 20 kr (children free) to walk around the castle grounds and view the sculptures; after hours, drop your coins into the box.

In the old water mill opposite the castle is **Tranekær Slotsmuseum**, which displays exhibits on the history of the castle and Tranekær village. It's open from 10 am to 5 pm Monday to Friday and from 1 to 5 pm on Sunday between mid-May and 30 September. Admission costs 15 kr (children free).

One kilometre north of the castle is **Tranekær Slotsmølle**, an attractive Dutch windmill dating from 1846. It's been re-stored as a museum and, wind permitting, still grinds flour. It has the same opening hours and admission charge as Tranekær Slotsmuseum.

Places to Stay & Eat The half-timbered village inn *Tranekær Gæstgivergaard* (☎ 62 59 12 04, Slotsgade 74, 5953 Tranekær), 200m south of the castle, dates from 1802 and retains its period ambience. Singles/doubles with bath cost 500/600 kr including breakfast.

Tranekær Gæstgivergaard's restaurant offers traditional Danish country dinners for around 150 kr. *Café Herskabsstalden*, a large café in the grounds fronting the castle, offers simple meals such as fish and chips, hot dogs and chicken dishes at reasonable prices. It's open in summer from noon to 10 pm and in spring and autumn from noon to 5 pm.

SOUTHERN LANGELAND

Southern Langeland has the island's best beaches, several passage graves and a couple of bird sanctuaries.

Heading south from Rudkøbing you'll pass a number of small villages. Three kilometres south-east of Lindelse is **Skovsgaard**, an estate managed by a conservation group, Danmarks Naturfredningsforening; it contains an old manor house and a large organic farm complete with a windmill and thatched farm buildings. Visitors are welcome, there's an organic food café and the stable has been converted into a carriage museum with 25 horse-drawn vehicles, ranging from a wedding carriage to farm wagons. You can stroll around the grounds free of charge; the museum is open Monday to Friday from 10 am to 5 pm and on Saturday from 1 to 5 pm (admission 20 kr).

A few kilometres away, just south of Kædeby, is **Kong Humbles Grav**, the largest long dolmen on Langeland. Dating from approximately 3000 BC, the barrow is edged with 77 stones, extends 55m in length and has a single burial chamber. Its size has given rise to local folklore that a king was buried here, although historians give little credence to the tale. The dolmen is on private property in a field of grain and rapeseed, but visitors are free to walk to the site along a path that begins near the whitewashed church in Humble. To get to the dolmen walk north-east from the car park, which is just past the church, and bear left at the first intersection; follow that trail past the farmhouses. The walk takes about 20 minutes each way.

If the crops aren't too tall you can also see the site from route 305 about 150m south of Kædeby; the mounded dolmen is about 800m east of the road.

The village of **Humble**, the little commercial centre of southern Langeland, has a bank, a coin laundry, a pizzeria and a 24 hour petrol station. Humble is also the turn-off for Ristinge.

Ristinge, a little seaside village with thatched houses, is bordered by a long stretch of sandy beach backed by dunes and wild roses. Despite being the island's favourite bathing area Ristinge is pleasantly low-key, its main visitor facility being the camping ground.

At the southern end of the island is **Bagenkop**, an attractive fishing village that has a ferry service to Kiel, Germany. Just beyond Bagenkop at the southernmost tip of the island is **Dovnsklint**, an area of 16m-high cliffs and pebble beaches that's popular with birdwatchers during the autumn southern migration. About 500m north of the cliffs is **Gulstav Mose**, a marshy bird sanctuary that provides a habitat for hawks, herons, ducks, reed buntings and small songbirds. East of the sanctuary are the adjacent woodlands **Gulstav Skov**. All three sites are connected by footpaths. Another area of interest to birdwatchers is **Tryggelev Nor**, a coastal nature reserve with a sighting tower, midway between Bagenkop and Ristinge.

Places to Stay & Eat

Ristinge Camping & Feriecenter (☎ 62 57 13 29, fax 62 57 13 47, Ristingevej 104, 5932 Humble), a three star camping ground, is within walking distance of the beach

in Ristinge. Open from early April to early September, it has 250 tent sites, a few four-person cottages, a grocery shop and a snack bar.

The nearest hotel to Ristinge is the little *Humble Hotel (☎ 62 57 11 34, fax 62 57 11 24, Ristingevej 2, 5932 Humble)*, in Humble village centre. It has four rooms; singles/doubles with bath start at 495/595 kr including breakfast.

The larger villages, such as Humble and Bagenkop, have *bakeries*, *grocery shops* and at least a couple of places where you can stop and get a meal.

Ærø

Well off the beaten track, Ærø is an idyllic island with small villages, rolling hills and patchwork farms. It's a popular place to tour by bicycle – the country roads are enhanced by thatched houses and old windmills, and the island offers some ancient passage graves and dolmens for visitors to explore.

Environmentally-friendly energy generation the Ærø way: picturesque old windmills abound.

FUNEN

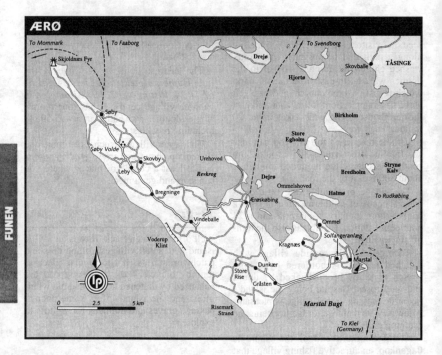

ÆRØ

Ærø is a favourite destination of yachters, and each of the three main towns – Ærøskøbing, Marstal and Søby – has a modern marina. Sailing is so popular that, with a total of 800 berths, there are four times as many yacht moorings as there are hotel rooms. Each of the three towns also has a commercial ferry harbour.

GETTING THERE & AWAY
Bus

Gråhundbus (☎ 44 68 44 00) operates a daily summer bus between Copenhagen's Ballerup S-train station and Ærøskøbing via Svendborg. The trip takes about 3¼ hours and costs 150 kr. Departure times vary with the day of the week.

Boat

Det Ærøske Færgetrafikselskab (☎ 62 52 40 00) operates year-round car ferries to Søby from Faaborg, to Ærøskøbing from Svendborg, and to Marstal from Rudkøbing. All run an average of five times a day, take about an hour and cost 64 kr for adults, 33 kr for children, 18 kr for a bicycle, 37 kr for a motorcycle and 142 kr for a car. These prices are one way; the return fare is 15% less than two one-way tickets. If you have a car it's a good idea to make reservations, particularly at weekends and in midsummer – even if you can only call a few hours before the sailing, do so, because at the dock priority will be given to those on the waiting list.

There is also a ferry (☎ 62 58 17 17) between Søby and Mommark (on Als in Jutland) which runs daily from 1 April to 30 September and at weekends during the rest of the year. The frequency, from two to six times a day, depends upon the season and the day of the week. The trip takes one hour and costs 60 kr for adults, 30 kr for children, 15 kr for a bicycle and 240 kr for a car with two people.

For information on the passenger ferry between Marstal and Kiel (Germany) see the Getting There & Away chapter.

GETTING AROUND
Bus
Fyns Amt (☎ 63 11 22 33) operates a bus service (No 990) from Marstal to Søby via Ærøskøbing. It runs hourly on weekdays from 5.30 am to 7.30 pm. Weekend buses are about half as frequent, with the first bus leaving Marstal at 8.30 am. It takes about an hour to get from one end of the island to the other. Fares range from 10 to 25 kr, depending on the distance, but there's also a pass for unlimited one day travel that costs 46/23 kr for adults/children.

Car & Motorcycle
Cars can be rented at the harbourside Q8 petrol station (☎ 62 53 18 55) and at Ærø Auto-Center (☎ 62 53 13 02), Skolevej 12, both in Marstal.

Bicycle
Cycle Routes There are three signposted cycle routes on Ærø. Cycle route 91 begins at Marstal and continues along the southern side of the island up to Søby, while cycle route 90 runs along the northern side of the island from Søby to Ærøskøbing and continues as route 92 from Ærøskøbing to Marstal. If you were to cover the entire route as a circular tour of the island you would cycle about 60km – a tough outing considering the island's hilly terrain.

Ærø's tourist offices sell an English-language cycling map (15 kr) of the island, listing sights along the routes. The county-wide cycle guide and map published by Cykelnetværk Fyn (see the under Cycle Routes in the introductory section of this chapter) also covers cycling on Ærø.

Rental You can hire bicycles in Ærøskøbing at Pilebækkens Cykelservice (☎ 62 52 11 10), Pilebækken 11; in Marstal at Nørre-

mark Cykelforretning (☎ 62 53 14 77), Møllevejen 77; and in Søby at Søby Cykelforretning (☎ 62 58 18 42), Langebro 4. The camping ground in Ærøskøbing and the island's two hostels also hire out bikes. The going rate is 40 kr per day, with a slight discount for longer rentals.

ÆRØSKØBING
A prosperous merchants' town in the late 17th century, Ærøskøbing has been preserved in its entirety. Its narrow cobblestoned streets are tightly lined with old houses, many of them gently listing half-timbered affairs with handblown glass windows, decorative doorways and hollyhocks along the streets.

In addition to its engaging historic character, Ærøskøbing has a central location and good accommodation options, which makes it an ideal base for a stay on Ærø.

Information
Tourist Office Ærøskøbing Turistbureau (☎ 62 52 13 00, fax 62 52 14 36, email turistar@post1.tele.dk) is opposite the harbour at Vestergade 1, 5970 Æøskøbing. Between June and August it's open from 9 am to 5 pm Monday to Friday, from 10 am to 3 pm on Saturday and from 11 am to 1 pm on Sunday; during the rest of the year it's open from 9 am to 4 pm Monday to Friday and from 10 am to 1 pm on Saturday.

Money There's an Amtssparekassen bank on Torvet and a branch of Den Danske Bank at Vestergade 56.

Post The main post office, on the northern side of town at Statene 6, is open from noon to 4.30 am Monday to Friday and from 10 am to noon on Saturday.

Things to See & Do
In keeping with the town's character, sights are low-key. The main attraction is **Flaskeskibssamlingen**, in the former poorhouse at Smedegade 22. This museum is dedicated to the lifetime work of Peter Jacobsen, a local sailor nicknamed Bottle Peter for the

1700 ships-in-a-bottle he created before his death in 1960 at the age of 86. In addition to the model ships, many of which are in handblown bottles, the museum contains other local folk art. Between May and September it's open from 10 am to 5 pm daily; between October and April it's open from 1 to 3 pm Tuesday to Thursday and from 10 am to 1 pm on Sunday. Admission costs 25 kr.

The **Ærø Museum**, Brogade 3, features antique furnishings and other historical items, including a collection of mid-19th century paintings. It's open daily, except Monday, from 10 am to 4 pm between mid-June and late August, and from 10 am to 1 pm in spring and autumn. Admission costs 15 kr.

Hammerichs Hus, a half-timbered house at Gyden 22, has antiques, china and period furnishings from Funen and Jutland collected by sculptor Gunnar Hammerich. It's open from 11 am to 3 pm daily, except on Monday, between 1 June and 31 August. Admission costs 15 kr.

If you want to visit more than one museum, ask about discounted combination tickets.

Otherwise, the main activity is wandering the quaint streets with their tidy houses – it's all a bit like winding the clock back a century or two. The oldest house in town dates back to about 1645 and is at Søndergade 36. Other fine streets for strolling are Vestergade and Smedegade; there's a particularly picturesque little house known as **Dukkehuset** (Doll's House) at Smedegade 37.

Places to Stay

The three star *Ærøskøbing Campingplads* (☎ 62 52 18 54, *Sygehusvej 40, 5970 Ærøskøbing*), open from 1 May to 30 September, is near a shallow beach just 1km from the town centre. Camping costs 44 kr per person, and four-person cabins with hotplates and refrigerator cost from 770 to 1155 kr per week, depending on the size. There's a kitchen, a laundry room, a TV lounge and facilities for disabled campers.

The 84 bed hostel *Ærøskøbing Vandrerhjem* (☎ 62 52 10 44, fax 62 52 16 44, *Smedevejen 15, 5970 Ærøskøbing*) is 750m from the town centre on the road to Marstal. It's open from 1 April to 30 September. Dorm beds cost 85 kr and rooms sleeping one or two people cost 210 kr.

Ærøskøbing Turistbureau maintains a list of islanders who rent out *rooms* in private homes around Ærø; singles/doubles cost 185/300 kr. Staff can also book *houses*, *cottages* and *flats* by the week, starting at around 3000 kr.

Det Lille Hotel (☎/fax 62 52 23 00, *Smedegade 33, 5970 Ærøskøbing*) is a cosy family-run hotel in a historic neighbourhood. There are six rooms with sink and desk costing 325/465 kr for singles/doubles, including breakfast. Bathrooms are off the hall.

The timber-framed, 30 room *Hotel Ærøhus* (☎ 62 52 10 03, fax 62 52 21 23, *Vestergade 38, 5970 Ærøskøbing*) has an old-fashioned character right down to its creaky hallways and fine china at the breakfast table. Singles/doubles cost 280/460 kr with shared bath, 460/670 kr with private bath; prices are about 15% cheaper from October to May. Breakfast is included in the rates. The hotel is part of the Dansk Kroferie association and accepts 'Inn Cheques' (see under Hotel Schemes in the Accommodation section of the Facts for the Visitor chapter for details).

For a homey country experience there's *Graasten Farm* (☎/fax 62 52 24 25, *Østermarksvej 20, 5970 Ærøskøbing*), a working dairy farm run by a Danish-English couple. On the main road midway between Ærøskøbing and Marstal, it has three guest bedrooms and lots of common space including a kitchenette and sitting area. Singles/doubles cost 215/330 kr including breakfast.

Places to Eat

On Vestergade, just west of the ferry dock, you'll find a small *grocery shop*, selling fresh bakery items, and the *Ærøskøbing Røgeri*, which serves inexpensive smoked fish and shrimp dishes. For fancy ice cream, there's **Vaffelbageriet** (*Vestergade 21*), specialising in freshly baked waffle cones. There are **bakeries** at Vestergade 44 and Vestergade 62.

Det Lille Hotel, in a former sea captain's house, has a small restaurant where lunch offerings, including chicken or steak dishes, cost from 50 to 85 kr.

Hotel Ærøhus has a pleasant dining room with a moderately expensive menu of Danish food. For the best value choose from the daily two course specials (98 kr) or from the snack menu, which has some filling dishes such as fish fillet and potatoes for around 60 kr.

MARSTAL

Marstal, at the eastern end of the island, is Ærø's most modern-looking town although it too has a nautical character, with a maritime museum, a shipyard and a marina.

Although Marstal is a quiet place today, until the 19th century it was one of the region's busiest harbours, with more than 300 merchant ships pulling into port annually. The sea was such an integral part of people's lives that even the gravestones at the seamen's church on Kirkestræde are engraved with maritime epitaphs, the most frequently quoted being 'Here lies Christen

Hansen at anchor with his wife; he will not weigh until summoned by God'.

Information
Tourist Office Marstal Turistbureau (☎ 62 53 19 60, fax 62 53 30 35), Havnegade 5, 5960 Marstal, is a five minute walk south from the harbour. Between mid-June and 31 August it's open from 9 am to 5 pm Monday to Friday and from 10 am to 3 pm on Saturday; in July it's also open from 10 am to noon on Sunday. Low-season hours are from 10 am to 3 pm Monday to Friday.

Money There's an Amtssparekassen bank on Kongensgade 28, the road that runs west from the harbour, and a branch of Den Danske Bank at Prinsensgade 8, one block inland from Marstal Turistbureau.

Post The post office, at Havnegade 1, is open from 11 am to 5 pm Monday to Friday and from 10 am to noon on Saturday.

Laundry Ærø Mønt-og Færdigvask is a self-service coin laundry at Kirkestræde 39.

Marstal Søfartsmuseum
The Marstal Søfartsmuseum, on the corner of Havnegade and Prinsensgade, has a

---

Soaking up the Sun

Ærø, with its many windmills, has a centuries-old tradition of harvesting renewable energy. It therefore seems fitting that Europe's largest solar power station, Solfangeranlæg, opened on the island in 1996. The facility, at the western outskirts of Marstal, encompasses an 8064 sq metre field of solar collectors that are capable of providing year-round heating for 270 homes.

The solar collectors have special glass faces that are designed to absorb heat from the sun, which is then transferred through a network of pipes to a heat exchange and generator installation, from where it enters the island's power grid. In all, the solar facility provides an annual output of power that previously required 350,000 litres of oil to produce.

Those interested in a guided tour of Solfangeranlæg can call ☎ 62 53 15 64; the tours are usually only offered to groups of at least 10 people, but if one is already scheduled you might be able to tag along. If you want to learn more about renewable energy efforts in general, contact the Ærø Natur og Energiskole, Smedevejen 13, 5970 Ærøskøbing.

collection of maritime paraphernalia including paintings and models of some of the schooners and brigs that filled the town harbour during its heyday. It's open daily, from 9 am to at least 5 pm in summer and from 10 am to 4 pm Tuesday to Friday the rest of the year. Admission costs 25 kr.

Activities

There's a reasonably good beach, half sandy and half rocky, on the southern side of town, about a 15 minute walk from the centre. Østersøens Surfcenter (☎ 30 34 81 29), at the beach, hires windsurfing equipment and offers windsurfing lessons.

Places to Stay

The three star *Marstal Camping* (☎ 62 53 36 00, Egehovedvej 1, 5960 Marstal) is behind the marina, 1km south of the ferry harbour. The camping ground occupies a quiet grassy area just minutes from the water. It's open from 1 April to 1 October. Camping costs 45 kr per person, and there are also cabins for rent from 770 to 1155 kr a week.

The 82 bed hostel *Marstal Vandrerhjem* (☎ 62 53 10 64, fax 62 53 10 57, Færgestræde 29, 5960 Marstal) is in a renovated municipal office on the corner of Havnegade and Færgestræde. It's a good central location, 500m south of the ferry harbour and within walking distance of restaurants and the beach. Dorm beds cost 80 kr, while private rooms sleeping one to four people cost from 200 to 320 kr. It's open from 1 May to 1 September.

Hotel Marstal (☎ 62 53 13 52, Dronningestræde 1A, 5960 Marstal), just a few minutes walk south-west of the harbour, has a handful of simple rooms above a restaurant, all with shared bath; singles/doubles cost 275/375 kr including breakfast.

Places to Eat

At the ferry harbour there's a small *food shop* and a *grill restaurant* serving inexpensive burgers, pizza and other simple eats.

For something a little more substantial, the restaurant at *Hotel Marstal* offers a two course daily special for 88 kr.

There's a *bakery (Prinsensgade 11)* about 200m west of Marstal Turistbureau, and a *Super Brugsen* grocery shop, which has a deli and good fruit and veg and wine sections, on the corner of Kirkestræde and Skovgyden, about 300m west of the ferry harbour.

For cheap beers head for *Minde (Kongensgade 13)*, a pub a few streets inland from the ferry harbour.

STORE RISE

The village of Store Rise, in the middle of the island, has an attractive **church** that dates from medieval times, although much of the current structure is from the 17th century. The churchyard is surrounded by a medieval circular wall and contains graves separated from one another by hedges. The church interior includes an ornately carved altar from the late Gothic period.

In the field behind the church is **Tingstedet**, a 54m-long Neolithic passage grave thought to be at least 5000 years old. The cup-like markings in the largest stone near the church indicate that the grave may have belonged to a fertility cult. It takes only a few minutes to get there along a footpath marked from the church.

A couple of kilometres south of the village is **Risemark Strand**, the best of Ærø's few sandy beaches.

SØBY

Søby has a shipyard which is the island's biggest employer, a sizable fishing fleet and a popular marina. It's a pleasant enough place with some thatched houses, but the town doesn't pack the same charm as Ærøskøbing and most of its visitors are yachters.

Information

Tourist Office In summer a branch tourist office (☎ 62 58 13 88) is open at Søby harbour from 10 am to 4 pm Monday to Saturday.

Post The post office, at Havnevejen 19, is open from 1 to 4.30 pm Monday to Friday.

Things to See & Do

Five kilometres beyond Søby, at Ærø's northern tip, is **Skjoldnæs Fyr**, a 19th century granite-block lighthouse with a narrow stairway; you can climb the lighthouse for a fine view of the sea. A few minutes walk beyond the lighthouse is a pebble beach.

Søby Volde are the mounded-over earthen ramparts that were once part of a 12th century fortress. They are along the main cross-island road, roughly 3km south of Søby.

Places to Stay & Eat

Søby Camping (☎ *62 58 14 70, Vitsø 10, 5985 Søby*), a small two star facility about 1km west of town, is open from May to mid-September. It charges 40 kr per person for camping and has huts costing 250 kr.

The town also has a small inn, the *Søby Kro* (☎ *62 58 10 06, Østerbro 2, 5985 Søby*). Singles/doubles with shared bath cost 210/360 kr.

Finn's Bageri (Nørrebro 2) sells fresh bread and pastries from 6.30 am. *Cafeteria Øen*, at the marina, has hot dogs, burgers and chicken with chips costing less than 50 kr as well as more expensive fish and beef dishes. There are also a couple of *fastfood kiosks* near the ferry harbour.

FUNEN

Southern Jutland

The Jutland (Jylland) peninsula, the only part of Denmark connected to the European mainland, was originally settled by the Jutes, a Germanic tribe whose forays included an invasion of England in the 5th century.

Jutland's southern boundary has long been a fluid one. It was last redrawn in 1920 when Germany returned part of the Schleswig region to Denmark following a postwar plebiscite on self-determination.

Southern Jutland has a number of well-preserved historic towns, the most notable of which is Ribe. However, many southerly towns tend to be modern and nondescript, in part due to the destruction unleashed during the border wars with Germany.

As is the case throughout Jutland, the bulk of the land is given over to fields and pastures, with only sporadic patches of woodland. The east coast of southern Jutland is cut by deep fjords whereas the west coast is bordered by marshland and moors.

ESBJERG

Esbjerg, the youngest city in Denmark, owes its rise to the territorial losses that beleaguered Denmark in the 19th century. Following the loss of the Schleswig and Holstein regions to Germany in 1864, farmers in Jutland suddenly needed a new export harbour for shipping grain to England. To serve that purpose the coastal town of Esbjerg was founded in 1868 on a site that had previously been farmland.

Esbjerg's port opened in 1874 and within only a few decades the town's population had grown to nearly 20,000. It's now Denmark's fifth largest city (population 83,000), the centre of Denmark's North Sea oil activities and the country's largest fishing harbour.

Although Esbjerg has its fair share of late-19th century buildings, it lacks the intriguing atmosphere found in the medieval quarters of other cities and isn't on the

Highlights

- Step back in time in Ribe, Denmark's oldest and best-preserved town
- Take an excursion to quaint Møgeltønder village and its lavish church
- Join the action on the island of Rømø, a haven for windsurfers
- Revel at Denmark's largest folk music festival, held in Tønder each August
- Tour Sønderborg with its seaside castle and 1864 battlefield sites
- Explore the unspoiled island of Fanø

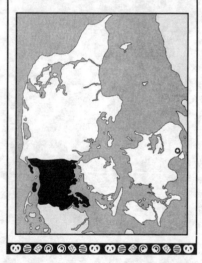

itinerary of most travellers unless they're travelling by ferry to or from the UK.

Orientation

Torvet, the city square where Skolegade and Torvegade intersect, is bordered by cafés, banks, the post office and the tourist office. The train and bus stations are about 300m

The seaside town of Sønderborg played a vital part in resisting the German invasion of 1864.

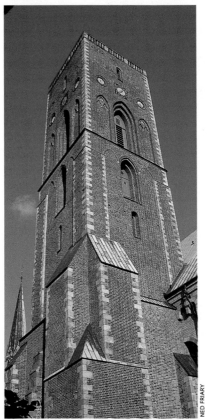

Ancient Ribe Domkirke dates back to 1150.

Koldinghus, a remarkable castle fortress.

Mennesket ved Havet, a landmark in Esbjerg.

CEES VAN ROEDEN/DANISH TOURIST BOARD

Denmark's oldest town is Ribe, where cobbled streets evoke bygone days and 1300 years of history.

NED FRIARY

Kristkirken in Tønder boasts impressive paintings and carvings including this intricately crafted pulpit.

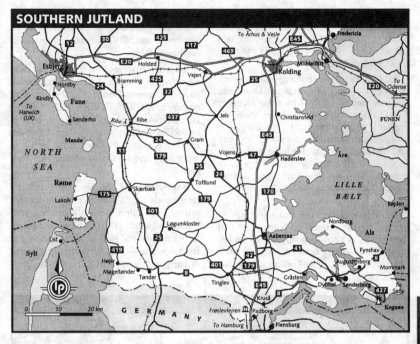

SOUTHERN JUTLAND

east of Torvet, while the ferry terminal is 1km to the south.

Information

Tourist Office The helpful Esbjerg Turistkontor (☎ 75 12 55 99, fax 75 12 27 67, email esbjerg.tourist.dk@post10.tele.dk) is at Skolegade 33, 6700 Esbjerg. In summer it's open from 9.30 am to 5 pm Monday to Friday and from 9.30 am to 3.30 pm on Saturday; during the rest of the year it's open from 10 am to 5 pm on weekdays and from 10 am to 1 pm on Saturday.

Money There are many banks in the centre, including Den Danske Bank south of the post office on Torvet and a Unibank around the corner on Kongensgade.

Post The post office, on Torvet, is open from 9 am to 5 pm Monday to Friday (to 5.30 pm on Thursday) and from 9 am to 1 pm on Saturday.

Library The library, at Nørregade 19, has a reading room containing foreign newspapers and magazines. It's open from 10 am to 7 pm Monday to Friday and from 10 am to 2 pm on Saturday.

Laundry There's a coin laundry on the corner of Danmarksgade and Englandsgade, just north-east of Torvet.

Medical Services Krone Apoteket, at Kongensgade 36, is open 24 hours.

Things to See & Do

There are a few local museums to explore, or you could pick up a free walking-tour map at Esbjerg Turistkontor and stroll along a route that traces Esbjerg's architectural development, unassuming as it is. Opposite the turistkontor, in the centre of Torvet, stands a **statue** of Christian IX, who held the throne in 1899 when Esbjerg obtained its municipal charter.

Esbjerg Vandtårn (Esbjerg Watertower), two blocks south of Torvet at Havnegade 22, was erected in 1897 by town architect CH Clausen, who incorporated medieval features in an attempt to give Esbjerg a more historic look. For a view of the city and harbour, you can climb the tower (admission 10 kr) from 10 am to 4 pm daily between June and mid-September and on Saturday and Sunday during the rest of the year.

Esbjerg Museum, three blocks north of Torvet on the corner of Nørregade and Torvegade, is known mostly for its amber collection featuring both ancient and modern pieces, but also has some minor his-

torical exhibits. It's open from 10 am to 4 pm daily (closed on Monday between September and May). Admission costs 20 kr (children 10 kr).

Esbjerg Kunstmuseum (Esbjerg Art Museum), near Esbjerg Vandtårn at Havnegade 20, features Danish paintings by 20th century artists of the COBRA (COpenhagen-BRussels-Amsterdam) movement, including Richard Mortensen, Robert Jacobsen and Per Kirkeby. It's open from 10 am to 4 pm daily and admission costs 30 kr (children free).

Bogtrykmuseet (Museum of Printing), Borgergade 6, is set up like a 19th century printing operation, with old printing machines and a manual type composing room. Between June and mid-September it's open from noon to 4 pm daily; during the rest of the year it's open from 1 to 4 pm Tues-

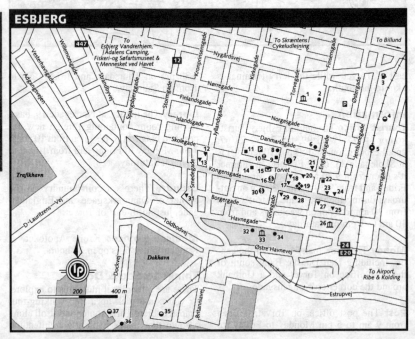

day to Sunday. Admission costs 15 kr (children 10 kr).

Fiskeri-og Søfartsmuseet (Museum of Fishing & Shipping) at Tarphagevej, 4km north-west of the city centre, has a 25 tank aquarium featuring mostly North Sea fish, an outdoor seal pool (feeding times at 11 am and 2.30 pm) and various fisheries exhibits. It's open daily, from 10 am to 6 pm in July and August and from 10 am to 5 pm during the rest of the year. Admission costs 55 kr (children 30 kr). Take bus No 1 or 6 from the train station; they run about once an hour.

West of Fiskeri-og Søfartsmuseet is Esbjerg's new waterfront landmark, **Mennesket ved Havet** (Man Meets the Sea), comprising four 9m-high stylised human figures created by Danish sculptor Svend Wiig Hansen to commemorate the city's centennial.

There's also an old wooden **lightship** down at the harbour that can be visited (10 kr) Monday to Friday from 10 am to 4 pm between May and September.

Places to Stay

Camping The nearest camping ground is the three star *Ådalens Camping* (☎ 75 15 88 22, fax 75 15 97 93, Gudenåvej 20, 6710 Esbjerg), 5km north of the city via route 447 or bus No 1 or 7. It charges 45 kr per person, has cooking facilities and a coin laundry and is open from 1 April to 1 November. There are also cabins costing 200 kr; these can accommodate from four to five people.

Hostel The 130 bed hostel *Esbjerg Vandrerhjem* (☎ 75 12 42 58, fax 75 13 68 33, Gammel Vardevej 80, 6700 Esbjerg) is in a former folk high school 3km north of the city centre. Dorm beds cost 85 kr and rooms range from 170 kr for a single to 340 kr for a quadruple. There's a kitchen, a TV lounge, bicycles for hire and sports facilities. It's open from 1 February to 15 December and is served by buses No 4 and 12.

Private Rooms Staff at the tourist office can book *rooms* in private homes, both in the city and in the surrounding countryside. The cost averages 125 kr per adult, 75 kr per child, plus 30 kr for an optional breakfast; there's no additional booking fee.

Hotels The 30 room *Hotel Bell-Inn* (☎ 75 12 01 22, fax 75 13 16 40, Skolegade 45, 6700 Esbjerg) is not terribly appealing but it does have the city's cheapest hotel rooms: single/doubles with shared bath cost 310/420 kr.

The best-value hotel is *Cab-Inn Esbjerg* (☎ 75 18 16 00, fax 75 18 16 24, Skolegade 14, 6700 Esbjerg), a member of the

SOUTHERN JUTLAND

ESBJERG

PLACES TO STAY					
9	Hotel Britannia	24	Café Bageriet	8	Hertz
11	Hotel Bell-Inn	25	You'll Never Walk Alone	10	Public Toilets
14	Hotel Ansgar	27	Super Brugsen Supermarket	15	Post Office
22	Cab-Inn Esbjerg	29	McDonald's; Sunset Boulevard	16	Den Danske Bank
		31	Føtex Supermarket	19	Midt-I Shopping Centre
PLACES TO EAT				26	Bogtrykmuseet
12	Sand's	**OTHER**		28	Krone Apoteket
13	Restaurant Munkestuen	1	Esbjerg Museum	30	Unibank
17	Café Chr IX; Papa's Cantina	2	Library	32	Esbjerg Vandtårn
18	Flannigan's	3	Petrol Station; Europcar	33	Esbjerg Kunstmuseum
20	Babylon Pizza	4	Bus Station	34	Musikhuset Esbjerg
21	Netto Grocery Shop	5	Train Station	35	Ferry to Harwich (UK)
23	Jensen's Bøfhus	6	Coin Laundry	36	Lightship
		7	Esbjerg Turistkontor	37	Ferry to Fanø

Copenhagen chain of the same name. The hotel, which occupies an attractive 100-year-old brick building, has been thoroughly renovated and offers 82 modern, comfortable rooms, all with bath, TV and phone. Singles/doubles cost 410/510 kr.

Hotel Ansar (☎ 75 12 82 44, fax 75 13 95 40, Skolegade 36, 6700 Esbjerg) is an older place that has 52 ordinary rooms with bath, TV, phone and minibar costing 495/700 kr for singles/doubles including breakfast. The hotel is a member of the Dansk Kroferie association; see under Hotel Schemes in the Facts for the Visitor chapter for details of their Inn Cheques discount scheme.

Hotel Britannia (☎ 75 13 01 11, fax 75 45 20 85, Torvet, 6700 Esbjerg) is a modern Best Western hotel in the centre of the city. All 79 rooms have bath, TV, phone and minibar; the hotel has a pub, restaurant and conference facilities. Standard rates, which include breakfast, are 795/880 kr for singles/doubles, but there's a summer rate of 695 kr per family room.

Places to Eat

Kongensgade A collection of eateries can be found east of Torvet on Kongensgade, the main pedestrian shopping street. *Café Bageriet (Kongensgade 7)*, a bakery just a couple of blocks south of the train station, is a good place for cheap coffee and pastries if you're stumbling off an early-morning train.

Jensen's Bøfhus (Kongensgade 9) offers courtyard dining and 39 kr steak lunches on weekdays from 11 am to 4 pm; at other times grilled chicken and steak dishes begin at about double that price.

You'll Never Walk Alone (Kongensgade 10) is an English-style pub complete with darts and live TV broadcasts of British football. It has English and Irish brews on tap and a few simple English snacks such as steak and kidney pie.

A block north of Kongensgade is *Babylon Pizza (Skolegade 28)*, where pizza slices cost just 10 kr and whole pizzas start at 35 kr.

There's a *Super Brugsen* supermarket on the corner of Kongensgade and Englandsgade. The *Midt-I* shopping centre on Kongensgade and Torvet houses a café-style bakery and a cafeteria. On the opposite side of the street, at Kongensgade 40, is a *McDonald's* and a *Sunset Boulevard*, serving ice cream and submarine sandwiches.

Torvet There are two adjacent restaurants – *Flannigan's* and *Café Chr IX* – on the eastern side of Torvet. On warm summer days both set out pavement tables right on the square and become popular beer gardens. Your best bet for lunch is Café Chr IX, where good salads, pasta dishes and hearty burger and chip meals cost 69 kr. Chr IX also has a pleasant basement restaurant called *Papa's Cantina* that offers a 69 kr Mexican lunch buffet from noon to 4 pm.

Elsewhere in Esbjerg *Restaurant Munkestuen (Smedegade 21)*, a cosy upmarket restaurant in a 100-year-old building, offers salads and light dishes that start at around 50 kr at lunchtime, and serves typical Danish dishes costing around 150 kr for dinner.

Sand's (Skolegade 60) is another traditional restaurant specialising in Danish cuisine. It serves good smørrebrød and various lunch specials for around 70 kr. For dinner there's a two course 'Danish nouveau' meal costing 169 kr.

Føtex, a modern supermarket near the harbour at the intersection of Havnegade and Kronprinsensgade, has a simple family restaurant serving inexpensive meals.

There's a *Netto* grocery shop in the town centre on Skolegade, just east of Esbjerg Turistkontor, and a *DSB Restaurant* at the train station.

Entertainment

You'll Never Walk Alone has live music – often blues, folk or soft rock – from Wednesday to Saturday. *Papa's Cantina* on Torvet turns into a nightclub at midnight on Friday and Saturday.

Musikhuset Esbjerg (Havnegade 18), a new performing arts centre designed by famed Danish architect Jørn Utzon, is the venue for classical music and big-name concerts of all types.

Getting There & Away
Esbjerg is 77km north-west of Tønder, 59km south-west of Billund and 92km west of the Funen-Jutland bridge.

Air Maersk Air (☎ 75 16 07 77) operates seven flights daily between Esbjerg and Copenhagen. The normal one-way fare is 710 kr but return fares start as low as 660 kr; see the Getting Around chapter for more details.

There are weekday flights from Esbjerg to the UK cities of Aberdeen and Edinburgh, operated by Business Air and bookable through Maersk Air. See the Getting There & Away chapter for details. These flights, geared to business travellers, tend to be expensive; return fares start at 2200 kr to Aberdeen and 2800 kr to Manchester.

Bus An express bus runs from Esbjerg to Frederikshavn (190 kr, five hours) about twice daily.

Train Trains run hourly between Copenhagen and Esbjerg (241 kr, 3¼ hours) throughout the day, with the last train in either direction leaving at 10 pm.

There's also a train service that runs north to Struer (128 kr, 2¼ hours) and south to Ribe (35 kr, 35 minutes) and Tønder (71 kr, 1½ hours), and another to Kolding (63 kr, 55 minutes).

Car & Motorcycle If you're driving into Esbjerg, the E20, the main expressway from the east, leads directly into the heart of the city and down to the ferry harbour. If you're coming from the south, route 24 merges with the E20 on the outskirts of the city. From the north, route 12 makes a beeline for the city, ending at the harbour.

There's a Hertz car rental office (☎ 75 12 60 88) by Hotel Britannia, an Avis office (☎ 75 13 44 77) at Exnersgade 19 and a Europcar office (☎ 75 12 38 93) at Jernbanegade 56. Europcar and Hertz also have booths at the airport.

Boat For details of ferry services to the UK see the Getting There & Away chapter. For information on boats to Fanø, see the following Fanø Getting There & Away section.

Getting Around
To/From the Airport The airport is 10km east of the city centre. Public bus No 9 runs about once an hour between the airport and the train station.

Bus Most city buses can be boarded at the train station. The cost is 11 kr per ride, or you can buy a 74 kr card valid for 10 rides.

Car & Motorcycle There's free central parking with a two hour limit west of Hotel Britannia (enter from Danmarksgade) and free parking with no time limit at the car park on Nørregade east of the library.

Bicycle Bikes can be hired from Skræntens Cykeludlejning (☎ 75 45 75 05) at Skrænten and Kirkegade to the north of the city centre. The tourist office provides free English-language brochures detailing suggested cycling tours.

FANØ
Fanø, just 15 minutes by ferry from Esbjerg, is a long flat island with a landscape dominated by heathland, dunes and broad sandy beaches. The two main villages, at opposite ends of the island, are Nordby and Sønderho, both of which have narrow streets and attractive period houses.

The best beaches are on the exposed north-western side of the island in the area around Fanø Bad and Rindby Strand. To the north of Fanø Bad is Soren Jemsens Sand, a 3km-long sand spit that can be explored on foot, while the packed-sand beach extending to the south is open to both pedestrians and cars. Windsurfers take to the beach south of Rindby Strand.

Fanø has attempted to hold onto its traditions more strongly than other parts of Denmark. As recently as the 1960s some of Fanø's elderly women still wore the traditional island costume, consisting of multiple skirts and a scarf that could be folded down as a face mask to protect against blowing sand. During island festivals, such as the Fannikerdage which takes place in Nordby in early July, you can see these costumes being worn and enjoy local folk music and dancing.

Information

Tourist Office The Fanø Turistbureau (☎ 75 16 26 00, fax 75 16 29 03), Havnepladsen, Nordby, 6720 Fanø, is at the ferry harbour in Nordby. Between early June and early September it's open from 8.30 am to 6 pm Monday to Friday, from 9 am to 7 pm on Saturday and from 9 am to 5 pm on Sunday. In the low season it's open from 8.30 am to 5.30 pm Monday to Friday, from 9 am to 1 pm on Saturday and from 11 am to 1 pm on Sunday.

Money In Nordby there's Den Danske Bank at Hovedgaden 74 and a Fanø Spare- og Lannekasse bank at Hovedgaden 51.

Post The post office, at Hovedgaden 15 in Nordby, is open from 10 am to 5 pm Monday to Friday and from 10 am to noon on Saturday.

Things to See & Do

Fanø has a surprising number of sights. In Nordby, 200m west of the turistbureau at Hovedgaden 28, is **Fanø Skibsfarts-og Dragtsamling**, a museum of model ships, maritime displays and local costumes. **Fanø Museum**, 300m to the east on the corner of Skolevej and Hovedgaden, is another local history museum, this one concentrating on period furnishings.

There are a few attractions in Sønderho's centre, within a few minutes walk of each other. **Fanø Kunstmuseum** is a small mu-

seum featuring paintings of Fanø; **Hannes Hus** is a 17th century sea captain's home complete with period décor. The 18th century **Sønderho Kirke** is known for its 14 votive ships. Five hundred metres north of Sønderho centre, on the road to Nordby, is a picturesque 100-year-old **windmill**.

Most of the sights on Fanø are seasonal; the hours fluctuate a bit, but all are open on afternoons in summer. Admission to Sønderho Kirke is free; admission to the other sights costs 15 kr, except for Fanø Kunstmuseum, where it costs 20 kr.

In the centre of the island, midway between Nordby and Sønderho, is a wooded area of 1162 hectares called **Fanø Klit-**

plantage crisscrossed by walking trails; it provides a habitat for deer, rabbits and birds.

Places to Stay

There are nine camping grounds on Fanø, most of which have cabins for rent in addition to the usual tent and caravan sites. About 1km north of Nordby is *Tempo Camping* (☎ 75 16 22 51, Strandvejen 34, Nordby, 6720 Fanø), open from mid-May to mid-September.

If you prefer to be a bit closer to the beach, *Feldberg Strand Camping* (☎ 75 16 24 90, fax 75 16 33 33, Rindby Strand, 6720 Fanø) is within walking distance of Rindby Strand and is open between mid-April and mid-September. *Camping Klitten* (☎/fax 75 16 40 65, Sønderho Strandvej 3, Sønderho, 6720 Fanø), on the western outskirts of Sønderho, is open from Easter to late October. All three have kitchens and coin laundries, and cost 45 kr per person.

The cheapest of the island's handful of hotels is the 12 room *Kellers Hotel* (☎ 75 16 30 88, Strandvejen 48, 6720 Fanø), north of Nordby on the beach road. Singles/doubles start at 200/300 kr with shared bath, 275/375 kr with bath, including breakfast. It's open from Easter to October.

An intimate, upmarket choice is the *Sønderho Kro* (☎ 75 16 40 09, fax 75 16 43 85, Kropladsen 11, Sønderho, 6720 Fanø), a small inn dating back to 1722. It's a member of the Relais & Châteaux chain and has eight rooms with bath; singles/doubles start at 645/780 kr.

Danland Feriehotel Vesterhavet (☎ 75 16 32 77, fax 75 16 61 04, Fanø Bad, 6720 Fanø), a three storey resort complex right on the beach, has 146 flats costing from 659 kr a day in summer, 490 kr in the low season.

For information on booking *summer holiday homes*, contact the turistbureau.

Places to Eat

There are *bakeries* and simple *cafés* in Nordby, Fanø Bad and Sønderho. At the *Tempo Center* at Strandvejen 27 in Nordby, near Tempo Camping, there's a supermarket, a coin laundry and an amusement arcade – a potentially convenient combo!

Danland Feriehotel Vesterhavet, on the beach at Fanø Bad, has a *Den Grimme Ælling* chain restaurant where all-you-can-eat buffets cost around 100 kr.

The *Sønderho Kro* has an expensive restaurant with traditional Danish décor and food.

Getting There & Away

Scandlines (☎ 33 15 15 15, 75 13 45 00) shuttles a car ferry between Nordby and Esbjerg from early morning until after midnight, departing two to three times an hour in the middle of the day. The return fare is 25 kr for adults, 12 kr for children, 25 kr for a bicycle, 75 kr for a motorcycle with rider and 280 kr for a car with up to five people.

Getting Around

Bus There's a local bus service from the ferry dock that runs about once an hour in summer, connecting Nordby with Fanø Bad (11 kr), Rindby Strand (11 kr) and Sønderho (15 kr).

Bicycle Bicycles can be hired in Nordby from Havnekiosken (☎ 75 16 21 20), at the harbour next to the turistbureau, and from Fanø Cykelhandel (☎ 75 16 25 13) at Hovedgaden 96. Fanø Cykelhandel also has branches in Rindby at Kirkevejen 67 and in Fanø Bad at Golfvej 1.

RIBE

Ribe, the oldest town in Denmark, is chock-full of historic sites. Recent excavations, which unearthed a number of silver coins, indicate that a market town existed on the northern side of the Ribe Å river as far back as 700. In 850 Saint Ansgar built the first church in Ribe and the town began to grow. During the Viking era Ribe, linked to the sea by its river, flourished as a centre of trade between the Frankish Empire and the Scandinavian states to the north.

In the 12th century the Valdemar dynasty fortified the town, building a castle and

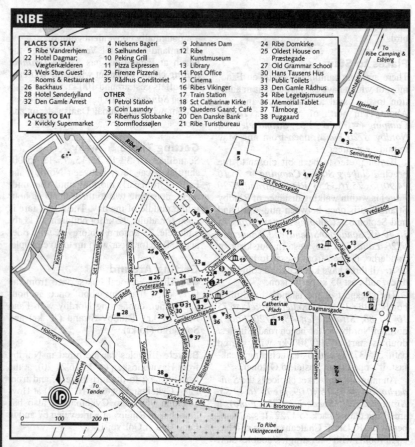

RIBE

PLACES TO STAY
5 Ribe Vandrerhjem
22 Hotel Dagmar;
    Vægterkælderen
23 Weis Stue Guest
    Rooms & Restaurant
26 Backhaus
28 Hotel Sønderjylland
32 Den Gamle Arrest

PLACES TO EAT
2 Kvickly Supermarket
4 Nielsens Bageri
8 Sælhunden
10 Peking Grill
11 Pizza Expressen
29 Firenze Pizzeria
35 Rådhus Conditoriet

OTHER
1 Petrol Station
3 Coin Laundry
6 Riberhus Slotsbanke
7 Stormflodssøjlen
9 Johannes Dam
12 Ribe
    Kunstmuseum
13 Library
14 Post Office
15 Cinema
16 Ribes Vikinger
17 Train Station
18 Sct Catharinæ Kirke
19 Quedens Gaard; Café
20 Den Danske Bank
21 Ribe Turistbureau

24 Ribe Domkirke
25 Oldest House on
    Præstegade
27 Old Grammar School
30 Hans Tausens Hus
31 Public Toilets
33 Den Gamle Rådhus
34 Ribe Legetøjsmuseum
36 Memorial Tablet
37 Tårnborg
38 Puggaard

establishing Ribe as one of the king's Jutland residences.

During the late medieval period, as power shifted to eastern Denmark, Ribe's importance declined. In 1580 a sweeping fire destroyed a third of the town's buildings and, in the century that followed, the incessant wars with Sweden strangled trade and further impoverished the town. Meanwhile the Ribe Å silted up and the town's population began to drop off. With the founding of the port city of Esbjerg in 1868, Ribe was completely bypassed as a trade centre.

Ironically, in terms of town preservation, Ribe's economic misfortunes have served to spare its historic buildings from modernisation. As a result the town centre, which surrounds an imposing medieval cathedral, retains a unique centuries-old character. With its crooked cobbled streets and half-timbered 16th century houses, Ribe is a bit like a living history museum. Indeed, the entire old town is a preservation zone, with more than 100 buildings registered by the National Trust.

Orientation

Ribe is a tightly clustered place, easy to explore. Everything, including Ribe Vandrerhjem and the train station, is within a 10 minute walk of Torvet, the central square.

Information

Tourist Office The helpful Ribe Turistbureau (☎ 75 42 15 00, fax 75 42 40 78), Torvet 3, 6760 Ribe, is conveniently located on Torvet. Between 15 June and 31 August it's open from 9.30 am to 5.30 pm Monday to Friday, from 9.30 am to 5 pm on Saturday and from 10 am to 2 pm on Sunday. During the rest of the year it's open from 9 am to 5 pm Monday to Friday (9.30 am to 4.30 pm between November and March) and from 10 am to 1 pm on Saturday.

Money Den Danske Bank is on Overdammen, just east of Torvet. It's open from 9.30 am to 4 pm on weekdays, except on Thursday when it closes at 6 pm. It has an outdoor ATM.

Post The post office, at Sct Nicolajgade 12, is open from 10 am to 5 pm Monday to Friday (to 5.30 pm on Thursday) and from 10 am to noon on Saturday.

Laundry There's a coin laundry by the Kvickly supermarket at Seminarievej 1.

Walking Tour

You can visit central Ribe's historic sights on a leisurely looped walk that takes a couple of hours.

The walk begins at Torvet and follows Overdammen east to Fiskergade, where you turn left. On Fiskergade you'll notice many alleys leading east to the riverfront. Take a look at the 'bumper' stones on the house corners; the alleys are so narrow that the original residents installed these stones to protect their houses from being scraped by the wheels of horse-drawn carriages.

At the intersection of Fiskergade and Skibbroen you'll find **Stormflodssøjlen**, a wooden flood column commemorating the numerous floods that have swept over Ribe. Note the ring at the top of the column indicating the water's depth (6m above normal!) during the record flood of 1634 which claimed hundreds of lives. Although these days low-lying Ribe is afforded more protection by a system of dikes, residents are still subject to periodic evacuation.

Continue north-west along Skibbroen, which skirts the old medieval quay, now lined with small motorboats. Here you'll also find the **Johanne Dan**, a replica of an 1867 sailing ship designed with a flat bottom that allowed it to sail the shallow waters of the Ribe Å; it's sometimes open for boarding.

From Skibbroen turn south onto Korsbrødregade and then head south-east on Præstegade. About halfway down on the right, you'll pass this street's **oldest house**, constructed in 1580, as noted on the plaque above the door; it was once the residence of the cathedral curate. Continue back to **Ribe Domkirke**, skirting around its western side and onto Skolegade.

On the corner of Skolegade and Grydergade is an **old grammar school** that first opened in the early 16th century. On the opposite side of Skolegade is the two storey **Hans Tausens Hus**, which dates from the early 17th century and is one of Denmark's oldest bishops' residences. A **statue** of Hans Tausen, who helped to spark the Danish Reformation, stands opposite in the churchyard.

From Skolegade continue south on Puggårdsgade, a cobbled street lined with older homes. The timber-framed **brick house** on the corner of Sønderportsgade and Puggårdsgade has an interesting 2nd storey that overhangs the road. A couple of buildings down on the left is **Tårnborg**, a 16th century manor house that now serves as a local government office. On the same side of the street, but a little farther south, is a half-timbered house dating back to 1550.

When you reach Gravsgade go right for about 50m and on the northern side of the street you'll find the brick **Puggaard**, a canon's residence constructed in about 1500. From there turn around and walk east on Gravsgade, then turn north onto Bispegade.

On the corner of Bispegade and Sønderportsgade you'll find a **memorial tablet** to Maren Spliid, burned at the stake on 9 November 1641, one of the last victims of Denmark's witch-hunt persecutions.

From that corner continue north past **Den Gamle Rådhus** (the Old Town Hall) and back to your starting point on Torvet, where you can finish off your walk with a frosty beer or an ice cream.

Ribe Domkirke

The town's dominant landmark, Ribe Cathedral, stands as a fine testament to Ribe's prominent past. The diocese of Ribe was founded in 948 but its original cathedral was a modest wooden building. In 1150 Ribe's Bishop Elias, with the financial backing of the royal family, began work on a more stately stone structure.

The new cathedral was constructed primarily from tufa, a soft porous rock quarried near Cologne and shipped north along the Rhine. It took a century for the work to reach completion. Although later additions included a number of Gothic features, the core of the cathedral remains decidedly Romanesque, a fine example of medieval Rhineland influences.

One notable feature is the original 'Cat's Head' door at the south portal of the transept, which boasts detailed relief work including a triangular pediment portraying Valdemar II and Queen Dagmar positioned at the feet of Jesus and Mary. At noon and 3 pm the cathedral bell plays the notes to a folk song about Dagmar's death during childbirth.

The interior décor is a hotchpotch of later influences. Among the highlights are an organ with a façade designed by the renowned 17th century sculptor Jens Olufsen and an ornate altar created in 1597 by Odense sculptor Jens Asmussen. You can find frescoes dating from the 16th century along the northern side of the cathedral, while in the apse are modern-day frescoes, stained-glass windows and seven mosaics created in the 1980s by artist Carl-Henning Pedersen.

For a towering view of the countryside, climb 27m up the cathedral tower, which dates back to 1333. A survey of the surrounding marshland makes it easy to understand why the tower once doubled as a lookout station for floods.

Ribe Domkirke is open from 10 am to 6 pm between June and August, from 10 am to 5 pm in May and September and from 11 am to 3 or 4 pm during the rest of the year. On Sunday and holidays throughout the year it opens at noon. The admission charge of 10 kr (children 3 kr) covers both the cathedral and the tower.

Sct Catharinæ Kirke

St Catherine's Church, about a five minute walk east of Torvet, was founded by Spanish Black Friars in 1228. The original church, built on reclaimed marshland, eventually collapsed and the present structure dates back to the 15th century. Of the 13 churches built in Ribe during the pre-Reformation period, Sct Catharinæ Kirke and Ribe Domkirke are the only survivors.

Sepulchral Monuments

In the Renaissance period, arranging for burial inside Ribe Domkirke became trendy among those wealthy enough to afford the floor space. Most of these graves are marked by simple carved stones in the aisles, but there are also more ostentatious memorials and chapels containing the remains of bishops and other distinguished citizens of the day. The highest ranked bones within the confines of the cathedral are those of King Christopher I, who was buried in 1259 directly beneath the great dome in the middle of the sanctuary.

In 1536 the Reformation forced the friars to abandon Sct Catharinæ Kirke and, in the years that followed, the compound served as, among other things, an asylum for the mentally ill and a wartime field hospital. The abbey is currently used as housing for the elderly.

In the 1920s Sct Catharinæ Kirke was restored at tremendous cost (due to its still-faulty foundations) and in 1932 it was reconsecrated. It boasts a delicately carved pulpit dating back to 1591 and an ornate altarpiece created in 1650. Sct Catharinæ Kirke is open from 10 am to noon and from 2 to 5 pm (to 4 pm in winter). Admission to the church itself is free; entry to the adjacent garden courtyard costs 3 kr.

Den Gamle Rådhus

This building, opposite the south-eastern corner of Ribe Domkirke, dates back to 1496, making it the oldest town hall in Denmark. In addition to being the site of council meetings it also houses a small collection of historical artefacts, including medieval weapons and an executioner's axe.

Before entering the rådhus, take a look at the highest point of its gable, which doubles as a nesting site for a pair of storks. It's open from 1 to 3 pm daily in summer and on weekdays only in May and September. Admission costs 15 kr (children 5 kr).

Quedens Gaard

On the corner of Overdammen and Sortebrødregade, this history museum is in a half-timbered former merchant's house, the oldest wing of which was built in 1583. Part of the house retains merchants' furnishings from the early 17th century; other rooms exhibit furniture and crafts from earlier periods plus trade and industry displays from more recent times. Between June and August it's open from 10 am to 5 pm daily; during the rest of the year it's open from 11 am to 3 pm (to 1 pm in midwinter) daily except Monday. Admission costs 20 kr (children 5 kr).

Stork Watch

A look at the top of Den Gamle Rådhus (the Old Town Hall) in Ribe will reward you with the rare sight of a large round nest built of sticks and reaching a couple of metres in diameter. Each year around the first of April a pair of storks returns to this nest. In the summer of 1998, reversing an infertile run, the pair produced four chicks. It is believed that in all of Denmark there are only eight pairs of nesting storks – so the multiple birth was celebrated by Ribe residents, who enthusiastically follow the comings and goings of these great birds each year.

Ribes Vikinger

The Vikings of Ribe, opposite the train station, is a well-presented 2500 sq metre museum featuring informative displays on Ribe's Viking and medieval history.

One exhibition hall reproduces a marketplace in 800 AD, complete with a cargo-laden Viking ship, while another hall has a late-medieval scene set in the town centre. There are also many interesting archaeological finds including pottery shards, glass and amber beads and an anchor from a Viking ship. Facilities include a museum shop and a café serving light eats. It's open from 10 am to 5 pm between 1 June and mid-September and from 10 am to 4 pm during the rest of the year (closed on Monday in winter). Admission costs 40 kr (children 15 kr).

Ribe Vikingecenter

The Ribe Vikingecenter, 3km south of the town centre at Lustrupvej 4, is affiliated with Ribes Vikinger. Open in summer only, the Vikingecenter has attempted to recreate a slice of life in Viking-era Ribe using various reconstructions, including a 34m Fyrkat-style longhouse. The staff, who dress in period clothing, cook over open fires and demonstrate Viking-era crafts such as pottery and leatherwork. There are also frequent demonstrations of the art of falconry involving various birds of prey.

Ribe Vikingecenter is open from 11 am to 4 pm daily except Monday between mid-May and late September. Admission costs 40 kr (children 15 kr).

Ribe Kunstmuseum

Housed in a 19th century villa at Sct Nicolajgade 10, Ribe Kunstmuseum is one of the oldest art museums in Denmark and has consequently acquired a good collection, particularly of works by the 19th century Danish 'Golden Age' painters. Exhibits include works by Abildgaard, Juel, Eckersberg, Købke and Lundbye. Among the museum's more notable paintings is Michael Ancher's *Barnedåb I Skagens Kirke* (Christening in Skagen Church). The museum is open from 11 am to 5 pm daily between mid-June and 31 August and from 1 to 4 pm Tuesday to Sunday during the rest of the year. Admission costs 30 kr (children aged under 16 free).

Other Attractions

A costumed **night watchman** makes his rounds from Torvet at 8 and 10 pm between June and August and you can follow him as he sings his way through the old streets. The tour starts in front of the Weis Stue restaurant and proceeds south from Torvet. It's an unabashedly touristy scene that's both fun and free. In May and during the first half of September the watchman makes the rounds once each night at 10 pm.

Ribe Legetøjsmuseum, just south-east of Ribe Domkirke, features a collection of 19th and 20th century antique toys, including porcelain dolls. It's open from 10 am to 5 pm daily in summer and in the afternoon only in winter. Admission costs 30 kr (children 15 kr).

Riberhus Slotsbanke, 1km north-west of the town centre, is the moated site of a former 12th century royal castle; it served as a fort until the 17th century and was then dismantled for its stones. In the south-western corner of the grounds is a statue of Queen Dagmar.

Places to Stay

Camping The nearest camping ground is *Ribe Camping* (☎ 75 41 07 77, fax 75 41 00 01, email ribe@dk-camp.dk, Farupvej 2, 6760 Ribe), in a field about 2km north of Ribe centre. A three star facility, it's open year-round and has a dozen insulated cabins. There's a laundry room, a TV lounge, a food kiosk and a cafeteria.

Hostel The modern 140 bed *Ribe Vandrerhjem* (☎ 75 42 06 20, fax 75 42 42 88, email ribedanh@post5.tele.dk, Sct Pedersgade 16, 6760 Ribe) has helpful management, comfortable rooms and an ideal location; it overlooks a quiet marsh and is within walking distance of the main sights. Dorm beds in a four or five bed room cost 90 kr. Private rooms cost 205/250 kr for singles/doubles, 300/350 kr for

You can follow Ribe's night watchman as he makes his rounds of the historic town.

triples/quads. All rooms have a bath and many are accessible to people in wheelchairs. Common facilities include a kitchen, sitting areas and a TV lounge. Breakfast is available for 40 kr. This is a popular hostel, so advance reservations are recommended. It's open to individual travellers from 1 February to 30 November.

Private Rooms Ribe Turistbureau provides a brochure listing about 20 *rooms* in private homes in the Ribe area. Some are in the town centre, others are on the outskirts and you will require your own transport to get to them. Rates are around 200/300 kr for singles/doubles in Ribe centre, 175/250 kr for places a few kilometres outside town. You can make the booking yourself or, for 20 kr, staff at the turistbureau will call around and find a place for you.

Hotels & Inns *Hotel Sønderjylland* (☎ 75 42 04 66, Sønderportsgade 22, 6760 Ribe), 300m west of Torvet, has five rooms above a small family-run pub. They vary a bit, but the rooms are generally old-fashioned with lace curtains in the skylights and bathrooms down the hall. Singles/doubles cost 250/450 kr including breakfast.

There are also two restaurants in town that rent similar 2nd storey rooms. *Weis Stue* (☎ 75 42 07 00, Torvet) has the lowest rates: singles/doubles cost 200/400 kr. *Backhaus* (☎ 75 42 11 01, Grydergade 12) has a fresh coat of paint and charges 250/500 kr. Rates at both places include breakfast.

The most unusual place to stay is *Den Gamle Arrest* (☎ 75 42 37 00, fax 75 42 37 22, Torvet 11, 6760 Ribe), in the old jailhouse opposite Ribe Domkirke. Originally built as a curate's residence, it was converted to a jail in 1893 and continued to serve that function until 1989. In 1992 it was renovated and converted into an 11 room hotel. There's a certain austere quaintness in entering your room through the old steel doors but, as might be expected, converted jail cells make rather cramped quarters. Rooms with individual washbasins, but with a shared bathroom off the hall, cost

from 370/490 kr for singles/doubles, while those with bath start at 520/640 kr. Rates include breakfast.

The red-brick *Hotel Dagmar* (☎ 75 42 00 33, fax 75 42 36 52, Torvet 1, 6760 Ribe), in the centre of Ribe east of Ribe Domkirke, dates back to 1581, giving credence to its claim of being the oldest hotel in Denmark. Carefully restored to retain its period character, it has 50 rooms with bath, TV, phone and minibar. Singles/doubles start at 695/895 kr including breakfast.

Places to Eat

On Nederdammen there's *Pizza Expressen*, which has long hours and serves large slices of pizza costing 20 kr, and *Peking Grill*, which offers good Chinese meals costing 39 kr; it's open from 11 am to 9 pm.

A pleasant sit-down Italian restaurant is *Firenze Pizzeria (Skolegade 6)*, open from noon to 10.30 pm. Pizza and pasta dishes start at 55 kr.

For a delightful old-fashioned dining experience try *Weis Stue*, a leaning half-timbered tavern with wooden plank tables, dating back to 1704. You can get a Danish beef plate throughout the day (85 kr); various dinner specials start at 125 kr.

Quedens Gaard Café (Overdammen 10), at the side of Quedens Gaard, has both indoor and pavement dining areas and is a pleasant place for light eats such as sandwiches or soup with bread (around 30 kr), as well as coffee and cappuccino.

Sælhunden (Skibbroen 13), opposite the harbour, offers generous servings of good Danish food. At this popular restaurant seafood and steak dishes cost around 100 kr at dinner, less at lunchtime. The fried plaice with shrimp and mussels (126 kr) is the local favourite. The kitchen is open from noon to 9.45 pm; on clear summer days you can dine outdoors.

The historic Hotel Dagmar has an elegant, expensive main dining room as well as a more affordable basement restaurant, *Vægterkælderen*, which shares the same kitchen but has less fastidious service and a simpler menu. In the basement light dishes cost around 85 kr, but the best deal is the 500g spareribs plate (99 kr) that can easily feed two. Vægterkælderen has an engaging atmosphere and is a popular spot for a relaxing drink. The kitchen is open from noon to 10 pm.

There's an *Underground Ice Cream stand* in Torvet near Hotel Dagmar in summer, when there are also simple café tables set up on the square where you can sit and enjoy a cold beer.

Rådhus Conditoriet, a couple of minutes walk south-east from Torvet at Hundegade 2, serves good takeaway and eat-in bakery items as well as coffee and simple eats. There's another bakery, *Nielsens Bageri*, and a *Kvickly* supermarket on Saltgade, in the same neighbourhood as Ribe Vandrerhjem.

Getting There & Away
Train Trains from Ribe run hourly on weekdays and slightly less frequently at weekends to Esbjerg (35 kr, 35 minutes) and Tønder (49 kr, 50 minutes).

Car & Motorcycle Ribe is 30km south of Esbjerg via route 24 and 47km north of Tønder via route 11.

Getting Around
Car & Motorcycle There's parking with a two hour limit at the southern side of Ribe Domkirke, parking with a three hour limit at Ribes Vikinger and parking with no time limit at the end of Sct Pedersgade near Ribe Vandrerhjem.

Bicycle Bicycles can be hired from Ribe Vandrerhjem; they cost 50 kr per day.

RØMØ
Rømø, the largest Danish island in the North Sea, extends 17km from north to south and about 6km across. Lying off the coast midway between Ribe and Tønder, it's connected to the Jutland mainland by a 10km causeway that passes over scenic marshland with grazing sheep and wading water birds. The causeway has a cycle lane.

For more than a hundred years Rømø, just 5km north of Sylt, Germany, has been a popular summer resort for German tourists, although in the low season it is a windswept sleeper.

The western side of the island, exposed to the North Sea, is lined with expansive sandy beaches that attract scores of windsurfers. The busiest beach area is at Lakolk, on the central west coast.

Lakolk 'village' is essentially a large strip-mall shopping centre and a camping

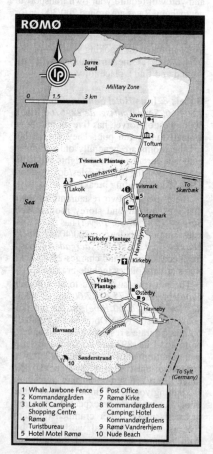

1 Whale Jawbone Fence	6 Post Office
2 Kommandørgården	7 Rømø Kirke
3 Lakolk Camping;	8 Kommandørgårdens
Shopping Centre	Camping; Hotel
4 Rømø	Kommandørgårdens
Turistbureau	9 Rømø Vandrerhjem
5 Hotel Motel Rømø	10 Nude Beach

ground on the inland side of the dunes. Although Lakolk is separated from the beach by just 100m, the beach itself is more than a kilometre wide, so it's a pretty hefty walk over the sand flats to the water's edge, particularly at low tide. Some people drive out, but be careful not to park your car in an incoming tide zone.

Despite a few unsightly caravan parking areas, most of Rømø is a rural scene with thatched houses, open spaces and the scent of the sea heavy in the air. The main settlements are on the east coast in the 7km stretch from the causeway bridge south to the harbourside village of Havneby.

Rømø is rich in birdlife and its west coast also provides a habitat for about 1500 seals, which haul themselves onto sandbanks to sunbathe during the day. The north-western corner of the island is a restricted military zone.

Information

Tourist Office The Rømø Turistbureau (☎ 74 75 51 30, fax 74 75 50 31), Havnebyvej 30, Tvismark, 6792 Rømø, is on the eastern side of the island, 1km south of the causeway. It's open from 9 am to 5 pm Monday to Saturday and from 10 am to 4 pm on Sunday (closed Sundays in winter). The Web site is at www.romo.dk.

Money There's a branch of Den Danske Bank west of Havneby harbour at Skansen 5 and another bank on the main road about 500m from the harbour.

Post The post office, 2km south of the causeway in Kongsmark, is open from 9 to 11 am and 1 to 4 pm Monday to Friday and from 9 am to noon on Saturday.

Things to See

Kommandørgården, a handsome sea captain's house dating back to 1748, retains much of its original décor, including 4000 Dutch wall tiles, and has displays on local history which, in Rømø, is strongly tied to the sea. In the 18th century a disproportionately high number of Rømø men served

as *kommandører* (sea captains) on German and Dutch whaling ships that hunted in the waters off Greenland. The museum (admission 15 kr), 1.5km north of the causeway at Juvrevej 60, is open Tuesday to Sunday from 10 am to 6 pm between May and September and from 10 am to 3 pm in October.

Another remnant of the whaling era, a **whale jawbone fence**, can be found 1km farther north on the eastern side of the main road in the village of Juvre.

At the rear of Rømø Turistbureau is a small **nature centre** (admission 15 kr) with modest displays on island flora and fauna. It's open from 10 am to 4 pm daily between May and October; hours are more limited in the winter. In summer the centre conducts **ecology tours** in Danish and German.

The island's 18th century church, **Rømø Kirke**, is on the main road in Kirkeby, about midway between Havneby and the causeway. It's noted for its unique Greenlandic gravestones erected by sea captains and decorated with reliefs of their boats and families; these stones can be seen lining the northern wall of the churchyard.

Walking

The inland section of this flat island has trails through both heathered moors and wooded areas, offering quiet hiking spots. There are three forest zones, each with a couple of kilometres of trails: Tvismark Plantage, along Vesterhavsvej, the main east-west road; Kirkeby Plantage, to the west of Kirkeby; and Vråby Plantage, a less diverse area dominated by pines, about 1km farther south.

Water Sports

Water activities are based largely along the west coast, with the main **windsurfing** zone south of Lakolk. Almost all windsurfers arrive with their own equipment so hired gear is not usually available, but try inquiring at the turistbureau or at Lakolk Camping.

There's a **nudist beach** in the Sønderstrand area, at the south-western tip of the island; to reach it, take Søndersvej to its western end, from where it's a 2km hike across the sand flats to the ocean.

Places to Stay

Lakolk Camping (☎ *74 75 52 28, fax 74 75 53 52, Lakolk, 6792 Rømø)*, on the west coast beach at Lakolk, charges 46 kr per person and is open from early April to mid-October. It also has some four-person huts costing 275 kr per day in the low season, 400 kr from late June to mid-August.

Kommandørgårdens Camping (☎ *74 75 51 22, fax 74 75 59 22)* in Østerby, adjacent to and managed by the hotel of the same name, charges 42 kr per person and is open year-round. Both places are three-star camping grounds with full facilities and have food shops and restaurants nearby.

The 91 bed *Rømø Vandrerhjem* (☎ *74 75 51 88, fax 74 75 51 87, Lyngvejen 7, 6792 Rømø)*, on the south-eastern side of the island near Havneby, is in a traditional building with a thatched roof. It's open from 15 March to 1 November and has dorm beds for 90 kr; double rooms cost 180 kr.

Hotel Motel Rømø (☎ *74 75 51 14, Gamle Færegevej 1, 6792 Rømø)*, 1km south of the turistbureau, is a simple motel-style place where good-value singles/doubles with bath cost 345/395 kr including breakfast.

Hotel Kommandørgårdens (☎ *74 75 51 22, fax 74 75 59 22, email info@komman doergaarden.dk, Havnebyvej 201, 6792 Rømø)* in Østerby is the biggest hotel on the island, with 80 units. Single or double rooms with bath cost 695 kr in the summer high season; singles/doubles start at 350/500 at other times, including breakfast. There are also huts and apartments costing from 1500 to 4500 kr per week, depending on the size and season. The hotel has a large pool, restaurants, tennis courts and a minimarket.

The vast majority of Rømø's accommodation is found in some 1300 *summer houses* scattered around the island. Prices vary, with rates for a simple six person, cabin-like place ranging from 1400 to 3000 kr per week, depending on the season.

A ritzier chalet would cost roughly twice that. The turistbureau can provide a catalogue with photos and prices of the houses and staff there can handle the bookings. Another agency specialising in summer rentals is Dansk Familieferie (☎ 74 75 55 00, fax 74 75 55 66), Søvej 2, 6792 Rømø.

Places to Eat

There are a couple of fast-food places near the harbour in Havneby but a better choice is the nearby *Rømø Røgeri* at Nordre Havnevej, which sells smoked herring and cooked shrimp by weight and has a small café with reasonably priced fish dishes. *Europa*, on Vestergade in Havneby, serves pizzas, other Italian food and Greek dishes at moderate prices. There's an all-natural *Underground Ice Cream kiosk* opposite Europa.

There's a *grocery shop* and a *bakery* in Østerby, within walking distance of Rømø Vandrerhjem. At *Café Therese*, in Hotel Kommandørgårdens in Østerby, burgers cost 35 kr and pizzas cost around 50 kr; there's live folk music on summer nights. There's also a more expensive sit-down restaurant in the hotel.

There's a *supermarket*, a *bakery* and numerous *eateries* at the shopping centre fronting Lakolk Camping; these include hot-dog stands, a café, a pizzeria and a cafeteria.

Getting There & Away

Bus No 29 runs from Skærbæk to Havneby (10 kr, 35 minutes) about once an hour on weekdays, less frequently at weekends. From Skærbæk there are trains to Ribe (35 kr, 19 minutes), Tønder (43 kr, 28 minutes) and Esbjerg (78 kr, 1 hour) about once an hour.

Rømø is 14km west of the town of Skærbæk, on route 175. It's a 30 minute drive on route 11 to either Ribe or Tønder.

The Rømø-Sylt Linie (☎ 73 75 53 03) operates car ferries between Havneby and the German island of Sylt (31 kr, one hour) several times each day.

Getting Around

Bus From late May to early September bus No 29/591 makes a 20 minute trip from Havneby up the east coast road and over to Lakolk. There are about 10 runs on weekdays and four at weekends. It costs 10 kr to go anywhere on the island.

Bicycle The best choice, if you don't have your own transport, is to rent a bicycle, as Rømø is notably flat and small enough to explore. You can hire bikes from the grocery shop opposite Lakolk Camping in Lakolk, from Garni at Nørre Frankel 15 in Havneby and at Hotel Kommandørgårdens in Østerby. The rate is 45/270 kr per day/week at Hotel Kommandørgårdens, 30/150 kr at the other two places.

TØNDER

Tønder, just 4km north of the German border, is an historic town that retains a few curving cobblestone streets lined with half-timbered houses.

Tønder's town charter was issued in 1243. Although it's surrounded by marshland today, it was once a busy market town with access to the sea. Because it's low-lying, Tønder has always been subject to serious flooding and in medieval times it was nearly swept away altogether. In the 16th century a network of dikes was erected to protect the town from flooding but the dikes also contributed to the alteration of the tidal flats and the seas eventually receded, leaving the town landlocked.

By the 18th century Tønder was again prospering: it had become the centre of a high-quality lace-making industry which, at its peak, employed some 12,000 workers in the greater Tønder area. Many of the town's finest houses were erected by wealthy lace merchants.

These days the high point of Tønder's year is the last weekend of August when the Tønder Festival (☎ 74 72 46 10), one of Denmark's largest folk festivals, attracts a multitude of international and Danish musicians for more than 40 concerts. The Web site is at www.tf.dk.

Information

The Tønder Turistbureau (☎ 74 72 12 20, fax 74 72 09 00) is in the centre of town at Torvet 1, 6270 Tønder. Between 15 June and 31 August it's open from 9.30 am to 5.30 pm on weekdays and from 9.30 am to 3 pm on Saturday; during the rest of the year it's open from 9 am to 4 pm on weekdays and from 9 am to noon on Saturday.

There are a couple of banks near Torvet, the central square. The post office is at Vestergade 83, a few minutes walk north of the train station.

Things to See & Do

Some of the town's most picturesque streets lined with period houses are off Søndergade, just a couple of minutes walk south of Torvet. The best-preserved is the cobbled Uldgade.

Tønder Museum exhibits objects relating to regional history, including a collection of delicate Tønder lace, period furniture and Dutch wall tiles. The adjacent **Sønderjyllands Kunstmuseum** (South Jutland Art Museum) features Danish surrealist and modern art, mostly by lesser-known artists. Both are at Kongevej 55, a 10 minute walk east of the train station, and are open Tuesday to Sunday from 10 am to 5 pm between May and October and from 1 to 5 pm in winter. Admission to both museums costs 30 kr.

Kristkirken, the large church on the northeastern side of Torvet, dates back to the late 16th century. The 47.5m-high tower, part of an earlier church that once stood on this site, doubled as a navigational marker in the days when Tønder was connected to the sea. The church interior boasts some impressive carvings and paintings, including a font from 1350, a pulpit from 1586 and a series of memorial tablets from around 1600. It's open from 10 am to 4 pm Monday to Saturday.

Det Gamle Apotek, on Torvet at Østergade 1, is noted mainly for its elaborate 1671 Baroque doorway which is flanked by two lions. Also worth a look is the old-fashioned interior, which was converted from a pharmacy to a gift shop just a decade ago.

You can hire **paddle boats and canoes** on the river near the Hostrups Hotel.

Places to Stay

Tønder Campingplads (☎/*fax 74 72 18 49, Holmevej 2, 6270 Tønder*), east of the town centre and adjacent to the hostel, is a three star facility with a coin laundry, cooking facilities, a food kiosk and cabins and bicycles for hire. It's open from 1 April to 1 October and is part of Tønder Fritidscenter (sports centre), which includes tennis courts, a swimming pool and squash courts.

Tønder Vandrerhjem (☎ *74 72 35 00, fax 74 72 27 97, Sønderport 4, 6270 Tønder)* is to the east of the town centre, about a 15 minute walk from the train station and just five minutes from Torvet. This hostel is a rather nondescript place but the rooms are comfortable, with four beds and a bathroom. Dorm beds cost 90 kr and singles/doubles cost 175/250 kr. It's open to individuals from 1 February to 30 November. There's a guest kitchen and bicycles for hire.

The turistbureau can provide a list of *rooms* in private homes in the Tønder area, which cost an average of 150/225 kr for singles/doubles. Some are in the centre, others on the outskirts.

The older *Hostrups Hotel* (☎ *74 72 21 29, fax 74 72 07 26, Søndergade 30, 6270 Tønder)*, a few minutes walk south-east of Torvet, has 23 rooms, most with bath, desk and TV. Singles cost from 380 to 575 kr, doubles from 490 to 700 kr.

Hotel Tønderhus (☎ *74 72 22 22, fax 74 72 05 92, Jomfrustien 1, 6270 Tønder)*, opposite Tønder Museum, is a modern brick building with 50 standard motel-style rooms with bath, TV and phone. Singles/doubles start at 475/575 kr including breakfast.

Places to Eat

Choices are limited and many people simply drive south to Germany where food is cheaper. Otherwise your best bet for restaurants is to look around Torvet.

Torve Bistroen, a café on Torvet, serves fish and chips, vegetarian omelettes and pasta for around 40 kr, as well as smørrebrød, burgers and salads. In the same building is *Torvets Restaurant*, an appealing place with a varied menu of meat and fish dishes costing around 100 kr. A short walk east of Torvet is *Pizzeria Italiano* (*Østergade 40*), where good pizza and pasta dishes start at around 60 kr. Immediately west of the pizzeria is a *bakery*. For cheap eats there's *Spisehuset Asian* (*Østergade 37*), offering Chinese dishes for 42 kr and some inexpensive grilled items.

Hagge's Musik Pub (*Vestergade 80*), opposite the post office, serves 'pub grub' and Danish and Irish draught beer; it's also a popular venue for live music, especially folk, blues and jazz.

There's a *market* selling fruit, vegetables and cheese at Torvet on Tuesday and Friday mornings and a *Fakta* grocery shop on Kongevej, opposite the post office.

Getting There & Away

Tønder is on route 11, 4km north of the border with Germany and 77km south of Esbjerg.

The train station is on the western side of town, 1km from Torvet via Vestergade. Trains run hourly on weekdays and slightly less frequently at weekends from Ribe (49 kr, 50 minutes) and Esbjerg (71 kr, 1½ hours).

MØGELTØNDER

If you're in the Tønder area, don't leave without first visiting the fetching village of Møgeltønder.

The centre of the village is the cobbled main street Slotsgade, lined with period brick houses sporting thatched roofs and colourful wooden doors. At the western end of Slotsgade is **Schackenborg**, a small castle that was presented by the Crown to Field Marshal Hans Schack in 1661 following his victory over the Swedes in the battle of Nyborg. Members of the Schack family occupied the castle until 1978, when it was returned to the Crown.

Since their marriage in 1995, Queen Margrethe's youngest son, Prince Joachim, and his wife, Princess Alexandra, have made Schackenborg their primary residence. Although the castle building is off limits to the public, the moat-surrounded grounds on the opposite side of the street have been turned into a small public park that's open to all.

At the eastern end of Slotsgade is **Møgeltønder Kirke**, which has one of the most lavish church interiors in Denmark. The Romanesque nave dates back to 1180 and the baptismal font is from 1200, but the church has had numerous additions – the Gothic choir vaults were built in the 13th century, the tower dates from 1500 and the chapel on the northern side was added in 1763.

The interior is rich in frescoes, gallery paintings and ceiling drawings. Here too is one of the oldest church pipe organs in Denmark, dating back to 1679. The elaborately detailed gilt altar dates back to the 16th century; it's flanked by a 17th century pulpit and a 'countess bower', a balcony with private seating for the Schack family, who owned the church from 1661 until 1970. Møgeltønder Kirke is open from 8 am to 5 pm daily between May and September, and from 9 am to 4 pm during the rest of the year.

Places to Stay & Eat

The *Schackenborg Slotskro* (☎ 74 73 83 83, fax 74 73 83 11, Slotsgaden 42, 6270 Tønder), in the village centre, has 11 comfortable but pricey rooms starting at 750/900 kr for singles/doubles. It has a small pavement café and an upmarket Danish restaurant.

There's a small *shop* at the western end of Slotsgade selling bakery items, ice cream and snack foods.

Getting There & Away

Møgeltønder is 4km west of Tønder on route 419.

Bus No 66 connects Tønder with Møgeltønder about once an hour on weekdays, less frequently at weekends; it takes 10 minutes and costs 10 kr.

HØJER

If you're heading directly onwards to the island of Rømø from Møgeltønder you'll pass right through Højer, a rural market town that once served as a port for shipping south Jutland cattle. Constructed only a few metres above sea level, Højer is bordered by marshland and is protected by an extensive network of sluice gates and dikes, some of which date back to the 16th century.

Although it's not a must-see town, Højer does have some distinctive red-brick houses with thatched roofs and claims the only **thatched town hall** in Denmark. The main site of interest, in the centre of town next to the tourist office, is a nicely restored **Dutch windmill** from 1857 that houses a little local history museum.

If you're interested in **birdwatching**, the coastal marshland west of Højer is a rich habitat for wading birds, sea birds and shore birds.

Getting There & Away

Højer is on route 419, 7km west of Møgeltønder. The Højer-Tønder bus connects Højer with Møgeltønder (10 kr) and Tønder (20 kr) about hourly.

KOLDING

Kolding is Jutland's fifth largest city, with a population of 59,000. Despite its industrial outskirts, Kolding has a pleasant centre with a castle and a few other historic buildings.

Information

Tourist Office The Kolding Turistbureau (☎ 75 53 21 00, fax 75 53 48 38), Akseltorv 8, 6000 Kolding, is open from 9.30 am to 5.30 pm Monday to Saturday, except in the low season when it closes at 1 pm on Saturday. The turistbureau Web site is at www.sima.dk/kolding.

Money & Post There's a branch of Den Danske Bank on the southern side of Akseltorv and a post office at the train station.

Central Sights

Akseltorv, the central square, is the site of **Borchs Gård**, a decorative Renaissance building which dates from 1595. Pedestrian streets radiate out from Akseltorv. Helligkorsgade, a few minutes walk south of Akseltorv at the end of Østergade, is a pleasant street for a stroll; you'll find Kolding's **oldest house** at No 18, a lovely timber-framed affair built in 1589. Just west of Akseltorv, on the other side of the rådhus, is **Sankt Nicolai Kirke**, a medieval church that was largely rebuilt in the 19th century. It's not grandly interesting but it does have a late-16th century altar and pulpit; admission is free.

Koldinghus

The town's main landmark is Koldinghus, a castle fortress immediately north of Akseltorv. The first fortress on this site was built in 1268 by Erik V to guard the border between Denmark and the Duchy of Schleswig. The oldest parts of the current castle, the north and west wings, date from around 1440. The distinctive tower was added in around 1600 by Christian IV, who spent much of his childhood at Koldinghus.

In 1808 Spanish troops stationed at Koldinghus during the Napoleonic Wars tried to fight off the chilly Danish weather by building a roaring fire in one of the castle's hearths; the fire got out of hand, engulfing a defective chimney, and the castle went up in flames. Koldinghus was left in ruins until 1890, when the north wing was restored to house a museum. The work continued piecemeal over nearly a century and in 1935 the Christian IV tower was rebuilt. The exterior now has an 18th century Baroque appearance while the castle interior retains some original Gothic and Renaissance influences innovatively fused with modern Scandinavian architecture.

Koldinghus, which displays church sculpture, paintings, period furnishings and historic exhibits, including one on the Schleswig wars, can be toured from 10 am to 5 pm daily. Admission costs 40 kr (children under 16 free).

Kunstmuseet Trapholt

Kunstmuseet Trapholt, at Æblehaven 23, is on the eastern outskirts of the city on the northern side of the Kolding Fjord. Opened in 1988, this is one of Denmark's largest museums dedicated to 20th century art. The fine arts collection includes works by Richard Mortensen, Anna Archer, Franciska Clausen and Per Kirkeby. The applied arts section shows the influence of Danish design on ceramics, textiles and furniture. It's open from 10 am to 5 pm daily between May and September and in winter it's open from noon to 4 pm on weekdays and 10 am to 4 pm at weekends. Admission costs 30 kr (children free). Bus No 4 runs between the train station and the museum about every 20 minutes.

Places to Stay

Vonsild Camping & Feriecenter (☎ 75 52 13 88, fax 75 52 45 29, Vonsildvej 19, 6000 Kolding) is a three star camping ground on the southern outskirts of Kolding that's open year-round.

The 92 bed *Kolding Vandrerhjem* (☎ 75 50 91 40, fax 75 50 91 51, email koldingv @post2.tele.dk, Ørnsborgvej, 6000 Kolding) is 1km north-west of the city centre. Dorm beds cost 80 kr and rooms cost from 160 kr for singles to 480 kr for six people. It's open from 1 February to 1 December.

Saxildhus (☎ 75 52 12 00, fax 75 53 53 10, Banegårdspladsen, 6000 Kolding), opposite the train station, is an older hotel with modernised rooms. Most of its 96 rooms are comfortable and have bath, phone, TV and minibar. Singles/doubles start at 625/775 kr including breakfast.

Places to Eat

There's a *food kiosk* and a *DSB Café* at the train station but the main cluster of eateries is on Akseltorv. Take Jernbanegade west from the station and it's just a 10 minute walk to Akseltorv; en route you'll find a **Jensens Bøfhus** steak restaurant at Jernbanegade 11 and a good bakery, **Skov's Bageri**, at Jernbanegade 6.

At the pizzeria **Den Italienske** *(Akseltorv 5)* there's a pizza buffet costing 39 kr from 11.30 am to 4 pm or whole pizzas at any time, costing from 49 kr.

Café Paraplyen on Adelgade, just west of Akseltorv, is a pleasant family-run café serving cheap eats including sandwiches for 8 kr and lasagne with salad for 25 kr. Opposite the café there's a fast-food place selling burgers and chicken. On the western side of Akseltorv is a *fruit and veg shop*.

Getting There & Away
Bus Bus No 34 runs to Haderslev (22 kr, 45 minutes).

Train There are regular train services from Kolding south to Padborg on the German border (78 kr, 70 minutes) and north all the way to Frederikshavn (215 kr, four hours). There's a second line to Esbjerg (63 kr, 55 minutes). Trains run roughly hourly, except for services to Padborg (every two hours).

Car & Motorcycle Kolding is 92km east of Esbjerg and 82km north of the German border. The E20 (which continues east to Funen) and the E45 connect Kolding with other major towns in Jutland. If you're travelling leisurely by road north to south, route 170 is a pleasant alternative to the E45.

HADERSLEV
Haderslev, which has a population of about 30,000, is a likeable town at the head of the Haderslev Fjord. Established as a market town in the 13th century, it has a nicely restored centre. In addition to the fjord the town also borders a lake, Haderslev Dam, which offers some good canoeing opportunities.

Information
The Haderslev Turistbureau (☎ 74 52 55 50, fax 74 53 46 67), Honnøkajen 1, 6100 Haderslev, is on the town outskirts, 1km east of the centre. It's open from 9.30 am to 4.30 pm on weekdays and from 9.30 am to 2.30 pm on Saturday but keeps a letter box stocked with tourist brochures when it's closed.

The turistbureau goes a long way to welcome visitors. Every day in summer the office schedules an outing at 10 am. On some days it's a free guided walking tour of the town, on others there's a canoe trip on the lake, a fishing expedition or a visit to a local dairy farm. The cost of each of these is 50 kr for adults, 25 kr for children. For outings outside the town, you'll usually need your own transport.

There are five banks along Nørregade, including a Jyske Bank at No 16 and a branch of Den Danske Bank at No 23. The post office is at Gravene 8, to the north of the town centre.

Walking Tour
The town's oldest quarters, in the streets surrounding Torvet, can be easily explored in a short walking tour. Before you start, you may want to stop by the turistbureau to pick up the free English-language brochure *A Stroll Through the Old Part of the City*, which describes every nook and cranny along the way.

Begin at the southern end of Højgade – you'll find some of the nicest **period buildings** along this short street and on **Torvet**, a cobbled square bordered by half-timbered buildings and filled with sculptures by Erik Heide.

Just north of Torvet, you can take the rear entrance into **Haderslev Domkirke** (detailed in the following section).

After that, a short stroll to the north-east will bring you to **Ehlers-samlingen** at Slotsgade 20, a museum specialising in Danish pottery dating from the Middle Ages up to 1900, when the regional distinctions in Danish pottery styles began to erode. The museum is housed in an attractive timber-framed building dating back to 1577 that retains some of its original decorative painted wall panels. It's open from 10 am to 5 pm on weekdays and from 2 to 5 pm at

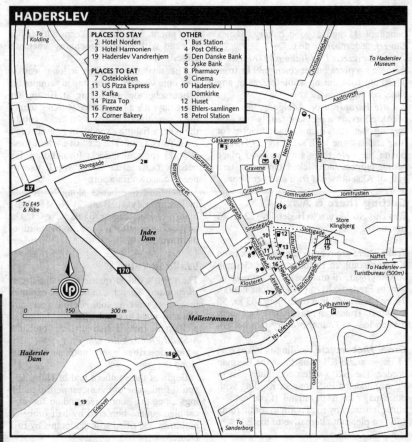

HADERSLEV

PLACES TO STAY
2 Hotel Norden
3 Hotel Harmonien
19 Haderslev Vandrerhjem

PLACES TO EAT
7 Osteklokken
11 US Pizza Express
13 Kafka
14 Pizza Top
16 Firenze
17 Corner Bakery

OTHER
1 Bus Station
4 Post Office
5 Den Danske Bank
6 Jyske Bank
8 Pharmacy
9 Cinema
10 Haderslev
   Domkirke
12 Huset
15 Ehlers-samlingen
18 Petrol Station

weekends; it's closed on Monday year-round and on Wednesday and Friday in the low season. Admission costs 10 kr.

If you return from Slotsgade via Store Klingbjerg and Lille Klingbjerg you'll pass by a few more handsome period houses.

Haderslev Domkirke

Haderslev's cathedral, on a knoll above Torvet, is the most imposing building in town. Parts of the building, including the transept and nave, date back to the mid-

13th century, while other additions were made in the centuries that followed. It's said that in 1525 it was the site of the first Lutheran teachings in Denmark.

Haderslev Domkirke has an impressive interior. Particularly notable is the altar, which has a crucifix dating back to about 1300 and alabaster figures of the 12 apostles created in around 1400. There's also a grand Sieseby organ and a baptismal font dating from 1485. The cathedral is open from 10 am to 5 pm (from 11.30 am on

Sunday) between May and September and from 10 am to 3 pm in winter; admission is free.

Haderslev Museum

This museum at Dalgade 7, 1km north-east of Torvet, features exhibits on southern Jutland's archaeological history as well as a small open-air museum with a windmill and a few other period buildings. It's closed on Monday but otherwise is open from 10 am to 4 pm between June and August and from 1 to 4 pm during the rest of the year. Admission costs 15 kr (children free).

Places to Stay

The 102 bed *Haderslev Vandrerhjem* (☎ 74 52 13 47, fax 74 52 13 64, Erlevvej 34, 6100 Haderslev) is about 1km south-west of the town centre, on the southern shore of the Haderslev Dam. Dorm beds cost 80 kr, while rooms cost from 145 kr for singles to 450 kr for six people. It's open from 1 February to 30 November and has a playground and canoes for hire.

At the 28 room *Hotel Harmonien* (☎ 74 52 37 20, fax 74 52 44 51, Gåskærgade 8, 6100 Haderslev) singles/doubles with bath, TV and phone cost 650/800 kr including breakfast. You can lower the cost of doubles to 720 kr by using an 'Inn Cheque,' which can be purchased at the turistbureau.

More upmarket is the 68 room *Hotel Norden* (☎ 74 52 40 30, fax 74 52 40 25, Storegade 55, 6100 Haderslev), about 500m north-west of Torvet. It has an indoor swimming pool and rooms with modern amenities including minibars and videos. Singles/doubles start at 725/825 kr. There's a bar, a restaurant and conference facilities.

Places to Eat

There are numerous places to grab a bite on or near Torvet, all of which are convenient for sightseeing.

Pizza Top, on the eastern side of Torvet, offers 30 kr pizzas as well as pitta-bread sandwiches, hot dogs and burgers. More upmarket is *Firenze*, on the southern side of Torvet, an Italian restaurant where pizza and pasta dishes cost 60 kr and meat and fish dishes cost about 120 kr.

On Nørregade, in the first block north of Torvet, you'll find *US Pizza Express*, which serves kebabs and pizza at moderate prices. Opposite, at Nørregade 6, is *Kafka*, a trendy alternative café serving good coffee and a variety of dishes costing 50 kr or less, including pasta, omelettes and chilli con carne.

On Apotekergade opposite the cathedral is *Osteklokken*, a substantial health food shop selling grocery items, fresh produce, cheeses and a full line of vitamins and teas. The *Corner Bakery*, a block south of Torvet on Lavgade, serves good pastries and filling brie baguettes (19 kr).

Huset (Nørregade 10), a music café just north of Kafka, serves up beer and wine with live rock and blues.

Getting There & Away

Bus Buses No 33 and 35 make the frequent 20 minute run between Haderslev and Vojens (20 kr), which has the nearest train station. Bus No 34 runs hourly between Haderslev and Kolding (22 kr), taking 45 minutes.

Train Services to Vojens, the nearest train station, run about hourly from Fredericia (43 kr, 45 minutes) and a bit less frequently from Sønderborg (43 kr, one hour).

Car & Motorcycle Haderslev is 31km south of Kolding via route 170 or the E45 and 51km east of Ribe via routes 24 and 47. There's a large free car park at the southern side of Sydhavnsvej with no time limit.

KRUSÅ & PADBORG

Kruså, an uneventful Danish outpost on the border with Germany, is lined with petrol stations and sex shops.

A more sombre landmark is found just west of Kruså at Padborg, the site of **Frøslevlejren** (Frøslev Camp), an internment camp opened near the end of WWII to detain members of the growing Danish

Resistance. Built to prevent the deportation of Danes across the border, Frøslevlejren held 12,000 prisoners during its nine months of operation.

The camp buildings now house a collection of displays and museums. The tower complex holds Frøslevlejrens Museum, which depicts the Danish Resistance movement and daily prison life at Frøslev, while other buildings house exhibits by Amnesty International, the United Nations and branches of the Danish defence forces. On a lighter note there's also an exhibit on local wildlife.

Frøslevlejrens Museum is open in the summer high season from 10 am to 5 pm daily and in the low season from 9 am to 4 pm Tuesday to Friday and 10 am to 5 pm on weekends; it's closed in December and January. Admission costs 25 kr. The camp's other exhibits are open from 9 am to 5 pm daily between April and October; admission to the UN museum costs 20 kr, the others are free.

Frøslevlejren is on the north-western outskirts of Padborg at Lejrvejen 83, 1km west of the E45 (take exit 76) and just 5km north of the German border.

SØNDERBORG

Sønderborg is an agreeable seaside town on the island of Als, with a population of nearly 30,000. It traces its origins back to medieval times when Valdemar I (the Great) erected a castle fortress along the waterfront. The town grew up around the castle and, with its good natural harbour, prospered as a fishing and trade centre.

Sønderborg played a notable role in Denmark's history as the site of the final battle in the German invasion of 1864. The Danish loss at the pivotal Battle of Dybbøl, fought on the western outskirts of town, marked the beginning of a German occupation in the region that continued until the end of WWI. One legacy of that 1864 battle is Sønderborg's predominantly modern appearance: the heavy artillery bombardment that took place during the fighting left much of the town in rubble.

Today Sønderborg has a distinctively peaceful appearance and caters in equal measure to German and Danish tourists.

Orientation

Sønderborg spreads along both sides of the Als Sund (Als Sound), which is spanned by two bridges. The town centre and Sønderborg Slot are to the east, on the island of Als, while the Dybbøl area and the train station are on the western side, which is part of mainland Jutland. There's a small sandy beach right in town by the southern side of the castle.

Information

Tourist Office The Sønderborg Turistbureau (☎ 74 42 35 55, fax 74 42 57 47, email soenderborg.info@inet.uni2.dk), Rådhustorvet 7, 6400 Sønderborg, is on the main town square. Between mid-June and mid-August it's open from 9 am to 7 pm Monday to Friday and from 9.30 am to 2 pm on Saturday; during the rest of the year it's open from 9 am to 5 pm Monday to Friday and from 9.30 am to 12.30 pm on Saturday.

Money & Post There's a post office, a branch of Den Danske Bank and a Unibank along the pedestrian street Perlegade, immediately north of Rådhustorvet.

Things to See & Do

The town's dominant sight is the waterfront **Sønderborg Slot**, a castle dating back to the 12th century, when it was constructed as a circular fortress to defend against marauding Wends. The deposed king Christian II was held captive here from 1532 to 1549 – not in the dungeon but in comfortable royal chambers. Sønderborg Slot has been rebuilt over the years, with its current Baroque design dating back to 1718. Of special interest is the chapel, built in 1568 by the dowager queen Dorothea, widow of Christian III, because it is Denmark's first Lutheran chapel and one of Europe's oldest preserved royal chapels.

The castle now houses **Museet på Sønderborg Slot**, featuring exhibits on the wars of 1848 and 1864, the maritime history of Sønderborg, medieval church art and the German occupation of Denmark. It's open from 10 am to 5 pm daily between May and September, with shorter low-season hours. Admission costs 25 kr (children 10 kr).

Dybbøl, on the western side of the Als Sund, was the site of the most important battle in the Danish-German war of 1864. The **Historiecenter Dybbøl Banke**, a museum at Dybbøl Banke 16, has a multimedia display commemorating the bloody battle that marked the fall of southern Jutland to the Germans. The reconstructed windmill **Dybbøl Mølle**, on the opposite side of the street, was damaged in the battle of 1864 and is now a national historic site. Admission costs 20 kr for Dybbøl Mølle and 40 kr for the Historiecenter. Both are open from 10 am to 5 pm between spring and autumn.

Places to Stay

Sønderborg Camping (☎/fax 74 42 41 89, Ringgade 7, 6400 Sønderborg) is set in a wooded area near the yacht harbour, 1km south-east of the town centre. It's a three star facility, open from mid-April to late September.

The modern *Sønderborg Vandrerhjem (☎ 74 42 31 12, fax 74 42 56 31, Kærvej 70, 6400 Sønderborg)*, 1km north of the centre, is almost motel-like with comfortable guest rooms, a lounge with a fireplace, a coin laundry, a sauna and sports fields. Most of the 44 rooms have just four beds, and all have baths and double-entry doors to ensure they are quiet. Dorm beds cost 90 kr and singles/doubles cost 200/250 kr. The hostel is accessible to people in wheelchairs and is open from February to November.

Sønderborg's cheapest hotel is the 13 room *Hotel Arnkilhus (☎ 74 42 23 36, Arnkilgade 13, 6400 Sønderborg)*, about 500m north of the centre. Simple singles/doubles cost 325/400 kr with shared bath off the hall, 350/500 kr with private bath.

Breakfast is included in the price and there's a TV lounge.

In a prime location opposite the castle is *Scandic Hotel Sønderborg (☎ 74 42 19 00, fax 74 42 19 50, Rosengade 2, 6400 Sønderborg)*, a top-end hotel with a restaurant, bar, sauna and indoor swimming pool. The 95 rooms, which each have a bath, phone, TV and minibar, cost 845/1045 kr for singles/doubles standard rate, including breakfast, but there are various schemes and holiday deals that can reduce the price.

Places to Eat

An atmospheric place to dine that won't burn a hole in your wallet is a branch of *Jensens Bøfhus (Løkken 24)*, a chain steakhouse, in a half-timbered building north of the centre.

A block to the east on the pedestrian street Perlegade you'll find, from north to south: *Aktiv Super*, a large grocery shop with a cheap cafeteria; *Restaurant Sønderjylland*, a moderately priced sit-down restaurant; an *ice-cream shop*; and a *fruit shop*.

If you continue walking south you'll reach the main square, Rådhustorvet, and *Byens Smørrebrød (No 3)*, which offers smørrebrød or a half-chicken and chips that costs 35 kr, and has a couple of pavement tables. Also with outdoor seating on the square is *Maybe Not Bob (No 5)*, which draws a young crowd with Kilkenny beer on tap and reasonably priced sandwiches.

Tortilla Flats (Brogade 2), north of Sønderborg Slot, is a popular place with decent Mexican food, good-sized servings and reasonable prices. A mixed lunch plate costs 58 kr while various combination dinner dishes cost about 100 kr.

Getting There & Away

Sønderborg is 30km north-east of the border crossing at Kruså, via route 8.

Air The airport is 6km north of town. The commuter airline Cimber Air offers daily direct flights to Copenhagen. For more information, see the Getting Around chapter.

SOUTHERN JUTLAND

Bus On weekdays bus No 13 departs from the bus station about twice hourly for Augustenborg (20 kr, 12 minutes) and bus No 11 runs about every two hours to Fynshav (20 kr, 30 minutes), from where there's a ferry service to Funen (see the Faaborg Getting There & Away section for details).

Train Sønderborg is connected by numerous trains a day to Kolding (96 kr, 1¾ hours) and the rest of Jutland. It's also possible to go from Sønderborg to Padborg (49 kr), changing trains in Tinglev; with a good connection it takes about an hour.

Getting Around

Bicycles can be hired from K Staugaard (☎ 74 42 33 75) on Kastanie Allé, a block north-east of Rådhustorvet, and at the Hydro petrol station (☎ 74 42 77 44) on Helgolandsgade, a couple of blocks west of Perlegade.

AROUND ALS

The 33km-long island of Als is separated from the Jutland mainland by the narrow Als Sund. Its only large town, Sønderborg (see the previous section), sits at the south-western corner of Als; the rest of the island is a quiet provincial region of small farming villages. There are more than a dozen camping grounds spread along the coast and the best beaches are in the south. Tourist sights are limited but many of the villages have small churches of varying antiquity that can be visited, and there's a dolmen and a Viking burial site on the eastern coast at Blommeskobbel.

Augustenborg, 8km north-east of Sønderborg along route 8, is one of Als' more easily accessible and interesting villages. It has a compact centre, of which the main street begins at the gate of **Augustenborg Slot**, an 18th century Baroque palace that now serves as a psychiatric hospital. The grounds are open to all, as is the small exhibition in the gatehouse and the courtly palace chapel (should the chapel door be locked, ask to borrow the key from the hospital caretaker). The Augustenborg Turistbureau (☎ 74 47 17 20) is at Storegade 28, just 300m west of the palace in a picturesque house dating back to about 1769. Nearby you'll find a bakery and a couple of cafés where you could grab something to eat.

For those with their own transport the area around **Kegnæs**, the island at the southern tip of Als, can make an enjoyable destination for a short outing, with its gently pastoral countryside and sandy beaches. Fifteen kilometres south-east of Sønderborg via route 427, Kegnæs is connected to the rest of Als by a short causeway. At the north-east of the causeway there's a long sandy beach and Als' most popular seaside camping ground, *Drejby Camping* (☎ 74 40 43 05, Kegnæsvej 85) in Skøvby, which has 500 pitches, some cabins, a grill-style eatery and a minimarket. On Kegnæs, 1km west of the causeway, is a hilltop **lighthouse** that can be climbed (admission 5 kr) for a coastal view. If you want to try your luck at angling, the fishing is said to be good at the western end of Kegnæs; otherwise the only place on the island that you're likely to find any company is at the beach.

Getting There & Away

On weekdays bus No 13 leaves from the Sønderborg bus station about twice hourly for Augustenborg (20 kr, 12 minutes), and bus No 11 runs about every two hours from Sønderborg, via Augustenborg, to Fynshav (20 kr, 30 minutes), from where there's a car ferry service to Funen (see the Faaborg Getting There & Away section for details). There's also a ferry from Mommark to Søby on Ærø (see the Ærø Getting There & Away section in the Funen chapter for details).

As bus services in the more rural parts of Als are sketchy, a pleasant alternative for those without their own transport is to hire a bike in Sønderborg. The Sønderborg Turistbureau sells a map with suggested cycling tours for 10 kr.

Central Jutland

Central Jutland covers a broad swath of Denmark extending from Fredericia in the south to the Limfjord in the north. The western side is an expansive plain of windswept moors, bordered by a coastline of beach flats and sand dunes. Although this western region was predominantly wild heathland until the 19th century, much of it has now been turned into pasture and sugar beet fields. The more protected eastern side of central Jutland has fertile soil, small farms, a coastline indented with shallow fjords, and the largest cities and towns.

East Central Jutland

This section of Jutland has two significant – but quite dissimilar – tourist destinations. Children who have grown up playing with Lego will undoubtedly want to make a beeline for Legoland, Jutland's most visited attraction, while adults travelling without kids may be more interested in Jelling, one of Denmark's most important historic sites.

FREDERICIA

Fredericia is an industrial city of 29,000 people that's notable mainly for its old fortified ramparts. The town dates from 1650, when Frederik III began construction of the fortress to guard the narrow sound between Jutland and Funen. Over the centuries the Fredericia fortress played a significant role in the frequent wars between Denmark and its neighbours. In the winter of 1657 to 1658 Swedish troops, en route to Copenhagen, overran the fortress and killed the entire garrison before marching across the frozen waters of the Lille Bælt. The most celebrated battle fought here took place two centuries later when, in 1849, the successful defence of Fredericia from German assault halted the northward advance of Schleswig-Holstein troops.

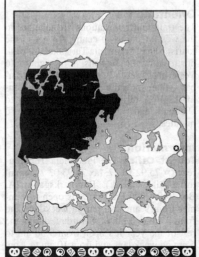

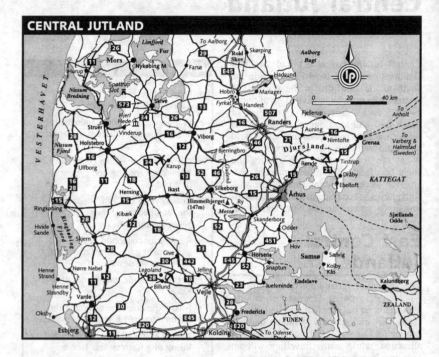

CENTRAL JUTLAND

Orientation

The train and bus stations are together to the west of the town centre. To get to the tourist office, Fredericia Turistbureau, walk north from the stations, turn right onto Vesterbrogade and follow it to the ramparts, then enter the old town gate at Danmarks Port through the rampart wall to Danmarksgade. The walk takes about 10 minutes.

Information

Tourist Office The Fredericia Turistbureau (☎ 75 92 13 77, fax 75 93 03 77, email turist@dk-7000.dk), Danmarksgade 2A, Box 248, 7000 Fredericia, is open in summer from 9 am to 6 pm on weekdays and from 9 am to 3 pm on Saturday; during the rest of the year it's open from 9.30 am to 5 pm on weekdays and from 10 am to 1 pm on Saturday.

Money & Post The Unibank at Gothersgade 5 and Den Danske Bank at Gothersgade 18 are a few minutes walk south-east of the turistbureau. The post office is to the north of the train station.

Things to See & Do

The old earthen **ramparts** of the Fredericia fortress remain largely intact, forming a mounded park-like green belt around the oldest section of the city. The ramparts extend about 2km and are topped with scattered war memorials, cannons and a footpath. You can get the best overview of it all from the top of the rampart wall at the western end of Danmarksgade, where there's a water tower that can be climbed in summer. A free English-language brochure detailing the history of different parts of the wall is available at the nearby turistbureau.

The other main sight is the **Fredericia Museum** (admission 20 kr), which displays local military and civilian history exhibits in an attractive collection of historic buildings at Jernbanegade 10, just a few minutes walk south of the train station. It's open from 11 am to 5 pm daily in summer, from noon to 4 pm Tuesday to Sunday during the rest of the year.

Places to Stay

The new 120 bed *Fredericia Vandrerhjem (☎ 75 92 12 87, fax 75 93 29 05, Vestre Ringvej 98, 7000 Fredericia)* is in a green area about 1km north-west of the train station. It's a comfortable five star facility; each guestroom has its own bathroom and there's a laundry, a guest kitchen and billiards. Dorm beds cost 90 kr and private rooms cost 275 kr for singles or doubles. It's open from 15 January to 15 December.

A reasonably priced city hotel is *Fredericia Sømandshjem (☎ 75 92 01 99, fax 75 93 25 90, email fsh@image.dk, Gothersgade 40, 7000 Fredericia)*, not far from the harbour. There are 32 straightforward but adequate rooms costing 300/420 kr for singles/doubles with shared bath, 460/580 kr with private bath; all prices include breakfast.

Places to Eat

The train station has a *minimarket*, a *DSB Café* and a cheap *snack bar* where you can get burgers and sandwiches.

In the town centre, you'll find a number of places to eat near the corner of Danmarksgade and Købmagergade, including *Lille Italia (Danmarksgade 31)*, an unpretentious hole in the wall serving good cheap pizza, and *Halis Pizza & Kebab Express (Danmarksgade 50)*, which offers sandwiches as well as pizza. For moderately priced dining there's *Bøf & Vino (Danmarksgade 36)*, a pasta and steak restaurant, and *Djengis Khan (Danmarksgade 33)*, which features Mongolian barbecue meals.

A few blocks south from Danmarksgade is the English-style pub *You'll Never Walk Alone (Gothersgade 39)*, which offers British draught beers, sandwiches and snacks.

Getting There & Away

Train Fredericia has good train connections, being on both the north-south line between Padborg and Frederikshavn and the Copenhagen-Århus route. Train fares are 63 kr to Odense (25 minutes), 92 kr to Padborg (75 minutes) or Århus (1 hour) and 203 kr to Copenhagen (2 hours).

Car & Motorcycle Fredericia is north of the E20, 80km from Nyborg and 92km from Esbjerg.

VEJLE

Vejle, at the head of the Vejle Fjord, has a population of 50,000. In the 19th century, after the railway was extended here, Vejle became a centre for iron foundries, cotton mills and food processing plants.

Information

The Vejle Turistbureau (☎ 75 82 19 55, fax 75 82 10 11), Søndergade 14, 7100 Vejle, is in the town centre on the main pedestrian street, a short walk west from the train station.

Things to See

Although most foreign travellers in Vejle are simply passing through on their way to Legoland or Jelling, there are two adjacent museums in the town centre on Flegborg, a few blocks north-west of the turistbureau. **Den Smidtske Gård**, a 1799 merchant's house, holds the local history collection, while **Vejle Kunstmuseum** exhibits Danish and European art. Admission to both is free.

More interesting, if you haven't already seen one of the 'bog people' in Århus or Silkeborg, is the corpse of an **Iron Age woman** dating back to 450 BC. She can be seen through a glass-topped case at Sankt Nicolai Kirke on Kirkegade, a 10 minute walk from either the train station or turistbureau.

CENTRAL JUTLAND

Places to Stay & Eat

If you need to break for the night, Vejle has a *hostel* (☎ 75 82 51 88, *Gammel Landevej 80*) about 5km south-east of the city, where dorm beds cost 90 kr; there's a *camping ground* (☎ 75 82 33 35, *Hellingkildevej 5*) about 4km north-east of the city. Staff at the turistbureau can book *rooms* in private homes and there are a few moderately priced *hotels* in the centre.

You'll find the usual array of *bakeries*, *cafés* and *restaurants* in the central streets around the turistbureau and in the neighbourhood of Rådhustorvet.

Getting There & Away

Vejle is off the E45, 73km south-west of Århus and 30km north of Kolding.

Vejle has frequent train departures because it's on both the main Jutland line and the north-westward line to Jelling, Herning and Holstebro. From Vejle it's 45 minutes (71 kr) to Århus, 36 minutes (49 kr) to Kolding and one hour (63 kr) to Herning.

JELLING

Jelling is a small town with a rich history. Although its sleepy rural character provides few hints to its past, Jelling once served as the royal seat of King Gorm the Old, the first in a millennium-long chain of Danish monarchs that continues unbroken to this day. The site of Gorm's ancient castle remains a mystery but other vestiges of his reign can still be found at Jelling Kirke.

Information

The Jelling Turistbureau (☎ 75 87 13 01) is west of Jelling Kirke at Gormsgade 4, 7300 Jelling. It's open between June and August from 10 am to 4 pm (to 6 pm in the summer high season).

Jelling Kirke

Jelling Church, erected in about 1100, is one of Denmark's most significant historical sites. Inside this small whitewashed church you'll find some vivid (although

The ancient rune stones outside Jelling Kirke were erected by Denmark's first kings.

unauthentically restored) 12th century **frescoes** that are among the oldest in Denmark. The main attractions, however, are the two well-preserved **rune stones** just outside the church door.

The smaller stone was erected in the early 10th century by Gorm the Old in honour of his wife. The larger one, raised by Gorm's son Harald Bluetooth, is adorned with the oldest representation of Christ found in Scandinavia and reads:

Harald king bade this be ordained for Gorm his father and Thyra his mother, the Harald who won for himself all Denmark and Norway and made the Danes Christians.

Harald Bluetooth did, in fact, rout the Swedes from Denmark and begin the peaceful conversion of the Danish people from the pagan religion celebrated by his father to Christianity. The larger stone, commonly dubbed 'Denmark's baptismal certificate', not only represents the advent of Christianity but also bids a royal farewell to the ancient gods of prehistoric Denmark. One side of the stone, which depicts a snake coiled around a mythological creature, is thought to symbolise this change of faith.

Two huge **burial mounds** flank Jelling Kirke. The barrow to the north was long believed to contain the bones of Gorm and his queen Thyra but when it was excavated in 1820 no human remains were found. In 1861 Frederik VII oversaw the excavation of the southern mound but, again, only a few objects were found, with no mortal remains among them.

In the 1970s a team of archaeologists excavated beneath Jelling Kirke itself and this time hit pay dirt. They found the remains of three earlier wooden churches, the oldest of which is thought to have been erected by Harald Bluetooth. A burial chamber was also unearthed at this time and human bones and gold jewellery were discovered. The jewellery was consistent with pieces that had been found earlier in the northern burial mound.

Archaeologists now believe that the skeletal remains found beneath the church are those of Gorm, who had originally been buried in the northern mound but was later reinterred by his son. Presumably Harald Bluetooth, out of respect, moved his parents' remains from pagan soil to a Christian place of honour within the church. The bones of Queen Thyra have yet to be found.

Items found during the excavation are displayed in Nationalmuseet in Copenhagen. The Jelling burial mounds, church and rune stones are a designated UNESCO World Heritage Site.

Jelling Kirke is open from 8 am to 5 pm Monday to Friday and from 8 am to 2 pm on Saturday; the grounds are open outside these hours. It's in the centre of town, right on route 442 and just a two minute walk due north from the train station along Stationsvej.

Places to Stay & Eat

The three star facility *Friluftsbadets Camping* (☎ 75 87 16 53, fax 75 87 20 82, *Mølvangvej, 7300 Jelling*) is in town, 1km west of Jelling Kirke. It's open from early April to mid-September.

At the *Jelling Kro* (☎ 75 87 10 06, fax 75 87 11 76, *Gormsgade 16, 7300 Jelling*), opposite the church, a daily two course meal costs 128 kr; there are six rooms

with shared bath costing 335/495 kr for singles/doubles, including breakfast.

You can get an inexpensive meal at *Jelling Pizza & Kebab* on Møllegade, 200m south of Jelling Kirke. The *Super Brugsen* supermarket, just west of the church on Mølvangvej, has a delicatessen selling takeaway items.

Getting There & Away

Jelling is 10km north-west of Vejle on route 442.

Bus There's an hourly bus service between Vejle and Jelling (bus No 211), but it takes a few minutes longer than the train.

Train Jelling is on the railway line between Vejle and Struer; trains run at least hourly on weekdays, slightly less frequently at weekends. From Vejle to Jelling the train takes 15 minutes and costs 20 kr.

LEGOLAND

Legoland, 1km north of the small inland town of Billund, is Denmark's most visited tourist attraction outside Copenhagen. A 10 hectare theme park built from plastic Lego blocks, Legoland has hosted some 28 million visitors, more than half of them from outside Denmark, since it opened in 1968.

Legoland has its own bank, post office, tourist office, hotel and restaurants, and even its own airport.

Information

Tourist Office The Billund Turistbureau (☎ 76 50 00 55, fax 75 35 31 79), Legoland Parken, 7190 Billund, is inside Legoland but has an entrance that faces the road and is open year-round. During the Legoland season it's open daily from 9 am to 8 pm (to 9 pm in July and August). Winter hours are shorter.

Money & Post There's a branch of Den Danske Bank at the turistbureau, open daily from 10 am to 5.30 pm (to 7.30 or 8.30 pm

Lego

Lego got its start more than 60 years ago when a local carpenter, Ole Kirk Christiansen, tried his hand at making wooden toys to earn money during a Depression-era construction slump. In 1934, after a couple of years of making pull-toys and piggy banks, Ole selected the business name Lego, a contraction of the Danish words *leg godt*, meaning 'play well', and expanded his line to four dozen toy designs.

In the late 1940s Lego became the first company in Denmark to acquire a plastics injection-moulding machine and began making interlocking plastic blocks called 'binding bricks', the forerunner of today's Lego blocks. In 1960, when Lego's wooden-toy warehouse went up in flames, the company decided to concentrate solely on plastic toys. By that time Lego blocks had become the most popular children's toys in Europe.

Lego continued to expand. In 1969 it created the Duplo series for younger children, with bricks twice as long and twice as wide as basic Lego blocks. Later, it introduced little vehicles, wooden families and complex theme sets of trains, pirate ships and the like. Although there are now advanced kits incorporating motors and fancy gadgets, the basic appeal of Lego continues to be the simple interlocking blocks that can be snapped together in endless creative combinations.

Lego is still a family-run business, today headed by Ole Kirk's grandson, but it's grown into one of Denmark's best-known companies and Europe's largest toy manufacturer. Lego now has 50 branches on six continents. It's estimated that in the past 50 years some 300 million children worldwide have at one time or another played with Lego toys. In addition to Denmark's Legoland, there are now Legoland parks in Windsor (UK) and California (USA).

in the high season). The park's post office franks mail with a special Legoland stamp.

Things to See & Do

The park's main attraction is a Lilliputian world of 45 million plastic blocks arranged into miniature cities, plus scenes with Lego pirates and safari animals. Most replicas are on a scale of 1:20 and include the medieval town of Ribe, Amalienborg Slot in Copenhagen and a handful of easily recognisable international cities and sights such as Amsterdam, Bergen and the Acropolis.

At times the park employs as many as 30 'builders', who spend their days snapping together the creations. The tallest piece, a model of the American Indian chief Sitting Bull, reaches 14m in height and contains 1.4 million Lego blocks. The most elaborate piece is the 3.5-million-block Copenhagen Harbour exhibit, which features electronically controlled ships, trains and cranes.

Legoland also features numerous amusement rides. Most of the rides are along the lines of merry-go-rounds, miniature trains and mechanical boats geared to children but there are a few, like the water slide, that can be fun for adults as well. All are included in the admission price except for the children's traffic school (25 kr), a driving course with little electric cars.

There's also an antique doll collection, a children's theatre and a Mindstorms Center, where visitors can build programmable robots. The various theme-park sections include Legoredo, a small Wild West town with a few costumed gunslingers and Indians in feather headdresses; Pirateland, with ships and swordplay; Castleland, featuring a train ride through a castle; and Duplo Land, with gentle rides for very young children.

Legoland (☎ 75 33 13 33) is open daily from early April to late October; the exact dates vary a bit each year. Opening hours

Stallholders peddle their wares in Telefon Torv, Århus.

Lake District paddle steamer.

In Legoland, visitors tour a world in miniature; Little Amsterdam, constructed from small plastic bricks.

Quaint thatched cottage, Boes.

Reconstructed historic buildings in Den Gamle By, Århus.

Doorway of half-timbered house, Den Gamle By.

Fishing boat at anchor in Ebeltoft harbour.

Make hay while the sun shines – idyllic fields in the fertile land of Central Jutland's Lake District.

are from 10 am to 8 pm (until 9 pm in the high season between late June and late August). High season admission costs 120 kr for children aged from 3 to 13 and 130 kr for adults. Its Web site is at www.legoland.dk.

Note that the activities and rides usually shut down two hours before Legoland closes and there's no admission charge after the rides stop. In this evening period when it is open gratis to the public you can still view the Lego block sights – so for those just curious to see what the park is all about it's an ideal time to swing by for a free stroll.

Places to Stay

In the high season places to stay near Legoland are often fully booked so advance reservations are advised. Nonetheless, even then staff at the turistbureau can usually find you a hotel, or a room in a private home (150 kr per person), though sometimes you may have to go 10 to 20km outside town. There's no booking fee for the service.

Billund FDM Camping (☎ 75 33 15 21, fax 75 35 37 36, Ellehammer Allé 2, 7190 Billund), just 400m east of the Legoland gate, is one of Denmark's largest camping grounds, with 550 sites. This three star facility has a coin laundry, lounges and playgrounds. The camping charge is 54 kr per person; cabins sleeping two to six people cost from 220 to 500 kr. It's open year-round.

The 228 bed *Billund Vandrerhjem* (☎ 75 33 27 77, fax 75 33 28 77, Ellehammer Allé, 7190 Billund), a modern five star facility, is adjacent to Billund FDM Camping. Dorm beds cost 90 kr, while family rooms cost from 325 kr for one person to 425 kr for five people. It's open year-round, except from 15 December to 15 January, and is accessible to people in wheelchairs.

Opposite Legoland, but connected to it by an overhead walkway, is *Hotel Legoland* (☎ 75 33 12 44, fax 75 35 38 10, Aastvej 10, 7190 Billund), the area's largest hotel. The staff are helpful and the rooms are comfortable with bath, TV, phone and minibar. Singles/doubles start at 875/995 kr including breakfast.

A cheaper option is *Hotel Svanen* (☎ 75 33 28 33, fax 75 35 35 15, Nordmarksvej 8, 7190 Billund), a motel-style place 600m south-east of Legoland, in the same neighbourhood as Billund Vandrerhjem and Billund FDM Camping. It has 24 modern rooms with bath, phone and TV starting at 575/625 kr including breakfast.

One kilometre south-west of Legoland is the *Billund Kro* (☎ 75 33 26 33, fax 75 35 31 91, Buen 6, 7190 Billund), near route 28. Part of the Dansk Kroferie association, it has 30 rooms, each with bath, phone and TV; singles/doubles cost 520/595 kr, though for that double rate you'll need to buy an 'Inn Cheque' at the turistbureau.

Places to Eat

Legoland contains about a dozen food stands and restaurants. Among them are the *Waffle Bakery*, which serves home-made waffles and Danish pastries; *Oasen*, which offers hot dogs, burgers and ice cream; the *Drive Inn*, with pizza, French-bread sandwiches and salads; the *Grill House*, specialising in grilled steaks, chicken and salmon; the *Saloon*, serving spareribs, apple pie and draught beer; and the *Cafeteria* which, not surprisingly, cooks up cafeteria fare.

A bit pricier is *Hotel Legoland*, which does good lunch and dinner buffet spreads. *Billund Vandrerhjem* has its own café serving three meals a day.

Getting There & Away

Billund is on route 28, 59km north-east of Esbjerg and 28km west of Vejle. There's no train service. If you're travelling by train, the most common route is to get off at Vejle and catch a bus from there.

Air Billund's airport, which sits right outside Legoland's gate, not only serves Legoland but, because of its central Jutland location, has grown into Denmark's second-busiest airport.

CENTRAL JUTLAND

Maersk Air (☎ 75 33 22 44) operates numerous daily flights to Billund from Copenhagen costing around 700 kr. It also provides daily international services to Billund from Amsterdam, Brussels, Frankfurt, London, Newcastle and Stockholm, as well as a weekly summertime service from the Faroe Islands.

In addition, British Airways (☎ 86 36 30 60) flies to Billund from Manchester, Gothenburg and Oslo; KLM-Royal Dutch Airlines (☎ 32 51 26 26) flies from Amsterdam; Sabena (☎ 75 33 21 77) flies from Brussels; Braathens (☎ 75 35 44 00) flies from Oslo; and Lufthansa Airlines (☎ 33 37 73 33) flies from Frankfurt.

Bus Seasonal bus tours, which include same-day return fares and entrance to Legoland, are available from a number of Danish cities. From either Vejle (☎ 75 82 97 66) or Esbjerg (☎ 75 12 33 77) the cost is 165/130 kr for adults/children.

There's also a frequent public bus service from Vejle to Legoland (39 kr, 30 minutes) and a bus about every hour from Esbjerg to Legoland (60 kr, 90 minutes).

In addition you could hop onto one of the airport buses, timed to meet scheduled flights, between Billund airport and Århus (100 kr, 1½ hours), Esbjerg (60 kr, 55 minutes), Fredericia (60 kr, 1¼ hours) and Kolding (50 kr, 45 minutes).

Car Four international car rental agencies have booths at the airport: Avis (☎ 75 33 29 99), Budget (☎ 75 35 39 00), Europcar (☎ 75 33 15 33) and Hertz (☎ 75 33 82 50).

Århus

Århus, Denmark's second largest city, has just over a quarter of a million residents. The cultural centre of Jutland, it's a lively university city with one of Denmark's best music and entertainment scenes, offering everything from symphony performances and theatre to a thriving night-owl café life.

Århus boasts a well-preserved historic quarter and plenty to see and do, ranging from good museums and intriguing old churches in the city centre to woodland trails and beaches along the city outskirts. Some of the highlights are: Den Gamle By, a quality open-air museum; Vor Frue Kirke, which contains Denmark's oldest chapel; Århus Domkirke, Denmark's largest church; and the Forhistorisk Museum Moesgård, which has notable Bronze and Iron Age collections and an enjoyable trail through a landscape rich in prehistoric sights.

History

In the middle of Jutland's eastern coast, Århus has been an important trade centre and seaport since Viking times; it was originally named Aros, meaning 'at the river mouth'. Archaeological excavations indicate that Århus was founded in around 900, when a semicircular rampart was constructed at the waterfront. The rampart, only a few city blocks in diameter, encompassed the area where the current cathedral, theatre and casino stand. Remnants of the original city can be seen in the excavated basement of the Unibank west of Århus Domkirke.

In medieval times Århus' central location often left it in the thick of conflict with neighbouring states; King Sweyn II of Denmark and King Magnus of Norway engaged in a major battle off Århus in 1043 and just a few years later, in 1050, Århus was ravaged by the Norwegian warrior-king Harald Hardrada. In the decades that followed its prosperity was kept in check by raids from other rival Vikings and attacks by fearsome Wend pirates.

Over the following centuries stability was slowly achieved and Århus grew as a centre of trade, art and religion. Its large, protected harbour became increasingly important. In the 18th century Århus flourished as a transport hub for central Jutland and, to this day, virtually all regional roads and railway lines lead to the city.

A lengthy dispute between Århus and the national government led the city to found its own university in 1928, but by the time the new campus was ready to open its doors in

1933 the national government had come around to recognise and support the university. Today students at Århus University, along with those at Århus' engineering college, dental school, business college, music academy and school of architecture, account for nearly 40,000 of the city's 265,000 residents.

Orientation

Århus is fairly compact and easy to get around. The train station (Århus Hovedbanegård) is south of the city centre. The pedestrian shopping streets of Søndergade and Sankt Clements Torv lead to Århus Domkirke in the heart of the old city. The small streets north-west of the cathedral are filled with cafés and restaurants.

Information

Tourist Office Tourist Århus (☎ 86 12 16 00, fax 86 12 95 90), Rådhuset, 8000 Århus C, is inside the rådhus on Park Allé. Between mid-June and early September it's open from 9.30 am to 6 pm Monday to Friday, from 9.30 am to 5 pm on Saturday and from 9.30 am to 1 pm on Sunday. During the rest of the year it's open from 9.30 am to 4.30 pm Monday to Friday (to 5 pm from May to mid-June) and from 10 am to 1 pm on Saturday. Its Web site is at www.aarhus-tourist.dk.

Money There's a Sydbank at the front of the train station and many more banks along Søndergade. There's also a Unibank near Århus Domkirke at Sankt Clements Torv 6 and a Midtbank near the harbour on the corner of Åboulevarden and Mindebrogade.

Post & Communications The main post office is beside the train station. It's open from 9 am to 6 pm Monday to Friday and from 10 am to noon on Saturday.

Gay & Lesbian Travellers Landsforeningen for Bøsser og Lesbiske (LBL; ☎ 86 13 19 48), the national organisation for gays and lesbians, has its Århus branch at Jægergårdsgade 42; it's open from 5 to 7 pm.

Travel Agency Kilroy Travels (☎ 86 20 11 44), Fredensgade 40, specialises in youth and discount travel.

Bookshops The GAD bookshop, at Søndergade 20 opposite Salling department store, has a good English-language travel section as well as novels and general-interest books about Denmark. The English Book Store, Frederiks Allé 53, specialises in both new and second-hand English-language books.

Library & Newspapers You can read international newspapers at the main public library, a large modern facility off Vester Allé. International newspapers are sold at the DSB kiosk in the train station.

Laundry Quick Vask, a coin laundry at Guldsmedgade 27, is open from 7.30 am to 9.30 pm.

Medical Services A conveniently located pharmacy is Jernbane Apotek, opposite the train station. For service after hours contact the Løve Apotek (☎ 86 12 00 22), opposite Hotel Royal at Store Torv 5, which is open 24 hours.

Emergency Dial 112 for police or ambulance. Århus Kommunehospital on Nørrebrogade has a 24 hour emergency ward. Krisecenter for Voldsramtekvinder (☎ 86 15 35 22) helps women in crisis and can provide a safe haven overnight.

Central Museums

Den Gamle By The Old Town is a picturesque open-air museum comprising 75 restored buildings brought here from all over Denmark and reconstructed as a provincial town, complete with a functioning bakery, silversmith, bookbinder and so on. Most of the buildings are half-timbered 17th and 18th century houses but there's

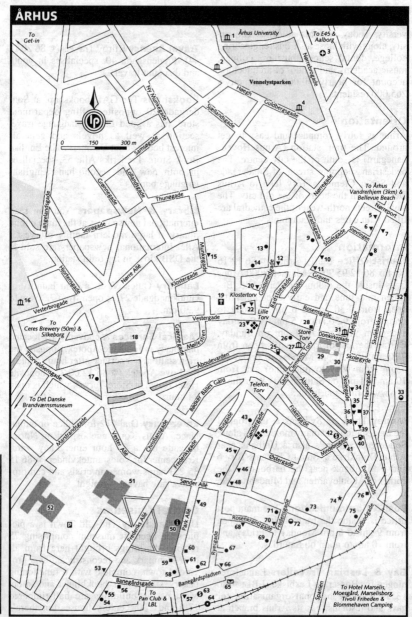

ÅRHUS

To Get-in

Århus University

To E45 & Aalborg

Vennelystparken

To Århus Vandrerhjem (3km) & Bellevue Beach

Nørreport

0   150   300 m

To Ceres Brewery (50m) & Silkeborg

To Det Danske Brandværnsmuseum

Lille Torv

Klostertorv

Vestergade

Domkirkeplads

Store Torv

Telefon Torv

Bakker Bailes Gård

Banegårdspladsen

Sender Allé

Rosenkrantzgade

To Pan Club & LBL

To Hotel Marselis, Moesgård, Marselisborg, Tivoli Friheden & Blommehaven Camping

CENTRAL JUTLAND

ÅRHUS

PLACES TO STAY		47	Super Brugsen Supermarket	29	Århus Domkirke
28	Hotel Royal;	48	China Wok House	30	Århus Teater
	Royal Scandinavia Casino	49	Bakery	31	Besættelses-Museet; Kvinde-
37	Århus City Sleep-In	53	Føtex Supermarket		museet; Museumscafeen
56	Eriksens Hotel	55	Sundhedskost	32	Crazy Daisy
59	Plaza Hotel Århus	57	Fruit Stand	33	Ferry to Kalundborg
60	Hotel Ritz	61	Guldhornet	35	Fatter Eskil
76	Hotel Atlantic	66	Loft Konditori	40	Petrol Station
		68	Jensen's Bøfhus	42	Midtbank
PLACES TO EAT		70	China Town	43	GAD Bookshop
5	Kulturgyngen; Musikcaféen			44	Salling Department Store
6	Gallorant Kif-Kif	OTHER		50	Århus Rådhus; Tourist Århus
7	Hornitos	1	Naturhistorisk Museum	51	Musikhuset Århus
10	Café Kindrødt	2	Steno Museet	52	Scandinavia Center Århus
11	Café Drudenfuss	3	Århus Kommunehospital	54	English Book Store
12	Emmery's	4	Århus Kunstmuseum	58	Scandinavian Airlines (SAS)
15	Naturkost	8	Sappho		Ticket Office
20	Pizza Hut	9	Øst for Paradis Cinema	62	Jernbane Apotek
21	Café Smagløs	13	Quick Vask (Coin Laundry)	63	Sydbank
22	Munkestuen	14	Blitz/Rokken	64	Train Station
23	Jacob's Bar BQ; Pita Bar	16	Den Gamle By	65	Post & Telegraph Office
34	Rosita's Cantina	17	Musikteater	67	Cine City Cinema
36	Melrose Place	18	Library	69	Asmussen Cykler
38	Bone's	19	Vor Frue Kirke	71	Kilroy Travels
39	Asian House	24	Magasin du Nord	72	Bus Station
41	Italia	25	Paddy Go Easy	73	Europcar
45	McDonald's	26	Løve Apotek	74	Police Station
46	Greengrocer	27	Vikinge-Museet; Unibank	75	Train (Nightclub)

also a watermill, a windmill and a few buildings from the late-19th century.

Den Gamle By is on Viborgvej, about 1.5km west of the city centre. It's open daily year-round: from 9 am to 6 pm between June and August, from 9 am to 5 pm in May and September, from 10 am to 4 pm in the shoulder season and from 11 am to 3 pm in winter. Admission costs 50 kr (children 15 kr).

After these hours, however, you can walk through the old cobbled streets for free – this is a delightful time to visit because the crowds are gone and the light is ideal for photography, but you won't be able to enter individual buildings. Bus Nos 3, 14 and 25 pass the museum.

Vikinge-Museet Pop into the basement of the Unibank, Sankt Clements Torv 6, for a look at artefacts from a Viking village excavated at this site in 1964 during the bank's construction. The excavated artefacts, which date from 900 to 1400, indicate that this neighbourhood was one of the earliest settlements in Århus. The display includes photos of the excavation, a skeleton, a reconstructed house, 1000-year-old carpentry tools and pottery. It's open during banking hours: from 9.30 am to 4 pm Monday to Friday and from 9.30 am to 6 pm on Thursday. Admission is free.

Besættelses-Museet The old rådhus at Domkirkeplads 5, which served as the Gestapo headquarters during WWII, now contains the Occupation Museum. Located in the basement of the building, it details the Danish Resistance movement through photo displays, tableaus, guns and a few instruments of torture. Besættelses-Museet is generally open from 10 am to 4 pm daily in summer and on weekends only during the rest of the year, but opening hours can be

Århus Pass

Århus has a nifty city pass that allows unlimited transport on municipal buses and admission to most city sights, including Den Gamle By, Århus Kunstmuseum, Forhistorisk Museum Moesgård, the two university museums, Det Danske Brandværnsmuseum, Kvindemuseet and Tivoli Friheden.

The cost for a two day pass is 110 kr for adults and 55 kr for children aged 15 and under. A seven day pass costs 155/75 kr for adults/children. The pass can be purchased from hotels and Tourist Århus (the tourist office).

⊗⊜✿⊘ ◉✿⊜⊗ ⊗⊜✿⊘ ◉✿⊜⊗

uneven because they depend upon the availability of a dwindling corps of volunteers. Admission costs 15 kr (children 5 kr).

Kvindemuseet Also at Domkirkeplads 5 is the Women's Museum, which features changing exhibits on the culture and history of women. This is also a good place for women travellers to get acquainted with Danish women involved in the feminist movement. Kvindemuseet is open from 10 am to 5 pm daily between June and September and from 10 am to 4 pm Tuesday to Sunday during the rest of the year. Admission costs 20 kr, or 15 kr for teenagers aged over 16 (children aged 15 and under free).

Århus Kunstmuseum This museum at Vennelystparken, south of the university, contains a comprehensive collection of 19th and 20th century Danish art. There's also a foreign collection, predominantly of German and American art, and periodic special exhibitions. It's open from 10 am to 5 pm Tuesday to Sunday. Admission costs 30 kr, except during special exhibitions when it's 40 kr. Take bus No 1, 2, 3 or 6 to Nørreport.

University Museums There are two museums in Universitetsparken, the grounds of Århus University. **Naturhistorisk Museum** features a large collection of domestic and foreign stuffed birds and animals, many set in dioramas. There are also displays on Danish ecology, evolution and minerals. Opening hours are from 10 am to 5 pm in July and August, and from 10 to 4 pm during the rest of the year; it's closed on Monday from November to March. Admission costs 30 kr (children free).

Steno Museet, a science history museum, features exhibits on medicinal herbs, anatomy and medicine. It's open from 10 am to 4 pm Tuesday to Sunday. The museum also has a planetarium with shows at 11 am and 1 and 2 pm. Admission to the museum costs 30 kr (children 10 kr). The planetarium shows cost 30 kr (children 20 kr).

Numerous buses go to Århus University, including Nos 2, 3 and 11.

Churches

Århus Domkirke Århus Cathedral is Denmark's longest, with a lofty nave spanning nearly 100m. Its construction began in around 1200 and took 100 years to complete. In the 15th century the cathedral was transformed from its original Romanesque style to its current Gothic one. At that time the roof was raised over the nave, the landmark clock tower was erected, high Gothic windows were installed and the chancel was extended.

Like many other Danish churches, Århus Domkirke was once richly decorated with frescoes that were painted to convey biblical parables to illiterate peasants. After the Reformation in 1536 Church authorities, who felt the frescoes embodied Catholicism, had them all whitewashed. Many of these frescoes, which range from tormented scenes of hell to fairytale-like paintings, have now been uncovered and painstakingly restored.

Our favourite painting, just north of the altar, is of a chipper St George, the patron saint of knights, slaying a dragon as a grateful princess looks on; the Arabic numbers in the corner date it to 1497.

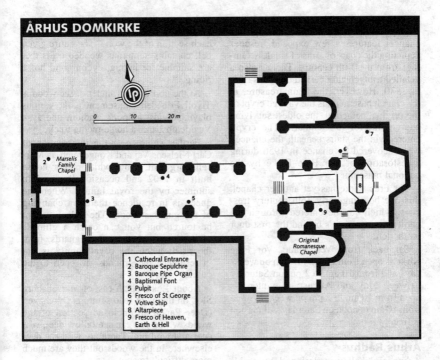

ÅRHUS DOMKIRKE

1 Cathedral Entrance
2 Baroque Sepulchre
3 Baroque Pipe Organ
4 Baptismal Font
5 Pulpit
6 Fresco of St George
7 Votive Ship
8 Altarpiece
9 Fresco of Heaven, Earth & Hell

A focal point of the cathedral is the ornate five panel gilt altarpiece (pentaptych) made in Lubeck by the renowned woodcarver Bernt Notke in the 15th century. In its centre panel, to the left of the Madonna and child, is a gaunt-faced St Clement, to whom Århus Domkirke was dedicated. Clement, rather ironically, became the patron saint of sailors by having the inauspicious fate of drowning at sea with an anchor around his neck. The anchor, which has come to symbolise St Clement, can be found in many of the cathedral decorations.

Other items worth special attention are the bronze baptismal font dating from 1481, the finely carved Renaissance pulpit created in 1588, the magnificent Baroque pipe organ made in 1730, the large 18th century votive ship and the Baroque sepulchre in the Marselis family chapel.

Århus Domkirke is open from 9.30 am to 4 pm between May and September and from 10 am to 3 pm between October and April. It's closed on Sunday. As with all churches, no visits are allowed during funerals, wedding and other services. Admission is free.

Vor Frue Kirke This church is like one of those Russian *matryoshka* dolls, opening to reveal multiple layers beneath the surface. It was here that the original Århus cathedral was erected shortly after 1060 when Sweyn II, bent on weakening the power of the archbishop who led the Danish church, divided Denmark into eight separate dioceses, one of which was Århus. The cathedral was constructed from rough stone and travertine and stood until about 1240, when it was replaced by the current Vor Frue Kirke.

CENTRAL JUTLAND

Built of red brick, the church has a largely whitewashed interior although the chancel features a few exposed frescoes depicting the coats of arms of wealthy families from the 14th century. There's also a detailed triptych altar carved by Claus Berg in 1530. However, the main treasure, in the church basement, is the vaulted crypt of the original cathedral, the oldest surviving church interior in Denmark. The crypt, entered via the stairs beneath the chancel, was uncovered by chance in 1956 during a restoration of Vor Frue Kirke by the national museum.

Vor Frue Kirke has yet another chapel, this one boasting early 16th century frescoes, which can be entered through the garden courtyard; it's behind the first door on the left.

Set back from Vestergade, Vor Frue Kirke is open from 10 am to 4 pm on weekdays and from 10 am to 2 pm on Saturday between May and August; in winter it's open from 10 am to 2 pm on weekdays and from 10 am to noon on Saturday. Admission is free.

Århus Rådhus

Århus city hall was designed by architect Arne Jacobsen, a pioneer of Danish modernism, and completed in 1942. This controversial building has a ponderous, functional design and is topped by a rectangular clock tower, the outer skeleton of whichresembles forgotten scaffolding. The outer façade is of dark Norwegian marble, while the inside has light open spaces. In summer at noon and 2 pm on weekdays you can take the lift (5 kr) up the tower for a view, or at 11 am take a guided tour (10 kr), which includes the tower.

Southern Outskirts

Marselisborg About 2km south of the city centre is the start of a large wooded area that stretches down along the coast for nearly 10km. The various parts of the wood have several different names, but generally the northern end is known as Marselisborg, the midsection as Moesgård

and the southern part as Fløjstrup, names taken from the estates that once owned each section of the wood. The entire green belt contains numerous wooded trails that are suitable for hiking, cycling and horse riding.

At the northern perimeter of the wood is Tivoli Friheden amusement park, various playing fields, a sports stadium and Jysk Væddeløbsbane, a horse-racing track.

Farther south, near the intersection of Carl Nielsens Vej and Kongevejen, is **Marselisborg Slot**, a big white manor house built in 1902 and occasionally used in summer by the royal family. When the queen is in residence there's a changing of the guard at noon. The palace cannot be toured but you can catch a glimpse of it, along with the palace guards, from the road; when the royal family is not in residence the grounds are open to the public.

About 1.5km south-east of Marselisborg Slot, on the main road south, is **Dyrehaven** (Deer Park), an enclosed section of the woods where you can see fallow deer, sika deer and wild pig. There are wild roe deer elsewhere in the woods but they are much more difficult to spot.

To get to Marselisborg from the city centre take Spanien (route 451) south to Strandvejen, the coastal road. Bus No 19 runs south from Århus train station along the coastal road.

Tivoli Friheden If you're travelling with children who are getting tired of old churches and museums, consider a skip to this amusement park 2km south of the city centre. It's on Skovbrynet, at the northern edge of the Marselisborg woods, and is reached via Strandvejen; you can get there via bus No 4, 18 or 19. The park contains fairground rides, clown shows, flower gardens, fast-food eateries, cafés and a small casino section with slot machines for wayward adults. It's open from 2 to 10 pm daily between late April and mid-August, and from 1 to 11 pm in midsummer. Admission costs 35 kr (children 15 kr).

Moesgård The Moesgård area, 8km south of the city centre, makes for an absorbing half-day outing. The main focal point is the **Forhistorisk Museum Moesgård** (Moesgård Prehistoric Museum), which features quality displays from the Stone Age to the Viking Age including flint axes, tools and pottery and a roomful of **rune stones**.

The museum's most unique exhibit, displayed in a glass case, is the 2000-year-old **Graubelle Man**, found preserved in a nearby bog in 1952 (see the boxed text below). The dehydrated, leathery body is amazingly intact, right down to his red hair and fingernails. The museum is open daily from 10 am to 5 pm between May and September and from 10 am to 4 pm Tuesday to Sunday during the rest of the year. Admission costs 35 kr (children free).

An enjoyable **trail** dubbed the 'prehistoric trackway' leads from behind the museum through fields of wildflowers, grazing sheep and beech woods down to **Moesgård Strand**, Århus' best sandy beach. The trail, marked by red-dotted stones, passes reconstructed historic sights including a dolmen, burial cists and an Iron Age house. Before you start off pick up a trail brochure at the museum. You can walk one way and catch a bus from the beach back to the city centre or follow the trail both ways as a 5km loop.

If you happen to be at Moesgård Strand during the last weekend in July, a Viking Moot re-enactment takes place along the waterfront – an ideal opportunity to combine a day at the beach with some historical enrichment.

Bus No 6 from Århus train station terminates at the museum year-round, while bus No 19 terminates at Moesgård Strand during the summer season; both buses run about twice an hour.

Det Danske Brandværnsmuseum

The Danish Fire Brigade Museum is one of the largest museums of its kind in Europe, housing more than 100 antique fire-fighting vehicles, both horse-drawn and engine-driven. It's open from 10 am to 5 pm Tuesday to Saturday. Admission costs 40 kr (children 15 kr). Located at Tomsagervej 23, 5km west of the city centre and just off Viby Ringvej, the museum can be reached on bus No 12 or 18.

Hiking & Cycling

The Århus Kommune distributes the handy detailed brochure *Nature Around Århus-South*, which maps out suggested hiking and cycling tours of the green space south of the city. This brochure (10 kr), which includes short but interesting titbits on local flora, fauna and history, can be picked up

---

Graubelle Man

Grauballenmanden (Graubelle Man), now displayed at Forhistorisk Museum Moesgård, was discovered in April 1952 in a peat bog near the village of Graubelle, 35km west of Århus. Graubelle Man died in around 80 BC, a slash across his throat indicating he may have been the victim of a murder or execution. One theory is that he was the object of a ritualistic sacrifice, perhaps killed as an offering to one of the pagan gods thought to be responsible for warding off plagues and assuring abundant harvests.

Graubelle Man was about 30 years old when he died. Tannic acids and iron deposits in the bog preserved his body and literally tanned his hide, giving his skin a brown, leather-like appearance.

Two millennia after Graubelle Man's last supper, scientists were able to discover a great deal about his eating habits by examining his stomach, which contained remnants of a porridge of barley and rye as well as 66 different types of seeds.

at Tourist Århus. Be sure to ask for the English-language version.

Specifically for cyclists is the *Cyclist Turistkort*, a detailed map produced by Århus Amt (Århus County). The county has 1200km of cycling routes over a mix of surfaced secondary roads, forest paths and abandoned railway tracks. The cycling map, available in English, details various countywide touring routes, including those in the immediate Århus area, the Lake District and the Grenaa/Ebeltoft region. It also gives information on things to see and do en route and has some useful tips and the addresses of cycle repair shops. The map costs 80 kr and can be purchased at tourist offices and bookshops.

Swimming

There are sandy beaches on the outskirts of Århus. The most popular one to the north is Bellevue, about 4km from the city centre (take bus No 6 or 16), while the favourite to the south is Moesgård Strand, 8km from the centre on bus No 19.

Windsurfing

Windsurfers will find suitable spots in Århus bay to the north of the city centre near Risskov and to the south at Marselisborg. For more on windsurfing, including information on classes, call the Surfline on ☎ 86 17 67 65.

Other Sports

Tourist Århus has a Tourist Sport programme (☎ 86 12 16 00); staff can help to arrange a variety of sporting activities including sailing, tennis, golf, ice-skating and windsurfing.

Organised Tours

Ceres Brewery Tours of the Ceres Brewery, on Vesterbrogade opposite Den Gamle By, are given year-round on Wednesday at 2 pm. From late June to early August tours are also given on Tuesday and Thursday at 9 am. Passes (5 kr) are distributed at Tourist Århus; pick them up as soon as you arrive

in Århus as the tours commonly book out days in advance.

Sightseeing Tour For a good overview of the city consider taking the guided 2½ hour public bus tour that leaves from Tourist Århus daily at 10 am between mid-June and early September. Conducted by knowledgeable multilingual guides, it gives a drive-by glimpse of the main city sights and a more detailed tour of Århus Domkirke. At 45 kr this is a great deal because it includes entry into Den Gamle By and also leaves you with a 24 hour bus pass. Not surprisingly the tour often fills to capacity, but you can secure a seat by booking in advance at Tourist Århus.

Places to Stay

Camping The nearest camping ground is *Blommehaven Camping* (☎ 86 27 02 07, fax 86 27 45 22, Ørneredevej 35, Århus), which has a nice beachside setting in the Marselisborg woods, 6km south of the city centre. Rated three star, it has cooking facilities, a coin laundry, a minimart, and cabins and caravans for rent. It's open from early April to mid-September. From Århus train station you can take bus No 19 (which stops in front of Blommehaven Camping) or No 6 (which stops 400m away).

Hostels & Private Rooms The 145 bed *Århus Vandrerhjem* (☎ 86 16 72 98, fax 86 10 55 60, Marienlundsvej 10, 8240 Risskov) is in a renovated 1850s dance hall in the midst of the Risskov woods, 4km north of the city centre. Dorm beds cost from 75 to 85 kr; family rooms are available, costing from 225 kr for one or two people to 425 kr for five people. Take bus No 1, 6, 9 or 16; from the bus stop it's a 300m walk east along Marienlundsvej. It's open from 20 January to 20 December. There are hiking trails through the woods and down to the ocean.

Århus City Sleep-In (☎ 86 19 20 55, fax 86 19 18 11, Havnegade 20, 8000 Århus C) is a great alternative place to stay. Run by the same people who operate Kulturgyngen, the city youth and culture centre, it has a good central location near the harbour. The building was originally a seamen's hotel, so the sleeping quarters are hotel rooms rather than large dorms. A dorm-style shared room costs 85 kr. You can also get a private room with shared bath for 200 kr or with your own bath for 250 kr; the private rooms cost the same for singles or doubles. If you don't have a sleeping sheet you'll need to rent linen for an additional 30 kr. There's a guest kitchen, a TV room, a pool table and laundry facilities. Breakfast is available and costs 25 kr. Reception is open 24 hours and advance reservations are accepted.

Staff at Tourist Århus can book *rooms* in private homes; singles/doubles cost 150/250 kr, plus a 50 kr booking fee.

Hotels The new 36 room *Get-in* guesthouse (☎ 86 10 86 14, fax 86 10 86 24, *Jens Baggesensvej 43*), near Århus University, is midway between a hostel and a hotel in both style and price. The rooms are clean and adequate but simple – most contain just a bed, a chair and a small desk. Common space includes a TV room and guest kitchen. Singles/doubles cost 250/300 kr with shared bath, 300/350 kr with private bath. To get there take bus No 7 from the train station.

Eriksens Hotel (☎ 86 13 62 96, fax 86 13 76 76, *Banegårdsgade 6, 8000 Århus C*) is a pleasant family-run hotel about 500m west of the train station. The 18 rooms are straightforward but have desks and washbasins; baths are off the hall. Singles/doubles cost 330/420 kr; breakfast is included in the single rate and is available for an optional 30 kr more per person for doubles. Rooms facing the rear are quieter.

For something more upmarket in the centre, try the 170 room *Plaza Hotel Århus* (☎ 87 32 01 00, fax 87 32 01 99, *Banegårdsplads 14, 8100 Århus C*). The hotel has recently been renovated and has full facilities including a fitness centre, sauna and parking. Singles/doubles with bath start at 520/690 kr. There are also four unadvertised rooms with shared bath for 410 kr.

Opposite the Plaza Hotel Århus and just north of the train station is *Hotel Ritz* (☎ 86 13 44 44, fax 86 13 45 87), *Banegårdsplads 12, 8100 Århus C*). A member of the Best Western chain, this older 70 room hotel has ordinary rooms and a 1950s look. Singles/doubles cost 695/775 kr.

More modern is *Hotel Atlantic* (☎ 86 13 11 11, fax 86 13 23 43, *Europaplads 12, 8000 Århus C*), between the bus station and the harbour, which has 102 pleasant rooms with bath, TV, phone and minibar. The standard rates are pricey at 960/1160 kr for singles/doubles but there's a 695 kr rate in summer and at weekends (including Sunday) year-round. If you have kids they'll usually put you into a roomy suite for the same price. Breakfast is included in the rates and there's free parking for guests.

The historic *Hotel Royal* (☎ 86 12 00 11, fax 86 76 04 04, *Store Torv 4, 8100 Århus C*), on the same square as Århus Domkirke, is the city's most expensive hotel. Its casino and deluxe rooms cater to high rollers; singles/doubles, frilled up with amenities including a private fax, cost 1500/1750 kr. There are also 'standard' rooms costing 1195/1345 kr with minibar, TV, video and the like.

Hotel Marselis (☎ 86 14 44 11, fax 86 11 70 46, *Strandvejen 25, 8000 Århus C*) is in a well-to-do suburb 3km south of the city centre. A member of the Best Western chain, this 100 room hotel fronts the beach and is backed by forest. The rooms, which have modern amenities including ocean-view balcony, TV and minibar, cost 1025/1240 kr for singles/doubles from Sunday to Thursday. On Friday and Saturday there's a weekend rate of between 695 and 995 kr, depending on the season, which covers two adults and two children. All rates include breakfast. The hotel has a pool, a sauna, a bar and a restaurant.

Places to Eat

Train Station Area There are a number of eating options within easy walking distance of the train station.

The station itself houses a small *supermarket*, open daily until midnight, as well as the usual *DSB chain eateries* serving up cafeteria fare, hot dogs, burgers and beer. There's a *fruit stand* at the front while across the street is *Loft Konditori*, a good bakery with a small dining room that opens for breakfast at 7 am every day except Sunday.

A two minute walk north of the station is *Guldhornet*, a pavement solarium restaurant near Hotel Ritz offering a lunch special of steak and potatoes, served until 4 pm, for just 35 kr. Dinner costs around 100 kr.

China Town (Fredensgade 46), opposite the bus station, has 10 daily lunch specials costing less than 50 kr served until 4 pm each day. For dinner there's a multicourse meal costing 95 kr and an à la carte menu with standard Chinese dishes averaging 75 kr. It's open from noon to 11 pm daily.

Jensen's Bøfhus (Rosenkrantzgade 23) offers the chain's usual 39 kr steak or chicken lunch deals and a salad bar for 29 kr; for dinner, dishes cost around 100 kr.

You'll find a good selection of health-food items at *Sundhedskost (Frederiks Allé 49)*, which is open on weekdays only. The *Føtex* supermarket, diagonally opposite Sundhedskost, has a bakery and a deli that can provide the elements of a cheap takeaway meal.

Central Area The *China Wok House (Sønder Allé 9)* is a casual Chinese restaurant with inexpensive deals, including a three item takeaway box costing 20 kr.

In the first block of the pedestrian street Søndergade there's a *Super Brugsen* supermarket, a *greengrocer* and a *McDonald's*. *Salling* department store, a bit farther north on Søndergade, has a supermarket and deli in its basement, a bakery on the ground floor and an upstairs 'bistro' with good croissants, tempting sandwiches and a small salad bar.

Italia (Åboulevarden 9) is an Italian restaurant with a wood-fired pizza oven. There's a pizza special costing 35 kr until 4 pm; otherwise pizza and pasta dishes are priced from about 50 kr and meat and fish dishes start at 100 kr. It's open from noon to 11 pm daily, except on Sunday when it opens at 5 pm.

The following restaurants, south-east of Århus Teater, are all within a few minutes walk of each other and open from 5 pm nightly. *Rosita's Cantina (Skolegade 21)* is a long-established restaurant offering a full menu of Mexican dinners served with rice and beans, costing around 100 kr; there's live music at weekends. *Melrose Place (Skolegade 27)* is a new café featuring a nightly buffet that includes salad and hot dishes and costs 69 kr. At the popular *Bone's (Skolegade 33)* good spareribs and steaks, served with a helping from the fresh salad bar, start at 100 kr. For Cantonese food there's *Asian House (Mindebrogade 2)*; three-course dinners cost around 100 kr.

Northside Cafés & Restaurants The narrow streets of the old quarter north of Århus Domkirke are thick with cafés serving Danish, Middle Eastern and other international cuisine at moderate prices. *Café Drudenfuss*, on the corner of Graven and Studsgade, is one of the more popular meeting places; it serves inexpensive sandwiches, empanadas and drinks. The nearby *Café Kindrødt (Studsgade 8)* offers candlelight dining; salads and pasta dishes cost around 50 kr.

More upmarket is *Emmery's*, on the corner of Klostergade and Guldsmedgade, a trendy café serving tapas, organic bakery items, cakes, sandwiches, salads and light meals. It's open from 7.30 am to midnight except on Sunday when it closes at 6 pm.

Munkestuen (Klostertorv 5), a smoky hole-in-the-wall café, serves excellent Danish food at affordable prices, including daily specials at lunch (50 kr) and dinner (80 kr). Meals are served from noon to 8 pm, though the bar stays open later. If Munkestuen is full, *Café Smagløs* next door serves reasonably priced fare: a spinach salad or chilli con carne costs 40 kr. On the opposite side of the same square is a *Pizza Hut*, which serves the chain's standard pizzas, pasta and salads from 11.30 am to 11 pm daily.

Jacob's Bar BQ (Vestergade 3), in an historic merchant's house, is a bustling place known for its grilled steaks, which start at around 100 kr. There are also fish, lamb and kebab dishes priced from around 80 kr. It's open from 11 am to 1.30 pm daily.

The *Pita Bar*, beneath Jacob's, is a smart café where good pitta-bread sandwiches cost 27 kr; it's open from 11 am to at least 2.30 am.

Naturkost (Gammel Munkegade 4), a small health-food shop, sells a good selection of natural products including juices, vitamins and snacks.

Kulturgyngen (Mejlgade 53), the youth and culture centre, serves hearty portions of good food, offering a different vegetarian meal and a different fish or meat meal each night for around 50 kr. There are lunch specials for 30 kr, as well as cakes, coffees and other drinks. Meals are served from 11 am to 5 pm and 6 to 9 pm Monday to Saturday but it's open for drinks and conversation until at least midnight and commonly until 2 am.

Nearby, *Gallorant Kif-Kif (Mejlgade 41)* is open nightly; Middle Eastern dishes such as couscous or shish kebab with salad and hummus cost around 85 kr.

Hornitos (Mejlgade 46B), inconspicuously tucked into a corner at the end of the courtyard, makes authentic Chilean empanadas for takeaway only. These delicious pies, which come in chicken, lamb, beef and vegetarian spinach versions, cost 25 kr. There are also enchilada or burrito meals costing 40 kr. It's open from 11 am to 9 pm on weekdays and from 5.30 to 9.30 pm on Saturday and Sunday.

The cosy *Museumscafeen (Domkirkeplads 5)* at Kvindemuseet is an inviting place for women to meet in. The menu includes wine, coffee, cakes, salads and sandwiches – all at reasonable prices. It's open the same hours as Kvindemuseet, from 10 am to 5 pm daily in summer and from 10 am to 4 pm Tuesday to Sunday in winter.

Entertainment

Being a university city, there's always a lot happening in Århus. For detailed listings of current events, music and other entertainment pick up *Kulturguide Aarhus*, *Musik Kalenderen* or the tourist office's *What's On in Århus*, all of which are free.

Music Clubs Much of the vibrant music scene is centred around backstreet cafés such as *Fatter Eskil* (☎ 86 19 44 11, *Skolegade 25*), which typically has jazz, blues or funk music from 10 pm most nights.

Musikcaféen and *Gyngen* (☎ 86 19 22 55, *Mejlgade 53*) are part of Kulturgyngen, a youth and culture centre that occupies a renovated factory to the north of the city centre. Both places offer an interesting alternative scene with a wide range of music including jazz, rock, techno and world music. Admission is sometimes free, often 20 to 50 kr, and occasionally higher if someone special is performing.

There's usually something going on at *Musikteater* (☎ 86 12 26 77, *Vester Allé 15*), which is part of Huset, a dynamic cultural centre. It stages rock, pop and ethnic music concerts; the cover charge is generally from 40 to 70 kr.

The hottest new place in town is *Train* (☎ 86 14 11 55, *Toldbodgade 6*), which features good rock, pop and soul bands from Denmark, the UK and the USA. Admission prices range from 50 kr on nights with a disco to about 150 kr when big-name bands are playing.

Blitz/Rokken (☎ 86 12 94 11, *Klostergade 34*) is a dance spot that bustles at weekends to both live rock music and disco. You'll also find a lively crowd bent on dancing at *Crazy Daisy* (☎ 86 18 08 55), a disco on a boat in the harbour.

Paddy Go Easy (☎ 86 13 83 33, *Åboulevarden 60*), an Irish pub, has live music at weekends, including a Sunday jam session. It's also the spot to watch football games on big-screen TV.

Musikhuset Århus Århus' modern concert centre, *Musikhuset Århus*, is in the city centre off Frederiks Allé. It contains two concert halls, the larger of which seats 1500, and is the arena for numerous events including dance performances, operas, musicals and concerts. Offerings range from performances by the city symphony orchestra to concerts by international pop and jazz stars. The foyer, which houses the ticket office and a café, occasionally has some sort of free musical performance, so if you're strolling by it's worth checking out. A monthly programme schedule is available from the ticket office (☎ 89 31 82 10), which is open from 11 am to 9 pm daily.

Theatre The *Århus Teater* on Bispetorv, south of Århus Domkirke, is a splendid 100-year-old building richly embellished with gargoyles and other decorative elements, including a scene from a Ludvig Holberg play painted across the front gable. Jutland's largest theatre, it has five stages, a permanent theatre troupe of 35 actors and an affiliated drama school. During the season, from early September to mid-June, there are also performances by students of the drama school and visiting actors. For schedule information call ☎ 89 33 26 22.

Gay & Lesbian Venues The main gay and lesbian hangout is the *Pan Club* (☎ 86 13 43 80, Jægergårdsgade 42), a café and disco a short walk south-west of the train station. The café is open from 6 pm to 1 am Monday to Thursday, from 8 pm to 6 am on Friday and Saturday and from 8 pm to 1 am on Sunday. The disco is open from 11 pm to 3 am Wednesday to Saturday and from 10 pm to 2 am on Sunday.

Gatherings for lesbians are sometimes held at *Sappho (Mejlgade 71)*, a women's centre that's open from 3 to 11 pm Tuesday to Friday.

The *Men's Club*, for gay men who are into leather, stages periodic discos and other events; call ☎ 86 19 10 89 for information.

Cinema There are several cinemas in Århus that show films in their original languages with Danish subtitles. The five

screen *Cine City* (☎ 86 13 70 90), centrally located at Sankt Knuds Torv 15, generally features first-run Hollywood movies. *Øst for Paradis* (☎ 86 19 31 22), a multi-screen cinema at Paradisgade 7, shows both European and American films.

Casino If you have extra cash burning a hole in your pocket, the *Royal Scandinavia Casino* (☎ 86 19 21 22) is at the Hotel Royal. It has slot machines and other electronic games as well as American roulette, French roulette and blackjack. Entrance requires proper dress but men can borrow a jacket at the door for 40 kr. It's open from 3 pm to 4 am daily. Admission costs 50 kr.

Shopping
Department Stores & Speciality Shops
The city's largest department stores are the huge Magasin du Nord, which takes up an entire block between Vestergade and Åboulevarden, and Salling at Søndergade 27, which has 30 departments. Both stores stock just about anything you can

imagine, from gourmet foods to designer clothing, Danish silverware and tax-free gift items.

Søndergade, a busy pedestrian shopping street, has numerous speciality shops, many selling fashionable clothing. Other shops and boutiques specialising in both Danish design and imported clothing are thick along Badstuegade and Volden, streets that run north from Lille Torv.

If you're interested in antiques, there are a couple of shops north of Århus Domkirke on Graven that stock everything from old furniture, silver and china to rare books.

Crafts Telefon Torv, a small pedestrian square off the northern end of Søndergade, has a few open-air stalls where immigrants and university students sell carved pipes, jewellery and other simple handicrafts.

More traditional items, including pottery, hand-blown glass and wooden toys, can be found in shops along Møllestien, a cobbled street east of the library. These include Glasmenageriet, a glassworks gallery at No 48; Gavlhuset, a shop that sells its own Danish and raku-style earthenware at No 53; and a mixed crafts shop at No 57. All are open on weekday afternoons and generally from 10 am to 1 pm on Saturday.

Getting There & Away

Air Århus airport, which is in Tirstrup, 44km north-east of Århus, is primarily a domestic airport; Scandinavian Airlines (SAS) provides numerous daily flights to and from Copenhagen. The one-way fare is 818 kr but there are return fares for only about 15% more. SAS also operates a daily afternoon flight from Århus to London (see the Getting There & Away chapter for details).

Billund airport, 1½ hours (100 kr) from Århus by bus, is the main link between Jutland and the rest of Europe, with direct flights to many cities in continental Europe and the UK. For information see under Getting There & Away in the Legoland section earlier in this chapter.

The SAS ticket office, on Park Allé near Århus train station, is open from 9 am to 4.30 pm on weekdays.

Bus All long-distance buses stop at Århus bus station, 500m north-east of the train station. The bus station has lockers (10 kr), a small grocery shop and an inexpensive café.

Express buses (☎ 86 78 48 88) run a few times daily between Århus and Copenhagen's Valby station, take 3½ hours and cost 190 kr. There are also a few daily (except Saturday) express buses to Aalborg (99 kr, 2¼ hours).

Train Trains to Copenhagen (241 kr, 3¼ hours), via Odense, leave Århus about hourly from early morning to midnight. There's also an hourly train service to Frederikshavn (156 kr, 2½ hours) as well as trains east to Grenaa, west to the Lake District (see those sections for more details) and south to Vejle (71 kr, 45 minutes) and Fredericia (92 kr).

Car & Motorcycle The main highways to Århus are the E45 from the north and south and route 15 from the west. The E45 curves around the western edge of the city as a ring road. There are a number of turnoffs from the ring road into the city, in-cluding Åhavevej from the south and Randersvej from the north.

Boat Scandlines (☎ 33 15 15 15) runs car ferries three to four times a day on weekdays between Århus and Kalundborg. The trip takes 3¼ hours and costs 290 kr for a car plus up three people and 160 kr for a motorcycle and rider.

Faster and much more frequent is Scandlines' Cat-Link, a sleek catamaran hydrofoil that takes just 1½ hours to get from Århus to Kalundborg and runs every hour or two. The passenger fare is 170 kr for adults and 85 kr for children. It costs 435 kr for a car plus up to four passengers and 210 kr for a motorcycle with up to two riders.

Getting Around

To/From the Airport The airport bus from Århus airport to the train station costs 50 kr; the service is synchronised with flight schedules, departing from Århus 70 minutes before domestic flights and 80 minutes before international flights.

Bus Århus has an extensive public bus system with frequent services throughout the city. Most city buses stop in front of the train station or around the corner from it on Park Allé. Tickets are bought from a machine in the back of the bus for 13 kr and are valid for unlimited rides within the time period stamped on the ticket (about two hours); you can change buses during that time as often as you like. You can also buy a 24 hour pass valid for bus travel in Århus municipality alone (45 kr) or one that is valid throughout Århus County, which includes Grenaa and the Lake District (for 85 kr). There are also discounted *klippekort* (clip card) tickets valid for nine rides. The klippekort tickets and the passes can be bought at newsstands and at Tourist Århus. For information on bus routes and departure times call ☎ 89 46 56 00.

Car & Motorcycle A car is quite convenient for getting to sights such as Moesgård on the city outskirts, though the city centre is best explored on foot.

Århus has numerous *billetautomats* (parking meters) along its streets. Parking generally costs 1 kr per six minutes, with a three hour maximum, from 8 am to 6 pm Monday to Thursday, from 8 am to 8 pm on Friday and from 8 am to 2 pm on Saturday. Outside those hours you can park free of charge.

There are several car parks around town, including large ones in front of and beneath the conference centre Scandinavia Center Århus.

Cars can be rented from:

Avis
    (☎ 86 16 10 99) Jens Baggesensvej 88A
Europcar
    (☎ 86 12 35 00) Sønder Allé 35
Hertz
    (☎ 86 19 18 12) Silkeborgvej 4

Taxi Taxis are readily available at the train station. You can also order a taxi by phoning ☎ 89 48 48 48 or 86 16 47 00.

Bicycle You can rent bicycles at Asmussen Cykler (☎ 86 19 57 00) at Fredensgade 54 near the bus station; they cost 50/250 kr per day/week. It also sells quality bikes and accessories.

Århus City Sleep-In hires out bicycles for 50 kr per day.

The Lake District

The Lake District (Søhøjlandet), the closest thing Denmark has to hill country, is a popular active holiday spot for Danes, offering good opportunities for canoeing, cycling and hiking. The scenery is pretty, but placid and pastoral rather than stunning. The district contains Gudenå, Denmark's longest river; Mossø, Jutland's largest lake; and Yding Skovhøj, Denmark's highest point – none of which are terribly long, large or high!

SILKEBORG

Silkeborg, population 35,000, is the Lake District's largest and youngest town. It was founded in 1846 when Michael Drewsen – whose statue graces Torvet – built a paper mill on the eastern side of the river. The mill and other industries still form the backbone of the economy. Because of its modern façade, the town may seem a bit bland but it has a pretty setting, bordered by both a river (Remstrup Å) and a lake (Silkeborg Langsø). If you're strolling through the town at night, walk down by the rådhus, where a colourfully-lit fountain spurts up from the lake.

Information

Tourist Office The Silkeborg Turistbureau (☎ 86 82 19 11, fax 86 81 09 83), Åhavevej 2A, 8600 Silkeborg, is north-east of the Silkeborg Museum. Between mid-June and

31 August it's open from 9 am to 5 pm Monday to Friday, from 9 am to 3 pm on Saturday and from 9.30 am to 12.30 pm on Sunday. During the rest of the year it's open from 9 am to 4 pm on weekdays, to noon on Saturday. Its Web site is at www.tourist.silkeborg.dk.

Money There are a number of banks on Vestergade, a block west of Torvet, including a Unibank at Vestergade 13 and a Jyske Bank at Vestergade 16.

Other Facilities The post office is on Drewsensvej, just east of the train station. There's a pharmacy at Vestergade 9 and a coin laundry at Hostrupsgade 21.

Silkeborg Museum

This quality regional museum of cultural history is housed in the 18th century Hovedgården manor house, the oldest building in town. Its Bronze and Iron Age collections include pottery, flint daggers and jewellery, most found in nearby peat bogs.

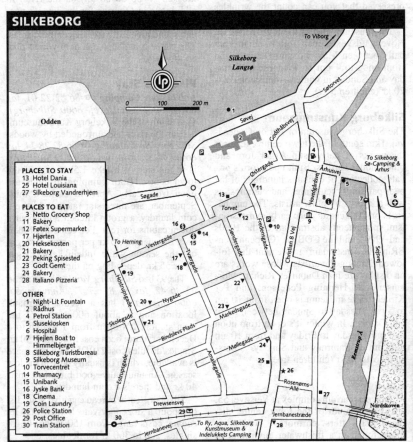

SILKEBORG

To Viborg

Silkeborg Langsø

Odden

0   100   200 m

Søvej

Sætorvet

To Silkeborg Sø-Camping & Århus

Århusvej

Østergade

Goddthåbsvej

Søgade

Torvet

To Herning

Vestergade

Søndergade

Fredensgade

Christian 8 Vej

Ahavevej

Selsvej

Hostrupsgade

Tværgade

Nygade

Markedsgade

Skolegade

Bindslevs Plads

Estrupsgade

Amaliegade

Møllegade

Remstrup Å

Rosenørns-Allé

Drewsensvej

Jernbanevej

To Ry, Aqua, Silkeborg Kunstmuseum & Indelukkets Camping

Jernbanestræde

Nordskoven

PLACES TO STAY
13 Hotel Dania
25 Hotel Louisiana
27 Silkeborg Vandrerhjem

PLACES TO EAT
3   Netto Grocery Shop
11 Bakery
12 Føtex Supermarket
17 Hjørten
20 Heksekosten
21 Bakery
22 Peking Spisested
23 Godt Gemt
24 Bakery
28 Italiano Pizzeria

OTHER
1   Night-Lit Fountain
2   Rådhus
4   Petrol Station
5   Slusekiosken
6   Hospital
7   Hjejlen Boat to Himmelbjerget
8   Silkeborg Turistbureau
9   Silkeborg Museum
10 Torvecentret
14 Pharmacy
15 Unibank
16 Jyske Bank
18 Cinema
19 Coin Laundry
26 Police Station
29 Post Office
30 Train Station

CENTRAL JUTLAND

There are also trade workshops from the end of the 19th century, including those of a cooper, a dentist and a shoemaker, and a good glass collection.

The museum's main attraction, however, is **Tollund Man**, an Iron Age man who met an untimely end in his late 30s in 200 BC. His blackened, leather-like body, complete with a rope still around his neck, was discovered in a nearby bog in 1950. He was apparently hanged as a sacrifice to the gods. When discovered, Tollund Man was wearing only a sheepskin cap and a simple leather belt. The face is so amazingly well preserved that you can count the wrinkles on his forehead.

The museum, east of the town centre on Hovedgårdsvej, is open from 10 am to 5 pm daily between May and mid-October, and from noon to 4 pm on Wednesday, Saturday and Sunday in winter. Admission costs 20 kr (children 5 kr).

Silkeborg Kunstmuseum

The Silkeborg Museum of Art on Gudenåvej, 1km south of the town centre, features the works of native son Asger Jorn and other modern artists. Built upon Jorn's private collection, it contains hundreds of his own paintings, sculptures and etchings, as well as works by other artists. The emphasis is on 20th century art: early expressionism, spontaneous abstract art of the 1930s and 1940s, and the COBRA (COpenhagen-BRussels-Amsterdam) movement that followed. Among the artists whose works are on display are Jean Dubuffet, Richard Mortensen Carl-Henning Pedersen, and Per Kirkeby. The museum is open from 10 am to 5 pm Tuesday to Sunday between April and October. In winter it's open from noon to 4 pm Tuesday to Friday and from 10 am to 5 pm on Saturday and Sunday. Admission costs 30 kr (children free).

Aqua

Aqua, an aquarium complex at Vejsøvej 55, about 2km south of the town centre, displays fish, otters, cormorants and other fauna found in a freshwater environment.

It's open from 10 am to 6 pm daily between June and August, and from 10 am to 4 pm daily (to 5 pm at weekends) in winter. Admission costs 55 kr (children 30 kr).

Hiking & Canoeing

To get to **Nordskoven**, a beech forest with hiking and cycling trails, simply walk over the old railway bridge at the eastern end of Jernbanestræde.

You can hire **canoes** for about 50/250 kr per hour/day at a few places around town, including the camping grounds and Slusekiosken (☎ 86 80 08 93) on the river. In addition to just touring for the day, it's possible to paddle through the Lake District and spend nights at lakeside camping areas. The canoe hire shops can help you to plan an itinerary.

Places to Stay

Indelukkets Camping (☎ 86 82 22 01, fax 86 80 50 27, Vejlsøvej, 8600 Silkeborg), 1km south of the Silkeborg Kunstmuseum, is near the river and surrounded by woods. *Silkeborg Sø-Camping* (☎ 86 82 28 24, fax 86 80 44 57, Århusvej 51, 8600 Silkeborg) is at the side of a lake 1.5km east of the town centre. Both camping grounds are open from early April to at least mid-September, are three star rated and have a coin laundry, a group kitchen and about a dozen cabins for rent. For camping, Silkeborg Sø charges 50 kr per person throughout the season while Indelukkets charges 45 or 55 kr, depending on the month.

The 93 bed *Silkeborg Vandrerhjem* (☎ 86 82 36 42, fax 86 81 27 77, Åhavevej 55, 8600 Silkeborg) has a scenic riverbank location and is about 600m east of the train station. It's open from 1 March to 1 December; dorm beds cost from 75 to 90 kr. Singles/doubles cost 210/255 kr when space is available, which is usually only in the low season. An unusually good breakfast costs 40 kr and there's a coin laundry.

Silkeborg Turistbureau can give you a list of about a dozen private homes that let *rooms*; costs range from 150 to 200 kr for singles, 200 to 300 kr for doubles.

Hotel Dania (☎ *86 82 01 11, fax 86 80 20 04, Torvet 5, 8600 Silkeborg)* is an old-fashioned hotel with front rooms overlooking Torvet and quieter rear rooms that overlook the lake. The rooms are large and all have bath and TV, but they are pricey at 910/1095 kr for singles/doubles including breakfast.

Also in the town centre is the stylish *Hotel Louisiana* (☎ *86 82 18 99, fax 86 80 32 69, Christian 8 Vej, 8600 Silkeborg)*, part of the Best Western chain. It has 27 commodious rooms with the usual comforts, including bath, satellite TV, phone and minibar. Singles/doubles cost 815/1015 kr but there's a good-value weekend rate of 695 kr per room. Breakfast is included in the rates. There's a sauna, fitness facilities and a restaurant.

Places to Eat

There are a cluster of affordable Asian restaurants on Søndergade. The best of them is *Peking Spisested (No 16)*, offering reasonably priced Chinese and Vietnamese dishes; three-course meals start at 60 kr and there are inexpensive grilled items such as burgers or chicken with chips.

At *Godt Gemt (Markedsgade 14)*, a Danish family restaurant specialising in beef, herring and salmon dishes, simple items start at around 60 kr and more elaborate meals cost from around 100 kr.

Hjørten (Tværgade 4) is a decent steak restaurant with dark wood and ceilings with exposed beams. From 11.30 am to 5 pm there are beef or chicken lunch specials for 58 kr, including a helping from a good salad bar. At dinner the same type of meal costs about double that.

Italiano Pizzeria (Frederiksberggade 1) is open for dinner only, serving moderately priced pizza and pasta.

The *Føtex* supermarket at Torvet has a cafeteria serving good-value specials – you can get a solid meal for just 30 kr.

You'll find *bakeries* on the corner of Søndergade and Møllegade, at the north-eastern corner of Torvet, and on Hostrupsgade just south of Nygade. *Heksekosten* *(Nygade 28)* sells health food, natural teas and vitamins.

Getting There & Away

Silkeborg is 37km south of Viborg on route 52 and 43km west of Århus on route 15.

Bus Long-distance buses leave from outside the train station. Express bus No 913X makes the 48 minute run between Silkeborg and Århus (42 kr) a couple of times daily; the frequent regional bus Nos 112 and 113 also go to Århus but they take 1¼ hours.

Train Hourly trains connect Silkeborg with Skanderborg (34 kr, 30 minutes) and Århus (49 kr, 45 minutes) via Ry.

Boat The paddle steamer *Hjejlen* sails from Silkeborg to Himmelbjerget daily during the summer; see under Getting There & Away in the Himmelbjerget section for details.

Getting Around

You can park along the streets in the town centre and in numerous car parks, including to the west of rådhus and at Torvecentret on Fredensgade.

Bicycle Bicycles can be hired at the camping grounds and Silkeborg Vandrerhjem; they cost around 50 kr per day.

RY

A smaller town in a more rural setting than Silkeborg, Ry is a good base from which to plan your exploration of the Lake District. Although there aren't really any notable sights in the town centre, there are lots of options for activities and excursions into the surrounding countryside.

Information

Tourist Office The Ry Turistbureau (☎ 86 89 34 22, fax 86 89 35 52, email ryturist @post6.tele.dk) is in the train station at Klostervej 3, 8680 Ry. It's open from 9 am to 4.30 pm Monday to Saturday between mid-June and August; during the rest of the year it's open from 9 am to 4 pm on week-days and from 9 am to noon on Saturday.

Other Facilities The post office is north of the train station and there's a branch of Den Danske Bank nearby at Klostervej 2.

Hiking

Ry Turistbureau sells an English-language brochure (20 kr) that maps out and briefly describes 10 hikes in the Ry area. One of the nicest hikes from Ry is the two hour, 7km walk to Himmelbjerget. The starting point for the hike is the dirt road that begins off Rodelundvej about 400m south of the Ry bridge. The path, which is signposted, leads to the Himmelbjerget boat dock before climbing the hill to the tower.

Cycling Tour

A good half-day outing is the cycle ride from Ry to **Boes**, a tiny hamlet that boasts an array of picturesque thatched houses and bounteous flower gardens. From there con-tinue through the countryside to **Øm Klos-ter**, the ruins of a medieval monastery. There are just enough bricks and rocks left to show what the monastery was once like. In the underground tombs, where the high altar once stood, you can peer through glass-topped enclosures at the 750-year-old skeleton of Bishop Elafsen of Århus and the bones of many of his abbots. There's also a small museum with more skulls and monastery artefacts.

Between May and September Øm Klos-ter is open from 10 am to 5 pm (to 6 pm in the summer high season). In April and October it's open from 10 am to 4 pm; it's closed in winter and on Monday year-round. Admission costs 25 kr (children 10 kr). The whole trip from Ry and back is about 18km.

Other Activities

If you want to explore the surrounding lakes and rivers on your own, Ry Kano-fart (☎ 86 89 11 67), Kyhnsvej 20, has canoes for hire; they cost 50/250 kr per hour/day.

To join a group, AktivitetsBureauet (☎ 86 89 08 28) offers kayak and mountain bike outings as well as windsurfing lessons.

Places to Stay

The closest camping ground is the lakeside *Sønder Ege Camping* (☎ 86 89 13 75, fax 86 89 02 07, Søkildevej 65, 8680 Ry) 1km north of town. Rated three star, it has full fa-cilities, including a coin laundry, a TV room and cabins for rent. It's open from early April to late September.

On the same bathing lake, fronting a popular beach, is *Ry Vandrerhjem* (☎ 86 89 14 07, fax 86 89 28 70, Randersvej 88, 8680 Ry). To get there from the train station cross the tracks, turn left and walk 2.5km, or take the infrequent bus No 104. Dorm beds cost 90 kr; private rooms for either one or two people cost 340 kr in summer, 200 kr at other times. It's open year-round and hires out canoes.

Ry Turistbureau can book *rooms* in about a dozen homes around Ry; they cost around 200 kr for a single, 250 to 300 kr for a double, and there's no booking fee. Staff at the turistbureau can also help you to book *cottages* in the Ry area, most of which sleep four people and cost from 2200 kr a week.

The *Ry Park Hotel* (☎ 86 89 19 11, fax 86 89 12 57, Kyhnsvej 2, 8680 Ry), in the centre of town, has 80 rooms with modern amenities, including TV, phone and mini-bar. The hotel has an indoor swimming pool, sauna and restaurant. Rates range from 445 to 695 kr for singles and from 645 to 895 kr for doubles, including breakfast.

Places to Eat

Ib & Gydas Slagter, a butcher shop oppo-site the train station, sells cheeses and fried fish by the piece and a few other takeaway items. There's a *bakery* next door to the butcher shop. At *Pizzeria Italia* (Skander-borgvej 3), 300m from the train station on the eastern side of the tracks, pizza and pasta dishes start at 50 kr.

The restaurant at the *Ry Park Hotel* of-fers traditional Danish food; starters begin at 65 kr and main dishes start at 100 kr.

Sønder Ege (Søkildevej 69), near Sønder Ege Camping, has a nice view; Danish and German meat dishes start at around 100 kr.

Getting There & Away
Ry is on route 445, 24km south-east of Silkeborg and 35km west of Århus.

The bus from Århus costs 38 kr and takes one hour. Hourly trains connect Ry with Silkeborg (22 kr, 20 minutes) and Århus (34 kr, 30 minutes).

Getting Around
Ry Cykel (☎ 86 89 14 91) at Skanderborgvej 19 hires out bikes for 50/250 kr per day/week.

HIMMELBJERGET
The Lake District's most visited spot is the whimsically named Himmelbjerget (Sky Mountain) which, at just 147m, is one of Denmark's highest hills. The hilltop is crowned with a 25m tower erected in 1875 which offers a fine 360° view of the lakes and surrounding countryside, which is part woodland, part farmland. On a clear day it's quite a lovely vista. Admission to the tower costs 5 kr.

There are marked hiking trails in the area, including one that leads 1km down to the lake, where there's a boat dock and a cafeteria that has live music in summer.

The parking area for Himmelbjerget is next to a hotel, a restaurant and souvenir kiosks. It's a five minute walk from the car park to the hilltop tower.

Places to Stay & Eat
Hotel Himmelbjerget (☎ 86 89 80 45, fax 86 89 87 93, Ny Himmelbjergvej 20, 8680 Ry) is a pleasantly rustic lodge with 18 rooms with shared bath, costing 290/450 kr for singles/doubles, including breakfast.

The *restaurant* at the hotel has a nice view of the woods and reasonable prices. There's also a kiosk selling fast food.

Getting There & Away
Bus No 104 runs from Ry train station to Himmelbjerget a few times a day, but check the schedule first with Ry Turistbureau because not every bus makes the stop. Himmelbjerget is a 10 minute drive west of Ry on route 445. It can also be reached by a pleasant 7km hike from Ry or by a scenic boat ride from either Ry or Silkeborg.

Boat Hjejlen (☎ 86 82 07 66), a paddle steamer that sails from Silkeborg to Himmelbjerget daily during the summer, leaves

---

A Paddle Steamer Cruise

The *Hjejlen*, one of the world's oldest operating paddle steamers, has been faithfully plying the waters of the Lake District since it was first launched in 1861. King Frederik VII was among the passengers on that inaugural cruise.

Built by the Burmeister & Wain shipyard in Copenhagen, the boat is such an antique that, when it was time for an engine overhaul a few years back, an engineer had to be called out of retirement to do the work.

These days the boat makes a couple of daily runs shuttling tourists from Silkeborg to Himmelbjerget during the summer season. The 15km route takes in a wealth of river and lake scenery along the way and is one of the most popular outings in the Lake District.

Silkeborg at 10 am and 1.45 pm. The trip takes 1¼ hours and costs 69 kr return or 46 kr one way; children's tickets are half-price. The same company also operates an ordinary boat on this route up to six times a day, so be sure to request *Hjejlen* when you book.

Ry Turistbåde (☎ 86 82 88 21) operates boats from Ry to Himmelbjerget daily in summer, leaving Ry at 10 am, noon and 2 pm and leaving Himmelbjerget one hour later. The fare is 35 kr one way, 50 kr return, 20/30 kr for children.

Djursland & Mols

Djursland and Mols are the names, respectively, of the northern and southern halves of the large peninsula north-east of Århus. It's a pleasant area of gently rolling hills and farmland interspersed with patches of woodland. There are small villages and a scattering of old manor houses throughout. The main destinations are the towns of Ebeltoft and Grenaa with their fine white-sand beaches which attract summer tourists.

There are a handful of other sites around the peninsula that could also be toured. The southern town of Rønde contains the ruins of **Kalø Slot**, a coastal brick fortress erected in the early 14th century. The Swedish king Gustav Vasa was a prisoner here in 1519. Although those who like to soak up history should enjoy this site, all that's left is the outline of the fortress foundation and the partial remains of one of the towers.

For a different sort of experience, there's **Djurs Sommerland**, an amusement park featuring water chutes and slides and other recreational activities geared towards children. It's about 20km west of Grenaa on Randersvej 17 in Nimtofte.

There's some particularly pretty countryside along the eastern side of the peninsula. If you're travelling by bicycle or car between Ebeltoft and Grenaa, consider taking the unfrequented rural route that leads through Dråby and continues as the easternmost through-road north.

EBELTOFT

Ebeltoft is an enjoyable tourist town with a centre of cobbled pedestrian streets lined with souvenir shops, cafés and ice-cream stands.

In medieval times Ebeltoft was a successful market town trading with Zealand, Germany and Sweden. The town's prosperity came to an abrupt end in 1659 when the Swedish navy sacked Ebeltoft and torched its merchant fleet. It wasn't until the 1960s, when the Swedes reinvaded (this time as tourists), that the economy shook off three centuries of stagnation. The central town quarters are more historic than modern, the streets around the old rådhus thick with period timber-framed buildings topped with red-tiled roofs.

The town sits on a calm, protected bay fringed with white-sand beaches; you'll find a nice stretch right along Strandvejen, the coastal road that leads north from the town centre. Another bathing area begins at the southern side of Ebeltoft, just below the harbour.

Orientation

The turistbureau, the *Fregatten Jylland* and the harbour are along Strandvejen. From the harbour walk east on Jernbanegade to reach Adelgade, the main shopping street. Torvet, home to the rådhus and its museum, is at the southern end of Adelgade. All of these places are within a five minute walk of each other.

Information

Tourist Office The Ebeltoft/Mols Turistbureau (☎ 86 34 14 00, fax 86 34 05 28) is at Strandvejen 2, 8400 Ebeltoft. Between mid-June and August it's open from 10 am to 6 pm Monday to Friday, from 10 am to 5 pm on Saturday and from 10 am to 2 pm on Sunday; during the rest of the year it's open from 10 am to 4 or 5 pm on weekdays and from 10 am to 1 or 2 pm on Saturday. Its Web site is at www.ebeltoftturist.dk.

Money There are four banks on Jernbanegade, including a Unibank at No 7, about 100m east of the turistbureau.

Post The post office, on the waterfront north of the turistbureau, is open from 9.30 am to 5 pm Monday to Friday, to noon on Saturday.

Things to See

Ebeltoft's old rådhus, which claims to be Denmark's smallest town hall, is a quaint half-timbered building erected in 1789. Located on Torvet, it now houses the **Ebeltoft Museum**, a worthwhile little collection that exudes a sense of the town's history. It's open from 10 am to 5 pm daily in summer and from 11 am to 3 pm Tuesday to Sunday in spring and autumn. Admission costs 20 kr (children 5 kr).

At the harbour is **Fregatten Jylland**, a 19th century wooden frigate that has undergone an extensive restoration. You can visit it, along with a retired lightship, daily from 9 am to 7 pm in summer and from 10 am to 5 pm in the low season. Admission costs 50 kr (children 20 kr).

Ebeltoft Kirke dates back to at least 1301, when the town received its charter from Erik VI. The church has a 13th century sandstone font and a few simple early 16th century frescoes, including a drawing of the *Maria*, a Danish warship that was used to attack Sweden in 1517. Ebeltoft Kirke is about a 10 minute walk south from Torvet via Overgade; the door is generally unlocked during the day and admission is free.

Missers Dukkemuseum, a little doll museum, is just west of Ebeltoft Kirke at Grønningen 17. It's open from 10 am to noon and 2 to 4 pm daily; admission costs 20 kr (children 10 kr).

Another attraction is the **Glasmuseum**, Strandvejen 8, which displays both decorative and functional works in glass. It's open from 10 am to 5 pm daily (until 9 pm in July) and admission costs 40 kr (children 5 kr).

Places to Stay

There are several camping grounds in the Ebeltoft area. *Vibæk Camping* (☎ 86 34 12 14, fax 86 34 55 33, Strandvej 23, 8400 Ebeltoft) is on a white-sand beach 1km

north of town. Open year-round, it's a three star facility with the usual amenities, including a laundry room, kitchen and cabins for rent.

The 72 bed *Ebeltoft Vandrerhjem* (☎ 86 34 20 53, fax 86 34 20 77, Søndergade 43, 8400 Ebeltoft) is a small hostel in a residential neighbourhood south of the centre, a 10 minute walk from the harbour and Torvet. Dorm beds cost 80 kr and private rooms cost from 170 kr for one person to 420 kr for six people. It's open year-round.

Hotel Ebeltoft (☎ 86 34 10 90, Adelgade 44, 8400 Ebeltoft), a small hotel in the town centre, has 10 straightforward rooms with shared baths. Singles/doubles cost 300/450 kr including breakfast.

Ebeltoft also has a couple of expensive hotels with modern facilities, including pools, saunas and restaurants. The 72 room *Hotel Ebeltoft Strand* (☎ 86 34 33 00, fax 86 34 46 36, email ebelstra@pip.dknet.dk, Nedre Strandvej 3, 8400 Ebeltoft) is on a rocky shoreline 500m north of the town centre. Singles/doubles with bath, TV, telephone, minibar and a terrace or balcony cost 740/1065 kr, but there's a summer price of 875 kr covering two adults and two children. Breakfast is included in the rates.

The 98 room *Hotel Hvide Hus* (☎ 86 34 14 66, fax 86 34 49 69, Strandgårdshøj 1, 8400 Ebeltoft), a few minutes walk from the waterfront north of the centre, has similarly appointed singles/doubles costing 850/1050 kr including breakfast.

Places to Eat

You'll find a few places to eat along Adelgade between Jernbanegade and Torvet, including *Gryden* (No 32), which serves pizza, burgers and pitta-bread sandwiches at the usual prices. *Torvet Burger* (No 6) offers cheap fast food including chicken and fish dishes and there's an *Underground Ice Cream shop* (No 4) serving natural ice cream.

For a place with more atmosphere, try *Mellem Fyder* (Juulsbakke 3), in a half-timbered house just south of Torvet and the old rådhus, which serves traditional Danish food; from noon to 4 pm lunches cost a reasonable 58 kr. At dinner, à la carte dishes begin at 75 kr.

Café Bageriet (*Adelgade 60*) is a pleasant place with good lunch deals: steak costs 39 kr and half a chicken with chips or pasta salad costs 45 kr.

Getting There & Away
Ebeltoft is on route 21, 54km east of Århus and 35km south-west of Grenaa.

Bus Bus No 123 runs between Århus and Ebeltoft about hourly on weekdays, less frequently at weekends; it takes 1½ hours and costs 42 kr. There's also a regular bus service (No 351, 30 kr) between Ebeltoft and Grenaa.

Boat Mols-Linien (☎ 89 52 52 52 in Ebeltoft, ☎ 59 32 32 32 in Zealand) operates a state-of-the-art hydrofoil car ferry between Ebeltoft and Sjællands Odde in north-western Zealand. The service runs 13 to 16 times a day and takes just 45 minutes. The cost is 110 kr for adults, 55 kr for children, 210 kr for a motorcycle with two riders and 435 kr for a car and up to five people. If you don't mind eating on the fly, the boat's restaurant offers good buffet spreads.

The same company also operates a slower boat that runs about half a dozen times a day, takes 1¾ hours and charges 375 kr for a car with passengers; other fares, however, are the same as on the express boat.

Getting Around
Bicycles can be hired from LP Cykler (☎ 86 34 47 77) at Nørreallé 5 and from Drevland Cykeludlejning (☎ 86 36 10 68) at Havnevej 10.

GRENAA
Grenaa, at the eastern tip of Jutland, is a relatively young town, having largely taken its present form in the late 19th century when its commercial harbour was dug and a rail link was established with the rest of Jutland.

It now serves as a port for ferries to Sweden.

Grenaa is divided into two sections. The centre of town, 3km inland from the harbour, has Torvet, an engaging main square, with the rådhus, the town church and the usual mix of shops, restaurants and bakeries. The train station is two blocks east of Torvet. A second commercial area has built up along the inland side of the harbour and has similar services, including banks and eateries. The harbour is a sizeable complex with a popular marina, the ferry docks and a fishing port.

A wide inviting beach, backed by gentle sand dunes, runs south from the harbour for nearly 7km. The inshore waters are shallow and popular with families who flock here on warm summer days.

Information
Tourist Offices The Djurslands Turistforening (☎ 87 58 12 00, fax 87 58 12 12, email dt@djurslands-turistforening.dk), Torvet 1, 8500 Grenaa, is open from 9 am to 5 pm on weekdays and from 9.30 am to 1.30 pm on Saturday between mid-June and August; during the rest of the year it's open from 9 am to 4 pm on weekdays and from 10 am to 1 pm on Saturday.

There's also a branch tourist office (☎ 86 30 93 88) opposite the harbour, open from 10 am to 4 pm Monday to Saturday between June and August.

Money There's a branch of Djurslands Bank at Strandgade 2, opposite the fishing harbour, and a couple of other banks on Torvet in the town centre.

Post The post office is at Stationsplads 2, west of the train station; it's open from 9 am to 5 pm on weekdays and from 9 am to noon on Saturday.

Things to See & Do
Although the main tourist draw is the beach, the town offers a couple of attractions to help keep visitors occupied during cloudy days.

Kattegatcentret at the harbour, north of the marina, is a modern aquarium housing several tanks of cold-water and tropical fish, including sharks. It's open daily from at least 10 am to 6 pm in summer and from 10 am to 4 pm in winter. Admission costs 65 kr (children 40 kr).

The regional history museum, **Djurslands Museum & Dansk Fiskerimuseum** at Søndergade 1, in a timber-framed merchant's house on the south side of Torvet, features antique toys, ceramics, coins, local archaeological finds and displays on the Danish fishing industry. It's open from 10 am to 4 pm Monday to Friday and from 1 to 4 pm at weekends in summer; winter opening hours are from 1 to 4 pm Tuesday to Friday and on Sunday. Admission costs 20 kr (children free).

Places to Stay
Polderrev Camping (☎ 86 32 17 18, fax 86 32 38 77, Fuglsangvej 58, 8500 Grenaa) is opposite the beach about 2km south of the harbour. Open from late March to mid-October, it has a three star rating and a grocery shop, a restaurant, a large group kitchen and a laundry room; there are also cabins for rent.

The 108 bed hostel, *Grenaa Sportel og Vandrerhjem* (☎ 86 32 66 22, fax 86 32 12 48, Ydesvej 4, 8500 Grenaa), is at a sports centre about 1.5km south-east of the town centre. Dorm beds cost 85 kr, family rooms cost from 250 kr for singles to 340 kr for four people. It's accessible to people in wheelchairs and serves three meals a day. The hostel is closed for a couple of weeks during the Christmas and New Year holidays.

The tourist office can provide a list of private *rooms* in the Grenaa area, with rates starting at around 120 kr per person. Staff can also provide information on beach-side *holiday cottages* to rent by the week in summer.

At *Hotel Grenaa Strand* (☎ 86 32 68 14, Havneplads 1, 8500 Grenaa), a small 16 room hotel opposite the harbour, singles/doubles cost 275/425 kr with shared bath

and start at 375/550 kr with private bath; prices include breakfast. Many of the rooms have TV and phone and there's a reasonably priced restaurant.

Places to Eat
In the town centre you'll find a number of places to eat on Lillegade, the street that runs north-west from Torvet. These include *Otto's Bageri* (No 10), a bakery-café combo offering tempting croissants, pizza sandwiches and a salad bar, and *Orient* (No 11), an inexpensive Chinese restaurant. *Den Gyldne Krus* (No 18) is a pub-style grill restaurant with a summertime pavement café. *Alberto's* (No 22) offers moderately priced pizza and pasta, and *Ibs Bageri* (No 31) is a typical Danish bakery.

Just inland from the harbour is *Glimmer Grill (Strandgade 7)*, a fast-food place offering inexpensive hot dogs and burgers; half a chicken and chips costs 42 kr. A block west is a *Dagli Brugsen* grocery shop, on the corner of Strandgade and Strandstræde; there's a bakery, *Strandbageriet*, next door.

Getting There & Away
Grenaa is 63km north-east of Århus on route 15, and 57km east of Randers along route 16.

Bus & Train Both bus (No 121 or 122) and train services run throughout the day between Århus and Grenaa, cost 50 kr and take about 1½ hours.

Boat For information on boats between Grenaa and the Swedish cities of Varberg and Halmstad, see the Getting There & Away chapter.

Getting Around
You can catch buses and get bus schedules at the DSB train/bus station at Stationsplads 4.

Bicycles can be hired from Viggo Jensen (☎ 86 32 06 83) at Strandgade 14 for 40 kr per day.

GAMMEL ESTRUP

Gammel Estrup, at Randersvej 2 in the village of Auning, 33km west of Grenaa, is an impressive estate dating back to the 14th century. It could make an interesting detour if you want a historical perspective on rural Danish life or if you haven't yet toured one of Zealand's castles.

The moat-encircled manor house, along with its period furnishings, tapestries and paintings, has been turned into a museum, the **Jyllands Herregårdsmuseum**. Visitors can wander through numerous rooms, including the kitchen, chapel, reception halls and sleeping quarters.

The estate farm buildings, adjacent to the manor house, have been set aside as a separate farming museum, **Dansk Landbrugsmuseum**, which depicts the more earthy lives of those who worked the land. Its halls are packed with farm tools, old tractors and carriages, milk jugs and the like; in summer there are often demonstrations of farm trades such as blacksmithery.

Both museums are open from 10 am to 5 pm between 1 April and 30 October. A combination ticket to both sites costs 50 kr (children free). Bus No 119 from Århus and bus No 214, which operates between Grenaa and Randers, stop at the front of the estate; both run about hourly.

The Interior

This area has some small industrial towns and cities, as well as wooded areas and farmland. The most interesting places are the 1000-year-old Fyrkat Viking ring fortress in Hobro and the Rebild Bakker national park, part of Rold Skov, Denmark's largest public woodland.

RANDERS

Randers is the fourth largest city in Jutland, although it has a population of just 60,000. Situated at the spot where the river Gudenå and the Randers Fjord merge, Randers' central location has made it an important trading town since it was founded in 1302. In the 19th century, after the railway linked Randers with the rest of Jutland, heavy industry developed and lofty smokestacks are still a dominant feature of the skyline. Because so many main roads and trains pass through Randers there's a good chance you'll pass through as well.

Orientation

The train station is west of the city centre, about a 15 minute walk from Randers Turistbureau (go east on Jernbanegade and Tørvebryggen) or 10 minutes from Rådhustorvet via Vestergade.

Information

Tourist Office Randers Turistbureau (☎ 86 42 44 77, fax 86 40 60 04), Tørvebryggen 12, 8900 Randers, is open in summer from 9 am to 6 pm Monday to Friday and from 9 am to 3 pm on Saturday; during the rest of the year it's open from 9.30 am to 4.30 or 5 pm Monday to Friday and from 9 am to noon on Saturday. Its Web site is at www.randers.dk.

Money The Jyske Bank on Rådhustorvet has an ATM that accepts major credit cards and operates until midnight.

Post The post office, north of Rådhustorvet at Nørregade 1, is open from 9.30 am to 5.30 pm Monday to Friday and from 9:30 am to 1 pm on Saturday.

Things to See & Do

By far the most interesting part of the city is its central area, where there is a cluster of period brick and half-timbered buildings. Among the most interesting, all dating from the late 15th century, are **Paaskesønnernes Gård**, a three storey brick building on Rådhustorvet; **Helligåndshuset**, once part of a medieval monastery, at Eric Menveds Plads; and **Sankt Mortens Kirke** on Kirketorvet. All three are within a few minutes walk of each other.

The local history and art museums are at **Kulturhuset** to the east of the city centre at Stemannsgade 2, a 10 minute walk from either Rådhustorvet or the turistbureau. The history museum has a prehistory section and collections of church art, period interiors, weapons and glass. The art museum features Danish paintings from the late 19th century to the present. Each museum is open from 11 am to 5 pm Tuesday to Sunday; admission costs 20 kr (children free).

The city's newest attraction is **Randers Regnskov**, a dome-enclosed tropical zoo at Tørvebryggen 11, about 300m west of the turistbureau. Trails within the sultry domes pass enclosures housing crocodiles, monkeys, pythons, iguanas, orchids, hibiscus and other rainforest flora and fauna. It's open daily from 10 am to 6 pm between May and August, to 4 pm during the rest of the year. Admission costs 50 kr (children 35 kr).

Places to Stay
The *Randers Vandrerhjem (☎ 86 42 50 44, fax 86 41 98 54, Gethersvej 1, 8900 Randers)* is just west of the city centre, a 10 minute walk north of the train station. It has 138 beds in 33 rooms. Dorm beds cost 77 kr and singles/doubles cost 157/214 kr. There's a coin laundry and rooms accessible to people in wheelchairs. It's open from 15 February to 1 December.

The turistbureau can provide you with a list of private homes with *rooms* for rent in the Randers area; prices vary, but expect a double to cost around 250 kr.

Hotel Kronjylland (☎ 86 41 43 33, fax 86 41 43 95, email hotelkronjylland@dk-online.dk, Vestergade 53, 8900 Randers), a five minute walk east of the train station, has 33 modern rooms with bath, TV and phone; singles/doubles start at 495/645 kr including breakfast.

The pleasantly old-fashioned *Hotel Randers (☎ 86 42 34 22, fax 86 40 15 86, Torvegade 11, 8900 Randers)*, in the city centre, has 79 comfortably renovated rooms with bath, TV, phone and minibar. The regular singles/doubles rate is 815/925 kr but there's a weekend rate of 695 kr per room; rates include breakfast. There's a restaurant, a lounge and free parking.

Places to Eat
There are some good food options in the town centre around Rådhustorvet. For atmosphere you can't beat *Kloster Konditoriet*, right on the square, which serves reasonably priced cakes and coffee in the basement of Randers' oldest building. *Belvedera Pizza*, just north of Rådhustorvet and opposite the post office, has late hours and serves large pizza slices (20 kr).

A block south-west of Rådhustorvet is *Café Borgen*, in an historic candlelit building on Eric Menveds Plads; it serves inexpensive sandwiches and lasagne (35 kr) during the day and turns into a mellow wine-and-dessert café at night. Also on Eric Menveds Plads is *China House*, which offers a Chinese lunch buffet from noon to 4 pm for 49 kr; a dinner buffet costs double that.

Storegade, which starts north-east of the turistbureau and runs towards Rådhustorvet, has a number of restaurants and pubs. A budget option is *Grilletten (No 6)*, which serves burgers and pitta-bread sandwiches. For something upmarket, try *Niels Ebbesen's Spisehus (No 13)*, which occupies a charming period building and offers moderately expensive steaks.

Getting There & Away
All trains between Århus and Aalborg stop in Randers. The fare is 49 kr to Århus and 71 kr to Aalborg.

Randers is 76km south of Aalborg and 36km north of Århus on the E45 and 57km west of Grenaa and 41km east of Viborg on route 16.

Getting Around
Jørgen Schmidt Cykler (☎ 86 41 29 03) at Vestergade 35 hires out bicycles for 50 kr per day.

HOBRO
Hobro is best known as the site of Fyrkat, an intact 10th century Viking ring fortress.

The town, which sits at the head of the Mariager Fjord, is otherwise a rather utilitarian place, being a mix of small industry and commercial facilities serving the farms and villages in the surrounding district.

The train station is at the western edge of town; to get from the station to the town centre, which is 1km away, walk east on Jernbanegade.

Information

Tourist Office The Hobro Turistbureau (☎ 98 52 56 66, fax 98 52 28 70), Sondre Kajgade 16, 9500 Hobro, is at the head of the Mariager Fjord. Between mid-June and 31 August it's open from 9 am to 5 pm on weekdays and from 9 am to 2 pm on Saturday; during the rest of the year it's open from 9 am to 4 pm on weekdays and from 9.30 am to 12.30 pm on Saturday. Its Web site is at www.hobro.dk.

Money & Post There's a branch of Jyske Bank at Adelgade 10. The post office is at Adelgade 8.

Town Centre

Over the centuries, fires have robbed Hobro of its finer buildings. The oldest remaining structure is a merchant's house erected in 1821. Located at Vestergade 21, it now houses the **Hobro Museum** (admission 20 kr), which displays local history exhibits, including excavated items from Fyrkat; it's open from 11 am to 5 pm Tuesday to Sunday between April and mid-October.

Fyrkat

Although it's somewhat smaller than the better-known Trelleborg in southern Zealand, the 1000-year-old Fyrkat fortress outside Hobro so closely resembles Trelleborg that both are presumed to have been built by the Viking king Harald Bluetooth in around 980.

Fyrkat was part of a farmer's overgrown field until the 1950s, when archaeologists from the national museum excavated the site. Items found during the excavation indicate that Fyrkat not only quartered about 800 Viking soldiers but that women and children were also part of the camp life. Many of the finds were singed, suggesting that the wooden longhouses that sat within the rampart walls had been destroyed by fire, probably within a few years of the fortress' completion, and that the site was then abandoned.

Today you can walk out onto the grass-covered circular ramparts for an impressive

Viking Play

Fyrkatspillet, a local amateur theatre troupe, presents a Viking play at Fyrkat annually during a two week period from late May to early June. A new play is performed each season, with the staging and production handled by members of the Aalborg Teater.

The plays are performed at the reconstructed Viking house. Although the performances are in Danish, the general theme is usually easy to follow and someone will gladly provide you with a little rundown on the plot before the action begins.

Themes commonly involve Viking kings; one play depicts the marriage of Sweyn Forkbeard and the strong-spirited Polish princess Swietoslawa, which was undertaken in a contrived effort to unite Denmark and Poland against the German kaiser. Whatever the storyline, you can expect beautiful damsels, sword-wielding Viking warriors, conflicts and resolutions, and lots of light-hearted laughter.

It's all quite a pleasant event with the inviting spirit of a neighbourhood party. On Friday and Saturday the performance is accompanied by a dinner featuring lamb roasted over an open spit. Admission to the play alone costs 60 kr; with dinner it costs 130 kr. Tickets can be reserved through the Hobro Turistbureau.

view of the fort's symmetrical design. The four cuts in the earthen walls, all formerly gates, face the four points of the compass. Within the rampart walls the fortress is divided into four equal quadrants, each of which once had four symmetrical buildings surrounding a central courtyard. Stone blocks placed within the fortress show the foundation shape of these elongated buildings, which once housed the inhabitants of Fyrkat. Sheep grazing in the fields add a certain timeless backdrop to it all.

No structures now stand within the ramparts but just outside is a replica Viking house built of oak timbers using a stave-style construction technique.

At the entrance to Fyrkat there are also some period farm buildings, including a functioning 200-year-old water mill and a half-timbered house with a pleasant old-fashioned restaurant.

Fyrkat (☎ 98 51 19 27) is 3km south-west of Hobro town centre via Fyrkatvej, and about a 75 kr taxi ride from the train station. If the weather is good, stop at the Viking farmstead (detailed in the following section) and then walk the last kilometre to the fortress site. During some summers there's an infrequent public bus service to Fyrkat but due to low passenger numbers it doesn't run every year.

Admission, which includes entrance to the water mill, the replica Viking house and Vikingegården Fyrkat (detailed below), costs 35 kr for adults and 15 kr for children. Opening hours are from 10 am to 5 pm daily between Easter weekend and mid-October.

Vikingegården Fyrkat To augment the Fyrkat fortress site, a Viking-style farmstead is currently under construction along Fyrkatvej, 1km north of the fortress. It is believed that farms such as this sat outside the fortress walls and served to provide food for the soldiers encamped within.

The goal is to construct at least nine Viking farm buildings but, since period-authentic materials and hand tools are used in the construction, the work is expected to

take another five years to complete. So far five buildings have been erected. The most impressive, a 33m longhouse, was built with a frame made of oak hewn by hand using an adze, a roof constructed of reeds fastened by willow shoots, a ridge of local peat and walls made of a mix of cow dung, blue clay and straw. Unfortunately the long-house was destroyed in 1998 by a fire of suspicious origin, and the elaborate process of rebuilding it has just begun.

Costumed interpreters give demonstrations of wool spinning, silverwork, archery and other Viking activities. You can even sample *mjød*, a fermented Viking brew of water, honey and spices.

The farmstead area has the same opening hours as Fyrkat and is included in the fortress admission fee.

Places to Stay

The three star *Hobro Camping Gattenborg* (☎ 98 52 32 88, fax 98 52 56 61, Skivevej 35, 9500 Hobro) is 1km south of the train station. It's open from early April to late September and has a swimming pool, a TV lounge and a few cabins for rent.

The 116 bed *Hobro Vandrerhjem* (☎ 98 52 18 47, fax 98 51 18 47, Amerikavej 24, 9500 Hobro), a modern hostel at a sports centre, is 1.5km east of the town centre. Dorm beds cost 90 kr and singles/doubles cost 235/260 kr. It's open from 1 February to 1 December.

Staff at the turistbureau can provide a list of *rooms* in private homes; doubles cost around 250 kr.

Hobro's cheapest hotel is *Motel Hobro* (☎ 98 51 02 12, fax 98 51 02 27, Randersvej 60, 9500 Hobro), about 1km south of the town centre. Singles/doubles with bath cost 300/400 kr, including breakfast.

Places to Eat

Although Hobro's restaurants tend to be spread out, there are a few eateries on Adelgade, the pedestrian street running through the town centre. *Bæch's Conditori (No 38)*, a bakery with café tables, sells pastries and sandwiches. The *Kvickly Cafeteria (No 14)* offers simple meals at inexpensive prices.

Musikcaféen at the harbour, west of the turistbureau, has good, reasonably priced Danish food and occasional live jazz.

An atmospheric option is *Fyrkat Møllegaard*, the restaurant at Fyrkat, which offers Danish country meals; lunch costs around 100 kr, dinner about twice that price.

Getting There & Away

Route 180 runs straight through Hobro, connecting it with Randers, 27km to the south-east, and to Aalborg, 49km to the north. The speedier E45 runs along the outskirts of Hobro, connecting it with the same cities.

Hobro is on the main Frederikshavn-Århus railway line. There are trains about twice hourly between Hobro and Randers (28 kr, 20 minutes) and between Hobro and Aalborg (49 kr, 34 minutes).

MARIAGER

Although it's a bit out of the way Mariager can be an interesting stop for those who want to unwind. This quiet little fjordside town has a solid grip on the past. Not only are its cobblestone streets lined with picturesque centuries-old buildings but it's home to two other relics, a vintage steam train and a paddle steamer.

Information

The tourist office (☎ 98 54 13 77, email mariager@post9.tele.dk), in the old rådhus on Torvet, is open from 9 am to 5 pm Monday to Friday and from 9 am to 2 pm on Saturday between mid-June and August, closing an hour or two earlier in the low season. Also on the square is a Sparekassen bank with an after-hours ATM.

Things to See & Do

You'll find the best collection of old buildings around Torvet, the central square, a 10 minute walk south of the harbour. The **Mariager Museum**, Kirkegade 4, just a minute's walk south of Torvet, occupies an 18th century merchant's house and contains the usual collection of historical artefacts. It's open from 1 to 5 pm daily in summer and admission costs 15 kr.

The 21m-long **paddle steamer** *Svanen* (☎ 98 54 14 70) plies the Mariager Fjord in summer, running a return journey between Mariager and Hobro four times a week. The schedule varies a bit but it typically operates between the two towns every Sunday from mid-May to mid-September and also on Monday, Thursday and Friday from late June to mid-August. The one-way/return fare is 45/70 kr for adults; children pay half price.

On Sunday from June to August a smoke-belching steam train, the **Veteranjernbane** (☎ 98 54 18 64), is taken out of mothballs to carry passengers on a 45 minute joyride to the village of Handest, where it stops for 30 minutes before making the return journey. The outbound departures from Mariager are usually at 11.30 am and 3.30 pm. The cost for the return journey is 40 kr for adults, 20 kr for children.

Places to Stay

The fjordside *Mariager Camping* (☎ 98 54 13 42, fax 98 54 25 80, Ny Havnevej 5A, 9500 Mariager), a three star camping ground, is open from April to mid-October. It has a shop and cabins for rent and is just a few hundred metres west of the boat dock and steam train station.

Hotel Postgaarden (☎ 98 54 10 12, fax 98 54 24 64, Torvet, 9550 Mariager), in a restored 300-year-old half-timbered building right on Torvet, has 14 rooms with bath, TV and phone; singles/doubles cost 450/600 kr including breakfast.

Places to Eat

Opposite the harbour there's a *grill* serving hot dogs and burgers, as well as a *Super Brugsen* grocery shop.

On Torvet you'll find a *bakery*, an *ice-cream shop* and a *pizzeria*. A fun place to soak up the village atmosphere is at *Hotel Postgaarden*, where a lunchtime special of traditional Danish fare costs 89 kr; it has tables right on the cobbled square.

Getting There & Away

Mariager is 15km east of Hobro on route 555. Other than the vintage tourist steam train, there's no train service to Mariager. Buses run every couple of hours from Hobro (18 kr) and hourly from Randers (26 kr); both routes take about 30 minutes.

REBILD BAKKER

Rebild Bakker, with its rolling heathered hills, is Denmark's only national park. In 1912 a group of Danish-Americans purchased 200 hectares of property at this site and presented it to the Danish government with three provisions. First, that it would remain in a natural state; second, that it would be open to all visitors; and third, that it would be accessible to Danish-Americans for the celebration of US holidays.

To augment the park area the Danish forest service acquired adjacent woodland tracts that are now set aside as nature reserves. Collectively the area, referred to as Rold Skov, is the largest forest in Denmark. Still, don't expect a vast wilderness, as it doesn't take much to lay claim to being Denmark's largest forest – the entire area accounts for only 77 sq km and at its greatest width can be walked across in a matter of hours.

Rebild Bakker is a pleasant area in which to stroll, its hills covered with heather, juniper, crowberry, blueberry, cranberry, mountain tobacco and club moss, while its scrubby woods contain European aspen, beech and oak trees.

Things to See & Do

The **Lincoln Log Cabin**, just west of the car park at the start of the trails, contains bits of Americana as seen through Danish eyes, plus displays on Danish emigration to the USA. The building, supposedly modelled on the log cabin that US president Abraham Lincoln grew up in, is itself a replica, the original having been destroyed by arsonists in 1993. Admission costs 15 kr (children free).

At the car park is **Spillemandsmuseet** (Fiddlers' Museum), a simple regional mu-seum featuring a varied collection of exhibits including fiddles, guns and traps, textiles and a 19th century kitchen. Admission costs 15 kr (children 3 kr).

There are numerous walking **trails** criss-crossing the park. One pleasant 4km route begins in a sheep meadow west of the car park. It goes past Tophuset, a small century-old thatched house that was built by the first caretakers; the Lincoln log cabin; a large glacial boulder called Cimbrerstenen, sculpted in the form of a Cimbrian bull's head by Anders Bundgaard; the hollow where the 4 July celebrations are held; and the Sønderland, the park's highest hill at 102m. It's a particularly lovely area in

Danish-American Festivities

Every 4 July thousands of Danes and Americans gather at Rebild Bakker to celebrate US Independence Day. The festivities, known as the Rebild Festival, have occurred annually since 1912 except during the two world wars, and are the largest US Independence Day celebrations held outside the USA. Many of the American participants are descendants of Danish immigrants, some 300,000 of whom went to the USA in the Danish emigration boom of the late 19th and early 20th centuries.

The festivities include singing, square dancing and country music as well as speeches by prominent Danes and Americans. Among the keynote speakers in recent times have been members of the Danish royal family, US presidents Bush and Reagan, and actors Richard Chamberlain and Danny Kaye.

Although the main celebration occurs at Rebild, in the days preceding the event there are also receptions and various activities in Aalborg, where most of the participants are accommodated. More information about the Rebild Festival can be obtained from the Aalborg Turistbureau.

summer and autumn when the heather adds a purple tinge to the hillsides.

Places to Stay

Safari Camping (☎ 98 39 11 10, fax 98 39 17 94, Rebildvej 17A, 9620 Skørping) is just a few minutes walk from the entrance to Rebild Bakker. This three star facility is open year-round and has 150 pitches as well as a few cabins.

The thatched *Rebild Vandrerhjem* (☎ 98 39 13 40, fax 98 39 27 40, Rebildvej 23, 9520 Skørping) has a handy location right next to the park entrance. There are laundry facilities and bicycles for hire, and it's accessible to people in wheelchairs. Dorm beds cost 80 kr and singles/doubles are 170/220 kr. The hostel has 100 beds and is open from 1 March to 1 November.

The *Scanticon Comwell* (☎ 98 39 12 22, fax 98 39 24 55, email hotel@scanticon comwell-rebild.dk, Rebildvej 36, 9520 Skørping) is a modern hotel opposite Rebild Vandrerhjem. The 151 rooms each have bath, TV, phone, minibar, desk and balcony. Singles/doubles cost 730/960 kr including breakfast, but there's a good-value summer price of 525/685 kr. The hotel has an indoor swimming pool, a sauna, a fitness room, tennis courts, a restaurant and a bar.

Places to Eat

At the Rebild Bakker car park you'll find a *kiosk* selling ice cream, hot dogs and sandwiches, and a *cafeteria* offering somewhat more substantial food such as lasagne or meatballs and potatoes for around 50 kr. Here too is *Rebild Hus*, a sit-down restaurant where a daily meal special costs 100 kr.

Skørping, the nearest town to Rebild Bakker, has a *bakery* and a *pizzeria* on the main road just east of the train station.

Getting There & Away

Route 180 runs through the Rold Skov forest, connecting Rebild Bakker with Hobro, 23km to the south.

From Aalborg, Århus-bound trains stop in Skørping (33 kr, 16 minutes), from where it's 3km west to Rebild Bakker. Bus No 104

runs between Aalborg and Rebild Bakker (33 kr, 45 minutes) via Skørping 12 times daily on weekdays, four times daily at weekends. There are also frequent trains from Hobro to Skørping (28 kr, 15 minutes).

VIBORG

Viborg's history can be traced back to the 8th century. In 1060 it became one of Denmark's eight bishoprics and a century later, in 1150, the town was granted its municipal charter. Viborg grew into a major religious centre and, prior to the Reformation, had 25 churches and abbeys, though ecclesiastical remnants from that period are few.

The old part of town consists of the streets around Viborg Domkirke. Sankt Mogens Gade, which is between the cathedral and the turistbureau, has some handsome old homes, including Hauchs Gård at No 7 and the Willesens House at No 9, both dating back to around 1520.

Viborg has a pleasant setting, bordering two lakes and surrounded by woods and moors. If you have your own transport, the Hald-Viborg reserve 6km south-west of Viborg has trails through the woods, a manor house with a natural history exhibit and the ruins of a castle.

The train station is about 1km south-west of the turistbureau.

Information

The Viborg Turistbureau (☎ 86 61 16 66, fax 86 60 02 38), Nytorv 9, 8800 Viborg, is in the centre of town. It's open from 9 am to 5 pm Monday to Friday and from 9 am to 3 pm on Saturday in summer; it closes at 4 pm on weekdays and at 12.30 pm on Saturday in winter.

Churches

The twin-towered cathedral, **Viborg Domkirke**, a two minute walk down the hill from the turistbureau, is one of Denmark's largest granite churches. Archaeological excavations in 1974 indicate that the first church on this site was a wooden structure dating back to Viking times. A series of stone

Skagen Fortidsminder highlights seafaring history.

Shipshape Viking grave, Lindholm Høje, Aalborg.

A bustling port since Viking times, Aalborg's economy is still heavily reliant upon its maritime culture.

JON DAVISON

The tower of the Tilsandede Kirke (Buried Church) rises eerily from the dunes south of Skagen.

NED FRIARY

The Kattegat and Skagerrak meet at the curving spit of Grenen, Denmark's northernmost point.

churches followed and, although there are traces of the first stone crypt dating from 1130, the current cathedral was virtually rebuilt in its entirety in 1876. The interior is splashed with grand frescoes painted over a five year period (1901-06) by artist Joakim Skovgaard. The frescoes in the nave depict scenes from the Old Testament, those in the transept depict the life of Christ, and the choir frescoes feature scenes from the Resurrection and Ascension. Viborg Domkirke is open from 10 am to 5 pm Monday to Saturday between June and August, and from 11 am to 3 pm in the low season; on Sunday it's open from noon year-round.

Also notable is **Søndre Sogns Kirke**, two blocks south of the cathedral. This church was built in 1230 as part of a Dominican monastery and, although it's been much altered over the centuries, the original nave remains largely intact. The most interesting interior feature is an ornately carved Dutch altarpiece from 1520. It's open from 9 am to 1 pm on weekdays, to noon on Saturday.

Museums

Skovgaard Museet, to the south of Viborg Domkirke at Domkirkestræde 4, features works by Joakim Skovgaard, the painter of the cathedral frescoes, but here the scenes are more varied and include nudes, portraits and landscapes. Works by friends and family members, including his father, PC Skovgaard, and his brother, Niels Skovgaard, are also on display. It's open from 1.30 to 5 pm year-round, and also from 10 am to 12.30 pm between May and September. Admission costs 10 kr.

There's a local history museum, the **Viborg Stiftsmuseum** at Hjultorvet 9, a minute's walk south-west of the turistbureau. It's open from 11 am to 5 pm daily between June and August; low-season hours are shorter. Admission costs 15 kr (children free).

Places to Stay

Bus No 707 (9 kr, seven minutes) can take you from the train station to DCU-Camping and Viborg Vandrerhjem, which are adja-

cent to each other on the eastern side of Søndersø.

The three star **DCU-Camping Viborg Sø** (☎ 86 67 13 11, fax 86 67 35 29, email viborg@dcu.dk, Vinkelvej, 8800 Viborg) has full facilities including a group kitchen, a coin laundry and bicycles and cabins for rent. It's open from late March to late September.

The modern **Viborg Vandrerhjem** (☎ 86 67 17 81, fax 86 67 17 88, email vibhoste @post8.tele.dk, Vinkelvej 36, 8800 Viborg) is a pleasant 137 bed hostel where dorm beds cost 90 kr and singles/doubles cost 195/250 kr. It's open from 1 March to 30 November. Bicycle and canoe hire can be arranged.

Staff at the turistbureau can book **rooms** in private homes; they cost from 110 to 150 kr per person, plus a 25 kr booking fee.

For a moderately priced central option try the **Palads Hotel** (☎ 86 62 37 00, fax 86 62 40 46, Sankt Mathias Gade 5, 8800 Viborg), a short walk north of the train station. A member of the Best Western chain, it has 75 rooms with baths and the usual amenities. The hotel offers a weekend and summer family rate of 695 kr for up to two adults and two children, including breakfast. At other times singles/doubles cost a hefty 895/995 kr.

Places to Eat

Pizzerias are thick on the ground in the town centre. There are places to grab a quick meal on Vestergade, the short pedestrian street west of the turistbureau. These include the bakery **Tougaard** (No 12) and **Santa Maria Pizza & Kebab Huset** (No 3).

If you walk south down the alley opposite Santa Maria, you'll reach a courtyard containing **Bone's** (Preislers Plads 3), a popular spareribs restaurant. You can get a good salad (21 kr) to take away, or sit down and eat your fill of ribs and potatoes for 79 kr.

Getting There & Away

Viborg is 66km north-west of Århus on route 26 and 41km west of Randers on route

CENTRAL JUTLAND

16. Trains from Århus (84 kr, 70 minutes) run hourly on weekdays, less frequently at weekends.

HJERL HEDE

Seven kilometres east of the small village of Vinderup is Hjerl Hede (☎ 97 44 80 60), a large open-air museum that traces the development of a Danish village from 1500 to 1900. Scenically set against a lake and moors, it has a collection of about 40 period buildings, many of them timber-framed with thatched roofs, which were brought here from around Jutland. You can wander around and visit a forge, a dairy, a grocery shop and even a village school.

From mid-June to late-August about 100 traditionally costumed men, women and children arrive at around 1 pm to 'inhabit' the village and perform traditional tasks such as dipping candles and tilling the fields. There's also a small settlement where 'Stone Age people' in costume make flint instruments and pottery and practise spear fishing from dugout canoes. Additionally, Hjerl Hede has a **forestry and bog cultivation museum** with an old steam engine and the remains of a narrow-gauge railway.

It's open from 9 am to 5 pm daily between 1 April and 31 October. Because of the activities, the summer high season is by far the most interesting time to go. Admission costs 60 kr (children 25 kr). The nearest train station is at Vinderup. There's no bus service from Vinderup, but a taxi costs around 90 kr. Trains run hourly between Viborg and Vinderup (35 kr, 55 minutes).

SPØTTRUP SLOT

In the countryside 20km west of Skive, on route 573, is Spøttrup Slot. It was built in the 1500s by Jørgen Friis, the region's last Catholic bishop, at a time when the Church was under siege by the impending Lutheran Reformation. Not surprisingly, the heavy brick structure, encircled by a high rampart and double moats, more closely resembles an austere fortress than a castle. Although it may lack the grand scale and splendour of other Danish castles, Spøttrup is unique in that it has survived the centuries without significant alteration and is one of the best-preserved medieval castles in Denmark.

The national government, which took over Spøttrup Slot and restored it about 50 years ago, still maintains it today. You can walk around the entire castle, which is pur-

---

Cycling on the Old Military Road

Denmark's best-known cycling route extends the length of Jutland, from Padborg on the German border to Skagen at the northernmost tip of Denmark, much of the way along an historic route called Hærvejen (Old Military Road). Established as Denmark's first national cycling route in 1989, this 440km trail roughly traces a path that has been used for 1000 years by nomad hunters, kings' armies, cattle herders and pilgrims. The ancient roadway follows the ridge of Jutland, providing broad views and minimising the need to cross rivers and fjords.

Although today parts of Hærvejen have been swallowed up by modern motorways, there are still many stretches that maintain their ancient character as field tracks. En route, cyclists pass through landscapes of heath and woodlands and find traces of earlier wayfarers, including barrows, old churches and rune stones.

Going at a relaxing pace, the entire route generally takes about a week – although many people opt for a smaller slice. The Dansk Cyklist Forbund produces a series of inexpensive maps (1:100,000 scale) that cover the route and detail the sights along the way. For more information see the special section 'Cycling in Denmark' in the Facts for the Visitor chapter.

posely kept in its original state with minimal furnishings and décor.

Spøttrup Slot (☎ 97 56 16 06) can be toured daily from 10 am to 6 pm between May and August, to 5 pm in September and to 4 pm in October. Admission costs 25 kr (children 5 kr).

The nearest train station is in Skive; from there you can take bus No 43 or 44, which cost 20 kr and leave about hourly on weekdays, less frequently at weekends. Trains run hourly between Skive and Viborg (28 kr, 26 minutes).

HOLSTEBRO & HERNING

Holstebro is roughly 50km west of Viborg on route 16; Herning is an equal distance south-west of Viborg on route 12. Both Holstebro and Herning are industrial towns with populations of about 30,000 and both are on the railway line from Silkeborg.

Holstebro is a long-established market town that reached its heyday in the early 18th century thanks to a large cattle market and its convenient location on the river Storå. It has a couple of small museums, but fire has claimed most of its historic buildings.

More interesting is Herning, a town that developed in the late 19th century when the railway came chugging through. Textile mills followed but have since been largely replaced by the wood processing and computer technology industries. The community has a keen interest in the arts; there are sculptures around town and the general ambience is enlivened by the presence of a music school. **Herning Museum**, Museumsgade 32, 300m south-west of the train station, features period furnishings and a collection of prehistoric items. Herning **Kunstmuseum**, 2km east of town at Birk Centerpark 3, has a decent collection of modern Danish art, including works by Asger Jorn, Richard Mortensen and Carl-Henning Pedersen.

The Herning tourist office (☎ 97 12 44 22) is on Bredgade 2, the main shopping street, two blocks north-west of the train station. The Holstebro tourist office (☎ 97 42 57 00), Brotorvet 8, is on the southern side of the river and is about a 20 minute walk south of the train station.

Herning has an HI hostel (☎ 97 12 31 44) and both Herning and Holstebro have camping grounds and a few hotels.

From Silkeborg, trains run about hourly to Herning (43 kr, 45 minutes) and Holstebro (63 kr, 1¼ hours).

Central West Coast

The central west coast, north of Esbjerg, is lined with sandy beaches, making it a popular summer holiday destination. One area particularly thick with summer cottages is Holmsland Klit, the thin neck of sand and dunes stretching nearly 35km from north to south, separating the North Sea from the Ringkøbing Fjord. This sandy neck, only about 1km wide, has its appeal but don't expect the drive to be overwhelmingly scenic as the dunes block the ocean view almost the entire way.

The Ringkøbing Fjord attracts scores of windsurfers with conditions that are suitable for all levels, including beginners, while the North Sea side of Holmsland Klit offers more challenging action for advanced windsurfers.

HENNE STRAND

Henne Strand is a small seaside resort especially popular with German visitors. The road into the village, Strandvejen, ends at the beach and is lined with a touristy collection of souvenir shops, boutiques, restaurants, discos and pizzerias, all in a row one after the other. The grassy dunes that separate the village from the beach are dotted with summer holiday homes, including some attractive thatched cottages.

The beach itself is long and lovely. On warm summer days when the wind is calm swimmers take to the waters, although caution should be used as strong North Sea undertows can be experienced anywhere along the west coast. The northern end of the beach is a popular spot for nude sunbathing.

CENTRAL JUTLAND

Places to Stay & Eat

Henne Strand Camping (☎ 75 25 50 79, Henne Strandvej 418, 6854 Henne Strand), a three star facility, is open from early April to late October. Located 300m east of the village centre, it's about a 10 minute walk from the beach. There's a coin laundry, cooking facilities and cabins. The site also has a 'tropicland' with a swimming pool and water slide.

The little 44 bed *Henne Strand Vandrerhjem (☎ 75 25 50 75, Strandvejen 458, 6854 Henne Strand)* is right in the village, just minutes from the beach. It's open from late June to late August and dorm beds cost 75 kr. Because it's so small, private rooms are rarely available, but when they are, singles/doubles cost 135/190 kr.

Henne Strand Feriehusudlejning (☎ 75 25 56 00, fax 75 25 51 20, Strandvejen 436, 6854 Henne Strand) can book *summer houses* costing from around 1800 to 6000 kr a week.

Along Strandvejen you'll find a *grocery shop*, *hot dog stands*, a couple of *bakeries* and numerous eateries where you can get a meal for between 40 and 75 kr.

Getting There & Away

Henne Strand is at the end of route 465. Almost all visitors arrive by car but it is possible to get there by public transport. The easiest way is to take a train to Henne Strandby from Varde (32 kr, 30 minutes) and from there catch a taxi, which will cost about 100 kr. Alternately you could take the train to the more northerly Nørre Nebel (32 kr, 45 minutes) and catch one of the infrequent buses that run from there to Henne Strand.

HVIDE SANDE

The town of Hvide Sande came into existence in 1931 with the opening of a sluice channel and lock between the Ringkøbing Fjord and the North Sea. The sluice regulates both the water level and salinity of the Ringkøbing Fjord and protects the fields on the inland side of the fjord from being flooded. The lock, which is 16.5m wide, allows ships to enter the fjord, which is otherwise sealed off from the sea. The channel cuts across the centre of town and you can get a view of it all from the bridge.

Hvide Sande has a busy deep-sea fishing harbour, with lots of trawlers, fish processing factories and an early morning fish auction. There's also a little fishing museum adjacent to the tourist office. Most visitors, however, aren't here for the fish but for the wind.

Information

The Holmsland Klit Turistforening (☎ 97 31 18 66, fax 97 31 28 80) is at the Fiskeriets Hus Museum, Nørregade 2, 6960 Hvide Sande, on the northern side of the channel. It's open from 9 am to 5 pm Monday to Friday and from 9 am to noon on Saturday; in summer it's also open from 10 am to 1 pm on Sunday.

Windsurfing

Ringkøbing Fjord has ideal wind and water conditions, and Hvide Sande attracts scores of windsurfers. Surfcenter Hvide Sande Nord (☎ 97 31 25 99, Gytjevej 15), a Westwind operation on the northern side of Hvide Sande, offers a three hour introductory course for 400 kr as well as more comprehensive classes. It also hires out gear, including wetsuits costing 120 kr per day and boards with rigs starting at 300 kr per day; weekly rates are equivalent to about three times the daily rate.

There's a good Web site on windsurfing in the area at www.ringkobingfjord.dk /windsurfing.

Places to Stay

The two star *Beltana Camping (☎ 97 31 12 18, fax 97 31 33 11, email beltana@dk-camp.dk, Karen Brandsvej 70, 6960 Hvide Sande)* is to the south of town opposite a popular windsurfing beach. There are cooking and laundry facilities; cabins are also available to rent. It's open from early April to mid-October. There are other camping grounds to both the north and south of Hvide Sande.

The new **Hvide Sande Vandrerhjem** (☎ 97 31 21 05, fax 97 31 21 96, Numitvej 5, 6960 Hvide Sande) has a central location at a sports centre on the northern side of the harbour. The 88 bed hostel has 23 modern rooms, half with their own shower and toilet. Dorm beds cost 90 kr and singles/doubles cost 230/270 kr. The centre has a large indoor swimming pool, plus handball and badminton courts.

Holmsland Klit Turistforening can provide information on private **rooms** and **summer cottages** to rent.

The in-town hotel **Hvide Sande Sømandshjem** (☎ 97 31 10 33, Bredgade 5, 6960 Hvide Sande) is on the southern side of the harbour. There are 15 straightforward singles/doubles with bath for 300/450 kr including breakfast.

Places to Eat

There are **bakeries** on the southern side of town on the corner of Metheasvej and Stormgade and on the northern side of town at Nørregade 50.

Edgar Madsen (Metheasvej 11), near the waterfront street Auktionsvej on the southern side of town, sells smoked fish by the piece and a few other takeaway items.

Two blocks to the south of Edgar Madsen is **La Barca** (Søndergade 3), where you'll find moderately priced pizza and pasta, though it's best known for its steaks and spareribs.

If you're looking for an upmarket place to eat, **Restaurant Slusen** (Bredgade 3) near the harbour has a good reputation for its fresh seafood.

Getting There & Away

Hvide Sande is on route 181. Bus No 58 runs to Hvide Sande from Ringkøbing train station (20 minutes) and Nørre Nebel train station (35 minutes) about once an hour on weekdays, half as frequently on weekends.

RINGKØBING

Ringkøbing, on the northern side of the Ringkøbing Fjord, is an old market town that was granted its municipal charter in 1443. The town originated as a North Sea port but, from the 17th century, shifting sands caused the mouth of the fjord to slowly migrate south and threatened to cut off Ringkøbing's access to the sea. It wasn't until the lock at Hvide Sande was built in 1931 that the town was once again assured a reliable North Sea passage.

Ringkøbing now has 8500 residents, a shipyard, some industry and the county administrative offices.

Information

The Ringkøbing Turistbureau (☎ 97 32 00 31, fax 97 32 49 00), Torvet, 6950 Ringkøbing, is in the town centre next to the church. It's open from 9.30 am to 5 pm Monday to Friday and from 10 am to 1 pm on Saturday.

There are two banks on Torvet. The post office is to the west of the train station.

Things to See

There are a few **period buildings** in the centre of town around Torvet, the oldest of which is Hotel Ringkøbing; its timber-framed wing dates from about 1600. The church north-west of the hotel dates in past from medieval times and has a sundial from 1728 on its western buttress.

The **Ringkøbing Museum**, on Østerport east of Torvet, features displays on the Greenland expedition (1906-08) of Mylius Erichsen and such intriguing local items as a chastity belt from 1600. It's open from 11 am to 5 pm daily in summer, with shorter hours during the rest of the year; admission costs 15 kr.

Places to Stay

The three star **Ringkøbing Camping** (☎ 97 32 08 38, fax 97 32 52 08, Vellingvej 56, 6950 Ringkøbing), on the eastern side of town, is open from April to October.

The **Ringkøbing Vandrerhjem** (☎ 97 32 24 55, fax 97 32 49 59, Kirkevej 28, 6950 Ringkøbing) is a modern hostel at a large sports centre 1.5km north of the train station via Holstebrovej. Open year-round, it has 120 beds in 24 rooms, most with bath.

Dorm beds cost 90 kr and singles/doubles cost 250/300 kr.

The historic *Hotel Ringkøbing* (☎ 97 32 00 11, Torvet 18, 6950 Ringkøbing) has 15 rooms; singles/doubles with bath start at 375/550 kr.

The Best Western *Hotel Fjordgården* (☎ 97 32 14 00, fax 97 32 47 60, Vesterkær 28, 6950 Ringkøbing), in the western part of town, has 98 modern rooms with bath, cable TV and minibar, and there's a sauna and indoor swimming pool. Singles/doubles cost 815/1015 kr; from mid-June to mid-August there's a summer rate of 695 kr per room.

Places to Eat

You can get a reasonably priced meal at *Rogeriet Sorte Louis*, at the harbour, which sells smoked fish and deli salads to eat in or take away.

A central supermarket is *Super Brugsen* (Torvegade 9), on the street leading west from Torvet. There's a *bakery* at Østergade

17, east of Torvet, and another at Vester Strandgade 10, south of Torvet.

Algade, which heads east from Torvet, is lined with small shops, including *Ristorante Pizzeria Italia* (No 11), serving pizza, pasta and Italian meat dishes at moderate prices.

There's a fine-dining restaurant specialising in fish at the *Hotel Ringkøbing* on Torvet and another expensive, but rather more contemporary, restaurant at the *Hotel Fjordgården*.

Getting There & Away

Ringkøbing is on route 15, 46km west of Herning and 9km east of the North Sea.

It is on the railway line between Esbjerg (71 kr, 1¼ hours) and Struer (63 kr, one hour). Buses to Hvide Sande leave from the train station.

There's a little seasonal ferry, the MF *Sorte Louis*, that sails across the Ringkøbing Fjord between Ringkøbing and Hvide Sande; call ☎ 97 32 06 66 or check at the turistbureau for the current schedule.

Northern Jutland

Northern Jutland, which is separated from the rest of Jutland by the Limfjord, has a coastal landscape dominated by heathlands, dunes and sandy beaches.

The region has only one large city, Aalborg, and a handful of mid-sized towns. Although road maps are peppered with the names of numerous smaller villages, these are often little more than a string of roadside houses broken by farmland and fields of grazing sheep.

Among the most interesting places in northern Jutland are the Lindholm Høje Viking burial ground on the northern outskirts of Aalborg, the vast shifting sand dunes of Råbjerg Mile and the arty resort town of Skagen, the sandy tip of which marks Denmark's northernmost point, called Grenen.

AALBORG

Strategically situated at the narrowest point of the Limfjord, the long body of water that slices Jutland in two, Aalborg has been a bustling port since Viking times.

Today Aalborg is the second-largest city in Jutland, with a population of 155,000. An industrial and trade centre, Aalborg's economy is reliant upon shipbuilding, cement and steel. It is also well known to bar hoppers as the leading producer of Danish schnapps, *akvavit*.

Although it's skipped over by most foreign travellers Aalborg has a few worthwhile sights, the paramount attraction being Lindholm Høje, Denmark's largest Viking burial ground.

Orientation

Aalborg spreads along both sides of the Limfjord, its two parts linked by bridge and tunnel. The heart of the city and most services are on the southern side, including the turistbureau and the cathedral, which are about 1km north of the train and bus stations along Boulevarden.

Highlights

- Reflect on the past at the Viking burial ground at Lindholm Høje (Aalborg)
- Get lost in vast stretches of deserted beaches
- Explore the extensive sand dunes of Råbjerg Mile
- Wander about seaside Skagen with its distinctive houses, museums and artists' community
- Cycle out to the 'buried church' in the dunes south of Skagen
- Taste the windsurfing action at Klitmøller

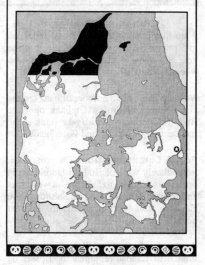

Information

Tourist Office The Aalborg Turistbureau (☎ 98 12 60 22, fax 98 16 69 22) is at Østerågade 8, Postboks 1862, 9100 Aalborg; its Web site is at www.tourist-aal.dk. Between mid-June and mid-August it's open from

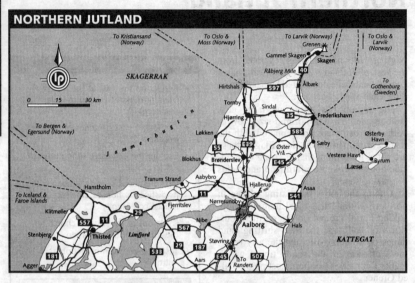

NORTHERN JUTLAND

9 am to 6 pm Monday to Friday and 9 am to 5 pm on Saturday; during the rest of the year it's open from 9 am to 4.30 pm on weekdays and 10 am to 1 pm on Saturday.

Money There are a number of banks in the city centre including a Unibank opposite Budolfi Domkirke and a Jyske Bank at the intersection of Nytorv and Østerågade.

Post & Communications The post office, immediately west of Budolfi Domkirke, is open from 9.30 am to 5.30 pm on weekdays and from 9.30 am to noon on Saturday. You can also send faxes or access the Internet here.

Gay & Lesbian Travellers The Aalborg branch of Landsforeningen for Bøsser og Lesbiske (LBL), the national organisation for gays and lesbians, can be reached at ☎ 98 16 45 07.

Bookshop Ginnerups Boghandel, Boulevarden 12, has a stock of maps and books on Denmark.

Laundry There's a coin laundry on the corner of Vesterbro and Borgergade.

Pharmacy Budolfi Apotek (☎ 98 12 06 77), on the corner of Vesterbro and Algade, is open 24 hours.

Danish Emigration Archives Udvandrerarkiv Det Danske (Danish Emigration Archives; ☎ 99 31 42 20), Arkivstræde 1, behind Vor Frue Kirke, keeps records of Danish emigration history and is set up to help foreigners of Danish descent trace their roots. It's open from 9 am to 4 pm Monday to Thursday and from 9 am to 2 pm on Friday and Saturday. Its Web site is at www.cybercity.dk/users/ccc13656.

Budolfi Domkirke

This whitewashed cathedral, which dates from the 12th century, marks the centre of the old town. As you enter the cathedral interior from Algade, look up at the foyer ceiling to see colourful frescoes. The interior boasts some beautifully carved items, including a gilded Baroque altar and a richly detailed pulpit. Interestingly, despite their different appearances, both were created by Danish sculptor Lauridtz Jensen; apparently the altar, carved in 1689, was too flashy for the parish so in 1692 Jensen used an older Renaissance style for the pulpit. In summer Budolfi Domkirke is open from 9 am to 4 pm Monday to Friday (to 2 pm on Saturday); in winter it closes an hour earlier. Admission is free.

Aalborg Historiske Museum

On the block west of Budolfi Domkirke is the Aalborg Historiske Museum, a local history museum featuring excavated artefacts, the requisite Renaissance furnishings and fine collections of glassware and ancient Danish coins. It also displays some interesting oddities, such as a mid-18th century hearse embellished with skull and crossbones motifs. It's open from 10 am to 5 pm Tuesday to Sunday. Admission is free on Tuesday and costs 10 kr (children 5 kr) on other days.

Other Central Sights

The alley between the Aalborg Historiske Museum and Budolfi Domkirke leads to the rambling **Helligåndsklostret**, or Monastery of the Holy Ghost, which dates from 1431. The interior can only be visited on a guided tour arranged through the turistbureau (see under Organised Tours).

East of Budolfi Domkirke on Østerågade are three noteworthy historic buildings: the Baroque-style **old rådhus** (circa 1762), the five storey **Jens Bangs Stenhus** (circa 1624), and **Jørgen Olufsens House** (circa 1616) at Østerågade 25. The latter two are lovely Renaissance buildings, one built by a wealthy merchant, Jens Bang, and the other by a wealthy mayor, Jørgen Olufsen.

In addition, the neighbourhoods of half-timbered houses around **Vor Frue Kirke** on Peder Barkes Gade are worth strolling through, particularly the cobbled street Hjelmerstald. **Aalborghus Slot**, near the waterfront, is more an administrative office than a castle but there's a small dungeon you can visit (admission free).

Ask at the turistbureau for the English-language *Good Old Aalborg* booklet, which maps out two suggested walking tours and provides details of buildings and sights along the way.

Nordjyllands Kunstmuseum

This regional museum of modern and contemporary art, at Kong Christian Allé 50, is in a marble building designed by Finnish architect Alvar Aalto. It has a fine collection of Danish art dating from the late 19th century to the present day, including works by JF Willumsen, Asger Jorn, Richard Mortensen and Edvard Weie. It's open from 10 am to 5 pm Tuesday to Sunday year-round; in July and August it's also open on Monday. Admission costs 30 kr (children free).

To get there take the tunnel beneath the train station, which emerges into Kildeparken, a green space with statues and water fountains. Go directly through the park, cross Vesterbro and continue through a wooded area to the museum, a 10 minute walk in all.

Aalborgtårnet

The hill behind Nordjyllands Kunstmuseum is topped with Aalborgtårnet, an ungainly tower offering a panoramic view of the city's steeples and smokestacks. The tower is open from 11 am to 5 pm between April and October (from 10 am to 7 pm in summer), weather permitting. The ride up costs 20 kr (children 10 kr).

Aalborgtårnet sits at the edge of an expansive wooded area, **Mølleparken**, which has walking trails, views and the Aalborg Zoo.

Aalborg Zoo

This zoo in Mølleparken, to the south-west of the city centre, has some pleasant aspects including a wooded setting and a children's zoo with goats and other tame creatures. In all, Aalborg Zoo is home to more than 800 animals including elephants, zebras, tigers, giraffes, orang-utans, crocodiles and polar bears. There are also golden-lion tamarins,

AALBORG

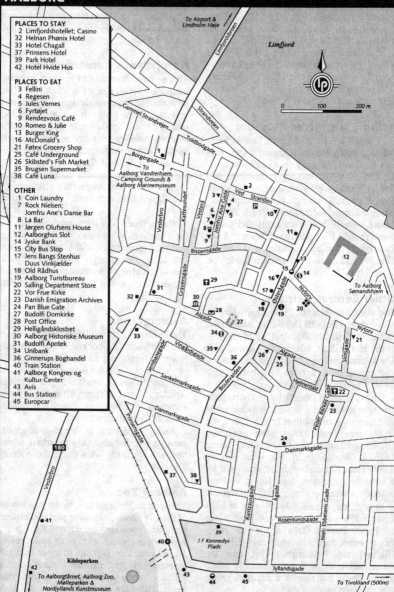

PLACES TO STAY
2 Limfjordshotellet; Casino
32 Helnan Phønix Hotel
33 Hotel Chagall
37 Prinsens Hotel
39 Park Hotel
42 Hotel Hvide Hus

PLACES TO EAT
3 Fellini
5 Regesen
5 Jules Vernes
6 Fyrtøjet
9 Rendezvous Café
10 Romeo & Julie
13 Burger King
16 McDonald's
21 Føtex Grocery Shop
25 Café Underground
26 Skibsted's Fish Market
35 Brugsen Supermarket
38 Café Luna

OTHER
1 Coin Laundry
7 Rock Nielsen;
   Jomfru Ane's Danse Bar
8 La Bar
11 Jørgen Olufsens House
12 Aalborghus Slot
14 Jyske Bank
15 City Bus Stop
17 Jens Bangs Stenhus
   Duus Vinkjælder
18 Old Rådhus
19 Aalborg Turistbureau
20 Salling Department Store
22 Vor Frue Kirke
23 Danish Emigration Archives
24 Pan Blue Gate
27 Budolfi Domkirke
28 Post Office
29 Helligåndsklostret
30 Aalborg Historiske Museum
31 Budolfi Apotek
34 Unibank
36 Ginnerups Boghandel
40 Train Station
41 Aalborg Kongres og
   Kultur Center
43 Avis
44 Bus Station
45 Europcar

To Airport &
Lindholm Høje

Limfjord

0   100   200 m

Gammel Strandvejen

Strandvejen

Toldbodgade

Borgergade

To
Aalborg Vandrerhjem,
Camping Grounds &
Aalborg Marinemuseum

Ved Stranden

Vesterbro

Kattesundet

Vesterå

Jomfru Ane Gade

Bispensgade

Gravensgade

Algade

Vingårdsgade

Jernbanegade

Sankelmarksgade

Boulevarden

Danmarksgade

Prinsensgade

Østerågade

Nytorv

Nytorv

Slotsgade

To Aalborg
Sømandshjem

Hjelmerstald

Algade

Peder Barkes Gade

Rosenlundsgade

Niels Ebbesens Gade

Danmarksgade

Rantzausgade

Agade

Jyllandsgade

Vesterbro

180

Kildeparken

42

To Aalborgtårnet, Aalborg Zoo,
Mølleparken &
Nordjyllands Kunstmuseum

J F Kennedys
Plads

To Tivoliland (500m)

almost extinct in the wild, which have been successfully bred here. The zoo is open daily from 9 am to 6 pm between May and August, from 10 am to 4 pm in April, September and October, and from 10 am to 2 pm during the rest of the year. Admission costs 60 kr (children 30 kr). There's a cafeteria serving moderately priced food. Bus No 1 runs there from the city centre.

Tivoliland

This amusement park on Karolinelundsvej, to the east of the city centre, has a roller coaster, a carousel, bumper cars and about 70 other rides and attractions as well as the usual carnival-style food. It's open from April to September; opening hours vary, but are from 10 am to 10 pm at the height of the season. Admission costs 40 kr (children 20 kr), not including rides.

Aalborg Marinemuseum

This waterfront museum at Vestre Fjordvej 81, 3km west of the city centre, features a 54m submarine, a torpedo boat, model ships and other maritime exhibits. It's open from 10 am to 6 pm in summer and from 10 am to 4 pm in winter. Admission costs 40 kr (children 20 kr). Bus Nos 2 and 8 stop nearby.

Lindholm Høje

On a hill-top pasture overlooking the city, Lindholm Høje is the site of 682 graves from the Iron Age and Viking Age. Many of the Viking graves are marked by stones placed in an oval ship shape, with two larger end stones as stem and stern. Interpretive plaques on the grounds provide historical insights. It's an intriguing place to walk around; there's something almost spiritual about the site.

Lindholm Høje Museet, by the site's car park, features archaeological displays that attempt to recreate a sense of life during Viking times. The museum is open from 10 am to 5 pm daily between April and October, and from 10 am to 4 pm Tuesday to Sunday in winter. Admission costs 20 kr (children 10 kr). The museum complex has

a café serving simple sandwiches and salads at reasonable prices.

The field containing the gravestones is open from dawn to dusk; admission is free.

Lindholm Høje is 15 minutes from Aalborg on bus No 6; cross the fence 50m beyond the bus stop and you're in the burial field. If you have your own transport, head north from the city centre over Limfjordsbroen to Nørresundby, following Lindholmsvej north to Hvorupvej. After Hvorupvej intersects with Vikingevej take the first left, which will bring you up the driveway to the museum.

Organised Tours

In summer a convenient three hour city bus tour, with a guide speaking both Danish and English, is run at 1 pm on Monday, Wednesday and Friday. It cruises past the city's main sights and stops for visits at the Nordjyllands Kunstmuseum and at Lindholm Høje and its Viking museum. Tickets, which include admission to the museums, can be bought in advance from the turistbureau; they cost 60 kr (children 25 kr).

The turistbureau also organises a tour of the 15th century Helligåndsklostret on weekdays at 1.30 pm. The tours cost 25 kr (children 10 kr); the guides on Tuesday and Thursday speak English.

Places to Stay

Hostel & Camping The hostel *Aalborg Vandrerhjem* (☎ 98 11 60 44, fax 98 12 47 11, Skydebanevej 50, 9000 Aalborg), at the marina 4km west of the centre, has 35 rooms, each with four beds and a bath. Dorm beds cost 90 kr; during the low season singles/doubles cost 200/300 kr. There's a TV lounge, table tennis and billiards. It's open year-round except from mid-December to mid-January. Bus No 8, which operates about twice an hour from 6 am to almost midnight, stops in front.

The hostel also runs the adjacent *Fjordparken*, a three star camping ground with full facilities. It costs 50 kr per person and is open from 15 May to 1 November. There are also heated fjordside cabins that can sleep up to five; the cost for two people ranges from 275 to 335 kr.

Strandparkens Camping (☎ 98 12 76 29, fax 98 12 76 73, Skydebanevej 20, 9000 Aalborg) is on the eastern side of the marina, 300m from Fjordparken and also reached by bus No 8. It has the same rating and comparable amenities, including laundry and cooking facilities, but cheaper rates at 40 kr per night. Cabins are also available. It's open from Easter to mid-September.

Private Rooms Staff at the turistbureau can book *rooms* in private homes; singles/doubles cost 150/250 kr plus a booking fee of 25 kr.

Hotels All of the following hotels include breakfast in their rates.

The centrally located **Prinsens Hotel** (☎ 98 13 37 33, fax 98 16 52 82, Prinsensgade 14, 9000 Aalborg) has 37 rooms with TV, phone and minibar. The rooms are comfortable enough but many are on the small side. Weekday rates are 375/520 kr for singles/doubles with shared bath (there are only a couple of rooms) and from 595/795 kr with private bath; there's a small discount at weekends and in summer.

The traditional **Park Hotel** (☎ 98 12 31 33, fax 98 13 31 66, email ccc20331@vip .cybercity.dk, Boulevarden 41, 9000 Aalborg) has a good location opposite the train station. Rooms are very comfortable, some with deep bathtubs and all with a TV, a hairdryer and soft down quilts. Ask for one of the courtyard rooms, which are the quietest. Singles/doubles start at 635/755 kr.

The following top-end hotels are in the city centre. In addition to the regular rates listed here, all of these hotels sometimes offer discounted rates at weekends, in summer or when business is slow, so it's worth inquiring.

Hotel Chagall (☎ 98 12 69 33, fax 98 13 13 44, email chagall@aix1.danadata.dk, Vesterbro 36, 9000 Aalborg) has 72 rooms with bath, TV, phone and minibar; singles/

doubles cost 750/970 kr. There's a sauna, a jacuzzi and an exercise room.

Hotel Hvide Hus (☎ 98 13 84 00, fax 98 13 51 22, email hhhaalb@pip.dknet.dk, Vesterbro 2, 9000 Aalborg) is a modern 200 room Best Western hotel with all the usual amenities. There's a fitness room, a sauna, an outdoor pool and a restaurant. The regular rate is 820/1020 kr for singles/doubles, but there's a summer rate of 695 kr for a family room sleeping two adults and two children.

Limfjordshotellet (☎ 98 16 43 33, fax 98 16 17 47, email limhotel@pip.dknet.dk, Ved Stranden 14, 9100 Aalborg) is best known as the site of the local casino. The 180 rooms, some of which are set aside for nonsmokers, are modern and have private bath, minibar and TV. Singles/doubles cost 875/1095 kr.

The old-fashioned **Helnan Phønix Hotel** (☎ 98 12 00 11, fax 98 16 31 66, email hotel @helnan-phonix-hotel.dk, Vesterbro 77, 9000 Aalborg) has 180 rooms with bath, TV, phone and minibar; singles/doubles cost 950/1150 kr. There's a bar, a restaurant, a sauna and a fitness room.

The **Aalborg Sømandshjem** (☎ 98 12 19 00, fax 98 11 76 97, Østerbro 27, 9000 Aalborg), about 1km east of the city centre, is part of a small hotel chain originally geared to seamen but now open to all. It has 54 rooms with bath, TV and phone; singles/doubles cost 450/595 kr. There are also a few single rooms with shared bath costing 290 kr. The hotel has a fitness room and free parking.

Places to Eat

Jomfru Ane Gade The best place to head at mealtimes is Jomfru Ane Gade, a boisterous pedestrian street lined with restaurants and cafés with outdoor tables. In the afternoon you'll find lots of lunch deals costing less than 50 kr, while three course dinners cost from 70 to 100 kr.

A good approach is to simply stroll the street and see what catches your fancy. Some of the choices, listed from north to south, are detailed here.

Water of Life

Akvavit (or aquavit), which means water of life, is the most popular spirit produced in Denmark. There are nearly 30 types of Danish akvavit on the market, most made from fermented potato mash. During the distilling process this dry spirit is flavoured with herbs, berries or spices, the most common being caraway seeds.

Akvavit is served in special long-stemmed glasses and is not sipped but swallowed straight in one gulp. The bottle is commonly kept in a freezer and the liquor served so ice-cold that it frosts the glass when it is poured. In Denmark, akvavit is often followed by a chaser of beer and is usually not drunk as an aperitif but as a complement to traditional Danish meals such as smørrebrød or herring.

Most akvavit is 40% alcohol and all varieties produce a strong fiery sensation on the way down the throat. The city of Aalborg has been producing akvavit since the 17th century and its namesake Aalborg brand is the world's most famous.

Fellini (Jomfru Ane Gade 23) is a popular Italian restaurant where lasagne or pizza costs 39 kr until 4 pm. At dinner, pizza begins at 54 kr, pasta dishes at 69 kr.

For traditional Danish fare, visit *Regesen (Jomfru Ane Gade 16)*, where a three course dinner special costs 84 kr.

At *Jules Vernes (Jomfru Ane Gade 14)*, which spices up its menu with international dishes, a three course set lunch (69 kr) is served until 6 pm.

If the weather is threatening rain, consider *Fyrtøjet (Jomfru Ane Gade 17)*, which has a glass-roofed courtyard and competitive prices.

The *Rendezvous Café (Jomfru Ane Gade 5)* offers light lunches and inexpensive pasta and salads.

Elsewhere The train station has a small *grocery shop* and a *DSB Restaurant*, and there's a *cafeteria* at the bus station.

Café Luna, a couple of minutes walk north of the train station on Boulevarden, is a pleasant place with long opening hours and reasonably priced lasagne, quiche and salads.

Algade, a pedestrian shopping street a block south of the turistbureau, has a few good inexpensive options. *Skibsted's Fish Market (No 23)* has fresh takeaway salmon-burgers and fish and chips, while *Café*

Underground (No 21) serves natural ice cream as well as crêpes and sandwiches.

There are a few fast-food restaurants in the city centre on Østerågade, including a **Burger King** and a **McDonald's**. The basement supermarket at *Salling* department store, 100m to the east on Nytorv, contains a deli selling smoked fish, salads and cheeses to take away. The *Føtex* grocery shop, a few minutes farther east at Slotsgade 8, contains a bakery, a fast-food kiosk serving pizza slices (13 kr) and a cafeteria where a filling meal of the day costs 30 kr.

Romeo & Julie (Ved Stranden 5), a pleasant pizzeria, offers a lunch buffet of pizza, pasta and salad for 59 kr and a three course dinner for 99 kr.

A superb way to cap off the evening is with a glass of wine at the smoulderingly romantic *Duus Vinkjælder*, a 300-year-old candlelit wine cellar in Jens Bangs Stenhus on Østerågade. Open until at least midnight from Monday to Saturday, it has surprisingly reasonable drink prices and offers a few cheap light eats such as burgers, chips and sandwiches.

Entertainment

Jomfru Ane Gade is a popular spot for nightlife. You'll find drinks, music and dancing along this street at *Rock Nielsen* and at the nearby *Jomfru Ane's Danse Bar*. For cheap drinks *La Bar*, just a few metres to the south, is the hot spot.

Aalborg Kongres og Kultur Center (☎ 99 35 55 55), on Vesterbro north of Kilde-parken, is the venue for classical music, opera and ballet performances.

Pan Blue Gate (☎ 98 12 22 45, Dan-marksgade 27A), a gay bar and dance club, is open at night from Tuesday to Saturday.

Limfjordshotellet has a *casino* with roul-ette, blackjack and poker. Admission costs 50 kr and is restricted to people aged 18 and over; it's open from 8 pm to 4 am daily.

Getting There & Away

Air Scandinavian Airlines (SAS; ☎ 70 10 20 00) operates 10 weekday and five week-end nonstop flights between Aalborg and Copenhagen. The one-way fare is 710 kr but discounted return fares, aimed at busi-ness travellers but open to all, are as low as 420 kr (maximum stay two days) or 560 kr (30 day stay).

The airport is 6km north-west of the city centre; cross Limfjordsbroen and follow the signs for *lufthavn*.

An airport bus (23 kr) coinciding with flight times runs between the airport and the bus station on Jyllandsgade. A taxi between the airport and the city centre costs about 100 kr.

Bus Express buses (☎ 70 10 00 30) run daily to Copenhagen (190 kr, six hours), Århus (98 kr, 2¼ hours) and Esbjerg (156 kr, 3½ hours).

Train Trains run about hourly to Frederik-shavn (61 kr, one hour) and a little more frequently to Århus (121 kr, 1½ hours).

Car & Motorcycle Aalborg is 112km north of Århus and 65km south-west of Frederikshavn. The E45 bypasses the city centre, tunnelling under the Limfjord, while route 180 (which links up with the E45 both north and south of the city) leads into the centre.

To get to Lindholm Høje or points north of the centre of Aalborg, take route 180 (Vesterbro) which crosses Limfjordsbroen.

Rental Hertz, Avis and Europcar have booths at the airport. Avis (☎ 98 13 30 99) has an office at the train station and Europ-car (☎ 98 13 23 55) is at Jyllandsgade 4.

Getting Around

Bus Almost all city buses leave from Østerågade and Nytorv, near Burger King. The standard bus fare is 11 kr, or you can buy a 24 hour tourist bus pass (70 kr). The detailed city maps found in the turistbu-reau's free *Aalborg Guide* show bus routes in blue; there's a bus information line (☎ 98 11 11 11) if you need further assistance.

Car & Motorcycle Apart from a few one-way streets that may have you driving in circles a bit, Aalborg is easy to get around by car. There's free parking along many side streets, and metered parking in the city centre. If you're unable to find a parking space, there are several large com-mercial car parks, including one at Ved Stranden 11.

Taxi Taxis line up at the train station and are usually plentiful at the airport around flight times. You can also order one (☎ 98 10 10 10, 98 12 12 12).

FREDERIKSHAVN

Frederikshavn, with a population of 26,000, is the largest town north of Aalborg and Jutland's busiest international ferry port.

Frederikshavn is a young town, quite modern in appearance and with few historic attractions. It has an industrial waterfront of boat terminals and shipyards, while the town centre is chock-a-block with super-markets selling liquor, canned hams and frozen meats to Swedes and Norwegians on shopping excursions.

Although overtaxed Scandinavians may be drawn here for bargains, Frederikshavn is not terribly appealing to most other foreign travellers who generally pass right through without pause. If you have time to spare, there are a couple of local sights you could visit, the most interesting being Bangsbomuseet.

Orientation

An overhead walkway leads from the ferry terminals to the turistbureau, which sits at the edge of the central commercial district. The train station and adjacent bus terminal are a 10 minute walk north from the ferry terminals.

Information

Tourist Office The Frederikshavn Turist-bureau (☎ 98 42 32 66, fax 98 42 12 99, email turistbureau@frederikshavn-tourist .dk) is opposite the harbour at Brotorvet 1, 9900 Frederikshavn. Between mid-June and mid-August it's open from 8.30 am to 8.30 pm Monday to Saturday and from 11 am to 8.30 pm on Sunday; in the low season it's open from 9 am to 4 pm on weekdays and from 11 am to 2 pm on Saturday.

Money There are several banks in the town centre spread out along Danmarksgade, and a 24 hour ATM is outside the Damsgaard Supermarket on Havnegade.

Post The post office, beside the train station, is open from 9.30 am to 5 pm on weekdays and from 9.30 am to noon on Saturday.

Things to See

If you're waiting for a train you might want to climb the nearby whitewashed **Krudttårnet** (gunpowder tower), a remnant of the 17th century citadel that once protected the port. Until 1974 this squat round tower stood 270m to the east but an expansion of the shipyards necessitated its move farther inland. Within the tower's 2m-thick walls are a few displays of antique swords, helmets and guns, and a steep stairway leads to a top galley mounted with cannons. Between June and September, it's open

from 10.30 am to 5 pm daily; admission costs 10 kr.

Frederikshavn Kirke, the church opposite the train station, dates from 1892 and has an altarpiece painted by Skagen artist Michael Ancher. The doors are open from 9 am to noon Tuesday to Saturday.

On Parallelvej, 500m west of the train station, there's a **cultural complex** with a modest art museum, swimming pools and the public library.

Bangsbomuseet

Bangsbo Museum, 3km south of Frederikshavn town centre, is an old country estate with an eclectic mix of collections. The manor house holds local history exhibits, Victorian furniture, antique dolls and a peculiar collection of ornaments woven from human hair.

The farm buildings contain old ship figureheads, military paraphernalia and exhibits relating to the Danish Resistance to the German occupation during WWII. The most intriguing exhibit is the **Ellingåskib** (Ellingå Ship), the reconstructed remains of a 12th century Viking-style merchant ship that was dug up from a stream bed 5km north of Frederikshavn.

If you're up to a walk, a gate just outside the museum leads into Dyrehaven, a wooded area that's home to red, fallow and sika deer. Bangsbomuseet is open from 10.30 am to 5 pm daily, except on Monday in winter; admission costs 25 kr. Bus No 3 stops near the entrance to the estate; from there it's an enjoyable 500m walk through the wood to the museum.

Places to Stay

The closest camping ground is *Nordstrand Camping* (☎ 98 42 93 50, fax 98 43 47 85, Apholmenvej 40, 9900 Frederikshavn) near the coast, 4km north of the town centre. It has a four star rating, a full range of amenities and cabins for rent. It's open from April to mid-September. Skagen-bound buses and trains (11 kr) stop near the camping ground.

The *Frederikshavn Vandrerhjem* (☎ 98 42 14 75, fax 98 42 65 22, Buhlsvej 6, 9900

Frederikshavn), about 1.5km north-west of the train station, has 130 beds and is open from 1 February to 20 December. Dorm beds, mostly in rooms with eight to 12 beds, cost from 53 to 65 kr. There are also four-bed family rooms with bath (160 kr) that are available as doubles when it's not busy. From the ferry harbour it's a 30 minute walk or a 50 kr taxi ride.

Staff at Frederikshavn Turistbureau can book you one of about 50 private *rooms*, most within a 15 minute walk of the town centre. Singles cost from 115 to 165 kr and doubles from 225 to 275 kr. There's a 25 kr booking fee.

Hotel 1987 (☎ 98 43 19 87, fax 98 43 19 42, Havnegade 8E, 9900 Frederikshavn) is a friendly place with 28 comfortable rooms, each with bath, TV, phone and minibar; singles/doubles cost 460/560 kr including breakfast. It's behind the Damsgaard Supermarket, a two minute walk from the turistbureau.

Frederikshavn Sømandshjem (☎ 98 42 09 77, fax 98 43 18 99, Tordenskjoldsgade 15B, 9900 Frederikshavn) has 40 rooms with bath and TV; singles/doubles start at 485/650 kr including breakfast. It's just a few minutes walk from the train station and the ferry terminals.

Hotel Jutlandia (☎ 98 42 42 00, fax 98 42 38 72, Havnepladsen 1, 9900 Frederikshavn), a modern multistorey hotel opposite the harbour, has comfortable if undistinguished rooms with bath, TV and phone; singles/doubles cost 740/910 kr. At weekends and in summer you can opt to buy a Scan Hotel Pass (90 kr) and then pay just 650 kr for the room, single or double.

Places to Eat

The train station contains a *kiosk* selling fruit and snacks and there are simple eateries at both the train station and the ferry terminals.

There are large grocery shops near the waterfront geared to travellers who want to stock up on cheap Danish food and liquor before they leave. One of these, *Havne Super (Sydhavnsvej 8)* at the ferry harbour,

is open from 7.30 am to 9 pm daily and has an upstairs cafeteria, open for lunch and dinner.

The *Damsgaard Supermarket (Havnegade 10)*, beside Frederikshavn Turistbureau, has an inexpensive 2nd floor cafeteria with a daily lunch special (30 kr) and a harbour view.

There are a number of places to eat on Lodsgade, one street to the north of Havnegade, as well as on the nearby streets of Danmarksgade and Søndergade. At *Europa (Lodsgade 5)*, a steakhouse and pizzeria, pizza and pasta dishes start at around 60 kr and a daily steak special costs 80 kr. *Bacchus (Lodsgade 8A)* specialises in meat and fish dishes costing from around 100 kr, while *Los Gringos (Lodsgade 4)* offers enchiladas or burritos for 89 kr.

In the same neighbourhood, just to the west, you'll find three pizza and pasta restaurants: *Venezia (Danmarksgade 73)*, *Firenze Pizzeria (Danmarksgade 84)* and *Toni Pizzeria (Søndergade 3B)*. *Ruen Thai (Søndergade 15C)* offers an all-you-can-eat Thai lunch buffet for 59 kr. For dessert, try *Is-Caféen (Danmarksgade 77)*, which sells Underground natural ice cream.

Getting There & Away

Bus & Train An express bus runs a couple of times daily from Frederikshavn and Esbjerg (190 kr, five hours).

Frederikshavn is the northern terminus of the Danske Statsbaner (Danish State Railways; DSB) railway line. Trains depart about hourly south to Århus (156 kr, 2½ hours) and Aalborg (61 kr, one hour), and on to Copenhagen (272 kr, five hours).

Nordjyllands Trafikselskab (NT) runs both a train (40 minutes) and a bus service (one hour) north to Skagen (33 kr). NT sells a *klippekort* (clip card) costing 68 kr and valid for 110 kr-worth of travel; several people can clip the same card.

NT also sells a 24 hour ticket valid for unlimited travel along its bus and train routes, which take in most of northern Jutland including Skagen, Råbjerg Mile, Hirtshals, Hjørring and Løkken (note that some of the beach routes operate in summer only). The ticket costs 70 kr (children 35 kr).

Car & Motorcycle Frederikshavn is 65km north-east of Aalborg on the E45 and 41km south of Skagen on route 40.

As Frederikshavn is a major port of entry, there are several car rental offices. These include:

Avis
  (☎ 98 43 19 77) Paradiskajen 1
Europcar
  (☎ 98 42 31 33) Havnepladsen 5A
Hertz
  (☎ 98 42 86 77) Danmarksgade 15

Boat For detailed information on ferries from Frederikshavn to Gothenburg in Sweden and to Oslo and Larvik in Norway see the Getting There & Away chapter. For information on the ferry to Læsø, see the following Læsø section.

LÆSØ

Læsø, 28km south-east of Frederikshavn, is a quiet island with 2400 inhabitants. Although it measures only 25km at its greatest width, this 114 sq km island is the largest in the Kattegat. It has a landscape of small farms, heathlands, coastal meadows, dunes and sandy beaches.

According to legend Queen Margrethe I, saved from a shipwreck off Læsø in the 14th century, rewarded her rescuers with a lovely dress and gave them the right to adapt it as an island costume. Although such regional customs had largely disappeared elsewhere in Denmark by the 19th century, Læsø women wore their traditional island dress up until the post-WWII period and continue to wear the costume today on special occasions.

Another island tradition continues in the making of Læsø salt, once an island export; it's now sold in small bags as a tourist souvenir.

The Læsø Turistbureau (☎ 98 49 92 42, fax 98 49 92 83), Vesterø Havnegade, 9940 Læsø, is 200m east of the ferry terminal in Vesterø Havn; its Web site is at www.laeso-tourist.dk.

Læsø is free from large resort hotels and attracts visitors looking for a low-key summer holiday. The island has a few small towns, two medieval churches, a straw-roofed maritime museum and a seaweed-roofed farm museum.

Places to Stay & Eat

There are two three-star camping grounds on Læsø. *Østerby Camping (☎/fax 98 49 80 74, Campingpladsvej 8, 9960 Østerby Havn)* is on the north-eastern side of the island right in the village of Østerby Havn. *Læsø Camping (☎ 98 49 94 95, fax 98 49 94 55, Agersigen 18, 9950 Vesterø Havn)* is on the north-western side of the island, 1.5km from the ferry terminal. Both charge 50 kr per person, are open from May to October and have food kiosks and cabins for rent.

The 90 bed *Læsø Vandrerhjem (☎ 98 49 91 95, fax 98 49 91 60, Lærkevej 6, 9950 Vesterø Havn)* is 500m south-east of the ferry harbour. It's open from mid-April to October and charges 70 to 85 kr for dorm beds, 215 kr for a single room and 340 kr for a room sleeping four.

Læsø Turistbureau can provide information on *holiday cottages* and *flats* available around the island.

There are *bakeries*, *food markets* and small *restaurants* in the main villages. In the evening you can get pizza or a dinner (75 kr) served with a helping from the salad bar at Læsø Vandrerhjem.

Getting There & Away

AndelsFærgeselskabet Læsø (☎ 98 49 90 22) ferries sail two to six times a day between Læsø and Frederikshavn year-round. The crossing takes 1½ hours. The return fare is 130 kr for adults, 65 kr for children, 400 kr for a car, 200 kr for a motorcycle and 45 kr for a bicycle. There's also a great 225/130 kr same-day return ticket for a car or motorcycle. Note that the aforementioned vehicle fares don't include drivers or passengers.

Getting Around

Bus A public bus runs about hourly on weekdays and every couple of hours at weekends between the villages of Vesterø Havn, Byrum and Østerby Havn.

Bicycle Bicycles can be rented from Jarvis Cykelservice (☎ 98 49 94 44) at Vesterø Havnegade 29 in Vesterø Havn and from the camping grounds.

SKAGEN

A fishing port for centuries, Skagen's luminous heath-and-dune landscape was discovered in the mid-19th century by artists and, in more recent times, by summering urbanites.

The town's older neighbourhoods are filled with distinctive yellow-washed houses, each roofed with red tiles edged with white lines. Skagen is half arty and half touristy, with a mix of galleries, souvenir shops and ice cream parlours. The peninsula is lined with fine beaches, including a sandy stretch at the eastern end of Østre Strandvej, a 15 minute walk south-east from the town centre.

Sankt Laurentii Vej, Skagen's main street, runs almost the entire length of this long thin town and is never more than five minutes walk from the waterfront.

Information

Tourist Office The Skagen Turistbureau (☎ 98 44 13 77, fax 98 45 02 94) is in the station (which serves both trains and buses) at Sankt Laurentii Vej 22, 9990 Skagen; its Web site is at www.skagen-tourist.dk. Between late June and early August it's open from 9 am to 7 pm daily; during the rest of the year it's open from at least 9 am to 4 pm on weekdays and from 10 am to 1 pm on Saturday.

Money There are a number of banks in the town centre, including an Egnsbank Nord opposite the station and a branch of Den Danske Bank on the corner of Sankt Laurentii Vej and Havnevej.

Post The post office is at Christian X Vej 8, 400m west of the station.

Museums

Skagens Museum This fine museum, at Brøndumsvej 4, displays the paintings of PS Krøyer, Michael and Anna Ancher and other artists who flocked to Skagen between 1830 and 1930 to 'paint the light'. Take a close look at *Johannisfeuer*, Krøyer's early-20th century work that shows a bonfire on Skagen beach; among the notable Skagen residents depicted on the left side of the painting are Anna Ancher, in a blue cape, and Holger Drachmann, in a brown cloak with a white beard and cane. Skagens Museum, just a few minutes walk east from the station, is open from 10 am to 6 pm daily in summer, to 5 pm daily in May and September, with shorter low-season hours. Admission costs 40 kr (children free).

Michael & Anna Anchers Hus The house that Michael and Anna Ancher purchased in 1884 was turned into a museum following the death of their daughter Helga in the 1960s. Preserved to look much as it would have during the artists' lifetimes, it is of note mainly to those with a particular interest in the Anchers. It's at Markvej 2, 300m north-east of the station, and is open from 10 am to 5 pm daily between May and September (to 6 pm in the summer high season), with shorter low-season hours. Admission costs 30 kr (children 10 kr).

Drachmanns Hus The house where poet/artist Holger Drachmann lived from 1902 until his death six years later is now a museum dedicated to his life. At Hans Baghs Vej 21, near Sankt Laurentii Vej, to the west of the town centre, it's open from 10 am to 5 pm daily in summer, with shorter low-season hours. Admission costs 20 kr (children free).

Skagen Fortidsminder Evocatively presented, this worthwhile open-air museum depicts Skagen's maritime history. It features interesting displays on Skagen's life-

A Mariner's Nightmare

The waters off northern Jutland have always been extremely treacherous for mariners and have claimed many hundreds of ships over the centuries. Not only are the waters tempestuous and the currents strong, but the land is flat and devoid of landmarks, offering few reference points by which ships can be guided.

Historically, when ships did wash up on shore, local residents would go straight to work pillaging the contents and dismantling the ships for their timber. Some unscrupulous souls are even said to have hung lanterns in such a manner as to imitate waterways and in so doing would lure captains into venturing too close to the shoreline, where they would strand on shallow shoals.

The situation got so out of hand that in 1521 a decree was passed to control salvaging. Gallows were erected along the coast to remind would-be pillagers of the new penalty for the looting of shipwrecks.

At the same time, simple wooden seesaw-style 'lighthouses' called *vippefyret* were erected along the coastline. Each had a basket that could be pulled down and filled with coal, and a counterweight that raised the basket high where it burned throughout the night. These forerunners of present-day lighthouses helped to guide ships safely around the point. Although none of the original coal lights still exist, there's a reconstructed one at Skagen above the beach at the north-eastern end of Østre Strandvej.

---

boat rescue service, including dramatic photos of ships in distress, as well as the preserved homes of fisherfolk with their original furnishings, and a picturesque Dutch windmill.

Skagen Fortidsminder is a 15 minute walk from the station west down Sankt Laurentii Vej, then south on Vesterled. Between May and September it's open from 10 am to 5 pm daily; in March, April, October and November it's open from 10 am to 4 pm on weekdays. Admission costs 25 kr (children 5 kr).

Grenen

Denmark's northernmost point is the long curving sweep of sand at Grenen, 3km north-west of Skagen town centre. From the car park at the end of route 40, the path to the beach crosses rose-covered dunes and at its highest point passes the grave of poet Holger Drachmann (1846-1908).

It's a 30 minute walk out along the vast beach to its narrow tip where the waters of the Kattegat and Skagerrak clash and you can put one foot in each sea. Swimming is not allowed near the point, however, because strong currents have been responsible for sweeping unsuspecting bathers out to sea.

If you're short on time you might want to walk one way and take the Sandormen in the other direction. This tractor-drawn 'bus' drives out to the point from the Grenen car park every half-hour in summer, spending 15 minutes at the site before returning. The cost is 10 kr one way, 15 kr return.

At the car park is the **Grenen Kunstmuseum**, an art gallery exhibiting contemporary Danish paintings with an emphasis on the seascapes created by Axel Lind, who founded the museum 20 years ago. It's open from 10 am to 6 pm daily in summer and from 10 am to 4 pm daily in May and September. Admission costs 20 kr (children 10 kr for children). The 35m-high bronze sculpture east of the museum is *God on the Rainbow*, created by Swedish sculptor Carl Milles.

Tilsandede Kirke

The Tilsandede Kirke (Buried Church) is a whitewashed medieval church tower that still rises up above the sand dunes that buried the surrounding village and farms in the late 18th century. The church itself, once the largest in the county, was closed in 1795 because of drifting sand that obscured the doorways, and in 1810 the main part of the church was finally torn down. The lofty tower, however, was left standing to serve as a navigational landmark.

The picturesque church tower and the surrounding area comprise part of Skagen Klitplantage, a nature reserve. It's 5km south of Skagen, well signposted from route 40. The nicest way to get there is by bike; take Gammel Landevej from Skagen. The tower interior is open from 11 am to 5 pm daily between June and August. Admission costs 8 kr (children 3 kr).

Places to Stay

Camping There are two three-star camping grounds about 1.5km north-east of Skagen's centre, both charging 55 kr per person in the high season, 45 kr in the low season. *Grenen Camping* (☎ 98 44 25 46, fax 98 44 65 46, email grencamp@post6.tele.dk, Fyrvej 16, 9990 Skagen) has a fine seaside location, some semi-private tent sites and pleasant four-bunk cabins. It's open from early May to early September.

Poul Eegs Camping (☎ 98 44 14 70, fax 98 45 14 60, Batterivej 31, 9990 Skagen) is inland from the beach but, like Grenen Camping, has full facilities, including guest kitchens and cabins to rent. It's open from early May to 31 August.

Hostel & Rooms The modern 112 bed hostel *Skagen Ny Vandrerhjem* (☎ 98 44 22 00, fax 98 44 22 55, Rolighedsvej 2, 9990 Skagen) is 1km west of the town centre on the southern side of the road to Frederikshavn. Dorm beds cost 85 kr, while doubles range from 275 to 400 kr. It's open from 15 February to 30 November but reception closes as early as 6 pm outside of summer. The facilities are accessible to people in wheelchairs.

Staff at Skagen Turistbureau can book private *rooms* for you; singles/doubles cost 150/300 kr plus a 35 kr booking fee.

Hotels & Pensions At *Clausens Hotel* (☎ 98 45 01 66, fax 98 44 46 33, Sankt Laurentii Vej 35, 9990 Skagen), opposite the station, singles/doubles cost 450/595 kr with shared bath, 550/795 kr with private bath, including breakfast.

The 12 room *Marienlund Badepension* (☎ 98 44 13 20, fax 98 45 14 66, Fabriciusvej 8, 9990 Skagen), out on the older western side of town near Skagen Fortidsminder, has singles/doubles with shared bath for 260/490 kr including breakfast.

The 30 room *Skagen Sømandshjem* (☎ 98 44 30 28, fax 98 44 25 88, Østre Strandvej 2, 9990 Skagen), near the harbour, charges 280/530 kr for simple singles/doubles with shared bath and 450/635 kr with private bath, including breakfast.

Finns Pension (☎/fax 98 45 01 55, Østre Strandvej 63, 9990 Skagen) is a popular gay-friendly pension in the town centre. The half-dozen rooms, which have shared bath, cost 325/575 kr for singles/doubles, including breakfast.

Places to Eat

In general, Skagen tends to be a pricey place to eat. Havnevej, the main road connecting the harbour and the centre, has the main cluster of affordable spots, with half-a-dozen pizzerias and grills.

At *Italia* (Havnevej 5), takeaway pizza and pasta costs 49 kr; sit-down meals including the same items are in the 50 to 70 kr range. You'll find similarly priced pizza, as well as more expensive fish and meat dishes, at *Firenze* (*Havnevej 9*) and *Alfredo* (*Havnevej 13*). *Blue Burger* (*Havnevej 4*) offers burgers or a half-chicken and chips (40 kr), while *Vaflen*, opposite Alfredo, is the place for ice cream.

Just 200m west of Havnevej is a branch of the steak restaurant chain *Jensen's Bøf-hus* (*Sankt Laurentii Vej 63*), which offers inexpensive lunch deals and reasonably priced dinners.

For more atmosphere, *Clausens Hotel*, opposite the station, offers a café lunch menu (78 kr) from 11 am to 5 pm that includes a smørrebrød plate or a half-lobster with salad, plus a glass of wine or beer; a 300g steak with chips costs 89 kr.

A good fish place right at the harbour is the popular *Pakhuset* (*Rødspættevej 6*), which has an expensive upstairs restaurant as well as a ground-floor café serving similar fare at lower prices, including a nice saffron fish soup (78 kr).

For a cheap harbourside eat, try *Havne-grillen*, opposite Pakhuset, which has hot dogs, burgers, beer and picnic tables.

There's a *bakery* opposite the rådhus at Sankt Laurentii Vej 82 and another farther west at Sankt Laurentii Vej 104. The central *Super Brugsen* grocery shop, at Sankt Laurentii Vej 28, is a two minute walk west of the station

Getting There & Away

Skagen is 41km north of Frederikshavn on route 40 and 49km north-east of Hirtshals via routes 597 and 40.

Bus & Train Either a bus or a train leaves the Skagen station for Frederikshavn (33 kr) about once an hour.

NT's seasonal Skagerakkeren bus (No 99) runs about half a dozen times daily from Skagen to Hirtshals (27.50 kr, 1½ hours) between mid-June and mid-August. That bus also continues on to Hjørring and Løkken.

Boat Color Line provides a ferry service between Skagen and Larvik in Norway. For

details, see the Sea section in the Getting There & Away chapter.

Getting Around

Bus In summer, buses run between Skagen station and Grenen (11 kr) hourly until 5 pm.

Taxi Taxis, available at the station or by calling ☎ 98 43 34 34, charge about 50 kr from Skagen town centre to Grenen.

Bicycle Cycling is a good way to get around. Both camping grounds hire out bicycles, as does Skagen Cykel (☎ 98 44 10 70), a stand at the western side of the station.

GAMMEL SKAGEN

Old Skagen, 4km west of Skagen, is an upmarket summer cottage community on the Skagerrak coast, known for its lovely evening sunsets. It was a fishing hamlet in centuries past, before sandstorms ravished this windswept area, forcing many of its inhabitants to move to Skagen on the more protected east coast.

Gammel Skagen is also known as Højen. Højensvej, the main road, leads right to the main beach and sunset spot.

Places to Stay & Eat

Gammel Skagen Vandrerhjem (☎ 98 44 13 56, fax 98 45 08 17, email glskagen@post1 .tele.dk, Højensvej 32, 9990 Gammel Skagen) has a variety of rooms, including some bright sunny ones. Dorm beds cost 85 kr and singles/doubles start at 150/240 kr. Because this hostel is no longer affiliated with Hostelling International, an HI membership card is not required. It's open from 1 March to 1 November. There's a kiosk on the beach where you can buy ice cream and snacks.

Getting There & Away

Bus No 79 between Frederikshavn and Skagen stops in Gammel Skagen every hour or two; there's a bus stop in front of Gammel

Skagen Vandrerhjem. From Skagen town centre the fare is 11 kr.

RÅBJERG MILE

Denmark's largest expanse of shifting sand dunes, these undulating 40m hills are almost large enough to disappear in and good fun to explore. The dunes, which are carried eastward about 10m a year by prevailing west winds, are a legacy of the 17th century deforestation and overgrazing that left northern Jutland susceptible to the ravages of sandstorms. While other dunes in northern Jutland have been stabilised by the planting of beach grasses, the dunes at Råbjerg Mile have purposely been left in a migratory state.

Råbjerg Mile is 16km south-west of Skagen, off route 40 on the road to Kandestederne. Between mid-June and mid-August, Nordjyllands Trafikselskab runs its Skagerakkeren bus No 99 six times daily from Skagen station to Råbjerg Mile (16.50 kr, 25 minutes) and on to Hirtshals. The dunes themselves are a 750m walk from the Råbjerg Mile bus stop.

HIRTSHALS

Hirtshals, with a population of 7000, takes its character from its commercial fishing harbour and ferry terminal. The main street is lined with supermarkets catering to Norwegian shoppers who pile off the ferries to load up with relatively cheap Danish meats and groceries.

The town boasts an impressive aquarium with the largest tank in Europe, and a small local history and liquor museum that serves samples of schnapps. There are coastal cliffs and a lighthouse on the more scenic western side of Hirtshals but if you want beaches and dunes head south to Tornby Strand.

Information

Tourist Office The Hirtshals Turistbureau (☎ 98 94 22 20, fax 98 94 58 20), 1km south of the ferry harbour at Nørregade 40, 9850 Hirtshals, has brochures on the entire region. Summer hours are from 9 am to

5 pm Monday to Saturday, and in the summer high season it's also open from 10 am to 1 pm on Sunday; during the rest of the year it's open from 9 am to 4 pm Monday to Friday (to noon on Saturday). Its Web site is at www.hirtshals-tourist.dk.

Money You'll find banks on Jørgens Fiblers Gade, a block south of the train station. At the ferry terminal there's a currency exchange machine that changes foreign notes into Danish kroner, as well as a regular ATM.

Nordsømuseet

The main sight in town is Nordsømuseet, where visitors can view North Sea marine life in a new four storey state-of-the-art oceanarium that holds 4.5 million litres of sea water. The huge oceanarium attempts to recreate the ocean ecosystem as closely as possible. The main viewing area is an amphitheatre that looks into the circular tank through an 8m-high window as feeding sharks and schools of herring, mackerel and other pelagic fish swirl by.

There are also educational displays on fishing and marine biology as well as a children's section and an outdoor seal pool with feedings at 11 am and 3 pm. The museum, 1km east of the town centre on Willemoesvej, is open from 10 am to 10 pm daily between May and August, and from 9 am to 5 pm daily during the rest of the year. Admission costs 90 kr for adults and 45 kr for children aged from four to 12; it's free for children aged under four.

Hirtshals Museum

This little historical museum at Sophus Thomsensgade 6, in the town centre, features period furnishings and displays on the town's fishing history. At the museum's schnapps exhibit you can taste your way through the various concoctions and make a sailor's swagger back to the streets. It's open from 10 am to 4 pm daily in summer and from 10 am to 4 pm (to 1 pm on Friday) on weekdays only in spring and autumn. Admission costs 10 kr.

Places to Stay

The three star *Hirtshals Camping* (☎ 98 94 25 35, fax 98 94 33 43, Kystvejen 6, 9850 Hirtshals) is in an open field on the coast. It's open from 1 May to mid-September and has bicycles for hire and cabin rentals.

The 72 bed *Hirtshals Vandrerhjem* (☎ 98 94 12 48, fax 98 94 56 55, Kystvejen 53, 9850 Hirtshals) is 1km from the train station to the south-west of town, 150m north of Hirtshals Camping. The hostel is open from March to November; dorm beds cost 90 kr and rooms sleeping three people cost 295 kr.

Staff at Hirtshals Turistbureau can book *rooms* in private homes; they cost from 100 to 150 kr per person plus a 25 kr booking fee.

The cheapest hotel in town, *Sømands-hjemmet* (☎ 98 94 53 33, Havnegade 24, 9850 Hirtshals), has clean, comfortable rooms and a convenient location opposite the ferry terminal. Singles/doubles cost a reasonable 200/395 kr with shared bath, 280/480 kr with private bath.

The *Skaga Hotel* (☎ 98 94 55 00, fax 98 94 55 55, Willemoesvej 1, 9850 Hirtshals) is a pleasant, modern hotel on the eastern side of town opposite Nordsømuseet. Each of the 108 rooms has full amenities including bath, phone and cable TV; singles/doubles start at 495/650 kr. There's an indoor pool, a sauna, a fitness room and a restaurant.

Places to Eat

You'll find cafés at the northern end of Hjørringgade, including the local favourite *Restaurant Lilleheden (Hjørringgade 2)*, which serves simple dishes as well as a daily special whcih costs 50 kr. *Sundbæk Bageri*, on the corner of Hjørringgade and Mikkelsgade, makes tempting pastries and sandwiches (15 kr); there's another recommendable *bakery* opposite the turistbureau. The harbourside hotel *Sømandshjemmet* has an inexpensive cafeteria popular with local fishers.

Getting There & Away

Hirtshals is 49km south-west of Skagen via routes 40 and 597 and 41km north-west of Frederikshavn via the E39 and route 35.

Bus There's a regular bus service from Hirtshals station to Hjørring (16.50 kr) but it takes twice as long as the train. From mid-June to mid-August the seasonal Skagerakkeren bus runs between Hirtshals station and Skagen (27.50 kr) six times daily.

Train Hirtshals' main train station is 500m south of the ferry terminal, but trains connecting with ferry services continue down to the harbour. A private railway, operated by Hjørring Privatbaner, connects Hirtshals with Hjørring (16.50 kr), 20 minutes to the south. Trains run at least hourly, with the last departure from Hjørring to Hirtshals at 10.25 pm. At Hjørring you can connect with a DSB train to Aalborg or Frederikshavn.

Boat Color Line runs ferries year-round to the Norwegian ports of Oslo, Moss and Kristiansand. See the Sea section of the Getting There & Away chapter for detailed information.

TORNBY STRAND

Tornby Strand, 5km south of Hirtshals, is a lovely undeveloped stretch of beach and dunes. It generally has good swimming conditions in summer, which is the only time you can expect to find much company.

The beach sand is packed hard enough to drive on and indeed many visitors park their cars right on the sand at the spot where they sunbathe. It's possible to drive south on the beach for about 4km, at which point a river slices across the beach en route to the sea. Use caution however, as it's possible to misjudge the tides or hit a soft spot.

There are plenty of possibilities for hiking on the beach, along the high mounded dunes and in the coastal woodlands that back the southern side of the beach. Other than a bit of sea bird watching there's nothing more to see or do here – which is

NORTHERN JUTLAND

what makes Tornby Strand an attractive little getaway.

Places to Stay & Eat

The family-run *Munch Badepension (☎ 98 97 71 15, Tornby Strand, 9850 Hirtshals)* is right on the beach at the end of Tornby Strandvej. It has a handful of rustic rooms with dune views and shared bath costing 275 kr for a double. The management also books *cottages* in the dunes, sleeping four to six people; these cost 1400 kr a week in the low season and 2600 kr in the summer high season. Munch Badepension has a *food shop* as well as a reasonably priced *restaurant* with an ocean view.

Getting There & Away

Tornby Strand can be reached from Hirtshals via route 55 and Tornby Strandvej. In summer the bus from Hirtshals to Hjørring stops en route at Tornby Strand six times daily; the fare from Hirtshals is 11 kr.

HJØRRING

Hjørring is an old market town with a population of 24,000; it's the capital of Vendsyssel county and a regional centre, with the district hospital and central rail connections.

It's a tidy town with streets and walkways enlivened by some 150 statues and bronze sculptures. The oldest part of Hjørring is built around the central squares: Springvandspladsen, where the municipal offices are located, and the nearby Sankt Olai Plads, which is bordered by three medieval churches. Springvandspladsen is a five minute walk north from the train station along Jernbanegade; continue 200m farther north on the pedestrian walkway Strømgade to reach Sankt Olai Plads.

Although Hjørring is not a very exciting destination in itself, it has an engaging small-town character and can be an enjoyable place to spend a few hours (or break for the night) if you are leisurely touring the region.

Information

Tourist Office The Hjørring Turistbureau (☎ 98 92 02 32, fax 98 92 04 52) is on Markedsgade 9, 9800 Hjørring, 750m east of the train station. It's open from 9 am to 4 pm on weekdays and from 9 am to noon on Saturday, except in summer when it closes at 5 pm on weekdays and 2 pm on Saturday. You can also pick up a tourist map of the town at the ticket window in the train station.

Money & Post There's a branch of Den Danske Bank on Springvandspladsen and many other banks nearby on Østergade, just east of its intersection with Jernbanegade. The post office is to the west of the train station.

Churches

Hjørring is unique in that it managed to retain three medieval churches despite the consolidations that occurred throughout Denmark following the Reformation. All three churches are within 200m of each other, on the northern side of Sankt Olai Plads.

The oldest, **Sankt Olai Kirke**, dates from the 11th century and has a Romanesque chancel and a 16th century altarpiece. **Sankt Catharinæ Kirke**, the current parish church, retains traces of its medieval beginnings in the transept and has a 13th century Gothic crucifix, although the church has been altered over the centuries and was largely rebuilt in the 1920s. Entry to Sankt Catharinæ Kirke is through the side door marked 'adgang for besøgende'. The Romanesque **Sankt Hans Kirke** has a nave built from medieval brick, a fresco painted in 1350 and an altarpiece and pulpit dating from the early 17th century.

Museums

The **Vendsyssel Historiske Museum** occupies an old deanery and a couple of 19th century school buildings on Museumsgade, about 250m south of Sankt Catharinæ Kirke. It features local history exhibits from prehistoric times, as well as an ecclesiastical art collection, period furnishings and displays on farming. In July and August it's open from 10 am to 5 pm daily; between April and June and in September and October it's open from 11 am to 4 pm daily. During the rest of the year it's open from 11 am to 4 pm on weekdays only. Admission costs 25 kr (children 5 kr).

There's also an art museum, the **Hjørring Kunstmuseum**, a five minute walk northeast from the train station at Brinck Seidelinsgade 10, devoted to regional art and crafts. It's open from 10 am to 4 pm Tuesday to Sunday. Admission costs 10 kr (children free).

Places to Stay

Both the camping ground and hostel are about 2.5km north-east of the train station and can be reached by local bus. *Hjørring Campingplads* (☎ 98 92 22 82, fax 98 91 06 99, *Idræts Allé 45, 9800 Hjørring*) has a three star rating, an outdoor swimming pool and two and four-bunk cabins for rent. It's open from early May to mid-September.

The *Hjørring Vandrerhjem* (☎ 98 92 67 00, fax 98 90 15 50, *Thomas Morildsvej 11, 9800 Hjørring*) is a modern hostel open from 1 March to 1 October. It has 116 beds in 28 rooms, each with bath. Dorm beds cost 90 kr and family rooms range from 210 kr for one person to 490 kr for six people.

Staff at Hjørring Vandrerhjem can book *rooms* in private homes costing from 120 to 240 kr for singles and 240 to 360 kr for doubles, plus a 35 kr booking fee.

Hotel Phønix (☎ 98 92 54 55, fax 98 90 10 37, *Jernbanegade 6, 9800 Hjørring*), a few minutes walk north of the train station, has 70 comfortable rooms with bath and TV. Singles/doubles cost 525/690 kr including breakfast.

Places to Eat

The train station contains a *café* and a *kiosk*. There's a small *cafeteria* at the bus station and a number of restaurants nearby on Jernbanegade, including three *pizzerias*

and *Peking Grill*, where Chinese dishes with rice start at 35 kr.

You'll find a *Føtex* supermarket selling good inexpensive pastries on Springvandspladsen and a *Jensen's Bøfhus* steak restaurant on Sankt Olai Plads offering lunch specials for 39 kr.

For an upmarket choice, *Hotel Phønix (Jernbanegade 6)* has a solarium dining room and traditional Danish dishes, including smørrebrød at lunchtime.

Getting There & Away

Hjørring is 35km west of Frederikshavn on route 35 and 17km south of Hirtshals on route 55 or the E39.

Bus & Train Hjørring is served by NT, which operates bus services to Skagen, Løkken, Frederikshavn and Hirtshals. The bus station is 200m north-east of the train station, near the intersection of Jernbanegade and Asylgade.

The town is on the Århus-Frederikshavn railway line (DSB) and is the terminus of a private railway line to Hirtshals. The fare is 16.50 kr to Hirtshals, 35 kr to Frederikshavn, 49 kr to Aalborg and 156 kr to Århus.

LØKKEN

Fronted by a broad sandy beach, Løkken is a small town of 1300 residents that's packed each summer with an invasion of beachgoers. Not surprisingly, its character is that of a popular resort area, more commercial than quaint, with a bustling centre of shops, ice-cream stands and cafés. Although the beach is the major attraction there's also a summertime museum in a former sea captain's house at Nørregade 12 that features exhibits on the town's history as a trading and fishing port.

Information

The Løkken Turistbureau (☎ 98 99 10 09, fax 98 99 11 59), Møstingsvej 3, 9480 Løkken, is on the southern side of Torvet, the central square. There's a Jyske Bank on the northern side of Torvet with an after-hours ATM.

Places to Stay

There are five camping grounds in the southern part of town either on or near Søndergade; all are open in summer only. Right in the centre, a five minute walk south of Torvet, is *Midtbyens Camping* (☎ 98 99 11 52, Jyllandsgade 2, 9480 Løkken), a small two star place that has a slightly longer season than the competition, opening from 1 May to 15 September.

One kilometre south of the centre is the three star *Løkken Campingcenter* (☎ 98 99 17 67, fax 98 99 26 80, Søndergade 69, 9480 Løkken), where camping costs 59 kr per person and there are 32 four-bed cabins, each with an equipped kitchen, starting at 1300 kr a week.

The nearby three star *Josefines Camping* (☎ 98 99 13 26, Søndergade 57, 9480 Løkken) charges 53 kr per person and mainly accommodates caravans and tents but also has a few cabins.

Løkken's cheapest central hotel is *Hotel Litorina* (☎ 98 99 10 44, fax 98 99 10 76, Søndergade 15, 9480 Løkken). It has 26 straightforward rooms; singles/doubles cost 235/315 kr with shared bath, 265/395 kr with private bath. These prices are liable to increase by about 35% during the month of July.

Most other hotels and apartment complexes in Løkken are geared to holiday-makers planning longer stays and offer their best prices for weekly bookings. The turist-bureau can provide a booklet with a brief description of each place and a detailed price list.

Places to Eat

There are numerous places to eat around Torvet and along Nørregade, which leads north from Torvet. *Café Søborg (Nørregade 1)* is popular for Danish fare, while *Løkken Snack Bar (Nørregade 18)* serves up inexpensive pizza and other light eats. For something fancier, the restaurant in the *Løkken Badehotel* overlooks Torvet and

has some reasonably priced specials including a steak lunch costing 49 kr. There's a *bakery* on Søndergade, a block south of Torvet.

Getting There & Away

Løkken is on route 55, 18km south-west of Hjørring. Buses run every couple of hours between Løkken and Hjørring (22 kr, 30 minutes) and between Løkken and Aalborg (44 kr, one hour).

HANSTHOLM

Hanstholm is a new town built around a large commercial harbour, completed in 1967; it's now one of Denmark's largest fishing ports. It was originally thought that the population would quickly reach 20,000, but to date Hanstholm has only about 3000 residents.

Information

The Hanstholm Turistbureau (☎ 97 96 12 19, fax 97 96 21 54), Bytorvet 2, 7730 Hanstholm, opposite Hanstholm Centret and about 1km inland of the harbour, is open from 8.30 am to 4 pm on weekdays and from 9 am to noon on Saturday, with slightly later closing times in summer. Hanstholm Centret, a shopping complex, contains banks, the post office, a library, a pharmacy and eateries.

Things to See & Do

There's no real reason to come to Hanstholm unless you're planning to take a ferry to Norway or Iceland. Those who do find themselves here might want to visit the **lighthouse**, which claimed to beam the world's most powerful beacon when erected in 1843 and now displays local history exhibits.

Early risers scratching for something to do might want to watch the harbourside **fish auction**, held at 7 am on weekdays. There are also some remnants of the German occupation during WWII in Hanstholm and in the village of Vigsø to the east, which has a coastline of concrete **bunkers** that are slowly being washed into the sea.

Places to Stay & Eat

The nearest camping ground is *Hanstholm Camping* (☎ 97 96 51 98, fax 97 96 54 70, Hamborgvej 95, 7730 Hanstholm), about 5km east of the harbour, midway to Vigsø. It's open from 1 April to 30 September and offers the usual three-star facilities.

At the harbour is the *Hanstholm Sømandshjem* (☎ 97 96 11 45, fax 97 96 27 80, Kai Lindbergsgade 71, 7730 Hanstholm). This seamen's hotel is a utilitarian place but the 19 rooms are adequate, each with bath and TV. Singles/doubles start at 345/450 kr.

The modern 74 room *Hotel Hanstholm* (☎ 97 96 10 44, fax 97 96 25 84, Christian Hansens Vej 2, 7730 Hanstholm) is inland from the harbour and close to Hanstholm Centret. Singles/doubles with bath, TV and phone cost 375/595 kr including breakfast. The hotel has a restaurant and a swimming pool.

Hanstholm Sømandshjem has a cheap *cafeteria* (open to 10 pm) that's a popular hang-out for local fishers but, like the town itself, doesn't draw many tourists. There's a *supermarket* just to the west of the hotel and a *grill* serving ice cream and hot dogs down by the harbour.

Hanstholm Centret has a *bakery*, a *cafeteria*, a *fast-food grill* and a *Super Brugsen* supermarket.

Getting There & Away

Hanstholm is at the terminus of routes 181, 26 and 29.

Bus & Train Thisted, 21km to the south via route 26, has the nearest train station. Bus No 40 makes the 45 minute run to Thisted train station from Hanstholm harbour about hourly on weekdays, a little less frequently at weekends.

Boat There are car ferries from Hanstholm to the Norwegian cities of Bergen and Egersund, as well as to Iceland and the Faroe Islands. See the Sea section of the Getting There & Away chapter for details.

Amber

Amber is fossilised tree resin, translucent and brittle. It's usually a golden yellow colour but can appear in other hues, most notably reddish-brown. Some pieces of amber contain fossilised ferns or insects that were trapped inside the resin aeons ago, when it was still sticky.

In Denmark, amber is most commonly found on the west coast of Jutland. The best time to hunt for amber is in the wake of a storm or strong gale, when the amber gets stirred up from the seabed, bobs to the surface and is washed ashore. Look for it up on the beach mixed with other lightweight items such as driftwood and seaweed.

Amber is not easily found by novices, however, and most first-time collectors end up with a pocketful of small yellow stones instead. There are two key identification points: amber is significantly lighter than rock and it floats in salt water; it also collects a small negative charge when rubbed and will warm to the touch after being held.

Professional amber collectors have their own tools of the trade, primarily a meshed net on a long frame with which they can snatch the amber as it's tossed around in breaking waves.

Amber is often polished and made into jewellery, particularly pendants, beaded necklaces, earrings and rings. If you're unable to find your own pieces, they can be readily purchased at jewellery shops all over Denmark.

KLITMØLLER

Klitmøller is a small fishing village that attracts lots of windsurfers, both German and Danish, with some of North Jutland's best wind conditions. The main windsurfing spot is right in town; follow the main road, Ørhagevej, to the waterfront. When the winds are down there's good swimming at the beaches north and south of the village.

The landscape around Klitmøller, dunes backed by stark heathlands, continues for more than 10km to the north and south. The section between Hanstholm and Klitmøller looks particularly barren as you zip along the road, but there are bogs and ponds inland and the entire area is an important bird reserve known as Hanstholm Vildtreservat; human access is restricted.

Windsurfing

Those interested in windsurfing can contact Windsurfing Klitmøller (☎ 97 97 56 56), near the beach at Ørhagevej 152, which hires out equipment and gives windsurfing lessons. In addition to the challenging North Sea waters, Vandet Sø, a lake to the east of Klitmøller, is a popular spot, with windsurfing conditions suitable for all levels.

Places to Stay & Eat

Most visitors to Klitmøller stay in one of the three camping grounds right in town; the first two listed are just a few minutes walk from Ørhagevej. The two star *Klitmøller Camping* (☎ 97 97 50 20, fax 97 93 11 12, Vangvej 16, 7700 Thisted) charges

40 kr per person. *Nordsø Camping* (☎/fax 97 97 50 71, Vangsåvej 25, 7700 Thisted) has a three star rating and more elaborate facilities and charges 49 kr; it also has the longest camping season, extending from 1 April to 30 October. The third and largest camping ground is the three star *Nystrup Camping* (☎ 97 97 52 49, fax 97 71 05 71, Trøjborgvej 22, Klitmøller, 7700 Thisted), which charges 51 kr per person. All three places have cabins for rent, minimarkets and grill-style *eateries*.

There's a *burger bar*, an *ice-cream shop*, a *bakery*, a *food market* and a few *cafés* and *restaurants* along Ørhagevej within 1km of the waterfront.

Getting There & Away

Klitmøller is 10km south-west of Hanstholm on route 181 and 15km north-west of Thisted on route 557. From Klitmøller, bus No 22 goes to Thisted, which has the nearest rail connections. Bus No 24 connects Klitmøller and Hanstholm. Both bus services average about eight runs a day during the week and three runs a day at weekends.

Language

Together with Swedish, Norwegian, Icelandic and Faroese, Danish belongs to the northern branch of the Germanic language group. Consequently, written Danish bears a strong resemblance to all these languages. Spoken Danish on the other hand has evolved in a different direction, developing sounds and quirks of pronunciation not found elsewhere.

Grammatically, Danish has the same general rules and syntax as the other Germanic languages of Scandinavia. There are two genders: common (or 'non-neuter'), and neuter. Articles are suffixed to the noun: *-en* for common singular nouns and *-et* for neuter singular nouns. Plural nouns take the suffixes *-ne* (indefinite) and *-ene* (definite), regardless of gender.

Danish has both a polite and an informal mode of address (where English uses the universal 'you'); the polite uses the personal pronouns *De* and *Dem*, the informal, *du* and *dig*. The translations in this chapter are mostly in the informal, except where it is appropriate and/or wise to use the polite form. In general, use the polite form when speaking to senior citizens and officials, and the informal in all other instances.

Most Danes speak English, and many also speak German. However, an effort to at least learn the basics, such as memorising the Danish words for 'Thank you', 'Goodbye', 'Hello' and 'I'm sorry', will be appreciated. With an increased command of the language, you'll be rewarded by gaining a greater insight into the country and its people.

Note that Danish has all of the letters of the English alphabet plus three others, æ, ø and å. These come at the end of the alphabet and we have used this order throughout the book.

Pronunciation

You may find Danish pronunciation difficult. Consonants can be drawled, swallowed and even omitted completely, creating, in conjunction with vowels, the peculiarity of the glottal stop or *stød*. Its sound could be compared with the 'ottle' in a Cockney's pronunciation of 'bottle'. Word stress in Danish usually falls on the first syllable or the first letter of a word. As a general rule, the best way to pick up the language is to listen and learn from the experts, the Danes themselves.

Vowels

a	as in 'father'
a, æ	as in 'act'
å, o &	
u(n)	as the 'a' in 'walk'
e(g)	as the 'i' in 'high'
e, i	a short, flat 'e', as in 'met'
i	as in 'marine'
æ	as the 'e' in 'bet'
ø	as the 'er' in 'fern', but shorter
o, u	as the 'oo' in 'zoo'
o	a short 'o', as in 'pot'
o(v)	as the 'ow' in 'vow', but shorter
o(r)	as in 'or' but with little emphasis on the 'r'
u	as in 'pull'
y	a long, sharp 'u'; purse your lips and say 'ee'

Semiconsonants

w	similar to the 'v' in 'Volkswagon'
j	as the 'y' in 'yet'

Consonants

Consonants are pronounced as in English with the exception of the following:

sj	as the 'sh' in 'ship'
ch	as in 'cheque', but sharper
c	as in 'cell'
(o)d	as the 'th' in 'these'
ng	as in 'sing'
g	before vowels, a hard 'g' as in 'get'
h	as in 'horse'
k	as in 'kit'
b	as in 'box'
r	a rolling 'r' abruptly cut short

Greetings & Civilities

Hello. | *Goddag/Hej.*
(polite/informal)
Goodbye. | *Farvel.*
Yes. | *Ja.*
No. | *Nej.*
Could I please have ...?. | *Jeg vil gerne bede om ...?*
Please ... (when making a request) | *Vær så venlig at ...*
Please (sit down). | *Værsgo (at sidde ned).*
Thank you. | *Tak.*
That's fine/ You're welcome. | *Det er i orden/Selv tak.*
Excuse me (Sorry). | *Undskyld.*
May I/Do you mind? | *Må jeg/Tillader De?*

Language Difficulties

Do you speak English? | *Taler De engelsk?*
Does anyone speak English? | *Er der nogen, der kan tale engelsk?*
I understand. | *Jeg forstår.*
I don't understand. | *Jeg forstår ikke.*

Small Talk

What's your name? | *Hvad hedder du?*
My name is ... | *Jeg hedder ...*
Where are you from? | *Hvorfra kommer du?*
I'm from ... | *Jeg er fra ...*
How old are you? | *Hvor gammel er du?*
I'm ... years old. | *Jeg er ... år gammel.*

Getting Around

What time does the ... leave/arrive? | *Hvornår går/ ankommer ...?*
boat | *båden*
bus (city) | *bussen*
bus (intercity) | *rutebilen*
train | *toget*

I'd like a ... | *Jeg vil gerne have ...*
one-way ticket | *en enkeltbillet*
return ticket | *en tur-retur billet*
1st class | *første klasse*
2nd class | *anden klasse*

Directions

Where is ...? | *Hvor er ...?*
I want to go to ... | *Jeg vil gerne til ...*

Signs

INDGANG	ENTRANCE
UDGANG	EXIT
INFORMATION	INFORMATION
ÅBEN/LUKKET	OPEN/CLOSED
FORBUDT	PROHIBITED
POLITISTATION	POLICE STATION
TOILETTER	TOILETS
HERRER	MEN
DAMER	WOMEN

Can you show me (on the map)? | *Kan De vise mig det (på kortet)?*
Go straight ahead. | *Gå ligeud.*
Turn left. | *Drej til venstre.*
Turn right. | *Drej til højre.*
near/far | *tæt på/langt væk*

Around Town

I'm looking for ... | *Jeg leder efter ...*
a bank | *en bank*
the city centre | *centrum*
the ... embassy | *den ... ambassade*
my hotel | *mit hotel*
the market | *markedet*
the museum | *museet*
the police | *politiet*
the post office | *postkontoret*
a public toilet | *et offentligt toilet*
the telephone centre | *telefoncentralen*
the tourist office | *turist-informationen*

beach | *strand*
castle | *slot*
cathedral | *katedral/domkirke*
church | *kirke*
main square | *hovedtorv/torvet*
monastery | *kloster*
old city | *den gamle bydel*
palace | *palads*
synagogue | *synagoge*

Accommodation

Where is a cheap hotel? | *Hvor ligger der et billig hotel?*
What is the address? | *Hvad er adressen?*

Could you write down the address, please?	*Kunne De være så venlig at skrive adressen ned?*
Do you have any rooms available?	*Har I ledige værelser?*

I'd like ...	*Jeg vil gerne have ...*
a single room	*et enkeltværelse*
a double room	*et dobbeltværelse*
a room with a bathroom	*et værelse med bad*
to share a dorm	*plads i en sovesal*
a bed	*en seng*

How much is it per night/ per person?	*Hvor meget koster det per nat/ per person?*
Can I see it?	*Må jeg se værelset?*
Where is the bathroom?	*Hvor er toilettet?*

Shopping

How much is it?	*Hvor meget koster den/det?* (common/ neuter)

bookshop	*boghandel*
camera shop	*fotohandel*
clothing store	*tøjforretning*
delicatessen	*delikatesse*
laundry	*vaskeri*
market	*marked*
newsagency	*aviskiosk*
souvenir shop	*souvenirbutik*
stationers	*papirhandel*

Health

I'm sick.	*Jeg er syg.*
My friend is sick.	*Min ven er syg.*

I'm ...	*Jeg er ...*
diabetic	*diabetiker*
epileptic	*epileptiker*
asthmatic	*astmatiker*

I'm allergic to antibiotics/ penicillin.	*Jeg er allergisk overfor antibiotikum/ penicillin.*
I need medication for ...	*Jeg behøver et medikament imod ...*
I have a prescription.	*Jeg har en recept.*

I have a toothache.	*Jeg har tandpine.*
I'm pregnant.	*Jeg er gravid.*

antiseptic	*antiseptisk*
aspirin	*aspirin*
chemist	*apotek*
condoms	*kondomer*
contraceptive	*præventiv*
dentist	*tandlæge*
doctor	*læge*
hospital	*hospital*
medicine	*medicin*
nausea	*kvalme*
soap	*sæbe*
sunblock cream	*solcreme*
tampons	*tamponer*
vitamins	*vitaminer*

Time & Dates

What time is it?	*Hvad er klokken?*
It's ... o'clock.	*Klokken er ...*

today	*i dag*
tonight	*i aften/i nat*
tomorrow	*i morgen*
day after tomorrow	*i overmorgen*
next week	*næste uge*
yesterday	*i går*
in the morning	*om morgenen*
in the evening	*om aftenen*
early	*tidlig*

Monday	*mandag*
Tuesday	*tirsdag*
Wednesday	*onsdag*
Thursday	*torsdag*
Friday	*fredag*
Saturday	*lørdag*
Sunday	*søndag*

January	*januar*
February	*februar*
March	*marts*
April	*april*
May	*maj*
June	*juni*
July	*juli*
August	*august*
September	*september*
October	*oktober*
November	*november*
December	*december*

Emergencies

Help!	*Hjælp!*
Call a doctor!	*Ring efter en læge!*
Call the police!	*Ring efter politiet!*
Go away!	*Forsvind!*
I'm lost.	*Jeg har gået vild.*

Numbers

0	*nul*
1	*en*
2	*to*
3	*tre*
4	*fire*
5	*fem*
6	*seks*
7	*syv*
8	*otte*
9	*ni*
10	*ti*
11	*elleve*
12	*tolv*
13	*tretten*
20	*tyve*
21	*enogtyve*
30	*tredive*
40	*fyrre*
50	*halvtreds*
60	*tres*
70	*halvfjerds*
80	*firs*
90	*halvfems*
100	*hundrede*
1000	*tusind*
one million	*en million*

FOOD & DRINK

I'd like today's special, please.	*Jeg tager dagens ret, tak.*
I'm a vegetarian.	*Jeg er vegetar.*
breakfast	*morgenmad*
lunch	*frokost*
dinner	*middag*
menu	*spisekort*
set menu	*dagens middag*
children's menu	*børnemenu*
daily special	*dagens ret*
dishes, courses	*retter*
starters, appetisers	*forretter*
main dishes	*hovedretter*
dishes for diabetics	*diabetes mad*
self-serve buffet	*tagselvbord*

Food & Drink Glossary

abrikos	apricot
agurk	cucumber
agurkesalat	sliced cucumber with vinegar dressing
alkoholfri	nonalcoholic
ananas	pineapple
and, andesteg	duck, roast duck
ansjoser	anchovies
appelsin	orange
asparges	asparagus
bagt	baked
bagt kartoffel	baked potato
banan	banana
benfri	boneless
blomkål	cauliflower
blomme	plum
blæksprutte	octopus
blødkogt æg	soft-boiled egg
blåbær	blueberry
bolle	soft bread roll, also a meatball or fishball
brombær	blackberry
brød	bread
bønner	beans
champignon	mushroom
chokolade	chocolate, also hot chocolate
citron	lemon
citronvand	lemonade
crème fraîche	sour cream
dampet	steamed
dild	dill
dyresteg	roast venison
eddike	vinegar
engelsk bøf	steak, commonly served with onions
fadøl	draught (draft) beer
fersken	peach
fisk	fish

fiskefilet	fish fillet	*hvidløg*	garlic
fiskefrikadelle	fried fishball	*hytteost*	cottage cheese
fiskeretter	fish dishes	*høns/hønsekød*	hen/chicken meat
fiskesuppe	fish soup, usually creamy	*hønsebryst*	chicken breast
		hønsekødsuppe	chicken soup
flute	type of French bread	*hårdkogt æg*	hard-boiled egg
flynder	flounder		
flæskesteg	roast pork, often served with crackling	*ingefær*	ginger
		ingefærbrød	gingerbread
flæskeæggekage	scrambled eggs with bacon	*is*	ice cream, ice
		iskold	ice cold
fløde	cream		
flødeost	cream cheese	*jordbær*	strawberry
flødeskum	whipped cream	*jordnød*	peanut
forårsrulle	spring roll, egg roll	*jordnødsmør*	peanut butter
forel	trout		
frikadelle	fried meatball	*kaffe*	coffee
frisk	fresh	*kage*	cake
friturestegt	deep fried	*kalkun*	turkey
fromage	a pudding	*kalvekød*	veal
frugt	fruit	*karry*	curry
fyld	stuffing	*kartoffel*	potato
fyldt	stuffed	*kartoffelmos*	mashed potatoes
fårekød	mutton	*kartoffelsalat*	potato salad
		kirsebær	cherry
gennemstegt	well-done	*klar suppe*	clear soup
glasur	glaze, frosting	*klipfisk*	dried salt cod
grapefrugt	grapefruit	*koffeinfri*	caffeine-free
grilleret, grillstegt	grilled	*kogt*	boiled
gryderet	casserole or stew	*kold*	cold
grøn bønne	green bean	*kotelet*	cutlet
grøn salat	green salad	*krabbe*	crab
grøntsager	vegetables	*kringle*	type of Danish pastry
gulerødder	carrots	*kryddere*	crispy bread rolls
gule ærter	split pea soup served with pork	*krydderi*	spice
		kryddersild	herring pickled in various marinades
gås	goose		
		kuller	haddock
hakkebøf	ground-beef burger	*kylling*	chicken
hakket	chopped, minced	*kærnemælk*	buttermilk
haresteg	roast hare	*kød*	meat
hasselnød	hazelnut	*kødbolle*	boiled meatball
helleflynder	halibut	*kødretter*	meat dishes
hindbær	raspberry	*kål*	cabbage
hjemmebagt	home-baked		
hjemmelavet	home-made	*lagkage*	layer cake
honning	honey	*laks*	salmon
hummer	lobster	*lamme, lammekød*	lamb
hvide	white (as in white potatoes, rice etc)	*lammesteg*	roast lamb
		letmælk	low-fat milk

LANGUAGE

lever	liver
leverpostej	liver pâté
løg	onion
majs	corn
makrel	mackerel
mandel, mandler	almonds
marineret	marinated
marineret sild	marinated herring
mellemstegt	medium cooked
mineralvand	mineral water
musling	mussel
mælk	milk
nudler	noodles
nødder	nuts
oksehaleragout	oxtail stew
oksekød	beef
oksemørbrad,	fillet of beef,
oksefilet	tenderloin
oksesteg	roast beef
olie	oil
oliven	olive
ost	cheese
ovnstegt	roasted
pandekage	pancake or crepe
parisertoast	toasted ham and
	cheese sandwich
peber	pepper
pebermynte	peppermint
peberrod	horseradish
persille	parsley
pocheret	poached
pommes frites	French fries, chips
porre	leek
purløg	chives
pære	pear
pølse	sausage, hot dog
rejer	shrimp
remoulade	mayonnaise-based
	tartar sauce
ris	rice
ris à l'amande	rice pudding with
	almonds
ristet	toasted
rugbrød	rye bread
rundstykke	crispy poppy-seed roll

rødbeder	beets, commonly
	served pickled
rødkål	red cabbage
rødspætte	plaice
røget	smoked
røget laks	smoked salmon
røget sild	smoked herring
røræg	scrambled eggs
rå	raw
salat	salad, lettuce
saltet	salted, cured
selleri	celery
sennep	mustard
sild	herring
skaldyr	shellfish
skinke	ham
skive	slice
skummetmælk	skimmed (nonfat) milk
sky	meat juice (for gravy)
smør	butter
smørrebrød	open sandwich
snittebønner	string beans
sodavand	soft drink, carbonated
	water
sovs	gravy/sauce
spejlæg	fried egg, sunny
	side up
spinat	spinach
stegt	fried
stegeretter	fried dishes
sukker	sugar
suppe	soup
surt	pickled cucumbers
svinekød	pork
syltetøj	jam
sød	sweet
sødmælk	whole milk
søtunge	sole
te	tea
tilberedt	cooked
torsk	cod
torskerogn	cod roe
tun, tunfisk	tuna
tunge	tongue
tykmælk	a pourable yoghurt
tærte	tart
vaffel	waffle
valnød	walnut

vand	water	*æggeblomme*	egg yolk
vandmelon	watermelon	*æggekage*	scrambled eggs with
vanilleis	vanilla ice cream		onions, potatoes and
varm	warm, hot		bacon
vegetar/	vegetarian	*ærter*	peas
vegetarianer			
vildt	game	*øl*	beer
		ølebrød	beer and bread soup
wienerbrød	Danish pastry	*ørred*	trout
		østers	oyster
æble	apple		
æg	egg	*ål*	eel

Glossary

Note that the Danish letters æ, ø and å fall at the end of the alphabet.

adgang forbudt – no trespassing
amt – county
apotek – pharmacy, chemist

bageri – bakery
bakke – hill
bibliotek – library
billetautomat – automated parking-ticket dispenser
bro – bridge
bugt – bay
by – town
børnemenu – children's menu

campingplads – camping ground

dagens ret – special meal of the day
damer – lady; often seen on toilet doors (or as 'D')
Danmark – Denmark
Dannebrog – Danish national flag
Dansk – Danish
domkirke – cathedral
DSB – abbreviation for Danske Statsbaner (Danish State Railway), Denmark's national railway

EU – European Union

Fyn – Funen, both a county and an island
færegehavn – ferry harbour

gade – street
gammel – old
god tur – literally 'good trip' (ie have a pleasant journey)
gård – yard, farm

have – garden
havn – harbour
herrer – gentleman; often seen on toilet doors (or as 'H')
HI – Hostelling International, the main international hostel organisation (formerly IYHF)
hygge – cosy

IC – intercity train
ICLyn – business class train
IR – inter-regional train

jernbane – train
Jylland – Jutland

keramik – ceramic, pottery
kirke – church
kirkegård – churchyard, cemetery
klint – cliff
klippekort – a type of multiple-use transport ticket
kloster – monastery
konditori – bakery with café tables
kro – inn
København – Copenhagen
køreplan – timetable

lur – Bronze Age horn

museet – museum
møntvask – coin laundry

nord – north

plantage – plantation, tree farm, woods
privat vej – private road

røgeri – fish smokehouse
rådhus – town hall, city hall
rundkirke – fortified round church, found on Bornholm

samling – collection, usually of art
Sjælland – the island of Zealand
skov – forest, woods
slagter – butcher
slot – castle
smørrebrød – open sandwich
strand – beach, shoreline
stykke – piece
sund – sound

syd – south
sø – lake

torv, torvet – square, marketplace
tårn – tower
turistbureau – tourist office

vandrerhjem – youth and family hostel
vej – street, road

vest – west

ø – island, usually attached as a suffix to the proper name
øl – beer
øst – east

å – river

LONELY PLANET

Mail Order

Lonely Planet products are distributed worldwide. They are also available by mail order from Lonely Planet, so if you have difficulty finding a title please write to us. North and South American residents should write to 150 Linden St, Oakland, CA 94607, USA; European and African residents should write to 10a Spring Place, London NW5 3BH, UK; and residents of other countries to PO Box 617, Hawthorn, Victoria 3122, Australia.

ISLANDS OF THE INDIAN OCEAN Madagascar & Comoros • Maldives • Mauritius, Réunion & Seychelles

MIDDLE EAST & CENTRAL ASIA Arab Gulf States • Central Asia • Central Asia phrasebook • Iran • Israel & the Palestinian Territories • Israel & the Palestinian Territories travel atlas • Istanbul • Jerusalem • Jordan & Syria • Jordan, Syria & Lebanon travel atlas • Lebanon • Middle East on a shoestring • Turkey • Turkish phrasebook • Turkey travel atlas • Yemen
Travel Literature: The Gates of Damascus • Kingdom of the Film Stars: Journey into Jordan

NORTH AMERICA Alaska • Backpacking in Alaska • Baja California • California & Nevada • Canada • Florida • Hawaii • Honolulu • Los Angeles • Miami • New England USA • New Orleans • New York City • New York, New Jersey & Pennsylvania • Pacific Northwest USA • Rocky Mountain States • San Francisco • Seattle • Southwest USA • USA phrasebook • Washington, DC & the Capital Region
Travel Literature: Drive Thru America

NORTH-EAST ASIA Beijing • Cantonese phrasebook • China • Hong Kong • Hong Kong, Macau & Guangzhou • Japan • Japanese phrasebook • Japanese audio pack • Korea • Korean phrasebook • Kyoto • Mandarin phrasebook • Mongolia • Mongolian phrasebook • North-East Asia on a shoestring • Seoul • South-West China • Taiwan • Tibet • Tibetan phrasebook • Tokyo
Travel Literature: Lost Japan

SOUTH AMERICA Argentina, Uruguay & Paraguay • Bolivia • Brazil • Brazilian phrasebook • Buenos Aires • Chile & Easter Island • Chile & Easter Island travel atlas • Colombia • Ecuador & the Galapagos Islands • Latin American Spanish phrasebook • Peru • Quechua phrasebook • Rio de Janeiro • South America on a shoestring • Trekking in the Patagonian Andes • Venezuela
Travel Literature: Full Circle: A South American Journey

SOUTH-EAST ASIA Bali & Lombok • Bangkok • Burmese phrasebook • Cambodia • Hill Tribes phrasebook • Ho Chi Minh City • Indonesia • Indonesian phrasebook • Indonesian audio pack • Jakarta • Java • Laos • Lao phrasebook • Laos travel atlas • Malay phrasebook • Malaysia, Singapore & Brunei • Myanmar (Burma) • Philippines • Pilipino (Tagalog) phrasebook • Singapore • South-East Asia on a shoestring • South-East Asia phrasebook • Thailand • Thailand's Islands & Beaches • Thailand travel atlas • Thai phrasebook • Thai audio pack • Vietnam • Vietnamese phrasebook • Vietnam travel atlas

ALSO AVAILABLE: Antarctica • Brief Encounters: Stories of Love, Sex & Travel • Chasing Rickshaws • Not the Only Planet: Travel Stories from Science Fiction • Travel with Children • Traveller's Tales

Index

Text

Bold indicates maps.
Italics indicates boxed text.

Boxed Text

MAP LEGEND

BOUNDARIES

·—·—·—··	International
—— — —	State

HYDROGRAPHY

	Coastline
	River, Creek
	Lake
	Swamp

ROUTES & TRANSPORT

	Motorway
	Highway
	Major Road
	Minor Road
	City Motorway
	City Highway
	City Road
	City Street, Lane

=======	Under Construction
	Pedestrian Mall
⇒ = = = =	Tunnel
+—+—●—+	Train Route & Station
—●Ⓜ●	S-Train & Station
— — — —	Walking Track
· · · · · · ·	Walking Tour
— — — —	Ferry Route

AREA FEATURES

	Building
✿	Park, Gardens

+ + + +	Cemetery
	Market

	Beach or Sand Dunes
	Urban Area

MAP SYMBOLS

○ CAPITAL	National Capital	❸	Bank	←	One Way Street
● City	City	⚲	Beach	🅿	Parking
● Town	Town	⛢	Bicycle Track	⛽	Petrol Station
● Village	Village	⚲	Bird Sanctuary	★	Police Station
		⚔	Castle or Fort	✉	Post Office
■	Place to Stay	✚ 🕆	Cathedral, Church	❖	Shopping Centre
Δ	Camping Ground	⌒	Cliff or Escarpment	🏛	Stately Home
		✪	Embassy	🏊	Swimming Pool
▼	Place to Eat	⛳	Golf Course	🕍	Synagogue
🍺	Bar or Pub	✚	Hospital	🚻	Toilet
		🕇	Lighthouse	❶	Tourist Information
✈	Airport	☀	Lookout	◔	Transport
⌒	Ancient or City Wall	⚑	Monument	⛵	Windsurfing
∴	Archaeological Site	▲	Hill	🐗	Zoo
		🏛	Museum or Art Gallery		

Note: not all symbols displayed above appear in this book

LONELY PLANET OFFICES

Australia
PO Box 617, Hawthorn, Victoria 3122
☎ (03) 9819 1877 fax (03) 9819 6459
email: talk2us@lonelyplanet.com.au

UK
10a Spring Place, London NW5 3BH
☎ (0171) 428 4800 fax (0171) 428 4828
email: go@lonelyplanet.co.uk

USA
150 Linden St, Oakland, CA 94607
☎ (510) 893 8555 TOLL FREE: 800 275 8555
fax (510) 893 8572
email: info@lonelyplanet.com

France
1 rue du Dahomey, 75011 Paris
☎ 01 55 25 33 00 fax 01 55 25 33 01
email: bip@lonelyplanet.fr
minitel: 3615 lonelyplanet *(1,29 F TTC/min)*

World Wide Web: www.lonelyplanet.com *or* AOL keyword: lp
Lonely Planet Images: lpi@lonelyplanet.com.au